*The Violin Family and its Makers
in the British Isles*

The Poor Fiddler's Ode to his Old Fiddle.

Torn,
Worn,
Oppressed I mourn
B a d,
S a d,
Three-quarters mad:
Money gone,
Credit none,
Duns at door,
Half a score,
Wife in lain,
Twins again,
Others ailing,
Nurse a railing,
Billy hooping,
Betsy crouping,
Besides poor Joe,
With festered toe.
Come, then, my fiddle,
Come, my time-worn friend,
With gay and brilliant sounds,
Some sweet, tho' transient solace lend.
Thy polished neck, in close embrace,
I clasp, whilst joy illumes my face,
When o'er thy strings I draw my bow,
My drooping spirit pants to rise;
A lively strain I touch — and, lo!
I seem to mount above the skies.
There, on Fancy's wing I soar,
Heedless of the duns at door;
Oblivious all, I feel my woes no more;
But skip o'er the strings,
As my old Fiddle sings,
"Cheerily, oh! merrily go!
"PRESTO! good master,
"You very well know,
"I will find Music,
"If you will find bow,
"From E, up in alto, to G, down below."
Fatigued, I pause, to change the time
For some *Adagio*, solemn and sublime.
With graceful action moves the sinuous arm;
My heart, responsive to the soothing charm,
Throbs equably; whilst every health-corroding care
Lies prostrate, vanquished by the soft mellifluous air.
More and more plaintive grown, my eyes with tears o'erflow,
And resignation mild, soon smooths my wrinkled brow.
Reedy Hautboy may squeak, wailing Flauto may squall,
The Serpent may grunt, and the Trombone may bawl,
But my Poll,* my old Fiddle's the Prince of them all.
Could e'en Dryden return, thy praise to rehearse,
His Ode to Cecilia would seem rugged verse.
Now to thy *case*, in flannel warm to lie
Till call'd again to pipe thy master's eye.
  * Apollo.

FROM THE 'MUSICAL WORLD', OF AUGUST 5, 1841

The Violin Family and its Makers in the British Isles

An Illustrated History and Directory

BRIAN W. HARVEY

CLARENDON PRESS · OXFORD
1995

Oxford University Press, Walton Street, Oxford OX2 6DP
Oxford New York
Athens Auckland Bangkok Bombay
Calcutta Cape Town Dar es Salaam Delhi
Florence Hong Kong Istanbul Karachi
Kuala Lumpur Madras Madrid Melbourne
Mexico City Nairobi Paris Singapore
Taipei Tokyo Toronto

and associated companies in
Berlin Ibadan

Oxford is a trade mark of Oxford University Press

Published in the United States
by Oxford University Press Inc., New York

© Brian W. Harvey 1995

All rights reserved. No part of this publication may be reproduced,
stored in a retrieval system, or transmitted, in any form or by any means,
without the prior permission in writing of Oxford University Press.
Within the UK, exceptions are allowed in respect of any fair dealing for the
purpose of research or private study, or criticism or review, as permitted
under the Copyright, Designs and Patents Act, 1988, or in the case of
reprographic reproduction in accordance with the terms of the licences
issued by the Copyright Licensing Agency. Enquiries concerning
reproduction outside these terms and in other countries should be
sent to the Rights Department, Oxford University Press,
at the address above

This book is sold subject to the condition that it shall not, by way
of trade or otherwise, be lent, re-sold, hired out or otherwise circulated
without the publisher's prior consent in any form of binding or cover
other than that in which it is published and without a similar condition
including this condition being imposed on the subsequent purchaser

British Library Cataloguing in Publication Data
Data available

Library of Congress Cataloging in Publication Data
Harvey, Brian W.
The violin family and its makers in the British Isles : an
illustrated history and directory / by Brian W. Harvey.
  p cm.
Includes bibliographical references (p.) and index.
1. Stringed instruments, Bowed—Construction—British Isles.
2. Stringed instrument makers—British Isles—Directories.
I. Title.
ML755.H35 1995   787.2'1941–dc20   94–31872
ISBN 0–19–816259–6 (acid-free paper)

Set by Hope Services (Abingdon) Ltd.
Printed in Great Britain
on acid-free paper by
Bath Press Ltd
Bath, Avon

Dedication

To Her

> . . . . . . dont l'âme emmène des autres
> Sur le pont du fleuve des rêves,
> Son archet à vie presse les fibres
> De l'essence de l'existence,
> Et fait vibrer les cordes du coeur
> Et résonner un écho, un rappel
> De la musique des sphères celestes.

And to the memory of Him, . . .

> Whose youthful Prelude was a journey
> Towards the soul of the Violin,
> The firstfruits of a pilgrim mind
> 'Voyaging through strange seas of thought, alone',
> And whose apt and chosen Postlude ran—
> *'Not on sad Stygian shore, nor in clear sheen*
> *Of far Elysian plains shall we meet those*
> *Among the dead whose pupils we have been,*
> *Nor those great shades whom we have held as foes*
> .   .   .   .
> *Who's right, who's wrong, t'will all be one to us,*
> *We shall not even know that we have met;*
> *Yet meet we shall, and part and meet again*
> *Where dead men meet—on lips of living men.'*
>   (From a Sonnet of Samuel Butler)

Preface and Acknowledgements

WALTER MAYSON, one of the 'heroes' of this book, opened the brief Preface to his work on *Violin Making* by saying: 'I do not like Prefaces.' His brief argument is to the effect that rather than waste time by explaining motives and giving foretastes of the meal to follow, both author and reader should plunge straight into the text. Readers may then draw their own conclusions.

There is much to be said for this approach when writing about an essentially narrowly focused topic such as how to make a violin. I claim a little more indulgence for my own work because the canvas on which the *scenae* which follow are depicted is a forbiddingly large one. I have tried to describe not only Britain's most eminent makers and their work, but the musical, economic, and social context of their activity. These factors include the inspiration given by leading contemporary players, exhibitions of instruments, and the written word, all of which motivated makers and interacted with them. Put another way, I have tried to suggest answers to the type of questions most owners and players of instruments of any age sometimes ask themselves—'I wonder who made this instrument, what the maker's other work is like, why, from the economic point of view, the maker chose to be a violin-maker, who influenced or taught the maker, what sort of prices were charged for instruments like this down the years, and what sort of reputation does the maker have now'—and so on. Others, not necessarily players, may be interested in the progress of the violin family in the British Isles as an aspect of British musical, economic, and social history—a subject, surprisingly not hitherto analysed in any detail. Questions are easily asked. Answers may depend on substantial research into the musical, economic, social, and cultural history of the city or county where the instrument was made and into the maker's working life, often ill recorded.

Some members of the violin-making and dealing fraternity are, perhaps unjustly, regarded by others as having a certain narrowness of vision. How will a book be received which tries to show that there is more to the subject of violin and bow-making than just making violins and bows? There comes to mind an old review of D. H. Lawrence's *Lady Chatterley's Lover* in *Field and Stream*:

This pictorial account of day to day life of an English gamekeeper is full of considerable interest to outdoor minded readers, the apprehending of poachers, ways to control vermin, and other chores and duties of the professional gamekeeper. Unfortunately, one is obliged to wade through many pages of extraneous material in order to discover and savour these highlights on the management of a Midlands shooting estate, and in this reviewer's opinion the book cannot take the place of J. R. Miller's book *Practical Gamekeeping*.

All the present author can hope is that the wider dimensions discussed in this book do help to explain the context of an activity which can easily become too introverted.

When I embarked on this journey it became apparent in terms of the sheer number of people, books, and periodicals to be consulted why no one had tried this approach before. A surprising number of other people, however, realizing that outside the standard dictionaries little of substance had been written on the history of the violin family in Britain, have since told me that some sort of project was on their agenda when there should be time. But in the absence of any real precedents I have simply done the best that I can with the help of a good many friends, experts, and also writers who have gone before. It will, I hope, bring pleasure and, perhaps, even some enlightenment to the many non-specialist enthusiasts that there are known to be world-wide for books about the violin as a musical instrument and its development in one particular country, whether they are players, makers, dealers, collectors, passive enthusiasts, or students of the subject from a more academic perspective. It is also my earnest hope that where deficiencies in knowledge are revealed, or opinions given prove controversial, these matters act as a springboard for further scholarly research. This is how a fuller understanding develops.

For technical reasons, and as will be seen from the chapter headings, the earlier chapters concentrate on the development of the violin and its music in England, particularly London. Chapter 8 then seeks to sketch in the often very dissimilar musical and violin-making situation in Wales, Scotland, and Ireland since the seventeenth century. Thereafter the book deals with the position in the British Isles as a whole. The Directory at the end attempts to be the most comprehensive list possible of professional makers, living and dead, from the four parts of the United Kingdom and also from the Republic of Ireland.

There is just one important point about sources which should be made. On the whole older books about the violin family have been very remiss in failing to give references. Many of these works contain numerous 'facts' or opinions whose authors are unattributed. I have tried to be scrupulous in this respect. If a fact or opinion is thought to be doubtful, at least its source should be apparent. I have also reproduced some quite lengthy passages from some of the 'classical' texts discussed in these pages, partly because they are interesting in what is said and the manner in which it is said by those nearer in time than we are to the matter described; partly also because many of these books are long since out of print, very difficult to find except in specialist libraries, and inordinately expensive if, as rarely happens, they can be spotted in a second-hand or antiquarian bookshop. They are in practice unavailable to the ordinary reader despite their historical interest.

Those who have helped to a greater or lesser extent are too numerous to mention comprehensively, and include many people who have contributed to the Directory of Makers at the end. Over the last two decades I have visited many workshops and attended many auctions—both fora being fertile ground for the exchange of opinions and discussion with practising makers and experts. The following have been exceptionally kind in answering detailed questions and in many cases reading parts of the book and letting me have their comments: John Basford, Hamilton Caswell, Albert Cooper, John Dilworth, Charles Beare and his colleagues, Juliet Barker and her teaching staff at Cambridge, Norman Rosenberg, Professor Cyril Ehrlich (whose published work on the history of the piano and of the music profession showed how it should be done), Andrew Hill—who was most helpful in correcting and amplifying the vital chapter on the Hill family,—Dr D. I. Lloyd, Jeannie Martin, Patricia Naismith, the late Edward Stollar and Philip Scott both of Messrs Phillips, Graham Wells of Messrs Sotheby's, Francois Bignon, John Stagg (bow-maker), Professor Basil Deane, Professor Robin Stowell, the late Stanley Johnson of Redditch, the cellist Bernard Gregor-Smith, and the inextinguishable octogenarian and historian of music, Dr Percy Young. On the Welsh scene I am grateful for help received from Roy Saer (Welsh Folk Museum), and John Teahan (National Museum of Ireland) on the Irish one. Ivor Jones was a source of much hitherto unrecorded information on his astonishing grandfather Edward Heron-Allen (together with Jan Morris and the others mentioned in the discussion of Heron-Allen's life). Daphne Bradley of Tottenham was equally helpful about her grandfather, William Atkinson. Helen Wallace, formerly editor of the *Strad*, has not only been helpful beyond all reasonable limits but provided encouragement where the project began to look impossibly daunting. For such faults as remain, needless to say I take full responsibility and this applies *a fortiori* to opinions expressed.

I am also immensely grateful to Messrs Phillips, Sotheby's, and Christie's, the eminent auctioneers of London, for allowing me access to their splendid photographic archives and permission to reproduce samples. The contribution of Phillips is particularly notable and reflects the interests in and knowledge of Messrs Stoller and Scott for British work over the years. Their enthusiasm and encouragement have been of the greatest value to me. The *Strad* itself deserves particular acknowledgement, not only because of the extent to which I have drawn on its unique repository of illuminating articles over the years but also because of the unfailing co-operation of its staff in the completion of this project. My thanks, too, to the staff of the Oxford University Press, Arts and Reference Division, for their patience, tolerance, and encouragement; the British Academy who made me a personal research grant which was invaluable in getting the project started; the librarians of the Music Library, University of Birmingham, the Bodleian Library,

Oxford, and the Royal College of Music, London, who were all helpful and accommodating; and Mrs Pam Kimmins who did sterling work over some four years in getting the text into something like presentable form, almost taking a maternal interest in it.

I would also like to thank my colleagues in the Faculty of Law for their slightly puzzled tolerance. They will find a little legal history here and there, but particularly in Chapter 11 where the possible criminal liability of such makers as the Fendts and Lotts in the early nineteenth century is discussed. My colleague Peter Cook pointed me in the right direction, for which I am grateful.

It will be inferred from the above that the book took some four years physically to write, but the gestation was far longer than this. The writing was preceded by many years of looking at instruments, collecting and playing a few of them, reading, talking, learning the elements of making, and listening to experts' opinions on the British violin-making scene. This took, in all, some fifteen years. When the time came to write the book the priorities of a demanding job in a dissimilar area made it necessary to work at weekends and late into the small hours. I hope the smoke of midnight oil is not too apparent. But the real point is that I am most grateful to all my family for living with this for so long and for their indulgence and unfailing support.

B. W. H.

Faculty of Law,
University of Birmingham,
B15 2TT, UK
St George's Day, 1994

Contents

List of Plates in Text xiv

1. THE INTRODUCTION OF THE VIOLIN FAMILY INTO ENGLAND: MUSICAL AND HISTORICAL CONTEXT   1
Artistry and Acoustic Design 1 · *The Violin World* 2 · *The Significance of Demand and Supply* 3 · *A Note on Sources* 3 · *The Problem of Tone: Old Versus New* 5 · *Pre-Restoration String Music and Musicians* 7 · *Origins of the Violin Family* 8 · *Early Bowed Instruments of the Violin Type* 10 · *Introduction of the Violin into England* 12 · *The Musical Scene at the Restoration* 17 · *The Promotion of Chamber Music* 20 · *String Music and Music Publishing* 22 · *Musical Education* 23 · *The Meeting of Demand for Stringed Instruments in England* 26 · *The Viola, Cello, and Double Bass in England* 29 · *The Cello* 32 · *The Double Bass* 34

2. CONSTRUCTION METHODS, MATERIALS, AND TECHNIQUES OF THE OLD ENGLISH MAKERS   37
Introduction 37 · *The Body* 38 · *Scroll and Button* 40 · *Other Distinguishing Features of Older Instruments* 42 · *Varnish* 44 · *Technical Constituents* 46 · *Varnish and English Violin-Makers* 48 · *Wood* 52 · *Purfling* 55 · *Accessories* 56 · *Strings* 60 · *Tools* 61 · *Tone* 61 · *Conversion from Baroque to 'Romantic' Violin* 62

3. ENGLISH VIOLIN-MAKERS OF THE SEVENTEENTH CENTURY AND THEIR DISTINGUISHING FEATURES   66
Geography and History 66 · *John Bunyan's Violin* 70 · *Leading Seventeenth-Century London Violin-Makers* 72 · *Early English Makers* 74 · *Authenticity Problems* 80

4. THE ECONOMIC AND SOCIAL ORGANIZATION OF VIOLIN-MAKING AND RETAILING IN ENGLAND   82
The Medieval Tradition 82 · *The Apprenticeship System* 84 · *Violin Factories* 85 · *The Piano in England: A Comparison* 87 · *Family Craft Businesses* 88 · *Retailers and Outworkers* 89 · *Merlin: The Ingenious Mechanick* 91 · *Other Retailers* 94

5. ENGLISH MUSIC AND MAKERS IN THE EIGHTEENTH CENTURY   95
Musical Developments 95 · *A Group of Early Eighteenth-Century Violin-Makers* 100 · *Barak Norman and Nathaniel Cross* 100 · *John and Joseph Hare* 105 · *John*

Barrett 106 · William Pryor 107 · Daniel Parker 108 · Other Eighteenth-Century Makers in England 113 · Unscrupulous Attributions 119

6. Prices and Economic Background to English Violin-Making from 1750   121

Why the Economic Background is Important 121 · *The Domestic Market* 122 · *The Impoverished Players* 124 · *The French Scene* 124 · *The German Scene* 125 · *The Effect of Competition* 126 · *Free Trade* 126 · *Cheap 'Tools'* 127 · *Cheap Musical Instruments* 128 · *The Struggle to Compete* 129 · *Prices* 129 · *Comparing Prices* 132

7. The Development of the Demand for Strings in England from 1760 to the Present   136

Handel's Legacies 136 · *Salomon's Enterprises* 138 · *The Cello and its Players* 139 · *Forster's 'Royal George'* 140 · *Other Cello Patrons and Players* 141 · *Viotti and the Stradivari Cause* 142 · *Paganini and his Guarneri* 143 · *The Bow* 146 · *Later Developments in the English Musical Scene* 146 · *Henry Hill and his Circle* 149 · *Money and Numbers* 152 · *J. T. Carrodus* 154 · *Proselytizers and Institutions* 155 · *Schools and Strings* 156 · *Music of the People* 159 · *Producing the Players* 160 · *Women and the Violin* 160 · *The Provincial Colleges* 162 · *Enthusiasm and Poverty* 162 · *Modern Times* 163

8. The Violin and its Votaries in Wales, Scotland, and Ireland   165

Introduction 165 · *Wales* 166 · *Scottish Violin-Makers: Cultural Background* 172 · *Scottish Violin Writers* 177 · *Ireland* 182 · *Thomas Perry* 183

9. The Hills and the Development of the Violin and Bow Industry   186

The Stainer Preference 186 · *Hart's View of the Development of English Taste* 186 · *The Panormo Influence* 188 · *The Work of the Hill Family* 189 · *Haweis's Portrait of William Ebsworth Hill* 192 · *The Sons of William Ebsworth* 193 · *The Later Hills* 195 · *English Bow-Making and the Hill Influence* 199 · *The Tubbs Connection* 201 · *Later Hill Bow-Making* 204 · *Physical Identification* 204 · *The Retford Collection* 208 · *Other English Bow-Makers* 208 · *Restoration Work and Dealing* 208 · *The Export Trade* 211

10. Eminent Dealers, Collectors, and Connoisseurs   215

The London Dealing Fraternity 215 · *Collectors* 217 · *The Gillott Collection* 219

11. The Great Copyists of Nineteenth-Century London   223

The Stradivari Influence 223 · *The Fendts* 224 · *The Lotts* 224 · *Forgery and the Criminal Law* 227 · *Retrospect* 230

12. Some Leading Lights in the Victorian Gloom 232
Was there a Dark Age? 232 · *Two Victorian Makers of the North Country* 234 · *The Life and Fortunes of Walter Mayson* 237 · *William Atkinson* 245 · *Violin-Makers: Saints or Sinners?* 250

13. Great Exhibitions and Victorian Values 252
Nineteenth-Century Developments 252 · *Motivating Factors* 255 · *Technical Instruction* 255 · *The Great Exhibitions* 256 · *Collecting British Violins* 261

14. The Power of the Pen: Heron-Allen and his Legacies 265
Working in a Vacuum 265 · *Periodical Literature* 265 · *Earlier Books* 266 · *A Violin-Makers' 'Bible'* 269 · *The Hidden Heron-Allen* 271 · *From Fiddles to Fossils and Fantasy: Assessing Heron-Allen's Achievements* 279 · *Tailnote to Heron-Allen* 280 · *Towry Piper* 280 · *William Meredith Morris and William C. Honeyman* 281 · *William Henley* 281

15. The Twentieth Century: Prospect and Retrospect 284
Introduction 284 · *Amateur or Professional?* 285 · *The Example of James Parkinson* 286 · *The Early Twentieth Century* 287 · *The Judgements of Frank Thistleton* 288 · *A British Tour* 291 · *Victor Fidicularum?* 292 · *George Wulme-Hudson* 292 · *T. E. Hesketh* 293 · *John Owen* 295 · *Arthur Richardson* 295 · *Alfred Vincent* 295 · *The Challenge from the Continent* 296 · *How to 'Cheat'* 298 · *The Contemporary Scene* 299 · *Retrospect and Prospect* 301 · *Survey of English Instruments used in Professional Orchestras in Britain* 303

London Map 1800 — 308

Appendix 1: A Directory of Violin- and Bow-Makers in the British Isles — 310

Appendix 2: Facsimile Labels — 407

Explanatory Notes to Plates — 412
Select Bibliography — 421
Index — 427

List of Plates in Text

Plates appear between pages 240 and 241

1. 'Tools for Violin Makers' (Ernest Kohler & Son, Edinburgh, leaflet, *c.*1900).
2. Violin Wood and Fittings' catalogue (Ernest Kohler & Sons, Edinburgh, leaflet, *c.*1900).
3. Frontispiece from catalogue of W. E. Hill and Sons (*c.*1920).
4. John Askew
5. William Atkinson
6. J. W. Briggs
7. Georges Chanot
8. George Craske, from a watercolour by John H. Leatherbrow, 1876 (reproduced by courtesy of Phillips, London).
9. J. J. Gilbert
10. George Hart
11. Thomas Earle Hesketh
12. William Ebsworth Hill
13. Walter Mayson
14. John W. Owen
15. H. H. Saby, with his Fendt bass
16. Alex Smillie
17. James Tubbs
18. Edward Withers
19. Edward Heron-Allen, FRS, 1928 (from a painting by Hardman).
20. W. Meredith Morris
21. Towry Piper
22. The Musical Union Artists of the 1851 Season.
23. J. T. Carrodus
24. Marie Hall
25. Beatrice Harrison
26. Albert Sammons

27. John Bunyan's violin (reproduced by courtesy of the Trustees of Bunyan Meeting, Bedford).
28. Head of William Forster's 'Royal George' cello (reproduced in full on front cover).
29. B. S. Fendt, decorated cello head, c.1840.
30. Front, side, and back of one of the two known violins made by Edward Heron-Allen when a pupil of Georges Chanot in London, c.1886, Strad model (reproduced by courtesy of Pat Naismith, London Guildhall University).

Chapter One

❦ *The Introduction of the Violin Family into England: Musical and Historical Context*

Artistry and Acoustic Design — The Violin World — The Significance of Demand and Supply — A Note on Sources — The Problem of Tone: Old Versus New — Pre-Restoration String Music and Musicians — Origins of the Violin Family — Early Bowed Instruments of the Violin Type — Introduction of the Violin into England — The Musical Scene at the Restoration — The Promotion of Chamber Music — String Music and Music Publishing — Musical Education — The Meeting of Demand for Stringed Instruments in England — The Viola, Cello, and Double Bass in England

Artistry and Acoustic Design

MODERN biologists assert that anything which can be said to have been 'designed' is either living, has lived, or is an artefact created by a member of one of those two classes. Blake spoke of the 'fearful symmetry' of the 'Tyger! Tyger! burning bright'. The bodies and organs of living creatures have this quality of symmetry. But the creativity of man is unique in the animal kingdom. Tools were his first invention. Musical instruments followed at a surprisingly early stage. They were, and are, an advanced test of man's ability to design for the dual purpose of producing an efficient acoustic artefact which is also a pleasure to look upon—and that pleasure is tied in closely to its symmetry. The basis of this symmetry as regards the violin, and its relationship to Greek architectural principles (involving the 'golden section' and other rules of proportion), are graphically explained by Kevin Coates in *Geometry, Proportion and the Art of Lutherie* (Oxford, 1985).

Many would consider the violin, in all its apparent simplicity, as the most potentially beautiful of all these dual-purpose challenges to the designer—'potentially' because it is cruelly difficult to produce an instrument which is both ultra-efficient acoustically and entirely satisfactory aesthetically when examined by the most critical eye. It is the achievement of this dual purpose which has been the motivating factor in the lives of many violin-makers of Europe and its former colonies and dominions, often leading them to a life of comparative poverty.

The search for the Holy Grail of the perfect violin, or even for something to match the perfection achieved in eighteenth-century Italy, has proved elusive. But, as in the story of *Turandot*, there never seems to be a lack of candidates prepared to try their luck at considerable risk, and violin-making in England is no exception to this noble propensity amongst suitably talented artistic people. Admittedly, the necessity of making at least something of a living has in England, as elsewhere, led to the periodic debasement of standards of both workmanship and honesty, but many a maker has given testimony that the challenge and innate satisfaction to be derived from making a fine instrument or bow more than counterbalance the natural tendency to maximize profits at the expense of standards. It is this feature which makes it such an elevating and interesting task to try to analyse the social, cultural, and economic background to the work of individuals who are often eccentric, sometimes very talented, but seldom dull.

The Violin World

As the editor of any violin periodical soon finds out, the 'violin world' consists of many different constituencies. There are, for instance, professional players, professional teachers, makers, dealers, collectors, and addicted listeners. The musical side of the instrument will be pre-eminent for some. For others the craftsmanship side will be the exclusive preoccupation. Some makers despise dealers, thinking of them as parasites, perhaps, or rag-and-bone men in smart suits. A maker may have little interest in or knowledge of old instruments; dealers may have little or no experience of the process of making and be largely uninterested in new instruments.

Yet all these categories of votary need one another. They have an economic function as well as a social one. Without new violins the stock would not be replenished. New violins will sooner or later come on to the market, and the dealer, as the intermediary, will have a powerful say in their valuation and marketing. The fact that a new violin can be sold to its first owner for a price which reflects the maker's outlay in (primarily) time and (secondarily) materials is an acknowledgement of the achievement of dealers in helping to establish the market for stringed instruments of all ages and antecedents. Even the player cannot be considered the final link in the chain because professional players need audiences from whom the resource will come to enable the player to invest in and live by his or her instrument in the first place.

The Significance of Demand and Supply

At first glance a study of makers of the violin family in the British Isles might appear to be comparatively straightforward. There already exists a number of directories either wholly or partially devoted to makers of the British Violin School, and full reference to their sometimes conflicting and often obviously derivative views will be made later on in this book. From these sources may be deduced brief biographical details of the makers and features of some of their instruments. But a closer scrutiny reveals a good many gaps in existing knowledge. In any modern study the reader deserves more than simple biographical details and a very often subjective account of the characteristics of makers' instruments. We need to know the answer to the basic question: *what was the demand* for bowed string instruments made locally? For without *demand* there can be no commercial *supply*. In turn, demand has to be deduced (in the absence of firmer economic data) from the likely requirements of players at any particular time. This in turn prompts us to ask: who were the players and how were they educated and trained? For what forces did the composers being played at any particular time write their music? And where did those players go to purchase their instruments? In what circumstances did they prefer to buy locally rather than to buy from makers on the continent of Europe—particularly Italy? What prices would these makers have been able to charge in the light of market conditions at any particular time?

It must be emphasized that there is virtually no existing published account of most of the answers to these questions. Indeed, owing to the passage of time, some of the questions can only be answered in a hypothetical way—but nevertheless some attempt must be made to do so. This is why the early parts of this book concentrate on the *context* in which music for the violin family was written and performed. It is from this context that we can deduce the reasons why stringed instrument making in England is so variable and fascinating an art.

A Note on Sources

It is a regrettable feature of almost all of the 'directories' (details of which appear in the Directory) or quasi-historical accounts of violin-makers that the authors do not reveal their sources. Sandys and Forster are better than most and the unassuming Eliza Cecelia Stainer, the daughter of Sir John Stainer, whose *Dictionary of Violin Makers* was compiled in Oxford and completed in 1896, is refreshingly honest: 'It was, of course, necessary that this small work should largely depend on the fruits of other people's labours, as personal research was out of the question.' But the latter author both corresponded with contemporary violin-makers, 'thereby ensuring accuracy', and fully acknowledged the work of Vidal, Hart, Coutagne, Berenzi, Hill, and others. The book is also preceded by a respectable bibliography. More modern dictionaries such as Vannes and Henley generally give no indication of the source of their information, though this can sometimes be traced without too much difficulty from one to the other! W. Meredith Morris's *British Violin Makers* (editions of 1904 and 1920) bears the stamp of careful personal investigation, though since it was written perspectives have changed and reputations have either died or been enhanced. Unique in terms of scholarship is the third volume of von Lütgendorff's work on *Die Geigen- und Lautenmacher* by Thomas Drescher (1990), which is scrupulous in citing sources both from books and periodical literature.

A serious 'health warning' should be given about these very intensively used but in the main essentially unscholarly productions. A writer who simply copies some other source, often itself second- or third-hand, is just as likely to perpetuate mythology as truth. Unless a modern scholar can retrace the steps of the author being studied, the original source may never be found and, in the world of violin-makers, may become entirely untraceable. In any event, the major subject-matter of these dictionaries is not really 'violin-makers' as such; it is *the fruits of their labour*. And if their instruments have been correctly identified the primary evidence needed for an assessment of the maker's contribution to the art of lutherie is readily to hand.

As a recent example of the general point, Albert Cooper, in his monograph on the Salisbury maker Benjamin Banks,[1] has established, by careful examination of the record of trade apprenticeships in the Public Record Office, that the widely held belief that Benjamin Banks served an apprenticeship under Peter Wamsley (sometimes 'Walmsley') or another London maker is erroneous.[2] Banks was in fact the apprentice of William Huttoft, musical instrument maker of New Sarum, from 1741 for seven years. Yet this myth had become almost biblical apparently for no better reason than the fact that Wamsley's maturity coincides with Banks's youth.

Although, as a matter of record, the standard dictionaries have been proved wrong on this point, there may, in fairness, be another side to the question. Huttoft was not a violin-maker. There are some similarities of style between Wamsley and Banks. Despite the apprenticeship arrangement in Salisbury, Banks may have spent some time in Wamsley's workshop in his early years. He must have been taught the craft somewhere. But in this situation authors should at least discriminate between fact and speculation, however informed the latter may be.

---

[1] *Benjamin Banks, The Salisbury Violin Maker* (Haslemere, 1989).

[2] See e.g. W. Henley, *Universal Dictionary of Violin and Bow Makers*, 2nd edn. (Brighton, 1973), 75: 'Studied the art of Peter Wamsley in London.'

So, although the present author must disclaim with other authors, such as Miss C. Stainer, any pretence of having reinvestigated every relevant biographical detail, an attempt has been made to make the source of each fact or opinion or quotation of any importance clear, and the value of that source can be assessed by the reader. Meanwhile none of the received wisdom on British makers should be taken on trust. As the Directory contained in this book shows, and the main text frequently suggests, fine instruments have been made by makers traditionally meriting a low rating and the output of many makers is very variable. It was commonplace to charge differentially according to quality of materials and workmanship. The most objective barometer of a maker's overall reputation is prices obtained at auction, and in the Directory this information is so far as possible indicated. Auctions are not infallible as regards correct identification and mistakes can still be made.[3] But taken overall, they reflect informed demand for a particular maker's products.

The Problem of Tone: Old Versus New

To some extent the quality of tone is necessarily a subjective matter. But the fact that one violin when played by a competent soloist is readily audible over a full orchestra whereas another one is not is beyond argument. Numerous attempts have been made and described to differentiate between old and new, good and not so good. For example, Paolo Peterlongo in *The Violin: Its Physical and Acoustic Principles* deals at some length with the acoustical evaluation of violins. As the author comments: 'The present writer has more than once witnessed the enthusiasm of distinguished performers for a modern instrument which sounded superb in the restricted space of a workshop. Great was their disappointment when they heard the same instrument in a large hall where numerous experiments were carried out with the help of a variety of players. Surprises of this kind are particularly unwelcome when a deal over an instrument has already been concluded.'[4] His work includes the results of experiments showing the average frequency curves (mean acoustical intensity) of six good classic violins compared to six good modern violins and six average modern violins. These experiments show the superiority of the classical Italian violins which evinced a good intensity of sound with a high-quality fundamental timbre. A 1717 Stradivari was found to have a peak resonance at around 400 Hz, corresponding to the natural resonant frequency of the volume of air in the resonance chamber. The sonority of old violins in the lower frequencies

---

[3] See, for example, Anne Inglis, 'Profile of Roger Hargrave', *Strad* (June 1992), 532–7. Roger Hargrave himself found his own copy of a Joseph Guarneri filius Andreae advertised for sale as genuine in a Viennese auction-house in March 1992. It is understood that brands had been removed and that the instrument was accompanied by a spurious certificate.

[4] (London, 1979), 95. See also Bernard Richardson, 'The Physics of the Violin' in Robin Stowell, (ed.), *The Cambridge Companion to the Violin* (Cambridge, 1992), ch. 2.

ensures that they possess the sound and the characteristic timbre associated with classic Italian instruments. In the higher frequencies they are found to have good penetrative power without too much wastage of sound emitted in phase opposition. Another feature observed was that in double-stopping the higher note always tends to dominate the lower one in modern violins, whereas with old violins the ear perceives a more balanced evenness between all four strings.

Nevertheless, it must be added in fairness that a well-made new violin is often infinitely preferable to an indifferent old one. And Peterlongo's thesis has been challenged, one recent writer arguing that the high reputation of old Italian violins is not a matter of physics or psycho-acoustics but a mixture of psychology and shrewd commercial marketing. 'The sound of a good violin does not depend on who made it, or whether it is old or new, but rather on how it is played.'[5]

We find a curious pre-echo of the preference of many musicians for older violins given by Thomas Mace in his delightfully idiosyncratic book *Musick's Monument* (London, 1676) conveying advice about acquiring a viol:

Your best provision, (and most compleat) will be, a Good Chest of Viols; six in number; viz. Two Basses, two Tenors, and two Trebles: All truly and Proportionably suited. Of such, there are no better in the world, than those of Aldred, Jay, Smith, (yet the Highest in Esteem are) Bolles and Ross (one Bass of Bolles's I have known valued at a hundred pounds). These were Old; but we have now, very excellent good Workmen, who (no doubt) can work as well as those, if they be so well paid for their work, as they were; yet we chiefly value Old Instruments before new; for by experience, they are found to be by far the best.'[6]

Mace's statement is valuable not only for its demonstration of the antiquity of the belief in the virtues of older instruments, but because of the listing of English viol-makers who were considered by the, perhaps partial, author to be worthy of note. Luckily there are beautiful surviving examples of some of the old viol-makers' work, particularly the bass viols by or attributed to John Rose (spelled 'Ross' by Mace), which are in the Hill Collection in the Ashmolean Museum in Oxford. One of these (*c.*1600) has double-purfled edges, with back and ribs of rosewood. The intricate purfled inlay of tulip-wood on the back is a very English feature, often used in subsequent violin-making in the next two centuries to add interest to relatively unfigured wood. The pegbox is intricately carved. This and other instruments surviving from this period[7] are strong evidence of the truth of the claim that English instruments were amongst the finest and most sought-after in Europe.

---

[5] W. Güth, 'The Physics of Violins, Ancient and Modern', *Strad* (Aug. 1991), 688.

[6] pp. 245–6. Jean Rousseau (of Paris) also makes it clear in his *Traité de la Viole* (Paris, 1687) how esteemed in Europe English makers of viols were. Ian Woodfield in 'the Viol in 16th-Century England', ch. 6 of his *The Early History of the Viol* (Cambridge, 1984), points out that John Rose sen. received the high price of 40s. for a viol of 'the finest sort' in 1552 (226).

[7] The collection of 17th-cent. viols in the Victoria and Albert Museum, London, includes examples by Rose and Henry Jaye (1667).

There is another reason why Mace's opinion is far from being of purely antiquarian significance. It was because the market has always favoured old instruments that many makers have been tempted to 'antique' their anonymous instruments so that they can be passed off (either to the purchaser or by the purchaser) more easily as having age and perhaps pedigree. As will be seen, John Lott, one of England's finest makers, was an adherent to this view. Activity in the field of false labelling has been with us since the earliest days of commercial dealings in the violin family and is certainly still with us today.[8] There remains a delicate line, however, between a fine facsimile which never pretends to be anything else and the reproduction designed to defraud.

Pre-Restoration String Music and Musicians

Thomas Mace's statement also serves to remind us that, although this present study formally starts just before the Restoration of Charles II in 1660, there is an important 'prehistory' of bowed string music in England. An analysis of this is beyond the scope of this work but it is a historical fact that the Tudor monarchs, particularly Henry VIII and Elizabeth I, were skilled and appreciative musicians whose courts created a highly sympathetic environment for the performance of all types of music. Polyphonic vocal music from the time of Thomas Tallis to the death of William Byrd (a period spanning, say, 1500 to 1623) represented a golden age in English musical history. Although Byrd was a master of a cappella music for voices, both he and Orlando Gibbons used viols instead of (or sometimes with) the organ as an accompaniment to some of their work.[9] In the early part of the seventeenth century Thomas Weelkes brought out his 'Madrigals of Five and Six parts, apt for the Viols and Voices', Dowland his 'Songs or Ayres', with tablature for the lute or orphorion, with the viola da gamba, and Morley his 'First Booke of Ayres or Little Short Songs to sing and play to the Lute with the Bass-Violl' (1600). Charles I was a patron of music and apparently a fine player on the bass viol, especially in 'those incomparable Fancies of Mr. Coperario to the organ'—Charles being a pupil of Coperario, (sometimes 'Coprario') the Italianized name of one John Cooper who himself excelled as a performer on the viol da gamba. Charles maintained a band in 1625 consisting of over forty players, eleven of whom are described as 'Musicians for the Violins'.[10] One of the later acts of Charles I

---

[8] See Ch. 11 and the Brian W. Harvey, *Violin Fraud: Deception, Forgery, Theft, and the Law* (Oxford, 1992). Mace refers to 17th-cent. false labelling of 16th-cent. lutes.

[9] See Edmund H. Fellowes, *English Cathedral Music*, 5th edn., ed. J. A. Westrup (London, 1969) 71, 74, 163.

[10] Peter Holman, *Four and Twenty Fiddlers* (Oxford, 1993) 229; William Sandys and Simon Andrew Forster, *The History of the Violin and other Instruments played on with the Bow from the Remotest Times to the Present* (London, 1864) 138.

was to grant a charter to Nicholas Lanier and others so as to incorporate them into the style of 'Marshall Wardens and Cominalty of the Arte and Science of Musick in Westminster, in the County of Middlesex', giving them many privileges.[11]

During this period there is abundant evidence of great activity as regards the use of bowed stringed instruments, not only in music for the court and church but also, of course, for dancing purposes. Indeed, it was the indelible association of stringed instruments, particularly 'the fiddle', with both the devil and dancing, that led to the abandonment of string music for ecclesiastical purposes in the Commonwealth period following the execution of Charles I.[12] But as twentieth-century scholars have shown, the two decades prior to the Restoration, although imbued with the deadening spirit of Puritanism, to some extent pushed the performance of music 'underground' and in these years chamber music continued to thrive.[13] Oliver Cromwell himself is reputed to have had a liking for music and Colonel Hutchinson is said to have enjoyed all sorts of music and to have given his children the kind of education which included 'music, dancing, and all other qualities befitting their father's house'.[14] And the eminent publisher John Playford (1623–86), a Norwich-born stationer with a business in London, published in 1651 *The English Dancing Master*, which itself suggests that even at this time people were not averse to music as a form of recreation.

Origins of the Violin Family

There has been a great deal of scholarly writing about the time and place of the birth of the violin. It seems likely that in the early part of the sixteenth century experimentation took place with the shape of bowed stringed instruments which could be held against the upper part of the body and were reasonably portable. Most experts now accept that the first recognizable violins emanated from northern Italy, probably Brescia. Credit is traditionally given to Gasparo da Salò as the founding father of the instrument (in its present recognizable form) between the years 1550 and 1610, though more modern research antedates its birth to about 1530, judging by contemporary literary references and pictures.[15] Gasparo da Salò was certainly an accomplished maker of viols and, according to Hart,[16] 'in his works may be traced the gradual development of the system upon which his followers

---

[11] Sandys and Forster, *History*, 140.
[12] See the discussion of John Bunyan's fiddle in Ch. 3.
[13] See Percy A. Scholes, *The Puritans and Music* (London, 1934).
[14] See E. D. Mackerness, *A Social History of English Music* (London, 1964), 80, citing Lucy Hutchinson, *Memoirs of the life of Colonel Hutchinson*, 292.
[15] David Boyden, writing in *The Violin Family* (The New Grove Musical Instruments Series; London, 1989), ch. 1. See also George Hart, *The Violin: Famous Makers and their Imitators* (London, 1885), 157; and John, Dilworth, 'The Violin and Bow: Origins and Development', in Stowell (ed.), *Cambridge Companion* 14–15.
[16] *The Violin: Famous Makers*, 158–9.

built their reputation, viz, a well-defined model, excellent materials, and choice of varnish. It is to be regretted that his immediate followers, with the exception of Paolo Maggini, departed from the path so successfully trodden by this great pioneer.' Hart also credits Gasparo da Salò with having commenced with a high-modelled form 'and gradually, as experience taught, lowered it'.

By the middle of the sixteenth century, the focus shifts from Brescia to Cremona where the first significant member of the Amati family, Andrea, had set up his workshop. Andrea Amati's most famous products were the set of (reputedly) thirty-eight violins (twelve large- and twelve small-patterned), six violas, and eight cellos made for Charles IX, which, Hart informs us,[17] 'were kept in the Chapel Royal, Versailles, until October 1790, when they disappeared. These were probably the finest instruments of Andrea Amati. On the backs were painted the Arms of France and other devices with a motto, "Pietate et Justitia".'[18] The date of these instruments is given by Hart as 1572, though the fine specimen at present on display in the collection at the Town Hall at Cremona is dated 1566, though not by the maker. This instrument bears on its back traces of the original gold coat of arms of the Kings of France and on its ribs the above-quoted motto. It is described in the museum's literature as having 'a strong and brilliant voice, and stands as a very rare example since it is one of the only five surviving ones of the group of historical instruments proving the great art of this master'. (The instrument does not in fact have an original label but is described as 'Authenticated and signed by the restorer Nicholas Lupot'.)

There are two further examples from this series in the Hill Collection, Ashmolean Museum, Oxford. The violin with a body-length of only $13^{7}/_{16}$ in. (342 mm), is dated 1564 and the very large viola (body-length $18^{1}/_{2}$ in., 470 mm) is dated 1574.[19] Another example is in the City Museum of Carlisle, also of 1574. The English maker Bernard Simon Fendt made a fine copy of a cello from this set in about 1830, which was sold in the London sale-rooms in 1991. This is illustrated in Plate C.

Although there is still some disagreement, the origin of the violin is thought to be from the lira da braccio, the rebec, and the fiddle, rather than the viol family which is regarded as a separate and distinct development. 'We can only say with certainty that by about 1550 the four-string ("true") violin must have been a familiar part of the European musical scene, since the instrument and its tuning were described in detail by Philibert Jambe de Fer in his *Epitome Musical* (Lyons), 1556.'[20]

[17] Ibid. 77.
[18] See also Boyden in *Violin Family*, 21.
[19] David D. Boyden, *Catalogue of The Hill Collection of Musical Instruments in the Ashmolean Museum, Oxford* (London, 1969), 17, 18.

[20] Dominic Gill (ed.), *The Book of the Violin* (1984), 15. See also John Dilworth in Stowell (ed.), *Cambridge Companion* 5–8 and the accompanying illustrations; and the survey in Agnes Kory, 'A Wider Role for the Tenor Violin', *Galpin Society Journal*, 47 (1994), 123.

Probably the key factor in the development of the design and structure of the modern violin family was the simple fact that the old viols could not supply sufficient volume of tone to compete with a well-trained choir or to fill a large building such as a cathedral, church, or theatre. The search for a full and penetrating tone must have been in the forefront of the minds of the early designers of the instruments from Brescia and then Cremona and Venice (for example the Linarolo family) to answer the contemporary demand from the royal courts of Europe and the Venetian churches. Exactly the same problem must have occurred in England where after 1660 the need increasingly was for orchestras in the cathedrals and theatres which could provide a convincing accompaniment and context to performance of anthems and operas by trained singers. The human voice cannot have varied much over the centuries in terms of tone and intensity. It provides a ready and unchanging measure of the volume and intensity of sound which needs at least to be matched by an economic number of string players.

Early Bowed Instruments of the Violin Type

The ancestry of the violin is a topic which is separate and distinct from a study of musical instrument makers of the seventeenth century. Makers obviously concentrated on producing what instruments were in demand, and in the context of bowed string instruments in London in the mid-1600s these were viols and violins. But owing to the confusion on the subject of ancestry a word of explanation may be helpful.

There are many representations in the medieval wood carvings of English church and cathedral pews and in roof bosses of figures playing instruments often of a guitar-like shape and held against the body (i.e. the chest or collar-bone) as distinct from being straddled by the legs or resting on the lap. Some of these have been classified indiscriminately as 'viols'—for example by Sandys and Forster.[21] By the sixteenth century there are a number of references to 'fiddles' in the literature of the period. An example occurs in *Gammer Gurton's Needle* (c.1551), where Diccon says:

> Into the town will I, my Frendes to vysit there,
> And hether straight again to see th' end of this gere;
> In the meantime, felowes, pype up your fiddles, I say take them
> And let your frendes here such mirth as ye can make them.[22]

[21] *History*, ch. 5, which reproduces many examples. An easily accessible one, formerly the constant companion of the author, will be seen carved on the pew adjacent to the Decani Bass Stall in Worcester Cathedral, presumably the one reproduced by Sandys and Forster on p. 29. See also Holman, *Four and Twenty*, ch. 1.

[22] Cited in Sandys and Forster, *History*, 106.

Sandys and Forster remind us that by the seventeenth century a company of fiddlers was accorded the disparaging, if evocative, collective noun 'a noise'. In Marston's *The Dutch Courtezan* the following dialogue ensues: 'O Wife! O, Jacke how does thy mother? Is there any fidlers in the house?' *Mrs Mul*: 'Yes, Mr. Creake's Noyse.' *Mul*: 'Bid 'em play, Laugh, make merry.'[23]

Representations of fiddles with between three and six strings, variously named by early writers fidel, fideile, viddle, viele, vielle, viula, etc. and often show features in common with the rebec and Renaissance fiddle, are plentiful.[24] It was probably the need for easy portability combined with better acoustic penetration for dancing and minstrelsy purposes that led to an instrument that was tonally bright, and physically light, small, and shallow enough to be held easily against the breastbone, or even tucked under the chin.

Structurally the *lira da braccio* (held in the arm), evolving from the fifteenth-century fiddle, whilst being distinct from the violin in having two 'sympathetic' strings running off the fingerboard, as well as five or so stopped strings, resembles the violin in having an arched back, an outline not too dissimilar to the violin, normally overlapping edges, 'f' rather than 'C' soundholes, and a soundpost. A good example can be seen in the Ashmolean Museum in Oxford in the Hill Collection, made in Venice, *c*.1525.

The viol family, strictly so-called, had a much earlier birth-date than the violin (probably as a bowed guitar-like instrument in Valencia, *c*.1450, according to modern scholars) but evolved separately; it is the rebec, the fiddle and the lira da braccio that are the more direct ancestors of the violin family; alternatively the lira da braccio may have developed contemporaneously with the violin. The subject is complicated by the confusion between the French word *violon* (= violin) with Italian *violoni* (= viols). Later terminology became stabilized as *violin* (England), *violino* (Italy), *violon* (France), *Violine* or *Geige* (Germany). The German expression for viola, *bratsche*, appears to derive from the Italian *viola da braccio* or 'arm viola'. The 'crwth' or 'crouth' associated particularly with Wales is known also as the 'croud' or fiddle, and there are many references to 'crouds' in English, Welsh, and Scottish literature of the sixteenth and seventeenth centuries (and occasionally earlier).[25]

---

[23] Ibid. 133.

[24] See the illustrations in Mary Remnant, *English Bowed Instruments from Anglo-Saxon to Tudor Times* (Oxford, 1986) and the same author's *Musical Instruments: An Illustrated History* (London, 1989), ch. 2; also in Anthony Baines (ed.), *Musical Instruments Through The Ages* (Harmondsworth, 1961), 112;) id., *The Oxford Companion to Musical Instruments* (Oxford, 1992), esp. under 'Fiddle', 109–10; and David Rubio, 'The Anatomy of the Violin', in Gill (ed.), *The Book of the Violin*, particularly the 'family tree', 22–3. Holman makes the bold statement that an alarming number of old instruments on which violin evolutionary theory is based are turning out to be forgeries (*Four and Twenty*, 1). This is certainly the verified position in a few cases; see L. Libin, 'Early Violins: Problems and Issues', *Early Music*, 19 (1991), 5–6.

[25] See the examples cited by Sandys and Forster, *History*, 30–1 and in Remnant, *English Bowed Instruments*. The crwth is discussed in more detail in Ch. 8.

Introduction of the Violin into England

Although by the middle of the sixteenth century the violin, viola, and bass were well established in France and Italy, it is now necessary to look for evidence as to when these instruments were introduced in England. Both nineteenth-century writers on this topic and modern scholars[26] have identified a number of references apparently to 'violins' (often 'vyolens'), both in estate inventories and in literature, including dramatic productions of the period such as *Gammer Gurton's Needle* already mentioned. One of the best-known is the direction of the commencement of the dumb show to the first act of the early tragedy *Gorboduc* (1561). This states: 'Firste the musicke of Violenze began to play, duryng whiche came in uppon the Stage sixe wilde men clothed in leaves.' Raynor remarks that this play was presented in the Inns of Court as part of the Christmas celebrations of 1561–2: 'Whether the authors meant violins, instruments at that time very new to English music, or viols, is not clear; violins were rare, but a wealthy audience like that to which Gorboduc was first acted might well have been able to afford violinists.'[27] The position is complicated by the existence of arm-held 'fiddles' and other rebec-type instruments played with a bow and having some of the features but none of the refinement of the genuine violin.

The conventional view is that almost all the native compositions for, or requiring accompaniment, by strings in England during the sixteenth and early seventeenth centuries were written for viols, including the treble viol. Interesting exceptions to this are Dowland's *Lacrimae or Seaven Teares figured in seaven passionate Pavans* (1605), for 'lutes, viols or violons', and Anthony Holborne's *Pavans . . . for Viols, Violins or other Musicale Winde Instruments*.[28] Thurston Dart has described a manuscript from a similar date which includes 'Fancyes | of 2 & 3 parts to ye organ | of Mr. Gibbons, and Mr. Coperario | with ye viol and violin too ye organ' and suggests that from about 1612 the combination of two violins, bass viol, and chamber organ was the one Orlando Gibbons and his contemporaries had in mind for court performances.[29] Peter Holman in his *Four and Twenty Fiddlers* exhaustively analyses the composition of early string consorts, often formed at court from immigrant musicians, and sees evidence from the music for these, and from numerous cited archival materials, of the much more extensive use of the violin than has hitherto been suspected.

---

[26] See particularly Sandys and Forster, *History*, ch. 8, and Holman, *Four and Twenty*.

[27] See Henry Raynor, *A Social History of Music* (London, 1972), 149–50.

[28] 'Other' here must mean 'otherwise'—see Ernest Walker, *A History of Music in England*, 3rd edn. by J. A. Westrup (Oxford, 1952), 86.

[29] 'Purcell and Bull', *Musical Times*, 104 (1963), 31, and 'The Printed Fantasies of Orlando Gibbons', *Music and Letters*, 37 (1956), 342.

There can be no doubt that instruments described as 'violins' were employed in Elizabethan court and aristocratic circles. At the other extreme 'violins' were used by waits and for dancing purposes. But the (scant) evidence from contemporary paintings seems to throw some doubt on whether there is sufficient identity to qualify these instruments as violins as now understood. One of the best-known is the frieze at Gilling Castle, York, painted in about 1580 and illustrated by Galpin in his book on *Old English Instruments of Music*, Pl. 55, by Van der Straeten in his *History of the Violin* (p. 41), and in the *Cambridge Music Guide* (1985), Pl. 7. These 'violins' appear to be five-stringed, played against the breast, and in outline, as Van der Straeten points out, more like a known lyra da gamba of Tieffenbrucker of Padua dated 1590. Van der Straeten also illustrates[30] two bowed stringed instruments of a guitar-like outline, held against the shoulder, taken from a painting of a wedding (or some similar celebration) at Horsleydown in 1590 by Hoefnagel, a painter at the English court.

It may be objected that to insist on an instrument having 'f' holes, corners, and four strings before classifying it as a 'violin' is too narrow a view. Whether such an instrument has, internally, a soundpost and bass bar may be just as important, but is impossible to tell from pictures. What is undeniable is that instruments which are identical to the violin as we now know it were in production in Brescia and Cremona by the mid-sixteenth century and these would almost certainly have had important acoustical differences from the cumbersome instruments depicted above. Both pictures remind us of the inventiveness of makers at this date before the design of the 'violin' proper had really settled down. They do not support the argument that the violin *as now understood* was used in the sort of circumstances depicted. Furthermore, if the violin was in more general use from about 1560 onwards, England's distinguished viol-makers appear, paradoxically, to have ignored it. The tangible evidence for this is that whilst a number of sixteenth- and seventeenth-century viols are preserved, as we shall see there appear to be no English violins or violas known prior to about 1640. (Cellos came later in any event.)

The preponderance of the literary, artistic, and musical evidence favours the view that the viol retained a firm hold on the affections of the musical public in England (at least outside court circles) for longer than was the case in Italy and France. Returning to the pages of *Musick's Monument* by Thomas Mace, writing as late as 1676 the author makes a number of disparaging references to the violin. In the context of the deplorable 'new fashion' of using violins and thus, in his opinion, unbalancing the texture of the music, he comments: 'What injury must it needs be, to have such things played upon instruments unequally suited, or unevenly numbered. viz. one small, weak-sounding bass viol and two or three

---

[30] *History*, i. 65; also in Remnant, *English Bowed Instruments*, Pls. 152–3. Holman, *Four and Twenty*, 116–17, discusses two Elizabethan paintings which may show dancing accompanied by 'a violin consort'.

violins, whereas one (in reason) would think that one violin would bear up sufficiently against two or three common sounding basses. . . . or suppose a theorboe lute, the disproportion is still the same. The Scoulding violins will out top them all.'[31] The only concession that the author makes to the violin, in the context of the gentleman's provision for musical instruments, is that 'you may add to your Press, a Pair of Violins, to be in Readiness for any Extraordinary Jolly, or Jocund consort-occasion; But never use them, but with this Proviso, viz. Be sure you make an Equal Provision for them, by the addition, and strength of basses; so that they may not Out-cry the Rest of the musick . . .'[32]

J. M. Fleming, writing in 1883, restated the conventional view of the slow introduction of the violin in England, relying primarily on Roger North and Anthony Wood.[33] Roger North, a distinguished lawyer who was born in 1650 and whose valuable *Memoires of Musick* bears the date 1728, comments:

But in the reigne of King Jac.I, and the paradisicall part of the reigne of King Cha:I, many musick masters rose up and flourished. Their works lay most in compositions for violls; but at that time the lute was a monopolist of the ayere kind, and the masters, gentlemen and ladyes, for the most part use it. . . . The violin was scarce knowne tho' now the principall verb, and if it was anywhere seen, it was in the hands of a country croudero, who for the portability served himself of it.

This is a valuable and significant reference to the strong association of the violin with itinerant musicians playing primarily for the dance—the reference to a 'croudero' meaning (at least originally) an itinerant crouth-player, the crouth (as mentioned above) being another ancestor of the violin. And Anthony à Wood, in the *Diary of his Life*, states 'But before the restoration of K. Ch.II, and especially after, viols began to be out of fashion, and only violins used, as treble violin, tenor, and bass violins, and the King according to the French mode, would have twenty-four violins play before him while he was at meals, as being more airey and brisk than Viols.' And the same author explains that before the Restoration gentlemen attending music parties played on Viols, 'for they esteemed a violin to be an instrument only belonging to a common fiddler, and could not endure that it should come among them, for feare of making their meetings vaine and fidling'.[34]

---

[31] Thomas Mace, *Musick's Monument*, London, 1976 233.

[32] Ibid. 146.

[33] James M. Fleming, *Old Violins and their Makers* (London, 1883), 195. The following quotations are from pp. 194–5.

[34] Cited in Francis W. Galpin, *Old English Instruments of Music*, 4th edn., rev. Thurston Dart (London, 1965), n. 70. Peter Holman in ch. 6 of *Four and Twenty Fiddlers* regards North and Wood as 'not necessarily reliable witnesses' on the early history of the violin in England. Simon McVeigh writes that 'though the violin was known (in England) in the sixteenth century, the viol retained its status well into the next century'—a balanced statement of the likely position, see *Cambridge Companion*, 47.

A slightly later view is put by Sir John Hawkins, writing in 1776, who states in his *A General History of the Science and Practice of Music* as follows (incorporating his posthumous notes into the text):

It has already been mentioned that the practice of singing madrigals, which had prevailed for many years throughout Europe, gave way to concerts of viols, such as are above described; but the Languor of these performances, which consisted of Fantazias of five and six parts, was not compensated by that sweet and delicate tone which distinguishes the viol species; the violin, though it had long been in the hands of the vulgar, (Dr. Tudway, in his letter to his son, says that within his remembrance it was scarce ever used but at Wakes and Fairs, and that those who played on it travelled about the country with their instrument in a cloak-bag), and had been so degraded that the appellation of Fiddler was a term of reproach, was found to be an instrument capable of great improvement; and the softness and delicacy of the violin tone, and the occasional force and energy of the instrument itself, were such recommendations of it as determined the Italian masters, about the beginning of the 17th century, to introduce it into practice.

Hawkins then mentions that the modern violin had assumed the form which it now bears almost as early as the beginning of the seventeenth century and that the *Orfeo* of Claudio Monteverdi represented at Mantua in 1607 'prefixed on the names and numbers of the instruments used in the performance; and among the latter occur "duoi Violini piccoli alla Francese"'. The *violino piccolo*, typically with a body length of approximately 75 per cent of a standard full-size violin (between 270 and 355 mm), formed part of a consort of violin-family instruments and was tuned a fifth higher than the standard violin. One view is that this was the instrument called for by Monteverdi in his opera *Orfeo* (1607).[35] David Boyden in *The Violin Family* takes the view that these were 'boat-like pochettes' tuned an octave higher than the violin and treated as a transposing instrument in Monteverdi's notation. The *Violino Ordinario* meant the violin proper.[36]

Hawkins continues:

It is certain that at the beginning of the 16th century the practice of the violin was cultivated in Italy with uncommon assiduity; so that in a few years after it became the principal of concert instruments. From Italy it passed into France, and from thence into England. At first it was used in accompaniment with the voice, and was confined to the theatre; but the good effects of it, in giving to the melody a force and expression that was wanting in

---

[35] See M. O. Banks, 'The Violino piccolo', *Early Music*, 18 (1990), 588.

[36] p. 20. See also the well-known illustration showing types of violin-like instruments in the early 17th cent. in Michael Praetorius's *Syntagma Musicum* (Wittenberg, 1620), illustration xxi, and Lenz Meirot, 'Small is Beautiful', *Strad* (Dec. 1993), 1181. The 'Kit' or 'Pochette' designed to be pushed into the dancing-master's pocket was the only one of these small-form instruments to continue to be used for about another two hundred years and there are many attractive examples by English 18th-cent. makers. Stradivari made one in 1717, now in the Paris Conservatoire.

the sound of the voice and extending the limits of the harmony in the chorus, recommended it also to the church'.[37]

Hawkins also remarks on the 'Violins of Cremona, so long celebrated for the beauty of their shape and fineness of tone', and goes on in a note to say 'The violins of Cremona are exceeded only by those of Stainer, a German, whose instruments are remarkable for a full and piercing tone.'[38]

This stated preference for the Stainer model was to a large extent reflected in the practice of English makers from about 1700 onwards. Indeed, the Hills make the point that this opinion was one found throughout Europe, and go on to say:

The work of Romans, Venetians, Florentines, Genoese, Mantuans, and Neapolitans—especially the earlier work—was all strongly touched by a mixed Amati–Stainer influence; and it took years to eradicate their errors and to return to the earlier teachings upheld and emphasised by Stradivari. In England, France, Germany and Holland it was the same; especially in England, as Stainer influence was early imported here—soon after 1700. How much richer we should be in old English instruments of merit had Stradivari's precepts obtained the firm footing acquired by those of his rivals![39]

The study of the violin was undoubtedly given great impulse by the arrival in England of the first recorded virtuoso violinist—Thomas Baltzar. Baltzar was born in Lübeck in about 1630 and came over to England in 1655/6 with the reputation of being the first to practise the use of the whole shift. John Evelyn records in his diary as follows (4 March 1655/6):

This night I was invited to Mr. Robert L'Estrange to hear the incomparable Lübicer[40] on the violin. His variety on a few notes and plaine ground with that wonderful dexterity, was admirable. Tho' a young man, yet perfect and skilful, that there was nothing, however cross and perplext brought to him by our artists, which he did not play off at sight with ravishing sweetnesse and improvements, to the astonishment of our best masters. In sum, he plaid on that single instrument a full concert so as the rest flung down their instruments acknowledging the victory. As to my own particular, I stand to this hour amazed that God should give so greate perfection to so young a person. There were at that time as excellent in their profession as anywhere thought to be in Europe, Paul Wheeler, Mr. Mell, and others, until this prodigie appeared.[41]

Baltzar was made the leader of King Charles II's 'Twenty-Four' violins at the Restoration and died (of dissipated habits, we are told) in July 1663, being buried in the cloister adjoining Westminster Abbey.[42]

---

[37] See pp. 687–9 in the 1875 Novello edition.
[38] Ibid. 687–9.
[39] W. H., A. F., and A. E. Hill, *Antonio Stradivari: His Life and Work*, (London, 1902), 254–5.
[40] That is, the violinist from Lübeck.
[41] Cited in Fleming, *Old Violins*, 196.
[42] Ibid. 196–7; Sandys and Forster, *History*, 152–3; and Holman, *Four and Twenty*, 268 ff.

The Musical Scene at the Restoration

Charles II had no doubt inherited a knowledge of music from his father. As Percy Young remarks: 'He was aware that style in music had changed and he was insistent that English composers should accommodate themselves to the standards to which he had become accustomed in France.'[43] In fact Hawkins in a note to his text speaks rather disparagingly about Charles's musical ability:

He understood the notes, and sang, to use the expression of one who had often sung with him, a plump bass; but it no where appears that he considered music in any other view than as an incentive to mirth ... His taste for music seems to have been such as disposed him to prefer a solo song to a composition in parts; though it must be confessed that the pleasure he took in hearing Mr. Gostling, is a proof that he knew how to estimate a fine voice ... King Charles II could sing the tenor part of an easy song; he would often times sing with Mr. Gostling; the Duke of York accompanying them on the guitar.[44]

Whatever the King's musical ability, the restoration of the monarchy released energies which had been under heavy restraint during the earlier Cromwellian Commonwealth period. It is thought that Charles II became an admirer of the violin upon the occasion of a visit to Paris in about 1651 when he heard the band of twenty four belonging to the court of Louis XIV. One of Charles's first musical actions was to form his own celebrated band of 'Twenty Four Violins', which in fact consisted of 'six violins, six counter tenors, six tenors, and six basses, with salaries varying from forty pounds to a hundred pounds per annum'.[45] As already mentioned, Baltzar was the first 'leader'. The band was used in the performances of anthems and services in the Chapel Royal, replacing the wind instruments that had been used earlier in the century. Their effect in the ecclesiastical setting was not much to the liking of John Evelyn, who records in his diary in 1662: 'One of His Majesty's chaplains preached, after which, instead of the ancient, grave and solemn wind music accompanying the organ, was introduced a Concert of twenty-four Violins between every pause, after the French fantastical light way, better suiting a tavern or play house than a church.'[46]

---

[43] *A History of British Music* (London, 1967), 228.

[44] Hawkins, *General History*, 693.

[45] Sandys and Forster, *History*, 146. Burney describes it as 'a band of violins, tenors and basses, instead of viols, lutes and cornets of which the court band used to consist' (Charles Burney, *A General History of Music* (London, 1726–89), ii. 402. Galpin in his *Old English Instruments of Music* (4th edn. by Thurston Dart) gives them as 'six Treble, six Counter-Tenor, six Tenor and six Bass Violins—the Treble and Counter-Tenor being identical, like our First and Second Violins' (p. 71). Holman appears to be of the same view (*Four and Twenty*, 318); Simon McVeigh describes the original 'Vingt-quatre violons du Roi' as a five-part string orchestra with three viola lines ('The Violinists of the Baroque and Classical Periods', in Stowell (ed.), *Cambridge Companion*, 47).

[46] See Fleming, *Old Violins*, 195, and Holman, *Four and Twenty*, 397. Pepys first noted this development on 14 Sept. 1662—see below.

Charles II also granted to Guido Gentileschi a licence to build a theatre for a body of Italian musicians, six in all, costing the King £1,700 a year. They were granted the sole right of performing opera in the theatre for six years.[47] In these days there was an active principle of 'Freedom of Establishment' which was particularly beneficial to European musicians who were able to move between Italy, the Low Countries, France, Germany, and England in particular as the market suited—a situation which we are only just beginning to re-achieve under the impetus of the principle of freedom of movement within the European Community. It has been remarked that between about 1670 and 1750 there were a greater number of Italian musicians working in London than anywhere else outside Italy except Vienna.[48]

So, with the violin in the ascendant and with able Continental exponents of the instrument, music for the violin started to thrive. In England Henry Purcell is particularly significant in this context. His music reflected the new fashion, for not only does he use the violin family with great effect as the string accompaniment to a number of his anthems but he also used strings extensively in his operas and chamber music. Purcell had able English contemporaries such as John Jenkins, who was primarily a treble viol player and writes for that instrument, and William Young whose sonatas and dance movements for violins, bass viol, and continuo were published in Innsbruck as early as 1653.[49]

This compositional activity brought in its wake an increased demand for violins, though not necessarily English ones. It is interesting to note that John Banister, one of the most eminent of English native violinists at the time of the Restoration and who was installed as one of the 'violins in Ordinary for the King's Private Musick' at £100 a year, paid £40 for two Cremona violins (and £10 for strings for two years) under a warrant dated 24 October 1662.[50]

At the Restoration Henry Cooke was made master of the Chapel Royal, and since it was through the choir schools that musical education was primarily conferred to the young, as such 'had the main responsibility for rebuilding the main structure of English musical education'.[51] 'Composers for the violin' at the Restoration were initially George Hudson, Matthew Locke, and Henry Purcell the Elder, though by 1665 John Banister was charged with the responsibility of selecting and instructing the court band of stringed instruments. Meanwhile,

---

[47] Raynor, *Social History*, 246.
[48] Ibid. 247–8; and see Peter Walls, 'The Influence of the Italian Violin School in 17th-Century England', *Early Music*, 18 (1990), 575.
[49] Only one copy of the latter survived. See Walker, *History of Music in England*, 170; Sandys and Forster, *History*, 158, and Young, *History*, 216. Holman, *Four and Twenty*, exhaustively explores the role of John Jenkins in his chapter on 'The Violin and Court Music 1625–1663'.

[50] See Sandys and Forster, *History*, 154, and Edmund S. J. Van der Straeten, *The History of the Violin* (London, 1933), 64. This is not the earliest reference to the purchase of a 'Cremona' for use in England. In Jan. 1637/8 a musician, Woodington, was paid £12 (a hefty sum) for a 'Cremonia vyolin to play to the Organ'; see Holman, *Four and Twenty*, 214.
[51] Young, *History*, 229.

Cooke guided the musical studies of his pupils who included John Blow, Michael Wise, Pelham Humfrey, William Turner, and Henry Purcell.

Pelham Humfrey (1647–74) was given an education designed to reinforce the Continental influence on English music. Leaving the choir of the Chapel Royal in 1664 he was sent abroad by Charles II supported by an allowance of £200 out of the Secret Service Fund for travel expenses in Italy and France. It seems probable that he was a pupil of Lully in Paris and came into contact with musicians of the French court. He probably also visited Italy, as planned, and was in any event influenced by his master, Cooke, who taught his choristers to sing Italian songs. However, the French fashion prevailed, so much so that on his return to Whitehall in 1667 Pepys, meeting him at a tailor's establishment, called him 'an absolute Monsieur'.[52] A number of his verse anthems, which at their best compare with the work of Purcell, are orchestrated for strings, and some include orchestral introductions and ritornellos.

The importance of the use of the violin family in the sacred music of the Restoration composers (of whom Henry Purcell is, of course, pre-eminent) must not be overestimated since it is quite clear that performances of this sort occurred rarely, if ever, outside London. The movement in London was, as has already been stated, the result of the King's conviction that the new style of verse anthem might be greatly improved if symphonies and ritornellos, introduced on the plan that had become familiar to him in France, were incorporated in England by the English composers then writing for the Anglican liturgy. It was for this reason that the 'Twenty Four Violins', referred to earlier and established on the model of Louis XIV's 'Vingt-quatre violons du Roi' (founded in 1626 in Louis XIII's court) were given the additional duty of playing in services in the Chapel Royal. This development probably first occurred on 14 September 1662 which was, according to Pepys, 'This first day of having vialls [sic] and other instruments to play a symphony between every verse of the anthem.'[53] Hawkins remarks:

In cathedrals that were amply endowed, as St. Paul's for instance, in which a maintenance is assigned for minor canons and lay singers, the performance was little inferior to that at the Royal Chapel: in other cathedrals, where the revenues were so small as to reduce the members of the church to the necessity of taking mechanics and illiterate persons to assist in the choral service, it was proportionably inferior.[54]

To gauge the extent of musical activities we need also to look at the theatre and concert scene. For the Restoration theatre new buildings were erected (e.g. the

---

[52] *Diary*, 15 Nov. 1667; and see Edmund H. Fellowes, *English Cathedral Music*, 5th edn., London, 1969 134–5.

[53] Ibid. 132. But as Thomas Tudway, writing much later (in 1716), recorded: 'This however did not Oblige the Cathedrals throughout England, to follow such an Example; for indeed such an Example was very improper for their imitations; because they had none of the fine voices, which his Majesty had in his Chappell, to perform light solos . . .' (Cited ibid. 133).

[54] Hawkins, *General History*, 693.

new theatre in Dorset Gardens and the Theatre Royal in Drury Lane) and in time English composers co-operated with dramatists to provide plays with music, masques, and modest operas. In 1674 there was a performance of the masque *Calisto* by John Crowne and Nicholas Staggins. The orchestra comprised two harpsichords, two theorbos, four guitars, three bass viols, four trumpets, timpani, four recorders, four oboes, and 'an augmented band of strings'.[55] Again, Matthew Locke contributed the instrumental music to a version of *The Tempest* at the theatre in Dorset Gardens, the stage direction to which reads: 'The Front of the Stage is opened and the Band of 24 Violins with the Harpsichords and Theorboes which accompany the voices, are plac'd between the Pit and the Stage. While the Overture is playing, the Curtain rises, and discovers a new Frontis piece joined to the great Pilasters, on each side of the stage.'[56] This is possibly the first stage direction clearly showing the position of the orchestra and giving, in this case, pride of place to either the band, or at least a band, of 'twenty-four violins'. Purcell subsequently contributed three 'near-operas' in *Dido and Aeneas* (c.1689), *King Arthur* (1691), and *The Fairy Queen* (1692). There is no doubt that this significant increase of activity in the musical theatre would have provided greatly enhanced employment opportunities for the musicians of the time, strings then as now forming the backbone of most ensembles.

The Promotion of Chamber Music

No dictator has found it possible to eliminate music, even if the desire were there, and it has already been mentioned that during the period of the Commonwealth there was no animus against music as such. It was the use of music in worship that particularly offended the Puritans. This resulted, during the outbreak of the Civil War, in the dismissal of Royal musicians and distinguished organists of our cathedrals and collegiate chapels. A particularly tragic casualty was Thomas Tomkins, potentially one of England's leading composers of the time, whose house at Worcester was destroyed during the first siege of that city in the Civil War, and who was reduced to retiring to the nearby village of Martin Hussingtree in 1656. The organs at a number of cathedrals were destroyed or dismantled. Some, usually from the smaller churches, were tactfully removed to taverns where they formed the basis for a certain amount of 'underground' music during this period.

When Charles I transferred his capital to Oxford in 1641 he was followed by a number of outstanding musicians. Concerts by way of informal music meetings in private houses were held under the auspices of, for example, Edward Lowe, organ-

---

[55] Young, *History*, 237–8.   [56] Ibid.

ist of Christ Church, and in various colleges.[57] Thomas Baltzar of Lübeck, already mentioned, made a number of appearances in recital and, as we have seen, inspired listeners by his virtuoso violin-playing. Meanwhile in London an embryonic concert life sprung up in a number of taverns, assisted by the removal of church organs from church to inn. Pepys writing in his diary at this period mentions music to be heard at the Dolphin, the Cock, the Green Dragon, the King's Head at Greenwich, the Bluebells, the Dog, and the Black Swan.[58]

The real impetus towards public chamber-music concerts of the sort that we would now recognize, came from the rapid career of John Banister, born in London in 1630, the son of one of the Waits of St Giles' in the Fields. He first comes to notice as a violinist in the orchestra with Thomas Baltzar in the performance of Sir William Davenant's *Siege of Rhodes* (an embryonic opera whose music is now lost) in 1656. He became one of the King's musicians at the accession of Charles II and was sent to France 'on special service and to return with expedition'. In 1663 he was installed as one of the 'Violins in Ordinary for the King's Private Musick', with orders to instruct and direct twelve players chosen from the band of twenty-four violins as a special band, for which he received the fee of £600 to be divided amongst them. Because of continual troubles about the musicians' salaries, which were always in arrears, and allegations against Banister of misappropriating payments, his position was in 1667 taken over by Louis Grabu (which Banister obviously resented).[59]

Banister's reaction was to boost his income by freelance activities. He was not alone in this. As Raynor remarks: 'Charles II knew, as Elizabeth I had known, that to deny the freedom of his musicians to earn money outside court would have been to make it impossible for any first rate composer or instrumentalist to accept a position in the King's service.'[60] For whatever reason these concerts were, on the whole, very successful and must have greatly enlarged the public's appreciation of music for strings (as well, of course, as for voices, woodwind, etc.). Virtuosi from the continent of Europe came to London and pre-eminent amongst these was the Italian violinist Nicolò Matteis. He arrived in about 1672 and attracted the very favourable attention of John Evelyn who referred to his talent as 'stupendous'.[61]

Although the account of the concert scene in London by Hawkins has been criticized as giving too much of the credit to John Banister,[62] it does provide a revealing account of musical activity in London at the time and a few samples are worth reproducing:[63]

---

[57] Ibid. 223.
[58] Raynor, *Social History*, 243; also Mackerness, *Social History*, 80–1.
[59] See Van der Straeten, *History of the Violin*, 64; Holman, *Four and Twenty*, ch. 12.
[60] *Social History*, 257.
[61] *Diary*, 19 Nov. 1674. See also Walls, 'Influence of the Italian Violin School'.
[62] See for example Raynor, *Social History*, 257.
[63] All cited from Hawkins, *General History*, 762–3.

Numb. 742. Dec. 30, 1672. 'These are to give notice, that at Mr. John Banister's house (now called the Musick-school) over against the George tavern in White Fryers, this present Monday, will be musick performed by excellent masters, beginning precisely at 4 of the clock in the afternoon, and every afternoon for the future, precisely at the same hour.'

Numb. 1154. Dec. 11, 1676. 'On Thursday next, the 14th instant, at the Academy in Little Lincoln's-Inn-fields, will begin the first part of the Parley of Instruments, composed by Mr. John Banister, and perform'd by eminent masters, at six o'clock, and to continue nightly, as shall by bill or otherwise be notifi'd. The tickets are to be deliver'd out from one of the clock till five every day, and not after.'

Numb. 1356. Nov. 18, 1678. 'On Thursday next, the 22d of this instant November, at the Musick-school in Essex-buildings, over-against St. Clement's church in the Strand, will be continued A consort of vocal and instrumental musick, beginning at five of the clock every evening, composed by Mr. John Banister.'

Banister died in 1679, but his son John also became a prominent violinist.

String Music and Music Publishing

The latter half of the seventeenth century in English music is overshadowed by the giant, but tragically short-lived, figure of Henry Purcell (1659–95). Purcell was always generous in acknowledging the Italian (in particular) and French influences on himself and other English composers.[64] He also looked back to the first half of the century in composing his contrapuntal Fantasias and In Nomines, and these, partly because of the advocacy of Benjamin Britten for these pieces, are now better known than they were—particularly the Chaconne in G minor. They were almost certainly written for viols. More material to our immediate concern are Purcell's compositions for two violins and bass (to the organ or harpsichord) of 1683, being sonatas of the *da chiesa* pattern. The twenty-four-year old Purcell openly acknowledged his debt to 'the most fam'd Italian Masters'. A posthumous set of ten such sonatas, published by Purcell's widow in 1697, includes the well known 'Golden' Sonata.

These works were rather overshadowed by the pathfinding compositions of Arcangelo Corelli to which subsequent historians such as Burney compared Purcell's work unfavourably. The Corelli sonatas were certainly readily available by September 1697 when Ralph Agutter advertised 'Twelve Sonatas (newly come over from Rome) in three parts: composed by Signor Arcangelo Corelli'. In turn Purcell's work has rather overshadowed that of his precursors. Playford in 1655 had published *Court ayres; or Pavins, Almaines, Corants and Sarabands, treble and basse*,

[64] See Young, *History*, 248.

for Viols or Violins, and in 1662 there was a similar collection containing works by John Jenkins, Davis Mell, and John Banister. John Jenkins published a number of works for two violins and bass from about 1660 onwards, long (but apparently erroneously) believed to be the first of the sort known in England.[65] Percy Young calls these works 'Prototype Sonatas'.[66] As Hawkins remarks:

> notwithstanding that Jenkins was so excellent a master, and so skilful a composer for the viol, he seems to have contributed in some degree to the banishment of that instrument from concerts, and to the introduction of music for the violin in its stead. To say the truth, the Italian style in music had been making its way into this kingdom even from the beginning of the 17th century; and though Henry Lawes and some others have affected to contemn it, it is well known that he and others were unawares betrayed into an imitation of it; . . .'[67]

Musical Education

There is apparently an almost complete absence of knowledge on the vital question of how aspirant violinists received the education and training necessary to render them competent to perform in public at this period. Hart[68] identifies the earliest violin instruction work published in England as being the 'Introduction to the playing on the Treble-violin', in Playford's *Introduction to the Skill of Musick* of 1655. Van der Straeten in his *Romance of the Fiddle*[69] states that the first edition of this appeared in London in 1654, as does Heron-Allen in his *Violin-Making*. The *New Grove Dictionary* confirms this, but gives the treble violin material as first appearing in the 1657 edition. (The book went through many editions to 1730.) Playford states in the later 1674 edition that 'The treble violin is a cheerful and spritely instrument, much played of late, some by book, and some without.' The author describes a method of holding the violin as follows: 'First the Violin is usually play'd above hand, the neck thereof being held with the left hand; the lower part must be rested on the left breast, a little below the shoulder; the bow between the ends of the thumb and the three fingers, the thumb being stayed upon the hair of the nut, and the three fingers resting upon the wood.'[70]

Later in the century John Lenton, a member of William and Mary's state band, published *The Gentleman's Diversion, or The Violin Explained* (1693). A second edition was published under a different title (*The Useful Instructor of the Violin*) in 1702. Lenton agrees with Playford's advice that the instrument should rest on the

---

[65] See e.g. Sandys and Forster, *History*, 158, from Hawkins and Burney; but Young (*History*, 216–17) indicates that this opinion was founded on a misleading MS annotation.
[66] *History*, 216.
[67] Hawkins, *General History*, 213.
[68] *The Violin and its Music* (London, 1881), 457.
[69] (London, 1911).
[70] Quoted in Van der Straeten, *Romance*, 70, from the 1674 edn.

breast and not be held 'as low as the girdle' as was the Italian street minstrels' practice. Hart confirms what is visible from contemporary illustrations and 'beard-marks' on the older instruments themselves: 'The mode of holding the instrument among good Italian players, differed only from the present manner in placing the chin on the reverse side of the tail piece.'[71] (There were, of course, no chinrests used before the nineteenth century.)[72]

It is not apparent from this at what age it is recommended that the aspirant violinist should start. We take for granted these days that the process should commence as early as possible. There are extant a few 'small-sized' instruments of the old masters—for instance the Stradivari of 1683, beautifully inlaid, in the Hill Collection in Oxford. But as its body-length is still 13³/₁₆ in. (334 mm) it seems more likely to have been a 'small-patterned violin' rather than a child's. Indeed, in Haweis's description of how he learned the violin (in the middle of the nineteenth century) very strong advice is given *against* starting with a reduced size. This is based on the brain's difficulty in adjusting finger-stretch to accommodate differing intervals according to the instrument's string-length. The author does refer, though, to his first 'small red eighteen penny fiddle and stick' which ended up as firewood.[73] But Mozart certainly started on a small violin. His childhood instrument is preserved in the Mozarteum in Salzburg and has a body-length of 10⁵/₁₆ in. (262 mm). It is the work of Andreas Ferdinand Mayr of Salzburg.[74]

There is in fact early evidence that some seventeenth-century children had violins of a suitable size and price. There are references in Customs records of the mid-seventeenth century to the importation of children's violins. In particular there is a reference in an Act of Parliament raising import and export duties in 1660 to 'Fiddles for Children, the dozen IV.s'. The same Act lists 'viols, per piece XIII.s.IV.d.'. These references are interesting also because the average *ad valorem* duty on musical instruments was five per cent, and so a rough approximation of the wholesale value of these instruments can be obtained.[75]

Other positive evidence that children may have been taught bowed stringed instruments during the early years of the violin comes from the knowledge that those choir schools which were active and progressive included instrumental

---

[71] Hart, *The Violin: Famous Makers*, 458.

[72] See also David Boyden, 'Violin Technique', in *Violin Family*, 39: '... the player commonly placed his chin at the right of the tailpiece'. For the early use of the chinrest, see Robin Stowell, *Violin Technique and Performance Practice in the Late Eighteenth and Early Nineteenth Centuries*, (Cambridge, 1985), 29–30. Spohr is thought to have been its first inventor.

[73] H. R. Haweis, *My Musical Life* (London, 1902), 18. Possibly the mandolin, with its identical intervals and convenient size, has in the past been used for initial learning.

[74] See Peter Walls, 'Mozart and the Violin', *Early Music*, 20 (1992), 7–28. See also M. B. Banks, 'The Violino Piccolo and other Small Violins', *Early Music*, 18 (1990) 588–96 (which contains illustrations), and Leopold Mozart's views on undersized violins in his *Treatise on the Fundamental Principles of Violin Playing* (Augsburg, 1756; trans. London, 1951), 10: 'But it is advisable, if the boy's fingers permit, to accustom him to a full-sized violin, so that he may hold his fingers in a consistently even position, harden them and learn to stretch them.'

[75] See Guy F. Oldham, 'Import and Export Duties on Musical Instruments in 1660', *Galpin Society Journal*, 9 (1956), 97.

tuition in the educational regime of the boys. As early as 1602 a commentator wrote: 'These boys have special preceptors in the various arts, and in particular excellent instructors in music... For the whole hour preceding the play one listens to the delightful entertainment on organs lutes, pandoras, viols and flutes...'[76]

Views on the educational merit of the teaching of music at this time varied. One suggestion was that music was a valuable study because it is 'very comfortable to the wearied mind, a princess of delights and the delight of princes'.[77]

At the end of the Elizabethan period it appears that there was a decline in music teaching and there was no perceptible revival until after the Handelian period. This contrasted sharply with the attention paid to music in German schools and the belief in Italy that the best way to prepare an orphan for the business of life was to train him as a musician.[78] In Italy in particular musicians were trained to fulfil the demands of the courts and the new opera-houses as well the services of the leading churches. The apprentice was not put at the expense of a master under the apprenticeship system familiar in England and elsewhere. It was this factor, perhaps, which enabled Italy to supply Europe with skilled musicians during this period.[79] We must assume that in England at this time, the instrument was more generally learned during early maturity, but there is little available evidence and certainly few, if any, early child's-size English violins (as opposed to dancing masters' pochettes) have survived.

A little later, one known example of an infant prodigy in the early part of the eighteenth century is Matthew Dubourg (b. London 1703, d. 1767). His grandson, G. Dubourg, states in his *History of the Violin*[80] that 'when quite a child' he played a sonata by Corelli at one of Thomas Britton's concerts, being 'made to borrow elevation from a joint stool' for greater visibility. A pupil of Geminiani, he later achieved considerable fame, not least as leader of the orchestra which was involved in the first performance of Handel's *Messiah* in 1742. It is said that on a subsequent evening Dubourg, playing a cadenza to a ritornello of an aria, modulated so wildly that when he at length reached the final shake Handel called out in the hearing of the audience: 'Welcome home, welcome home, Mr. Dubourg'.[81]

---

[76] C. W. Wallace, *The Children of the Chapel in Blackfriars*, cited in Raynor, 150. It has been suggested that the lute, cittern, and consort MSS of Mathew Holmes, probably compiled at Christ Church, Oxford, in the 1590s, may have been the teaching materials of a cathedral singing-man; they involve four of the five instruments just referred to. See John M. Ward, *Sprightly and Cheerful Musick: Notes on the Cittern, Gittern & Guitar in 16th- and 17th-Century England*, The Lute Society Journal, 21 (1979–81), 30–3. See also ibid. 104–6 for an account of instrumental tuition at an English college in France. Further discussion in Woodfield, *The Early History of the Viol*, (Cambridge, 1984), ch. 14.

[77] Cited Raynor, *Social History*, 141, from Mulcaster of St Paul's School, late 16th cent.

[78] Ibid. 140.

[79] Ibid. 141.

[80] 1st edn. (London, 1836), 185.

[81] Ibid. 187.

The Meeting of Demand for Stringed Instruments in England

As already explained, in England throughout the seventeenth century, and particularly from 1660 onwards, there was a steady increase in the performance of church music with orchestral accompaniment, opera, and chamber music. The modern music-lover has to make an effort of imagination to appreciate how good music could be promulgated without the assistance of broadcasting, the record, and the tape. These media did not become an effective means of musical communication until well into the twentieth century. In London, by the late eighteenth century educated members of the middle class or aristocracy would have taken opportunities to hear good music in the churches and theatres. We know, for instance, that Samuel Pepys enjoyed 'fiddling' (on both viol and violin, it seems) as a pleasant diversion, and the diaries of John Evelyn are full of enthusiastic references to chamber music concerts that he attended. The crucial question is, from where did the instruments come?

Italy, with its established network of workshops in Brescia and Cremona in particular, was an obvious source of high-quality instruments, although some evidence suggests that makers such as Stradivari operated to a large extent on commissioned work, and, as John Dilworth points out, 'the violins which left the city were almost invariably passed through priests or were commissions for other Catholic courts'.[82] But Gasparo da Salò's tax return in 1588 bears comment on falling exports of instruments to France, indicating a long-standing export trade.[83] The Hills mention one case where, if the story is true, Cervetto, the cellist (1682–1783), brought a consignment of instruments direct from Stradivari and imported them to England. The story, as relayed by Sandys and Forster,[84] ends by stating that the instruments had to be returned since the seller was unable even to get £5 for a cello. (William Corbett may also have been a direct customer, as mentioned below.) But if it was usually difficult to buy instruments direct from the makers, with perseverance it was clearly possible to procure instruments through third parties and there is evidence, as mentioned below, that a significant number of Italian instruments reached England. So far as the nobility and gentry were concerned, it was common practice for those who could afford to do so to undertake a 'grand tour' on the Continent of Europe and visit, at least, the major cities of France and Italy. Many of England's stately homes were furnished with the fruits of these expeditions. Lord Burlington is said to have arrived home from one of these tours with 848 pieces of luggage containing his art souvenirs.

[82] 'Vain, Golden Age', *Strad* (Sept. 1991), 768–70. See also Holman, *Four and Twenty*, passim.
[83] See David Boyden, 'The Violin', in *Violin Family*, 21.
[84] *History*, 227–8. See also Hill, *Stradivari*, 246.

As already mentioned, from the middle of the sixteenth century onwards there was a generous influx of Italian, French, and German musicians into London. Some, such as the Bassanos, were of Jewish origin, part of the *kletzmorim*. Spanish and Portuguese Jews had settled in Cremona since 1250 but were expelled from there in 1597. Many went to Amsterdam by 1650 and played in the brothels there.[85]

The playing of Nicolò Matteis, the distinguished Italian violinist who arrived in London about 1672, was, as mentioned above, particularly admired. Fleming remarks that:

With the arrival of the elder Matteis, who was said to have been the inventor of the half shift, the furore for the fiddle—which was originally introduced to this country from France—reached an intensity to which it had not previously attained, and Italian violins came into as high repute as Italian music, the latter having made here great advances in public favour through the importation of Corelli's works, some of whose compositions were first published at Rome in 1683.[86]

The fashion of travelling in Italy had its influence on the development of this taste, and North (writing in the early eighteenth century) states that most of the young nobility and gentry who had been there 'affected to learn of Corelli and brought home with them such favour for the Italian music as hath given it the possession of our Parnassus. And the best utensil of Apollo, the violin, is so universally courted and sought after to be had of the best sort, that some say England hath dispeopled Italy of violins.'[87] The obvious conclusion from all this is that English native makers must have had a ready source of Italian models from which to take inspiration from earlier times. Since the Austro-German influence of Stainer and Klotz could not have been established until about 1670—Stainer was made 'Maker to the Emperor' in 1669 and the derivative Klotz dynasty did not become established in Mittenwald until about 1680—those English makers already flourishing by 1660 must have been heavily influenced by the instruments then coming from northern Italy, not least those of the well-established Amati family. Emigré makers, such as Jacob Rayman, probably of Tyrolean extraction, naturally brought their own variations on the predominantly Italian theme, via Austria, France, and the Low Countries. (These makers are discussed in Chapter 3.)

On the formation of Charles II's twenty-four violins, Sandys and Forster draw attention to a warrant dated 24 October 1662 under which John Banister had an order for £40 for two Cremona violins bought by him with £10 for strings for two years.[88] This is another indication of the continuing ascendancy of the Cremona

---

[85] See Dilworth, 'Vain, Golden Age', 769, and Holman, *Four and Twenty, passim.*
[86] Fleming, *Old Violins*, 198.   [87] Ibid.   [88] *History*, 154.

school. As we have seen, as early as 1638 £12 was paid for 'a Cremonia vyolin' for the court of Charles I.[89]

For a perhaps more significant illustration of taste at the time it is interesting to see the inventory of the estate of Thomas Britton, the 'Musical Small-Coal Man' whose enterprise and initiative was so important to the foundation of chamber-music concerts in London in the latter half of the seventeenth century. Many of his effects, including instruments, were sold by auction in December 1714 at Tom's Coffee House, Ludgate Hill. The catalogue of instruments is as follows:

INSTRUMENTS

1. A fine Guitar in a case. 2. A good Dulcimer. 3. Five instruments in the shape of a fish. 4. A curious ivory Kitt and bow in a case. 5. A good Violin by Ditton. 6. Another very good one. 7. One said to be a Cremona. 8. An extraordinary Rayman.[90] 9. Ditto. 10. Ditto. 11. Ditto. 12. One very beautiful one by Claud Pieray of Paris, as good as a Cremona. 13. One ditto. 14. Another very good one. 15. Another ditto. 16. A very good one for a high violin. 17. Another ditto. 18. An excellent tenor. 19. Another ditto by Mr. Lewis. 20. A fine viol by Mr. Baker of Oxford. 21. Another excellent one, bellied by Mr. Norman.[91] 22. Another said to be the neatest that Jay ever made. 23. A Fine bass violin, new neck'd and bellied by Mr. Norman. 24. Another rare good one by Mr. Lewis. 25. A good harpsichord by Philip Jones. 26. A Rucker's Virginal, thought to be the best in Europe. 27. An Organ of five stops, exactly consort pitch, fit for a room, and with some ornaments may serve for any chapel being a very good one.

N.B. There is not one book or instrument here mentioned that was not his own: and as it will be the best sale that hath been made in its kind, so it shall be the fairest. All persons that are strangers to pay 5s. in the pound for what they buy, and to take away all by Friday night following.

There are a great many books that Mr. Britton had collected in most parts of learning, the whole consisting of 14 or 1500 books which will shortly be sold at his late dwelling-house. But the manner and method of sale is not yet concluded on.[92]

Trespassing into the eighteenth century, the Hills' monograph on *Stradivari* states that William Corbett, the violinist (1668–1748), brought back a collection of Cremona instruments from a visit to Italy in 1710—the price then being charged by Stradivari being four Louis d'Or (estimated by the Hills as £10 in 1902). In 1724 Corbett, probably unsuccessfully, offered his instruments for sale and the inventory included instruments by the Amatis, 'Old Stradivarius of Cremona', Maggini, and Gasparo da Salò of Brescia. The familiar reference to 'Old Stradivarius' leads the

---

[89] Young, *History*, 214; See also examples in Holman, *Four and Twenty*.

[90] 'Jacob Rayman dwelt in Bell-Yard, Southwark about the year 1650. The tenor violins made by him are greatly valued.' (Hawkins's footnote)

[91] 'Barak Norman was one of the last of the celebrated makers of viols in England: he lived in Bishopsgate and afterwards in St. Paul's churchyard. He had two daughters who were actresses of the lower class at the theatre in Goodman's field.' (Hawkins's footnote)

[92] Hawkins, *General History*, 793.

Hills to speculate that Corbett might actually have met *il vecchio Stradivari* on his Italian tour of 1710.[93]

The evidence summarized above shows that taste in England in the mid- to late seventeenth century veered towards the Italian master makers, primarily, perhaps, the Brescians but with an acknowledgement of the merits of Cremona. But Thomas Britton's inventory also suggests an interest in 'extraordinary' Rayman instruments and those of other English makers. There must have been many players, unable to afford the expense of a trip to Italy, and the attendant costs of transporting luggage, perhaps by separate conveyance, who bought instead from local makers. To these players the native English or immigrant craftsman must have offered an economic alternative, based on a firm tradition of distinguished viol-making and an awareness of the Italian violin-making tradition.

A further crucial point to remember is that although attempts were undoubtedly made to import Italian instruments,[94] carriage, particularly of the highly vulnerable cello, would have been a cumbersome and dangerous business. This factor must have encouraged the local production of cellos and basses. It perhaps explains the superiority to all but the best Italian instruments which is claimed for choice English cellos and basses throughout the eighteenth century and which is more fully discussed later in this book.

The Viola, Cello, and Double Bass in England

The Viola

There is considerable academic debate as to whether the birth of the viola preceded or succeeded the birth of the violin. This debate matters not as regards English instrument-making because, as we have seen, the violin was late in establishing itself in England and the same applies to the viola, which can probably trace its birth to northern Italy at about 1535 (along with the cello).[95] In fact, in music of the sixteenth and seventeenth centuries in Italy and France (in particular), the viola was used as 'the instrument of the middle'—i.e. for both alto and tenor registers of four- or five-part ensembles. It was probably for this reason that the makers of Brescia and Cremona tended to produce violas of two distinct sizes, the true tenor viola being so large that it is almost impracticable to play it on the arm—two examples being the viola for Charles IX by Andrea Amati, Cremona, 1574, having a body-length of 18½ in. (470 mm), and that by the 'brothers' Amati, Cremona, 1592, with a body-length of 17⅞ in. (454 mm). The more manageable

---

[93] Hill, *Stradivari*, 246–52.
[94] See, for example, ibid. 246.
[95] See *Violin Family*, ch. 5, and Kenneth Skeaping, 'The Viola', in Anthony Baines (ed.), *Musical Instruments*, 132 ff.

smaller viola was also being produced, the Hills[96] recording an A. & H. Amati, 1616, of 16¼ in. (413 mm) and two Stradivaris of 1672 and 1701 respectively both of 16³⁄₁₆ in. (411 mm). An even earlier Gasparo da Salò instrument is known of an unaltered body-length of 15¾ in. (400 mm). It is supposed that the reason why the size of violas varied in this way (a matter which puzzled the Hills in their book on Stradivari) was simply that the very large models were needed to play the deep tenor register and the smaller ones to play the alto register.[97]

In England the viol family had not been seriously challenged until about 1660 and it is generally accepted, even as regards Italy, that viola production markedly declined after this date since the popular chamber music of the time, as typified by Corelli's 'forty-eight trios for two violins and bass', supplied no part for the viola. It is easy to forget that Haydn did not start to establish the string quartet using the viola as the tenor part until about 1755, and only a minority of Boccherini's fifty-two string trios (*c.*1768) are written for violin, viola, and cello. There were enough instruments in circulation largely to satisfy such demand as there was. But 'tenors' (as they were frequently called in England until recent times) were certainly being made at this time in England. Tom Britton's estate included two, one of which was made by Lewis.

As Kenneth Skeaping points out,[98] orchestral music from 1750 onwards made few demands on viola players. The viola had not overcome its low status. The expectation was that the player would be of poor quality, perhaps a 'demoted' violinist. For the purposes of string quartet playing, however, quite a different picture presented itself, and it is not without significance that Haydn was a trained string-player and Mozart, with his almost superhuman all-round ability, was an accomplished player on the instrument. They both made it their business to include interesting and independent viola parts.

The viola player Henry Hill (born 2 July 1808, died 11 June 1856) is a brilliant exception in the rather depressing English scenario. The son of the violin-maker Henry Lockey Hill, he not only played to the composer's acclaim the solo viola part in the first English performance of Berlioz' *Harold in Italy* in England (London, 7 February 1848), but participated with Joachim in quartet playing. He was a founder member of the London Beethoven Quartet Society and 'Principal Tenor' at the Royal Italian Opera and the Philharmonic Concerts. (See further Chapter 7.)

---

[96] *Stradivari*, 296.

[97] See David Boyden, 'The Viola', in *Violin Family*, 141; some authorities now take the (surely counter-intuitive) view that they played the same part whatever the size. Violas may also have been used in equal number with violins, for the 'country music' of the time and for fairs, weddings, and feasts. Their lower pitch might have suited accompanying male-voice singing better than the violin. See also Agnes Kory, 'A Wider Role for the Tenor Violin', *Galpin Society Journal*, 47 (1994), 123, in which she examines the significance of instruments tuned an octave below the violin and probably either arm-held or played like a cello, according to size.

[98] In Baines (ed.), *Musical Instruments*, 133.

But to be enjoyed chamber music did not in those days require, and was not intended for, large concert-halls. The smaller-sized viola was both easier to handle and acoustically satisfactory. Orchestral players also preferred smaller instruments. Even the valiant attempts of Paganini to induce interest in the viola as a solo instrument (his first viola recital being in London in 1834) met with little success and most viola-players were widely regarded simply as incompetent violinists. It was Berlioz in the mid-nineteenth century in France who persuaded the Paris Conservatoire to take viola training seriously. At the same time he saw the advantage in terms of orchestral tone of larger-sized violas than were then customarily being used.

Orchestral standards in England were generally far from high in the nineteenth century and, as Skeaping points out, it is significant that it was the viola-players of the Philharmonic Society in London in 1894 who protested because Tchaikovsky's *Symphonie Pathétique* had a viola part which was thought to be unplayable. But by then European composers had realized the importance of a rich viola sound and makers responded by experimenting with viola design. In Britain, perhaps the most notable attempt to introduce uniformity was the 16¾ in. (425 mm) model designed and advocated by Lionel Tertis and first made in the 1930s by Arthur Richardson and a few others internationally.[99] Although the question of viola design and body-length has not been conclusively settled, it is probably true to say that most professional players would regard a body-length of between 16 in. and 16¾ in. (406 mm to 425 mm) as being ideal, the resonance of the bottom C-string and the alto-like quality of the top A-string being the prime considerations.

English viola design of the classical school, i.e. to about 1800, reflected the uncertainties outlined above. As a general rule violas made between about 1700 and 1800 are of the smaller variety, between 15 in. and 15¾ in. (381 mm to 400 mm). English makers tended to understand the acoustical importance of interior air volume, and an attempt to compensate for smaller length is often met by increasing the depth of the ribs or of the arching. As Cooper points out in his discussion of the violas of the Banks family,[100] the depth of rib varies considerably, usually in relation to the height of the arching.

There were some exceptions to the smaller-size norm. The magnificent Brescian-style viola of 1650 by (or firmly attributed to) Jacob Rayman, sold by Sotheby's for £11,000 in November 1980, measured 16 9/16 in. (421 mm). This is illustrated in Pl. 92. Two large-model violas of or attributed to Daniel Parker have been described in the *Strad*,[101] measuring 16⅛ in. (410 mm) and 17 in. (432 mm)

---

[99] Richardson's model is illustrated in Pl. 93. For further details of the development, see Lionel Tertis, *Cinderella No More* (London, 1953), and Maurice W. Riley, *The History of the Viola* (Ypsilanti, Mich., 1980), 233–5 and ch. 13.

[100] *Benjamin Banks*, 85–6.

[101] (Dec. 1973), 454 and (June 1969), 54 resp.

respectively. But more typical are the violas of Benjamin Banks loosely following the designs of Stainer or Amati, and having body-lengths varying between 15⅛ in. (384 mm) and 15⅜ in. (391 mm) with a stop (distance from upper edge to notch in soundhole) of 8¼ in. (211 mm).[102] In terms of general craftsmanship, makers who excelled in violin-making such as Benjamin Banks also made beautifully constructed and internally carefully finished violas. The reverse consideration applied to those makers who produced 'for the trade' or for the bottom of the market, where one finds the familiar ink purfling and internal roughness often matched by a certain grotesque bulbousness. Violas exceeding 16 in. (406 mm) came into more common, but far from universal, production from about 1820—Henley, for instance, recording an instrument of Henry Lockey Hill, presumably of about this date, having a body length of 16⅛ in. (411 mm).

The Cello

The cello[103] occupies a particularly important place in English stringed instrument making, as will be pointed out frequently in the text. In a similar way to the viola, early Italian instruments of the sixteenth century tend to have been considerably larger than the standard modern cello (approximately 30 in. (762 mm)), although many of these early specimens have been 'cut down', having been born as 'bass violins'. The key factor in enabling players to avoid excessive string-length, as was the case with the viola, and therefore unwieldy size, was the winding of gut strings with a metal covering, initially silver, thus giving far greater sonority than a pure gut string would have given.

The earliest English cello-maker of consequence appears to have been Barak Norman, discussed further in this text, though individual instruments have been traced to earlier makers. In an article on the violin family in an early edition of Grove's *Dictionary of Music and Musicians*,[104] which is something of an edited hotchpotch but in which Edward Heron-Allen had a hand, the following statement is made: 'The first English violoncellos date from about the Restoration. The oldest one known is undoubtedly the work of Edward Pamphilon. It is of a very primitive pattern being extremely *bombé* in the back and the belly, the arching starting straight from the purfling, which is double.' The writer then goes on to say that the cello must have been kept out of general use by the fact that it was tuned in fifths and the fingers of the performer, being only able to stretch a major third, found difficulty in commanding the scales. It is suggested that it was not until the middle of the eighteenth century that its difficulties were sufficiently

---

[102] See Cooper, *Benjamin Banks*, 85–6.
[103] See generally Elizabeth Cowling, *The Cello* (London, 1975); also Klaus Marx, 'The Violoncello', ch. 6 of *Violin Family*.
[104] Vol. v, ed. J. A. Fuller Maitland (London, 1910), 302.

overcome to enable it practically to supplant the viola da gamba in the orchestra. Nevertheless the writer expresses the view that the earlier violoncellos in England date not long after those of Italy, the French and German ones somewhat later. The attribution of the first cello to Pamphilon[105] is rather weakened by the subsequent statement[106] that 'no Pamphilon violoncello is known to exist'. The instrument illustrated (Pl. 34), by William Baker of Oxford, is certainly one of the earliest English cellos known, and Edward Lewis is also thought to have made cellos in the 1690s.

The cello production of distinguished individual English makers will be discussed in the appropriate context later, but as regards the makers of the Old English School, most instruments by the mid-eighteenth century have a body-length averaging about 29 in. (737 mm) with a stop of 15¼ in. (387 mm). If the work of Benjamin Banks is taken as being typical, and certainly as being representative of some of the best English cello-making of the period, we see that his copy of the Stradivari of 1730 has a body-length of 29⅜ in. (746 mm) whereas his Amati copies tend to be about 28¾ in. (730 mm).[107] An instrument dated May 1817 of Charles Harris of Woodstock, Oxford, having a back-length of 30⅛ in. (765 mm), is exceptionally large for this period.[108] Plates illustrate, with body-lengths, cellos by William Baker (Pl. 34), Barak Norman (Pl. 83), Cross (Colour Pl. A), Banks (Pl. 36), and Harris (Pl. 65), amongst others.

Cellos, as will be seen, appealed particularly to the musical aristocrat (including Hanoverian) in England. English makers such as the Hills and Forsters lavished their best attentions on their higher-quality cellos, and some of these instruments are now becoming more widely appreciated. Indeed, one of the recurring themes of this book is a celebration of the English cello.

At the other extreme of the market, locally made or otherwise unsophisticated cellos alternated with bassoons as the favoured bass instrument of those parish-church choirs which used a band rather than an organ to accompany them. Many a wormy English cello started life in this way, particularly during the period approximately 1700–1860.[109] One such cello by John Barrett, dated 1720 and known as the Berkswell Cello, is illustrated and discussed in an article in the *Galpin Society Journal* in 1984.[110]

It is apparent, incidentally, that violins were also sometimes played in these church bands. One rustic instrument by Thomas Lewis, thought to have been a Gloucestershire cobbler, bears an inscription on the wood 'Made by Thomas Lewis, in 1823. Played it in the Chire in 1824. Its a good fiddle when I plays.'[111]

---

[105] Ibid. 304.
[106] Ibid. 305. This inconsistency is very untypical of Heron-Allen, as will be inferred from Ch. 14.
[107] Cooper, *Benjamin Banks*, 117.
[108] See Lot 206 of Phillips's sale of 21 Nov. 1991.

[109] See N. Temperley, *The Music of the English Parish Church* (Cambridge, 1979), ii. 196 ff.
[110] Eric Halfpenny, 'The Berkswell Cello', *Galpin Society Journal*, 37 (1984), 2.
[111] Henley, *Dictionary*, 706.

This delightful character might have stepped out of the pages of a Thomas Hardy novel; there is a well-known description of a rural church band in his *Under the Greenwood Tree*.

The Double Bass

If controversy attended and still attends the design of the viola, the same is even more true of the double bass. Its basic design owes much to the instrument's ancestor, the bass viol, and one type of model accordingly has a flat back with the top part sloping towards the neck, and sometimes 'C' rather than 'F' holes. Other instruments are more like the violin in design and have rounded backs. In terms of body-length 45¼ in. (1150 mm) is probably the orchestral norm, though 'full-size' instruments may have a body-length up to 55 in (1400 mm). There are also a number of stories of double basses of such a height that the neck had to be let through the ceiling and the tuning took place in a room in the floor above, the bow being equally huge. Such an instrument is recounted by Sandys and Forster as belonging to one Martin who kept a public house,[112] and one monstrous specimen built in 1851 by J.-B. Vuillaume can be seen in the museum of the Paris Conservatoire, while Dragonetti's large instrument is in the Victoria and Albert Museum, London. (Dragonetti played on Gasparo da Salò's instruments primarily, and several double-basses of this period associated with Dragonetti were displayed at the Special Exhibition in London of 1872. See further Chapter 13.)

Again, where a particular English maker excelled in producing double basses this will be mentioned in context. But at this stage it is worth noticing that *The Violin Family*[113] picks out Forster, Kennedy, Lott, and Tarr. One could add that one of the earliest English double basses has been attributed, c.1720, to John Barrett (the Chandos Inventory), and the Panormo family in London were also of great importance in this connection. Henley in his *Universal Dictionary* goes so far as to say that double basses were the speciality of Vincenzo Panormo (who worked in London from 1789) and 'one or two of them rank as the finest in the world'.

As to 'Forster', this was a family of violin-makers and it is fortunate that the work on the *History of the Violin* by Sandys and Forster (1864) contains some details (whose accuracy is debatable) of individual instrument production. The distinguished maker William Forster ('Old Forster') who died aged 68 in 1808, somewhat significantly describes himself on his card as 'violin, violoncello, tenor and bow-maker' without mention of the double bass. He is credited as having made only four double basses, three of which were made by the command of George III, apparently to a large design.[114] According to Sandys and Forster these double

---

[112] *History*, 165.   [113] Rodney Slatford, 'The Double Bass, 190.
[114] See Sandys and Forster, *History*, 315–16.

basses were made in the same shape as a cello, without being tapered off and bevelled at the fore-end of the sides and the back. But Towry Piper, commenting on this, states that

a significant commentary on the reliability of the book [Sandys and Forster] may be seen any day at Boulangier's in Frith Street, in the shape of a splendid double-bass of full size and the ordinary form with sloping shoulders ... specially built to the order of a medical man, an amateur ... There is no mistake about the instrument, which is a typical "Forster", beautifully finished in every detail and finely varnished. The back is modelled and the corners are strengthened externally after the manner of some of those of John Lott and other members of the English School.[115]

The son of 'Old Forster', William Forster also, again primarily made violins, 'tenors' (i.e. violas), and cellos, charging £3. 3s. 0d. (£3.15) for an ordinary tenor and an unknown price for 'best tenors', according to Sandys and Forster. As is clear from the authors' rather laconic account of theatre playing conditions at the time, the safety of both player and instrument was far from guaranteed. This Forster is recorded as having made

five or six double-basses, of second-class workmanship, ... made chiefly for letting out on hire; and there was one of the best work finished for a person named M'Calla, which instrument was destroyed either when the Royalty Theatre, at the east part of London, was burned down in 1826, or crushed to pieces when the roof of the Brunswick Theatre unfortunately fell in, killing several of the performers whilst at rehearsal, on 28 February, 1828. The latter is believed to be the cause of its destruction. These double-basses were all made of the same shape as violoncellos.[116]

The last Forster of significance, Simon Andrew Forster,[117] lists three double basses (of the first class), dating from between 1833 and 1836, together with one unsold instrument from about this year. No 'second class instruments' in the double bass category are mentioned. His instruments are made in the traditional English outline in the manner particularly of his father and John Lott.

Undoubted impetus was given to the study of the double bass by the arrival in England (in 1793) of the Venetian player Dominique (or Domenicus) Dragonetti who often played with his contemporary, the distinguished cellist Robert Lindley. It was said of Dragonetti: 'The richness and power of his tone were marvellous; and his execution such that he would play the violoncello or violin part of a quartett on his unwieldy instrument, or even join in a violin duett.'[118] As the New Grove *Violin Family* mentions, Dragonetti's success was such that for over fifty

---

[115] 'Concerning Double Basses', reprinted with a commentary from the *Strad* of 1911 in *Strad* (Feb. 1991), 120–8, and referred to below.
[116] Sandys and Forster, *History*, 339–40.
[117] Joint author of the oft-quoted work by Sandys and Forster.
[118] Sandys and Forster, *History*, 194.

years he was an indispensable part of any significant musical gathering and was acquainted with composers from Haydn and Beethoven to Liszt.[119] He died in 1846.

One writer has said of London makers of the double bass in the early part of the nineteenth century that they were 'as a group the most prolific and gifted craftsmen to ever work in a single place (London) simultaneously'.[120] The same writer deservedly praises Towry Piper's series of articles in the *Strad* in 1911 which both surveys the Italian School of makers (and the players who used their instruments) and the main bass-makers of the English School at the time, including Bernhardt Fendt, John Frederick Lott ('the high watermark'), the Forster family, John Taylor of Drury Lane (c.1800), the hitherto unnoticed Baker of Brighton (*fl.* 1820–30), James Brown of Spitalfields (d. 1860), and William Valentine, a clever workman with John and George Hart. Towry Piper's much-praised work on this topic is reproduced with scholarly comment in the 1991 volume of the *Strad* with illustrations of various fine double basses including one by William Forster II.[121]

Double basses were occasionally used, perhaps as an alternative to the cello, in parish church bands. Towry Piper recounts (in 1911) that just before a Sunday evening service was due to begin at an ancient church on the east coast the blacksmith contrabassist announced from the gallery (normally at the west end of the church where the choir also forgathered): 'There won't be no anthem tonight. Some of those blasted boys has put beans or something in my bass—and she rattles!'[122]

The nineteenth-century orchestras demanded strong double-bass sections and perhaps the most remarkable specialist maker that England has produced was William Tarr of Manchester (1808–91). He is credited as having produced more than two hundred double basses, as well as a quantity of violins, violas, and cellos. His first double bass was made in 1834. Morris relates that he was also an excellent musician and for twelve years played the double bass in the Gentlemen's Concerts at Manchester. At a Dublin music festival in which Tarr performed, all nine double basses were made by him. He clearly had an unusually diverse and interesting life, for he also played the organ in New Orleans during a short residence in the United States and later became a prominent socialist, secularist, and anti-vaccinator. Miss Stainer in her *Dictionary* adds that he gave up violin-making to become a photographer. When he died in July 1891 he was buried in Manchester's Southern Cemetery with, as Morris pointedly remarks, secular rites.

[119] p. 196.
[120] D. Rosengard, 'Concerning Double Basses—Paying Tribute to Piper', *Strad* (Feb. 1991), 120.
[121] (Feb. 1991), 120–8. Towry Piper is discussed further in Ch. 14.
[122] See *Strad* (Feb. 1991), 121, the East Anglian words being slightly adjusted by the present author.

Chapter Two

❦ Construction Methods, Materials, and Techniques of the Old English Makers

Introduction — The Body — Scroll and Button — Other Distinguishing Features of Older Instruments — Varnish — Varnish and English Violin-Makers — Wood — Purfling — Accessories — Strings — Tools — Tone — Conversion from Baroque to 'Romantic' Violin

Introduction

You can no more describe the features of an English violin than you could describe a typically English face, and you would be inviting criticism from those who think a particular feature untypical or common to other nationalities if you were to try.

THIS type of comment was made forcibly to the author when discussing recognition factors of the Old English School. Nevertheless, taking courage in both hands and in the knowledge that Meredith Morris was the pathfinder in this respect, an attempt will be made. A caveat must be repeatedly borne in mind, however. What follows are generalities to which there will be exceptions. As it happens, if there are identifiable stylistic features of any particular era, they roughly follow the centuries. From 1650 to 1700 approximately, we expect to find English instruments influenced by a mixture of Brescian and Amati features with a strong dash of early 'Tyrolean' style in some cases. The period 1700–1800 saw the strong Stainer influence often referred to in this book at its height, with Amatise instruments appearing sporadically in the later part. The last decade began to show Stradivarian influences which gained ground in the nineteenth century. Only Daniel Parker and one or two other early eighteenth-century makers had taken much note of Stradivarian principles before. From 1800 onwards copyists prevailed and Italian models were almost invariably used, though materials and varnish (amongst other features) can still betray an instrument's origin in the nineteenth century.

This chapter primarily deals with features of the period *circa* 1700–90 except where earlier or later makers and their characteristics are clearly referred to. The

'Old English School' starts to lose its identity from about 1800 and the picture in some respects becomes more complex—paradoxically, as it also becomes more essentially imitative; the reasons for this are discussed in later chapters.

The Body

In Heron-Allen's seminal work, *Violin-Making as it Was, and is*,[1] he presents readers wishing to copy a Stradivari violin with an 'outside' mould 'which is cut out like a frame and *inside* which the fiddle is made'. This is contrasted with the Guarneri model which is constructed with the aid of an 'inside' mould 'which is solid, and *round* which the fiddle is made'.[2]

The received opinion with regard to instruments of the Old English School is that the back was first carved out and the instrument 'built up' from there. The Hills elaborate this point thus:

> Were it not known that Stradivari made use of moulds for the building up of the sides, we would have suggested that he, after first setting upon his design for the outline, and tracing it—probably from a cartridge pattern—on the slabs of maple and pine prepared for back and belly, roughly cut it out by a bow-saw; that then, after shaping the model, finally trueing up the curves of the outline and hollowing out the back to its correct thickness, he proceeded to glue on the six shaped blocks exactly in their respective places, and, when these were dry, bent the sides to them, thus dispensing altogether with a mould. This system, though obviously presenting greater difficulties, especially in the way of keeping the sides true, was that in use with all the old English makers (to whom we think moulds were unknown); and it certainly has the advantage of allowing unlimited freedom to continually alter the outline, a facility which is restricted by the use of a mould—i.e. if the same mould is utilised unaltered—as it cannot be too clearly understood that the outline has to follow the exact contour of the mould and vice versa.[3]

Morris takes a more cautious view and simply states that 'many of our second-rate and inferior instruments were probably built without a mould. So were a large number of Italian ones; but there is generally this difference in the result: the latter are often crude and sadly out of line; the former at the worst, are only a little rough and quaint looking.'[4] Albert Cooper, in his monograph on *Benjamin Banks*, states that this maker's work was built up from the back (rather than being constructed with an inside mould) and that this gave scope for journeymen, 'provided they had a good eye and were able to square the top, bottom and corner blocks

---

[1] (London, 1884).
[2] Ibid., chs. 14 and 21. Stradivari's inside mould used for the construction of the Tuscan set of instruments is illustrated in Hill, *Stradivari*, 194.
[3] Ibid. 193–4.
[4] W. Meredith Morris, *British Violin Makers*, 2nd edn. (London, 1920), 16.

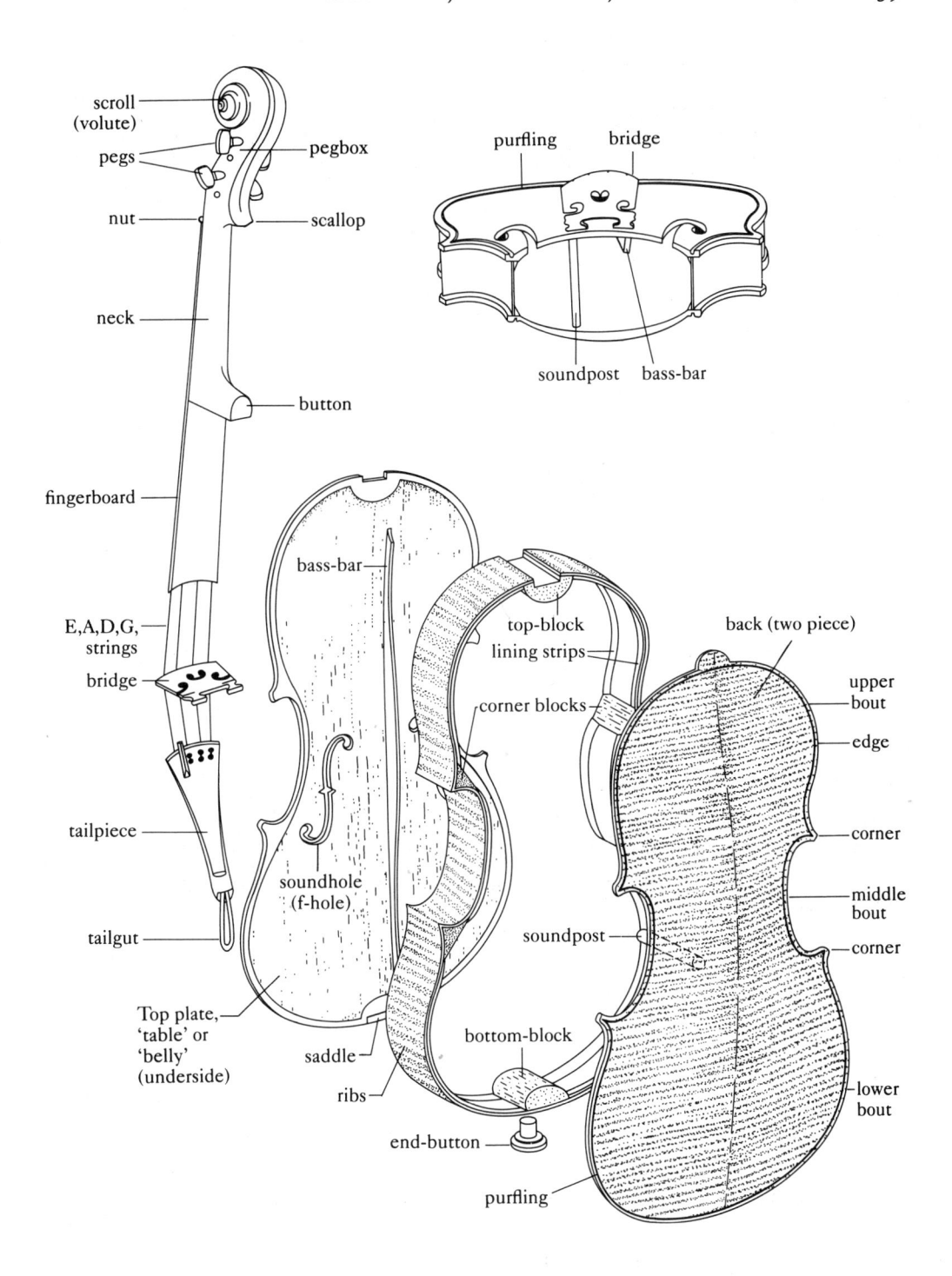

FIG. 1. An 'exploded' view of a modern violin.

accurately'.[5] The instruments of Benjamin Banks and his family were in demand (as new instruments) from about 1770 to 1830, the business moving from Salisbury to Liverpool. There seems good reason for thinking that the family ran a workshop which Banks, in his lifetime, would have superintended, and that he would have delegated some of the work to his sons or assistants. Cooper suggests that some of the scrolls were made in this way. 'Roughing out by others would be an obvious procedure when pressed for time.'[6]

It is clearly not possible to generalize. The earliest makers in England were, we have seen, influenced by both northern Italian and Austro-Germanic models and the use of moulds must have been a known skill. Stradivari used them despite changing his model materially several times during his working life. On the other hand, John Dilworth's view is that some early English makers, such as Rayman, Urquhart, Pamphilon, and Barak Norman 'used the Flemish method of construction, managing without a mould by setting the ribs into a channel cut into the back, allowing a greater flexibility of outline . . .'[7]

English makers of a later generation basing their work on Stainer or Amati would have had sound reasons for using appropriately shaped moulds. In the early nineteenth century when the modelling became more obviously copied from Stradivari or other classical Cremonese makers the use of a mould, usually an inside one, became more common, particularly if a series of instruments were to be made on the same model. But where an individual instrument was being copied a mould would probably have been regarded as unnecessary.

One prominent exception to the earlier tendency to do without moulds appears to have been Daniel Parker (and probably also Edward Lewis). John Dilworth records: 'Marks on the back of a dismantled Parker I have examined follow the inside of the ribs and can only have been made when the ribs were supported by an outside mould without blocks or linings. The corner blocks do not extend to the full length of the ribs, so must have been put in at a later stage and are slightly overlapped by the linings.'[8]

Scroll and Button

The 'head' of the instrument, by which for present purposes (terminology being non-uniform in various writings on this subject) we mean the scroll or volute, descending down the pegbox to the 'scallop' or 'shell' at the back of the bottom of the pegbox, is one of the most distinctive features of the luthier's art. The head has

---

[5] p. 31.   [6] Ibid.
[7] John Dilworth, 'Pioneer Spirit', *Strad* (Dec. 1986), 571.
[8] Ibid. 572.

no acoustic significance and makers or manufacturers wishing to produce a cheap product will inevitably economize in this part of the work. On the other hand the craftsman will make a particular point of achieving a satisfactory aesthetic effect. This will require considerable time and trouble in achieving a design which is satisfactory from whichever angle it is viewed and executing that design with the accurate use of the necessary tools, particularly the gouge.

As Kevin Coates has explained,[9] its classical design follows the volute of the Ionic order of classical architecture. Elaborate demonstrations of this can be seen in the illustrations in Coates's book, but from the layman's point of view the appearance of an Ionic volute is one of visual 'tidiness', since the curl of the curves, of which there are usually three starting from the 'eye' at the centre, increase proportionately in distance from the eye. Since a three-dimensional effect is obtained by making the eye the most protuberant point in the scroll, there must be extreme evenness between the two sides of the scroll, and the central 'tongue', exactly dividing the scroll in terms of width, should be carved so as to run the whole length lying on the top of the highest point of the pegbox. The volute should also be 'thrown' forward so that its frontmost point meets an imaginary straight line drawn as an extension of the bottom of the pegbox.

Old English instruments can often readily be recognized by their scrolls, but a word of warning is appropriate. Not all old instruments retain their original scrolls, almost all of which will in any event have been grafted on to the neck in the course of the modernization operations described in this chapter. Even where the scroll is original, many makers finished their work on the heads either better or worse according to the money they expected to receive for the instrument. So, for instance, although Morris states that 'Richard Tobin was the best scroll carver that Britain has ever produced',[10] examples of Tobin's work can be seen where the scrolls are far from impressive. And Morris goes on to state that, by contrast, Benjamin Banks, the English 'Amati', has left some scrolls which are rather feeble in design and execution.[11] Makers such as Banks are thought to have run small workshops and work on the heads may in some cases have been delegated. But taken as a whole there is little doubt that Morris's remarks about the scrolls of the Old English School still retain their validity:

Old British scrolls not infrequently show some strength and decision of character, but the curves are inclined to be stiff and the heads a trifle flat. The throat of the scroll is usually somewhat thick, and the head in consequence appears diminutive. Almost invariably the back of the peg-box diminishes rapidly right away from the scallop down to the first turn, where the volute begins. This is so persistent a characteristic of old English scrolls that an expert could pick one out from among a dozen others with his eyes shut. In all Italian

---

[9] *Geometry, Proportion and the Art of Lutherie.*
[10] *British Violin Makers*, 17.   [11] Ibid.

fiddles of the first water, the width of the back of the peg-box diminishes almost imperceptibly until it reaches the throat, where it diminishes much more rapidly: this arrangement of lines and curves gives the whole scroll a feeling of majesty combined with simplicity—a feeling wholly lacking in all but the very best of our old English fiddles.[12]

Morris does not mention another characteristic of the old English scroll, perhaps because it is related to what he states above. This is that the largest and topmost curl of the volute tends to be disproportionately thick compared to the smaller curls, and the most forward part of the volute tends to be carved rather flat. This is also a characteristic of German makers which, it has been suggested, results because the scrolls have been brought too far forward and so the curve was cut away till it came into line with the neck. The 'snail-like' appearance of, for example, the Klotz school's scrolls demonstrates the features discussed above in their most exaggerated form. This 'high forehead' feature can be seen in some of the illustrations of English instruments in this book and is well exemplified by the Forster cello head illustrated in Pl. 28.

The button is another valuable 'visiting-card' when identifying the nationality of a violin. It is the semicircular piece at the back which joins the neck of the violin and in some cases, as with the scroll, may not be original. Problems may well have been caused in the past when the neck has been removed from the body of the violin to effect repairs, and unless this is done carefully it may result in fracturing the button. Equally, problems are caused by restorers putting ebony crowns around the button, often when the instrument was modernized, and this disguises its true shape.

If the scroll tends to have Germanic characteristics, this cannot be said about the button of old English instruments. As a rule it is set on a true level with the back or may even stand proud of the back. It is a characteristic of the button of a German instrument that it is rather dome-shaped, and tends to slant back towards the rear of the neck. This gives a weak appearance to the instrument. English buttons tend to be semicircular and, particularly in quality instruments from the late eighteenth century onwards, tend to stand 'proud' and have two 'nicks' on either side where the button meets the back (Fig. 2).

Other Distinguishing Features of Older Instruments

Classic Italian violins tended to have their edges finished with a knife so that there was a flat surface between the sides and the protrusion of the edge. English makers, as with their French counterparts, tended to finish their edges with a file and

[12] *British Violin Makers*, 16–17.

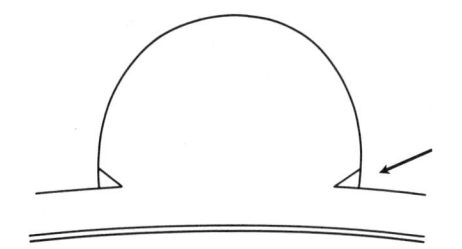

FIG. 2. The button of an English violin, showing the characteristic 'nicks' at the sides (arrowed).

sandpaper (or its predecessors, typically Dutch rush, as used by Grinling Gibbons, sandpaper not being in use until the nineteenth century) before gluing the plates to the ribs, thus giving a rounded appearance. Not infrequently the edges of the table are 'beaded', that is carved with slight indentations following the grain, giving the edge of the table a serrated appearance, as often found on English furniture—for example grandfather-clock cases. In some cases, too, the body 'stop'—that is the distance between the upper edge of the table and the notch on the soundhole—can be rather short, thus abbreviating the effective string-length. Cellos are particularly susceptible to this characteristic which, if exaggerated, can lead a player not used to the instrument to play slightly sharp.

Soundhole design is often referred to in the text. Through much of the eighteenth century and even in the seventeenth, when Brescian principles generally prevailed, soundholes tend towards the short, widely cut, and upright. Fluting of the wings of the soundholes, which lends a certain elegance to the design, is not usually to be found in routine instruments of this period (see Fig. 4).

It has already been observed that internally the work can be rough, with the linings, corner blocks, and end blocks rather crudely finished. But it must be emphasized that this is not uniformly the case, as can readily be perceived from the illustration of the interior of a Banks violin in Cooper's monograph.[13] But in some of the cruder instruments of other English makers the bass bar can actually be built in integrally to the table, rather than being independently made and subsequently attached. The neck and top block are commonly cut from the same piece of maple with the rib slotted into the sides. The omission of corner blocks entirely is more usually a German rather than an English characteristic, though the author's attention has been drawn to an early William Baker viola without corner blocks or linings. It is also the view of at least one expert that the nineteenth-century reworking of many old English instruments by restorers such as the Hills and Harts includes the fitting of corner blocks to instruments built originally without them. Blocks, where fitted, and linings are made of coarse pine and linings tend to be modest in height with a small chamfer on the top edge only. They are not mortised into the lower blocks in the manner of better Italian and French

[13] Cooper, *Benjamin Banks*, 62.

instruments. In cheaper eighteenth-century 'trade' instruments it is unfortunately the case that the purfling was done in ink rather than being inlaid. (Purfling, and its English characteristics, is mentioned below.)

Varnish

The vexed question of varnish

More ink has probably been spilled on the precise constitution of the varnish used by the classic violin-makers, particularly those of the Cremona school, than about any other of the constituent parts of the violin. The fact that it seems impossible to reproduce classic Cremona varnish and that its chemistry has never been disclosed assists the mystery. It is also well established that the so-called 'Cremona varnish' was known throughout the seventeenth century and for most of the eighteenth century to Italian violin-makers well removed from Cremona and, as the Hills remark,[14] even Jacob Stainer 'possessed the open secret of this varnish' as did some of the Salzburg makers, some of the early French and Dutch makers, and some English makers: 'All these men had, and at times used, a quite superior varnish, the constituents of which were similar to those employed by the Italians.' The Hills also go on to point out that the lute makers of the fifteenth and sixteenth centuries already used varnishes made from the standard gums, oils, and vegetable colours. There was probably considerable common ground between the varnishes used by the great Italian painters and those used by the great Italian violin-makers. (As will be seen later, this was also the view of the English late nineteenth- and early twentieth-century maker, William Atkinson.) Some commentators have seen similarities between the Cremona varnish and that used on Italian furniture and keyboard instruments during the period approximately 1680–1740.[15]

It is possible that the missing secret is discoverable amongst the numerous treatises which still exist from the sixteenth century onwards on the making of varnishes for many different purposes.[16] What is difficult to reproduce in the laboratory is the effect of light and wear over the centuries.

The purpose of varnishes is widely agreed to be the dual one of preserving the wood and presenting it to the eye in the most aesthetically satisfactory manner. Equally, whilst the varnish itself does not explain the secret of outstanding tone, it is generally believed that an unvarnished violin rapidly loses its tone and a good

[14] *Stradivari*, 171–2.
[15] See Ole Bull's 'Violin Notes' quoted in J. Broadhouse, *The Violin: How to Make it* (London, c.1910).
[16] See e.g. ibid. 99 and Heron-Allen, *Violin-Making*, ch. 10, where many of these recipes are given. See also George Fry, *Italian Varnishes* (London, 1904), and Joseph Michelman, *Violin Varnish* (Oh., USA 1946). More modern research is summarized in *Violin Family*, 226. Also Peter Forrester, 'Sticky Solutions', in *Strad* (Apr. 1988), 304. Modern thought on Stradivari's varnishes is mentioned *post*.

violin clothed in a bad varnish is tonally depreciated by this process. Even if an indifferent varnish does not adversely affect the timbre of the instrument, the Hills speaking from long experience say that commercially the instrument becomes much more difficult to sell. No doubt it was for this reason as well that the great makers have shown their individuality by choosing and mixing their varnishes with great care, particularly as to the inherent substance and colouring used, and would have wished to vary the colourings from one time to another. Most buyers of instruments are unschooled in the technicalities of their making and it is the varnish which is the first thing that catches the eye. More discrimination is needed by the buyer in search of an old instrument who, despite initial appearances, appreciates the time-marked presentation of what was once a very different-looking product.

Similar preoccupations affected English makers of all periods where, particularly in the nineteenth century, there was considerable interest in rediscovering the apparently lost Italian secret. Two examples of this may be given to demonstrate this point.

First, the Revd Charles L. Tweedale combined his work as Vicar of Weston, in Yorkshire, with enthusiastic making of violins. In his book *News from the Next World*[17] he states that he was actually in communication with the spirit of Stradivari who revealed to him the secret of violin construction and of the varnish. Although one modern directory[18] describes Tweedale's varnish as 'Fine oil varnish, soft, very transparent and generally applied with subtlety', the appearance of many (though not all) of Tweedale's instruments as seen in the sale-room today is a sorry sight indeed. Many of these instruments are remarkable for the amount of the varnish which has actually removed itself entirely from the body of the violin. Indeed, consistent results in varnishing techniques seem to have eluded all but a few of the British makers of the late nineteenth and early twentieth centuries.

The second example of the nineteenth-century obsession with the discovery of the Italian secrets is the experience of James Whitelaw, who is described by Honeyman[19] as 'The maker of one of the finest oil varnishes for violins that has been produced during this century' (i.e. the nineteenth century). As will be seen, many late nineteenth- and early twentieth-century makers used his products. The vouchsafing of the method of making 'Cremona Varnish' is related in Whitelaw's own words as follows:

I was lying in bed on the last Sunday morning of February 1886, about five o'clock, I think. Whether I was asleep or awake I could never be certain. Suddenly my bedroom seemed to be transformed into an old-fashioned-looking kitchen, in which was a large dresser with a

---

[17] (London, 1940). [18] Henley, *Dictionary*, 1172.
[19] William C. Honeyman, *Scottish Violin Makers: Past and Present*, 2nd edn. (Dundee, 1910), 97–101.

lighted candle at one end. Above the dresser, instead of crockery and household odds and ends, there were rows of fiddles handing on the wall. While I was looking at this display of fiddles, a very tall and majestic man came into the kitchen. He had on a little round white cap and a white leather apron, his hair was nearly white, and in little crisp curls. He had beautiful grey eyes, and a very pleasant expression. He spoke to me, and I asked him about the violins on the wall. He said they had all been made in Cremona, and among other things told me about the varnish being a secret.

He now took down a violin from the wall, and having removed the candle to the middle of the dresser, he held the violin up behind the flame at an angle of about forty five degrees, and moving it from side to side he asked me if I could see the beautiful satin-like glint which followed the candle flame. I said—'Yes'. 'Well!' he said, 'that is a peculiarity of the varnish'. After some conversation I asked him if amber was used in making the varnish. He said 'It is amber varnish, and the solvents are lead and lime'. Just at that moment the violin disappeared, and I awakened and found that during the awakening 'lead and lime', . . . by some mysterious process, had in my mind become converted into two quite different substances. Impelled by curiosity I got up at once, and hurried to my shop. It was now 7 am. I hastily fitted together some odd pieces of apparatus sufficient for the experiment, and before 8.30 I had the satisfaction of knowing that I could dissolve amber without chemical disintegration . . . I found out afterwards, it is one thing to dissolve amber but quite another matter to make it into a working varnish. It was fully a year before I had varnish to try on a violin, and nearly three years before I had a bottle ready for sale, so that the discovery was not completed without a considerable amount of trouble and anxiety.

The end of this story is disappointing. Whitelaw's varnish was widely marketed in his lifetime (he died in 1904) and thereafter as 'Cremona Amber Oil Varnish', and many an eager maker of the period saw it as the answer to his problems, probably putting it on (as Honeyman advocated) 'on the bare wood' without any preliminary sizing 'so as to get its claws into that wood to secure a firm grip'. Alas, in many cases seen today the grip has been anything but firm, resulting in a tawdry, blistered (or craquelled and 'crazed') appearance to the varnish of what might be a well-built instrument. Whitelaw sold two varieties, one to dry quickly and the other to dry moderately quickly—Honeyman advocating a modicum of patience combined with the latter. It would be interesting to ascertain by analysis whether the degenerative problem is intrinsic to Whitelaw's varnish, or if the mode of putting it on is partly to blame.

Technical Constituents

There has been a certain lack of discrimination in the use of terms applied to varnish materials in much of the writing on this subject. The term 'oil' is often used to signify linseed oil, but there are also 'fixed vegetable oils' such as poppy, nut, castor, and 'essential' oils like those of rosemary, spike, and turpentine, etc.; and mineral oils such as benzene, oil of tar, and naphtha. There have also been different names for such substances as 'amber' and 'sandarac', leading to confusion. For many centuries sandarac was the resinous basis of colourless or pale alcoholic varnishes. Because it was brilliant but friable, and lacked durability, it was often combined with other gums possessing greater pliability and toughness, particularly Manila copal or castor oil.[20]

Generally the old English violin-makers and most, but not all, of the classic violin-makers, used what is loosely described as 'oil varnish'. This has a basis of the oils described above, particularly linseed oil. The varnish then oxidizes over the years and gradually solidifies into an extremely tough, and often mellow and beautiful coating. Spirit varnish, on the other hand, is alcohol-based. It consists of solutions of the relevant gums in alcohol, often with the use of only modest heat. The principal resins and substances used are lac and sandarac and sometimes mastic, Manila copal, elemi, benzoin, and Venice turpentine.

The careful conclusion of writers such as Taylor[21] (now perhaps, somewhat dated) was that the Italian makers had two distinct varnishing processes, the first consisting of the covering of the wood with a substratum which was the real protective varnish, followed by the application of a brilliant, coloured superstratum for purely decorative purposes. Many makers preceded the process by applying a 'wash' of a transparent nature of perhaps a yellow or red tint. In the case of Stradivari, it is thought that in the first place he primed and prepared the wood with a waterproof, transparent, and shiny priming coat which also had the purpose of improving the acoustic properties of the wood. This substance is thought to have been potassium silicate (sometimes known as water-glass).

David Rubio, writing in *The Book of the Violin*,[22] states that the research of modern experts (for example S. F. Sacconi) has revealed traces of silicates in the wood possibly due to the use of dogfish skin as an abrasive or from particles of glass—ground glass being added to the varnish to provide added refraction and, if lead-based, to help the varnish dry more quickly. But Rubio agrees that this 'sealant' was likely to have been potassium silicate—a water-glass which would vitrify in the fibre of the wood and provide an indestructible sealant base.

After the primer the second stage then followed, and Rubio suggests that a pure pine-resin varnish was made by cooking the resin (Venetian turpentine or colophony) at very high temperatures. If this cooking took place in an iron pot that contained traces of rust (ferric oxide), a rich red colour would be obtained. After cooking, the resin would be reheated with linseed oil until it reached the right consistency and was then thinned with a suitable solvent for use. This varnish turns out to be flexible and transparent, and fluoresces a bright salmon colour

---

[20] See Joseph Taylor, *The Principles of Violin Construction* (London, 1926), 45–6.
[21] Ibid. 47.   [22] Gill (ed.), 35.

under long-wave ultraviolet light. Varnishing was completed with several layers of coloured varnish applied until the desired shade was reached. There would then have been several coats of clear varnish, which, when dry, was rubbed with pumice and tripoli powders until the surface was silken to the touch.[23]

Oil varnishes of this sort, which required long drying times, tended to be set aside in the nineteenth century (but not so much in England) in favour of quicker-drying spirit varnishes. These provide a characteristically glassy appearance and there is a continuing controversy as to whether they tend to stifle the tone of the violin.

Colouring matters were traditionally powdered and put in the turpentine to dissolve sometime before it was wanted for making the varnish. Yellows could be obtained by the use of aloes, gamboge, turmeric, or saffron. Red could be obtained by the use of madder or logwood. These, and many other colouring substances, were generally available in Italy from the sixteenth century, mainly due to the prosperous trade route between the East Indies and Venice. From the seventeenth century onwards the use of similar materials for finishing furniture and in fine art spread throughout Europe.[24]

Varnish and English Violin-Makers

As with all other aspects of the luthier's art in England, standards of varnishing have proved to be extremely variable—though English varnishes at their best are probably only excelled by those of the classic Italian makers. Because of this variability there appears to be no extensive study of the varnishes likely to have been used in England from the start of our period, i.e. 1650, onwards. Even the expert author of the recent monograph on Benjamin Banks contents himself with saying that Banks's varnish

is among the most successful of the eighteenth century English makers, in spite of the few early writers who claim that his varnish 'kills the grain', whatever they mean. Time has dealt unkindly with some deep top reds, they have oxidised into a dark texture, but look below all where this has been removed by natural wear and tear, the ground colours are as fresh as when applied. The golden red, rose red, and brown varnishes have not suffered in this way so that here the work of time has only enhanced their attraction.[25]

The author goes on to propose that there were probably two different methods of applying the varnishes, since sometimes the top varnish separates from the base

---

[23] Gill (ed.), 36.
[24] For a number of varnishes in use in Europe during the 15th and 16th centuries, many of them based on boiled and purified linseed oil plus powdered mastic, sandarac, and roche alum, see Forrester, 'Sticky Solutions', 304.
[25] Cooper, *Benjamin Banks*, 147.

and at other times the base colours blend better and show no sign of chipping. The author also observed that fading has not taken place where the varnish is exposed to light—it remains the same under and away from the fingerboard. But what was the formulation of this varnish? Albert Cooper has to settle for saying that 'Most likely a local chemist would have been involved as no varnishes exist that relate to the London makers except perhaps that found on some work of William Forster.'[26]

It is, of course, disappointing that we apparently have so little *concrete* information as to exactly how varnishes of the Old English School were made up. That many of them were oil-based varnishes is certain. And the Early English School has always attracted plaudits for varnishing standards. The varnishes of such makers as Urquhart (to whom Norman was allegedly apprenticed), Pamphilon, and Lewis were usually of high quality and sometimes taken for that of Italian makers. They are discussed in the next chapter in the context of the relevant maker.

The success of the earlier makers no doubt stems from the earlier tradition of varnishing lutes and viols, in respect of which (particularly as regards viols), as we have seen in Chapter 1, the English makers enjoyed an outstanding reputation. John Dilworth writes of the early English varnish that the local groups of violin craftsmen in Bishopsgate and St Paul's, and later Piccadilly and Holborn, seem to have shared a specific varnish which was obtained from the nearest varnish-maker, and was chosen for its availability rather than quality in many cases.[27]

To generalize about the position in the eighteenth and earlier part of the nineteenth century is never likely to be very satisfactory, but one summary by an anonymous writer states that

the varnish varies greatly in colour, but as a general rule various shades of yellow have been used. With the exception of yellow varnish, the English made their varnishes somewhat opaque, and their red tones were not successful. Their yellow-brown varnish was good and clear, but dark vandyke brown was hardly ever used. The quality of the English varnish used from 1750–1850 is really good; in some cases it is quite equal in texture, though not in colour, to that used by the celebrated Italian makers. Minor makers, who sold their instruments through the medium of small dealers, only used a thin, dirty varnish.[28]

Meredith Morris, writing in 1920 with the advantage of having seen numerous old English instruments, enthuses about the varnish. He described it as 'excellent as regards elasticity and adhesiveness. The oil varnish of our old makers will probably wear better than that of even the great classical makers themselves.' He states that the varnish on the instruments of such makers as Duke and Forster has lasted

---

[26] Ibid.

[27] Dilworth, 'Pioneer Spirit', 574. It is also understood from John Dilworth that analysis of varnish used by Cross and Norman done at the Rijksmuseum (Amsterdam) indicates a colophony-based recipe.

[28] Balfour & Co., *How to Tell the Nationality of Old Violins* (London, 1900; repr. 1983), 5, 6.

the years better than many Italian instruments, and he adds: 'I have seen a Dodd's cello varnished with the celebrated "original Cremona varnish", which had a hole knocked in one of the bouts, and the varnish around the scraggy edges had parted "clean". There was not a suspicion of a "chip" or transversal crack.' Morris continues by saying that it is remarkable that so few authentic recipes of old varnishes have been handed down to us and concludes that this may have been one of the 'mysteries' of the craft, confined by the master to his apprentice.

It has been seen already, however, that there are in fact a large number of recipes known for varnishes, though not necessarily specifically for stringed instruments, and the difficulty is not so much finding possible sources but analysing accurately, after this length of time, the constituent parts of the varnish. Morris concludes: 'Our old makers used both oil and spirit varnishes. The gums, resins, etc, which entered into their composition are perfectly familiar to us . . .', and he then refers to a comprehensive list of ingredients in Heron-Allen's book on violin-making.[29] By and large the remarks of the anonymous writer of Balfour & Co.'s Guide and of Morris can be seen to be borne out on inspection of the better class of instrument between 1660 and about 1850. The golden-brown varnish often seen on, for instance, a Lockey Hill cello is a thing of some beauty and bears out Morris in terms of its durability.

From about the second half of the nineteenth century onwards makers have shown less inclination to make their own varnish and a number have made use of proprietary products, many of which were made up from fossil amber in a solution of oil. Examples of these were 'Whitelaw's Varnish', already discussed and thought by Morris to be transparent, elastic, and fiery but actually rather brittle and prone to craquelle with age, 'Dr. Inglis Clark's varnish' (formerly available from manufacturing chemists in Scotland in colours ranging from golden-yellow to ruby red and purportedly not so inclined to crack or chip), and 'Anderson's Varnish', another Scottish product. Morris mentions all these, together with 'Harris's Varnish' from Gateshead-on-Tyne and 'Walker's Varnish' made by John Walker of Solihull (soft, elastic, and transparent, according to Morris). The latter is said to be subject to fading and this is an observable problem with varnishes on a number of more modern English instruments, of which Millington's Varnish (made by a chemist of Borrowash, Derbyshire), as used by the eminent maker Arthur Richardson of Crediton, Devon (awarded First Prize, best-toned British violin, London, 1919) is perhaps the best-known.

Even the Hills' firm advertised varnish, along with wood, tools, and accessories, available through the post. A catalogue, *c.*1925, gives charges of 3*s.* 6*d.* for spirit varnish and 5*s.* 0*d.* for oil—enough for one violin. The same catalogue also men-

---

[29] Morris, *British Violin Makers*, 12–15.

tions the availability of violins in the white, 'for amateur varnishes', 10s. to £3 each. These were probably Mirecourt imports, but the item emphasizes the point made later in this book, that 'makers' could easily cheat, if they had a mind to do so, by buying the unvarnished factory-made model, only varnishing it (the oil varnish would make it look less French) and then inserting their own label.

Despite the existence of these proprietary varnishes, most of the more eminent English makers of the period from 1850 onwards undoubtedly followed the tradition of making up their own recipes and keeping that recipe secret, William Atkinson being a good example of this (see Chapter 12.) Many were clearly obsessed with the problem of varnish, presumably because it was thought to be critical in reproducing Cremona tone. In retrospect, few makers of this later era achieved really fine and enduring results.

To conclude these thoughts on the use and abuse of varnish, David Laurie gives an amusing and revealing glimpse of how famous makers can apparently exploit their varnishing secrets without actually giving anything away. Vuillaume in a typically cunning way epitomized this particular accomplishment. Laurie describes how in Vuillaume's garden there stood a greenhouse in which, for the edification and entertainment of his visitors on Thursdays, he gave a demonstration of varnishing a fiddle.

Here they might view him at work, as, attired in his working blouse, he stood, a fiddle in one hand, a brush in the other and pot of varnish on the bench. At the other end of the bench were bottles filled with varnish for sale and he would dip into his pot of varnish and one of the bottles alternately, as he varnished the fiddle before their admiring eyes. This was done in order to show the similarity of the varnish in the pot and bottle.

Laurie then followed Vuillaume back to the attics above the first floor of his château and there, to Laurie's astonishment,

he carefully removed from the fiddles he had varnished in the greenhouse, every drop of varnish he had put on, and at last I asked him why he did this. He laughed uproariously at my amazed looks, and said that, while the varnish he sold was good varnish and would make a fine job of a fiddle if put on according to the directions given, he could hardly be expected that he would give away his own varnish.[30]

To sum up, the appearance of an older English violin is often greatly enhanced by its durable varnish. This usually lacks the characteristic iridescence of a fine Italian varnish and can often deteriorate to a murky brown or even darker colour. But at its best it can be transparent, elastic, durable, and calculated to enhance the appearance of the instrument. Instruments of the late nineteenth and earlier twentieth century may suffer from varnish degeneration problems, as described.

[30] David Laurie, *The Reminiscences of a Fiddle Dealer* (London, c.1924), 49.

Comments are made on the varnishing methods of various specific makers throughout the text where this is appropriate.

Wood

Almost as much space has been taken by writers on the description and analysis of wood used for violin-making as for varnish. The general principle is well known even to non-experts. The table of the violin is of a resonant nature, softer to work than the wood used for the back, and normally of pine or spruce. The table wood of the classic Italian makers probably came from the Tyrol or what became northern Yugoslavia or Switzerland, trees growing at a considerable height being needed. The modern view is that the most suitable wood comes from trees growing at 2500 metres above sea-level in soil discouraging rapid growth, aged about 200 years with annular rings of between 1 mm and 2 mm.[31]

As the Hills say in the context of Stradivari, 'All our information goes to prove that this wood used by the Brescian and the Cremonese makers up to the time of Stradivari was of local growth, and no difficulty could have been experienced in obtaining it. The demands of a few cabinet and fiddle makers could not absorb the produce of many trees, and it must therefore have been both easily and cheaply procurable.' The back of stringed instruments, together with ribs, neck, and scroll, must be of hard wood, preferably nicely figured with acoustic resonance. Maple coming from southern Europe was the wood most generally used, and this was produced in the Italian Tyrol, Dalmatia, Czechoslovakia, southern France, Germany, and Switzerland, amongst other European sources. Pear wood was also sometimes used by the earlier Italian makers, but English makers generally relied upon native sycamore.

It is quite clear that trade was sufficiently advanced in England by the middle of the seventeenth century to allow the importation of a wide variety of comparatively exotic foreign woods. These were primarily used for the fine furniture which was then starting to be produced in England. Timber-yards abounded, and before specifically selected violin wood as such became commonly exported to England in the nineteenth century one would have expected the earlier English makers to make use of their local timber-yards. English timber-yards were major *importers* of all the woods needed for the high-quality furniture made in the eighteenth century. The *London Tradesman* c.1740 stated: 'Furnished with Deal from Norway; with Oak and Wainscot from Sweden, and some of the Counties of England; with Mahogany from Jamaica; with Walnut-Tree from Spain.'[32] Maple, though not in

---
[31] See Rubio in Gill (ed.), *Book of the Violin*, 25.
[32] See Bernard Price, *The Story of English Furniture* (London, 1982), 90.

the list, must have been available too. In the case of Banks there was a large timber-yard adjacent to his workshop. So there may well have been some choice as between native and foreign wood.

The extent to which the older English makers in fact used foreign maple in their instruments' backs was hotly debated in the pages of the *Strad* in correspondence between the prolific article-writer and dealer Arthur Dykes and George Wulme Hudson. Alfred Hill intervened, with his unique authority,[33] and supported Hudson's view that English sycamore was largely used:

Richard Duke, senior, as well as junior, invariably used English sycamore in the construction of their instruments; the Forsters frequently made use of it, and for their best instruments; it was likewise employed by John Betts, John Dodd, the Fendts, Panormo, Banks, Hill, and others, and I very much doubt that in the XVIII century, foreign maple was imported into the country in any considerable quantity . . . As a matter of fact, violin-making has never been a remunerative craft, and the old English fiddle-makers, not being in affluent circumstances, naturally made use of the wood obtainable at the cheaper price and I would add, fine English sycamore such as is procurable from time to time, compares very favourably with foreign maple, which latter wood, taken as a whole, is obviously superior to the former; it is, however, incorrect to affirm that an instrument made of maple should, on that account, prove superior to one in the making of which sycamore had been employed, inasmuch as it is the happy combination of certain recognised features which goes to make the perfect instrument.[34]

As the nineteenth century progressed there was more of a tendency to use imported Continental maple, *Acer platanoides*. The belly wood, readily available in the pine forests of Scotland, northern England, and elsewhere, perhaps had a tendency to a 'softness' which, some writers have stated, explains the comparatively 'chamber music' acoustic quality of many of these instruments. The trees were certainly on lower ground than was desirable for correct growth. But, again, particularly as foreign violin craftsmen settled in this country at the turn of the nineteenth century, there was much more resort to straight and closely reeded Continental pine.[35] On some of the early English instruments much less attention is given to the pattern of the grain on the table, which should be straight and tend to widen towards the flanks. The grain in some of the more cheaply produced English instruments can be decidedly 'wild' and erratic.

In the case of both maple and pine, traditionally the tree should have been from the south side of the forest (and thus exposed to the sun), cut in midwinter at a time when the sap has ceased to flow, cross-cut to the desired lengths and figuration, and then seasoned for six or seven years before use.[36] Unfortunately some

---

[33] See Albert Cooper, 'Trade Secrets', *Strad*, (Feb. 1985), 753–9.
[34] Ibid. 757.
[35] This is usually Norway spruce, *Picea abies*.
[36] See the discussion in Heron-Allen, *Violin-Making*, 128 ff.

French and English makers, more concerned with volume than quality, have tried to expedite this process by baking or chemically treating the wood. This process may be discoverable on opening the instrument when a baked and brittle quality is discernible.

Meredith Morris states his view that old English makers for the most part used 'maple and pine of the orthodox kind', with occasional experiments. 'Old' Forster used common deal for the tables of many of his second-class instruments, and others produced very plain but acoustically satisfactory backs. Owing to the tendency of many of the older English makers to be on the verge of insolvency, the yardstick used must often have been the best available wood for the very modest expenditure involved. Such considerations did not trouble Stradivari and his Cremonese colleagues, though one can see the same tendency to economy in instruments of such Milanese makers as Testore and Grancino. By the second quarter of the nineteenth century many of the leading London makers were using Tyrolean pine and Continental maple to match the figure of good Italian instruments.

There is also a long-running controversy on *how* wood should best be seasoned for violin-making purposes. Meredith Morris states that the older tradition was to submerge the wood in water for an extended period, followed by exposure to dry air for a similar or longer period. He states that he had observed the practice of sinking newly sawn planks in deep water for two years and afterwards stowing them in open sheds. This is a tradition which is alleged to go back to the days of the Romans, and Morris stated that the timber used in English cathedrals and ancient churches was all seasoned in this manner.[37] But modern scientific investigation of small particles of old Italian instruments has not confirmed this 'ponding' theory. In fact the investigators found most of the wood samples to be indistinguishable from modern air-dried spruce of musical instrument quality.[38]

To summarize, as with varnish the choice of wood in the older English instruments is variable. At its best it is certainly acoustically satisfactory though there is a tendency to use plainer native materials for the back. There must also be a question mark over the acoustical properties of the table wood, particularly if of native growth. But no generalizations are possible since the illustrations in this book show that magnificent material can also be found in use from a comparatively early date for making highly flamed backs. Where the wood was plain some makers 'enhanced' it by decorative purfled patterning which can be quite attractive. Acoustically, most experts are of the view that English sycamore is little, if any, different from the more traditional maple. At the other end of the aesthetic spectrum, English makers of the older school also tended to prefer for the ribs and

---

[37] *British Violin Makers*, 24–6.
[38] See C. Y. Barlow and J. Woodhouse, 'Was Italian Spruce Soaked?', *Strad* (Mar. 1991), 234 and 'Bordered Pits in Spruce from Old Italian Violins', *Journal of Microscopy*, 160 (1990), 203–11.

back wood cut 'on the slab', and there are some beautiful cello backs in existence from the school of Lockey Hill and his contemporaries where the one-piece back is cut 'on the slab'. This expression means that the wood, instead of being 'quarter-sawn' (cut as a wedge, like the traditional slice of birthday cake), is divided by parallel cuts into slabs of equal thickness. This produces a wavy, circular pattern and it is an attractive feature of many English instruments' ribs as well as backs. For 'cellos, the size of tree needed to produce this effect must have been quite considerable, though if it is to be a one-piece back at all, a slab-cut one is of course easier to produce than one cut 'on the quarter' (see Fig. 3).

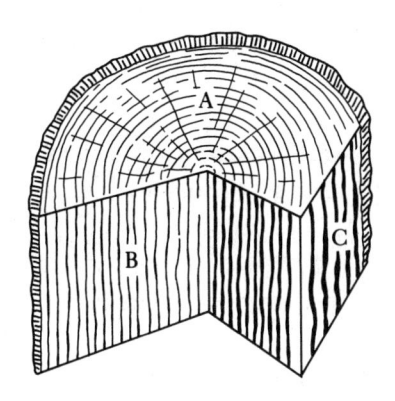

FIG. 3. Segment of sawn timber, showing: (*a*) end surface with growth rings and medullary rays; (*b*) 'quarter sawn' surface or 'edge grain'; (*c*) 'slab-cut' surface or 'on the slab'.

As to *glue*, practices have not changed, and the use of an animal gelatin-type, to some extent hydroscopic (from rabbit skins or horse's hooves), and applied when heated is virtually universal for securing the wooden parts to each other. This has many advantages: for example, it facilitates opening without damage for restoration purposes, with a sharp knife between table and ribs; and the glue, whilst strong and neat, can be cleaned off later with hot water.

Purfling

Purfling is the decorative inlay which follows the contour of the front and back of the instrument equidistant from the outer edge, throwing the form of the instrument into relief. Great makers such as Stradivari took considerable pains to mitre the corners and to point the 'bee-sting' towards the corner's highest point rather than its centre, a style copied by most modern makers of all nationalities since.

Purfling consists of a white piece of wood (or whalebone in some cases) sandwiched between two pieces of ebony, or other wood dyed black. In modern making it is possible to buy these purfling strips ready-assembled (perhaps made out of dyed white hawthorn), but the traditional maker would plane them out himself.

Lower-grade Italian makers, particularly the Milanese, sometimes omitted purfling or 'scratched' or 'scribed' it on, and inked imitation purfling became commonplace in Germany and England to save cost where, perhaps, a student instrument was required. John Barrett (*fl.* 1714–33, London) was one of the first English makers intermittently to adopt this practice, as did even members of the Forster family for cheaper-range instruments. Of course, discerning purchasers could then get their unpurfled instruments purfled and thus less easily distinguishable from the maker's higher-grade products. Simon Andrew Forster is actually driven to complain about 'the deceit and fraud practised by persons getting them purfled, and selling then as "genuine Forsters", for a larger sum than they were really worth'.[39] But in such purchasers' defence, the purfling does also have a functional purpose in helping to prevent cracks from running to the edge of the instrument.

It is a feature of many eighteenth-century English instruments that the purfling 'sandwich' is distinctly uneven, the middle white strip being much wider than the two outer black strips. Illustrations of this can be seen in some of the plates of eighteenth-century instruments featured in this book. It is not suggested that this feature is unique to English makers, but it is a sufficiently persistent feature to be significant for present purposes.

The Hills point out that modern makers usually insert the purfling at a relatively early stage, after cutting out the outline but before adjusting thicknesses. They add that old English makers followed the Cremonese practice of not dealing with the purfling until the body was assembled. This enabled inequalities of curvature of back and belly first to be 'corrected', but the Hills believe a consequence of this practice to be the 'inequalities of thicknesses of many of the old Italian instruments'.[40]

Accessories

Accessories in more recent times have been almost universally bought in by makers from specialist suppliers—for example, bridges (before final shaping) from Mirecourt, France. In England in earlier centuries some parts were made by the

FIG. 4. (*a*) Edge and soundhole of violin by Robert Cuthbert, London, 1676.
   (*b*) Edge and soundhole of violin branded 'Simpson', London, *c.* 1780.

[39] Sandys and Forster, *History*, 317.   [40] Hill, *Stradivari*, 196–7.

METHODS, MATERIALS, AND TECHNIQUES 57

A

B

maker himself, and others probably supplied by cabinet-makers. This particularly applies to the innocent little tail-button, whose function is to hold the tailpiece in place against the strong tension of the strings. Many of these old tail-buttons are preserved and it will be seen that they are beautifully turned and made of an attractive hardwood, often boxwood. Alternatively they can be made of ivory, sometimes decoratively inlaid with circular black lines or a miniature picture. These must have been readily obtainable by ordering them from a specialist manufacturer of furniture, where somewhat similar accessories were produced as handles for the small drawers of, for example, writing-desks. The top nut, over which the strings go from the pegbox to the fingerboard, is often made of ivory in the older English instruments, particularly violins. Saddles, over which the tail-gut joining the tailpiece to the tail-button runs, were also sometimes of delicately carved ivory. These features could greatly add to the attractiveness of an otherwise rather plain instrument. In old English instruments the saddle was often let into the bottom rib to just above the tail-button, the top being almost flush with the table.

Traditionally English pegs are made of boxwood, the attractively light-coloured but hard-grained wood of the box tree. After about 1800 the use of ebony or rosewood became much more common and the firm of Hills was a specialist supplier of these important fittings.[41]

Few bridges survive from the seventeenth or eighteenth centuries, but makers would normally have made their own bridges from odd pieces of hardwood not needed for the backs. As is the case with Stradivari's bridges, illustrated in the Hills' work on Stradivari, bridges of the older instruments were thinner and lower than those of today. Throughout Europe, as it became more important to maximise tonal penetration by use of the best possible wood, makers of the nineteenth century onwards tended to leave the manufacture of the outline bridge to specialists and buy these 'blanks' in. Considerable care would then be employed on making the bridges an exact fit, so that the feet fit the curve of the belly and the bridge is of the correct height, camber, and graduated thickness.

Looking at the older bridges made by Daniel Parker and others,[42] these are quaintly cut out but, as Morris remarks, are neither geometrically precise nor highly finished. Morris continues by saying that 'the claims of the modern bridge were advanced in this country chiefly by the labours of William Ebsworth Hill, who made hundreds of bridges, using only the very best wood, and finishing his work with the utmost care'. Messrs Hart of Wardour Street and Withers of Leicester Square are also mentioned by Morris as being makers of high-class bridges of the finest, well-seasoned wood and of simple but beautiful design, in the nineteenth century. Cooper[43] remarks that up until the early nineteenth century

---

[41] See Cooper, *Benjamin Banks*, 148. [42] See Morris, *British Violin Makers*, 34–7.
[43] *Benjamin Banks*, 148.

bridges were made from maple or sycamore offcuts. He states that their design showed great skill and dexterity but little thought was given to acoustics. Spotted maple is now the preferred material for high-class bridges.

Fingerboards in the baroque era were not necessarily the ebony to which we are now used. A baroque fingerboard was approximately 2 in. (50 mm) shorter than the modern fingerboard and often made of offcuts of maple. The better eighteenth-century makers, particularly those of Cremona, carefully designed the fingerboards, by inlaying a line of purfling or stringing which could be composed of ivory or ebony. Tailpieces were made of similar material.[44] From the late eighteenth century onwards all old instruments of any merit tended to be altered so as to increase tonal capacity and allow far greater string tension. This was done usually by removing the head from the neck, and substituting a longer neck inclined at a slight angle, grafting back the head onto the new neck, and exchanging the old shorter bass bar for a new stronger one. This matter is discussed in more detail later.

Most of the original fingerboards and baroque-style tailpieces have disappeared. However, Cooper in his book on Banks illustrates an attractive ivory fingerboard, a number of nineteenth-century violin and viola tailpieces with silver and mother-of-pearl decorations, as well as a selection of decorative cello bridges.

So far, at least, as the fingerboard is concerned, the originals have almost uniformly been replaced by modern full-length ebony ones which have the requisite hardness to mitigate the tendency for 'ruts' to be formed where the strings have been held down by the fingers in the course of long use.

Again, many of the accessories which have survived from the eighteenth and early nineteenth centuries show a high standard of craftsmanship consistent with the excellence of the cabinet-making carried on by firms all over the country at this period—and we should therefore not be surprised by the standard of work.[45]

There is now a considerable international industry in the making of copies of instruments in their original baroque form so as to reproduce as far as possible the authentic sound of an eighteenth-century (or early nineteenth-century) instrument as appropriate for music of the period. It is probably fair to say that the models are usually Italian rather than English, with fittings to match, a uniformity which is perhaps regrettable. A number of makers mentioned in the Directory specialize in exquisite reproduction baroque instruments.

---

[44] See Hill, *Stradivari*, 205.

[45] An advertisement presumably of the mid-18th century by Thomas Cahusac of The Strand, London, is reproduced in Cooper, *Benjamin Banks*, 168. The advertisement lists, amongst other things, bridges, pegs or pins, and tailpieces for violins or basses.

Strings

The history of the technique of string-making has a technical importance in violin-making since, in particular, the resonance of the bottom string of any instrument of the violin family is greatly affected by whether it is a plain gut string or overspun with a strand of thin metal, a technique introduced in the mid-seventeenth century.[46] It is generally thought that from the introduction of the violin in England up to about 1750, all-gut stringing was used by most players (in common with their Italian and German counterparts). Only French violinists used an overspun close-wound G-string and an open-wound D, with the usual close-twisted plain gut A-string and thin plain gut E.[47] Throughout the nineteenth century most players used gut on the three upper strings with an overspun close-wound G. A metal E-string appeared and became popular during the first half of the twentieth century.

The centres of string-making from about 1660 were Bologna and Venice. English players used 'Venice catlins', the gut in fact being made from the intestines of sheep or rams. Lyons also became a noted centre for French string-making.

String manufacture took place in England but English strings appear not to have had a good reputation. Haweis, writing in the latter part of the nineteenth century and probably reflecting contemporary opinion in England, states:

> The English make a good, serviceable, dull green looking string, durable, uneven, and not unfrequently false.[48] To my mind English strings are only fit for rank-and-file orchestra fiddling, but not good enough for the leader. Mr. Heron Allen, who has given great attention to such details, says that the best strings in the market are imported from ... Naples, and I have always had a weakness for Roman strings.[49]

Meredith Morris disagrees with the Haweis view about the indifferent quality of English strings. Morris states that after a test of Italian, French, German, American, English, and even Russian and Indian strings, 'the relative merits of strings of foreign and native manufacture are very slight indeed'. He goes on to allege that some strings in fact manufactured in England were dressed up as Italian, thus disguising their origin. 'It passes one's comprehension why the British public, or a large section thereof, should be forever acclaiming everything of foreign origin and denouncing everything British. That sort of thing has too long been prevalent in Britain, and it is about time we had done with it.'[50] Morris then

---

[46] For a good summary of string-making techniques, see Rubio, 'The Anatomy of the Violin', in Gill (ed.), *The Book of the Violin*, 37 ff.

[47] Ibid. 39.

[48] 'False' here presumably means not producing perfect fifths when the same finger stops two contiguous strings.

[49] H. R. Haweis, *Old Violins and Violin Lore* (London, 1898), 158.

[50] Morris, *British Violin Makers*, 40. A case of *plus ça change*?

gives an account of how strings were made at the time in England, notably in the factory of G. A. Parker, 94 Burghley Road, Kentish Town, London NW, where he inspected the process of making gut and metal-wound strings. Morris's prediction that 'the British artist and the British fiddle are coming to their own, and British strings will not tarry long'[51] has not significantly come true.

Gut strings produced in England during the twentieth century and in the author's possession include 'Conservatoire', 'King', 'New England' by 'R.M. & Co., London', 'Lyra' ('unequalled for value and quality'), 'Cathedral' by 'British Music and Tennis Strings Ltd., London', 'Millward', and 'Diana'. Most strings used by professional players today have been manufactured on the continent of Europe, particularly Germany.[52] Austria, France, Denmark, and the USA are also significant exporters.

Tools

Tools for violin-making were fairly standard throughout western Europe in the seventeenth century and beyond. They have not changed for handcrafted work very much since, and a typical set of violin-makers' tools is illustrated in Pl. 1.

Tone

An assessment of tone is difficult because the phenomenon of 'tone' is the most elusive of concepts. For a start, in any violin a great deal will depend on how carefully it has been set up. The comparative positions of the bridge and soundpost are particularly critical, as is the density and quality of the bridge wood itself.

In the opinion of Meredith Morris, old English instruments tend to have the reputation of 'a tone approximating to that of the Amatis'.[53] Morris goes on to say:

the tone of old English fiddles is neither loud nor piercing: it is rather small, but bright, silvery and responsive . . . the very best work of Banks, Forster, Duke, Parker, and a few others, rivals all but the very best Italian work, and I submit that in the supremely important matter of tone production, our old makers take rank next to the Italians . . . The tone of our old fiddles is not powerful, and it may not fill our large modern music halls, but it carries well, and ought to win, where it fails to conquer, by its purity and sweetness.[54]

---

[51] Ibid. 41.
[52] 'Pirastro' strings, made since 1798, originate from Germany.
[53] *British Violin Makers*, 18. [54] Ibid. 19–20.

These remarks are naturally generalizations. It is well known, for instance, that the better instruments of Daniel Parker have been used successfully as concert violins.

Conversion from Baroque to 'Romantic' Violin

In the case of those English violins made very approximately between 1700 and 1800 in the highly arched pattern of Stainer or Amati, these instruments are likely to share the same tonal problems under modern playing conditions as those attributed to their models. This point, which is speculative but probably well founded, needs elaboration and to understand it fully it is necessary to understand the radical alterations which have been made to all better-quality violins of this period to suit them better to modern playing conditions (as already outlined).

The musical background to this development has already been mentioned. Briefly, the increase in orchestral concerts and in public music-making generally led to the use of larger concert-halls. Audibility was required over a far greater area as the late eighteenth and nineteenth centuries progressed. Furthermore players increasingly desired to play in the highest positions which required the fingerboard to be lengthened.

From about 1780, thanks to the development of the bow by Tourte and Dodd, it became a much more powerful weapon in the hands of the artist to produce dynamic and tonal variation. A challenge was now thrown at the feet of the violin-makers and restorers to produce instruments capable of responding to the new demands.

A further factor which required bowed stringed instruments to be modified was the changing concert pitch. The question of pitch is a difficult one and it is apparent that there were quite significant variations from country to country. Clues are obtainable from diagrams of organ-pipes whose given dimensions produce a stated pitch.[55] The general opinion is that much of the music of the eighteenth century is properly performed at an interval of approximately a semitone below current concert pitch, now giving *a* at 440 cycles per second and then about 415 cycles per second. Since 1800 there has been a gradual raising of the pitch to its present level, probably for psycho-acoustic reasons. Singers often find that the tessitura of eighteenth- and earlier nineteenth-century choral works is much more comfortable at this lower pitch. The human voice can be assumed not to have changed significantly in terms of its natural range. But a raise in pitch seems to add to aural 'excitement'. The increased string tension which raising of the pitch causes inevitably imposes structural strain on the instrument. This strain is exacerbated

---

[55] See the copy formerly in the library of St Michael's College, Tenbury, and now in the Bodleian Library, Oxford, of Tomkins's *Musica Deo Sacra* (1668).

by the use of covered G and D strings and steel E strings or all-metal strings (as opposed to the traditional gut stringing throughout).

The violin family was accordingly altered or redesigned in a number of important aspects. First, the neck of late seventeenth-century instruments was typically about ¼ in. (6 mm) shorter and rather wider than the modern one. The old-style neck was set with the face level with the edge of the table. A wedge-shaped fingerboard was then required to raise the angle of the top surface towards the bridge so that the strings could be played on for the fingerboard's entire length. The neck was glued flat on to the top block, nails being driven through the block into the base of the neck. Old necks measured, typically, between 4¾ in. (120 mm) and 5 in. (127 mm). The modern neck is about 5⅛ in. (130 mm) to 5¼ in. (133 mm) and is mortised into the top block. This enables the nails to be dispensed with and the shoulders or base of the neck to be reduced and shaped more elegantly. The raised face of the neck enables the old wedge which had previously lifted the fingerboard to be dispensed with. The bass bar, whose function is partly acoustic and partly structural, also needed to be replaced with something longer and stronger. A typical measurement for an old bass bar would be about 9½ in. (241 mm) long, with a central depth of ¼ in. (6 mm) and a width of 3/16 in. (5 mm). The modern average equivalent would be 10½ in. (266 mm) × 7/16 in. (12 mm) × ¼ in (6 mm). (These measurements were not universal. Cooper describes Benjamin Banks's violin bass bars as 10⅛ in. (257 mm) in length; 3/16 in. (5 mm) width; ⅜ in. (9 mm) height.)[56]

In order to allow more pressure to be brought upon the strings by the modern bow, modern bridges tend to be rather higher and more acutely arched so as to reduce the chance of inadvertently catching adjacent strings. The fingerboard, whose function is not acoustic, has been lengthened, by a somewhat gradual process, from an average length of 8 in. (203 mm) to a modern length of 10½ in. (266 mm).[57] Soundposts are usually thicker and more substantial than those previously in use.

Finally, the open-string length on a modern violin is approximately 13 in. (330 mm). Occasionally this string-length was produced in baroque instruments with shorter necks by virtue of the nut being placed further back in the pegbox and the bridge being placed further towards the tailpiece than is now normal.[58]

By about 1800 modernization was in full swing. Hart's view was that 'short necks were dispensed with in Paris towards the end of the [eighteenth] century, and doubtless Viotti was the chief instigator with regard to the change'.[59] It can

---

[56] *Benjamin Banks*, 52. See also Kenneth Skeaping, 'A Baroque Violin from Northumberland', *Galpin Society Journal*, 14 (1961), 45, where the author's measurements of the unaltered bass bar (*c*.1720) were similar to the above.

[57] An English violin of a design transitional between baroque and modern, which was in the author's possession, had a fingerboard of about 9 in. (228 mm).

[58] 'Footprints' showing a variety of stop-lengths can often be detected on old violins.

[59] George Hart, *The Violin: Famous Makers*, 151 relying on Vincenzo Lancetti, *Biographical Notices* (Milan, 1823).

hardly be coincidental that it was at about this time that Stradivari's position as a superior maker to the previously much-revered Stainer and Amati family became established. As has already been indicated, this appears to have been largely due to Viotti's spectacularly successful concert appearances with his Stradivari violin. The implication is that the higher string tension on the heavier bass bar inserted into Stradivari's robust and flatly arched model awakened the full power of these instruments. On the other hand, this extra pressure on the more highly arched Amatese and Stainer models simply 'overloaded' them. Stainers and Amatis failed to develop the additional power reserve needed to respond to the new bow and the new concert-hall. Most modern artists agree that this still remains the position except, of course, where a 'baroque' sound and style is needed for authenticity. The more highly arched models of Amati and Stainer are inferior in terms of tonal flexibility and dynamic range to, for example, Stradivari and Guarneri del Gesù where comparisons are made with modernized instruments.[60]

A record exists[61] of a scholarly and informed trial of an unaltered Stainer dating from 1668 as compared with an unaltered instrument made in London, c.1750, by Charles and Samuel Thompson. Both these instruments had been played with a normally placed bridge and tuned to a pitch varying from half to three-quarters of a tone below present standards. The Stainer had an open-string length of just 12¾ in. (323 mm) and the Thompson of 12⅞ in. (326 mm). The string rise from nut to bridge was much more pronounced on the Thompson—a shade under 2 in. (51 mm), whilst that on the Stainer was about 1½ in. (38 mm). Bass-bar measurements were not known, though the Thompson bass bar was much deeper than the Stainer. Messrs Hills, from whom the instruments came, on opening the Thompson violin found that it was integral to the table rather than being separately made, which is quite a common feature of English instruments of this period. Nevertheless, in the comparisons which follow it should be borne in mind that the products of the Thompson family are not regarded as typical of the best English making of the time.

Kenneth Skeaping's reactions on playing these instruments in a baroque fashion and with a baroque bow was that 'the Stainer yields a beautiful tone, thick and rich in quality and of a dark colour, though neither so loud or so brilliant as the violin of today . . . in general character the Thompson violin is similar, although it lacked the free resonance and subtle flavour of the tone of Stainer's masterpiece'. Kenneth Skeaping concluded that the thesis advanced by the Hills, namely that the popularity of the Stainer instruments arose from their tonal resemblance to 'the nasal, wiry quality of the treble viol', then familiar to the seventeenth-century violin-

---

[60] This material is based in part upon data in Kenneth Skeaping's article 'Some Speculations on a Crisis in the History of the Violin', *Galpin Society Journal*, 8 (1955), 3 ff.
[61] Ibid.

player, was incorrect. Their popularity declined from the failure of the Stainer and Amati patterns to respond to the structural changes above described. It happened that the more powerful arching and flatter modelling of the Stradivari–Guarneri instruments produced the acoustic response that modern players now expect.

The same judgements should apply to the flatter modelling of the earlier Brescian makers such as Maggini, as repopularized by such players are Charles de Bériot, but there are so few of these instruments in circulation that it is not possible to be dogmatic. The point here being made is that since most, though not all, English makers from 1700 to about 1800 followed the higher arched modelling of the Stainer–Amati type, these instruments on modernization will demonstrate the same defects as the originals in terms of tonal response.

These remarks cannot apply so much to those few makers, such as Daniel Parker, who went some way in copying the flatter Strad modelling, nor can they apply to those many good-quality instruments made after (approximately) 1800 in England whose makers had learned the advantages of flatter modelling.

The present author tentatively suggests that there is often a more 'open' sound in English instruments, even quite modern ones, as opposed to a 'reedier' tonal quality in Italian ones, most easily perceived in the almost nasal quality of Italian cellos of quality. Singers who need to project their voices over the orchestra adopt a technique of bouncing the voice off the hard palate and using sinus cavities for resonance. English 'open' tone can carry too, but is it too fanciful to contrast the vocal tone of the English oratorio singer and the Italian opera singer by way of analogy?

A significant number of soloists and professional ensemble players use English instruments, cellos made between about 1780 and 1850 being particularly popular, and this suggests that these instruments can be tonally very satisfying in today's concert-halls. As examples, the violinist Tasmin Little at her Promenade Concert Debut in 1990 used a violin by Henry Lockey Hill made in about 1815 which can be heard on her gramophone recordings of the Bruch and Dvořák violin concertos and her recital of the music of George Lloyd.[62] The great violinist Alfredo Campoli owned a John Lott (in addition to a famous Strad and three Roccas). He used the English violin for his last (so far apparently unpublished) recording.[63] As will be shown later, instruments from the British Isles both ancient and modern are popular in British professional orchestras to an extent not hitherto realized.

---

[62] See *Strad* (Aug. 1990) 617. Information also supplied by the artiste to the author. She now uses a Guadagnini.
[63] See *Strad* (Sept. 1991), 740.

Chapter Three

English Violin-Makers of the Seventeenth Century and their Distinguishing Features

Geography and History — John Bunyan's Violin — Leading Seventeenth-Century London Violin-Makers — Early English Makers — Authenticity Problems

Geography and History

THE thesis argued in this book is that violin-making came fairly late to England, and the main reasons for this are suggested in Chapter 1. English makers were therefore susceptible to the examples of their predecessors in Italy in particular, and also probably in the Low Countries and in France. The story of the evolution of violin-making in England would have been more straightforward if it had been possible to say that there was a distinct school of English makers, building on their viol-making tradition, who developed their own models and flourished independently of their Continental counterparts. Unfortunately this is certainly not the case. And it is therefore easier to appreciate the *mélange* of influences which were brought to bear in England by the influx of immigrant craftsmen in the seventeenth and early eighteenth centuries if the main trends of European history at the time are appreciated.[1]

Immigration on a significant scale tends to be caused by people wishing to remove themselves from an unstable or hostile environment in favour of a more friendly one. The period 1550–1700 was a time of great turbulence throughout Europe. Much of this turbulence was caused by the religious wars stemming from the Reformation in Europe which is usually dated from 1517, when Martin Luther posted his ninety-five theses on the church door at Wittenberg. Germany's econ-

---

[1] Immigrant violin-makers continued to play an important role in English violin-making up to fairly modern times, as will be seen later in this book.

omy was seriously damaged by the struggle between Protestants and Catholics known as the Thirty Years War, which took place in the Holy Roman Empire, and particularly in what is now Germany, between 1618 and 1648. The Peace of Westphalia brought a compromise solution. After 1648 Germany became fragmented into some 300 small states and free cities. There was consequential political disruption and the great German banking houses of Welser and Fugger went bankrupt in 1614 and 1627 respectively. Much of the land was devastated. The population declined from some 21 millions in 1618 to around 13 millions in 1648. England, which was seen as a comparatively stable Protestant country, was no doubt a beneficiary of this movement of people.

Perhaps better documented, however, is the emigration of Protestants from, in particular, France, throughout this period. The French protestants, known as Huguenots, were primarily followers of Calvin. Despite persecution, by 1560 there were some 400,000 Huguenots in France. They proved themselves doughty fighters and had by 1570 established a measure of independence. However, by a singular act of treachery usually attributed to Queen Catherine de Medici, some 2,000 Huguenots, gathered in Paris for the marriage of Henry of Navarre, were massacred on St Bartholomew's Day 1572. The Paris massacres were followed elsewhere in France, accounting for a total of perhaps 5,000 or 6,000 Huguenots. It is from this time onwards that it is possible to trace a significant emigration of Huguenots from France into England and other Protestant countries. Within France itself the Huguenots had their privileges restored by the Edict of Nantes in 1598. Nearly a hundred years later, in 1685, Louis XIV took the disastrous decision to revoke the Edict of Nantes, which again led to large-scale emigration. Over 400,000 Huguenots fled from the persecutions that followed and settled in Holland, Switzerland, America, and the British Isles.

The Huguenots' influence on the English economy has been well documented.[2] Their contribution to the textile industry is particularly notable, as it was to watch- and clock-making and to silversmithing.[3] Such contemporary firms as Cartier have Huguenot origins. Significantly, it is to the Huguenots in England that is attributed the development of joinery in furniture with new techniques of decoration. 'We see for the first time the emergence in England of the cabinet maker.'[4] Added to this immigration from Germany and France was an identifiable stream of German and Dutch cabinet-makers who came over from Holland to England on the accession of William III.

It is possible to hypothesize that some of the early English violin-makers may

---

[2] See e.g. R. D. Gwynn, *Huguenot Heritage: The History and Contribution of the Huguenots in Britain* (London, 1985).

[3] Take, for example, the work of Paul de Lamerie (1688–1751) the son of Huguenot parents who came to England as refugees when he was a baby. John Larqueir and John Quett were making lute strings in 1684, having emigrated from Nîmes. Ibid.

[4] Price, *The Story of English Furniture*, 41.

have come from this source. The Pamphilon family might seem to be good candidates, but this hypothesis is much weakened by evidence that a Pamphilon family, associated with violin-making, had long been established in Essex.[5] Some apparently English names had been rapidly anglicized from the French—for instance De la Croix became Cross, and Boulanger became Baker. Of the early English makers Barak Norman is probably the strongest candidate for a Huguenot origin. In the eighteenth century the Cahusac family made wind instruments and sold stringed instruments in London. This family is also of Huguenot descent, from Languedoc.[6] Although Thomas Perry is more correctly classified as an Irish maker it is fairly certain that his family were of Huguenot descent and related to Claude Pierray, the Parisian violin-maker.

Even if the Huguenot thesis were provable it would not solve the problem of tracing the predominant national influences brought to bear on the early makers in England. This is partly because German, Dutch, and French immigrant workers would themselves have been influenced by previous makers, particularly those in Italy and the Tyrol. It has been suggested that the way the body of the instrument was built up in England generally without a mould came predominantly from Flemish practice.

The economic history of the time can also throw some light on the context of this problem. The development of violin-making in northern Italy was intimately connected with the then existing trade routes. In the thirteenth century the natural Alpine barriers had been breached by the opening of the Septimer and St Gotthard Passes, and the Brenner Pass into the Austrian Tyrol was also particularly important. One of the main trade routes was from Genoa through Milan to Augsburg in southern Germany and from then either to the Baltic ports or to northern France and the Low Countries. Industry was concentrated in the narrow corridor running north–south from Antwerp and Bruges through Augsburg to Milan or France. Later, with the development of the metal and woollen economy of the lower Rhine and Saxony, the great trading cities of northern Italy lost their economic importance. The cities of northern Europe, including London and Paris, began to predominate both in terms of economic production and population. But up to about 1700 the trade routes founded in medieval times, together with the fairs regularly held in the larger towns in or near trade routes, were an important determinant in the distribution of musical instruments from northern Italy and the Tyrol. While Flemish influences would not be surprising in the light

---

[5] The name Pamphilon and derivatives such as Pamplin may come from the French word *pamphilion*, a multi-coloured coat, or possibly *papillon*, butterfly. For the Essex connection, see the Directory, App. 1; see also Michael Coyne, *Pamphilon: An Essex Family* (Essex [sic], 1992), esp. 91–106. The family is traced back to Spanish immigrants in the 15th century and includes other members flourishing c.1690 who were violin or 'instrument' makers in Essex, the main one besides Edward being Nicholas (d. 1727).

[6] See Cooper, *Benjamin Banks*, 152.

of the volume of trade between Britain and the Netherlands, it is difficult to identify migrant workers in the violin-making field from this source. Only the little-known John Grice is, by his labels, thought to have connections with Antwerp amongst other cities and his work shows a Flemish/Brescian influence.

The other important factor in the development of the craft of violin-making, one which can flourish on the simplest of raw materials and which is not dependent on mineral wealth or the wool off a sheep's back,[7] is the availability of suitable wood. It is in large part for this reason that northern Italian and Tyrolean violin-making centres were within reach of the south Tyrolean Alps (for example Mathius Alban (1621–1712) worked in Bolzano) and that the infant German violin-making industry chose such towns as Mittenwald in the Karwendel mountains, now on the southern boundary of Bavarian Germany and Austria. After the Thirty Years War Markneukirchen and Klingenthal established themselves as violin-making centres further to the north-east on what became the border of Czechoslovakia, and Füssen in the Bavarian Alps. The centre of the French violin industry, Mirecourt, is conveniently placed in the foothills of the Vosges mountains.

It may be argued that since within the British Isles there was at that time an abundance of forests, including pine forests, there should have been the incentive to develop a parallel industry here. But, as was argued in the first chapter, musical development and social expectations in Britain until the middle of the seventeenth century were not such as to encourage this development. English violin-making was almost certainly greatly helped in its infancy by makers and players originating from continental Europe and then using the local materials that they found available. Since, as has been shown, the main supplier countries of immigration were Germany, France, and the Low Countries, it is not surprising that the development of the art of lutherie did not proceed in the same way as was occurring in Italy. In so far as the Italian influence exists this is because the makers then in England tended to copy the instruments, particularly of the Brescian makers, brought over by visiting players or, in a few cases, imported. But by 1700 or so the Brescian influence, such as it was, had diminished and the Austro-Germanic traditions were firmly established.

Stradivari's influence on the old English school was not at first significant, with one or two apparently isolated exceptions. It cannot be that his instruments were unknown. The Hills record in their book on Stradivari that in 1682 a complete set of his instruments were destined to be presented to James II of England.[8] In Chapter 1 other evidence was given of the esteem in which he was held by connoisseurs travelling in Italy. The dates of work of Daniel Parker are controversial,

---

[7] But the sheep's intestines were traditionally used for strings.   [8] Hill, *Stradivari*, 37.

but if current belief that Parker was producing copies of the 'long Stradivari' pattern as early as about 1700 is correct, Parker must have been one of the first European makers to follow this model. Joseph Hare's work shows a similar influence. Another non-Italian copyist was the French maker De Comble of Tournay, who flourished between 1720 and 1750.[9] But it was not until the mid-eighteenth century that Richard Duke and Joseph Hill started inserting copies of Stradivari's labels in their instruments. Tradition has it that the real impetus to the spread of Stradivari's fame was a visit of Viotti to Paris in 1782, and to England a few years later, playing apparently to great effect his Stradivari made in 1712.[10]

At this juncture, some attempt must be made to summarize the sources of what became a distinctive old English style of making. A fundamental point is that London, by the seventeenth century, already had a distinguished viol-making tradition amongst its native makers. The introduction of the violin family occurred cautiously, reflecting the changes in musical taste already outlined. Meanwhile, throughout the seventeenth century, immigrant makers came to London and elsewhere bringing high standards of craftsmanship and sophistication to allied crafts, particularly furniture-making. Jacob Rayman has been fairly confidently identified as both an immigrant from Germany and the founding father of serious violin-making in England. Foreign players abounded and a pool of mainly London makers slowly transferred their allegiance from the viol to violin-making. Some, such as Barak Norman, continued throughout the latter part of the seventeenth century to make both. Foreign players brought in Italian, mainly Brescian, instruments as well as those from Germany, Austria, and the Netherlands. Some such instruments were imported too, as the customs records showed. Native makers no doubt restored and then copied these instruments. Buyers followed fashion in their preferences and the Stainer model started to prevail as the preferred model from shortly after the turn of the eighteenth century, by which time a distinct violin-making craft industry is readily identifiable in London. The use of native materials and distinct varnishes helps, with the construction methods used, to identify an instrument from this era. Originality in construction or acoustic principle cannot be claimed, but the various influences described did merge into a distinctive national style from heterogeneous beginnings.

John Bunyan's Violin

The violin attributed to, and almost certainly made by, John Bunyan is of particular interest since it is one of the earliest known violins in conventional shape made

---

[9] Hill, *Stradivari*, 256. [10] See Ch. 7 and Hill, *Stradivari*, 153.

in England and still extant.[11] From the illustration (Pl. 27) it can be seen that there is a distinctly Brescian cut to the soundholes. Its history has been researched.

The instrument was found amongst the 'rubbish' comprised in the estate of an old lady who is believed to have dwelt in a cottage at Milton Keynes, and was acquired by one Alfred Bullard of Newport Pagnell. Mr Bullard sold the instrument to Thomas Blagg FSA in 1916, and he in turn to John Beagarie of Hitchin in 1928. The instrument was eventually presented to the trustees of the Bunyan Meeting in 1935 by Sir Leicester Harmsworth and is now in their museum in Bedford.

John Bunyan was born in 1628 and followed his father's calling of a tinker. In the days prior to his 'conversion' in about 1650 Bunyan was known to be exceptionally fond of music and dancing and this took him, we are told, 'a year's hard struggle' to give up as a sinful occupation. Bunyan joined the army as a soldier on the side of Cromwell in 1644 at Newport Pagnell (where the violin was later found). It was partly because of a lucky escape in the Civil War—he was drawn for the siege of Leicester, but a companion volunteered in his stead and shortly afterwards, while acting as a sentry, was shot through the head with a musket-ball—that Bunyan felt compelled to abandon such pursuits as dancing for a holier life. Mr Blagg gave careful thought to the dating of the violin and its attribution and is firmly of the opinion that 'the fiddle is a genuine relic of Bunyan's earlier days, of his illiterate, unregenerated days . . . made with his own hands . . .'[12]

The violin is inscribed on its back 'JOHN BUNYAN, HELSTOW'. Helstow (or sometimes Helstowe) was the then colloquial way of describing Bunyan's place of birth, Elstow. There is a very similarly inscribed brazier's anvil, also in the Bunyan museum, which is iron, quadrangular, with a flat circular top and pointed foot. It is incised on three sides with the inscription 'J. Bunyan | Helstowe | 1647'. It is significant that in 1647 John Bunyan was released from the army and resumed his trade as a tinker.

Careful examination has been made of the inscription in capital letters on the back of the violin. It is thought that the letters were produced by zig-zagging with a graving tool, a method known as 'wriggling' which was frequently used for engraving ornament on pewter in the seventeenth century. It was the opinion of Mr W. W. Watts, FSA, who was for many years Keeper of Metal Work at the Victoria and Albert Museum, that it would be most unlikely that this work would

---

[11] An earlier strangely shaped instrument credited to one 'Pemberton', now regarded as spurious, is mentioned later. Sandys and Forster, *History*, 254, quote a label of Jacob Rayman in Southwark as dated 1641, a date which has since been repeated in the standard reference works and is still thought to be correct by some modern experts. If this is really so, the Rayman violin in question would pre-date Bunyan by a few years. Hart in *The Violin: Famous Makers*, 315, states that Rayman settled in London about 1620, but instruments by English makers of the violin family as early as this have not been traced by the author, nor are any identified specifically in any reliable published source.

[12] Quoted in Reginald Hine, *Relics of an Un-Common Attorney* (London, 1951), 143.

have been forged. Mr Watts's opinion was as follows: 'I see no doubt that the fiddle is of the seventeenth century, and the signature goes to prove that it was at least the property of John Bunyan; while, from the fact of his being a tinker and a musician, I am strongly inclined to the opinion that he was also the maker of this instrument.' In 1917 the instrument was inspected by Mr Arthur Hill of the firm of William E. Hill & Sons who stated that 'so far as its design and characteristics were concerned there is no reason why it should not belong to the latter half of the seventeenth century'.[13]

It is, of course, unusual to find a violin of this period constructed of metal. In the latter part of the eighteenth century, violins were, occasionally, fashioned of iron plate, brass, copper, silver, or even tortoiseshell, but Canon Galpin opined that Bunyan's must have been one of the earliest metal instruments.[14] There seems no reason why a tinker should not make a violin for dancing purposes out of the material in which he habitually worked. This leaves only the date controversial. But it seems, on the balance of probabilities, that the violin would date from the same time as the anvil, namely about 1647 (and not later, as Mr Hill opined). Bunyan would hardly have made, or even used, an instrument so closely associated with dancing as a fiddle after his conversion in about 1650. If, then, the violin is from not later than 1647 it gives an invaluable insight into the type of the model which an English maker might have used at that period, particularly for use not at court but for the music and dancing enjoyed by the common man. No other English instrument of the violin family is known by the author to survive from before about 1640, and violins and violas are very rare in the British Isles before 1660, as discussed in Chapter 1.

Leading Seventeenth-Century London Violin-Makers

Almost all the makers of consequence flourishing in England between 1660 and the end of the seventeenth century had their places of work in London. In Britain as a whole London was clearly the centre of both commerce and art, though in the latter respect Edinburgh provided some significant competition. But in England itself there is but little evidence of makers of the violin family at this period working outside London. Exceptions were William Baker and (probably) his son John, who worked at Oxford, primarily, but not exclusively, on viols.[15]

By the middle of the seventeenth century London had grown from being, in

---

[13] *Relics of an Un-Common Attorney*, 144.
[14] Ibid. 145.
[15] Francis Baker, thought to be John's brother, also specialized in viols and is one of many makers in the last few decades of the 17th century and early 18th century who practised in the neighbourhood of St Paul's Cathedral—in Francis Baker's case, St Paul's Churchyard. The first identified cello made in England is thought to be by William Baker, 1672.

feudal times, a walled city stretching from the River Fleet on the west to Aldgate and the Tower of London on the East. London Bridge by now had a significant number of buildings erected on it. In this quarter are thought to have worked Thomas Urquhart, Edward Pamphilon, and Edward Pemberton (who may have been the son of the Pemberton said to have been the maker of the instrument presented to the Earl of Leicester by Queen Elizabeth I and of curious shape, now thought to be spurious).[16] Some of these buildings were damaged by the Great Fire in 1666. The houses on London Bridge were all cleared away between the years 1757 and 1759, having fallen into dereliction and being thus accounted a public nuisance.

In the early eighteenth century a number of makers congregated around St Paul's Cathedral, particularly in St Paul's Alley in the corner of St Paul's Churchyard. Other makers were turning westwards, for example Wamsley to Piccadilly, and by the turn of the nineteenth century the area around Soho and Leicester Square was the main violin-making and violin-dealing centre. The map of eighteenth-century London reproduced in this book shows the place of work of some of the leading makers.

A word might be said also about the trade signs by which the early makers identified their workshops. For instance, Barak Norman worked from the 'Bass Viol' in St Paul's Alley, London, and a little later Peter Wamsley worked from 'Ye Golden Harp in Pickadilly' and 'The Harp and Hautboy in Pickadilly'. From c.1762 Joseph Hill worked at the 'Harp and Flute' in the Haymarket and the sign became the trade mark of the firm. But the trouble with signs was that they tended to break off in high winds to the peril of passers-by. One sign fell in Bride Lane in 1718 and though this was followed by an official enquiry no action was then taken. Paris banned them in 1761 and this probably inspired the City of London to make a proclamation in 1762 ordering the removal of hanging signs. This was followed by a similar proclamation for the City of Westminster. Soon houses and shops were given numbering for identification purposes which, though much less picturesque, was safer for the public.[17]

---

[16] This was exhibited in the 19th century in the Victoria and Albert Museum and is illustrated and fully described in Sir John Hawkins's *General History*, (iv, 342); see also Heron-Allen, *Violin Making*, 5–6. Michael Coyne, in researching his data for *Pamphilon: An Essex Family*, told the author that exhaustive searches in the Guildhall Record Office, which holds the records of rentals for the Bridge, failed to reveal any evidence of either a Pamphilon or an Urquhart as tenants. A token 'coin' exists reading 'Edward Pamphilon—living at Clavering' (Essex). It dates from between 1648 and 1672. It is possible, therefore that there might have been purely a retail establishment on London Bridge.

[17] See generally Sir Ambrose Heal, *The Sign Boards of Old London Shops* (London, 1957, repr. 1988).

Early English Makers

It is difficult to identify anyone who might be called the 'founding father' of the early English violin school. As has already been explained in Chapter 1, London was renowned for its makers of the viola da gamba, and, apart from one or two isolated examples which have survived, there is no evidence of significant activity in the violin-making field much before 1660. Hart[18] mentions in the context of the making of viols, in particular, the work of Jay (or Jaye), Smith, Bolles, Ross (or Rose), Addison, and Shaw (whose label ran 'John Shaw att the Goulden harp and Hoboy nere the May pole in the Strand 1656').[19]

A number of viols from the sixteenth- and early seventeenth-century English makers survive and specimens can be inspected in museums. For example the Ashmolean Museum has two instruments by or attributed to John Rose and a small bass viol by Richard Blunt, London, 1605. Occasionally examples of bass viols converted into cellos come on to the market, one such being attributed to Richard Meares whose label is given by Henley as running 'Richard Meares, without Bishopsgate, near to Sir Paul Pinder's, London'.[20] Morris makes this interesting comment: 'Richard Meares (1680) adopted the Brescian model, and made excellent violins on the lines of Maggini. This old maker probably made the first English violoncello.'[21] As mentioned above, the earliest such cello identified by the author is in fact by William Baker of Oxford, 1672.

The earliest English violin on public view in a museum in England (other than the Bunyan example) is thought to be the 'baroque violin' in the Victoria and Albert Museum, dated to the last third of the seventeenth century. It is an unusual instrument, having an elaborately carved back with the royal coat of arms on the upper bout, suggesting that the instrument may have been that of Charles II or James II. The back is made of one piece of sycamore and the scroll is also elaborately carved. The instrument was exhibited in the Special Exhibition of 1872 in the Museum, item 122*a*, where it is described as early seventeenth century—'said to have belonged to James I'. Modern assessment has adjudged it as being later and it appears that the table may be alien to the instrument. Interesting though the instrument is, it serves to underline the point that it is a tragedy that no museum exhibits instruments of the violin family made by, and typical of, British makers through the centuries. This specimen is certainly very untypical.

In the absence of firmer historical data, the earliest identified maker of violins

---

[18] *The Violin: Famous Makers*, 279.
[19] See Sandys and Forster, *History*, 251. Of these, the work of John Rose (the elder) of Bridewell, London, and his son of the same name, who had an even higher reputation, is regarded as outstanding. See Ian Woodfield, *The Early History of the Viol* (Cambridge, 1984), 223.
[20] See Sotheby's, 22 Nov. 1984, lot 73. Sir Paul Pinder owned a large house in Halfmoon Alley, off Bishopsgate.
[21] Henley, *Dictionary*, 9.

and violas is Jacob Rayman, whose labels are given by Sandys and Forster, copied by Henley, as running: 'Jacob Rayman dwelling in Blackman Street, Long—Southwark, 1641' and 'Jacob Rayman at ye Bell Yard, in Southwarke, London 1648'.[22] Sir John Hawkins in his *General History of Music* states that Rayman was still living at Bell Yard in 1650. Rayman was unusual in working across London Bridge, 'the other side of the river'. (Later, some members of the Hill family worked in the same area.) Dates on labels of seventeenth-century instruments should be regarded with caution, but if correctly dated to the 1640s he is certainly the earliest identifiable specialist violin-maker in London or elsewhere in Britain.

'Quaint' is the word which springs to mind as an appropriate description of Rayman's work. Hart notices with characteristic perspicacity that

there is a German ring in the name which makes me think that he came from Germany, and, if so, brought with him the semi-Italian character of work common to the makers who live so near Brescia. If the work and style of Rayman be carefully examined, it will be seen that it has much in common with the inferior Brescian makers. The outline is rugged, the soundhole is of that gothic form peculiar to Brescia; the head is distinct from that of the early English type.[23]

Morris states that 'the workmanship was very neat (with the exception of the inlaying of the purfling) and the tone was clear, responsive, and silvery'.[24] Sandys and Forster comment:

it has been asserted by some persons that he made violins of a large size, but those which have been seen are small, and not of an elegant outline or model; the fore-bout being wide, the short-bout long, and out of all proportion with the lower part of the instrument. However, he was a maker of talent and ability; the tone was clear, penetrating and silvery; not possessing the reedy quality of the Cremona violins, but partaking more of the Brescia character; and his instruments were highly prized.[25]

In Chapter 1 reference is made to the catalogue of musical instruments for sale from the estate of Thomas Britton, and lot 8 was 'an extraordinary Rayman'. Sir John Hawkins comments on this that 'the tenor violins made by him are greatly valued'. Sandys and Forster continue:

notwithstanding the purfling is done indifferently yet the work, generally, was neat and good, the fluting at the edge where the purfle is inlaid is deep and acute. The soundhole is rather small, like that used at times by Steiner [sic]; the varnish very good, and of a yellowish-brown colour with a little tinge of red, and the vehicle used appears to be oil.[26]

---

[22] See also Hart, *The Violin: Famous Makers*, 315; 'settled in England about 1620'; Fleming, *Old Violins*, 204.
[23] Hart, *The Violin: Famous Makers*, 280. It is understood that modern scholarship has traced Jacob Rayman's place of birth to Füssen in the Bavarian Alps of Southern Germany, a town with a long tradition of first lute-making and then violin-making.
[24] *British Violin Makers*, 224–5.
[25] Sandys and Forster, *History*, 253.
[26] Ibid. 253–4.

76 THE VIOLIN FAMILY

Instruments of this maker which can be authenticated with any degree of confidence (because inevitably there have been copies and nondescript Tyrolean instruments falsely labelled) conform to the consensus of opinion given above. His violins are usually undersize—13¾ in. (349 mm) is a representative length of back. Although Fleming, writing in 1883, was able to say that 'his work does not appear to be either scarce or dear'[27] his instruments now but rarely surface in the auction room. A splendid and valuable viola of Rayman's (or, at least attributed to him by Sotheby's without qualification) is illustrated in Pl. 92, though it may not be typical of his work.

Thomas Urquhart flourished between about 1650 and 1680, and both Scotland and England have a claim. Tradition suggests that he may have come from Scotland to London at the invitation of Charles II. Honeyman in his book on *Scottish Violin Makers* boldly states that he was born in 1625 and confirms that 'his violins are all dated from London Bridge, thus showing that he belonged to that select caste of Londoners then living on London Bridge buildings, who are said to have said to have looked down upon all other Londoners as inferior beings'. Honeyman adds that:

his violins are of two sizes, the small much in the style of Stainer [this, of course, being an anachronism], the larger so much resembling the grotesque and much bulged violins of Edward Pamphilon that it is highly probably that Pamphilon, who also lived on London Bridge, learned the art with Urquhart. There is still another resemblance between their works in the fine oil varnish common to both, which is sometimes of a pale brown colour, and sometimes inclining to red, and quite equal to the Italian varnish in transparency and flexibility. The wood used by both is of that kind commonly imported from the Baltic, and the tone of their violins is frequently of surprising excellence; indeed, these violins are often mistaken by novices for the works of Gasparo da Salo and Jacob Stainer . . . It is probable that Urquhart went to London from Scotland at the invitation of Charles II; who delighted in fostering art, and had also a warm heart towards Scotland.[28]

More modern commentators have noticed neat purfling placed close to the edge and quaint but nicely cut and graceful soundholes. There is sometimes a 'bat-wing' crescent-shaped incision on the base of the scallop of the scroll. This decorative work on the back of the pegbox, and black dotted incisions on the volute, are attractive features of some early English makers, including Pamphilon and Urquhart. Similar decorative work on the scallop of the scroll can be seen in the work of the seventeenth-century south German makers Frantz Straub and Hans Krouchdaler.[29] This is further evidence of the strong south German/Tyrolean

---

[27] *Old Violins*, 205.
[28] Honeyman, *Scottish Violin Makers*, 95; Henley, *Dictionary*, duly reproduces this (unattributed) opinion. The Hill Archive contains observations by the Hill family doubting the authenticity of this Scottish derivation. See further in the Directory.
[29] See the illustrations in Olga Adelmann, *Die Alemannische Schule* (Berlin, 1990), 40.

influence on English makers even at this early date, which soon predominated over the earlier Brescian ideas. Decorative purfling and pattern-work is not particularly associated with Stainer's own instruments—the tradition appears to stem from a different source. Charles Beare, writing in the *New Grove Dictionary of Musical Instruments*, comments on the fine quality of sound of Urquhart's instruments if well preserved and also on the almost Italian beauty of the varnish 'so that his instruments have often been sold as more important Italian instruments'.

Instruments of Urquhart now very rarely appear in the sale-rooms, but a violin or viola either by or attributed to Urquhart occasionally surfaces. Of those sold in 1991 from the Hill collection, two bore labels 'Tho. Urquhart' (with date). It is not known if these labels were authentic—one was in manuscript, one printed in Gothic. Soundholes measured on one specimen were 2½ in. (63 mm) extreme length, being short and upright. Although Urquhart is not credited with having made any cellos, at least one possible instrument by him has been identified.

Edward Pamphilon flourished in London, putatively on London Bridge, between the years 1670 and 1695. Miss C. Stainer,[30] reflecting turn of the century opinion, states that 'his instruments are much liked'. Poidras, writing in 1928, is of the contrary view: 'a bad, high make, coated with a fine yellow varnish'.[31] A more balanced opinion is probably that of Towry Piper, writing in 1916, who describes Pamphilon's work thus:

used a beautiful varnish of yellow colour, sometimes with a tinge of red. The fiddles are squarish, and stiff looking in outline. The scrolls small. The bottom of the shell is finished in a peculiar way. Some of the soundholes are more curious than beautiful, the lower turns having a very wide sweep. Double-purfling was generally, but not always, employed. The writer has seen a few specimens containing Maggini labels. His own tickets are very scarce and contain the day of the month when the instrument was finished in addition to the year.[32]

Jack Livoja-Lorius writing in the *New Grove Dictionary of Musical Instruments* confidently states that Pamphilon's violins and violas are invariably small, neatly crafted, and with a clear, responsive tone. The soundholes 'tend to be either too short or too long'.

Instruments of Pamphilon do occasionally come on the market. There were two (one 'attributed') in the Hill collection sold at Phillips in 1991. One is illustrated (Pl. 85), from an earlier sale.[33] One specimen measured by the author had rather Brescian soundholes (3 in. (76 mm) extreme measurement) and the above-described decorative work on the scroll. The varnish was of good quality but

---

[30] *Dictionary of Violin Makers*, 70.
[31] Henri Poidras, *Dictionnaire des Luthiers* (Rouen, 1928–30), i. 146.
[32] See Hidalgo Moya and Alfred Towry Piper, *Violin Tone and Violin Makers* (London, 1916), 222–3.
[33] See also the Maggini-influenced model with double purfling and purfled trefoils on the back illustrated in the *Strad* (Nov. 1971), 290.

lacking the true Cremona lustre. He is credited with small-patterned violas but no cellos are authenticated. His instruments nowadays are probably of more interest to the collector than to the practising player—though Sandys and Forster give their verdict thus: 'The violins—and no other instruments have been seen—are strong in wood, the tone clear, pure and penetrating. The professors of this period greatly approve of them for orchestral uses.'[34]

A maker flourishing towards the end of the seventeenth century and on to the early eighteenth, whose work stands in high repute, though extremely rare, is Edward Lewis. Morris gives his working dates as 1695–1730 and Henley, probably more correctly, 1687–1745. His possible connection with Daniel Parker is noticed below and it seems more likely that he flourished in the last two decades of the seventeenth century and the first three of the eighteenth. Sandys and Forster praise him as

pre-eminent for his good workmanship; his style was excellent, and the few violins which have been seen were varnished with a light yellow colour, however others assert that he also used a red colour with a golden ground. Be that as it may, there can be but one opinion that his violins, which are scarce, have much beauty, and are remarkable for their fine varnish.[35]

The estate of Thomas Britton, the inventory of which is reproduced in Chapter 1, included a 'tenor' (i.e. viola) as lot 19 and a 'rare good' bass violin by this maker. Henley refers to some models approximating to that of Maggini and a splendidly conceived and finely carved scroll. Morris, who has the virtue of direct visual testimony, states: 'I have seen only three violins of this make, one of which was on a model approximating to that of Maggini, the wood, workmanship, and tone being very fine indeed. The varnish was an oil one of a rich golden-red colour, perfectly transparent, and elastic.'

Of the known instruments of, or attributed to, Lewis there is a bass viol bearing the label 'Edward Lewis | in St. Paul's Allay in London 1687' in the Museum of the Paris Conservatoire, and a violin is described as measuring $14^{5}/_{16}$ in. (364 mm), with two-piece back and transparent elastic golden varnish. It is said to bear its original label of 1704, carries a Hill certificate, and was owned by a professional player who described its tone as 'full bodied, sweet and equal on all registers'.[36] The entry in the *New Grove Dictionary of Musical Instruments* refers to a specimen branded 'E. Lewis 1742', but one suspects both that Lewis's work may have been copied and some of his originals passed off as Italian. A small cello with very worn varnish in a recent London sale was identified by the author as being by Lewis and

---

[34] Sandys and Forster, *History*, 255, written in 1864. Pamphilon's family background from Essex and his absence from the record of tenants of London Bridge buildings is discussed above.

[35] Ibid. 258.

[36] See *Strad* (June 1966), 46, where this instrument is illustrated. The scroll is visibly compatible with the highest Italian standard of the time.

bearing his handwritten label from 'over against Earls Court Drury Lane, London', dated 1732. The varnish was of the thin, yellow variety. Lewis is one of a group of distinguished English makers the absence of whose better work from any museum in Britain is a national tragedy.

Christopher Wise (*fl.* 1660) is categorized by Morris as 'chiefly a maker of viols'. Piper comments that 'a violoncello attributed to this maker was seen by the writer in London recently, but was not a very interesting specimen. The violins are occasionally met with and have very good varnish. Size rather small.'[37] Hart simply comments: 'Yellow varnish, neat workmanship, flat model, small pattern.' Henley speaks in a complimentary fashion of his work, though again referring to 'small dimensions'.

Wise's labels indicate that he worked in 'Half-moon alley, without Bishops-Gate, London', and in Vine Street in the same area. He may have produced instruments in the decade before the accession of Charles II. The specimen illustrated in this book (Pl. 109) was from the Hill collection and is a particularly good example of the Brescian influence, not only in the shape of the soundholes but in its body shape, having very abrupt corners and narrow waist. The body length was $13^{13}/_{16}$ in. (352 mm) and the printed label ran 'CHRISTOPHER WISE Vine Court without Bishops-Gate, London 1663'.

Occasionally an instrument from this early period emerges in the sale-room which gives experts the chance of assessing the instrument against the accepted descriptions in the standard directories. Robert Cuthbert is a maker of whom almost nothing is known. Henley gives his working dates as 1650–70. Morris, who does not give Cuthbert's Christian name, states with commendable honesty that 'he was chiefly a maker of viols, and is not supposed to have made many violins. I have never seen any of his work,' though he refers in the text to an 'admittedly genuine' example of this maker being on the Maggini model.[38] Hart, commenting on his violins, states that many of them have merit: 'Model flat, and wood of good quality. Very dark brownish.'[39]

In their June 1987 sale Phillips described lot 136 as 'a violin attributed to and most probably by Robert Cuthbert, bearing the maker's label "at the White Horse in Russell streete, nigh Covent Garden, 1676"'. This instrument, which has been internally examined during the course of restoration, is illustrated in this book (Pl. 47). Its catalogue description was 'the two-piece back of medium flame ascending slightly from the joint, the ribs and scroll of similar curl, the table of narrow grain, the varnish a clear brown colour'.[40] The appearance of the violin is distinctly Italianate (or possibly Flemish) and the work is extremely neat and accomplished.

---

[37] Moya and Piper, *Violin Tone*, 276.
[38] Morris, *British Violin Makers*, 10.
[39] Hart, *The Violin: Famous Makers*, 289–90.

[40] The varnish is in fact of a translucent golden brown, contrary to Hart's description above.

The nearest equivalent model would be an Amati of similar period. Rather shorter soundholes, a narrower lower bout, and the distinct quality of the varnish are the main differentiating features. The corner blocks (probably original) are hollowed out in a 'v' shape as is sometimes the case with English instruments, possibly to lighten the weight. The other dimensions are similar to those of the small-form Amati instrument dated 1671 given in appendix 3 of the Hills' work on *Stradivari*. A comparison is given in Table 1.

TABLE 1

	Small-Form Amati, 1671	*Robert Cuthbert, 1676*
Body length	13 7/8 in. (352 mm)	13 7/8 in. (352 mm)
Max. width lower bout	7 15/16 in. (201 mm)	7 11/16 in. (195 mm)
Max. width upper bout	6 3/8 in. (162 mm)	6 3/8 in. (162 mm)
Bottom rib width (inner)	1 3/16 in. (30 mm)	1 3/16 in. (30 mm)
Top rib width (inner)	1 1/8 in. (28 mm)	1 1/8 in. (28 mm)
Soundholes max. length	?	2 13/16 in. (71 mm)
Circumference at bridge	?	12 in. (305 mm)

As would be expected from such a well-made and good-looking instrument, the tone of the Cuthbert is regarded as being similar to that of an Amati. The label is in neat, seventeenth-century manuscript calligraphy. Without the label this attractive violin might well have been passed off as a northern Italian or possibly a superior Flemish instrument. It shows the very high standards of which makers of this period were capable. The Hill Archive gives some further information on Cuthbert, a sample of whose work was long in the Hill's collection of English instruments. This information is summarized in the Directory.

Other distinguished, and better-known, makers such as Barak Norman are better left for discussion in the context of the eighteenth century to which the bulk of their work more properly belongs.

Authenticity Problems

As a final and rather fundamental point it has to be said that there remain severe difficulties in assessing the work of the makers of the seventeenth century, caused primarily by the suspicion that musical instrument dealing tended to go hand in hand with music publishing or music selling and makers whose names appear on labels may have bought their instruments in. Their source could have been local, anonymous makers—in which case the character of the wood used can be a useful indication. As we have seen, English native wood was the usual rule and looking at the rather plain wood used by makers such as Nathaniel Cross (considered later), their early eighteenth-century work sets the norm by which to judge authenticity in this period. But there were apparently exceptions to the use of rather plain wood and since, as already discussed, the importation of decorative timber was well established by the latter part of the seventeenth century, there seems no reason in principle why figured maple should not have been available from these sources. Some native sycamore is also handsome and not always easy to distinguish. But the suspicion remains that some provincial 'makers' may simply have been retailers who put their labels in London-made instruments, and that other instruments may have been imported from Italy, the Low Countries, or Germany before acquiring London labels.

On the other hand, indisputable masterpieces were not long before being made in the viol field, and why should not local makers try to match the Continental instruments of the violin family then being widely used by London players? We should surely give the new generation of violin-makers in London the benefit of the doubt and assume that they simply transferred and adapted their skills to meet the burgeoning demand. In this some of them were so successful that fully authenticated cases have arisen where a seventeenth-century English instrument has acquired an Italian label. It is transmigration *to* Italy rather than *from* it that was their more common fate.

Chapter Four

The Economic and Social Organization of Violin-Making and Retailing in England

The Medieval Tradition — The Apprenticeship System — Violin Factories — The Piano in England: A Comparison — Family Craft Businesses — Retailers and Outworkers — Merlin: The Ingenious Mechanick — Other Retailers

The Medieval Tradition

IT is one of the peculiarities of the craft of violin-making in England that its participants tend to fall outside the main patterns of commercial organization. For a brief illustration of more mainstream production patterns, England's main trade for many centuries, woollen manufacture, is typical. In the process of production of woollen garments there were involved the distinct crafts of woolcombers, carders, weavers, fullers, dyers, and drapers. Successive sales of partially finished goods, for example combers selling wool to the spinners, spinners selling yarn to the weavers, weavers selling grey cloth to the fullers and dyers, and so on, exploited both the efficiency to be gained by specialization and the capitalist–merchant employer co-ordinating the production process and marketing the finished goods. By contrast, in violin-making in England the completion of the finished product from the raw materials was often the work of one man alone. Although mass-production methods were employed from quite early times in Germany and France (discussed later), this did not occur in England. A major factor was that there was in existence no equivalent to the long-established woodcarving industry symbiotically related to the forests of Bavaria and the Vosges.

Nevertheless, the organization of craft work originating in medieval times did have some influence in the organization of the violin trade, particularly up to the eighteenth and early part of the nineteenth centuries. It is worthwhile, therefore, outlining the main features of the traditional system.

Medieval trade outside the agrarian industry was centred on the town. The weekly market of the town gave the opportunity for the exchange of non-agricultural goods for food and also the opportunity for trade outside the town. A town of any importance was anxious to run its own affairs and exempt its citizens from tolls and exactions of neighbouring towns. Securing the administration of justice and electing its own mayor was also an important objective. These liberties could best be achieved by obtaining the grant of a Royal Charter.

Frequently created by the town's charter was an organization known as the merchant guild. This was an association of merchants within the town whose object was to guarantee fair prices to buyers and a fair reward to the seller. These objectives went hand in hand with the monopoly of trading for members of the merchant guild within the town. Non-members were permitted to sell to guildsmen provided a toll was paid. A primitive form of welfare was practised between members by the guild helping those who fell into poverty and relieving the sick. The merchant guild was common to most towns, though London, probably because of the size of its activities and disparate nature of its economy, did not have one. During the twelfth and thirteenth centuries the organization of the merchant guild and the municipality of the town, though originally separate and distinct, tended to coalesce.

Within the short time of the establishment of merchant guilds, a separate but somewhat similar organization known as the craft guild became common. Craft guilds were associations of *particular* trades—contrasted with the merchant guild whose members were those who bought and sold within the town generally. Late in the twelfth century the earliest Guild was formed, that of the Weavers. By the end of the thirteenth century craft guilds were numerous and widely spread. Their members were often burgesses (town officials) and members of the merchant guild.

The object of the craft guild was to monopolize a particular industry. This was seen as a way of obtaining a fair living for the worker and a good standard of craftsmanship. The idea that making an article to the best of the workman's ability was a desirable object in its own right, even if a buyer would not suspect bad workmanship, was an enduring and deeply fixed one. There was a pride in craftsmanship for its own sake. But craft guilds also had religious functions, associated with prayers for the souls of deceased members, the performance of pageants and 'mystery' plays, a charge on their funds which together with welfare commitments did much to cause the disintegration of the guild system by the sixteenth century.

The Apprenticeship System

An important feature of the guild system, common throughout western Europe, was apprenticeship. A boy or a girl who wished to follow a particular trade, for example a hatter, a fishmonger, or a weaver, applied to become a member of the relevant guild. This would involve an apprenticeship to a master. A boy would bind himself, usually on payment by his parents of a fee to the master, for a period of time which typically was seven years. During this time he would work for and live with the master craftsman, learning the 'mysteries' of the trade and receiving payment, if at all, only during the last year or so. The master's obligation was to feed, house, and clothe the apprentice as well as to teach the apprentice the trade. The advantages of the system were that the production of skilled workmen was continued and generations of craftsmen proud both of their craft and their town were produced, leaving, for example, the great medieval cathedrals of England as a monument to their building and craftsmanship skills.

The concept of apprenticeship continued to be important long after the disintegration of the guilds from about 1500 onwards, when it became apparent that in many trades bands of self-employed and under-capitalized workers were incapable of producing the volume and variety of goods required by commerce. In many trades the 'domestic' or 'putting-out' system under which an 'employer' found capital and gave out work to wage-earners working in their own homes, often outside the town so as to secure freedom from the restrictive practice of the guilds, replaced the system under which the workers controlled their own output. During the fifteenth century the success of the new system is evidenced in England by the beautiful 'wool' churches arising in the Cotswold villages and other areas of the country associated with the wool industry, at the time England's most important trade.

But the apprenticeship system persisted, since in the days before any organized teaching of skills in schools and colleges it was the only way by which the 'mysteries' of a particular trade could be passed on. The economic incentive to a master was the prospect of a number of years' free labour from his apprentice. The disincentive, which in time was to prove near fatal, was the prospect of a skilled apprentice setting up in competition on his own in due course.

The legal basis of apprenticeship was to be found in the Elizabethan Statute of Apprentices (1562–3). By the old common law, it was 'not legal to prohibit any man to work in any lawful trade or in more trades than one (at his pleasure)'.[1] But the Elizabethan Statute contained a restraining clause which stated 'it shall not be lawful to any person, to set up, occupy, use, or exercise, any craft, mistery or occu-

---

[1] Richard Burn, *Justice of the Peace* (London, 1758), i. 71.

pation now used or occupied within the realms of England or Wales, except he shall have been brought up therein seven years at the least as an apprentice by this Statute, nor to set any person on work therein except he shall have been apprentice as aforesaid, or else having served as an apprentice will become a journeyman . . .' Although there were many exceptions to this restraint, the spirit of the Statute continued to dominate actual practice in both trades then current and trades, such as violin-making, established afterwards. Subsequently developed trades were held to be outside the letter of the Statute as early as *Tolley's Case* in 1615. The Statute, after much judicial and political disapproval of its restrictive effects, was repealed in 1814. Nevertheless conventional progression involved satisfactory service as an apprentice followed by a period as a journeyman before, under the beneficent supervision of overseers of the guild, the craftsman himself became a master.

It is significant that in Germany to this day a similar system applies, for instance, in the town of Mittenwald in the violin-making school originally established there by Matthias Klotz. There the *Geigenbauschule*, which offers twelve places per annum, involves a three-and-a-half-year apprenticeship for *der Lehrling* who then becomes a journeyman (*der Geselle*) and then, after a further three years' work under a master craftsman (*der Meister*), takes a final examination known as *die Meisterprüfung*.[2]

Although, as will be seen, the apprenticeship system (also known as an articled pupilship) did occur in eighteenth- and nineteenth-century violin-making in England, apprenticeship was never by law compulsory. Anyone could set up in the trade. Indeed, it was probably difficult for an outsider to obtain an apprenticeship. Families, sometimes making reciprocal arrangements, had something of a monopoly. It was not surprising that this rather undernourished stock was refreshed by a supply of Continental trained craftsmen, particularly after 1800.

Violin Factories

In England, however, 'violin factories' of the sort which were by the eighteenth century well established in Mirecourt in France and in the German violin-making towns were for all practical purposes unknown. It is strongly suspected that the reason for this lack of industrialization in the violin-making process in England was partly the relative lack of demand owing to the slow progress of interest in music in that country (discussed in later chapters). Where there was a need to

---

[2] Edward Heron-Allen translated *The Arts and Crafts Book of the Worshipful Guild of Violin Makers of Markneukirchen for the Years 1699–1772* in a pamphlet published in 1894. This reveals many similar features to the type of system typical of the English craft guild two centuries earlier. For the Swiss four-year apprenticeship system current at Brienz, see 'The Violin Making School in Brienz', *Strad* (Feb. 1993) 151.

produce cheap instruments in England in general, and in London in particular, the tendency was for an individual, or perhaps a small team in a workshop, to make instruments (by hand) of different grades, the cheapest being very crude work indeed.

Later on at least one attempt to establish a 'factory' in England has been recorded. This comes from the evidence relayed by the Revd W. Meredith Morris who in his book *British Violin Makers* (1920) discussed an apparently short-lived 'Violin Makers' Guild' as follows:

This is a Guild or school of violin making established at 35 South End Road, Hampstead, London, N.W. Its full title is 'The British Violin-Makers' Guild,' and it is described in the pamphlet explanatory of its object as 'The only *all British* manufactory producing violins, violas, violoncellos, and basses at competitive Continental prices.' Its managing director, Mr. Albert J. Roberts, in a letter in the press writes that 'arrangements are being made for the employment of disabled soldiers and sailors,' and that 'there are also vacancies for improvers and a few articled pupils desirous of learning the art of violin-making under the guidance of a skilled staff of English, French and Russian instructors, now engaged.' I visited the institution, or factory, in August of the year 1915, when the managing director was good enough to take me over the workshop, and to explain to me that the Guild had two definite objects in view: (1) to teach violin making, and (2) to produce a high-class factory violin at a price that would enable them (the Guild) to compete successfully with the foreigner. Every patriot will agree that the objects are very sensible and praiseworthy. There is not a shadow of doubt about it, the fiddle factory has come to stay. The connoisseur may fling his scorn and utter his malediction, but the British public will smile at him and purchase its thirty shilling fiddle. Well, since there must be factory fiddles, let those used in Britain, I say, be of British manufacture. I express myself thus in all sincerity, firm believer in universal brotherhood though I be, for my sense of brotherhood does not bid me love my neighbour (the foreigner) *better* than myself (i.e. my own nation).

The time is propitious for the founding of an industry of this description, and all its promoters need to make it a success in organization, concentration, co-operation, and a reasonable belief in themselves.[3]

On the other hand, in continental Europe, particularly Mirecourt in France and the German towns of Mittenwald, Klingental, and Markneukirchen, where local wood-carving industries were closely related to the forested and mountainous terrain, it is clear from at least the beginning of the eighteenth century that violin-making guilds were formed and the division of labour practised. Specialist buyers found violin-making and bow-making wood which was purchased in bulk from the appropriate sources and ready cut for piece-work production. 'Boxmakers' made the bodies of the instruments and others specialized in scrolls, fingerboards,

---

[3] Morris, *British Violin Makers*, 247–8. This enterprise disappeared without trace within a few years. This type of mechanical production should be distinguished from the 'craft workshop' organization of, for instance, the Hills at Hanwell, discussed in Ch. 9.

and the other accessories of violin- and bow-making. Mirecourt was particularly jealous of its own privileges and 'know-how', producing instruments of well-figured wood often superior to the German product and using apprentices and assistants almost exclusively employed from Mirecourt. Families specialized in, for example, the varnishing process which is such a distinctive feature of these violins. When both France and Germany began to lower unit costs further by employing machines in the manufacture of stringed instruments in the nineteenth century, this, together with the lightening or complete removal of customs duties on imported goods, was prejudicial to the always small violin-making industry in England. These matters will be more closely explored later in the book. But the threat to 'home' industry from cheap German imports started in the eighteenth century, as is clear from the following revealing passage in Sandys and Forster writing in about 1864:

> After pioneering through the account-books of this violin-maker[4] from 1786 to 1816 it is found that a list of the instruments manufactured cannot be produced even approaching tolerable accuracy, therefore it is abandoned. Four different classes of instruments were made by William Forster (3), assisted by his son and workmen; and about the year 1786-7 the German fiddles of cheap and common workmanship, were introduced into England, it is believed, by Astor, of Wych Street, Strand, of whom tales could be told connected with German clocks and German musical wind instruments; and entries are seen in the books for fiddles as low as nine shillings, which were mostly sold to dealers; but others have participated in the low prices. Moreover, there are many exchanges and re-purchases of instruments, so that it is very probable the same instrument may have been disposed of more than once.[5]

The Piano in England: A Comparison

This reluctance to contemplate the use of available woodworking machinery was echoed in the development of the far bigger piano industry in England. By 1851 Broadwood's in London employed over 300 workmen, and an elaborate division of labour was practised involving about forty different specialist workmen. Existing machinery was practically ignored, as Cyril Ehrlich shows in his comprehensive analysis of the economic history of the piano. So, although annual output was about 2,500 instruments, productivity per man was only about seven. As the USA and a little later Germany and France began to make better and cheaper pianos by developing a more mechanized production system well suited to this particular instrument, the consumer was for some time denied much choice, owing to a combination of factors such as financial ties between manufacturers and retailers

---

[4] i.e. William Forster (3).   [5] Sandys and Forster, *History*, 336.

restricting supplies, social snobbery, and an innate belief in the superiority of the English product from the design and tonal point of view.[6]

Family Craft Businesses

As already mentioned, in violin-making, whether in France or Germany or England, there was a persistent tradition of passing the skills involved down from father to son. In England, the Hill family, the Forster family, the Kennedy family, the Duke family, and the Banks family were eminent examples. In this very convenient system trade secrets and working methods are kept within the family, and the industry was small enough to allow business to prosper in this way without the need for capital infusion from outside. Retailing was either done direct from the maker's workshop, particularly if the maker had a retail general music establishment too, or through dealers, usually in London, who had a tendency to 'own-brand' their wares.

The life and business organization of Benjamin Banks of Salisbury has now been well documented by Albert Cooper.[7] As mentioned in Chapter 1, that author has established from the apprenticeship ledgers kept to record the stamp-duty on articles of apprenticeship that Banks was apprenticed in 1742 to William Huttoft, self-styled instrument maker, of Salisbury, for seven years. Banks was related to the Huttoft family, William being his uncle. Although this does not reveal where Banks in fact learned his instrument-making skills, since Huttoft himself is not known to have possessed any, when taken with the history of other English dynastic makers such as the Hills, it suggests that apprenticeship to a family member was often the preferred start of an English violin-maker's career.

Before Banks became established as a violin-maker in his own right in Salisbury it is clear that he had a commercial relationship with such London retail establishments as Cahusac's and Longman and Broderip, the latter becoming his London agents. He may, therefore, have been introduced to other makers using the same retailing connections. There is some evidence that Banks's subsequent production, once he had acquired and developed his skills, was at least in part shared by other members of his family and employees. Cooper infers from the stereotyping of the scrolls on Banks's instruments that these may be the product of one craftsman, whilst others have roughed out the bodies ready, perhaps, for the master craftsman to put the finishing touches. (Banks's sons eventually continued the business in Liverpool.)

---

[6] See generally Cyril Ehrlich, *The Piano: A History* (London, 1976), esp. chs. 1 and 2.   [7] *Benjamin Banks*

This system worked well enough if there was a family instrument-making tradition. An example of an eighteenth-century apprenticeship to a violin-maker outside the family circle was that of Samuel Gilkes, much patronized as a maker and dealer in his lifetime (1787–1827). Gilkes was apprenticed to Charles Harris the elder, along with Charles Harris the younger. Sandys and Forster explain that Gilkes, born in Northamptonshire, was 'sent to London to learn fiddle-making'. Gilkes's apprenticeship was finished about 1810 and he then became a journeyman to William Forster (3) before setting up on his own.[8] W. E. Hill was also apprenticed to the Harris family, but this was no doubt a friendly arrangement between families based on mutual respect.

Retailers and Outworkers

To revert to the London scene with which a provincial maker even of the calibre of Banks was necessarily connected, there are other examples of retailers who used local and usually anonymous violin-makers as outworkers. Amongst these establishments were Goulding and Co., a firm (proprietor George Goulding) which flourished from about 1785 to 1798 and whose instrument-supplying business included piano-making and organ-building.[9] The trade name is branded under the button of otherwise anonymous stringed instruments emanating from this trading concern, which also apparently bought in French and German instruments.[10] Those instruments without a label are generally discernible as English work, though the actual makers are not known. (The Goulding production is discussed further in the Directory.)

The firm of Longman and Lukey, later Longman and Broderip, already mentioned above, who dealt in Cheapside between 1741 and 1798, bought all their instruments in and put their trade label inside, also usually branding the instrument on the back below the button. Benjamin Banks and Henry Jay (1740–76) as well as Lockey Hill and Joseph Hill for violas, have been associated by experts with this firm. Longman and Broderip were musical-instrument 'makers' and dealers, music sellers, and publishers of 26 Cheapside, London, and operated there between 1776 and 1798, succeeding Longman Lukey & Co. from 1769. In 1798 the firm became bankrupt and the partnership was dissolved.[11] Many of their instruments were made to sell cheaply, being unpurfled and crudely constructed—redeemed only, perhaps, by a certain charm.

---

[8] Sandys and Forster, *History*, 276, 348.
[9] This firm later became Goulding and D'Almaine, music sellers and publishers and military musical-instrument makers, from about 1798.
[10] See Henley, *Dictionary*, 480.
[11] See generally C. Humphries and W. C. Smith, *Music Publishing in the British Isles* (London, 1954).

The eighteenth-century music publisher and instrument-maker Thomas Cahusac, in business between 1755 and 1798 at the sign of the 'Two Flutes and Violin' in the Strand, also bought in work of very variable quality.

One of the best-known London 'makers' who made few instruments himself was John Edward Betts (1755–1823). 'Old Betts the Fiddle Maker' was himself a pupil of Richard Duke but the authorities agree in ascribing to his business the work of such artists as the Panormos, John Carter, his nephew Edward ('Ned') Betts, Bernhard Fendt, and Richard Tobin. But, as Morris states, 'there is quite a number of instruments about bearing the label of Betts, which could not have been made by the artists just named: they are of inferior workmanship, and not a few of them have a poor tone. These were possibly the work of apprentices or "improvers".'[12]

Often given as an indication of the shrewdness of J. E. Betts as a businessman is a frequently related story of his acquisition of the famous 'Betts Strad', a fine and handsome instrument. Fleming recounts it thus:

Some person sold a violin over the counter to one of the Messrs. Betts, in their shop at the Royal Exchange—No. 2—one of the shops, probably, which at present face the front of the Bank of England. The price asked, or agreed upon, for the instrument was twenty shillings [£1], the person selling it, not having, of course, the slightest idea of its value. Mr. Betts, however, knew what it was, and bought it, keeping it beside him for years, and declining very handsome offers of as much as five hundred guineas [£525] for it.[13]

Morris excoriates Betts for this unconscionable transaction:

It is deplorable that writers treat this sort of thing as though it were nothing but an exceptionally interesting and clever bit of fiddle dealing. Clever it may be, but more clever than honest . . . If business morality in Britain were generally on a level with the 'Betts Strad' transaction, the day would not be far distant when prisons and workhouses would be as numerous as schools and churches.[14]

In English law in the latter part of the twentieth century one could add that if Betts had falsely denigrated the instrument (which is not proven) the transaction would be likely to infringe the Trade Descriptions Act 1968 which includes within its ambit trade *buyers* who in the course of a trade or business apply a false trade description to goods.[15] But the story also points to the economic truth that traders such as Betts in early nineteenth-century London were beginning to find it more profitable to import and trade in classic Italian instruments than to subsist primarily on the production of new, home-made, ones.

---

[12] *British Violin Makers*, 106.
[13] J. M. Fleming, *The Fiddle Fancier's Guide* (London, 1892), 42.
[14] *British Violin Makers*, s.v. 'Betts, John'.
[15] See *Fletcher* v *Budgen* (1974) and Harvey, *Violin Fraud*.

Merlin: The Ingenious Mechanick

Another entrepreneur trading in eighteenth-century London was John Joseph Merlin. Fortunately his life has been subjected to meticulous research and this shows that his association with violin-making was but a very minor part of an extraordinary career.[16] Merlin was born in 1735 in what is now Belgium, possibly of Huguenot extraction. His occupation can best be described as 'inventor'. His first invention appears to have been developed in Paris, the 'Fauteuil ... pour ceux qui ont la goute au [sic] jambes' (a chair for those suffering from gout in the legs). He came to London in the household of a Spanish nobleman and his first recorded commission there was as a participant in the construction of the mechanical organ at Carlton House, made for the Princess of Wales. This was described by a viewer in 1763 as having 'seventeen barrels of eighteen inches (diameter) by four feet, a weight of 400lb. for the three bellows and another of 250lb. for the movement...'[17]

Although he was closely associated with music he was best known in his lifetime for the Mechanical Museum which he opened in Princes Street, Hanover Square. The museum was intended both to provide innocent amusement for those who were fascinated by clockwork automata and other ingenious gadgets, and also to offer articles for sale. One group of articles comprised musical instruments, some of these being self-playing.

Merlin's mechanical genius was more appropriately matched with the production of keyboard instruments, and indeed he took out patents for and manufactured ingenious combinations of pianofortes and harpsichords, one of which is now in the Deutsches Museum in Munich and is said to have been owned by Catherine the Great. Such instruments as survive by him and bear his inscription on the name board are not only mechanically ingenious but demonstrate exquisite cabinet-making skills. During his lifetime Merlin mixed in distinguished musical circles, being particularly friendly with the Burney family. J. C. Bach is known to have played one of Merlin's instruments during public recitals in 1774 in the Hanover Square Rooms, London's most fashionable concert-hall and near to Merlin's own exhibition rooms in Princes Street (later becoming the 'violin street' named Wardour Street).

So far as stringed instruments are concerned, Merlin's name is not only associated with the conventional violin family, but also with at least one guitar-shaped tenor or small cello and a 'pentachord' made in about 1775 for Sir Edward Walpole. This is a cello-like instrument with an additional treble string.

With or without justification Merlin appears in the standard violin directories as

---

[16] See *John Joseph Merlin: The Ingenious Mechanick* (London, 1985), being a catalogue of an exhibition.
[17] Ibid. 85.

a London maker of violins. Indeed, his museum catalogue included advertisements for both violins and 'bass viols'. The description of the former runs as follows: '*New Violins* made equal to the best Cremonas, with new-indented Pegs and Tailpieces which prevent the strings from slipping. Price from 5 to 10 Guineas.'[18]

The price of the similarly described 'bass viols' was from twelve guineas to twenty. Merlin also undertook to 'improve' old violins, presumably those made in the Stainer tradition, to make them sound more like the instruments of the Cremonese makers which were now becoming popular. His advertisement ran: 'The tone of *old Violins* and *Bass Viols* improved to great Perfection. For improving the Tone of a Violin and adding the new-indented Pegs and Tailpieces £1.16s.'[19] It is unfortunate that Merlin's newly invented anti-slip pegs, and also the advertised tailpieces, have not come down to us. The pegs were presumably designed to prevent a phenomenon still depressingly familiar to string players, and one which, incidentally, Thomas Mace writing in the seventeenth century in *Musick's Monument* (as discussed in more detail in Chapter 1), wrote complainingly about in the context of slipping pegs on his lutes.

Both Morris and Henley in their standard directories do not suggest other than that Merlin's work was his own. However, this is extremely doubtful. The catalogue with the entry quoted above confirms that 'New Violins' were on sale and a typical label, as quoted by Morris, runs: 'Josephus Merlin Cremonae Emulus, No. 104, London (Londini), 1779, Improved. | 69 Queen Ann Street East, Portland Chapel'. The instrument shown in the GLC 1985 exhibition of his work has a similar label (No. 121, 1776).[20] It is not entirely clear whether these labels are intended to convey that these were existing instruments 'improved', or original instrument made according to Merlin's improved design. But whichever was the case, it seems inherently improbable that Merlin would have had either the skill or the time to make the instruments himself. They probably carried his newly invented pegs and tailpieces and perhaps bore the stamp of his overall design. But as a fashionable inventor and 'mechanical genius', he would have been tempted to exploit his own name and use 'outworkers' for the actual production of his instruments.

The 'pentachord' mentioned above has a letter associated with it stating that the maker of the instrument was John Carter, 'the assistant to Wm. Forster—the machinery by Mr. Merlin of the Museum of Mechanical Inventions', although it is clearly marked with Merlin's stamp. His will, made two months before his death in 1803, refers to 'the lease of my Messuage warehouses and Effects', and it seems a legitimate assumption that Merlin's extensive stock of a wide variety of items was safely secured away from his retail establishment in a warehouse before acquiring 'own-brand' insignia. Whether, in the case of violins, he always used the same

---

[18] *The Ingenious Mechanick* 93.
[19] Ibid. 92–3. [20] Their numbering was clearly erratic.

outworkers, remains obscure, but the few instruments that have survived generally reveal quite good workmanship in the Stainer tradition.[21] They seem typically English work of the period and could have involved the same outworkers as used by other London retailers. Commentators are virtually united, however, in condemning the tone. Sandys and Forster, for instance, comment laconically that 'the tone was of the usual quality of high-built instruments'.[22]

Merlin's association with the violin is linked with the well-known story of the episode which took place some time between 1761 and 1772, as related by Thomas Busby in his book *Concert Room and Orchestra Anecdotes of Music and Musicians Ancient and Modern*.[23] This reads:

One of his ingenious novelties was a *pair of skaites* contrived to run on small mechanic wheels. Supplied with a pair of these and a violin he mixed in the motley group of one of the celebrated Mrs. Cornleys' masquerades at Carlyle-house, Soho-square; when, not having provided the means of retarding his velocity, or commanding its direction, he impelled himself against a mirror, of more than five hundred pounds' value, dashed it to atoms, broke his instrument to pieces, and wounded himself most severely.[24]

This confirms Merlin's reputation as an eccentric genius, but the object of the exhibition was to demonstrate his ingenious new roller-skates which now, incidentally, reside in the National Museum of Roller Skating, Lincoln, Nebraska. It may be assumed that he was actually playing the violin at the time. Perhaps his technique on this instrument was better than that of his roller-skating.[25]

It is apparent that this very talented inventor's ingenuity lay primarily in working with scientific and mathematical instruments, horology, furniture design, and keyboard instruments. He gained sufficient fame to be painted by Thomas Gainsborough, a magnificent portrait now in the Ireagh Bequest, Kenwood. It is clear from the comparatively high price that he apparently successfully asked for 'new violins', five to ten guineas, and twelve guineas to twenty for 'bass viols' (presumably cellos rather than double basses), that his marketing was as successful as the ingenuity of his production methods. But the dealer who at a recent sale of one of Merlin's instruments was heard to observe that he did not think the instrument was 'right' was probably in one sense correct. The instrument would have come, in all likelihood, from one of the better class of workshop makers who rarely used their own labels but supplied a number of the retail establishments mentioned in this chapter. Some of these makers when using their own labels emphasized the point by stating, for example, 'Wm. Smith | Real Maker | London, 1771'.[26]

---

[21] See the instrument illustrated in the 1985 catalogue of the GLC exhibition.
[22] *History*, 277.
[23] (London, 1825).
[24] ii. 137.
[25] Henley suggests the violin was 'of his own make'—*sed quaere*.
[26] See Henley, *Dictionary*, 1081, who probably took it from Sandys and Forster, *History*, 282.

Other Retailers

A number of other retail establishments of a similar nature flourished in London during the latter part of the eighteenth century. For example, Henley probably correctly assumes that violins bearing the label 'Made by Norris and Barnes | Violin, violoncello, and bowmakers to their Majesties | Coventry Street, London' were made by employees and their bows by Dodd. Sandys and Forster had come to the same conclusion, ascribing one of their cellos to Edmund Aireton.[27] This business had an interesting subsequent history. Robert Barnes left the business and by 1794 appears to have set up on his own, his label running 'Robert Barnes, Violin maker, Windmill Street, Haymarket'.[28] John Norris died in 1818 and the business was succeeded to by 'the shopman' Richard Davis 'more as a dealer than a manufacturer'. His cousin William Davis then took over until 1846, 'more as a dealer than a maker', and he brought the eminent French maker Charles Maucatel to work for him. The business was then sold to Edward Withers, one of nineteenth-century London's best-known violin-makers and sellers.[29]

Poidras[30] states that 'Miller' (London, early eighteenth century) is not known as a maker but was probably a dealer who stuck his own label in instruments he bought. Henley does not confirm this judgement, merely stating that he worked at a shop signed 'At the citern' (presumably culled from Sandys and Forster who refer to printed literature advertising the music shop as being 'At the Signe of the Citern London Bridge')[31] and signed his instruments 'Miller, London'. And Thomas Dodd, brother of the eminent English bow-maker John Dodd, ran successful dealing businesses in Covent Garden, Charing Cross, and Berners Street during this period, employing, it is thought, the exceptional talent of John Lott and Bernhard Fendt. The latter names are a reminder not only that we are now trespassing into the nineteenth century, but how much violin-making in the British Isles owed at the end of the eighteenth century to workers whose origin was in Germany, Austria, France, and with the arrival of the great Panormo, Italy.

[27] *History*, 268.   [28] Ibid. 269.
[29] Ibid. 268. The firm is further discussed in the Directory.
[30] *Dictionary*, i. 145.   [31] *History*, 278.

Chapter Five

English Music and Makers in the Eighteenth Century

Musical Developments — A Group of Early Eighteenth-Century Violin-Makers — Barak Norman and Nathaniel Cross — John and Joseph Hare — John Barrett — William Pryor — Daniel Parker — Other Eighteenth-Century Makers in England — Unscrupulous Attributions

Musical Developments

THE period between the death of Henry Purcell in 1685 and the first arrival of Handel in England in 1710 is often referred to as a period of transition. There was no towering figure to replace Henry Purcell and English native composers proved incapable of supplying a home-made product which could compete with Italian opera.

Nevertheless the underlying trend in the country was one of significant expansion of musical activity. A necessary underpinning of this activity is a vigorous music-publishing industry, and John Playford's family publishing business was soon challenged by a number of rivals. Amongst these was Thomas Cross who set up in 1695 at the Golden Harp and Hautboy, near the Strand. He popularized music by issuing cheap instruction books for flute, violin, and voice, anthologies of songs, instrumental sonatas, and, later, operas. He went on to exploit the success of Handel.[1]

At the same time the manufacturing, retailing, and repairing of musical instruments expanded. This was often combined with the selling of sheet music. Percy Young notes that Ralph Agutter of London found the competition so intense that by 1707 he had moved to Edinburgh where he advertised the making of violin, bass violin, tenor violin, viol da gamba, lute, trumpet marine, and harp, the repair, setting-up, and stringing of all these instruments, and also keyboard instruments,

---

[1] See Young, *History*, 266.

'all at reasonable rates'.[2] Ralph Agutter later moved to Newcastle upon Tyne, an indication of how some musicians in the early part of the eighteenth century moved out to the provinces where competition was less intense. The author has inspected a violin from the early eighteenth century bearing Agutter's printed London label, presumably a workshop product.

The concert scene in London was improved when in 1685 York Buildings in Bow Street were adapted for concert-giving and were of a suitable standard to entertain visiting royalty. Other concert-halls in Charles Street, Sadlers Wells, Islington, and elsewhere in London were established at this time.[3]

Of particular significance too was the continued ascendancy of composers and instrumentalists of foreign descent. We have already seen the great effect that the arrival of Baltzar and Matteis had caused in London by their violin playing. Subsequent German musicians, such as Gottfried Finger and J. C. Pepusch, concentrated more on composition and the direction of musical activities. Italian musicians also arrived in significant numbers. Amongst these were Francesco Geminiani, a pupil of Corelli, Gasparo Visconti (a violinist mentioned later), Nicola Haym (a cellist and composer); and in 1714 the distinguished violinist Francesco Maria Veracini arrived in London to lead the opera orchestra, succeeding Corelli's pupil Castrucci.[4] It is impossible to overestimate the effect the playing of these gifted Italians had on the concert scene in England. They must have inspired many others to try their hand at a stringed instrument, the music and books of tuition now being readily available.

A steady traffic of foreign violinists,[5] often with other skills as conductors, composers, or keyboard players, continued throughout the eighteenth century, and this abiding phenomenon is discussed further in Chapter 7. A little later in the century Felice de Giardini (born Turin 1716, died Moscow 1796) made a particular impression in London from his début in 1751. In his work at the Opera he is reputed to have been the first to introduce uniform bowing. He wrote many violin concertos, operas, and other works, and on the copy of his violin solos, Op. 16, calls himself Music Master of the Duke of Cumberland.[6]

W. T. Parke in his *Musical Memoirs*[7] speaks of Giardini producing a tone more powerful and clear than any of his contemporaries. This 'knack' proved profitable to Giardini 'enabling him to sell his inferior instruments at a large price to gentlemen who, in his hands, admired the powerful tone, though they found afterwards,

---

[2] See Young, *History*, 267.
[3] Ibid. 268.
[4] Ibid. 302. See also Robin Stowell, 'The Sonata' in Stowell (ed.), *Cambridge Companion*, 171–2, and McVeigh, ibid., ch. 3.
[5] Not all were Italian. The Rotterdam-born Peter Hellendaal (1721–99) enjoyed a successful career as violinist and composer in London, King's Lynn, and Cambridge. He was a pupil of Tartini.
[6] See further Ch. 7 and Van der Straeten, *History of the Violin*, 19; also Simon McVeigh, *The Violinist in London's Concert Life, 1750–1784; Felice Giardini and his Contemporaries* (New York, 1989).
[7] (London, 1830), i. 155.

to their great surprise, that they could draw forth very little, apparently not aware that the tone came from the skill used, not from the fiddle'.[8] Giardini clearly enjoyed dealing in instruments as an avocation and one suspects that this was a comparatively common phenomenon at this time. Many good player–dealers have been able to produce poor tone when negotiating the purchase of an instrument and powerful 'selling tone' when passing the same instrument on. It sounds as if Giardini knew this trick.

In 1738 the Royal Society of Musicians was founded with the warm backing, moral and financial, of Handel. The Society provided invaluable funds 'for the support of decayed musicians and their families'.[9] The promotion of performance was materially assisted when in 1710 the Academy of Ancient Music was founded and many prominent musicians resident in England became members of it. This organization specialized in keeping alive the music of the great sixteenth-century masters, but also promoted works by contemporary composers.

Concert programming in the early part of the eighteenth century tends to pander to the then English tendency of wanting instant and easy diversion. The public required to be amused rather than intellectually stimulated. It was often thought appropriate to intersperse 'comic interludes' between acts of operas or movements of sonatas,[10] and the reluctance of concert promoters to risk boring the audience by too concentrated a dose of 'serious' music continued well into the nineteenth century, as can be judged by the numerous concert programmes surviving from these years. Nevertheless, to those who were serious about learning the violin an important event occurred in 1751, when Francesco Geminani published in London *The Art of Playing on the Violin*, containing 'all the Rules necessary to attain to a Perfection on that Instrument, with great variety of compositions, which will also be very useful to those who study the Violoncello, Harpsichord, etc.'. Although, as some music historians suggest, this was not the first such treatise, it was the first serious one. It was at that time only clearly exceeded in terms of thorough and conscientious instruction by Leopold Mozart's 'Complete Tutor' (*Versuch einer gründlichen Violinschule*) which appeared in Augsburg in 1756.

Handel's arrival in London in 1710 and its effect on musical activity both in London and in the provinces have been so well documented that little more needs to be said here. Suffice it to say that for the first twenty-five years or so of his residence in England Handel concentrated with early but diminishing success on the opera scene. The mounting of opera in London, with its particular appeal to the aristocratic and well-heeled, also resulted in the importation of numerous Italian singers and instrumentalists and laid the foundation for a British inferiority complex which lasted well into the twentieth century. Put bluntly, any singer,

---

[8] Cited in Hill, *Stradivari*, 261.   [9] E. Blom, *Music in England* (Harmondsworth, 1942), 104.
[10] See Walker, *History of Music in England*, 249.

instrumentalist, or conductor without an Italian (or possibly German) name had to disprove the presumption that he or she was not as good a performer as a foreign one. (As an astonishing reflection of British taste for foreign-sounding names, the conductor Basil Cameron (1884–1975) adopted the name Hindenburg in 1912, when conducting the Torquay Municipal Orchestra, for two years.)

But as enthusiasm for opera further diminished, something more permanently important occurred. It profoundly affected the music-making in England until recent times. This was the discovery by Handel that the oratorio, which could well have a semi-operatic 'plot', held mass appeal. This appeal was reflected not only in frequent performances of oratorio in London but also in the English provinces where by 1724 the Three Choirs Festival had become established in Gloucester, Worcester, and Hereford. As early as July 1713 there is a notice of a performance in Worcester Cathedral of 'Mr. Purcell's great *Te Deum* with the Symphonies and instrumental parts on Violins and Hautboys'.[11] Oratorio required the presence of an orchestra, and many professional musicians over the last two centuries in England, including Edward Elgar in his early days, have good cause to be thankful for the English predilection for this type of religious music. Handel died in 1759, the last composing period of his life having been primarily devoted to composition of oratorio and instrumental music. His most astonishing achievement, in retrospect, was perhaps the writing of the oratorio *Messiah* in three weeks during 1741. This work has received countless performances in the British Isles, involving choral and orchestral forces of widely varying sizes, ever since. Many British conductors, singers, and instrumentalists have found performing the work provides over the years a regular source of 'bread-and-butter' income.

An important factor in the promotion of the performance of music as a fashionable activity is the attitude of the landed aristocracy at the time. Undoubtedly most would have been inclined to regard the concert as a place to be amused—perhaps a pleasant occasion to relax with the ladies after some strenuous hunting. But it is worth observing that some of the nobility took a closer interest in music for more serious reasons. Some were responsible for bringing Italian musicians back to England—for example Lord Burlington, who brought Castrucci, and the Duke of Rutland, 'himself an amateur violinist of some quality', who brought back Carbonelli.[12] Noble patrons also sponsored private concerts, at some of which Handel would conduct. We are told that there were 'very frequently concerts for the Royal Family, at the Queen's Library in the Green Park in which the Princess Royal, the Duke of Rutland, Lord Cowper, and other persons of distinction per-

---

[11] See H. W. Shaw, *The Three Choirs Festival* (Worcester, 1954).

[12] See Percy M. Young, *The Concert Tradition: From the Middle Ages to the Twentieth Century* (London, 1965), 76.

formed'.[13] The predilection of amateur players amongst the aristocracy, including members of the Royal Family, for the cello in England is an important phenomenon which will often be noticed in this book, and had a vitally important bearing on English cello-making.

Other, more informal, concerts were established in less elevated surroundings, often taverns, after Thomas Britton's establishment had closed down. In 1724 there was a report that

one hundred gentlemen and merchants of the City, had lately form'd themselves into a musical society, the one part Performers, the other Auditors in St. Paul's churchyard ... As musick must be allow'd to be the most innocent and agreeable Amusement, and a charming Relaxation to the Mind when fatigued with the Bustle of Business, or after it has long been bent on serious Studies, this bids fair for encouraging the Science, and seems to be a very ingenious and laudable Undertaking.[14]

Although activity in London has been emphasized, mention has already been made of the growth of oratorio performance in the provinces, particularly those cities with cathedrals, which was also accompanied by the formation of music clubs. For example, Norwich had a 'Musick Meeting' beginning in the 1720s, Bristol had two music clubs by 1731, Oxford's Music Club was restarted in 1733 (under the revivifying effect of Handel), and fashionable Bath maintained a professional orchestra.[15]

Although Handel's music had been performed in, for instance, Lichfield, Bridgnorth, Walsall, and Chester during his lifetime, the great northern choral tradition became more securely established in the second half of the eighteenth century. This was so much so that in 1788 Charles Dibdin could write that 'more than one man in Halifax can take any part in choruses from *Messiah*, and go regularly through the whole oratorio by heart; and, indeed, that the facility with which the common people joined together throughout the greatest part of Yorkshire and Lancashire, in every species of choral music, is truly astonishing'.[16] In fact by the later part of the eighteenth century there were very few cathedral cities which did not have organized non-ecclesiastical music performances on a regular basis, and surprisingly small towns, such as Great Yarmouth (in the 1730s) developed 'meetings' or 'clubs'. Although some oratorios were performed with purely organ accompaniment, the bigger performances required the services of a 'band'. The string section would typically be a mixture of professional and amateur players.

The development of the musical scene particularly in London towards the end

---

[13] Quoted from a contemporary source in Young, *The Concert Tradition*, 76.

[14] Young, *The Concert Tradition*, 77, quoting the *Daily Post* of 17 Oct. 1724.

[15] See S. Sadie, *Concert Life in Eighteenth Century England*, Proceedings of the Royal Musical Association, 9 Dec. 1958; and Raynor, 'A Social History, 263.

[16] Charles Dibdin, *The Musical Tour of Mr. Dibdin* (Sheffield, 1788), quoted in E. D. Mackerness, *A Social History of English Music*, 113.

of the eighteenth century and beyond must now be left to a later chapter (see Ch. 7). Enough has been said to show that there was already significant demand for string-players. It now remains to look at a selection of makers whose work must have assisted in meeting that demand.

A Group of Early Eighteenth-Century Violin-Makers

In this section a group of distinguished violin-makers of the early part of the eighteenth century will be discussed, following the same method as before. Views of the leading critics in the past will be summarized as appropriate and some attempt made to come to a modern judgement. They make an interesting group, not least because of the variety of influences at work. Barak Norman's instruments show the waning influence of the Brescian school mixed with Tyrolean or Staineresque features more typical of this school as a whole. Isolated makers, particularly Joseph Hare and Daniel Parker, show the influence of early Stradivari work. The influence too of the work of the Amati family, whose instruments are very likely to have been in use in London by this time, is pervasive even if it was not long before the Stainer model, as already discussed, became by far the more popular choice of players. The Amati–Stainer–Tyrolean models all involved significantly higher arching than is associated with Stradivari and his followers.

Barak Norman and Nathaniel Cross

Hart[17] gives Barak Norman's dates as 1688–1740 and subsequent dictionary biographers have adopted the same dates. He is universally regarded as being among the best of the Old English School. As his name suggests (and as discussed in Ch. 3) he was probably of Huguenot origin. Most commentators agree that he is likely to have been a pupil of Thomas Urquhart (considered in Chapter 3). As Hart states, 'This opinion is strengthened upon examining his earliest instruments. We there find the same peculiarities which mark the individuality of Urquhart. Later in life he leaned much to the model of Maggini.'[18]

Earlier opinion was that 'no violins of his are known'.[19] However, a handsome violin, dated 1704, by this maker was illustrated in the *Strad*[20] coming from Messrs John and Arthur Beare and bearing its original handwritten label 'BARAK NORMAN, at the Bass Viol in St. Pauls Alley London Fecit 1704'. The instrument certainly

---

[17] *The Violin: Famous Makers*, 311.   [18] Ibid. 312.   [19] See Morris, *British Violin Makers*, 'Norman, Barak'.
[20] 'Barak Norman', *Strad* (Feb. 1979), s.v. 982.

looks Italianate. Other violins attributed to Norman appear in the sale-room from time to time.

It is known that Barak Norman's instruments sometimes copy Maggini features such as double purfling or soundholes with the lower circles smaller than the upper ones. There is also a tendency to use decorative purfling work on the back, particularly where the wood is plainer. The *Strad* article suggests that 'his work seems to have been influenced both by the Brescian School and the instruments of Stradivari, of which there were several examples in London around the beginning of the eighteenth century'.

As to Norman's other bowed stringed instruments, as Hart says 'his Tenors are fine instruments',[21] but it is for his cellos, violas da gamba, and violas d'amore that Barak Norman is best known. In these instruments he often demonstrates consummate woodworking craftsmanship.[22]

Discussing the detailed characteristics of Norman's violas and cellos, Hart states that the violas were made before he began the cellos, 'a fact which satisfactorily accounts for the marked difference in form peculiar to them. The build is higher, and the sound-hole German in character. The varnish is very dark.'[23] Later into the eighteenth century it appears that he adopted a flatter model. Cellos are usually of full size, i.e. at least 29 in. (736 mm). The exception to this is where a bass viol has been cut down, in which case the length is likely to be just under 27 in. (686 mm).

On his varnishing Sandys and Forster state the accepted view that 'it will be seen by the varnish that he adheres to early recollections of colour, similar to the lutes and viols of old, by using a dark brown with a blackish hue, as if produced by nitric acid and accelerated in drying by heat, which heightens the colour, after which a coat or two of oil varnish to enrich the whole and help to preserve the instrument. This tint or colour may be considered the one generally used by him.'[24]

Another key identification mark on many of Norman's instruments is the monogram 'NB' inlaid in purfling at the centre of the back or in the upper plate just under the wide part of the fingerboard (in the case of cellos). (Henley warns against 'painted' copies of this design on non-genuine instruments: 'these cheap reproductions are fairly widespread'.)[25] From about 1715 Barak Norman went into partnership with Nathaniel Cross at the same address: the sign of the Bass Viol, St Paul's Churchyard. Hart cites at least one example where the work (on a 'quaint gamba'), was done jointly by both partners.[26] In this type of case the label will be

---

[21] *The Violin: Famous Makers*, 312.
[22] See, for example, the carved heads of the viola da gamba of 1718 and 'the dragon' viola d'amore illustrated in the *Supplement to the Strad* of Dec. 1926.
[23] Hart, *The Violin: Famous Makers*, 312.
[24] Sandys and Forster, *History*, 259.
[25] Henley, *Dictionary*, 835.
[26] *The Violin: Famous Makers*, 313.

preceded by a Maltese cross and then, for example, 'Barak Norman | Nathaniel Cross | at the Bass Viol in St. Pauls Church Yard, | London | Fecit 1724'.

Barak Norman's instruments have been held in varying esteem over the years. As we have seen, Thomas Britton thought highly enough of his instruments for specimens to be in his collection and part of his estate. Sandys and Forster speak highly of the tone of both violas and cellos: 'deservedly held in esteem'. They mention a viola in the ownership of Frederick Ware 'celebrated for the great quality of tone he produced', in about 1800. Henry Hill, son of Henry Lockey Hill and an eminent viola-player of the first part of the nineteenth century whose work is discussed further in Chapter 7, also owned this instrument and there are many glowing accounts of its tone. Heron-Allen, writing in the Fuller-Maitland edition of Grove's *Dictionary*,[27] says; 'The viola by Barak Norman which was always used by Henry Hill the viola player changed hands a few years ago at £100, but this was to some extent a sentimental figure, though the instrument was an exceptionally fine one.'

There are a number of historical anecdotes about Norman's cellos which illustrate the value accorded to them in the past. Sandys and Forster relate how William Shield the composer and violinist (*c.*1748–1829) saw a small-sized cello of Barak Norman's at a humble shop in London 'suspended by the head outside the house, and blowing about in the wind'.[28] The appearance of the instrument nevertheless attracted him and he arranged for John Crosdill, the eminent cellist (1751–1825), to see it, and Crosdill ultimately bought the cello at a very small cost. On being cleaned and properly set up it proved to be a fine-toned instrument and became a special favourite of the owner. Crosdill provided tuition to the Prince of Wales, afterwards George IV. On one occasion it was taken to Carlton House where the Prince took a liking to it. However, Crosdill withstood several liberal offers. At a subsequent period, however, the Prince sent a page to collect it since he wished to use it the same evening. The cello was never returned. Crosdill was instead allowed to keep an Amati cello which had cost 70 guineas in lieu of it. He was also given a sinecure place of £100 per annum to soothe his disappointment and loss, which sinecure he retained until his death.

In more modern times, David Laurie tells the story arising out of his friendship with N. F. Vuillaume, at the time (*c.*1870) established in Brussels, and brother of the celebrated J.-B. Vuillaume. N. F. Vuillaume's sister had a house in which a room had been let to a good cellist by the name of Jansen. Jansen showed Laurie his cello which was unlabelled. The Vuillaume brothers agreed that it was an Italian instrument of the Amati School. David Laurie continues:

[27] Vol. v (1914), 307. [28] *History*, 259.

I looked at it again, examining its varnish and details, which did not seem to me to be Italian. I also noticed that on the table below the finger board, was an ornamental circle cut in the wood but not through it. I had seen in London, two instruments with this same circle on the table whose tickets bore the name of Barak Norman, and in this ornamental circle his initials were wrought in purfling . . . This cello of M. Jansen's was similar in all particulars and with some little hesitation I mentioned having seen these two other instruments, and drew his attention to the circle with the initials in it. M. Jansen seemed rather put out at my remarks though I did not assert that his was by the same maker, but suggested that possibly the English maker had copied his or some other Italian instrument. One thing was clear to me and that was that all three instruments had been made on a similar model. I passed the matter off, however, and came away. M. Jansen accompanied me downstairs and there told M. Vuillaume what I had said, but he only smiled and said that 'whoever made that cello, it was not an Englishman, and there could be no doubt that it was Italian'. But even this assurance did not restore its owner's equanimity, as, strange to say, neither he nor the brothers Vuillaume had ever noticed the circle on the table. I left Brussels shortly afterwards but was called there again a month or two later when I called on M. Vuillaume. He received me with a great amount of deference and immediately summoned M. Jansen, who was also most deferential. I was very much surprised, but they soon explained matters to me. It seemed that M. Jansen could not get my remarks on his cello out of his mind, and, in the hope of getting a clue as to its maker, he thoroughly overhauled its case. In one of the pockets he found a receipt from a London dealer to its previous owner in which it was referred to as a genuine Barak Norman cello . . . The fact that two such good judges could make a mistake with an instrument so characteristic of its maker will no doubt surprise many people in this country. It will surprise them more, however, to learn that the English school of makers was almost unknown abroad at the time to which I refer.[29]

Current values for Barak Norman's work are indicated in the Directory. It is mainly cellos that have come on the market and it must be borne in mind that because of their age and, in the past, the erratic regard in which Norman's instruments have been held by their owners, conscious perhaps of the huge discount at which English instruments retailed as against their Italian counterparts, their condition may not always be good. But Barak Norman's cellos have always been sought after by English connoisseurs and Sandys and Forster state that a 1718 cello was, 'in the year 1790, considered at the value of fifteen guineas, since that time they have realised much larger sums [*sic*].'[30]

Norman's partner Nathaniel Cross, where his work can be separately identified, is traditionally regarded as having been influenced by the style of Stainer. His early labels put 'Stainero' after his latinized name. 'The fluting round the edge where

---

[29] Laurie, *Reminiscences*, 18–19. Laurie then goes on to relay another story about the stubborn faith of French experts in the late 19th century that a Banks viola was an Italian instrument!
[30] *History*, 260.

the purfle is inlaid is very acute, and his instruments are beautifully worked in all particulars.'[31] Hart refers to his 'excellent scroll'.[32] Henley supports these descriptions and states that his cellos were invariably under normal length: 27 in. (685 mm) but with broad bouts. His instruments are marked on the inner back with his initials with a Maltese cross above. Both Henley and Morris agree that he worked in London until 1751, and amongst his known labels are ones giving his address as 'The George Inn, Aldersgate Street, London' and 'Pickadilly near St. James Church, London'. (There is some doubt whether his partnership with Barak Norman commenced in 1715 or a little later, but there is a general view that his work improved as he went on.)

There was until very recently little published information about Cross's violins. Fleming, however, made the interesting comment that 'in a violin by him the bass bar was cut out of the solid wall of the breast instead of being affixed to it in the usual way'.[33] This method of working was a characteristic feature of the cheaper range of English string instruments right through the eighteenth century, as is the painted purfling which can be found on some of Cross's instruments. It is sometimes the case that purfling has been added by another hand subsequently, but English painted purfling is distinct from the methods used by the 'Milanese cheapjacks' where imitation purfling is scratched into the wood.

A modern review of Nathaniel Cross has been undertaken by John Dilworth.[34] Dilworth summarizes that both Cross and Norman were pupils of Richard Meares, mainly known for his fine-quality viols, instruments still taken more seriously at this time in some circles than the violin, though this attitude was rapidly changing. Cross, as we have seen, worked with and was hugely influenced by Norman from about 1715, Norman having been established at the Bass Viol in St Paul's Churchyard since 1692. From about 1725 Cross made instruments under his own name. The partnership was at that time effectively dissolved but the reason for this is not known. Cross seems subsequently to have been something of a rolling stone, to judge by the varying addresses which his labels reveal, and much of his work suggests the need for economy in materials.

Nevertheless, Dilworth makes a good case for Cross having been consistently underestimated. His instruments have been passed off as that of the Carcassi school of Florentine masters or even possibly misattributed to Rogeri. Identification of Cross's work should be possible from inspecting the interior work. 'Buttress'-shaped linings, low but stout and chamfered to a steep angle rather than the Italian tapering angle, and generous blocks, with a generally strong and generous build, using plain wood of probably British origin have been pin-pointed by

---

[31] *History*, 260. [32] *The Violin: Famous Makers*, 289.
[33] James M. Fleming, *Old Violins and their Makers* (London, 1883), 205.
[34] 'Cross Examination', *Strad* (Aug. 1987), 592–4.

John Dilworth as characteristic features. He also mentions as a most reliable point of recognition that Cross did not use pins into the upper and lower blocks as did the Italians.

An opportunity to inspect the interior of an unaltered specimen in good condition (and typically with rather plain, native wood and brown varnish) occurred in 1992 and the author, with John Dilworth, observed the very clean and neat interior work. Joseph Pearce, writing in 1866, states that 'a violin of this maker which we have seen, has the great fault of having the bass bar cut out of the solid, instead of being glued in, thus contravening the established principles of the art'.[35] This certainly was not the case here. A carefully fashioned bass bar had been glued in.

Dilworth praises Cross's free adaptation of the Stainer model, reminding us also that the Hills mention in their book on Stradivari[36] that Cross was a 'possible exception' to the normal rule that English makers of this era never copied Stradivari. (It would be interesting to know on what evidence the Hills made this admittedly tentative statement.)

Sandys and Forster's description of Cross's varnish is quoted by Dilworth with approval: 'a light yellow colour, the vehicle or body varnish is considered to be made of one of the soft gums, mastic or sandarac dissolved in alcohol, which renders them of easy blemish and disfigurement by any slight scratch'.[37]

Cross also may have been the earliest English bow-maker. He worked in a style similar to Wamsley (who was almost certainly Cross's pupil), if the attribution in Pl. 10 of Anthony Baines's *Musical Instruments Through the Ages* is correct.

John and Joseph Hare

Although there was formerly some doubt on the matter, it is quite clear (from the Hill Archive; see Directory) that Joseph Hare was the son of John Hare. Both were in partnership but John Hare died in about 1725 and Joseph in 1733. John Hare's label reads 'John Hare, Viol and Flute, near | The Royal Exchange | in Cornhill London 17 . .' His modelling is highly arched, influenced by the Tyrolean style, and his instruments are generally regarded as rather crude affairs. Hart states that his labels indicate that he was in partnership with one Freeman. There was also a music publisher 'John Hare' at this time (connected with John Walsh), and it is now thought that the two were the same. It was not uncommon for musical-instrument dealing to go hand in hand with music publishing.

The instruments of Joseph are rather a different matter since Joseph Hare is

---

[35] Joseph Pearce, jun., *Violins and Violin Makers: Biographical Dictionary of the Great Italian Artistes, their Followers and Imitators, to the Present Time* (London and Sheffield, 1866), 27.
[36] p. 255.   [37] *History*, 261.

credited as being amongst the first of the English makers to have been influenced by Stradivari. Certainly the instrument from the Hill collection sold in London in April 1991 at Phillips (see Pl. 84) stood out from almost all the other contemporary English instruments by having a distinctly Cremonese build. This instrument was considerably more highly arched than a Stradivari but was greater in length (14$^{1}/_{16}$ in. (357 mm)) than a typical Amati. The one-piece back exhibited very pretty wood and, an unusual feature, the scroll and corners had been picked out with a black outline in the manner used by Stradivari[38] and widely copied by the French makers. This particular instrument had a printed engraved label reading 'Joseph Hare at the Viol and Hautboy, over against Urchin Lane in Cornhill, London' with the manuscript date 1723 added. Joseph Hare is also given by Henley as having worked at 'Ye Viol and Flute' (as per John) and 'at Ye Golden Viol in St. Pauls churchyard', London. He was clearly one of the more go-ahead and interesting of early English violin-makers, though his instruments are now sufficiently rare to make a definitive judgement difficult. Vannes[39] recorded a violin of his as late as 1738 but if this was an accurate observation it must have been a 'posthumous product' since it is tolerably certain that Joseph died in 1733. After that date his business was carried on by Elizabeth Hare and later by John Simpson.

John Barrett

Barrett worked in London about 1714–30. His instruments quite commonly come on the market and, unfortunately, in some cases exhibit features which bring English violin-making into disrepute. Morris summarizes his achievements by saying that he worked on a modified Stainer outline, long, narrow, much grooved, and highly arched. 'The tone is small and muffled.' Barrett often used ink lines instead of purfling and his varnish, Morris described as 'yellow and hungry looking and helps to give a cheap look to the instrument'. Although this judgement is largely correct, appraisers should be prepared to come across instruments from time to time much better presented than that indicated above. Barrett clearly made for the lower end of the market with the occasional much higher-quality instrument interspersed, a characteristic trading practice of later English makers in London. John Dilworth in his article on Nathaniel Cross mentioned above[40] states that 'John Barrett was also making fine Stainer copies at the "Harp and Crown" also in Piccadilly around 1722'. (His labels actually read 'at the Harp and Crown in Pickadilly, London'.) These are likely to be dated between 1714 and 1733.[41]

[38] See discussion in Hill, *Stradivari*, 40.
[39] René Vannes, *Dictionnaire Universel des Luthiers* (Brussels, 1985-8).
[40] n. 34.
[41] See Ch. 1 for a reference to a cello by Barrett.

William Pryor

Almost all the violin-makers of note at this time in England worked in London. Presumably the music festivals and activities associated in particular with the cathedral cities in the provinces had not yet grown so as to provide a sufficiently viable economic substructure to support makers of consequence. (Later in this century this was not the case, Benjamin Banks of Salisbury being the best-known example.) A case has, however, been made for William Pryor of Gateside (the same, according to some authorities, as Gateshead, County Durham) which (if correct) suggests that Pryor flourished between 1700 and 1740. He adopted a predominantly Brescian style and Henley's *Universal Dictionary* mentions an instrument of 1722. Jack Liivoja, writing in the *Strad* in 1981,[42] discusses and illustrates an instrument with a mutilated label dated 1712 which is 'a faithful copy of the Brescian style', is made with native sycamore and pine, and is covered with a thick coat of lustrous oil varnish of a golden yellow. Body length is $14^{1}/_{16}$ in. (scant) (357 mm).

The above is couched in cautious tones since John Dilworth, probably the most authoritative modern writer on the stylistic aspects of English violin-making, states: 'the finely finished instruments sold by William Prior [*sic*] of Newcastle, and labelled as his own work ... were most probably made by Lewis, conforming precisely to a violin of his labelled and dated 1709'.[43] Dilworth also remarks that 'a feature of the St. Paul's Alley group was the exchange of patterns and styles as well as labels, to the great confusion of the poor historian'.[44] However, that writer's views are understood to have been modified in the light of recent research and he now believes there to be a far stronger case for the possible existence of a group of talented makers working in the provinces, influenced by Brescian instruments which were at the time quite widely in use. (Contemporary records suggest that there were several members of the Pamphilon family engaged in instrument making in Essex, *c*.1700.)

The Hill Archive interestingly reveals the same puzzlement. A note by Arthur E. Hill in 1907 discusses an instrument he describes as follows: 'Strad outline with same type of Gothic top as in case of Parker. Model well hollowed out round purfling. F Holes lengthy, similar to Parker scroll neater and weaker. Varnish of a spirit nature, orange-brown, clearly Pryor was a professional maker. We have seen two examples of his work.' The photograph in the Archive shows an instrument extremely similar to those attributed to Parker and with the following dimensions given: body $14^{3}/_{16}$ in. (360 mm), top width $6^{9}/_{16}$ in. (167 mm), bottom $8^{1}/_{8}$ in. (206

---

[42] 'William Pryor (*c*.1700–40)', *Strad* (June 1981), 103.   [43] 'Pioneer Spirit', *Strad* (Dec. 1986), 571.
[44] Ibid. 572.

mm), ribs 13/16 in. (21 mm). (The instrument was sent to Liverpool for the firm of Rushworth and Dreaper to give a further opinion which, if received, is not recorded.)

Readers must come to their own conclusion as to how likely it is that a maker working in the far north of England should be producing models of the best London style. A more probable, if less charitable, explanation must be that (as John Dilworth thought originally) Pryor simply labelled distinguished works of other makers with his own label. A facsimile label from the Hill Archive is included in Appendix 2.

Daniel Parker

One thing can be agreed about this most enigmatic, and possibly greatest, early English violin-maker. That is that, as Morris states, 'the information which is usually given about this maker is misleading, and most writers content themselves with repeating early errors in almost the same words'.[45] Morris points out that earlier writers including Hart and Miss Stainer give his period as 1740–85. Joseph Pearce, writing in 1866, favoured *c.*1714. Davidson (1881) gives 1720–85.[46] Despite the difficulty caused by the great rarity of labelled instruments (or any other indicia of maker and date), it is now more generally accepted that Parker flourished in London between about 1710 and 1745. As Morris states, 'the earliest which I have actually seen and tried is dated 1712, a specimen which has been pronounced genuine by the Messrs. Hill, and the Messrs. Hart, and which I also think genuine, all except the scroll . . . I have in my possession a very beautiful violin of his make, on the Strad model, and in his best style, bearing a label dated 1719. This is genuine in all its parts and is of excellent tone'.

What other evidence is there of Parker's dates of making, since any proper biographical detail is completely absent? Alfred Langonet made a special study of this old English maker and owned no fewer than four violins by or attributed to Daniel Parker. One of these bore the label 'Edward Lewis | St. Paul's Alley in London 1704' in manuscript. From this Langonet assumed that Parker may have been a pupil or a close associate of Edward Lewis. But surely an equally tenable possibility is that Lewis, whose work is very little known but acknowledged to have been of high quality, made the instrument himself. Lewis was a fine maker—Thomas Britton's collection included his work—and his identified instruments are now very rare. (Lewis's work is discussed in Chapter 3.)

---

[45] Morris, *British Violin Makers*, s.v. 'Parker, Daniel'.
[46] Peter Davidson, *The Violin: Its Construction Theoretically and Practically Treated* (London, 1881), 248.

The Hills, in their book on the *Violin Makers of the Guarneri Family*, attempt to elucidate matters as follows:

There is reason to believe that a specimen of the distinct form of Stradivari violin, known as the 'Long Stradivari' was introduced to London audiences soon after 1700; that is, within some fifteen years of its construction, for the master did not originate this pattern until 1690.[47]

Our English maker, Daniel Parker, made from 1710 onwards some excellent violins, which embodied the special features of this particular type and other marked characteristics of Stradivari's style. The cause of Parker's departure from the orthodox Amati or Stainer models in vogue at the time can be traced, we believe, to the sojourn of Gasparo Visconti, the Cremonese violinist, in London, where he published in 1703 *Solos for Violin with thorough Bass*, dedicated to the Duke of Devonshire.

Fetis writes that Visconti's 'counsels greatly aided Stradivari in the manufacture of his instruments';[48] and it is quite conceivable that he played on a 'long Stradivari', and thus became the source of Parker's inspiration.

Although this is a remarkable piece of speculation on the part of the Hills, speculation it remains! It will be seen that the Hills assume that (1) Visconti played a Long Strad, (2) he had some reason to show it to a London violin-maker so that it could be copied, (3) Daniel Parker, of no known trading address, was either that maker or an associate of his and almost alone decided to make copies of the Strad violin which was then modern and unfashionable. This combination of chances appears at first sight somewhat mind-boggling. There is, however, a possible connection between Visconti and the Hares through the publication by Hare of his *Solos for Violin and Thorough Bass* referred to above.[49] Indeed, a more likely scenario is that Visconti, who was indeed born in Cremona in 1683 and by tradition was friendly with Stradivari, got to know the Hares, father and son, in London between about 1702 and 1705 when he played frequently there in public. It is clear that there was a close association between John Walsh, the eminent publisher, and the Hares between 1695 and 1730, owing to the quantity of works bearing the imprint of both Walsh and the Hares. Visconti happened to choose this firm for the first edition of his Corelli-influenced *Solos*, the second edition of which was published in Amsterdam also in 1703. Joseph Hare was one of the very few other London makers influenced by the Stradivari model (as we have seen). Assuming, then, that Parker must have seen a Long Strad, as must Joseph Hare, and also assuming that Visconti was in possession of one during his London sojourn, it is certainly not beyond possibility that Parker was working at this time

---

[47] W. H., A. F., and A. E. Hill, *The Violin Makers of the Guarneri Family* (London, 1931), 110.
[48] See *Nicolo Paganini*, Schott & Co, London, 1852 2nd ed, p. 17. (Hills' footnote)
[49] *Opera Prima*, pub. J. Walsh and J. Hare (London, 1703). For the business connection between John Walsh and the Hares, see C. Humphries and W. C. Smith, *Music Publishing in the British Isles from Earliest Times to the Nineteenth Century* (London, 1954), 170–2.

in association with the Hares and that both Joseph Hare and Daniel Parker took the opportunity of loosely copying this instrument while the Hare firm was involved with the business relationship with Visconti. A comparison of the illustrations in this book of the violins by Daniel Parker and Joseph Hare, the first unlabelled and the second labelled and dated 1723, will be found instructive.

An article in the *Strad* simply states that 'we know that he worked in London during the first half of the eighteenth century and that he died, or ceased to work, around 1730. It is not known where or from whom he learnt his craft.'[50] The same article goes on to describe a viola (one of at least three which had been discovered), which was said to bear its original label: 'Daniel Parker | London 1714'.

What other identification marks have there been? The great majority of Parker's instruments bear no label or other inscription at all. Writers have simply said that he 'made many violins for the trade', but a further mysterious feature if this is so is that 'the trade' in the early eighteenth century in London was a highly individual one and there appears to be no direct, independent evidence of one maker systematically making anonymously (except perhaps as an apprentice) for another at so early a date. There is though, *circumstantial* evidence that makers made (anonymously or otherwise) for London and provincial music-sellers and that those instruments then acquired alien labels; but it is likely that the same makers would make other instruments of a similar character which they would sign or label in the normal way. Nor would it be logical to make such an unfashionable model for a dealer, intent as always on a quick turnover, to sell. But Alfred Langonet stated that he identified several violas and violoncellos by Parker, all of which had been made for the trade and in some instances were signed at the lower part of the back or on the lower block. The scrupulous Towry Piper states: 'Writer has seen one or two labels in manuscript.'[51] Ideally, any such signatures should be scientifically compared to one another and Parker's calligraphic style established. No systematic photographic evidence of the relevant handwriting is known to the author. Until this task is undertaken, judgement must be suspended on the authenticity of some or all of these 'labels'.

In the best modern exploration of Daniel Parker's frustratingly mysterious working life, John Dilworth comes down firmly in favour of the earlier dates. Dilworth is able to reproduce an apparently printed label 'Daniel Parker London 1717' which he describes as having name, place, and date laid rather unevenly between two hand-drawn lines, and snipped carelessly to size. The enigma is if anything deepened by the author's remark that 'there is a strong suspicion that from the one or two good labels extant, which were handwritten by Parker in imitation of print, some shadowy figure has had a block made up with which to deco-

---

[50] 'Daniel Parker', *Strad* (Dec. 1973), 454.
[51] Moya and Piper, *Violin Tone*, 226.

rate every known copy of a Long Strad violin. If they are all to be believed, 1715 must have been a very busy year for him.'[52]

As will have been deduced, Parker's main claim to fame was that he was the first maker in England, with the possible exceptions of Joseph Hare and Nathaniel Cross (occasionally), to adopt broadly Stradivarian principles in his construction methods. In addition his instruments had (and continue to have) a fine tonal reputation, one having been owned by Fritz Kreisler; and Ruggiero Ricci is reported as having played a Daniel Parker violin for a televised broadcast.[53] Towry Piper described the tone of these instruments as 'large and brilliant'.[54]

With regard to dimensions of his violins, John Dilworth's 1717 example is given as body 14³⁄₁₆ in. (360 mm), stop-length 7⅝ in. (193 mm), width top bouts 6⁹⁄₁₆ in. (167 mm), middle bouts 4⅜ in. (112 mm), lower bouts 8³⁄₁₆ in. (208 mm), rib height 1⅛ in.–1¼ in. (29.5–31 mm). Parker is likely to have used native sycamore for back, head, and ribs.

Violins by or attributed to Daniel Parker not infrequently come on the auction market. One was sold as part of the Hill collection, unlabelled and described by the auctioneer as '*circa* 1750', and having a body-length of 14⅛ in. (359 mm).

Some writers had formerly asserted that no violas or cellos were known of this maker. A cello, unlabelled, with magnificent ribs and back, was illustrated in the *Strad*, September 1930. It was attributed to Daniel Parker, but on what evidence is not clear. Expert opinion is that this was a misattribution. As mentioned later, it was perhaps the work of Richard Duke. The labelled viola described in the *Strad*[55] had a body-length of 16⅛ in. (410 mm).

Stylistically there is general agreement that besides basing himself on Stradivarian models he also copied Stainer and Amati—though such copies are sufficiently individual to absolve him from any charge of being mechanical. There is also a consensus that Parker's varnish was sometimes spirit- and sometimes oil-based, but always richly coloured, often light red or orange-red.

As to the build, Morris simply states that 'his work is thoroughly British in character. It is solid, chaste, and very "correct" . . . The plates of the violins are well stocked with wood, and with due care the instruments may be expected to last in first class condition another hundred years at least.' Parker's choice of wood, too, tends to distinguish him from other English makers of about this era, the backs in particular being of finely figured sycamore as a rule. There is little to suggest an

---

[52] Dilworth, 'Pioneer Spirit', 571–5. See also the same author's analysis of a famous viola of Parker bearing 'an unquestionably authentic label' (dated 1715) in 'The Paragon of Parker's Violas', *Strad* (Feb. 1994), 124–5 and the fine illustrations of the viola in question.

[53] 'Daniel Parker', 454.

[54] Moya and Piper, *Violin Tone*, 225.

[55] (Dec. 1973), 454. See also the viola (body-length 421 mm) illustrated in John Dilworth's 'The Paragon of Parker's Violas', *Strad* (Feb. 1994), 124–5. The instrument shows a nice blend of Tyrolean and Italian influences, with its discreet decorative purfling of front, back, and pegbox.

English maker has been at work on the scroll either: scrolls are often of even and well-regulated craftsmanship in the Italianate manner. For all these reasons there must be little doubt that some of his instruments have been mislabelled in the past and have been traded as Italian.

It is perhaps the quality of the varnish, the robust construction of the corners and edges, and the tendency of the upper corners to 'droop' which puts the appraiser on notice that he is dealing with an English instrument by Parker. Morris simply states that 'they are easily recognised by the expert who has made a study of the work of the old English School'. The sharply downturned, 'drooping' corners of the upper bout John Dilworth finds to be a feature of this maker from his earliest instruments[56] (see Pl. 88).

The same author points to a number of other detailed characteristics (taken from the 1717 model under discussion) including separate ribs for bottom and top bouts (more usually at least the bottom rib is continuous in early English work), with rib corners jointed down the centre with no overlap, 'truly dramatic arching' (17 mm on both plates), soundholes more 'open' than the Stradivari modes with cuts made with the knife angled outward from the belly, nicks pointing diagonally across the body, the upper and lower circular holes of the soundhole of similar diameter and 'cut with a knife rather than a punch' and the unfluted, sharply pointed wings of the soundhole. The (comparatively weak) scroll has its 'wayward chamfer' blackened and the pegbox walls are cut thin. On this specimen the varnish was of a clear red transparent colour but lacking the glow and lustre of the Cremonese.[57]

It is exasperating that so little is known of this maker, particularly as some regard him as England's finest. Even now there is some controversy about the correctness of the dating of Parker's instruments, and opinions voiced about his having made for the trade, even sometimes not varnishing his instruments before sale, are not known to have any hard evidence to support them. It is easy to understand the case for dating his instruments to the middle part of the eighteenth century, rather than the early part. They have a maturity about them which, if the pattern of making throughout the eighteenth century is not too carefully analysed, may suggest a later era. And the 'made for the trade' theory also fits better at a time when volume trade in London was beginning to be established—i.e. from about 1750 onwards. On the other hand there are not dissimilar instruments from Joseph Hare which emanate from the early eighteenth century and by 1750 the Stainer or other high-built Tyrolean-influenced model was almost universal. But speculation one way or the other can only be checked by a much more critical evaluation of labels, genuine or (all too commonly) by attribution, and handwritten signatures,

---

[56] 'Pioneer Spirit', 573.   [57] Ibid. 574.

dates, and the like. Without being unduly cynical, it must be remembered that dealers have always found instruments of an identified maker easier to sell and have not hesitated to embellish an anonymous product. And if it can clearly be established that Parker was copying Long Strads as early as the Hills suggest, the achievement is the more remarkable. Few others in Europe were such early copyists.

It is always interesting to compare values in previous times. Sandys and Forster state that 'about 1793 the violins of this maker were valued at five guineas [£5.25], and in the beginning of the first half of the present [nineteenth] century they have realised twelve and fifteen guineas, but now are again reduced in amount, from the desire of performers to possess none but Italian instruments, and other causes which depress the manufacture of such articles'.[58] Henley simply repeats this information (without acknowledgement) and adds that they have been valued at £50 and upwards since 1920. The specimen sold in April 1991 by Phillips realized £9,000. We can assume from this that Parker, together with Banks and a few other particularly talented makers of the eighteenth century, continues to be held in the highest esteem. As with most English instruments, there is probably an element of undervalue when compared with not dissimilar products from the Italian and French Schools.

Other Eighteenth-Century Makers in England

From the middle of the eighteenth century onwards, the growth in musical activity in London and major provincial cities (often through the medium of festivals), described in Chapter 7, brought a parallel increase in the volume of violin-making activity. This must have been particularly so before the market threatened to become swamped with cheap 'factory' products from Germany and then France towards the end of this century, as mentioned in Chapter 4.

Accordingly individual violin-makers of merit became too numerous to attempt to assess individually in a text of this kind. Some makers such as Merlin are commented upon in the context of the economic history of the time (see Chapter 4). Details are given of all known professional makers in the Directory towards the end of this book. But a few key families or individuals are of such importance that their place in the developing scene has to be explained.

A major figure was Benjamin Banks of Salisbury (1727–95), whose work has recently been comprehensively described in Albert Cooper's affectionate monograph *Benjamin Banks, The Salisbury Violin Maker* (1989).

---

[58] Sandys and Forster, *History*, 256–7.

As already mentioned, Banks was apprenticed to his uncle William Huttoft, 'Musical Instrument Maker Old Sarum', on 24 June 1741 at a premium of £20 (with 10s. duty paid), and the entry confirming this is in the Public Record Office.[59] Huttoft in fact died in 1747, a year before the seven-year apprenticeship was due to end, but the mystery is really how Banks could have learned his violin-making skills from a master about whom there is no evidence as to his ever having made violins. It is more than likely that the Huttoft business in Salisbury was a retailer of music, keyboard instruments, woodwind, and, probably, 'English guitars' or citterns, since a cittern of 1757 was one of Banks's first recorded instruments on which, perhaps, some of his experience in apprenticeship had been spent. It is possible that Banks attached himself to the Wamsley workshop when in London in the 1740s. It was certainly one of the larger ones, judging by Wamsley's productivity, and it may be that there was a Wamsley connection, but not as formal as has been frequently alleged. Some experts detect great similarities of style between the two makers.

It was common in those days for retailers of the work of others to claim to be the maker of the relevant instrument. Benjamin Banks himself in an advertisement of 1768 claimed to have made 'harpsichords pianofortes and spinets'.[60] Cooper suggests that there may have been a 'reciprocal arrangement' between keyboard instrument makers and stringed instrument makers.[61] Certainly English bows were often stamped with the name of an instrument-maker who is likely to have had nothing to do with their creation. 'Own-branding' is nowadays a commonplace retail marketing practice amongst High Street multiples.

It seems probable that Banks exploited the contacts that his uncle would have had with the pool of London makers, many of whom made at least some of the time for 'the trade', and learned his skills under one or more of them at the time, himself contributing anonymous instruments for retailing on. Unfortunately this is the sort of detail, now of vital interest to us, which is likely to be unverifiable owing to absence of records. Partly this obscurity is due to the makers' desire to preserve trade secrets, and partly because the economic activities of the 'artisan class' were not usually thought worthy of any particular record.

Although Banks followed the fashion of copying Stainer in some of his work (much of this being for 'the trade', particularly for Longman and Broderip), it is his Amati copies that attract considerable admiration by connoisseurs—'wood, workmanship and varnish are almost faultless' according to Morris.[62] (Banks in fact loosely copied both the brothers Antonius and Hieronymus Amati and later Nicolò Amati.) Banks also made magnificent violas and cellos, copying models of both Stradivari and Andreas Guarneri, as well as Amati and Stainer. He used,

---

[59] Cooper, *Benjamin Banks*, 11.   [60] Ibid. 26.   [61] Ibid. 26–7.   [62] *British Violin Makers*, 98.

generally, a light brown or dark red-brown varnish generally of a typically 'Old English' fine quality, and his instruments are often branded by the tail-button and internally. Violins vary in measurement between 13⅞ in. and 14 in. (352–356 mm), violas are between 15⅛ in. and 15⅜ in. (384–391 mm) and cellos generally between 28¾ in. (734 mm) and 29½ in. (749 mm)—the latter being modelled after Andreas Guarneri, dated 1774.[63] Banks's reputation as the 'English Amati' is mentioned elsewhere in this book and readers may see examples of his work on display in the Salisbury and South Wiltshire Museum in the cathedral close (which also constructed an interesting tableau of his workshop). Cooper's book contains detailed illustrations of every feature of Banks's work.

It is interesting to read the opinion of a mid-nineteenth-century author on Banks, namely George Dubourg.[64] Dubourg writes in the context of a few sentences on English makers: '*Banks*, of Salisbury, also claims notice. His violoncellos . . . are of the finest quality of tone—not too strong and fiery as old Forster's, but, in sweetness and purity excelling them. Banks' are more adapted to the chamber and Forster's to the orchestra.'

One can summarize Banks's work by saying that it is precisely executed, externally and internally, and although some would inevitably criticize any design copied from tracings of Italian or other instruments as lacking spontaneous architecture, Banks was certainly no mere copyist. His designs are based on, rather than slavish copies of, Stainer, the Amatis, and occasionally Stradivari or members of the Guarneri family. Scrolls remain obstinately Anglo-Teutonic. Perhaps they were normally cut out by a particular member of Banks's family (or possibly even an employee) in the workshop. Banks ran a successful business with considerable demand for his instruments in London and the provinces. Production, though by hand, had to be commercial and involved the family team. But the care taken with production in his lifetime did much to raise the standard of English violin-making at a time when, at least at the lower end of the market, it too easily slipped into unpurfled, badly finished, shoddy examples. The Banks product could be relied upon to be of good quality and a durable investment for the first owner and successors.

Banks had three violin-making sons amongst his nine children. Benjamin Banks junior (1754–1820) moved to London, apparently without much success. His work, which is sparse, is not regarded as the equal of his father's. The two other sons, James and Henry, continued their father's business in Salisbury until 1811 when they removed themselves to the thriving city and port of Liverpool. Of these two, James is reputed to have been a violin-maker of real talent. Certainly, although the output of the brothers is variable—often descending to the crude 'workshop'

---

[63] See Cooper, *Benjamin Banks*, 117.   [64] *History of the Violin*, 273.

model—on occasions a fine instrument of theirs surfaces in the market.[65] James and Henry died respectively in 1831 and 1820.

Benjamin Banks senior's labels, when they are to be found, are, for example: 'Made by Benjamin Banks, Catherine Street, Salisbury, 1770'; 'Benjamin Banks, Musical Instrument Maker, In Catherine Street, Salisbury, 1780'; 'Benjamin Banks, fecit Salisbury'; 'B. Banks, Sarum'.[66]

Peter Wamsley (1715–51) is one of the best-known English makers of the mid-eighteenth century because he was a prolific worker (or probably ran a small workshop) and was one of Banks's putative mentors. Certainly his work is highly variable and modern auction prices reflect these disparities. At his best he turned out very careful and neat instruments, quite highly arched and copying, usually, the prevailing Tyrolese–Stainer pattern with short, upright soundholes. Some very substantial cellos exist which, although often too bulbous to be concert instruments, are popular for ensemble work. Henley accuses him of artificially ageing his wood chemically, or perhaps by baking; also of thinning the plates for more immediate tone-production at the expense of the instrument's future. But many of his instruments are still in regular use and this is perhaps Wamsley's best answer to his critics. He is also credited with being the master of Edmund Aireton (c.1727–1807) and Joseph Hill (1715–84, see Ch. 9), both makers of distinction.

One of the most interesting and enigmatic makers of this century was Joseph Collingwood who, according to Henley, worked in London from 1735 to 1779 at the sign of the Golden Spectacles. Morris only gives him his due in the postscript section of the second edition of his work, and this mainly because a friend showed him his Amati copy 'with an orange-coloured oil varnish of great lustre and transparency'. But other instruments inspected by Morris and which still bore their original label confirm the quality of this maker, who, in Morris's view, must rank with the finest work of Banks, Forster, Duke, and Parker. The enigma is that both Morris and Henley state that he copied 'Joseph' Guarnerius, as well as Amati, Stainer, and Stradivari. If this is so, and it is improbable, he must be the earliest English maker to have done so—some fifty years before Paganini brought his Guarneri del Gesù to popular attention. It is widely thought that Collingwood's labels have been removed on a large scale and some more seductive name substituted. This always adds to the difficulty of attribution.

Jacob Ford, who worked in London from about 1770 to 1795, produced excellent violins on the Stainer model but with exceptionally finely carved scrolls. An article in the *Strad* draws attention to his treatment of the moulded edge of one specimen examined. 'This is beaded with the purfling inserted immediately before the rise of

---

[65] See, for example, the cello sold by Phillips in London, 20 June 1991, lot 166, illustrated in the catalogue. The hammer price was £11,000.

[66] See Morris, *British Violin Makers*, 102.

the moulding of the edge, and is of the type found in many English violins of this period: a wide inner strip of white wood sandwiched between two narrow strips of black' (as opposed to the more usual more or less equally broad strips). His work if in good condition now commands respectable prices at auction.[67]

A much more prolific maker whose work emanates from Cheapside, London, between about 1745 and 1762 is John Johnson. One suspects a workshop team at the back of this production of violins, violas, and cellos (some without labels but in his style). Indeed, Hart points out that 'Old Johnson' was a sheet-music and general musical-instrument retailer.[68] Another Stainerite, at his best these instruments can hold their own with the better of his London contemporaries. He is believed (according to the article on him in the *New Grove Dictionary of Musical Instruments*) to have used maple rather than native sycamore for some of his work and, if so, this is unusual at this time.[69] Morris, who had obviously seen an inferior specimen, remarks on the very high arching and thin, dry, yellow varnish. More often it is of a deep brown colour. Some of his labels refer to the 'Harp and Crown', Cheapside.

Another retailing firm that quite possibly did not involve the proprietors in 'real' making was that of James and John Simpson. Henley's rather pejorative remarks on these 'makers' (for such he said they were) should be read with caution, not least because, as with the similar firms of Longman & Broderip and Norris & Barnes (discussed in Chapter 3), some good instruments emanated from the Simpsons. The firm was established as music publishers and instrument dealers in London from about 1735 under John Simpson the elder. His son James, and James's son John junior, commissioned most of the instruments branded 'Simpson' or labelled as 'J & J Simpson, Musical Instrument Makers at the Bass Viol and Flute in Sweeting's Alley, Opposite the East door of the Royal Exchange, London', during the period 1765–99. The actual makers are unknown but if the Simpsons did not do the work themselves owing to the pressure of business they must have employed anonymous workmen. The work is quite homogeneous, however, arguing considerable 'system'.

Some fine workmen worked in the 'pool' mentioned above, including for a time Aireton, Banks, and members of the Hill family. The Simpson model is both distinct and typically 'Old English' with characteristic short, wide, and upright soundholes, but comparatively flat-built. Some examples have very nicely done purfling and scrolls. The varnish is a typically durable light golden-brown. Good specimens are now becoming sought after. One from the Hill collection sold at auction in April 1991 (Phillips) for £2,600. Experience suggests that these instruments have satisfying, if discreet, tonal qualities.

---

[67] See 'Jacob Ford', *Strad* (Dec. 1954), 254, and the Directory for more detail.
[68] Hart, *The Violin: Famous Makers*, 307.   [69] The author has seen little evidence of this.

Richard Duke (c.1718–83) achieved a high reputation in his lifetime, being appointed musical instrument maker to the Duke of Gloucester in about 1768. His finest violins have long been regarded as being typical of the best of later English eighteenth-century work, so much so that his instruments were widely and crudely copied, complete with the brand 'Duke', by nineteenth-century German factories. Duke copied Stainer, Amati, and, on occasion, the long Strad model, apparently based on the 'Falmouth' Strad of 1692 which was in his possession and sold through his business. He may have been a pupil of Wamsley and he established his workshops in the High Holborn area, first in Lambs Conduit Passage and then, after a brief move to Red Lion Square, to a workshop described on the label as being 'Near Opposite Great Turn-Stile, Holborn, London'. Again, as with so many of the more productive makers in London in the late eighteenth century, there is every ground for thinking that Duke established a workshop with a number of apprentices and assistants, and his shop sold a variety of musical instruments besides stringed instruments—as his trade card makes clear. As a consequence instruments bearing his brand 'Duke, London', with or without his label, vary in quality, though unlike the case with some of his contemporaries, it is clear that when his business activities in retail and music publishing permitted, he was an able maker enjoying aristocratic patronage. His Amati and Stradivari copies in particular remain highly sought-after and well regarded by players in terms of evenness and quality of tone.

An occasional Duke viola surfaces, one so attributed seen by the author having a lengthy body with very narrow ribs. Cellos are unknown, though it is suspected that there may have been some Stradivarian lines which now bear attributions or false labels suggesting the work of other hands. There is even a theory that the 'Parker' cello on Stradivari modelling discussed above may in fact be the work of Duke.[70]

On his death in 1783 the business appears to have been succeeded to (by purchase from Duke's daughter) by John Betts who described himself as 'Late Foreman and Successor to Mr. Richard Duke, Deceased Musical Instrument Maker to His Royal Highness the Duke of Gloucester'. Indeed by training not only John Betts but John's nephew Edward, Richard Duke did much to pass on the torch to the next generation of makers.

His son, also Richard Duke, is thought to have been his father's pupil, but the son independently made and marketed inferior products, with a curved 'Duke' brand, up to about 1790. According to Henley his business deteriorated to such an extent that he was reduced to hawking his own and other instruments to neighbouring shops at knock-down prices. His father's will merely released his son's

---

[70] See John Dilworth, 'The Grand Old Duke of Lutherie, *Strad* (Mar. 1994), 249–55, in which the help of Messrs J. & A. Beare and especially Andrew Fairfax and Maureen Pestaille is specifically acknowledged.

indebtedness to him and gave him no other property, indicating that there was no love lost between father and son.

Finally, because late eighteenth-century makers appeared in London and the provinces in numbers too great for analysis here, a nod should be made in the direction of Richard Tobin, mentioned in Chapter 8 in the context of Irish makers. His dates (c.1771–1841) take him into the next century but his work may be briefly considered at this point. Few, if any, instruments bear his label but in a fine and minute analysis of his work John Dilworth has identified his signature in a number of instruments (usually under the belly against the bottom block, as inaccessible as possible). Sometimes the brand 'Tobin' appears by the tailpiece. This low profile was no doubt because his work was almost all produced for the major London workshops of Betts, probably until 1823, and then probably Dodd and Henry Lockey Hill. His varnishing is thought to be the work of others. He had been apprenticed to Perry of Dublin and influenced by his colleague there, Vincenzo Panormo, fleeing the French Revolution. He was hence one of the first 'English' makers to adopt Stradivari's mature style as the norm. (John Dilworth is surely correct in doubting whether, as some have said, Tobin copied Guarneri. It was still too early, and this remark *a fortiori* applies to Collingwood above.)

Tobin is famed for his usually finely carved scrolls with their deep, clearly carved throats and evenly regulated volutes, the chamfers usually having the black edging used by Stradivari so effectively to pick out the shape. Tobin was one of a number of British craftsmen of that time who died in their local poorhouse, and allegedly exacerbated his decline by alcoholism.[71]

Unscrupulous Attributions

As a tailnote to this chapter, readers less used to violin commerce might understandably be puzzled at the number of 'grey areas' revealed in discussing the work of many of the English classical makers. This in large part derives from the self-serving activities of dealers in Britain and elsewhere, in the past, who thought nothing of putting either a fabricated or a genuine label into an unlabelled instrument which perhaps reminded them of a particular maker. Buyers of the less sophisticated variety have always preferred their instruments to bear a label. Dealers obliged and found readier sales. Italian instruments, or those thought to be sufficiently Italianate to pass, were particularly prone to this dishonest treatment, but English instruments were by no means exempt. It will be seen that, when combined with a virtual or complete lack of any economic or industrial

---

[71] See John Dilworth, 'Alcoholic Anonymous', *Strad* (May 1987), 45.

records (the calling presumably being regarded as too workaday to be of interest), the problem of attribution can be acute. Knowledge can only be built up from admittedly genuine examples *if* they can be accurately identified. Otherwise whole edifices arise on completely unsound formulations. Luckily modern scholarship is much more scrupulous than it used to be and a more accurate picture of the work of this period is slowly emerging.[72]

[72] For a brief history of false labelling, see Harvey, *Violin Fraud*.

Chapter Six

Prices and Economic Background to English Violin-Making from 1750

Why the Economic Background is Important — The Domestic Market — The Impoverished Players — The French Scene — The German Scene — The Effect of Competition — Free Trade — Cheap 'Tools' — Cheap Musical Instruments — The Struggle to Compete — Prices — Comparing Prices

Why the Economic Background is Important

AT the start of Chapter 1 the fundamental question was asked: what was the *demand* for bowed stringed instruments made locally in England? It is then necessary to go on to ask what gave rise to this demand once identified. Clearly the musical environment of the country in any particular time is important, since if the esteem in which professional orchestral or chamber-music players are held is low, as it generally was in England from the mid-eighteenth century until fairly recent times, this would be reflected in those players' financial circumstances. And if we accept the thesis for the time being that players of real eminence would normally have looked towards Italy for their source of supply and the others would necessarily be seeking to economize in their choice of purchase, we are driven inexorably to the conclusion that much of the market for products of English stringed-instrument makers was composed of wealthy and interested amateurs. Their wealth would have been derived from sources other than professional music-making.

There is quite a significant amount of circumstantial evidence to suggest that from the late eighteenth century onwards, visiting violin virtuosi playing Cremonese instruments, and particularly the visits to England of Paganini (he first played in London at the King's Theatre on 3 June 1831), helped to stimulate the already burgeoning interest of collectors in fine Italian instruments. As will be seen, collectors were not usually professional musicians.

The Domestic Market

An example of the reluctance of eminent connoisseurs on the continent of Europe in the nineteenth century to give much credit to eighteenth-century English violin-makers has already been given in Chapter 3, relating to David Laurie's account of the Barak Norman cello. In fact, until the late nineteenth century, there is very little evidence of any systematic export of the work of English violin-makers. They appear to have worked almost entirely for the domestic market.

Evidence from the account books of William Forster (II), who died in 1808, does exist, and it can be seen from the details of the listed buyers that they are predominantly, if not entirely, identified as living in England or having very Anglo-Saxon names. There are a few Italian names but these are often identifiable as resident Italian players or artists. For instance, Cervetto the Younger had a cello of William Forster (II) which was burned when the Italian Opera House, Haymarket, was destroyed by fire on 17 June 1789.[1]

The account books[2] deal with instruments which were produced by William Forster (II) assisted by his son and workmen, though Sandys and Forster explain that the accounts are not complete. This is partly because three distinct classes of work were adopted. The commonest instruments, which were unrecorded, were not purfled and had oil varnish of an inferior quality. Unfortunately, as the authors remark, 'few of this class were made in consequence of the deceit and fraud practised by persons getting them purfled, and selling them as "genuine Forster's" for a larger sum than they were really worth'.[3] The intermediate class was much better finished, properly purfled, with a 'superior varnish'. The 'highest' style of workmanship was one in which 'everything was embodied to conduce to excellence, to beautiful appearance, and to the finest tone'. Most of the extant entries seem to relate to the latter two classes.

Looking at the list of buyers, one is struck by the number of instruments made for military, ecclesiastical, medical, and legal buyers as well as Fellows of the Oxford and Cambridge colleges. Aristocratic purchasers are particularly to be noted in the list of those requiring Forster cellos, about which Henry Hill, the eminent mid-nineteenth-century viola-player, wrote:

his instruments are second to none, but the best Europe has ever known; especially his *amber* coloured violoncellos, they are renowned for mellowness, a volume and power of tone, equalled by few, surpassed by none. His dark red coloured are not so much admired, though the difference in merit is scarcely discernible.[4]

---

[1] Sandys and Forster, *History*, 315.   [2] Ibid. 319.   [3] Ibid. 317.
[4] Ibid. 324. 'Red ones are more in favour to-day', in Morris's view (*British Violin Makers*, 152).

Amongst the cello buyers are His Grace the Duke of Richmond, Lord De La Warr, the Earl of Uxbridge, and Lord Archibald Hamilton. HM King George III is listed as having acquired a double bass in 1787, 1789, and again in 1805.

It may be felt surprising that the military also supplied an apparently ready market for such makers as Forster. But George Macdonald Fraser, always scrupulous about his historical detail, gives an unforgettable portrait of Major-General Sir James Hope Grant in the Peking expedition of 1860 who, despite having never read a line of the Bible, so inarticulate as hardly being able to say anything but 'charge!', and whose only concern of discipline was to flog anything that moved, was a cellist of very considerable ability—and also 'the best fighting man in the world'.[5] According to the authorities cited, Grant despite his fearsome military achievements was a kindly and gentle man, a cellist and a composer. It is said that he owed his early advancement to the fact that his commanding General was a keen violinist who wanted a cello player as a Brigade-Major![6] Grant owned a 1772 Forster cello which he lent to the Special Exhibition of Ancient Musical Instruments at South Kensington in 1872 (Item 195). This Exhibition is discussed in more detail in Chapter 13.

If the violin family was becoming more fashionable by 1800, as Forster's records suggest, it is remarkable that there are very few portraits in eighteenth- and nineteenth-century English novels of characters, ecclesiastical or otherwise, who are serious players of stringed instruments. Of those that exist perhaps the best known one is Trollope's Revd Septimus Harding. This Precentor of Barchester Cathedral had edited a collection of ancient church music, greatly improved the choir of the cathedral, and 'played the violoncello daily to such audiences as he could collect, or, *faute de mieux*, to no audience at all'.[7] As Trollope's portrait of Barchester Cathedral is in part founded on Salisbury, perhaps Septimus Harding's cello was by Benjamin Banks of that city—but history does not relate. It was not until John Meade Falkner wrote *The Lost Stradivari*, a minor masterpiece, in 1895 that the violin became a central theme of a significant novel by an English writer of consequence. There had been some earlier lesser works, such as Walter Mayson's *The Stolen Fiddle* (alluded to later in this book in the biography of Mayson) and Maud Des Champs De La Tour's virulently anti-Semitic and almost incoherent *The History of a Violin* (c.1878) about the 'Red Cross Knight' Stradivari.[8]

---

[5] See G. M. Fraser, *Flashman and the Dragon*, paperback edn., (London, 1986).

[6] Ibid. 308, citing Grant and Knollys, *Incidents in the China War*; Fortescue, *History of the British Army*, xii (1930), and *Dictionary of National Biography*. Query if he actually took his cello on campaign, as Fraser suggests.

[7] Anthony Trollope, *The Warden* (London, 1982), 6 (first pub. 1855).

[8] Conan Doyle's Sherlock Holmes became famous for his addictions to his violin and to cocaine.

The Impoverished Players

What was the average income of musicians in the early nineteenth century? Cyril Ehrlich has undertaken a minute examination of their economic circumstances from the evidence available. Quite clearly, the more eminent soloists, normally singers until Paganini changed perspectives, were capable of making a very handsome living indeed. But if we take an eminent operatic orchestral player such as Dragonetti, who first came to England in 1794, his salary at engagement was £250 per annum plus a benefit. Ehrlich estimates that at the peak of Dragonetti's earning capacity he made about £1,000 a year. Fashionable lawyers and doctors could earn ten times this sum. The Lord Chancellor earned, in 1810, £22,730.

Dragonetti's income was exceptionally good even for such an extraordinary player. £500 per annum would have been more typical.[9] The majority of musicians, who depended wholly or partly on teaching, were financially less favoured still. It is estimated (from censuses) that in England and Wales in 1794 there were about 1,500 practising musicians. In the course of the nineteenth century numbers steadily expanded from 6,600 in 1841 to 39,300 in 1901, by that time comprising almost equally men and women. In 1890 there are recorded 633 instrumentalists in London of whom 255 played the violin or viola, 45 the cello, and 43 the double bass. By 1920 these figures had undergone a remarkable expansion: 3,155 instrumentalists are recorded of whom 1,319 played the violin or viola, 340 the cello, and 235 the double bass.[10] It seems clear that this expanding pool of string-instrument players became increasingly reliant on Continental imports, rather than the English craftsmen, for their instruments. A serviceable German or French fiddle could be had for a price far more appropriate to the modest length of the musician's purse. By the end of the nineteenth century 'trade fiddles' from the factories of Mirecourt, Mittenwald, and Markneukirchen accounted for about 90 per cent of the world's supply. It is therefore instructive to look at the selling prices and selling methods of typical French and German factories.

The French Scene

The firm of J. Thibouville-Lamy was established in Mirecourt, in the Vosges area of France, in 1790. A wholesale trade catalogue from 1891 states that in 1890 'more than 35,000 violins, tenors, violoncellos, double basses, guitars and mandolins were made at our factory'. This astonishing figure gives some idea of the worldwide

---

[9] Cyril Ehrlich, *The Music Profession in Britain since the Eighteenth Century* (Oxford, 1985), 49.
[10] Ibid. Tables I, IV.

demand for these instruments from students, more serious players, and the many people who, before the days of television, sought to amuse themselves by learning a bowed stringed instrument or, perhaps, the guitar.

The wholesale price-list of these French violins for the trade and export in 1891 included, in US dollars:

Violin 'medio-fino' $2.75 and $3.50 according to whether or not they had Jerôme Thibouville's 'oriental varnish' or not.

A hundred violins 'medio-fino' were available packing-free for $264.

Full-sized purfled violins, labelled 'Companion', varied in price from $3.50 to $4.85.

Violins labelled 'Barnabetti', with brown varnish, were each $8.10 (or with extra-choice wood $11.25) and those labelled 'Virtuose' with 'oriental varnish' $25.

A variety of other violins was available, including violins with mosaic, being copies of Duiffopruggard, richly ornamented, for $48. Copies of most of the great Italian makers could be obtained, the most lavish being 'Fine Violins Oil Varnish' with Jerôme Thibouville's special varnish ('elastic, transparent oil varnish of great beauty, which reminds of the splendid Cremona instruments') from prices up to $128.[11] Thibouville-Lamy's broke down their production costs, in pounds sterling, as 5*d*. for wood, 6*d*. for labour, 1*s*. 1*d*. for machine cutting and shaping, 10*d*. for varnish, to which should be added 15 per cent profit, making a wholesale price of 4*s*. 6*d*, or 22½p in modern currency.[12]

The German Scene

Germany's production of trade violins etc. during the nineteenth and early part of the twentieth century exceeded that of France. Another trade catalogue gives an account of the production of what appears to be an American-owned violin factory in Leipzig, Saxony (the Stratton Violin Factory). The descriptive article, written in about 1873, states that 'the great demand for Violins is for those that cost the retailer not over $5'. In fact the cheaper grades would normally sell for $2 to $5 with the middle quality being $5 to $10. Describing factory procedures, the catalogue states that:

The most curious machines are those for turning out the tops and backs. These machines (there are four) attended by one girl at $2 per week, will turn out tops and backs for 150 violins per day.

---

[11] To convert to the then current value of the pound sterling the dollar should be divided by a little over 4.
[12] Cited Ehrlich, *Music Profession*, 101.

Six tops or backs is a good day's work for a violin maker, therefore as there are 150 tops, and 150 backs it would take fifty skilled workman to do the work of this one girl, which at $6 per week's wages, (a man's wages,) would cost just $300 instead of $2, and this is only one of the many labour-saving machines which Mr. Stratton has invented.[13]

The Effect of Competition

This 'Continental invasion' of cheap instruments coincided exactly with the growth in popularity of playing already noticed. But this development had a dire effect on native instrument-making. As Sandys and Forster say,[14] 'About the year 1786–7 the German fiddles of cheap and common workmanship, were introduced into England . . . and entries are seen in the books for fiddles as low as 9s, which were mostly sold to dealers; but others have participated in the low prices.' And in another passage[15] the authors say in the context of the work of S. A. Forster that no account was kept of 'second-class instruments, perhaps numbering not more than 24 violins, 4 or 5 tenors, and about 10 violoncellos'. An account was not kept 'as the interest in them experienced a check by the cheap and very common instruments from Germany, France, and other countries, which sadly interfered with the welfare of the English artisan, who could not compete in price, as this class of foreign goods could be purchased for a less sum than the materials cost for making them'.[16]

Free Trade

With Forster's very significant statement it is opportune to glance at the general economic expansion of the country during the nineteenth century and the effect which doctrines of free trade had on some types of manufactured goods, including musical instruments. To the accompaniment of expansion of trade and the lowering of customs duties, from about the middle of the eighteenth century onwards Great Britain saw the start of the first industrial revolution in Europe. This was due to a combination of circumstances. Industrial development was not unique to Britain. The swift increase in population, which was a marked feature within Britain, was also a common experience of other European countries. But Britain alone amongst the then developed nations of the world possessed huge overseas markets, an expanding commercial system, a growing population enjoying a rising

---

[13] See Roy Ehrhardt, *Violin Identification and Price Guide*, Bk. 2 (Kansas City, 1978) (being a collection of trade catalogues), 34–5.
[14] *History*, 336.   [15] Ibid. 347.   [16] Ibid.

standard of living, scientists of considerable inventiveness and sometimes genius, a stable political system, and a relative isolation from the constant political turmoil which affected most of the rest of Europe.

Foreign goods could be discouraged by protective tariffs, and for two centuries the creed had been that foreign trade must be regulated to assure a favourable balance—a central part of mercantalist theory. Numerous customs duties existed on imports of various kinds and Germany and France followed similar systems. The result was that trade in many commodities could not be conducted except by smuggling. The dire effects of this system were first conspicuously condemned by Adam Smith in his *Wealth of Nations* (1776). Smith pointed out the great advantages that would follow from division of labour and specialization internationally as well as nationally. Artificial restrictions on the free flow of goods were shown to be detrimental to national interests. British industrialists realized that if Britain lowered its tariffs other countries would be encouraged to do the same and Britain could only profit from wider markets.

The Napoleonic wars in the late eighteenth and early nineteenth centuries stopped what would otherwise have been a gradual liberalization of trade, but during the tenure of Huskisson as President of the Board of Trade (1823–7) and the Prime Ministership of Peel (1841–6) a large number of duties were either reduced or abolished. The Committee on Import Duties of 1840 had exposed an indefensible position. It was shown that duties on seventeen kinds of articles alone produced no less than 94.5 per cent of total customs revenue. Yet at this time there were nearly 900 kinds of articles on the customs list. Of the balance many duties were more expensive to collect than the net yield and many others produced a minimal amount of revenue. The Committee therefore proposed that customs duties should concentrate on those articles which yielded revenue and, by implication, should not be used to confer protection on home-manufactured goods. By 1842 a maximum of 20 per cent was levied on manufactured goods. It was left to Gladstone to complete the process, as described below.

Cheap 'Tools'

Free trade made a substantial contribution to the distribution of cheaper instruments. As late as 1853 the import duties on 'fancy articles', costly to collect, generating little revenue, encouraging smuggling, and generally raising costs and dampening trade were applied with bureaucratic punctiliousness to musical instruments:

Musical-boxes, small, not exceeding four inches in length, the air, 3d.: large, the air, 8d.: overtures, or extra accompaniments, the air, 2s. 6d.; pianofortes, horizontal grand, each £3:

upright or square, each, £2; musical harmoniums or seraphines, and not exceeding three stops, each 12s.: four stops, and not exceeding seven stops, each, £1 4s.: eight stops, and not exceeding eleven stops, each £1 10s.: exceeding eleven stops, each £2; musical instruments, not otherwise enumerated or described, for every £100 value, £10; accordians, commonly called Chinese, the 100 notes, 1s.; other sorts, including flutinas and common German square concertinas, the 100 notes, 5s.; concertinas of octagon form, not common German, each, 4s.; brass instruments, all sorts, the pound, 9d.[17]

Effectively this 10 per cent *ad valorem* duty on stringed instruments was finally swept away in 1860 at the time of the conclusion of the Cobden–Chevalier Treaty between Britain and France. The Treaty involved an agreement by Britain to abolish all duties on manufactured goods and reduce them on wines and brandy. France in turn abolished all prohibitions and lowered the duties on British imports. Britain then extended this system to all countries and for the next seventy years remained a country of free trade.

But the abolition of customs duty was only one element in the development of a highly competitive international market. Cheap labour and large-scale production of the type described above in the German factories was the route of the price challenge to English violin-makers. Added to this was the factor that firms such as Thibouville-Lamy were able to buy raw materials, notably their wood, very cheaply because of the economies of scale involved.

Cheap Musical Instruments

The prices of all musical instruments dropped and remained low until the early years of the twentieth century. Flutes, for instance, were available from Rudall Rose and Carte for £3 and clarinets for between £4 and £12 in 1854. By 1883 French flutes could be had for 32s. (£1.60), clarinets for £2. 14s. (£2.70), and trumpets for £5. Thibouville-Lamy's finished instruments wholesaled at 4s. 6d. (22½p). More specifically there is an advertisement at the end of the 1864 edition of John Bishop's translated version of F. J. Fétis's *Notice of Anthony Stradivari* (price 5s.) for Vuillaume's 'Renowned Copies of the Old Makers (some 2,000 of which have already been sold)' for £14. 14s. and Vuillaume's patent bows for between 10s. 6d. and 30s. (brazil wood). The agent was Robert Cocks & Co. of Burlington St., London. (Note that the violin was equivalent in price to about fifty-nine copies of the book—a comparatively small differential. A good instrument by J.-B. Vuillaume now fetches at auction in London about £40,000.)[18] Quality French violins during the later nineteenth century could be had for between £5 and £15 and

---

[17] Ehrlich, *Music Profession*, 100–1.
[18] See e.g. Phillips, 21 Nov. 1991, lot 171, a violin numbered 2771.

cellos from £9 to £27. (Compare the price of a Stradivari or Guarneri at the time which would have been between £200 and £500.) In 1904 Hill's sold their (imported) soundly made violins for the equivalent of £1.05, with bows at 25p and lined wooden case at 30p. The important effect of these very modest prices was to encourage parents of slender means to choose the violin as an instrument to learn because of the low outlay involved, as noted by Leopold Auer in his *Violin Playing as I Teach it*.[19]

The Struggle to Compete

In England in the latter part of the eighteenth century many makers and retailers such as Norris & Barnes and Longman & Broderip bought in cheap instruments from outworkers (who were often distinguished makers when they tried harder). The cheap, unpurfled products of the Kennedy family and Charles and Samuel Thompson frequently come on the market today. Most of these sources were capable of producing much better instruments, and did so from time to time, probably primarily in response to specific commissions. But even the cheapest lines were doomed. As Sandys and Forster pointed out, the cost of buying the raw materials was more than the price of the finished French or German product.

The market that existed was of the type described above: the cheap market for child, student, or low-grade orchestral instruments which had to compete with the Continental products of France and Germany, and the commissions for bespoke instruments from the more discerning players, often amateur, whose interest kept the craft alive. When it came to the better class of stringed instrument, particularly cellos which were more difficult to ship and import, the best of English work competed very favourably. This fact provided incentives for late eighteenth-century and early nineteenth-century makers who would otherwise have been driven to alternative employment.

Prices

Ascertaining the prices charged by the major English makers of the late eighteenth and early nineteenth centuries is a frustratingly difficult business. The accounts of the Forster family as reproduced in Sandys and Forster are demonstrably imperfect and reveal virtually nothing about prices actually charged other than, in the case of William Forster (III) a reference to 'violins at £3. 3s. 0d'.[20] (by implication the cheapest class of fiddle) and the reference that 'no account

---

[19] (London, 1921), 6; see generally Ehrlich, *Music Profession*, 101. [20] Sandys and Forster, *History*, 337.

whatever of instruments of 5 guineas value and less has been kept' in the context of the same maker's cellos.[21] We know from John Joseph Merlin's advertisements in about 1775 that he charged between 5 and 10 guineas for violins and from 12 to 20 guineas for cellos.

Merlin was a fashionable maker and his prices may be seen to be typical of the higher class of instrument available at the time. Again there is a disappointing lack of accounts apparently available to price the work of Benjamin Banks of Salisbury (1727–95). Albert Cooper, basing his opinion on somewhat tentative evidence, surmises that Banks probably charged £21 for a cello and sold violins and violas at £10 to £12 each. Cooper goes on to say that 'prices remained steady until the third quarter of the 19th century when a tremendous influx of trade instruments, mass-produced in France and Germany, played havoc with the home market'.[22] Nevertheless, there is evidence that there was still demand for good, hand-crafted British stringed instruments. George Hart, as good a judge as any, in writing in the first edition of his masterly *The Violin: Famous Makers and their Imitators* in 1875, speaks of £5 to £20 being given for English violins, 'while Violoncellos and Tenors commanded prices proportionately high'.[23]

For a time in the nineteenth century a good English cello could fetch premium prices. Sandys and Forster indicate that William Forster (II) made, probably as his last cello, an instrument for the eminent player Crosdill. On the sale of Crosdill's property on 9 May 1826 Lot 6 was described as 'a violoncello—of the long Stradivarius pattern—by Forster, Senior, the very last instrument manufactured by that justly celebrated maker, and most highly valued by Mr. Crossdill, with bow, in a most excellent dove-tail case, covered with leather, brass nails, lock and key'. This was bought for 46 guineas by Thomas Dodd, the dealer, for a private purchaser.[24]

Another cello made by the same maker in about 1772 was sold for 100 guineas and an Amati bass 'worth at least 50 guineas, in exchange' in 1787. The purchaser was apparently the Revd H. A. Hole, one of the best amateur performers on the cello of the day who had the distinction of lacking the first two joints of the forefinger on the left hand and therefore being compelled to use the thumb from the first position.[25] (Sandys and Forster relate that the surgeons removed the first joint of the finger but refused to operate on the second joint. Hole therefore excused himself, went to his dressing room, 'and cut off the injured part, with his penknife, at the second joint, and then returned to the surgeons to have the wound properly dressed'. The surgeons then acknowledged that it was right to amputate it to prevent future mortification!) While in Hole's ownership, an accident occurred to the cello, fracturing its back, at which time it was valued at £500.

---

[21] Sandys and Forster, *History*, 338.   [22] Cooper, *Benjamin Banks*, 162.   [23] p. 163.   [24] *History*, 323.
[25] Ibid. 326.

William C. Honeyman, writing in 1893, warned of the danger of English makers pricing themselves out of the market:

TO VIOLIN MAKERS
A friendly Warning

Before concluding let me utter a friendly warning to the British violin maker. Within the last 15 or 20 years this delicate art has sprung into life again in this country, and there is only one thing which is likely to crush it—that is, rapacity. Nearly a century ago English violin makers gradually screwed up the prices till Dodd and others were getting £25 for violins and £50 for 'cellos. The natural result was the death of the industry under the competition of cheap German work. Germany is still in existence and violin manufacture in that country has vastly improved, so it bids even more loudly for the patronage of the British violin player, and it will undoubtedly gain it if the old cause should step in to help on the disaster. Oil varnish and carefully selected wood are now the last hold which the British maker has against the German manufacturer, who has even learned to use a soft spirit varnish instead of a hard one. (Many of the second class old Italian makers did the same.) It is also painfully significant that the best dealers in the land now sell these German made instruments. Let the British violin maker, therefore, beware of Rapacity. He may fancy that he is being benefited by charging exorbitant prices, but it is a delusion. The policy is simply suicidal. In writing 'Scottish Violin Makers: Past and Present' (price 1s.), nothing amused me more than the prices of the different instruments submitted to me, some of which prices were simply horrifying. The fun did not come to me from the value put upon the violins by these makers, but from the fact that the violins, which were charged at very moderate prices, were almost invariably far superior in tone and in finish to the dear ones. If I were to name the highest prices stated by some of the makers, my readers would amazedly gasp out, 'What! Are they worth it?' To this question, having seen and carefully tested the instruments, I answer

THEY ARE NOT

Let the British violin maker be reasonable in his prices and he will prosper. If he cannot produce a good violin at £10 he should learn his business over again. Let him also remember the ever increasing thousands of old violins well preserved, which are constantly in the market, and competing with him in price and he will not accuse me of advocating a niggardly policy. Where is the ordinary orchestral player who can afford to give more than £10 for his violin? I have seen an old violin large in model, thick in wood, and about 100 years old which had never been fractured and had a large and telling tone, and was covered with a fine oil varnish, sold to one of these professional players for £7. Would the best new violin that could be produced beat that, for that particular kind of work?—namely, playing in a theatre orchestra. When a violin is of the right kind, age adds immensely to its value to the professional player. The amateur who often wishes more for an instrument pretty to look at and chiefly for drawing-room playing is not so particular, and if the tone sound large under his own ear he usually troubles himself little about its carrying powers.

But even to leave out the competition of old violins and instance a new one—I have seen a violin produced and sold for £10 which was exquisitely made and finished with a lovely and lustrous oil varnish, and which when fresh from the maker's hands was pronounced by the testers, who were all experienced judges, better than a well preserved violin by J. B. Vuillaume which belonged to one of the judges. 'Facts pinch,' says Brougham. Let our violin makers put on their thinking caps and decide whether this artistic industry is to live or to languish.[26]

Comparing Prices

In the course of this book there are numerous instances of prices being quoted at various times for makers' instruments, whether of the 'trade' or handcrafted variety. And it can be seen from the above that charging more than £10 for a violin in the 1890s was regarded by Honeyman as inviting economic suicide.

Another factor in assessing whether an instrument would be viewed as 'cheap' or 'expensive' by the average buyer would be to gauge what percentage of monthly or annual income the purchase would represent. For instance, according to Gregory King's estimate of the population wealth of England and Wales for 1696,[27] military officers had a yearly income per family of £60 and 'persons in the law' £140. In about 1750 labourers' wages in London varied from 9s. to 12s. a week, approximately £25 per annum. A fiddle would therefore have to be very cheap indeed to be affordable on this income. Skilled and rapid workmen on piece-work could earn from £1 to £4 per week in such trades as jewellery, chair carving, and the making of optical instruments (i.e. up to £200 per annum). A violin for, say, £10 would represent an outlay of only 5 per cent of gross income, which is more feasible.[28]

As to the profession of music, by 1857 a contemporary writer reckoned that whilst composers could expect practically nothing, a 'respectable London professor of the pianoforte would make from £400 to £800' and eminent teachers at least £2,000. London parochial organists got an average of £50, cathedral organists about £150 and sometimes a house.[29] These figures in fact sound rather optimistic when one compares them with the yields of music businesses actually advertised in the 1880s, one of which states net profits of £550 per annum, and another £160 per annum, the latter apparently involving tuning and teaching.

An example of a professional musician's contract (Henry Hill, principal viola player) is of interest in showing the fee offered to a leading mid-nineteenth-

---

[26] William C. Honeyman, *The Violin ... How to Choose One* (Dundee, 1893; 6th edn., repr. 1983), 22.

[27] Extracted from W. A. Speck, *Stability and Strife: England 1714–1760* (London, 1977), Appendix, and B. R. Mitchell and P. Deane, *Abstract of British Historical Statistics* (Cambridge, 1963).

[28] See M. D. George, *London Life in the Eighteenth Century* (London, 1966), ch. 4.

[29] Byerly Thomson, cited in Ehrlich, *Music Profession*, 43–4.

century string-player for eight engagements and eight rehearsals in the Philharmonic Society's Orchestra. It runs:

    PHILHARMONIC SOCIETY
    HANOVER SQUARE ROOMS

 Sir,
I beg to acquaint you that the Concerts of the ensuing Season will take place on the following Nights, viz.:-
 March .... 4 and 18,
 April .... 8 and 22,
 May .... 6 and 20,
 June .... 3 and 17,
the Rehearsals for which will be held on the Saturday Mornings previous, at Eleven o'Clock precisely; for your performance at which as Principal Tenor, I am directed to offer you the sum of Seventeen Pounds, including your gratuitous attendance at Two Trials, should they be required.

It must be distinctly understood that, in accepting the above, you strictly adhere to the following stipulations, any infringement of which will nullify your Engagement:-
 1. To be ready in your place in the Orchestra a Quarter of an Hour before the time of commencing the Rehearsals and Concerts.
 2. To be entirely under the control of the Director of the Orchestra, and not to leave your place during the Rehearsals and Performances without his permission.

              I am, Sir,
              Your obedient servant,
              G. W. Budd
              Secretary

January 10, 1850.
118 Pall Mall.
N.B.—You will please fill up the enclosed Form and return it to me on or before the 17th of January.
H. Hill Esqre.

Indices of prices[30] reveal that, taking a basket of consumer goods and ascribing the value of 100 to them in 1701, the index stood at 97 in 1725, 95 in 1750, 113 in 1775, 212 in 1800, and 128 in 1823. The fluctuations thus revealed are indicative of the disruption caused by agricultural and industrial depressions and wars. A similar index based on an aggregate of agricultural and principal industrial products gives a value of 95 in 1850, 117 in 1875, 91 in 1900, and 106 in 1913.

Since 1900, retail price indices show that it would take £40 in 1990 to equal the purchasing power of £1 in 1900, £30 today to equal £1 in 1930, and £10 to equal £1 in 1960. But this inflation masks the way that real prices of different and

---

[30] See Mitchell and Deane, *Abstract of British Historical Statistics*.

commonly used commodities actually change. So it has been calculated that in today's money the cheapest car available in 1900 appropriately grossed up would have cost £10,238, in 1930 £5,313, and in 1960 £4,940. The decreasing cost in real terms demonstrates economies in production. In similar terms the price of a Monet painting would have been £34,496 in 1900, £67,144 in 1930, £200,000 in 1960, and £4,000,000 in 1990. This shows the effect of increased demand for a unique item so that the price of the item rises in real terms. Similar considerations would apply in turn to both 'trade' and high-class violins, violas, cellos, and basses (and their bows).[31]

Bows also produce interesting price comparisons, even taken over the span of the twentieth century. The reputation of the firm of W. E. Hill & Sons has been particularly outstanding in this field (as is examined in Chapter 9). In the catalogue of Lyon and Healy of Chicago from about 1903–4 Hill bows are offered at $30 for silver-mounted with a plain frog, $35 for a handsome frog, better finish, $40 for a Dodd copy with an ivory frog and pearl slide, and $55 for a gold-mounted frog with very finest finish. In the same catalogue the 'world renowned' bows of James Tubbs of London with dark finish, round, and pure silver mountings are advertised for $38. The bows of A. Vigneron of Paris, also silver-mounted, are advertised for $20. (To reduce to pounds sterling at the then current exchange rate it is necessary to divide the sum in dollars by a little over 4.)[32] Many of these bows will now fetch at least £1,000 at auction in London, if in good condition.

The violins of W. E. Hill & Sons were marketed in the USA by Wurlitzer's, and their 1922 retail price list refers to their having been awarded a certain quota of violins 'but unfortunately the supply is exceedingly limited, as they are not made in commercial numbers'. The first model, being a copy of Stradivarius, is priced at $400 and the second model with 'superior wood and varnish, most artistic workmanship and finish' is priced at $600 in 1922.[33] This again is a warning to present-day appraisers that in common with many other producers Hills made their violins in significantly different qualities. This should, but it is suggested usually does not in fact, result in a differential value at today's prices, at least with violins. (It is easier to discriminate between one Hill bow and another, as is explained in Chapter 9.)

In the context of differential pricing it is refreshing to come across a price-list issued by William Atkinson of Tottenham, London in about 1905 which advertises his violins as 'one quality only—£15'; similarly, violas are £20 and cellos £30. George Wulme Hudson is also recorded as charging £10 for a violin in 1916, later increased to £15 (which meant that they became too expensive for his usual retailer, Edward Withers of Wardour Street).[34]

[31] See *Economist* 22 Dec. 1990, 128. [32] Ehrhardt, *Violin Identification*, 105. [33] Ibid. 68.
[34] See Albert Cooper, 'Trade Secrets', *Strad* (Feb. 1985), 753–9.

These data sufficiently indicate that the retail prices charged by the better makers changed little from about 1775 to the end of the First World War. Good violins of English makers were clearly available for about £10 and good cellos for £20–£30 for most of this period. Current auction prices averaged £2,000 to £3,000 for these instruments in 1990–1.

Chapter Seven

The Development of the Demand for Strings in England from 1760 to the Present

Handel's Legacies — Salomon's Enterprises — The Cello and its Players — Forster's 'Royal George' — Other Cello Patrons and Players — Viotti and the Stradivari Cause — Paganini and his Guarneri — The Bow — Later Developments in the English Musical Scene — Henry Hill and his Circle — Money and Numbers — J. T. Carrodus — Proselytizers and Institutions — Schools and Strings — Music of the People — Producing the Players — Women and the Violin — The Provincial Colleges — Enthusiasm and Poverty — Modern times

Handel's Legacies

HANDEL died in 1759 and though his musical contributions to the British musical scene were monumental, he also bequeathed a *hereditas damnosa* with two main features. One was the cultivation of English taste for the oratorio—admirable at first but as the oratorio tradition developed in such an overwhelming way, ultimately costive in its effect on the development of English music. The other less positive feature of the Handel era was the established dominance of foreign musicians. On this latter point, admittedly the same phenomenon was occurring elsewhere in Europe. German musicians substantially colonized Paris. Italian musicians predominated at the German secular courts and some of the ecclesiastically based ones such as Salzburg. The electoral band at Mannheim under the Bohemian Johann Stamitz (1717–57), which raised orchestral standards to a hitherto unmatched standard of excellence, also used talented non-German musicians. It was therefore hardly surprising that native musicians in England accepted, and probably expected, to be dominated by emigrant musicians of talent from the Continent of Europe. A national inferiority complex had set in, consciously or unconsciously, from which England suffered well into the twentieth century. Within living memory conductors and soloists with Anglo-Saxon names had to fight significant public prejudice.

The early development of the symphonic tradition was primarily introduced to England by J. S. Bach's youngest son Johann Christian, who had worked in Milan—so again there was a distinct pan-European tradition at work. J. C. Bach teamed up with his compatriot Carl Friedrich Abel of Leipzig, the latter being music master to Queen Charlotte since 1764. Bach and Abel began a series of concerts at Carlisle House in Soho Square under the aegis of Teresa Cornelys, an Italian singer. It was at one of that lady's masquerades at Carlisle House, it will be recalled, that Joseph Merlin did his celebrated roller-skating act in which he wounded both his instrument and himself (see Chapter 4).

Later on in the eighteenth century the Pantheon in Oxford Street, opened in 1772, and the Hanover Square Rooms, opened in 1775, became the preferred venues for concerts of this kind. Clementi, the Italian pianist, was brought to England in 1766 as a boy of 14 by an enterprising member of the Beckford family (associated with Fonthill Abbey). Having made a secure name for himself abroad, Clementi participated in the foundation of the Grand Professional Concerts held at the Hanover Square Rooms. He produced his first symphony at these concerts in 1786. The German–Jewish violinist Johann Peter Salomon started, as an impresario, an important series of rival subscription concerts in the 1780s in which he actively participated. It was he who introduced to the English public the symphonies of Haydn and Mozart.

It was also Salomon who invited Haydn on two visits to England (1791–2 and 1794–5), and, inspired by the immeasurably improved standard of orchestral playing in London, Haydn wrote the set of twelve 'Salomon' symphonies which are amongst his greatest. As was the tradition at the time, Salomon led from the first violin desk and Haydn sat at the keyboard. William Gardiner of Leicester (1770–1853) states that Salomon's violin 'was the celebrated one that belonged to Corelli, with his name elegantly embossed in large capital letters on the ribs'.[1] An interesting connection between Haydn and the London violin-making world was the contract entered into in 1781 for William Forster II to publish a large number of Haydn's symphonies and other works.

The scale of forces needed for the performance of these symphonies is now well known to modern audiences from contemporary baroque performances which reproduce as far as possible the original sound. Although the number of string-players involved was usually small, the example set for orchestral standards must have been of great national importance. By way of contrast Haydn attended the

---

[1] Jonathan Wilshere, *William Gardiner of Leicester* (Leicester, 1970), 17.

Handel Commemoration held in Westminster Abbey in 1791 which involved in excess of a thousand performers. And this was as nothing compared to the 3,625 performers who participated in the Sacred Harmonic Society's Festival in the Crystal Palace in 1862.

Percy Young also points out[2] that it was during the eighteenth century that the comparatively short-lived tradition of professionals playing with amateurs was established. The concerto grosso, popular in Britain, was ideal for mixed performance and gave the amateur an important part in the control of programme selection and organization of concerts generally. This phenomenon occurred not only in London but in many of the provincial cities and towns of Britain. Unfortunately amateur taste tended to be self-indulgent and this, perhaps as much as anything, led to the progressive sclerosis of English musical enterprise compared to what was happening, for example, under the more authoritarian tradition prevalent in Germany.

Salomon's Enterprises

As the eighteenth century turned to the nineteenth, interest in such events as Salomon's subscription concerts declined and proprietors were obliged to withdraw themselves from them with the loss of a great sum of money (according to a contemporary commentator).[3] Although the early members of the Royal House of Hanover were highly sympathetic to music, it appears that orchestral standards declined significantly at the beginning of the nineteenth century and fine players such as Robert Lindley (1776–1835) were driven to providing visual as well as aural entertainment—in Lindley's case of necessity playing the cello whilst protected by an umbrella against the leaks in the roof of St Andrew's Hall, Norwich.

The reaction against this decline lead Salomon and others to found, in 1813, the important Philharmonic Society on a proper professional basis. It promoted the performance of the major works of Mozart, Haydn, and Beethoven and gave the first performance in England of the *Eroica* Symphony in 1814. The Society commissioned important works including the Ninth (Choral) Symphony which Beethoven subscribed in his own hand to the Philharmonic Society. And it was Ludwig Spohr, directing one of his symphonies for the Philharmonic Society in 1820, who insisted on conducting from a conductor's rostrum with a baton for the first time, at least if Spohr's own statement in his autobiography is to be believed.

[2] *The Concert Tradition*, 103.   [3] Ibid. 165.

The Cello and its Players

As has been previously mentioned, the cello has always occupied a special place in English music-making. Perhaps because it is not associated with dancing and diablerie, the gentlemen and aristocrats of the latter part of the eighteenth century with a bent for music felt less inhibition about performing on it. In the case of George, the third Earl Cowper, he has gone down to history as depicted by the artist Johann Zoffany (in about 1800), playing his cello, surrounded by members of the Gore family including four elegant ladies. One of these accompanies him on the square piano, both players sharing the same music score. The fine, but unidentified, baroque cello is wedged between the legs and played with the bow held about a quarter of the way along the stick, as was then the manner.[4] This type of positive example helped develop a symbiotic relationship between player and maker, encouraging the production of fine English instruments, particularly between about 1700 and 1830.

The establishment of the cello into England (initially as the preferred alternative to the bass viol) was largely attributable to a small group of Italian musicians. Amongst these was Giovanni Bononcini whose reputation as a cellist is rather overridden by the notoriety of his habit of plagiarizing the work of others and passing it off as his own. It was he who sent in a madrigal to the Academy of Ancient Music for competition against Handel which was discovered to be the work of Antonio Lotti of Venice. He had arrived in London in 1720 and left, shortly after the above episode, in 1733.

But it was probably Giacomo Bassevi,[5] called Cervetto the Elder (born 1682 in Italy of Jewish parents), who deserved most credit for introducing the cello securely into the English concert scene. He came to London in 1728, initially as a dealer in Italian instruments, and as a cellist. Strangely, he failed to prosper as a dealer and so devoted himself instead to the cello (though he may have continued to dabble in the instrument market from time to time—his son certainly did). Historians give him the credit, together with Abaco, Pasqualini, and Caporale at about this time, for bringing the cello into favour and making musicians, according to Burney, 'nice judges of that instrument'. Cervetto the Elder became a highly popular performer, particularly as solo cellist at the Drury Lane Theatre where Garrick was in the middle of a triumphant career. He also became the manager of that theatre and is credited with a considerable fortune. He was affectionately known as 'Nosey' on account of his prominent proboscis. He is reputed to have offended Garrick by loudly yawning in the middle of a particularly touching speech by Garrick, which reduced the audience to violent laughter. When Garrick

---

[4] The painting, from the Yale Center for British Art, is reproduced in S. Sadie (ed.) with A. Latham, *The Cambridge Music Guide* (Cambridge, 1985), 321.

[5] Variously Giacomo, Jacopo.

upbraided him for this he is said to have commented: 'I beg ten thousand pardons, but I alway do so ven I am ver much please.'[6] He also composed for the cello and died in London at the age of 101 in 1783.

Cervetto was able to leave a fortune of £20,000 to his son James Cervetto (Cervetto the Younger), who was born in 1747 and appears to have been a finer cellist even than his father. He had been taught by his father and appeared at the age of only 13 at a concert in the Little Haymarket Theatre. (One of his fellow performers was a 9-year-old pianist, the celebrated Fanny Burney, daughter of Dr Burney, author of the country's first *General History of Music*, 1776–89.)[7] In 1771 James Cervetto was appointed cellist in the Queen's Private Band and published *Twelve solos for a Violoncello with a Thorough Bass for the Harpsichord* amongst other cello works. He died at the age of 90 in 1837. There is a fine portrait in oils of him tuning up, formerly in the possession of Messrs W. E. Hill & Sons and reproduced in Van der Straeten's book on the *History of the Violoncello*.[8] Cervetto the Younger was a keen buyer of stringed instruments from the increasingly fashionable William Forster II. As mentioned in the preceding chapter, a Forster cello of his was burned when the Italian Opera House, Haymarket, was destroyed by fire in 1789. Sandys and Forster relate that Cervetto never recovered from this loss and it caused his retirement.[9]

Probably the greatest player of the age was John Crosdill, born 1755, who started his career in music as a choirboy at Westminster Abbey. He appeared as an infant-prodigy cellist at the age of 9 and continued his studies in Paris. He became a great favourite in English aristocratic circles, and returned to London in about 1780, becoming a chamber musician to Queen Charlotte in 1782. An important step in his career followed when he was appointed teacher of the cello to the Prince of Wales (later George IV), and continued as his teacher for two years. This started a fashion for learning the cello from Crosdill, much to the remunerative benefit of that player. He followed the now familiar pattern of also managing his concerts and was frequently to be heard at the Hanover Square Rooms and the Three Choirs Festival, by now well established. Crosdill left seven cellos at his death, amongst which was a famous William Forster II instrument.

Forster's 'Royal George'

The Hanoverian dynasty was, despite its other manifest faults, exceptionally musical. The cello was particularly associated with two important members of the

---

[6] This account, one of a number of differing versions, is from E. S. J. Van der Straeten, *The History of the Violoncello* (London, 1925), 154.

[7] See generally ibid. 314–15.
[8] Ibid., pl. xxxiii.
[9] Sandys and Forster, *History*, 315.

Royal Family. Frederick Lewis, Prince of Wales, the son of George II (born in 1707 and died before accession in 1751), was an amateur cellist and a friend of Handel. There is an interesting painting by Philip Mercier of 1733 showing a music party in the gardens of Kew Palace. At the centre of the portrait is an excellent depiction of Frederick Lewis playing the cello (naturally of baroque specification, without a tail-pin) from an elegant music-stand and with, apparently, considerable concentration. The painting is in the National Portrait Gallery and also shows his sister, Anne, the Princess Royal, playing the harpsichord and Princess Caroline Elizabeth playing the mandolin.[10]

More eminent still in the role of aristocratic cellist was George Frederick, Prince of Wales, born in 1762, who ascended the throne as George IV in 1820. As already mentioned, he studied for two years with Crosdill and, along with his brothers the Duke of Gloucester (violin) and the Duke of Cumberland (violin, viola, and flute), was a keen amateur player and concert-giver. The English instrument most associated with George IV is a William Forster II cello bearing the Prince of Wales's royal coat of arms painted on the table of the instrument and the words 'Liberty and Loyalty' on the ribs. It has a back-length of 28⅞ in. (734 cm). The instrument became known as the 'Royal George'. (It has been suggested that there were two such instruments. Forster's accounts indeed show that in 1782 he produced two cellos for the Prince of Wales.)[11]

Other Cello Patrons and Players

The relationship between the Forster family of violin-makers and the eminent and aristocratic players of the time has already been mentioned. In particular William Forster II ('Old Forster'), assisted by his son and workmen, supplied two cellos to the Prince of Wales in 1782, a double bass for King George III in 1787 (specially commissioned and of large dimensions), and another in 1789 for the King's private band. A further cello was supplied to George III in 1795 and another double bass was so commissioned in 1805. The Prince of Wales had two concerts a day at his residence, in Carlton House. The morning concert was of chamber music and the evening one, to a larger audience, orchestral. The Prince played on his Forster instrument.[12] When Haydn, who had been listening was asked how he had played, Haydn is said to have diplomatically replied 'Vy, your 'ighness do play like a Brince.'[13]

[10] This picture is reproduced in Van der Straeten, *Violoncello*, pl. xxxiv.
[11] The 'Royal George' instrument was sold in 1903 at Christie's for 52 guineas. See Henley, *Dictionary*, 402. It was re-offered at Sotheby's in Nov. 1990 (lot 336, estimate £30,000 to £40,000) but not then sold. It is illustrated in Pl. 28.
[12] Van der Straeten, *Violoncello*, 317–18.
[13] Quoted in Haweis, *Old Violins*, 128.

Sandys and Forster credit William Forster (II) as probably making his last instrument 'by express wish for Mr. Crosdill'.[14] A Forster instrument owned by Crosdill was, in turn, bought by auction in 1826 by Robert Lindley, who went on to become the finest cellist of his era. He deserves a further word to himself.

Lindley (1777–1855) was another cellist who started professional life at the age of 9 years. At the age of 16 he became a pupil of James Cervetto the Younger and then played as principal cellist both at the King's Theatre and at the 'Ancient Concerts' and the Philharmonic Concerts. He is closely associated with his friend Dragonetti, the double bassist. He did much to keep to the fore the work of Corelli in the London concert scene, though a review of his performances reveals little inclination to tackle the mainstream repertoire of chamber music as we would now identify it. An exception occurred in 1817 when he participated in one of Mozart's string quintets. Robert Lindley died in 1855, some nine years after Dragonetti and after a very successful professional career.[15] The famous Forster cello, formerly owned by Crosdill and bought by Lindley in 1826, later became the property of General Sir Hope Grant (see Chapter 6) and was exhibited as Item 195 (the 'Royal George' being 196) at the Special Exhibition of 1873 in the South Kensington Museum.

Lindley did much to further the cause of Forster's cellos which came to be regarded in some circles as quite the equal of and possibly superior to 'Cremonas', though Albert Cooper, in his monograph on Benjamin Banks, suggests that Lindley's Forster purchases were probably for pupils and 'a Benjamin Banks Strad copy of which he was particularly proud was the instrument used for public performances until his retirement in 1851'.[16]

Viotti and the Stradivari Cause

Up to this point the text has focused on the role of a few eminent performers in England in promoting one important member of the string family, the cello. In musical histories the cello tends to be overshadowed by descriptions of the contribution to music in London of virtuoso violinists, Italian in particular, during this period. And it would indeed be perverse not to draw attention, for instance, to the career of Giovanni Battista Viotti (b. Piedmont 1755, d. London 1824).

Often looked upon as the father of modern violin technique, Viotti followed a distinguished career as a soloist at the royal courts of Europe and was in particular devoted to Marie Antoinette. However, the arrest of the King and Queen during the French Revolution caused him to emigrate to London in 1792 and he made his

---

[14] Sandys and Forster, *History*, 323.   [15] See generally Van der Straeten, *Violoncello*, 324–7.
[16] Cooper, *Benjamin Banks*, 156.

London début in 1793 playing his twenty-first violin concerto. He became leader of the Italian Opera at the King's Theatre and played frequently in public concerts. After being accused of revolutionary activities he fled to Germany but returned to London in 1801 and entered into an ill-fated venture as a wine merchant. He still performed as a soloist, giving the première of his twenty-third concerto in London in 1803, and then became one of the founders of the Philharmonic Society of London already mentioned. By 1818 the wine business had ruined him and after further unsuccessful ventures as an impresario in Paris he died in London in 1824.

Viotti's importance as a violin technician and composer is discussed in other works.[17] This book is primarily concerned with the relationship between performers, orchestral forces, and native violin-makers. In this context Viotti made one extremely important contribution to the development of English violin-making style. This was simply that Viotti is traditionally credited as having established the primacy of the instruments of Antonio Stradivari in both Paris and London. Viotti probably owned at least two instruments by this maker: the Hills in their work on Stradivari mention specimens of 1709 and 1712,[18] but they particularly praise a superb example of 1712 which they state was the violin used by Viotti until his death. It was then sent to Paris and sold by public auction. As the Hills remark:

The noble beauty of its tone seems to us to echo the elevated style of Viotti's compositions and his broad and impassioned playing. Viotti, we must recollect, was the first supremely great violinist and composer for the violin to introduce and prove to his audiences the merits of Stradivari violins; and we find his followers and admirers—Baillot, Habeneck, Kreutzer, Lafont, Rode and many others—all using Stradivaris, and permanently establishing their position in the world of music.[19]

It was left to Niccolò Paganini, who did not perform outside Italy until 1828, to make the case for Guarneri del Gesù.

Paganini and his Guarneri

So much has been written about Paganini and his astonishing impact on the West European musical scene that little needs to be added here. On his first tour of Britain, from his sensational début at the King's Theatre on 3 June 1831 and over the next ten months, he gave some 140 concerts. Of these, 49 concerts took place in the English provinces, 23 in Scotland, and 22 in Ireland. His fee for a Dublin

---

[17] See, for example, William Mann, 'The Nineteenth Century', in Gill (ed.), *Book of the Violin*, 116 ff.; Stowell (ed.), *Cambridge Companion*, *passim*.

[18] Hill, *Stradivari*, 153.
[19] Ibid. 153–4.

appearance was £500, enough, it was said, to relieve eighty Irish farms from the miseries of hunger during the ensuing winter.[20] He attracted a huge and adoring following and though the audiences objected to the high ticket prices more usually associated with opera evenings, they came in droves.

The impact of Paganini's London debut is graphically described by William Gardiner thus:[21]

I placed myself at the Opera two hours and a half before the concert began; presently the crowd of musicians and violinists filled the Colonnade to suffocation, all anxious to get the front seat, because they had to pay for their places, Paganini not giving a single ticket away. The concert opened with Beethoven's Second Sinfony, admirably performed by the Philharmonic band, after which Lablache sung 'Largo al Factotum' with much applause, and was encored. A breathless silence then ensued, and every eye was watching the entré of this extraordinary violinist; and as he glided from the side scenes to the front of the stage an involuntary cheering burst from every part of the house, many rising from their seats to view the spectre during the thunder of this unprecedented cheering—his gaunt and extraordinary appearance being more like that of a devotee about to suffer martyrdom than one to delight you with his art. With the tip of his bow he set off the orchestra in a grand military movement with a force and vivacity as surprising as it was new. At the termination of this introduction he commenced with a soft streamy note of celestial quality; and with three or four whips of his bow elicited points of sound as bright as the stars. A scream of astonishment and delight burst from the audience at the novelty of this effect. Immediately execution followed that was equally indescribable, in which were intermingled tones more than human, which seemed to be wrung from the deepest anguish of a broken heart. After this the audience were enraptured by a lively strain, in which was heard, commingled with the tones of the instrument, those of the voice, with the pizzicato of the guitar, forming a compound of exquisite beauty. If it were possible to aim at a description of his manner, we should say that you would take the violin to be a wild animal which he is endeavouring to quiet in his bosom, and which he occasionally, fiend-like, lashes with his bow; this he dashes upon the strings as you would whip with a walking switch, tearing from the creature the most horrid as well as delightful tones.

He has long legs and arms, and the hands in his playing often assume the attitude of prayer, with the fingers pointed upwards. The highest notes (contrary to every thing we have learnt) are produced as the hand recedes from the bridge, overturning all our previous notions of the art. During these effects a book caught fire upon one of the desks, which burnt for some time unobserved by the musicians, who could neither see nor hear, though repeatedly called to by the audience, anything but the feats of this wonderful performer.

Some few pieces were played by the orchestra that gave some repose to the admiring audience. He then entered upon his celebrated performance of the single string, intro-

---

[20] See Ehrlich, *Music Profession*, 46.

[21] William Gardiner, 1770–1853, was a hosiery manufacturer and keen violinist and musician, who wrote (amongst others) a book of reminiscences, *Music and Friends*, published in 3 vols. between 1838 and 1853. This passage comes from his *Music of Nature* (Boston, 1838), 214–17. The passage is also quoted in Haweis, *My Musical Life*, 382–3.

ducing the air of 'Nel cor più sento' (Hope told a flattering tale), in which he imparted a tone so 'plaintive and desolate, that the heart was torn by it;' in the midst of this he was so outré—so comic—as to occasion the loudest bursts of laughter. This feat was uproariously encored. He then retired to put on the three other strings, and ended this miraculous performance with the richest arpeggios and echoes, intermingled with new effects, that no language can describe. Though he withdrew amidst a confusion of huzzas and bravos that completely drowned the full orchestra, yet he was called for to receive the homage of the audience; and was so apparently affected, that he would have dropped had he not been supported by Laporte and Costa.

There was no trick in his playing; it was all fair, scientific execution, opening to us a new order of sounds, the highest of which ascended two octaves above C in alt.

Haweis's version of the same passage adds that 'it was curious to watch the faces of Lindley, Dragonetti, and the other great players, who took up places on the platform to command a good view of him during his performance—they all seem to have agreed that the like had never been heard before, and that in addition to his marvellous eccentricities and novel effects, he had transcended the highest level of legitimate art that had ever been reached'.

Although Paganini owned a number of instruments, including a quartet by Stradivari, for some 40 years he normally played his Guarneri del Gesù 'Cannon', of 1742 (by tradition presented to him early in his career by M. Livron, and eventually left by Paganini to his native town Genoa).[22]

Paganini brought the name of Guarneri del Gesù firmly to public notice and there was the inevitable demand for copies. But in England it is fair to say that as between the Stradivari and Guarneri models, nineteenth-century makers generally preferred to follow Stradivari (on abandoning the Amati–Stainer types). The Hills in their work on Guarneri[23] mention the Fendt family and George and John Lott as the primary English followers of the rival Guarneri model, but it is surely to John Frederick Lott junior (1805–71) that the palm must be given. Though often slightly larger than the genuine article, his fine copies were born duly 'antiqued' and soon acquired a reputation for tonal qualities too. They are now amongst the most valuable of all English-made instruments and are discussed in Chapter 11.

It is possible that Paganini's Scottish appearances helped to plant the Guarneri seed there, many more Scottish makers following the Guarneri pattern than their English counterparts. A few English makers in the twentieth century, such as Thomas Earle Hesketh and William Luff, show a predilection for Guarneri, and Heron-Allen presents his Guarneri as an alternative pattern to that of Stradivari in his immensely influential book on *Violin-Making*. (Heron-Allen's favourite instrument for playing purposes was his own Guarneri copy; see Ch. 14). Since

---

[22] See Hill, *Stradivari*, 276.   [23] Hill, *Guarneri Family*, 98.

Paganini, many notable artists (for example Ole Bull, Spohr, Sainton, Vieuxtemps, Carrodus, Auer, Wieniawski, and Heifetz) have owned Guarneris as their premier concert instruments.

The Bow

The important relationship between the bow and the virtuoso instrumentalist must not be forgotten. The invention of a concave bow, rather than an almost straight or actually convex bow-stick, is credited to the encouragement and promotion of Wilhelm Cramer (1745–99), who arrived in London as a virtuoso violinist from Mannheim in 1772 and held sway as the finest violinist available until Viotti's début in 1792. What is called the 'Cramer' bow has a slightly concave stick and a 'battle-axe' head. This type of bow, which was popular between 1772 and 1792, was made by a number of makers including Tourte père, Edward and John Dodd of London, and the firms of Forster and Norris & Barnes.[24] It was, on the other hand, with Viotti that the bows of François Tourte were associated and it was the superb design of the Tourte bow which gave rise to modern bows and which facilitated modern virtuoso violin technique. It has been pointed out, too, that it is possible that John Dodd (1752–1839), a contemporary of Tourte, arrived at the design associated with Tourte at about the same time. Dodd's bows are not however of the same quality and are slightly shorter in length. A contemporary illustration suggests that Viotti may have used a Dodd bow.[25] The development of the bow-making industry in England is examined in more detail in Chapter 9.

Later Developments in the English Musical Scene

It is not the purpose of this book to attempt a detailed history of the development of English music from 1800. The relevance of the subject here is simply to indicate the likely demand for stringed instruments whether by rich amateurs, poor amateurs, or professionals at a particular time. There are, however, a few features which should be noted since they all influence the general interest in music or public or private provision for encouraging players through appropriate musical education.

The foundation of the Philharmonic Society in 1813 has already been mentioned. Professional musicians such as the veteran violinist William Dance, the brothers Henry Smart (leader of the orchestra of Drury Lane Theatre) and Sir

---

[24] See *Violin Family*, 210–11, with illustrations.   [25] Ibid. 214.

George Smart (organist and conductor), and Clementi were all associated with this, while Salomon led at the first violin desk. Viotti was content to play as a subordinate violinist, so great was his enthusiasm for the project.

In the context of the times, the Philharmonic Society's promotion of new works by Beethoven in particular was remarkable. But composers such as Spohr, Liszt, and Mendelssohn were also associated with the Society as composers or performers. In 1833 the Society found a home in the Hanover Square Rooms. However, as Percy Young remarks, although the attendance figures for concerts were very satisfactory there was an instinctive dislike of so much professionalism and the need for musicians actually to be paid was apparently accepted only with great reluctance. This attitude may have led to the founding in 1834 of a Society of British Musicians to encourage, in particular, compositions by English, rather than foreign composers.[26] In the nineteenth century this was to prove a very uphill task.

Music in the provinces tended to flower on the rich loam of the by now well-established oratorio tradition. Often conveniently coupled with collections for charities such as hospitals, many of the major cities in England held regular festivals. One example was the Birmingham Festival, started in 1768 and becoming established on a triennial basis. Funds were collected in aid of the General Hospital. The Leicester Festival dated from 1827, the Norwich and Norfolk Festival was put on a triennial basis in 1824, and the Yorkshire Musical Festival was founded in 1791. Manchester and Liverpool sponsored 'Gentlemen's Concerts' more reliant on local amateurs and professionals.[27]

Programmes which did not take place in churches tended to be designed for box-office appeal and to modern tastes seem absurdly frivolous. Normally singers predominated and popular arias or duets from light opera were punctuated with glees, perhaps a violin or piano concerto, and lighter chamber music. No systematic attempt can be discerned in the provinces to introduce the public to, for instance, the symphonies of Beethoven—though they did occasionally appear on an individual basis. But more typical were the *concerts monstres* at the Royal Zoological Gardens which attracted crowds of many thousands to a diet of quadrilles, polkas, and operatic arrangements. Tickets ranged from 1s. to 2s. 6d. for this type of event. However frivolous, public demand led automatically to an increase in the size of a symphony orchestra, particularly after 1850. As Cyril Ehrlich explains,[28] whereas Salomon had mustered forty players for Haydn which included twenty-eight strings, by 1900 a symphony orchestra of 100 players was required to play the works of such composers as Richard Strauss. In between these dates, from a contemporary programme relating to a concert in the Queen's Concert Rooms in Hanover Square on the morning of 24 April 1850, the personnel

---

[26] See Young, *The Concert Tradition*, 170–5.   [27] Ibid. 185–6.   [28] *Music Profession*, 60.

TABLE 2

Violins	E. Perry	Hatton	Clarionets
Sainton	Simmons	Hausman	Lazarus
(Principal)	Thirlwall	Lavenu	Boosé
H. G. Blagrove	Watkins	W. Loder	Bassoons
W. Blagrove	Watson	Lucas	Baumann
Bradley	Westrop	Phillips	Larkin
Betts	Wilkins	Contra-Bassi	Godfrey
Bezeth	Willy	Howell	Horns
Bort	Zerbini	(Principal)	C. Harper
Brown	Tenors	Campanile	Jarrett
Cusins	H. Hill	Casolani	Rae
Dando	(Principal)	Castell	Keilbach
Deloffre	R. Blagrove	Griffiths	Trumpets
Doyle	Glanville	Mount	Harper
Dunsford	Hann	Pratten	T. Harper
Griesbach	Lyon	Rowland	Handley
Goffrié	Thompson	C. Severn	Trombones
Hill	Trust	Vaudrelon	Cioffi
Jay	Webb	Wilson	Antoine
Kelly	Westlake	Flutes	Healey
J. Loder	Violoncellos	Ribas	Ophicleide
Marshall	Lindley	Card, Jun.	Prospere
Mellon	(Principal)	Oboes	Drums
N. Mori	Goodban	Barret	Chipp
Newsham	Guest	Cooke	Side Drums
Patey	Hancock	Nicholson	Horton
Payton			Seymour

of the 'entire Band of The Royal Italian Opera and the Philharmonic Concerts (Conductor—Mr. Costa)', is as given in Table 2.

From this list it will be seen that the orchestra included such well-known players as Prosper Sainton (principal violin),[29] Henry Blagrove and other members of his family, Henry Hill (principal tenor (or viola), see below), and Thomas Lindley (principal cello). The battery of eleven double basses compares well with the biggest symphony orchestra of today. The predominantly gut stringing of the violin family until quite recent times, as well as differences in tone-production, meant that less volume per player was produced in orchestras of this period. This factor does something to explain the apparently liberal number of players, particularly in the bass section. It is a pity that the concert programme itself consisted of the

---

[29] Sainton was born in Toulouse in 1813 and died in London in 1890, it being said about him that at the last Birmingham Festival before his death, every violinist in the orchestra had been either a direct pupil of Sainton's or a pupil of a pupil; see Van der Straeten, *History of the Violin*, ii. 180.

usual mixture of songs, piano solos, and a Corelli trio, on either side of Beethoven's 'Grand Symphony in C Minor' (i.e. the Fifth Symphony).

Henry Hill and his Circle

Henry Hill, whose name appears elsewhere in this book,[30] was a violist of particular interest to us here. This was because he was a member of the famous Hill family, namely the son of Henry Lockey Hill, the distinguished violin-maker, and uncle of W. H., A. F., and A. E. Hill, the authors of the work on Stradivari. He was born on 2 July 1808 in London and died there on 11 June 1856, after a busy career as orchestral player, chamber-music player, and, occasionally, soloist. He is perhaps best known for playing the solo viola part in *Harold in Italy*, Berlioz's 'Symphony', at its first London performance on 7 February 1848. The brief biographical details available from established texts such as Sandys and Forster suggest that he studied under various teachers but his proficiency on the viola was primarily a result of self-critical study alone. He was also a scholar of some note since he not only wrote some unpublished materials on violin-makers but also contributed analytical programme notes to the proceedings of the London Beethoven Quartett Society of which he was a founder member. He was in addition a member of Her Majesty's Private Band, and principal tenor (viola) at the Royal Italian Opera and the Philharmonic Concerts.

Perusal of an almost complete set of programmes covering Henry Hill's comparatively short professional life reveals intense activity on all these fronts, plus, inevitably, frequent engagements with *ad hoc* orchestras to accompany oratorio performances. His life must have been stressful by any standards. But it is Hill's contribution to the growth of public appreciation of chamber music that is particularly distinctive.

Chamber music (in the sense that we now understand that term) was not much performed publicly until 1831 when the Müller Brothers String Quartet began touring Europe after leaving service at the court of the Duke of Brunswick.[31] One would expect London and the provinces to be somewhat stony ground for this type of high artistic activity, particularly where most audiences were attracted to large-scale orchestral and vocal extravaganzas. But by 1841 we see Hill joining in the Sixth Season Quartett Concerts in the Hanover Square Rooms where vocal items were interspersed with Beethoven's Quartet in B Flat Major, Op. 18 No. 1, and Mozart's G Minor Quintet. Hill's fellow players were Messrs Blagrove, Dando, and Lucas. J. H. B. Dando (1806–94, an enterprising and able violinist) in

---

[30] See Ch. 9.
[31] See Percy A. Scholes, *Oxford Companion to Music* (10th edn.; London, 1970), s.v. 'Chamber Music IV'.

fact sponsored a number of seasons of quartet concerts in the late 1840s and 1850s, in which Hill participated, in Crosby Hall, Bishopsgate, London. Quartets by Mozart, Haydn, and Mendelssohn feature quite frequently, though again the pill apparently had to be sweetened by the interposition of vocal arias.

Hill's partners varied from concert to concert. An outstanding series sponsored by Mr Lucas (the cellist) at his residence, 54 Berners Street, in the mid-1840s consisted, besides Hill, of the violinists Sainton and Guynemer, and Lucas on the cello. A series of four chamber-music concerts cost a subscription of 2 guineas and consisted purely of chamber music of fine quality, including Beethoven's middle- and last-period works—which must have been extremely testing both for the players and for the audience. A similar series to that of Mr Lucas was M. Scipion Rousselout's Beethoven Quartett Society series at 76 Harley Street or other venues in London. This extremely enterprising series usually involved a team of Sainton, Cooper, Hill, and Piatti (see below), but 'visiting players' would sometimes be accommodated, Joseph Joachim leading at the concert on 12 July 1847, for example. Rousselout himself, being an able cellist, quite frequently took that part. Mr Lucas's series, in particular, at 54 Berners Street quite often included the performance of a then contemporary quartet or quintet, such as one of George Onslow's many quintets or a new quartet in manuscript by William Horsley (1774–1858).[32]

Another set of chamber-music concerts in which Hill took part were those in Willis's Rooms, King Street, St James's, London. It was to one of these series in about 1848 that the young H. R. Haweis, then about 10 years old, subscribed. He left a short but valuable description of the playing standards and atmosphere:

It now happily occurred to my father to subscribe to certain quartet concerts then announced to take place at Willis's Rooms. In those days such things were novelties. With the exception of Ella's Musical Union, then in its early days, I believe no public quartets had been given in London, except perhaps as a rare feature in some chamber concert.

Sainton and Piatti were then in their prime. I remember them as young men with their hair jet-black. My father wrote to M. Sainton and asked whether he could admit me as a child half-price. M. Sainton wrote back with the utmost politeness to say that to make such a reduction was not in accordance with their rule, but that under the circumstances he should be glad to conform to my father's wishes, especially as my father's sacred office—that of a clergyman—always inspired him with the greatest respect. Accordingly I went. There were amongst the choicest performances I heard in my boyhood. Nor, in some respects, have they ever been excelled in London since. What a quartet caste that was! Sainton, Hill, Piatti and Cooper. Sainton, full of fire, brilliancy, and delicacy. Cooper with more tone, and a depth and passion which sometimes gave him the advantage over his brilliant French rival; but at the end of each concert we were always left balancing the

---

[32] Described as No. 2 in D major, it was performed under the auspices of the Society of British Musicians at the Hanover Square Rooms on 11 Dec. 1848.

merits of the two violinists, I inclining at times to the Englishman's fervour and *abandon*, but won back by the Frenchman's finish and execution. In Spohr's violin duets each had an opportunity for the display of his peculiar gift. Each was on his mettle; each gave his own reading to the same phrases in turn, and this friendly artistic rivalry was to me intensely exciting. Hill was a splendid tenor, full, round, and smooth in tone; and of Piatti, prince of violoncellists, it is needless here to speak . . . But everyone at Willis's Rooms was appreciative. The players all seemed to feel the atmosphere sympathetic and genial. Everyone played heartily, and the artists were the very best that could be got.[33]

The Quartett Association's series ran from 1852 to 1855 when the project was abandoned for lack of support, but other chamber-music concerts were held there too.[34] Ella's Musical Union had more snob appeal and ran from 1845 to 1880 with eight afternoon concerts per annum.

Hill, whose 'splendid tenor, full, round, and smooth in tone' is commented on by Haweis, no doubt had the run of a variety of valuable instruments from his family firm. His usual viola was, however, an 'incomparable instrument' (in the words of Hector Berlioz) by the English maker Barak Norman.[35] Haweis refers again to Henry Hill in his book on *Old Violins*[36] thus: 'Henry distinguished himself as an admirable quartet player, and well do I remember the splendid tone of his Barak Norman tenor as far back as I think 1848, when with Sainton, Piatti and Cooper—one of the best, as it was almost the earliest string quartet cast in London—he assisted in delighting and educating a select public in the mysteries of chamber music'.

It is a great pity that Hill's 'manuscript collections towards the history of the violin' were never published. Sandys and Forster[37] comment that 'he does not in general give any authorities, and his dates and names are in several cases doubtful; but his anecdotes and particular descriptions may probably be depended on'. These materials were obviously available to Sandys and Forster who occasionally refer to them, particularly in the context of classical Italian instruments. There is one longer quotation from his work, alluding to William Forster II, which makes one suspect that these materials were more useful to Sandys and Forster than they were prepared to admit. They must certainly have agreed with his views on the cellos of William Forster senior. Hill writes that Forster was

a highly justly esteemed maker of violoncellos, etc; it is said he was not originally bred to the occupation, but came to it by chance or accidental preference; if so, he must have possessed a rare talent for his instruments are second to none, but the best Europe has ever

---

[33] Haweis, *My Musical Life*, 23.
[34] See Robert Elkin, *The Old Concert Rooms of London* (London, 1955).
[35] See *New Grove Dictionary of Musical Instruments* (London, 1984), 221 (the material attributed to Arthur F. Hill), and Ch. 5 of this book. Hill certainly also owned an Amati, previously the property of Dragonetti and Alsager (a founder of the Beethoven Quartett Society); see *Violin Times* (1894), 36.
[36] p. 138.
[37] *History*, 198.

known; especially his *amber coloured violoncellos*; they are renowned for mellowness, a volume and power of tone, equalled by few, surpassed by none. His dark red coloured are not so much admired, though the different in merit is scarcely discernible. He was not so successful with his violins and altos; he does not appear to have given the same care and judgment to their production; he followed the grand Amati in his forms and model without being a mere copyist, and had a rare excellence in the facture of the violoncello particularly his own. The expression—*a true Forster tone*—is not a *jeux d'esprit* [sic].[38]

This almost contemporary assessment of Forster's instruments reinforces the opinion that in Hill's playing days Forster cellos, in particular, continued to be extremely highly regarded. Morris and other writers such as George Hart infer that Forster had a talent for marketing rare in the violin-maker's trade, and later on in the nineteenth century Forster's instruments became less expensive than in his lifetime, Italians or cellos of Banks or Duke being preferred. A contemporary judgement might be that a good specimen of an 'Old Forster' cello would be amongst the most valuable of any English string instruments. One was sold at Phillips in April 1991 (Lot 207) for £24,200 (1782).

Money and Numbers

How much were players of this time paid? Percy Young gives the figures for the Chester Music Festival of 1814.[39] Singers scooped the pool, the solo soprano being paid £420 out of the total singing bill of £1,508. The conductor, Greatorex, earned £105, £251 was paid to violinists, £72 to Tenors (violas), £108 to cellos, and £91 to double basses. With wind and percussion added the total orchestral bill was £931.

Cyril Ehrlich has ascertained that in 1821 front-desk strings of the Philharmonic Society received £52. 10s. for ten rehearsals and eight concerts. In the opera orchestra these generally ranged from three to five guineas and in the provinces fees were similar.[40] Ehrlich also estimates that very successful and distinguished solo players such as Dragonetti at the peak of his career made about £1,000 per year, about the same as a 'modestly capable physician'. Other leading instruments might have made £500 in a good year. Routine instrumentalists made much less than this and would have had to supplement their income by teaching.[41] Henry Hill's contract of January 1850, discussed further in Chapter 6, is for £17 for a series of Philharmonic Society Concerts in the Hanover Square Rooms (eight concerts, each preceded by a rehearsal)—a little over £2 per complete session, inclusive of 'Two Trials, should they be required'. Against these earnings it is instructive to compare the prices asked for their instruments by contemporary makers, as dis-

[38] See Sandys and Forster, *History*, 323–4.   [39] *History*, 428.   [40] Ehrlich, *Music Profession*, 49.
[41] Ibid.

cussed in Chapter 5, £10 for a violin and £20 for a good cello not being out of the way.

Cyril Ehrlich has also investigated the statistics of known professional musicians. He traces a huge increase in their numbers between 1870 and 1930. In 1840 there were approximately 7,000 musicians at work amongst the general population of 27 million. By 1930 the numbers had risen to 50,000 musicians throughout Britain and Ireland out of nearly 50 million people. In 1910 at least 1,017 violinists and 245 cellists can be identified though these are necessarily minimum totals of musicians. It is also clear from the census for England and Wales in 1851 that there were more male than female music teachers (2,800 as against 2,300), though by 1861 the position had been reversed; there were 3,100 women and 2,400 males.[42]

What are the reasons for this increase in the number of performers? It is clearly not linked with the unexciting production of compositions by English composers—a depressing factor which has tended to obscure the underlying vigour of the general musical scene. Even in the case of home-grown oratorios, quantity was the key, not quality. It was this lack of quality and the seeming national indifference to large parts of the symphonic, operatic, and chamber-music repertoire which caused a German critic to label England 'Das Land ohne Musik'. But the Victorian oratorio, long since buried, and although often dreary, religiose, insipid, uninspired, derivative, and generally lacking in profundity, was almost always scored for a large orchestra. Players were needed in relative abundance.

If English composers of this period failed, with rare exceptions, to produce works of any lasting value, English audiences were happy for their festivals to be spiced with the work of the great Continental composers, particularly Mendelssohn. And whether it was Mendelssohn or Handel, there were no inhibitions about using a large orchestra. The idea of reproducing original performing conditions would have been regarded as ludicrous, flying in the face of 'progress'.

Lowell Mason gives an account, as a visiting American musician, of some of the events in the Birmingham Festival of 1852. It had been for this festival that Mendelssohn had written his oratorio *Elijah* for production in 1846. In 1852 Mason was to state that a better band and chorus were brought together than on any previous occasion. There were 26 first violins, 26 second violins, 18 tenors, 18 cellos, and 18 double basses, plus a full complement of wind (including 1 ophicleide and 2 serpents) and percussion—in all 140 instruments. This excluded the great organ, which he described as one of the most powerful in the world.[43] Mason spends most of his letter in describing the qualities of the solo singers and chorus but he undoubtedly found the well-rehearsed 'band' impressive.

---

[42] Ibid. 53 and Table 1.
[43] This was in the Town Hall in the centre of Birmingham. It was used for City of Birmingham Symphony Orchestra concerts until the recent opening of the Symphony Hall in Broad Street.

When the same forces tackled Handel's *Messiah* under the baton of Mr Costa,[44] Mason described the precise effect of its commencement:

Think of the fugue led off by 26 violins, and answered by as many more; think of the roar of 36 violoncellos and double basses, and the coming in of the other instruments; imagine every point to be taken up with the most perfect accuracy, and the subject carried on without the slightest wavering or doubtfulness! It was a fugue indeed.[45]

Another factor in the creation of demand for players was the increasing prosperity of the country as a whole and the facilitation of travel by the development of the railway system. Seaside towns had their theatres and music-halls galore. Even though concerts were likely to centre around the presence of an eminent solo singer (such as Jenny Lind who in 1847 was paid in Brighton £500 for a single concert), supporting orchestras were needed. Later in the century operetta in general, and the inspired creativity of Gilbert and Sullivan in particular, encouraged the widespread development of amateur operatic societies whose productions could be greatly enhanced by a small professional, or perhaps mixed, orchestral band. If the casualty of all this was the development of anything approaching the serious musical attitude of composers and audiences in, particularly, Germany and Austria, and to some extent St Petersburg and Paris, string-players were still needed to satisfy public demand, however undiscriminating.

J. T. Carrodus

The most eminent native violinist of the late Victorian era was probably John Tiplady Carrodus, who was born in Yorkshire in 1836 and died in London in 1895. Carrodus was 'spotted' by the conductor Costa who was, as Carrodus remarks, 'the most thoroughly competent conductor under whom I have played'.[46] Carrodus combined a busy career as an orchestral leader with that of soloist and recitalist. Van der Straeten says that he remembers 'a remarkably fine performance by him of Bach's Ciaconna, at the Old St. James's Hall, remarkable for his powerful tone, perfect technique and purity of intonation'.[47] Carrodus himself states that 'in 1881 I gave a violin recital at St. James's Hall, interesting publicly, because it was the first violin *Recital* which had ever been given. I was the sole performer, being assisted only by an accompanist.'[48] Many of his recollections in his book are concerned

---

[44] Sir Michael Costa (b. Naples 1806, d. Brighton 1884) was one of the leading oratorio composers and perhaps the leading choral and orchestral conductor in England during this period.
[45] Lowell Mason, *Musical Letters from Abroad* (New York, 1854; repr. 1967), 230.
[46] J. T. Carrodus, *How to Study the Violin* (London, 1895), 41.
[47] *History of the Violin*, 299.
[48] Carrodus, *How to Study*, 49.

with the events of the various Three Choirs Festivals in which he played an important role as leader, soloist, and chamber-music player—'the work', he writes, 'is extremely arduous and the positions of importance are full of anxious responsibility'.[49] In the Hereford Festival of 1894 the Orchestra included his five sons, two of whom played violins and the others cello, double bass, and flute.

Carrodus's name was sufficiently well known for him to lend it to a brand of French trade violins marketed in London for Haynes & Co. between 1887 and 1910. But it is interesting to see what his own choice of instrument was, since it reflects English 'fashionable' thinking amongst the leading players of the time. Carrodus started his professional career with a Nicolò Amati which he described as 'a very splendid specimen of his work'. But in his later years he played a Guarneri del Gesù (one which Carrodus believed to have been gambled away by Paganini), and by his death Carrodus had acquired a second such Guarneri.[50]

Proselytizers and Institutions

Education played an important part in the increasing popularity of the violin family. A few leading pioneers, such as the Revd H. R. Haweis, had a strong belief in the improving qualities of music. This view is particularly expounded in his *Music and Morals* (1873) and *My Musical Life* (1884), both being books of immense influence at the time. As it happened Haweis was a talented and enthusiastic violinist whose writings on the violin did much both to popularize the intrinsic interest of the violin as an object of craftsmanship and to remove any stigma which was thought still to adhere to the playing of it. His views now appear pietistic and eccentric, but there is no doubt that he was extremely influential at the time, along with other well known mid-Victorian writers such as Charles Reade, as a catalyst in the process of the growth of interest and demand in the stringed-instrument world. Furthermore, though it is easy to scoff, the study and performance of good music has long been recognized educationally as imposing a strict discipline without stifling creativity, an ideal and arguably unique combination of qualities.

Institutionally the Royal Academy of Music in London started in an under-resourced way in 1822 and its achievements were disappointing.[51] Although eminent professional players were advertised as being associated with the teaching, this was in practice done by far humbler musicians and the Academy seemed incapable of insisting upon proper standards either among its staff or its pupils. For instance, several pianists were expected to practice *together* in the same room, and presumably a similar cacophony prevailed in violin practising. This was thought to

[49] Ibid. 92. [50] Ibid. 54, 56–9. [51] See Ehrlich, *Music Profession*, 80.

be an aid to the development of concentration![52] The Royal College of Music inherited the assets of the former National Training School in 1882. But that too produced a disappointing list of alumni and a lack of ability to invoke official support in terms of funds.[53]

Schools and Strings

At the lower level, musical education in schools in the greater part of the nineteenth century was either non-existent or, where a bow was made in music's direction, not designed to provide the country with distinguished instrumentalists. Admittedly there were important enthusiasts such as John Hullah who had particularly enlightened views. He saw the easiest entrée into serious music for the English schoolboy or schoolgirl to be through the tonic sol-fa system, with a heavy emphasis on the importance of singing and choral music. He accurately identified the philistinism rife amongst opinion-formers, inclined actually to boast of their musical ignorance. The practice of music tended to be regarded as an effeminate pursuit incompatible with prowess on the rugby field or cricket pitch. Nor was there any great tradition in previous centuries to which to appeal since, as we have seen, performing standards were largely dominated by 'foreigners' from whom eccentric behaviour was to be expected. Van der Straeten makes the same sort of point to explain the lack of eminent native cellists up to about 1850:

> The English nation is essentially a sporting nation, and sports and arts have very little in common with each other. During the early part of the eighteenth century, and even beyond the fifties, it was considered a sign of an effeminacy if a young gentleman employed part of his time in learning to play a musical instrument. This has vastly changed during the last fifty years, but it accounts for a numerically poor list of virtuosos on any musical instrument during that earlier period.[54]

In fact Hullah's emphasis on singing and particularly the development of singing at sight (albeit with a flawed system) was an undoubtedly beneficent influence on the philistinism prevailing at this time. A few private schools were enterprising enough to employ an inspirational director of music, of whom the most outstanding example was undoubtedly Paul David (1840–1932), for forty years the music master of Uppingham School. Paul David was the son of Ferdinand David who as a violinist gave the first public performance of Mendelssohn's Violin Concerto. Paul David was fortunate in finding an extremely enlightened headmas-

---

[52] See Percy A. Scholes, *The Mirror of Music 1844–1944* (London, 1947), 694; Ehrlich, *Music Profession*, 85.

[53] See the discussion in Ehrlich, *Music Profession*, ch. v.

[54] Van der Straeten, *Violoncello*, i. 309.

ter, Edward Thring, who despite being reputed to be tone-deaf believed in 'the refining and elevating influence of music'.[55] More typical was the experience of Joseph Barnby who on becoming precentor at Eton in 1865 was disappointed to find 'that these young patricians had by no means the natural ability that was to be found in the lower strata of life'. He estimated that hardly thirty per cent had the 'faintest notion of sound', whereas at least 70 per cent of the 'lower orders' were attributed with this quality.[56]

Matters did improve somewhat over the years when directors of public schools' music implemented the idea of treating music in the same way as the major sports and encouraged interest by running house competitions. The House Competition programmes at Eton in 1925 reveal considerable talent on the keyboard on the part of the boys (such works as Bach's Organ Prelude and Fugue in E Minor and the last (and difficult) movement of Beethoven's 'Moonlight' Sonata figuring amongst the many items played). However, the programmes for that year reveal no solo string pieces other than a number for the violin of a comparatively elementary character. Programmes of other major schools such as Clifton and Rugby also suggest a similar unevenly distributed pattern.[57]

If house music competitions exalted the soloist, usually a keyboard player as we have seen, school orchestras at least gave string pupils a chance of ensemble playing. The *Musical Times* first notices a concert by the Marlborough College Orchestral Society in 1893: 'the first school that has essayed the performance of symphonic music by a full orchestra'. Robert Berndt conducted them in Beethoven's *Egmont* Overture and Schubert's 'Unfinished' Symphony. The *Musical Times* expresses pleasure that 'the sons of the classes' were thus 'inoculated' with 'a taste for what is noble and exalted in music at an age when games and the grub shop too often occupy their entire leisure'.[58]

These fee-paying schools, along with the older grammar schools or cathedral schools to which cathedral choirs were attached, produced, certainly after the First World War, distinguished generations of organists. The organ was after all a necessary accompaniment to compulsory chapel and requires for its mastery very considerable concentration, physical co-ordination, and mental agility—admirable educational skills. And even within the author's memory, which centres on music at Clifton College in the years following the Second World War, it was undoubtedly keyboard playing that attracted the major talent.

There were a few individual string-players of merit (violins in the main, one or two cellos, and zero violas), but they tended not to get the major music scholarships, perhaps because such players were inherently rarer birds. The fundamental

[55] Scholes, *Mirror*, 627.
[56] Ehrlich, *Music Profession*, 72.
[57] See A. H. Peppin, *Public Schools and their Music* (Oxford, 1927).
[58] Cited in Scholes, *Mirror*, 627.

reason for this relative scarcity was that the choir schools or outstandingly musical primary schools from which the boys were chosen tended to lack suitable specialist teachers except on the keyboard. The teaching of stringed instruments, often by part-time staff, rarely rose above the routine. Skill on the keyboard was also a far more useful accomplishment for a choirboy to attain, particularly if he wished to continue his career in church music, or obtain an organ scholarship to one of the colleges of Oxford or Cambridge. Now, at New College, Oxford, for example, it is understood that boys are encouraged to learn keyboard and one other instrument, strings being preferred, for technical (breathing) reasons, to wind instruments.

The impression given at these boys' schools in the era immediately before and after the Second World War was that to the non-performer whose interests outside the academic syllabus centred more naturally on the sports fields, the best introduction to music was the vocal contribution to the annual performance of one of the great choral classics such as Bach's B minor Mass or one of Handel's oratorios.

Private Girls' Schools, where one might have expected a more sympathetic environment for string-playing development, seem primarily to have concentrated on singing. The *Musical Times* in 1890 comments on some 3,000 girls singing 'a meagre and somewhat sombre programme of unison songs'.[59]

At about this time, the distinguished musicologist and gifted violinist the Revd E. H. Fellowes was looked at askance by his collateral relatives when he showed a strong interest in music. His parents were enlightened enough to give him an Amati violin (price £100 with a Tourte bow in 1879), and the author remembers Fellowes playing the Brahms A major Sonata at St Michael's College, Tenbury (of which Fellowes was the Honorary Librarian) in the late 1940s on this instrument. But at school Fellowes had been forced to abandon music in term-time and could practise only in the holidays.[60] (The author also remembers the same Edmund Fellowes performing the 'Tallis Canon' by both singing and humming this canonic tune in canon—an astonishing accomplishment which he said at the time was regarded as a routine exercise by his own contemporaries when he was a boy chorister! If so, our assumptions about rising musical standards may be misplaced.)

The peculiarities of the privately educated classes probably present an untypical picture of interest in music in the country as a whole. John Hullah, already mentioned, was able to carry his proselytizing, at least for vocal music, more directly into the state schools when he was appointed a Government Inspector of Music in Schools for the United Kingdom in 1872. He was succeeded to his upgraded post by no less than John Stainer who became Inspector of Music in the elementary schools of England. The focus was on song, especially if the words were suitably

[59] Cited in Scholes, *Mirror*, 628.   [60] Ehrlich, *Music Profession*, 71–2.

patriotic or 'healthy'. Instrumental music was very much less welcomed. In the context of the public provision of school pianos the *St James Gazette* of 1890 enquired 'What must be the feelings of the middle-class householder when he is asked to take money out of his ill-lined pocket in order that the children of the "poor" may be taught to dance and sing under the auspices of smug philanthropists?'[61]

Music of the People

At the post-school or university level choral and operatic societies in the late nineteenth century and beyond provided many enthusiastic amateurs with an opportunity to absorb at least part of the then standard repertoire. In the middle of the nineteenth century a number of Mechanics' Institutes (in part predecessors of the modern Colleges of Further Education) held evening meetings where lectures on music for adults were promoted or vocal and instrumental tuition was given. Military bands had been established at least since the time of Charles II and throughout the succeeding century the better bands obtained the services of distinguished foreign musicians, such as Sir William Herschel (the great astronomer), to train them. The more popular movement associated with the growth of brass bands was probably not a direct offshoot of these military bands, though it must have been the case that many players obtained their early experience on their instrument whilst in military training. In the nineteenth century brass bands were associated with industrial towns, factory owners often encouraging music-making amongst their employees.[62]

Mackerness in his *Social History of English Music* dates the development of the brass band as a distinct feature of working-class life from about 1840. It was facilitated by the rapid growth of the railway system and improvements to the design of brass instruments which made them easier to play (for example the invention of the valve or piston).[63] Demand for brass instruments had an important economic effect in the retail trade, since it provided a broader base than simply the piano or stringed instruments for a successful retailing operation, such as that of the renowned Boosey and Hawkes in London (founded as a publishing house by Boosey in 1816). This firm's contribution to the supply of stringed instruments was based primarily on the mass importation of cheap but good-quality French work.

The most popular instrument for home use was undoubtedly the piano which from 'cottage' to grand became widely dispersed in British homes. Cyril Ehrlich estimates that by the early years of the twentieth century sales of new pianos per

[61] Young, *History*, 500.   [62] See Mackerness, *Social History*, 166.   [63] Ibid. 166.

head were three times higher than in 1850, and ownership of playable instruments may have been as much as one for every ten people. It was the piano which was the subject of the first hire-purchase case when the courts gave their blessing to a system which allowed a purchaser to pay for his or her instrument by instalments over, typically, three years without the seller losing his inherent security.[64] If a musical instrument figured at all in a nineteenth-century novel, it was likely to be a feminine character delighting her house guests with her expertise on the keyboard.[65]

Producing the Players

None of this begins to explain how within Great Britain during the nineteenth century violinists at least of the standard to maintain an orchestral part were produced. A few outstanding players such as Henry Blagrove (1811–72) had the determination and means to study privately with such eminent teachers as Spohr in Germany. The violin in particular seems to exert an irrepressible influence on those who succumb to its charms at an early age. These players, often because of unusually enlightened parents or other close relatives (as in the case of the Revds Haweis and Fellowes, both mentioned above), were provided with the tuition at an early age which they needed. Although the achievements of the Royal College of Music (founded 1882, formerly the National Training School for Music) and the Royal Academy were disappointing, they produced at least some players of competence. The number of such products increased with the founding of new music schools in London such as the Guildhall School of Music (1880) under the auspices of the able administrator and eminent violinist T. H. Weist Hill (1828–91) and Trinity College (1874).

Women and the Violin

A major new factor in the latter part of the nineteenth century was the growing social acceptance of the violin as a suitable instrument for women. Previously only the harp and the piano had generally been thought to be respectable. Before the 1850s 'no young lady ever thought of learning it or carrying a violin case about in the streets'.[66] A pervasive influence was undoubtedly the distinguished soloist

---

[64] See Ehrlich, *Music Profession*, 102 and the same author's *The Piano*. The case was *Helby* v. *Matthews* (1895) AC 471 (House of Lords) which involved a hiring agreement with a nominal option to purchase.

[65] See Ch. 6 for some exceptions.
[66] Ehrlich, *Music Profession*, 157, quoting from W. Ganz, *Memoirs of a Musician* (1913).

Wilma Neruda, from a Czechoslovakian family of musicians, who maintained her distinguished career as a soloist in England as Lady Hallé.[67] Ehrlich points out that by the 1890s Emile Sauret presided over a large violin class, well patronised by females, at the Academy where there was 'a perfect craze for learning the fiddle'.[68] Also influential was Marie Hall, born in Newcastle upon Tyne in 1884, the daughter of an impecunious harpist and violinist, who attracted the attention both of the violin-maker Walter Mayson (discussed subsequently) and of Elgar, who taught her for about a year. She subsequently studied under Max Mossel in Birmingham and Ševčík where, as Van der Straeten states 'she made such rapid progress that in 1902 she was ranked among the first virtuosos'.[69] She owned a fine Strad and played enterprising programmes including works by such English composers as Vaughan Williams and Rutland Boughton.

The cause of lady cellists was also particularly well served by the career of Beatrice Harrison who made her debut at 14½ years in the Queen's Hall in 1907. Not only was she a fine exponent of contemporary English composers (she introduced the Cello Concerto of Delius), but coming obviously from an elegant upper-middle-class background she set an important example of how women could master an instrument already socially acceptable (as we have seen above). Her sister, the violinist May Harrison, was equally distinguished and Delius had their playing in mind when writing his Double Concerto.[70]

Although a concert at the Royal Academy in 1893 which included eighty violinists playing Handel's Largo in unison might be a more typical indication of average achievement, it nevertheless became apparent by this time that women were becoming an increasingly formidable professional force in music in general and stringed-instrument playing in particular. They inevitably met male chauvinist opposition. They lacked 'firmness of attack' or 'power of tone'. A woman's weakness was thought to be inescapable because, 'according to physiologists, there is one muscle entirely absent from the female arm'![71] Perhaps the real reason was resentment that they were seen to be taking jobs from men with families to support. Furthermore, it was suggested that the rough language used in music-halls and theatres was unsuitable for refined and sensitive girls. But this did not stop women starting exclusively female string orchestras—Ehrlich mentions the Aeolian, Miss Clay's, Miss Grave's, Mrs Hunt's, and Madam Marie Levante's Ladies' Orchestras as advertising their services in 1899. He even notes a 'Royal Naval Ladies' Orchestra' operating in 1911.[72]

---

[67] She became the second wife of Sir Charles Hallé who founded the Hallé Orchestra in 1957. She was known as Mme Norman-Neruda.
[68] Ehrlich, *Music Profession*, 157.
[69] Van der Straeten, *History of the Violin*, 310.
[70] See T. Potter, 'May Harrison', *Strad* (Aug. 1990), 628; and on Beatrice, Patricia Cleveland-Peck, 'The Lady of the Nightingales', *Strad* (Nov. 1992), 1174; discography, ibid. 1178.
[71] Cited in Ehrlich, *Music Profession*, 158.
[72] Ibid. 159.

The Provincial Colleges

The aspiring provincial violinist was likely to be able to find a suitable neighbourhood conservatoire or an extra-mural award-conferring institution as the nineteenth century progressed. For instance, the Birmingham and Midland Institute School of Music was founded in 1886, the Huddersfield College of Music in 1887, the College of Violinists (a London extra-mural diploma-awarding institution with which such celebrities as Pablo Sarasate (Patron), Heron-Allen, and Albert Sammons were associated) in 1889, the prestigious Royal Manchester College of Music in 1893, and the City of Leeds School of Music in 1898. For the amateur, Rural Music Schools were established in 1929 with the object of developing musical activity in villages and small towns. Students were encouraged to become useful members of choirs, orchestras, quartets, and music clubs. Starting in Hertfordshire they spread through the whole country under the auspices of a National Council.[73]

Enthusiasm and Poverty

By 1920 censuses reveal something of a high-water mark of 1,319 violinists and violists, 340 cellists, 235 double bassists, and 5,546 music teachers in London.

Unfortunately, although composers such as Stanford, Parry, and (particularly) Elgar succeeded in writing music of which educated English people could legitimately be proud, pay and rations for musicians remained miserably small. In 1926 orchestras in Manchester, Bournemouth, Birmingham, Eastbourne, Hastings, Glasgow, and Edinburgh were all running at a loss.[74] Nor could any British orchestra compare in playing standards with the great German orchestras, as a visit in 1927 by the Berlin Philharmonic under Furtwängler showed only too clearly. Players supplemented their income by teaching or playing in more than one orchestra, making use of a deputy system. This made training an orchestra much more difficult since its personnel were constantly changing. But despite all these problems enthusiasm to learn stringed instruments never waned, helped as it was by the plentiful supply of cheap instruments from France and Germany. The handcrafted products of the increasingly successful English school of violin-makers (from about 1870 onwards) tended to find their purchasers amongst seasoned players, whether professional or the enthusiastic amateur.

---

[73] Scholes, *Mirror*, 633.   [74] Ehrlich, *Music Profession*, 207.

Modern Times

Recent decades have seen an unparalleled increase in enthusiasm for, and standards, in string-playing. The foundation of the National Youth Orchestra in 1947 by Dame Ruth Railton was undoubtedly of fundamental importance, not least because that orchestra became the cradle for many future professional orchestral or chamber-music players. There were also several specialist music schools founded since 1945, Chetham's in Manchester, the Purcell School, Wells Cathedral School, and the Yehudi Menuhin School being amongst the best known. England began to produce soloists of international calibre such as Jacqueline du Pré and Nigel Kennedy.

The private sector of education can only attract the musical offspring of impecunious parents by awarding realistic scholarships. The abiding importance of England's virtually unique choir-school tradition (where boy choristers often get full or substantial fee remission and free instrumental tuition) should not be overlooked. Paradoxically, the reputation of the country's finest collegiate and cathedral choirs is apparently better appreciated abroad than in Britain itself. Their records have a huge international market. The carol service from King's College, Cambridge was broadcast in 1992 to an estimated 190 million listeners and viewers world-wide. The best choirs perform work of often formidable difficulty, contemporary composers making no concessions to a treble line consisting of 8–13-year-olds. It is not surprising that a significant number of these choristers go on to become professional musicians, whether as composers, conductors, keyboard players, singers, or solo and orchestral instrument players.

In the state system of education many counties established County Youth Orchestras, playing to standards undreamed of in earlier years. Music now has its place in the National Curriculum but there remain worries as to whether central government will make available sufficient resources to enable standards of instrumental playing to be maintained. As a counterbalance to political indifference (as some perceive it) charities such as Music for Youth have for many years striven to keep music alive in schools, and MFY organizes (with the help of commercial sponsorship) the annual Schools Prom in the Albert Hall. Cultivation of the concert-going habit, largely confined to middle-aged middle-class listeners, has to be broadened. Simon Rattle and his CBSO, for example, make time to go into schools and encourage children, through creative work with them, to make the quantum leap from Madonna to the *Rite of Spring* with apparent success.

Statistics relating to the taking of graded performance examinations in the UK provide some guidance on the current likely demand for stringed instruments. The present position is indicated by the figures supplied by the Associated Board of the

Royal Schools of Music. The total numbers of UK candidates who have taken the Associated Board's exams in violin were as follows: 1970: 16,434; 1980: 36,071; 1990: 36,746.[75]

But there remains a less positive side. Sir Thomas Armstrong, writing in *The Times*,[76] whilst welcoming the achievements of many youth orchestras in Great Britain, points out that in a school of 1,000 pupils under a music director keen on conducting, less than 100 pupils might be influenced by the activity of the orchestra. He agrees with Professor Alexander Goehr's suggestion that other pupils regard those who play in the orchestra as 'a select and effete minority'. It is these remaining 900 who sadly remain unawakened musically. Sir Thomas points out that Zoltán Kodály set about reorganizing or creating musical education in Hungary beginning with village schools and relying on the human voice and the national heritage of folksong.[77]

It is certainly true that the current scene in England is confusing. On the one hand, youth orchestras seem to be maintaining extraordinarily high standards of playing in all departments. On the other hand there is concern about a perceived general diminution in state musical education, mainly for financial reasons, and much concern by leading professional musicians in the country that this could result in markedly reduced standards and enthusiasm. And whilst electronics and broadcasting have brought the opportunity for all to listen to fine music, the insidious 'pop culture' exerts a stultifying influence in the opposite direction which should not be underestimated. The 'classical violin' has no place in this alternative scheme of things. Much will depend on schools' and parents' ability to encourage children to apply themselves to the time-consuming, and for some years comparatively unrewarding, discipline of learning to play a bowed string instrument. The violin family has never yielded its secrets easily, but once communion between instrument and player is established an investment of great richness is made for life.

[75] Cited in *The Times*, 11 Feb., 1992.
[76] 14 Mar. 1992.

[77] Percy Young, himself a leading educationalist, suggested to the author that the Armstrong–Goehr views above were unduly pessimistic.

Chapter Eight

❦ The Violin and its Votaries in Wales, Scotland, and Ireland

Introduction — Wales — Scottish Violin-Makers: Cultural Background — Scottish Violin Writers — Ireland — Thomas Perry

Introduction

CORRECTLY speaking, the expressions 'English' and 'England' in the context of this book mean England as a geographical part of the United Kingdom of England, Wales, Scotland, and Northern Ireland ('the UK'). Because the Act of Union of England and Wales united Wales with England in the sense that the two areas share a single legal system, it is customary to bracket Wales with England when discussing English law, though Wales has its own language, identity, and culture which needs to be recognized in a work of this type. The expression 'Great Britain' or 'British' should refer to the island comprising England, Scotland, and Wales. The 'British Isles' as a geographical expression usually includes the whole island of Ireland (divided constitutionally in 1920 between the Republic of Ireland, an independent state, and Northern Ireland, part of the UK), the Channel Islands, and the Isle of Man.

Despite these legal proprieties, many an Irishman, Scot, or Welshman has been affronted by being indiscriminately classified as 'English' in foreign passport-inspection areas and the like, and outside the UK the word 'English' is not infrequently used as conterminous with 'British' in its broader sense. Vannes's *Dictionnaire Universel des Luthiers* (Brussels, 1988 edition) is a particularly bad offender in this respect. Meredith Morris, the Welsh writer discussed below, is described as 'écrivain anglais', the Irish maker (conceivably of French origin) maker Thomas Perry is described as 'considéré comme un des premiers luthiers de l'école anglaise', and the 'Scottish Stradivari' Matthew Hardie is 'considéré comme un des meilleurs luthiers anglais'. It must be added, though, that the three-volume dictionary of violin-makers by von Lütgendorff is much more scrupulous.

So whilst this book could legitimately confine itself to makers within England, or even London, alone, this would cut off important parts of the whole picture. For one thing, a few English makers spent part of their working lives in, for instance, Edinburgh or Dublin. Thus Urquhart, before settling at London Bridge, is supposed to have come from Edinburgh to London at the invitation of Charles II (at least according to William Honeyman). In the reverse direction, the interesting and little-known maker John Grice indicates on his label (according to Henley) that he moved from London to Edinburgh where he flourished *c*.1725. As already mentioned, he appears to have been another of the small group of makers at this time whose model was influenced by Stradivari. Tobin, born in Ireland *c*.1777, was associated with Perry of Dublin in his early years. The Sicilian Vincenzo Panormo is known to have worked for a short time in Dublin (and, it seems, Cork) before settling in London in 1789, assisting John Betts and others there. His instruments, though not in any real sense English and usually unlabelled, are important as exemplars of a more Italian style than was the norm in London at this time. John Dilworth sees a connection between Panormo, fleeing the French Revolution to the atelier of Perry (probably related to Claude Pierray, the Parisian violin-maker), and Perry's contemporary apprentice, Richard Tobin.[1]

Writers on the violin form an interesting study in themselves, and as will be seen below Wales and Scotland have produced important authors in this field.

Makers in Scotland, in terms purely of a biographical list of them, have been well served by William Honeyman's *Scottish Violin Makers: Past and Present* (Dundee, 1910) (amongst others), but a brief review of a few outstanding features of the Scottish violin-playing, collecting, and making tradition is included here since it is in some respects similar to and in others divergent from the English tradition. Ireland's position, whilst not dissimilar from Scotland's, really requires its own monograph, but again one or two outstanding features are mentioned. Wales, besides for centuries being closely linked economically and constitutionally with England, lacks the complexities of Scotland or Ireland in this field, and it is appropriate to start with that Principality.

Wales

In chronological terms, Wales is associated historically with the crwth, a precursor of the violin. Much debate has centred around the question whether the crwth could be regarded as a true ancestor of the violin and, if so, how it got to Wales. Heron-Allen, one of the earlier writers on this topic, states that

---

[1] John Dilworth, 'Alcoholic Anonymous', *Strad* (May 1987) 45. There is evidence from labels that V. Panormo also worked in Cork; see John Teahan, 'A List of Irish Instrument Makers', Galpin Society Journal, 16 (1962), 28.

the Romans, colonising the north-western part of Europe introduced their lyres, where in due course the use of the bow superseded that of the plectrum, the lyre becoming the rotta, and subsequently the crwth or chrotta. Meanwhile the Moors from Spain . . . drove the crwth before them, till it had to take refuge among the aborigines or earlier inhabitants of the north-west, lingering on till it died a natural death in the wilds of Cambria [i.e. Wales] (which, as we know, has remained more exclusively Celtic than any other part of the continent), until the last century.[2]

Heron-Allen's views may or may not represent those of modern scholars, who are driven to admit that the subject of the crwth is still replete with uncertainty. Joan Rimmer in the article on the crwth in *New Grove Dictionary of Musical Instruments* refers to comparable instruments surviving into the twentieth century in the Baltic area, particularly Karelia, Estonia, and Sweden. The crwth was originally three-stringed before becoming double-coursed, with putative tuning of $g'-g''-c'-c'-d'-d''$, the top string being as tightly drawn as possible without breaking and the Gs being off the fingerboard, plucked with the thumb.[3]

Heron-Allen also reproduces and describes[4] an example of the Welsh crwth in the South Kensington Museum (since 1900, the Victoria and Albert Museum). This is probably a later copy of the 1742 specimen in the Welsh Folk Museum, St Fagans, Cardiff. It is of (approximately) rectangular shape and is described as being formed of one solid block of sycamore wood—except the belly, which is of pine and glued on. The bridge is flat and curiously formed, one foot passing through the left soundhole to the back, and thus serving as a soundpost; it is set obliquely on the belly. Its dimensions are: length 22 in. (558 mm), width 9½ in. (241 mm), depth 2 in. (51 mm) at the extreme, fingerboard 10½ in. (267 mm) long. It has six strings, four of which are set along the fingerboard and vibrated with the bow. The other two lie off it to be played pizzicato with the thumb.

An interesting and revealing story belongs to this instrument. The original crwth was owned by the famous collector Carl Engel whose collection of instruments is in the Victoria and Albert Museum. Edward Heron-Allen, in his Inaugural Presidential Address to The Sette of Odd Volumes in 1927, related that the instrument had been sent for repair to Georges Chanot in Wardour Street, 'the last of the grand school of Violin makers and imitators, and my revered master in the art of Violin making. Chanot, for his own amusement, made a replica of it, a copy so amazing that when Engel saw the two together he was completely powerless to decide which instrument was his own original. Georges Chanot would never say which of the two Engel took away.'[5]

---

[2] Heron-Allen, *Violin-Making*, 66.
[3] See also Remnant, *English Bowed Instruments*, esp. ch. 6, 'The Crowd'. The crwth of Richard Evans of Llanfihangel of 1742 is illustrated there in pl. 154.
[4] *Violin-Making*, fig. 38, p. 64.
[5] *The Year-Booke of the Sette of Odd Volumes*, 25 (1929), 25–6. See also Heron-Allen, *Violin-Making*, 65 n. 5.

Besides the 1742 example in the Welsh Folk Museum there is another good example in the Warrington Museum and Art Gallery in Cheshire, *c*.1760.[6] The word *crwth* is thought to relate to the old English word *crowd* for 'fiddle', and *crowder* or *crowdero* (as in Butler's *Hudibras*), for 'fiddler'.

Meredith Morris, in discussing the crwth in Wales, states that 'there were numerous crwth-fiddles extant in the middle of the Eighteenth century . . . In converting a crwth into a fiddle, little more had to be done in addition to the removal of the two left or pizzicato strings, but the mongrel thus improvised was but a clumsy substitute at the best.' He goes on to suppose that Welsh makers turned their attention to the new instrument towards the close of the seventeenth century and the popularity of the violin overshadowed that of the crwth by about the middle of the eighteenth century. By the end of the first quarter of the nineteenth century the crwth had been completely vanquished.[7]

In fact, Wales, in common to a large extent with Scotland, illustrates in its rural culture how the violin (or some cruder bowed instrument serving a similar purpose) was both an essential provider of music for the dance and also—from around the seventeenth century onwards—very much looked down upon as a frivolous and almost pagan plaything. In Morris's own words:

> Wales was not particularly keen on fiddles. The great wave of religious enthusiasm which had already begun to gather in the latter half of the Eighteenth century, and which swept everything before it at the full-tide, bore on its crest the foam of hatred of high musical art and instruments. Telyn [the harp] and crwth were cursed by the 'saints', so that the poor Welsh minstrel became the outcast Barnum of the road.[8]

These itinerant 'fiddlers' clearly played an important part in rural entertainment, even though the instruments used for outdoor purposes were sometimes quite a long way from the traditional violin. Photographs exist of two well-known itinerants, Adolphus and Cornelius Wood, showing them bowing their 'fiddles' which are visibly made out of Fry's shilling chocolate boxes, thought to have been produced in the years 1897–1914. Saer states that examples of such fiddles exist today at the Cadbury archives in Keynsham, Bristol, and in a craft museum near Stevenage, Hertfordshire.[9] Such 'gipsy fiddlers' were apparently common till World War I in North Wales, and these two also performed with a third relative on a 'Grecian' harp, held in the Welsh manner against the left shoulder, the left hand uppermost.

---

[6] This is described in Jack M. Bevil, 'The Welsh Crwth, its History and its Genealogy (M. Mus. thesis, North Texas State University, 1973). See also C. Bevan, *Musical Instrument Collections in the British Isles* (Winchester, 1990), 104.

[7] From Morris's unpublished 'De Fidiculis', cited in *Famous Fiddlers by the Reverend W. Meredith Morris*, ed. D. Roy Saer (Cardiff, 1983), 4–5.

[8] Ibid. 5. 'Barnum' means 'showman'.

[9] Ibid. 34–5, which also reproduces two such photographs.

Welsh cultural tradition is also not one inherently sympathetic to the violin family proper. There is a long and outstandingly successful record of producing powerful singers, and the singing tradition adapted itself successfully to hymnody when the chapel movement developed in the eighteenth and nineteenth centuries, whether in the rural parts or in the coal-mining areas. The musical instrument most closely associated with Welsh folk-music is the harp, which has the advantage of being a more appropriate way of accompanying oneself when singing. As Morris himself says:

> It is very remarkable that Wales, the land of song . . . has produced so few violin-makers. This was probably due to the fact that she has cultivated vocal at the entire expense of instrumental music. The orchestra is all but *non est* in Wales. But then, the Welsh people have ceased to be an artistic people. Even their bards today know no other art than that of *cynghanedd*, and it is even doubtful if a quasi-esoteric use of numbers be a sufficiently important art to command the homage of the best talent. And where the orchestra is an unknown quantity, the art of fiddle-making may be denoted by zero.[10]

Morris's words were published in 1904 and do not represent a fair picture of the scene from approximately 1920 when music in Wales became perceptibly more eclectic. Arguably even before 1920, Morris does less than justice to the activities of such Welsh composers as Joseph Parry (1841–1903), who was born in Merthyr Tydfil but educated in London. His opera *Blodwen* was performed in at least three Welsh towns between 1886 and 1890, and his oratorio *Saul of Tarsus* was the centrepiece of the Cardiff Festival in 1892. All this is evidence of considerable *orchestral* activity (albeit in a subsidiary capacity). It is not without significance that Morris did not repeat the above passage in the second edition of his book in 1920. By then the National Council of Music for Wales, later the University Council of Music, with its Director Sir Walford Davies (1869–1941), had been founded (in 1919) and a determined effort was made to make mainstream European music more familiar in villages, churches, and schools throughout the Principality. Walford Davies, Professor of Music at University College, Aberystwyth and successor to Elgar as Master of the King's Music, encouraged instrumental tuition, including violin classes, from the centre of this activity, University College, Cardiff. Some commentators have suggested that interest in choral singing (usually taught using the tonic sol-fa system) declined after about 1950 and was replaced by a new enthusiasm for instrumental and orchestral music.[11]

Nevertheless it was true to say that Wales had not produced any outstanding violin-makers, no doubt owing to the factors suggested by Morris. The only maker

---

[10] Morris, *British Violin Makers*, 1st edn. (London, 1904), 233.

[11] See eg. Scholes, *Oxford Companion*, s.v. 'Wales'; Denis Arnold (ed.), *The New Oxford Companion to Music* (Oxford, 1983), 1958.

from Wales picked out by Morris in his first edition as worthy of any substantial mention is Benjamin Williams of Aberavon, 1768–1839. Morris was able to obtain direct information from the living grandson of that maker and supposes that Williams modelled his work on a Duke violin assumed to be in his possession. The model is similar to that of a Nicolò Amati with Stainer-type soundholes. Morris mentioned two 'local country-side fiddlers' who played effectively on fiddles made by this maker.

Nowadays Cardiff, Swansea, and other major towns have their Arts Festivals designed to appeal to an international audience and Wales plays host to a distinguished opera company and a high quality BBC orchestra. The Welsh cultural festival known as the National Eisteddfod moves around each year to different towns, visiting northern and southern Wales alternately. Between them these festivals not only succeed in encouraging the performance of orchestral and choral music to a high standard but also encourage Welsh composers and performers, whilst keeping traditional culture alive.

From the collection of 'Welsh lutherie' sold in London in 1991,[12] it is possible to discern evidence of a flowering of interest in violin-making in the first quarter of the twentieth century. The collection included an interesting instrument made by the Revd W. Meredith Morris himself in 1904 (which attracted a bid of £1,000), as well as instruments by James Parkinson of Llandudno, whose interesting work is discussed further in Chapter 15 (1922, £600) and John Edward Barton, who was born in Moulton, Lincolnshire, and moved to Llanelli (gold medallist at the Welsh National Eisteddfod, Barry, 1920, estimated at £300–£400), and a viola by Watkin Thomas of Swansea, dated 1896 (16³⁄₁₆ in. (410 mm), sold at £880). It is understood that the Parkinson and Thomas instruments are now in the National Museum of Wales, with one of Morris's—a good example which should be followed in England and Scotland. Instruments by a number of other Welsh makers of this period generally fetched bids of significantly less than £500, reflecting their rather routine workmanship.

It is the Revd W. Meredith Morris himself who merits special mention since he made the most outstanding contribution to the appreciation of the violin, not only in Wales but internationally as regards 'British' instruments. Little seems to be known of this scholarly man who produced the first edition of his work on *British Violin Makers* in 1904, and a second edition in 1920. He explains in his Preface to the first edition that

the following pages are the fruit of many years of patient labour. The author has spent nearly all the spare moments of his life in the active service of the King of Instruments, and the effort embodied herein is homage paid by a loyal subject to a worthy monarch.

[12] Phillips, 25 Apr. 1991, lots 84–98.

Part I of this major work discusses general matters such as the history of the model of the violin, its varnish, workmanship, and acoustical principles. Part II consists of a dictionary of violin- and bow-makers, classical and modern. Morris paid particular regard to accuracy (though he admits to the possibility of error) and had either visited or corresponded with the majority of the contemporary makers whom he discusses in his text, some of whom or whose work are illustrated with photographs.

A somewhat belated interest has been taken in Meredith Morris within Wales and some of his manuscript notes on 'Famous Fiddlers' in Wales have been reproduced in an edition, with instruction and notes, in the work referred to above, by D. Roy Saer.[13] This also contains some brief but valuable biographical information.

Although Morris does not appear in the *Dictionary of Welsh Biography down to 1940*, certain biographical details were obtained by Saer from Morris's near relatives. Morris described himself modestly as 'B.A.' on the title-page of his book, and more recent research indicates that this was an Arts degree from London University in 1900, externally—a fine achievement in the light of all his vocational and research commitments. There is no evidence that he obtained a Mus. Bac. degree as has been tentatively suggested in the above work, but he did become a Fellow of the Royal Historical Society. He was born in 1867 in North Pembrokeshire and becoming first a Baptist minister he later entered the Anglican church. The first edition of his book was written from Garth Parsonage, Maesteg, South Wales, and the second, revised and enlarged, edition in 1920 (the year before his death) was written from Clydach Vale Vicarage in South Wales. Morris's tragically early death in 1921 at the age of 53 was clearly a serious loss to Welsh scholarship since he wrote either for publication or for private study not only on violin matters,[14] but on the Welsh harp, Pembrokeshire dialect, Welsh hymnody, and South Pembrokeshire folklore.

Morris states in a manuscript of 1917 that:

For upwards of 30 years (since 1886) I have been an enthusiastic devotee of the Fiddle Cult—a humble worshipper at the shrine of old Antonio Stradivari. Love for the violin was awakened within me by contemplating the outline and arching of my grandfather's cello—an old Betts, of no great intrinsic value. At Haverfordwest, during my grammar school days, my youthful imagination was fired by the sweet strains of the old strolling fiddler, Dick of Dale, who visited all the principal fairs held in the town, and who used to delight the lads and lasses from the country that were assembled on St. Thomas's Green, or in Barn Street, for a dance ... I was bitten young, and have never got cured of the

---

[13] See n. 7 above.
[14] Besides his book on *British Violin Makers* he wrote a privately printed biography of Walter Mayson, the Manchester maker who was approximately a contemporary (see Ch. 12).

mania (if mania it is) to this day. And I neither expect nor wish to be cured at all. I was about twenty when I began to take an intelligent interest in the instrument, and to study it in real earnest. I have played a great deal, but from the start took greater interest in the construction and history of it, . . .[15]

As we have seen, Morris made occasional instruments, a very respectable instrument of his being sold in London in 1991 (as mentioned above), bearing the label 'Gulielmus Mereditus Morrisius Garthiensis Faciebat Anno 1904'. Another of his products is on display at the Welsh Folk Museum, St Fagans, Cardiff.

Morris appears also to have dabbled in the violin commercial world. An English violin, *c.*1770, unlabelled originally, was labelled by Morris thus: 'I certify this violin to be the work of Joseph Collingwood of London, fecit circa 1770. Wm. Meredith Morris November 1919; violin expert Ar air a Chydwybod.'[16]

Because of the great care with which Morris conducted his research over many years his findings are inevitably frequently quoted in this book, particularly in the Directory. His judgements have not always been vindicated by subsequent events, some of the makers confidently predicted to be outstanding having not stood the test of even quite brief time. But, despite these occasional failings and some rather high-flown language, most of Morris's opinions have proved sound and astute. It is to be hoped that the action of the National Museum of Wales in publishing parts of his manuscript on 'Famous Fiddlers'—an account of a number of folk-fiddlers from the eighteenth century onwards and some of the stories associated with them—will encourage greater interest within Wales in Morris's life and work.

As a sad tailnote to this brief survey of the violin in Wales, the Welsh Violin Making School in Abertridwr (Mid Glamorgan) closed in June 1991. It was founded in about 1978 by the late educationalist and violin enthusiast Aylwyn Jones, but the county education authority could not procure enough funding to continue it. However, it appears that most of the students came from outside Wales—indeed, outside the UK altogether. It had only two Welsh students throughout its existence.[17]

Scottish Violin Makers: Cultural Background

There is some evidence that in the dying years of the seventeenth century Edinburgh was the site of musical activity which, if it could not rival London, at least matched up well to the larger provincial cities in England. Aristocratic patrons could encourage the formation of an orchestra (Edinburgh could provide

---

[15] Morris, *Famous Fiddlers*, 3.   [16] See Sotheby's, June 1992, lot 21.
[17] B. Morgan, 'The Demise of Violin Valley', *Strad* (Aug. 1991), 676.

one in 1695 which included twelve violins, five cellos and viols da gamba, as well as woodwind), and the taste of such patrons was more often than not formed as a result of taking the grand tour and the consequential visit to Italy.[18] A commentator in 1721 suggests that Scottish taste in Edinburgh showed itself in programmes containing an admixture of Corelli with Scottish folksong. There is ample evidence from the work of other non-native composers that Scottish songs and folkmusic were recognized as having a distinctive character. John Playford's *Dancing Master* of 1651 (and other similar later collections) included 'several new Scotch tunes'—some undoubtedly being pseudo-Scottish.

There is a school of thought which identifies the germs of a promising, specifically Scottish (or Irish) creative musical tradition, but sees this tradition swamped by alien influences and the necessity of conforming with 'polite' society.[19] It is certainly disappointing that until the twentieth century was well advanced it is not possible to find any equivalent in Scotland to Norway's Grieg, Denmark's Nielsen, or Finland's Sibelius. The analogy with Grieg is particularly revealing, partly because he was of Scottish descent, though his early training was distinctly German. (It was Ole Bull, the distinguished Norwegian violinist, who persuaded Grieg to train in Leipzig.) Yet Grieg managed to integrate into his music distinctive Norwegian characteristics, including (for instance) in his Violin Sonata, Op. 13, the music of the Hardanger fiddle. In Scotland's case it may have been a diet of an excess of metrical psalmody and a Calvanist attitude to the pleasures of music, as well as the comparative local lack of advanced musical training, which helps to explain this disappointing phenomenon.

This is not to say that Scottish cities and towns remained without the advantage of being able to listen to fine music. Those cities and towns associated with the ancient universities were far from cut off from European tradition, in music, literature, or any other branch of knowledge. The northern choral tradition extended to Scotland and Percy Young traces as far north as Lerwick in the Shetland Islands a choir, accompanied by an orchestra, which was able to perform Mendelssohn's *Elijah* as soon as it was published; and the same society was able to perform major oratorios of Handel in the early part of the nineteenth century. New choral societies were established in some numbers in Edinburgh in the early years of the nineteenth century and there was a Choral Union in Glasgow by 1843. Aberdeen's Musical Society was founded as early as 29 January 1748.[20] Aberdeen was one of those cities benefiting from its close association with an internationally reputed university. Edinburgh's reputation as a city associated with outstanding musical scholarship was enhanced by the foundation of the University's Reid Chair of

---

[18] See Young, *The Concert Tradition*, 88.
[19] See ibid., ch. 7.
[20] Ibid. 91; see also Henry George Farmer, *A History of Music in Scotland* (London, 1947; 1970); Kenneth Elliott and Frederick Rimmer, *A History of Scottish Music* (London, 1973).

Music in 1839. One of the most distinguished professors there was Sir Donald Francis Tovey (1875–1940), who besides writing a formidable corpus of analytical material numbered amongst his compositions a cello concerto and solo sonatas for both violin and cello. Tovey was not, though, a native Scot. He was born in Eton, near Windsor.

But if these developments, viewed as a whole, suggest a country rather remote from the musical development of more central Europe, or even Scandinavia, there is another part of the picture which is highly significant. Scotland shares with Ireland, and to some extent Wales, a vigorous folk-fiddle tradition. Wilfred Mellers is able to trace a close relationship between the Norwegian Hardanger fiddle and its music and the fiddle tradition of the Shetland Isles.[21] A recent survey of music in the Shetland Isles suggests that it is still the case that the finest folk-fiddling in the United Kingdom is likely to be enjoyed there.[22] The context of this playing was the dance or some ceremony such as a wedding. Older fiddlers held their instruments against their chests or even on their arm and used a much flatter bridge than normal. As in Ireland, electronics technology has been the enemy of this traditional art. The community hall with its blaring disco or band of electric guitars and banjos offers to the young a seductive alternative. But for many centuries the folk-fiddle, along with the pipes, was the most important way of transmitting the folk-tunes of Scotland from generation to generation. Learning was transmitted almost entirely aurally. There was little, if any, formal instruction.

From where did the violins used for these activities come? The Scots were great travellers and many violins are thought to have been brought back as a result of visits to continental Europe. In later years cheap violins were available from the music shops and markets of the cities and towns of Scotland. But, significantly enough, Peter Cooke remarks that although it was possible in Lerwick to buy a violin for as little as 18 pence 'this did not stop numerous Shetlanders from building their own instruments and it was once said that the real test of a good carpenter in Shetland was that he should have made a violin. To-day few Shetland homes are without a violin and several craftsmen in the islands are making violins of very acceptable quality.'[23]

William Honeyman, in his discussion of Scotland's most important violin-maker, Matthew Hardie, remarks that Hardie's violins were 'mostly to be used for dance music and ballroom playing'.[24] Wilfred Mellers[25] remarks on the ambiva-

---

[21] See 'From Folk Fiddle to Violin' in Gill (ed.), *Book of the Violin*, 211 ff. Also Peter Cooke, 'The Violin: Instrument of Four Continents', in Stowell (ed.), *Cambridge Companion*, 234–48; David Johnson, *Music and Society in Lowland Scotland in the Eighteenth Century* (London, 1972), esp. ch. 6, 'Fiddle Music'; and M. A. Alburger, *Scottish Fiddlers and their Music* (London, 1983).

[22] See Peter Cooke, 'Tak a Tune oot o da Fiddle', *Strad* (Dec. 1991), 1108.

[23] Ibid. 1109.

[24] Honeyman, *Scottish Violin Makers*, s.v. 'Hardie, Matthew' ('The Scottish Stradivari').

[25] 'From Folk Fiddle to Violin', 220.

lence within Scotland in the eighteenth century in the context of violin music. On the one hand was the 'cultural sophistication' of such cities as Edinburgh. On the other were the fiddlers, folk-musicians playing with archaic reedy tone and traditional ornamentation, who then found that there was a demand for their services outside the bounds of the purely rural society. As Mellers remarks, 'Scots fiddle music became a middle-class phenomenon. Reels and Strathspeys, written down in manuscript books and later printed, were relished by the rising middle-class and even by the aristocracy.'[26]

The artist David Allen painted (in 1780) a graphic portrayal of a highland wedding at Blair Atholl in which the happy couple in the middle of a rural landscape dance the reel to the accompaniment of a violin and a cello while the bagpipe-player takes what appears to be liquid refreshment. Niel Gow[27] is regarded by many as being the earliest and most influential of the eminent folk-fiddlers and some of his music was published. Even more influential, because some of his playing survives on records, was James Scott Skinner (1843–1927), who received classical violin training in Manchester before returning to Scotland to pursue his career as fiddler-composer.

Mellers notes the characteristic ambivalence between modality (in the folk tradition) and modern tonality. The distinguished Orkney-based contemporary composer Peter Maxwell Davies cleverly bridges the two traditions in, for example, his children's opera *The Two Fiddlers*. Niel Gow and his colleagues undoubtedly inspired a number of Scottish violin-makers into creative effort during the later eighteenth and early nineteenth centuries. It is interesting to read from Honeyman that Joseph Ruddiman of Aberdeen (1730–1810) is thought to have repaired Niel Gow's Gasparo da Salò violin after it had been fractured by a fall in 1784, 'an accident to which violins were then more liable as they were carried in a green bag instead of in a fiddle case as now'.[28] One of Niel Gow's violins, thought to be of Scottish manufacture, is on display at Blair Castle.[29]

A perusal of the Directory will confirm the exceptional abundance of Scottish makers. Man for man (all being male) this achievement is almost certainly numerically proportionately greater than that of English makers. There must have been national enthusiasm for the art of violin-making, concentrated particularly in the major towns and cities such as Edinburgh, Glasgow, Aberdeen, and Dundee from the time of Matthew Hardie (c.1800) onwards. Clearly many thousands of handmade instruments have been produced.

An interesting theory is that the violin in Scotland might have benefited from

---

[26] Ibid. 221.
[27] Though Mellers states that Gow was born in 1827 his dates were in fact 1727–1807.
[28] *Scottish Violin Makers*, 2nd edn. (1910), 88–9.
[29] See the foreword by John Turner to the 1984 reprint of Honeyman's work (Scotpress and Fiddletree Music, Morgantown, Va.).

the attempted prohibition on the use of the bagpipes in Scotland proclaimed after the Battle of Culloden in 1746, when the Jacobites were finally crushed. Whilst this might well be so, the fiddle tradition seems already to have become well rooted before this date. Nor do most of the products of the earlier Scottish makers suggest that standards of making were significantly higher than in England, as might perhaps have been expected in the light of Scotland's long-standing cultural connection with the Catholic courts of France, Spain, and Italy. Urquhart, if he was Scottish (and the Hill Archive notes on him suggest that the theory rests on mistaken identity), was a maker of considerable sophistication, but if he was in fact based in Edinburgh he obviously decided that London offered a more sympathetic environment. Disappointingly, the few pre-1750 Scottish instruments inspected give the impression that their makers had the dance-floor rather than the court in mind. Joseph Ruddiman, who worked in Aberdeen *c.*1760–1800, is usually regarded as the first Scottish maker of some merit.

E. W. Lavender, one of the best-informed assessors of British violins in modern times and for many years editor of the *Strad*, singles out for special mention, in addition to Matthew Hardie (1755–1826), whose work is discussed by Honeyman in the extract reproduced later in this chapter, David Stirrat (Edinburgh, *fl.* 1810–20), John Anderson (Aberdeen, 1829–83), and James (he states 'John') Briggs, born in Wakefield, Yorkshire, 1855, pupil of William Tarr, who worked in Glasgow and is discussed in the Directory (surely an 'expatriate' English maker). William Smith, who was Briggs's pupil, believes the Markneukirchen-born Philipp Schreiber, who is known to have worked with Briggs in Glasgow from 1895, with some intervals, made many of Briggs's instruments other than the heads. Also mentioned are James Hardie (Edinburgh, 1826–1916, a prolific maker whose labels appear also to have got into cheap German and French productions, probably without authorization); and Alexander Smillie (Glasgow, 1844–*c.*1918).[30]

Although no short list of distinguished Scottish violin-makers is likely to be comprehensive, Lavender's omission of George Duncan (1855–?) is perhaps surprising, though the maker emigrated from Glasgow to Canada in 1892. Duncan obtained a gold medal for two of his violins in the International Inventions Exhibition in London in 1885, Béla Szepessy, obtaining the silver and John Askew, W. R. Pearce, and Anton Sprenger (Stuttgart, Germany) obtaining bronzes. Duncan was an important witness in a lawsuit against David Laurie concerning a Strad allegedly genuine in all its parts. Duncan's evidence helped to persuade the court that one of the ribs of the instrument was new. In his later instruments he used an oil varnish and he copied Stradivari and Guarneri models. He only made about forty violins while working in Glasgow but Honeyman and Morris in their

---

[30] See Lavender's chapter in Franz Farga, *Violins and Violinists* (London, 1950), 109–18, anomalously titled 'English Violin Makers'.

Directories both speak highly of workmanship and tone. Heron-Allen seems to suggest that Duncan's success might have been a flash in the pan: 'One hears nothing from players about his violins.'[31] In fact modern auction prices, as indicated in the Directory, suggest that Duncan's work attracts amongst the top prices for Scottish violins of this era.

Pejorative judgement cannot be made on the later work of John Marshall of Aberdeen (1844–1919), whose exquisite copies of Allesandro Gagliano (in particular), excellent choice of wood, beautifully cut soundholes, and lustrous oil varnish would put one in mind of Italian work were it not for the label. There is certainly nothing specifically 'Scottish' about this work. It measures up to the highest European standard of craftsmanship.

The Directory has given some indication of the large numbers of Scottish makers that have worked since c.1750. Between them they must have made many thousands of instruments. William Blyth, castigated by Henley as a 'pretender and charlatan', is nevertheless credited alone with about 2,000 violins.

Scottish Violin Writers

Scotland produced several interesting authors whose personality comes through very strongly in their writings. Pride of place must go to William Crawford Honeyman who was born on 30 January 1845 and died suddenly on 13 April 1919. Most of his writing was done from what served as both his home and the office of the Honeyman Publishing Company, namely Cremona Villa, Newport, Dundee, Fife in Scotland. His most valuable work is *Scottish Violin Makers: Past and Present*,[32] but he also produced *The Violin: How to Choose One* (1893) and his first work, *The Violin: How to Master it* (1880). This appeared first as a series of articles in *The People's Friend*, a journal for which he had written a number of stories and romances. He created the character Detective James M'Govan, which, in *The Wasp* of 3 November 1897, is taken to show the author's capacity to view 'the ways of criminals from a human and sympathetic standpoint'.

Honeyman was born at Wellington, New Zealand in 1845 of Scottish parents and brought to Edinburgh at the age of 4. His childhood combined study of the violin and music with explorations of literature and the learning of Latin and French. His musical activities led him into theatre orchestras as well as teaching and writing. In *Musical Scotland* by David Baptie[33] (1894) that author states that

His chief characteristics are unsparing diligence and activity, an original and versatile genius, a clear and felicitous style, and an unbounded enthusiasm for the violin. He is an

---

[31] 'Observations', *Violin Times* 1 (1894), 124, signed 'Observer'.   [32] (1899; 2nd edn. 1910; repr. 1983 and 1984).
[33] (Paisley, 1894).

accomplished solo player, with a fine tone and a graceful style, and is one of the leading violinists in the Dundee Philharmonic Society . . . His domestic life has been somewhat shadowed, and out of six children but one survives, his wife also having died in 1885.

Apropos of his own violin books, Honeyman, writing in 1910, states that during the past thirty years he had received not hundreds but thousands of letters from all parts of the world expressing delight, approval, and gratitude for benefits received from the study of these books.

All that I have done in this direction has been done through love of the subject and as a pleasing relief from my weekly grinding out of fiction, and the pleasure of putting players in the way of proper methods and their enthusiastic gratitude has been my sweetest experience in life. That these works have also been very profitable is a mere freak of fortune, and was quite unexpected by me.[34]

His work on *Scottish Violin Makers: Past and Present* contains biographies and assessments of the work of the major figures in Scottish violin-making accompanied by artistically drawn portraits of the majority of makers. As with so many writers of this period, his judgements are often somewhat dogmatic or idiosyncratic but the work remains a model of its kind and fundamentally sound.

An interesting discussion took place between Edward Heron-Allen (the doyen of English writers on the violin) and Honeyman in the pages of *The Violin Times* for June and July 1894 at a time when Heron-Allen was co-editor of that journal with E. Polonaski. This discussion reveals a good deal about contemporary making and is worth reproducing for that reason alone. Heron-Allen, writing as 'Observer', made the following comments:

In the 'Westminster Gazette' for the 16th May, there appeared a most high-flown article upon a local violin-maker who has just died at Glasgow. It alludes to the late Mr. James Gilchrist, and he is spoken of as the Scottish Stradivari. Mr. Gilchrist, with all his evident talents for many things was, as regards violin-making, but an amateur. He was essentially a local maker, inasmuch as his instruments are not known to the world at large, and we doubt very much whether his name is known far from Glasgow. Many clever mechanics have tried to make violins, and after all it is not a difficult task; in fact, any good cabinet-maker can make a violin, but without a special training—as essential in violin-making as in anything else—the result can be imagined. One fact seems, strangely enough, to have been overlooked by all these local and self-taught violin-makers, namely the necessity of being players as well as mechanicians. We consider that unless a maker is a player himself, he can have no proper means of testing the result of his own work; and we attribute the production of so many crudities by violin-makers of Mr. Gilchrist's stamp, who have sprung up all over the British Isles within the last ten years, to the fact of their not being players.

---

[34] Preface to 2nd edn. of *Scottish Violin Makers*.

Of all the violin-makers that Scotland has possessed, the only one whose work has stood the test of time is Matthew Hardie, who worked at Edinburgh about a hundred years ago. Many of his violins possess considerable merit, but they seem to be quite overlooked. What has become of the violins made by Mr. Duncan, of Glasgow, the maker who was going to take everything by storm, and who obtained a gold medal at the Inventions Exhibition? One hears nothing from players about his violins.[35]

This was answered in a published letter from Honeyman which neatly summarizes his views about Scottish making and the comparative merits of Scottish makers:

Dear Sirs,

The very sensible and just notes of 'Observer' in last month's *Violin Times*, tempt me to pen a word or two in confirmation of his opinion of the works of the late James Gilchrist of Glasgow. Someone said to me lately, 'Have you seen that account in the papers of the death of the great Scottish Stradivari?' I replied that there must be some mistake, as the great Scottish Stradivari was dead years before I was born (Matthew Hardie died in 1826), when I was told that his name was Gilchrist, which made me smile. A year or two ago this maker wrote to me asking if I would allow him to show me two of his works, adding something about their greatness and value, which did not surprise me or make him singular among violin-makers, each violin-maker, as a rule, fancying himself the pivot upon which the whole musical world revolves. I responded at once, and he brought the violins, one of which he said he had sold for £30. This one was a good solidly-made instrument of *Strad* model with something of the flatness of the *Guarnerius* in it, but it had been varnished first with spirit varnish (brown) and then with oil, so the tone was hard and brittle. I should have valued it at £7, though, possibly, some amateur might have given as high as £10 for it. The other was rather deeper in the back and decidedly tubby in tone, as I quickly told him. I should have valued it at from £5 to £6. The work was evidently that of a man accustomed to use tools skilfully, but it seemed to me to lack that subtle and artistic individuality which stamps the real artist in violin-making, and the same might be said of the tone. Violin makers, like poets and painters, are born not made.

Any man skilled in the use of tools can copy a violin, as a painter's drudge can copy a picture, but the man who can idealise the work must have the faculty in his brain and soul, not in his fingers alone. The mantle of Matthew Hardie, the real Scottish Stradivari, has never yet, so far as I have been able to discover, fallen upon any other man's shoulders, not even on those of his own son Thomas, whose violins are very attractive in appearance and very vile in tone. I have seen and tested many hundreds of violins, old and new, by different Scottish makers, but none of them even approach those of Matthew Hardie. Some of his violins seem to have been very hastily put together. His earlier ones are marked with imitation purfling (1796) and his varnish is poor stuff, yet in the whole of them there is apparent in every line that subtle *something* which no one can define, but which is seen as clearly in the roughest work of Guarnerius (del Jesu). It is the same with the tone. The trained ear at once notes the difference from the common-place tone, though it sometimes

[35] *Violin Times*, 1 (1894), 123.

takes a firm hand to show its real grandeur. I have noticed also that the *Asses' bridge* of the ordinary copyist of Stradivari, the third string—has no terrors for Hardie, for his third string has a large round tone of the finest quality. The ordinary *Strad* copyist limps dreadfully with his third string, and on it the note F natural or G in the first position almost invariably call forth a gasp of disappointment . . .

The nearest to Hardie in merit, among Scottish makers, is, I think, Thomas Ruddiman, of Aberdeen, who worked from about 1768. His wood is exceedingly fine; his model a deep Strad, with rather a sharp rise at the edge of the plates and the edge of the scroll; spirit varnish, brown and dark purple, of poor quality; tone large and telling, of fine quality and not quite so dry as that of Hardie's violins.[36]

Amongst other writers in Scotland, Peter Davidson also deserves particular mention. Born in 1834 in Speyside he was both a maker and a writer, his major work being *The Violin: Its Construction Theoretically and Practically Treated*.[37] Davidson migrated to Georgia in the United States in 1886 and died there in 1901. Henley's *Universal Dictionary* states: 'Reputed to have dabbled in occult science and to have made magic mirrors. Had a mind steeped in mysticism and Oriental lore.' His book, though little known nowadays, is in fact one of the most interesting products on this subject written in English in the nineteenth century.

The influence of esoteric religious doctrine does appear in Davidson's chapter on the 'Theoretical Principles of Construction' when he commends the idea of a relationship between music and universal harmony as propounded by the Rosicrucian Brotherhood, in turn based upon the opinions of the Cabbalists, Gnostics, Pythagoreans, and Platonists. But he goes on to give a succinct and well-illustrated detailed guide to the making of an instrument, and the history of various attempts to improve the design of the violin, long before Heron-Allen's book on violin-making, widely thought to be a pathfinding one, was written. Heron-Allen refers to Davidson's work in somewhat patronizing tones: '. . . Author of the above little work, which is not without its merit',[38] though he does commend Davidson's alphabetical list of makers (and rightly so), and later refers to his book as 'of great general merit'.[39] It is perhaps a pity that Heron-Allen was not more ready to acknowledge Davidson's quality as a writer.

Davidson deals with the violin specifically in Scotland only in passing, but he had clearly conducted research on Scottish collectors. He catalogues some fifteen Amatis as belonging to various Scottish owners (other suspected proprietors 'failing to render any information relative thereto'),[40] and in the context of Guarneri

---

[36] *Violin Times*, 1 (1894), 139. The letter goes on to doubt whether the recently deceased maker John A. Mann actually made his instruments personally. In his *Scottish Violin Makers* Honeyman relates that Mann had the opportunity of buying Stradivari's 'Messiah' violin (now in the Ashmolean Museum, Oxford) for £160 from J. B. Vuillaume. Unfortunately he dithered and Vuillaume changed his mind!

[37] (London, 1871; subsequent edns. 1880, 1881, 1895).
[38] Heron-Allen, *Violin-Making*, 2.
[39] Ibid. 170.
[40] Ibid. 140.

mentions in particular the eminent collector W. Croall of Edinburgh. Scotland boasted a number of Stradivari owners and Davidson states that he accidentally came upon such a one when travelling through the north-western Highlands 'which for many years had been suspended like a criminal upon the bare, sooty, and smoky walls of a highlander's hut amongst the mountains. It was in woful [sic] condition, having been literally plastered or bespattered with rosin or tar, to keep its back, breast, and sides from open rebellion by separation. The old proprietor would not hear of parting with it, it having descended as an heirloom amongst the family.'[41]

But it is clear that the more affluent of Scottish society did indulge in the collecting of fine Cremona instruments in the same way as their London counterparts.

This being so it is not surprising that one of the most distinguished experts and dealers within the British Isles in the latter part of the nineteenth century was based in the city of Glasgow. This was David Laurie, whose well-known work *The Reminiscences of a Fiddle Dealer* was published posthumously in 1925. Laurie was born in 1833, produced eighteen children from two marriages, developed one of the best-reputed violin-dealing businesses from his house at 36 Lansdowne Crescent, Glasgow, and died in 1897 in Brussels where he had made many interesting business contacts. He was a good violinist himself and attained a reputation as a violin expert probably only excelled by the Hill family. He was adversely involved in litigation when he sold a Strad as 'genuine in all its parts' where the instrument actually consisted of two 'cannibalized' Stradivaris, but this seems to have done nothing to diminish his reputation. Most of his business was done in the field of fine Italian violins and a number of Stradivaris and the like passed through his hands. His book contains a list of prices he obtained for such instruments between 1876 and 1880, a Stradivari violin of 1715 making £800 as did a Joseph Guarneri from 1740.

The book is also well worth reading for shrewd and revealing anecdotes relating to violin-dealing at the time, and is mentioned in other parts of this present text. The Hills in *Antonio Stradivari* state:

Of recent years, i.e. from 1865–1885, we have been more particularly indebted to the late Mr. David Laurie, of Glasgow, for the introduction to our shores of some of the finest existing examples of Stradivari's genius. Though in no way connected by tradition with our calling, Mr. Laurie developed a taste for high-class instruments which, added to a keen business capacity and rare energy, he soon turned to good account.[42]

---

[41] Ibid. 134. [42] Hill, *Stradivari*, 265.

Ireland

Although Ireland and the violin will to many people conjure up an image associated with a virile folk-fiddling tradition, Dublin has a long tradition of 'classical' music performances and it was in Dublin that on 13 April 1741 Handel gave the first performance of *Messiah*. Dublin occupied much the same position as Edinburgh, an important provincial capital but lacking a musical conservatoire to serve as an adequate base for the formation of permanent professional orchestras or to encourage native composers to work in the European tradition.

Nevertheless, Handel's entrée was to a Dublin already well used to choral entertainment. This was in the early days centred around the singing-men of Christchurch and St Patrick's Cathedrals. The choirmen participated in another performance of *Messiah* in 1742 under the auspices of the Philharmonic Society, the profits of which, as rapidly became the norm throughout the British Isles, were applied for the benefit of a local hospital.[43]

There was also a court at Dublin Castle and the Lord Lieutenant in the early eighteenth century maintained a Kapellmeister in the German tradition. Matthew Dubourg, a pupil of Geminiani, occupied this position until 1765. Dubourg was particularly associated with the performance of Handel's works (in which he played the first violin). In the middle of the eighteenth century Thomas Arne became involved with concert life in Dublin and Niccolò Pasquali, the violinist, lived in Dublin for a short time before moving to Edinburgh. As the century progressed Dublin's musical life was given impetus by the Earl of Mornington who became Professor of Music at Trinity College in 1764 and established a Musical Academy for 'Persons Moving in the Highest Sphere of Society', and excluding 'Professors and Teachers'.[44] The Orchestra of the Academy comprised seven violinists, one viola, four cellos, woodwind, and harpsichord. In the nineteenth century musical life there was enlivened by the activities of the emigrant Neapolitan Commendatore Michele Esposito (1855–1929), who besides being a publisher, a pianist, and a conductor was also a violinist.

Thereafter, although musical activity was never absent, the tendency was for Irish musicians of note to make their careers outside Ireland. John Field (1782–1837), William Balfe of *The Bohemian Girl* fame (1808–70), William Wallace (1814–65), originally a violinist, and later Sir Charles Stanford and Sir Hamilton Harty from Ulster, all became almost expatriot composers. There was in the sphere of musical creativity in any case nothing to match the literary brilliance of authors such as James Joyce and W. B. Yeats. It may have been the Act of Union of 1801 which was the kiss of death to Dublin's creativity, though as indicated

---

[43] Young, *The Concert Tradition*, 93. [44] Ibid. 95.

above, the nineteenth century was not an entirely barren period. The Royal Irish Academy of Music was founded in 1848 and operas and concerts continued to take place in the capital city.

Of much more Celtic or Irish interest is the development of the folk-fiddle in Ireland. It is in this field that the rich tradition of Irish Celtic music, which many would regard as the true music of Ireland, developed. The pipe and fiddle with, later, the accordion and button concertina, dominated rural music. This tradition continues into modern times, for the most part passed down aurally, and modern recordings of this traditional music have an enthusiastic following. Wilfred Mellers[45] mentions the art of Tommy Potts as being particularly outstanding. Most of this style of music is for the dance, to encourage it and to accompany it. The art involved in playing is summarized thus:

Good tone, in the accepted sense of the word, is not important, nor is it necessary to have a good fiddle. What makes a good fiddler is not too different, in many ways, from what makes a good piper: there must be rhythm and verve in the playing with just the right amount and mixture of ornamentation—of course in fiddling this includes bowing technique. Having said that, you have to realise that a good fiddler is so much more than the sum total of all the techniques and ornamentation.[46]

Witnesses of the older tradition speak of dancers who listened quietly to the fiddler's slow air and then, when the fiddle had established the rhythm to the dancers' satisfaction, joined in for reels, polkas, and the like.[47]

As is the case with Scotland, the demand for folk-fiddle music manifested itself throughout the rural parts of the whole island and encouraged both local making and the importing by retailers of cheap instruments from France and Germany.

Thomas Perry

It is against this background that the work of Thomas Perry of Dublin (c.1744–1818) has to be assessed. Perry's work is in fact of such quality that he must rank as one of the finest makers in the entire British Isles during this period. It is now widely accepted that he came from a Huguenot family and was related to Claude Pierray, the Parisian violin-maker, the surname having been adapted. Perry is first recorded as having worked at 6 Anglesea Street, Dublin, later moving to 4 Anglesea Street. John Dilworth, writing in the *Strad*, states that Thomas Perry

---

[45] 'From Folk Fiddle to Jazz Violin', in Gill (ed.), *Book of the Violin*, 215 ff.
[46] Ibid. 218, quoting Matt Crenitch.
[47] See also Dermot McLaughlin and Liz Doherty, 'Tin Fiddling', *Strad* (Aug. 1991), 696–9, being a detailed discussion of the construction of and music for the Irish fiddle, with illustrations of historic players.

took over his father's workshop on the latter's death in 1778.[48] It was during this period that Richard Tobin became his apprentice and Vincenzo Panormo worked with Perry prior to moving to London, as discussed above.

Tradition has it that Perry was able to copy an Amati lent to him by the Duke of Leinster, but his other models are of a more Tyrolean type or reminiscent of the work of Richard Duke in London (with whom some say that he was in his early days associated). Perry usually used attractive wood with a brown, reddish, or golden-amber varnish. Since he is credited with having made more than 3,000 instruments it is not surprising that his work is variable, but tonally they are generally highly regarded by professional orchestral players. Most of his violins are thought to have been numbered and branded 'THOMAS PERRY' under the button on the back. (The brand is often found on German forgeries.) One identifying characteristic is the soundholes which tend to have a small aperture at the top, the narrow stem gradually widening to the lower turn. Henley finds this gives a somewhat unbalanced look to the design. Although the majority of instruments were violins, violas and cellos are known and one double bass is mentioned by Meredith Morris. A fine cello labelled in manuscript 'Thos. Perry No. 6 Anglesey Street Dublin 1785' and branded 'Perry Dublin' sold for £7,500 in Phillips's London sale in April 1991. There is a fine quartet, and a double bass, of the 'Irish Stradivarius' in the National Museum of Ireland, Dublin.

Much has been made of the fact that although Perry's firm apparently continued to trade as 'Perry and Wilkinson' after 1818, Perry and Wilkinson were probably never in partnership, though William Wilkinson married Perry's daughter. The general view is that standards declined after 1818: 'a lamentable falling-off in workmanship, modelling and tone' (Henley). A fairer picture is perhaps that quality became much more variable. Some good work was produced from this workshop but owing to labelling problems it is not always clear what was sold after 1818 but made under Perry's direction beforehand.[49]

The workshop of Perry and Wilkinson appears to have been discontinued after 1839 and from then on, although violin-making by no means disappeared, there is an absence of any pre-eminent makers. As in Scotland there is considerable evidence that where an instrument could not be bought locally, somewhat rustic models were knocked up in the local carpenter's or wheelwright's workshop. The author was able to inspect one of these emanating from the late nineteenth century in County Donegal—an attractive instrument in its own way whose highly arched modelling produced the piping, penetrating tone that would have been appropriate

---

[48] See 'Father Figure', *Strad* (Apr. 1986), 932. See also the important earlier article on Perry by A. McGoogan, *Bulletin of the National Museum of Ireland* (1911–12), 11, drawn on and acknowledged by Morris, *British Violin Makers*, 2nd edn., 218.

[49] See e.g. Phillips, Apr. 1991, lot 176: 'A fine violin by Perry and Wilkinson bearing the maker's label Musical Instrument Makers No. 4 Anglesea Street Dublin 1809 No. 3592 L.O.B. 13^{15}/₁₆ in. (355 mm) branded PERRY DUBLIN' and realizing £2,500.

for the local ceilidh. But a survey would probably show that the majority of instruments played by folk-fiddlers from the middle of the nineteenth century onwards were common German or French imports.

Although Perry dominated the scene, there have been a number of other Irish makers worthy of notice and Meredith Morris refers to a booklet on Irish makers by the Revd Fr. Greaven, to whom he is obviously indebted. A contemporary of Perry's was John Delany, who followed the Amati model and Morris states that there is a fine example of his work in what is now the National Museum, Dublin. A man of what were then radical views, Delany's label, having given the maker's particulars, ends with the message 'LIBERTY TO ALL THE WORLD, BLACK AND WHITE'. Morris also says that there is a specimen of the work of one Molyneux, of Huguenot French extraction, working c.1800, in the Dublin museum. The exhibited instrument has Italian characteristics.

Of more modern makers, since at any one time there must always have been at least ten and perhaps up to twenty makers whose instruments circulate in trade, no brief account can be comprehensive. It is clear that, as in the rest of the British Isles, makers could gain encouragement and recognition by exhibiting their work at arts and crafts festivals and the like. One such was Edward Keenan of Dublin (1876–1935), who was able to copy the Stradivarius 'Vieuxtemps' owned by Professor Joshua Watson of Dublin and whose violin won first prize at the Royal Dublin Society Art Exhibitions of 1913, 1914, 1915, 1919, 1923, and 1925, and the highest award at the Aonach Tailtean Medal of Art in 1924 and 1928.[50]

Morris speaks particularly enthusiastically about the work of Robert Irvine who worked in Belfast from about 1893 to 1925. His models are along Stradivarian lines and attract considerable plaudits from both Morris and Henley. His instruments are dated and numbered. Morris also picks out the work of George Rogers, Conlig, Co. Down, who flourished about 1900. In this connection Morris makes the following characteristic comments, written in 1920, which appropriately close this chapter:

It is worthy of remark that the majority of Irish makers have a decided preference for the Strad model, whereas Scottish makers have a penchant for the Joseph [Guarneri] model. Perhaps the national temperament has something to do with the respective choice. The Irish are fervid, sympathetic and responsive; the Scotch dour, persistent, and practical. With the exception of Italy there is no soil in the world more rich in art productibility than Ireland. The country which produced the fine old artists of a century ago is capable of even greater things, and when the Emerald Isle is regenerated and its sorrows forgotten, the memory of fiddles that are yet unmade will gladden the land.[51]

---

[50] Poidras, *Dictionary*, ii. 90.

[51] Morris, *British Violin Makers*, 288. There are stated to be violin-making courses in Limerick and Cork: see W. Smith and Y. Boydell, 'Violin Making in Ireland', *Strad* (May 1981), 23. The Directory lists a number of contemporary makers working in Ireland. See also John Teahan, 'A List of Irish Instrument Makers', Galpin Society Journal, 16 (1962), 28.

Chapter Nine

The Hills and the Development of the Violin and Bow Industry

The Stainer Preference — Hart's View of the Development of English Taste — The Panormo Influence — The Work of the Hill Family — Haweis's Portrait of William Ebsworth Hill — The Sons of William Ebsworth — The Later Hills — English Bow-Making and the Hill Influence — The Tubbs Connection — Later Hill Bow-Making — Physical Identification — The Retford Collection — Other English Bow-Makers — Restoration Work and Dealing — The Export Trade

The Stainer Preference

THE predilection for Stainer-model instruments by most English makers from 1700, when the previous Brescian influence declined, has already been extensively described. This is not to say that developments in Cremona since the Amati family had settled there in the mid-sixteenth century had not been noticed in England. As has already been mentioned, William Corbett brought back a collection of Cremona instruments from a visit to Italy in 1710, and in 1714 at the sale of the effects of Thomas Britton, Item 12 is 'One very beautiful one by Claude Pieray of Paris, as good as a Cremona'—the inference is obvious. Furthermore, there are a few makers, of whom Daniel Parker is the best-known, who clearly copied, in his case, the early Stradivari pattern. English taste was nevertheless firmly in favour of the Tyrolean–Stainer model during the whole course of the eighteenth century.

Hart's View of the Development of English Taste

One of the best testimonies as to how English taste developed is that of George

Hart senior (1839–91), the son of John Hart (the founder of Hart & Son of London) and the author of the classic text *The Violin: Famous Makers and their Imitators* (1875). Hart was well placed to give his opinions. The Hills, in their work on *Antonio Stradivari*, state that the principal dealers in England during the mid-nineteenth century were A. and J. Betts, Corsby, John Hart, Davis, Fendt and Purdy, John Alvey Turner, and W. E. Hill. 'The foremost was Hart . . .'[1] His son George wrote an illuminating passage clearly drawing on a great deal of family experience and his own direct observation. What follows is a summary of his views, from the enlarged 1885 edition.[2]

Hart starts by pointing out that the introduction of Italian instruments into Britain was a matter of slow growth, and did not assume any great proportion until the beginning of the nineteenth century. London and Paris then became the chief cities for the distribution of old Italian instruments all over Europe.

At the same time the taste of the dilettanti in the fiddle world began to abandon the preference for the Stainer–Tyrolean, high-raised model, there having been in England 'an army of Stainer-worshippers', including 'Wamsley, Barrett, Benjamin Banks, the Forsters, Richard Duke, and a whole host of little men,' though Hart points out that Banks, Forster, and Duke did not copy Stainer steadfastly. Benjamin Banks, in particular, 'led the English makers to adopt the pattern of Amati'. This movement eventually led to English fiddle-fanciers becoming 'total ab-Stainers'.

From about 1800, then, attention became focused on the works of the Cremonese. The instruments by the Amatis were the most sought after and were obtainable at 'nominal prices'. 'The number in Italy was far in excess of the requirements.' William Forster II's day-book records the sale of a Nicolò Amati cello for £17. 17s. 0d. in 1799, and in 1804 the sale of an Amati violin for £31. 10s. 0d. 'These prices were probably less than those which William Forster received for many instruments of his own make.'

This situation did not last long. The call for Amatis became so clamorous that demand soon equalled and then exceeded the limited supply. At the same time the theory of the flat model was gaining ground. Players compared notes and it was found that the elevated model was inferior in every way to the Italian model. Of the Amati family, whose instruments had hitherto been valued equally, the work of Nicolò began to be preferred. 'Grand Amatis became the coveted Fiddles; they were put up frequently at twice the value of the smaller patterns.'

The taste for the flat form having developed, the fame of Antonio Stradivari became known outside the circle of royal orchestras, convent choirs, and private holders who had possessed them without fully appreciating their merits. 'Demand

---

[1] Hill, *Stradivari*, 262.   [2] Hart, *The Violin: Famous Makers*, 323 ff.

increased to an extent far beyond that commanded by the work of the Amatis at the height of their popularity . . . Among the artists of the early part of the [nineteenth] century who used the instruments of Stradivari were Boccherini [sic], Viotti, Rode, Kreutzer, Habeneck, Mazas, Lafont, and Baillot.'

Hart dates the interest in Giuseppe Guarneri from 1820, chiefly promoted through the instrumentality of Paganini. Other Italian makers then became sought after on the basis that 'if the master could not be had, the pupil must be found'. Makers quite unknown in England fifty years before became familiar to connoisseurs: Guadagnini, Gagliano, Grancino, Santo Serafino, Montagnana, and others 'passed from Italy into France and England, until the various schools of Italian violin manufacture were completely exhausted'. Within seventy-five years French and British players and collectors had 'continued to possess themselves of the finest specimens of Cremonese instruments, together with those of other Italian schools. We here have an example of the energy and skill that is brought to bear upon particular branches of industry when once a demand sets in. Men of enterprise rise with it unnoticed, and lead the way to the desired end. In the case of Italian Violins it was Luigi Tariso who acted as pioneer . . .'[3]

The Panormo Influence

A factor not mentioned by Hart, but referred to earlier in this work, was the coming to London of experienced makers from the continent of Europe who brought with them a much stronger attachment to the Cremona tradition. Foremost of these was Vincenzo Panormo who, having worked first in Paris and Dublin, joined the firm of John Betts at the Royal Exchange in the City of London in 1791 aged 57. Panormo worked with Betts until 1813 and was undoubtedly a key catalyst in persuading sellers and buyers of the superiority of the Stradivarius model. Although, as John Dilworth points out, 'working hours were literally dawn to dusk, and holidays were the eight days in the year when hangings took place at Tyburn',[4] this was at a time when the Napoleonic Wars had the beneficial effect of raising wages for skilled craftsmen as well as making to a large extent impracticable the importation of goods from continental Europe.

Panormo was not the only *émigré* to be drawn to London and to work with Betts. He was joined there by Bernhard Fendt, nephew of François Fent of Paris and also greatly influenced by the work of Stradivari.

---

[3] Tarisio's activities are discussed in the next Chapter.
[4] John Dilworth, 'Father Figure', *Strad* (Apr. 1982), 935.

The Work of the Hill Family

By the middle of the nineteenth century London shared with Paris the distinction of being the centre of the market for fine Cremona instruments. It was also remarkable for producing a number of distinguished violin-making and dealing families. The Forster family has already been described. But there were also the Fendt family, the Furber family, the Hart family, and the Kennedy family, to name those which extended to at least three generations. A number of others had stretched to at least two, for example the Duke, the Dodd, the Harris, and the Lott families. But by any reasonable judgement the family that quickly established its pre-eminence as violin-makers, dealers, bow-makers, and authors was the Hills. Their work has often been referred to previously in this text but at this point an attempt will be made to describe the astonishing achievement of the Hills up to the sad closure of their business in 1992.

The Hills themselves trace their family back to at least the diary entry of Samuel Pepys for 17 February 1660 which runs as follows: 'In ye morning Mr. Hill ye Instrument Maker & I consulted with him about ye altering my lute & my viall.' There is a further entry for 5 March 1660: 'Early in ye morning Mr. Hill comes to string my theorbo, which we were about till past ten o'clock, with a great deal of pleasure.' Whilst it is not entirely established that Pepys's Hill was connected, earlier members of the family being associated with Alvechurch in Worcestershire, the family tree can safely commence with Joseph Hill (1715–84). He was probably an apprentice of Peter Wamsley and became a well-known London maker working at the Harp and Flute in the Haymarket from 1762 to 1780 and previously to that at High Holborn from 1753 to 1756, at the Angel Court, Westminster, 1756–61, and Pall Mall in 1762. The charming street sign illustrating the harp and the flute, 1762, was for many years the firm's trade mark and was reproduced on the notepaper of W. E. Hill & Sons. Joseph Hill adopted the Amati–Stainer pattern and these days is particularly esteemed for his cellos.

Reference must now be made to the accompanying family tree from which it will be seen that there were four violin-making sons. Of these, probably the most distinguished was Lockey Hill, the fourth son (1756–1810), who worked at Islington, primarily for trade retailers such as Longman & Broderip (it is thought), and at Boro' in Southwark. The latter label, rectangular with clipped corners, is quite common but one has also been observed running 'Lockey Hill, MAKER, Islington, 1792'. William Hill (1748–90) of Poland Street, near Broad Street, Carnaby Market, also produced distinguished work. Joseph (II) and Benjamin spent most of their time assisting their father. The three brothers Joseph, William, and Benjamin are listed as playing in the orchestra of the First Handel Celebration, May 1784.

HILL FAMILY TREE

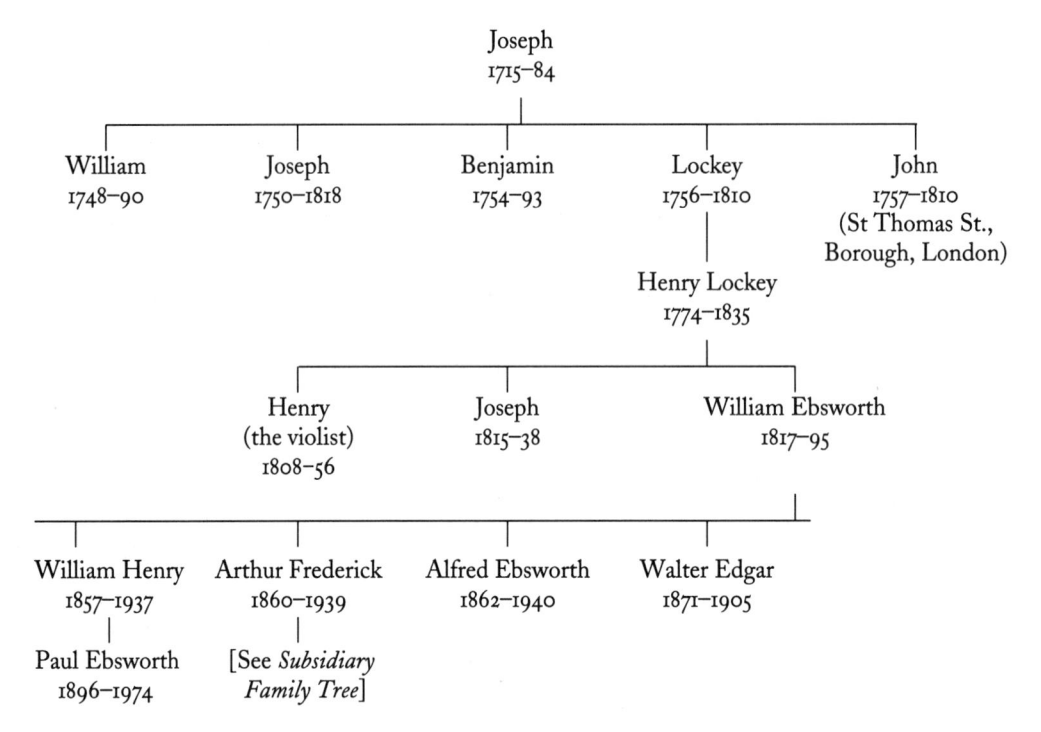

```
                          Joseph
                          1715–84
    ┌──────────┬──────────┼──────────┬──────────┐
 William    Joseph     Benjamin    Lockey       John
 1748–90    1750–1818  1754–93     1756–1810    1757–1810
                                   │            (St Thomas St.,
                                   │            Borough, London)
                              Henry Lockey
                              1774–1835
              ┌───────────────────┼───────────────────┐
           Henry              Joseph            William Ebsworth
          (the violist)       1815–38                1817–95
           1808–56                                     │
    ┌──────────────┬──────────────┬──────────────┐
 William Henry  Arthur Frederick  Alfred Ebsworth  Walter Edgar
 1857–1937      1860–1939         1862–1940        1871–1905
    │              │
 Paul Ebsworth  [See Subsidiary
 1896–1974      Family Tree]
```

NB: These dates are as extracted from the records in the possession of the Hill family. They do not always agree with the dates given in the standard dictionaries such as Henley. The Tree shows significant violin-making Hills only; there were many other members not connected with the trade or only peripherally so.

SUBSIDIARY FAMILY TREE

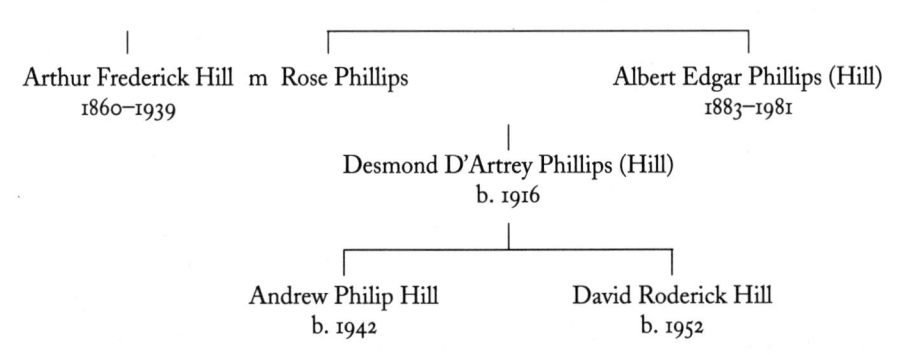

```
         ┌──────────────────────────────────┐
 Arthur Frederick Hill  m  Rose Phillips    Albert Edgar Phillips (Hill)
 1860–1939                                  1883–1981
                        │
              Desmond D'Artrey Phillips (Hill)
                        b. 1916
              ┌─────────────────┐
        Andrew Philip Hill    David Roderick Hill
           b. 1942               b. 1952
```

Lockey Hill's son, Henry Lockey Hill (1774–1835; often confused with his father), was arguably the finest maker of the entire family. He is generally regarded as being the first Hill to abandon the Stainer–Amati model and adopt that of Stradivari. His violins, violas, and magnificent cellos are now amongst the most valuable of English instruments.

W. Meredith Morris explains that Henry Lockey Hill was initially a pupil of his father and then worked for some time with John Betts. He later went into partnership with his father in Southwark (in Brandon Row, Newington Causeway) and Kent Street, Boro', Southwark (on his own account). Morris also draws attention to the fact that many of his instruments seem not to have labels or, in other cases, the label has been removed and an Italian one substituted. Morris continues:

the varnish, although of excellent quality, is not to be compared with that of Stradivari, and the purfling, which is carefully inlaid, is not in the manner of the master. Any one carefully examining the mitring at the corners will perceive the difference ... Hill frequently used a light-coloured varnish, which is perfectly transparent and elastic. I have seen only one of his violas, which was on a modified Amati model, with a widened waist, and not over-pronounced arching. The tone of this instrument was large and sonorous on the lower strings, but not quite so full and clear on the upper strings. The scroll was in the best Italian style, and the sound-holes well designed and carefully cut. Altogether, the work of Lockey Hill is very fine, and it is a pity there is not more of it.

Henry Lockey Hill had five sons of whom the eldest was Henry Hill, the violist discussed in Chapter 7. Joseph (III) died early, his dates according to the 'official' family tree being 1815–38. Occasional fine specimens of work attributed to him materialize. However, Henry Lockey Hill's brother (and W. E. Hill's uncle) was also called Joseph Hill (not included in the family tree) and family documents suggest that his name appears in an instrument dated 1818. There may therefore have been confusion between the two cousins of the same name.

By far the most eminent of the violin-making sons, William Ebsworth Hill (1817–95), was the founding father of the firm of W. E. Hill & Sons and he established its international reputation. He originally worked with his father, probably his uncle Joseph, and then for a short time with Charles Harris in Oxford. In 1838 he established himself in Southwark, London and then in Wardour Street and finally in New Bond Street. His output was not large but those instruments that he did make personally show the careful and educated work that one would expect.

Before long W. E. Hill experienced the conflict, familiar to many makers and restorers, between the necessity of running a growing business and the natural instinct to continue making instruments. And, as others have found, the economics of the situation dictated the course which his life had to take. London, with Paris, was rapidly becoming one of the two centres of trade in valuable Italian instruments, in the restoration and identification of which Hill rapidly established an élite reputation. Morris points out how sparing Hill was in the use of fresh material in his restorations. 'No artist ever deplored more deeply the necessary renewal of parts which could not be re-set. He restored faithfully because he preserved faithfully. And this is the essence of all true restoration of art work.'

Haweis's Portrait of William Ebsworth Hill

Morris also refers to the vignette of W. E. Hill by H. R. Haweis in his book *Old Violins and Violin Lore* published in London in 1898. Haweis first made Hill's acquaintance at his Wardour Street establishment, and in the light of the importance of Hill in the London violin trade at the time and his influence on it subsequently, Haweis's comments as a contemporary record are invaluable.

Ebsworth Hill was not, financially speaking, a business man—though he did all his own business. For years everything that came into the shop passed through his hands; he made every repair, doctored every fiddle, adjusted every screw, regulated or replaced every sound-bar and sound-post, and even strung the fiddles for his clients with his own hand—in short, he did or closely superintended everything; division of labour, to the extent to which it is now carried, being a thing unknown in those early days.

That such a system could not bring in large profits was obvious. Hill had many debts; his memory for fiddles was infallible, but his memory for accounts shocking, and he was cheated right and left.

His fame was so widespread that orders poured in which could not be executed; and when the old man's apparently inexhaustible powers of work began to give out, the sons, who had watched proceedings for years and slowly qualified themselves for every department, came in and broke up the one-man system—not before financially confusion was becoming worse confounded. They trained their workmen, distributed the work, kept proper accounts for the first time, and in a few years built up what is, perhaps, when considered in all its branches, the largest individual violin-dealing industry in the world.

Mr. Hill was a man of striking appearance: thin, spare, with light hair, and moustache early gone grey; blue-grey eyes, very keen; a thoughtful face, often lighted up with a whimsical smile—for the man was full of humour, though mostly of a genial sort.

He was very much more of an all-round man than people who merely conversed with him on violins would suppose. Highly educated, in the usual sense of the word, he was certainly not; but he had a great acquaintance with human nature, and an extraordinary insight into character . . .

He was frequently appealed to in doubtful cases, but was greatly opposed to litigation, and it was difficult to extract from him any opinion likely to lead to it.

Once in the witness-box he was what the lawyers call a dangerous customer. His manner was perfectly quiet, assured, and straightforward. He was absolutely decided, and would never budge from his opinion, and under pressure of cross-examination often raised a laugh at the expense of counsel . . .

His memory was as extraordinary as Tarisio's. On one occasion a claim was brought against a railway company for sixty pounds' damage to the belly of a violoncello. The company demanded a valuation, and damages to be assessed by Hill. The claimant at last angrily submitted. Hill reported on the instrument, which he repaired for about thirty shillings. Five pounds he thought would be very liberal damages. The owner was furious, and would not even accept fifteen guineas. Mr. Hill was at last called up, and made the following unpleasant statement: 'This instrument does not belong to this man at all. It is one of the instruments belonging to her Majesty, and used by members of the private band.' The *soi-disant* owner was perfectly dumbfounded, but was obliged to confess that he had actually borrowed the instrument when employed as deputy in the Queen's Band several years before, and had never restored it. Mr. Hill had only seen it once before.

A violin, said to be by F. Panormo [*sic*], was sold as such by a dealer in Pentonville Road. It came into Hill's hands many years afterwards, who was asked to take it in part payment for another violin. He said: 'This fiddle was not made by Panormo; it was made by my father about the year 1812 for my brother Henry, and owing to the difficulty of getting good foreign wood, my father made the back and ribs from English maple. It could not possibly have a good tone, but I should like to have it, and will allow £10 for it.' Mr. Hill immediately proceeded to remove the belly. On the inside was written in pencil, 'Made for my son Henry in the year 1812.'

Mr. Hill led an extremely abstemious life. His only relaxations were reading and long walks on Sundays. Towards the close of his life he found himself surrounded by his sons, superintending a large staff of workmen, and his workshops at Hanwell, adjoining his country home are well known. For some years before he died the direction of affairs had practically passed into the hands of his sons, whom he had so admirably trained to succeed him, and to them is entirely due the present great commercial prosperity of the firm.

William Ebsworth Hill sank gradually from senile exhaustion of brain power, and died in 1895, aged seventy-seven.[5]

The Sons of William Ebsworth

It is apparent from Haweis's description that William Ebsworth's sons (see family tree) took a strong grip on the successful but badly managed state of affairs. The firm became the partnership styled W. E. Hill & Sons, first in 1880 in Wardour Street and then at 38 New Bond Street (1882–96) and then 140 New Bond Street. The family tree indicates those members of the family most intimately connected with the firm, amongst whom were the authors of the standard texts on Stradivari and Guarneri often referred to in this book. As mentioned in the Directory, the firm began to employ skilled workmen, particularly those trained in Mirecourt, and from the mid-1880s produced semi-commercial instruments, which were nevertheless handmade. Their experience of handling priceless Italian instruments enabled them to make accurate copies of celebrated Stradivaris and the like. Morris mentions copies of the 'Messie', the 'Tuscan', the 'Betts', the 'Alard', the 'Rode', and 'Viotti'. 'The price of these instruments is £35.' As Malcolm Sadler states, the instruments changed little over the earlier years, except for the varnish.

[5] Haweis, *Old Violins*, 142–5.

The period 1914–20 is generally thought to have produced the most impressive examples, though varnishing problems were never consistently resolved.[6]

Sons going into the business tended to be trained in Mirecourt and the Hill production of instruments in the late nineteenth and early twentieth centuries has a decidedly French look about it (other than the varnish). It was also a Mirecourt connection which persuaded Alfred Ebsworth (1862–1940) in particular to promote the bow-making side of the business at a 'factory' established in Hanwell in 1890. This was a development of such importance that it is dealt with as a separate section of this chapter.

The other achievement of the Hill family, which is unique in the annals of international violin-making, is the production of a number of texts, exceptionally scholarly for their time, on the classic Italian violin-makers, for which the Hills were able to draw on their extensive family dealing experience. The authors of the texts on Stradivari and Guarneri were William Henry, Arthur Frederick, and Alfred Ebsworth Hill, the Stradivari text being first published in 1902, with a second, 'popular' edition in 1909. As the authors said apropos of the first edition in the Preface to the second, 'the one thousand copies of which the edition consisted, were sold within three years'. A third edition was contemplated but never achieved. The Guarneri text was produced in 1931. Both these books are mines of information not only on the makers mentioned but on the historical background to those makers' work. They are not, however, canonic in their authority as some enthusiasts believe. Thorough and exceptionally well-informed though they are, modern scholarship is inevitably likely to revise some of the biographical and instrumental information.

In addition to the above works, texts were produced on Stradivari's *'The Tuscan'* and *The Salabue Stradivari* (otherwise known as 'Le Messie'), both in 1891. William Ebsworth Hill and his sons William, Arthur, and Alfred also contributed to the book on Maggini, the titular author of which was Margaret L. Huggins, published in 1892.

During the later years of the nineteenth century the firm of W. E. Hill & Sons obtained gold medals at the National and International Exhibitions at London (1885), Paris (1889), and Brussels (1897). The firm was also given the Royal Warrant of Appointment as Violin and Bow Makers to the Kings of Italy and Portugal in 1908. In the 1920s and 1930s they could add in their beautifully printed catalogues 'By Appointment Violin and Bow Makers to the King'. It is ironic that with all the beneficence of this family to the Ashmolean Museum in Oxford in particular—the Hill Gift including arguably the most famous violin in the world

---

[6] See Malcolm Sadler, (ed.), *The Stradivari Influence* (London, 1987).

(Stradivari's 'Le Messie')—there appears to be no museum in England displaying good specimens of the Hill family's instrumental work.[7]

The Later Hills

As has been mentioned, two of the sons of William Ebsworth, namely Alfred Ebsworth and Walter Edgar, were trained both in the family firm and at Mirecourt. This reinforced an important connection which resulted in the employment of such distinguished French makers as the Langonet family (see Directory). They worked for three generations for the Hills, though both Charles Frank and Alfred Charles Langonet eventually set up their own business, the former after working for the firm of W. E. Hill & Sons for thirty-six years. Conditions in Mirecourt were poor, workers depending on ill-paid piece-work for the most part. It was not difficult for the Hills to tempt some good workmen to London.

The other two sons of William Ebsworth also went into the business, William Henry first following a career as a professional viola-player (giving the young Edward Heron-Allen at least one lesson) and Arthur Frederick specializing in the commercial side of the business. As the business developed and a 'violin factory', or, perhaps more appropriately, 'workshop', was opened and developed at Hanwell in the 1890s, the Hill business consisted not only in the making of fine instruments and bows, but the restoration of a very high percentage of the fine Italian instruments in circulation today, the making of fine cases, and the making of accessories. It was not the only such business in England—Rushworth and Dreaper a little later opened a violin-making workshop in Liverpool and there were other smaller-scale workshops in London—but certainly in the size of its activities and the distinction of its work it was unique in Britain and unsurpassed anywhere else in the world. Henley, who obviously inspected the Hanwell workshop, speaks of 'magnificently equipped workshops at Hanwell, where a large staff of skilled workmen are continually employed, several of them having previously been the "pick" of many Mirecourt-trained'.[8] It is still a pleasure to admire the bridges, pegs, chinrests, and even the routine but beautifully made wooden cello cases with their brass fittings, emanating from Hills during the last years of the nineteenth and much of the twentieth century. Special Hill mahogany cases in which to keep and show off particularly valuable instruments have long been appreciated for their outstanding craftsmanship. Even their catalogues were works of art, beautifully printed on fine-quality paper.

[7] There is, however, reputed to be a pretty instrument of William Ebsworth's in the Musée de Bruxelles (No. 237) (see Vannes, *Dictionnaire*, i. 161).
[8] Henley, *Dictionary*, 572.

The only grandson of William Ebsworth through the male line to enter the business was Paul Ebsworth, who studied with A. Delanoy (a pupil of J. B. Vuillaume) in Bordeaux and worked with his father from 1921. He was regarded as not suited to the business, however, and played little part in it. The present living generations of the Hill family descend through Albert Edgar Phillips (1883–1981), Arthur F. Hill's brother-in-law, himself a distinguished maker who had worked under Mangenot, a pupil of Paul Bailly, in Mirecourt and in Munich with Guiseppe Fiorini. The start of the Second World War saw the Hill business in some trouble with Arthur dying in 1939 and Alfred in 1940. The business was in effect sold by arrangement to Albert Phillips on condition that he changed his name by deed poll, which he did in 1941. Although the genetic line of the Hill family was then broken, violin-making cannot in actuality be a hereditary skill and it was fortunate that the firm descended to a proven master craftsman thoroughly acquainted with, and determined to uphold, the Hills' family ethics and reputation.

Albert Phillips Hill enhanced the firm's reputation not only as a craftsman but as a fine businessman. As Bill Watson, the bow-maker who worked at Hills for seventeen years from 1945, states: 'He took over in 1940 and the firm could have been flattened. The trade was at rock bottom—all the men had left.'[9]

Albert Phillips Hill is credited with between forty and fifty instruments since starting in 1900. He also specialized in fine bridges, including those for gambas. As his son, Desmond Hill, states: 'There was so much managerial work to be done that he didn't get much chance to work with instruments, although he used to spend three or four hours a day at the bench, between the wars.'[10]

Mary Anne Alburger in her book *The Violin Makers: Portrait of a Living Craft*, includes a valuable interview with Desmond Hill who had trained under Pierre Hel in Lille. This interview explains the workings of the business in the earlier part of this century and his contributions to it. Desmond explains that he made his first instrument in 1934, a violin, and probably made no more than a dozen altogether. He spent more time doing other things such as case design and general management. But the virtue of knowing how to do the basic work of the firm and being respected for it is clearly an advantage when dealing with skilled staff such as worked at the benches of the Hill workshop. Desmond Hill also explained that the firm had four separate departments, the Bow Shop, the Violin Shop, the Case Shop, and the Accessories Shop, with a manager over the entirety.

There was a large gap in the production of instruments for rather over thirty years, except for one or two special commissions. This was because of the impact of purchase tax (imposed at rates of around 30 per cent at its height) on the price

---

[9] See Anne Inglis, 'W. E. Hill & Sons: End of an Era', *Strad* (Apr. 1992), 298.
[10] Mary Anne Alburger, *The Violin Makers: Portrait of a Living Craft* (London, 1979).

of new instruments (old instruments being exempt from this tax). Purchase tax was first introduced in 1941 and imposed, inappropriately in the case of the Hills, on a notional wholesale price. When purchase tax was replaced by VAT on 1 April 1973, shortly after the United Kingdom's admission to the European Economic Community, the discrimination was eliminated and Desmond Hill states that the firm managed to finish off sixty instruments before moving from London to Great Missenden.

The move from Bond Street to Great Missenden in Buckinghamshire occurred in 1974 and only after the move was a limited company first formed. The rationale for the move was that the large house, 'Havenfields', which appears in all their advertisements from 1974, was big enough to house the entire enterprise including, a few years later, the workshops at Hanwell. It was close to London and convenient for the airports. Casual trade would be lost, but the trade in accessories and the like which took much of the time of the Bond Street establishment, though thriving, was not the most profitable part of the business. There were also other factors relevant to the decision, not least of which was the rent of the Bond Street premises. Having been £700 per annum until 1960 it then escalated to £4,000 and would have increased to an estimated £40,000–50,000. The freehold was denied to the firm. Fine, modern, workshops were installed at Great Missenden. In retrospect, although major dealing continued, the removal of the business from the centre of the national scene (and, arguably, the international one) was probably a mistake.

Desmond Hill goes on to explain other details of the Hill production. Inside moulds were always used for their instruments. Violins, violas, and cellos were made, the only problem being with violas because of the continuing controversy as to the optimum size. Accordingly, three different viola models were used, the Brescian, the Amati, and the Stradivari. Desmond also recalls an instrument made by William Ebsworth for Henry Hill, the violist: 'a jolly good model, with lots of sensible features. It is almost identical to a Lupot copy of a Stradivari which we have, and which was obviously the one W. E. Hill modified for his brother. So Lupot copied Stradivari and modified it slightly, and W. E. Hill modified that a little bit, and now we've taken it and changed it again.'[11]

For violins, the 'Alard' and 'Messie' copies were the most popular though the firm had complete patterns and moulds for about fifteen different Strads of various types and for several cellos. The favourite cello model was a modified Montagnana whose breadth was preferred to that of the Stradivari model.

Varnish was made in-house with colours from a medium gold through light brown, dark brown, bright red, to rich orange-red. All instruments were

[11] Ibid. 77.

scraper-finished and varnish was put on at weekly or fortnightly intervals. The thickness of the coats was the subject-matter of some experimentation. The formula used was 'traditional knowledge', but not the same used by the former Hill generation, which was a very soft varnish which took too long to dry. Something was needed which would dry more quickly.[12]

Prices in the late 1970s were about £1,400 for a viola, while for some violins, which were rather better finished, Hills asked from £2,000 upwards.[13]

Desmond Hill also mentions that initially violas took over 100 hours in the making but with some encouragement the workmen concerned got the time down to fifty or even forty hours. Part of the secret was using a 'belly gouge', a large tool which takes a great deal of wood out in one operation.

Working at Hills from the employees' point of view has been described by a number of those workers, particularly distinguished bow-makers. Arthur Bultitude, for example, explained that he spent his school-days near the Hill workshop in Hanwell and his school mentioned Bultitude's name to Alfred Hill since Bultitude was very interested in woodwork. Alfred Hill interviewed him and asked such questions as whether his father was honest, sober, and industrious and whether he was a member of the Church of England. Bultitude was then told to appear on Monday morning with a clean apron and his hair cut short. He spent the first six months in the case-making department, as was traditional, before being assigned to the bow-making department. There he worked under the watchful eye of William Retford, possibly the finest of all English bow-makers, but whom Bultitude regarded as 'a holy terror to work for'.[14]

Bultitude went on to see the advent of the Hill bow 'which became universally accepted as the top grade available'. Bultitude attributes this to the standards of Alfred Hill and the integrity of Retford who organized the bow department for many years. Retford had joined the firm in 1892 and opened the bow department in 1893. Bultitude started his apprenticeship in 1922 and worked for them for thirty-nine years before becoming self-employed.

One feature of the business is particularly distinctive. It was almost axiomatic that the partners should themselves be sufficiently skilled craftsmen to be able to judge, regulate, and where necessary improve the work of their employees. It was very much a 'hands-on' management tradition. Elliot Brunton, a foreman of the Hill workshop, is quoted as saying about the Hills as employers:

> They had a reputation for fairness and quality, and everyone trusted their judgment. If you bought an instrument with a Hill certificate, it was water-tight. When I first started the Hills were very good to me, and I enjoyed working on the great instruments. People will

---

[12] Alburger, *Violin Makers* 78.
[13] Ibid. 79. [14] Ibid. 190.

always knock a successful business but it is difficult to sort the wheat from the chaff. Name me a family that doesn't have problems. If I have a criticism it would be that the Hills were not all that open to new ideas. But it was probably that we had three or four people to deal with. Had there been just one person in charge it would have been more harmonious and they would have got more out of us.[15]

This perhaps explains the fundamental reason for the closure of the business in its long-established form in March 1992.

As an amusing testimonial for the firm of W. E. Hill & Sons in its prime, this is the advertisement, written in antique English, which the firm put in the *Musical Times* of 1 Dec. 1891:[16]

W. EBSWORTH HILL & SONS, Violin Makers and Sellers of ye Viol at No. 38, NEW BOND STREET, London, furnish all ye divers thyngs for Stringed Instruments, especially Bows & eke Cases, chastely wrought, & of excellent workmanship. All are made in theyre own Work-a-day Shoppes situate in Hanwell in ye fields, & ye best in Europe's Continent. There with hys famile dwells Master William Ebsworth Hill and supervyzes ye worke with ye assistance of hys four Sonnes, William, Arthur, Alfred, and eke Walter.

Ye Violoncellos made by W. Ebsworth Hill & Sons are of exceeding worth & everie Instrument repaired or sold by them is yielded up in perfect order for ye playing upon. Ye name of Hill & Sons has gained renown through Europe for theyre dealings in olde Instruments. Violins, Tenors & eke Violoncellos are to be found by everie Maker of Merit at times in theyre hands. With everie olde Instrument is given a certificate—proof of its age and Maker—& such is accepted as a bond of genuineness all ye wide world over. They will tell you what it will cost to have your Instrument mended, & there you willen eke hear of a Master for any Instrument now in use. There also monie can be had for all sorts of olde stringed instruments. Copies of beautiful books on Stradivari & Maggini & divers other matters of fiddle interest can be obtained.

English Bow-Making and the Hill Influence

It is a feature of the history of violin-making in Britain that, as a glance at the Directory will indicate, numerous keen amateurs and semi-professional makers have found themselves able to make instruments of the violin family, but few have taken to bow-making. On the other hand, a select band of English bow-makers, not least those associated with the firm of Hill, have given England a very high international reputation in this field, excelled only by the great French makers. Many distinguished professional players who would not use and never have used an English instrument nevertheless play with a Hill or a Tubbs bow.

---

[15] Inglis, 'W. E. Hill & Sons', 298. Subsequently to this two successor businesses have been established, so the Hill name will continue.

[16] No. 586, p. 3.

The making of a violin comes fairly naturally to a professional or amateur cabinet-maker or carpenter—the tools being to a large extent similar to those used for cabinet-making. But bows are rather a different matter. If the full bow is made, including the nut (or frog) (and to do anything else would be regarded by many as cheating), it requires in part a type of work met with more typically in the jewellery trade. Whether it is a matter of cutting the stick or making the accessories, the tools employed are different from those used in violin-making. It is not without significance that the Dodd family started as gun-lock and scale makers and members of the Tubbs family were associated with the jewellery trade.

The first 'modern' bows were what William Retford in his book on *Bows and Bow Makers*[17] calls 'Corelli' bows, straight-sticked or even convex-sticked early eighteenth-century bows with fixed frogs, often made of snakewood and light in weight, and often having 'pike's head' points or heads. Samples of these are on exhibition from the Hill Collection in the Ashmolean Museum. David D. Boyden in his catalogue of the Hill Collection notes that the term 'Corelli bows' does not allow for the marked differences of individual early bows, nor has anyone defined what a 'Corelli bow' is.[18] In England these bows were produced as necessary accessories of somewhat low status and often carry the name of the violin-maker, for example 'Wamsley', stamped on the frog (which is often of ivory). The actual maker is unknown.

There then evolved what Retford calls 'the semi-Corelli type', the stick being sprung in the modern way, but not to the full extent. In England these bows are often attributed to Edward Dodd (1705–1810), the founding father of a distinguished family of bow- and violin-makers in London discussed elsewhere in the text and also in the Directory. Retford remarks that 'many of these are of exceptional craftsmanship; few specimens were named, apparently being made and supplied to the trade'.[19] Edward's son John Dodd (1752–1839), formerly a gun-lock and scale maker by repute, is thought to have worked with his father for some years, producing English 'semi-Corelli' bows of a high quality. John Dodd is often compared to Tourte, the Parisian bow-maker of colossal distinction. Retford does not share this enthusiasm for the work of John Dodd:

The majority of Dodd violin bows are obsolete; no performer of the present age or time would consider using them . . . There is evidence of a more expert touch in the metal parts of the bow than that of the wood section, which frequently is uneven and irregular in the graduation of the stick. There are exceptions to this; occasionally a Dodd is seen in which the stick, apart from the length is equal to anything produced in France at that time.[20]

---

[17] (London, 1964).
[18] Boydon, *Hill Collection*, 27. See also *Violin Family*, ch. 8, for a history of the bow. Also Peter Walls, 'Mozart and The Violin', *Early Music*, 20 (1992), 5, esp. 13–21.
[19] Retford, *Bows*, 65.
[20] Ibid. 67.

Retford's reference to length reminds us that Dodd's bows are usually rather shorter than the modern preferred length adopted by François Tourte (1745–1835), working in Paris. But the modern view is that John Dodd probably began to make his bows between 1780 and 1790, later adopting the innovations occurring in French bow-making. (The length of bow adopted by Tourte, incidentally, was from 74 to 75 cm for violin bows, 74 cm for the viola bow, and 72–73 cm for cello bows. The weight of the violin bow averaged about 56 g.[21] The generally preferred weight in modern times is about 60 g for violins, 70 g for violas, and 80 g for cellos.)

In Dodd's time the design of the head began to resemble the modern 'hatchet' head, the stick became concave and longer, and the design for the movable nut or frog was developed, with a wider ribbon of hair. Of these developments the adoption of a concave stick, in substitution for the former (usually snakewood) convex or straight bow-stick, was a fundamental one which affected the playing potential of the instrument. An important catalyst for change was Wilhelm Cramer (1745–99), the Mannheim violinist who went to London in 1772. He is associated with the 'Cramer bow', transitional in type and having a 'battle-axe' head. These Cramer-model bows were in vogue between 1772 and 1792 when overtaken by the 'Viotti bow' developed by the Tourte family. Because of the concave design of the stick, the old 'pike's head' was found too low to provide sufficient clearance between hair and stick in the middle of the bow. The 'battle-axe', and then 'hatchet' heads were therefore developed in the late eighteenth and early nineteenth centuries to provide a solution to this problem.

The adoption of pernambuco wood, a type of Brazil-wood, for fine bows also became universal during this time. This dense, strong, but flexible wood is also intimately connected with the development of the type of technique required to play such display pieces as Paganini's Caprices.

The Tubbs Connection

In the latter part of the nineteenth century the two great bow-making families of London, the Hills and the Tubbs, interconnect. The first of the Hill family definitely to have made bows appears to be William Ebsworth, of whom Henley remarks that he 'produced many bows of very serviceable utility for average good soloists. Balance and workmanship completely excellent, though their style assumes no special ingenuity of creativeness. Round and octagon sticks . . .'[22]

But Henley also states that William Ebsworth 'employed' James Tubbs

[21] *Violin Family*, 212.   [22] Henley, *Dictionary*, 572.

(1835–1921), though William Watson is quoted as saying that 'The Hill bow-making dynasty really started with James Tubbs who worked for Hills, although he had his own business and was never employed there.'[23] Retford's account is probably the more accurate, since W. E. Hill discussed Tubbs with Retford. Apparently in about 1860 James Tubbs was unemployed, having worked in the textile trade. Nevertheless, he possessed the tools and appliances common to the Tubbs family of bow-makers and must have had some training. He persuaded W. E. Hill to employ him, although his first bow was described by W. E. Hill to Retford as 'like a dog's hind leg'. Retford then states that James Tubbs worked in W. E. Hill's workshop for probably a decade. During this time, Retford says, 'there was no division of labour here. Tubbs made the complete bow, this is obvious to one having knowledge of the craft.'[24] Retford adds that when one of these bows, made for 16 shillings probably on a piece-work basis, later came into the possession of Tubbs his practice was to stamp 'TUBBS' over W. E. HILL, and there were certainly reported disputes in the sale-room where Tubbs claimed authorship of a bow described as a 'Hill bow'. It seems a certain animus was mutual. The Hills regarded Tubbs as not entirely honest and with a tendency towards drink.

Retford thinks that Tubbs left the employment of W. E. Hill in 1870 and commenced working on his own account. Henley states that Tubbs's name became renowned when 'quartetists at the Monday popular concerts, London, used his bows from 1865'. Be that as it may, Tubbs moved into premises in King Street, Soho, and subsequently into Wardour Street from 1872. Although Tubbs continued to do repairs and rehairing at the behest of Alfred Hill, he stamped his bows 'J. Tubbs' and changed the design of the head more to the Tourte type. He also discarded the round-ended frog, introduced a silver face on the head of the bow, and adopted what Retford calls 'the excessively whippy stick'.[25]

Retford dates the birth of what is now recognized as the standard Tubbs bow to about 1875. 'Chamber music was a past-time [sic] of the aristocracy of Mayfair. A popular combination being an Italian fiddle and a Tubbs bow—the cost of the bow being 3 guineas.'[26] Retford states that the key to the mystery of the weak sticks is that they were needed to satisfy the demand of the wealthy amateur. His book includes a detailed analysis of the development of the work of James Tubbs, with diagrams, work which was to provide the major competition to the Hill family in the bow-making industry. Few of his bows are now left which retain the original hairing system, namely 150 hairs inserted into the ferrule of the frog, or nut, without a wedge. By his final decade of work, the whippy stick had been abandoned. As regards balance, Morris says that Tubbs developed his bows in accordance with

[23] Ann Inglis, 'Tales from the Chimney Corner', *Strad* (June, 1992,), 539.
[24] Retford, *Bows*, 72.
[25] Ibid. 73.
[26] Ibid. 74.

mathematical principles developed by W. S. B. Woodhouse, a scientist and musician. Weight and diameter had to ensure vibration throughout the length of the stick.

Retford's verdict on the work of Tubbs is this:

> The Tubbs bow is a straightforward product. Silly mannerisms are missing, the whole design being entirely practical and efficient . . . The Tubbs is justly recognised as being a first-class bow. Time was not spent on elaborate attention to detail. The head had no centre ridge and is of a type rapidly and easily fashioned. Doubtless, a Tubbs was made in the number of hours constituting a Victorian day, but not during the hours of any one particular day.[27]

The latter remark relates to the legend that Tubbs made one bow a day. John Stagg, the contemporary bow-maker trained at Hills, considers this to have been impossible and reckons that a skilled bow-maker would take about forty hours per bow, half this time being applied to the making of the stick and the other half to its accessories and finishing.

Meredith Morris called on Tubbs at his workshop on 5 August 1890, having first met him twenty-five years previously. He reported:

> He certainly looks good for another ten years' work. He is a man of medium height, rather spare but wiry figure, very shrewd and somewhat reticent and incommunicative in his manner. He seldom speaks except when spoken to, and his answers are usually brief and categorical. The enthusiast or scribbler who enters the little shop at 94 Wardour Street, with the intention of 'drawing' its occupant is certain to go away a disappointed man. Tubbs is invulnerable, and criticism or praise are equally lost upon him. On one point only is it possible to arouse his susceptibility: if you confuse his name with that of any other bow-maker of the name of Tubbs, you are likely to drop in for a warm time of it . . . He is a man of the good old school, plain, simple, straightforward, with a rather crusty exterior, but with a solid heart and plenty of sober sense. He is very different from the typical business man of-today, who is essentially a man of the world, with often a slice of the flesh and the devil thrown in.[28]

During his lifetime Tubbs sold his bows for 3 guineas each (or more, depending on the materials used and on the inherent quality). In the sale-room, the *Musical Standard* reported in 1908 that two silver-mounted bows by James Tubbs were sold for £2. 4s. 0d. and £2. 8s. 0d. respectively—sale-room prices of 'new' articles often being below retail price.[29] Heron-Allen, when writing his book on *Violin-Making as it Was, and Is*, produced in 1884, remarked that 'the bows of James Tubbs are even now much sought after, and will, in time to come, be valuable from their scarcity and sterling qualities'.[30] This was a prescient remark. In 1992 one major

---

[27] Ibid. 76–7.
[28] Morris, *British Violin Makers*, 242.
[29] Quoted in John Broadhouse, *The Violin: How to Make it* (London, c.1910), 133.
[30] p. 103.

auction-house estimates the value of a silver-mounted cello bow of this maker at £2,500–£3,500. Tubbs's output is estimated as being about five thousand bows. He was assisted by his son Alfred until the latter's death in 1912.

Later Hill Bow-Making

Tubbs was essentially someone who required to be appreciated on his own terms. Morris remarked how little he liked being bracketed with other makers of his family such as C. E. Tubbs, his brother, good though the work often was. All the descriptions and photographs of him with his hat and neck-scarf at his bench, indicate an unashamed individualist. By contrast, the subsequent history of the Hill bow-making industry involved an element of team-work. Essentially, the workshop having been established in Hanwell, one generation of bow-makers had apprenticed to it the next generation and the line continued unbroken until very recent years. Table 3 lists the known makers employed at Hills with their relevant working dates. Experts can often tell which particular maker was responsible for a specific bow both by the markings on the bow (see below) or by specific characteristics of the work, although all workmen were supplied with the same template. Arthur Bultitude gave some examples. He could, for instance, spot a fake bow supposed to be a Hill by Arthur Copley by finding that the forger had overlooked the fact that Copley was left-handed and had stamped the bow right-handed. Bultitude's own bows had two silver pins underneath the hair of a gold-mounted bow. William Napier and Sidney Yeoman both had eye defects so that they 'cleaned up' their heads with a different slope one side from the other. Retford's work was identifiable by the roundness and fullness with which he 'cleaned up' the head around the point.[31] But essentially all were Hill bows and it was never intended that they should be publicly associated with an individual employee.

Physical Identification

The earlier makers adopted a particular pattern of frog which is identifiable, or put marks on the face at the head of the bow. From about 1920 onwards until about 1970 most bows have a letter (and sometimes digits) stamped on the lower facet of the butt underneath the nut (or frog), and a mark or number is stamped on the face (the silver triangular lower part of the tip or head). The two numbers next to the letter on the stick beneath the nut indicate the year of manufacture—so, for

---

[31] Alburger, *Violin Makers*, 196–7.

example, 32 indicates 1932. When a letter is used, for example 'B', it indicated the exact matching of the nut and stick so marked. In addition, gold-mounted bows bear a serial number on the stick. Marks and numbers on the *face* of the bow do indicate the maker. The numbers are accordingly given in Table 3. In this connection, the veteran Hill bow-maker Bill Watson is quoted as saying that in the 1930s 'there was a division of labour. You might have Albert Leeson and Edgar Bishop working together, Leeson making the frog and Bishop making the stick, which is why No. 3 is marked on the frog and 2 on the face. This all stopped in 1945 when everyone became a complete bow-maker. There was a danger that they would be left with people able to make either a stick or a frog with no experience of the other half.'[32]

Prices from their catalogue *c*.1930 range from £15 for violin, viola, or cello bows mounted in gold and tortoiseshell (stamped with the firm's full name 'W. E. HILL & SONS'), £6. 6s. 0d. for violin bows mounted in silver and tortoiseshell, £5 if mounted in silver and ivory, £4. 4s. 0d. if in silver and ebony (all stamped as above), £3. 3s. 0d. for silver- and ebony-mounted bows stamped 'W. E. H & S', £2. 2s. 0d. for those stamped 'H & S', and £1. 11s. 6d. for those stamped 'HILL', all with silver mounts. These differences in price and quality are important since second-hand values are often graded appropriately.

The Hill firm also offered a rehairing service. 'A bow in daily service should be rehaired every three months', or the 'bite' will be lost, they explain. They stress the importance of entrusting bows to good workmen only, 'as in the hands of the incompetent, serious damage, often unperceived by the owner, is frequently done'. The charge in *c*.1930 was 3s. 0d., '(hair of the finest quality only being used)'. Wooden boxes with special india-rubber fittings to ensure the safe transit of bows through the post were 4s. 6d. 'Beautiful bow-boxes in oak, mahogany, walnut and satinwood, to take two, four or six bows' were also available at prices between 10s. 6d. and £5. 5s. 0d. 'Guinea bows', unstamped, are thought to have been made for the trade, particularly Hart & Sons and Beare's.

Hills made bows in various different qualities until about 1950. One particularly infamous batch from the 1930s, consisting of at least 1,000 bows, were 'slab cut' rather than being cut on the quarter. (The curl should show on the side of the bow, not on the top or underneath.) The consequence of this method of working the wood is that the head easily comes off. The firm, apparently on the initiative of the workshop manager, rather than scrapping these bows, bored a hole in the head and inserted a wooden peg. These bows bear a tiny W between the pernambuco and the metal face.[33]

---

[32] Inglis, 'Tales from the Chimney Corner', 539.   [33] Ibid. 544.

Superior bows of the Hills often carry a fleur-de-lis design on the frog. This was originally supplied by manufacturing jewellers and trimmed and inlaid at Hills. After 1945 it was not possible to continue to obtain work from that source and so Arthur Bultitude, the then foreman, decided that the job should be done 'in-house'. Bill Watson was the first to cut the fleur-de-lis, a job that initially took over three hours but was reduced to about seven minutes after a year's experience. (There is some Hill family scepticism as to the possibility of such speedy work.) Watson states that 'in those days a gold-mounted fleur-de-lys bow cost £14, Bond Street paid the workshop £28 in 100% mark-up and the bows were sold for £100'. This notional mark-up was not unconnected to the structure of purchase tax.

Of the many distinguished bow-makers in Table 3 associated with Hills, Samuel Allen, William Retford, and Arthur Bultitude call for specific comment. Samuel Allen (1848–c.1905) was a discovery of the Hill brothers in the 1880s. He was a musician and opera singer as well as a craftsman who repaired instruments for colleagues. He commenced bow-making some time before the Hill brothers saw his work. They were sufficiently impressed to employ him as a bow-maker and put him in charge of a section of their workshops at Hanwell. He remained there for about a decade before working on his own account at St John's Wood, London.[34] Retford describes his bows as 'wonderful specimens of high-class craftsmanship, made entirely without any division of labour—with one exception—his daughter hairing the bows'.[35] He was the originator of the style of bow known as the 'Hill bow', though opinion differs on whether the fleur-de-lis type was introduced by him, or later, about 1910. Allen copied many aspects of Tourte's style and is thought to have worked at one time with a member of the Bazin family in France. Allen also introduced the not universally popular whalebone lapping. Though Panormo had in fact used this in the past, the French fashion was for gold or silver tinsel to cover the stick where the player's fingers grasped it. Retford's verdict is that 'Allen's standard of craftsmanship bordered on perfection, yet he lacked knowledge vitally necessary for complete success in bow-making.' Andrew Hill's view, expressed to the author, is that this reservation is completely unfounded.

Retford, in his modest, idiosyncratic, chaotically designed, but fascinating book on *Bows and Bow Makers*, referred to in numerous places in this part of the text, gives no credit to himself for his own enormous contribution to English bow-making. Arthur Bultitude describes his early years under Retford as being remarkable for the perfection which was always demanded and Retford's complete integrity. 'If there was a bad piece of wood at Hills it went on the fire. Their materials were first class, and their metal work was far in advance of anything that had ever been used in a bow before, and they used stout gauge metal, high quality.'[36]

---

[34] Retford, *Bows*, 63.   [35] Ibid.   [36] Alburger, *Violin Makers*, 190–1.

Retford had come to the firm in 1892 and gone straight into the bow department after Samuel Allen had departed leaving one or two mysterious tools which nobody knew quite what to do with. Fortunately Hills had such a collection of fine bows through their hands that models were easy to come by. Retford himself had no known teacher as such. By the time William Watson arrived at Hills in 1945, Retford was already 77 years old, and Watson considers that Retford was the finest bow-maker the world has ever seen. He is described by Watson as being

a charming man. Arthur [Bultitude] said he was cantankerous, but I never found that. Maybe there was a clash of personalities—he was a stickler for having everything right, dead right. He didn't have time for people like William Napier and they were always at loggerheads. Napier made fine bows when he was younger but he came from Broadwoods, the piano people, and Retford always considered he made bows like a carpenter.'[37]

Retford is credited with always using the masculine, more popular Tourte–Peccatte type head rather than the Voirin–Sartory style, 'even if he always considered Voirin the best maker of all time'.[38]

Arthur Bultitude (1908–90) is the only bow-maker interviewed by Mary Anne Alburger in her book on *The Violin Makers*. He gives a long account of his work with Hills which is invaluable and from which quotations have already been made. Watson considers that the work of Bultitude was good in his younger days but suffered as a result of running a busy workshop. In 1961 Bultitude left Hills and continued his bow-making activities in Hawkhurst, Kent. During this period he again produced many fine bows, though his later bows may have been affected by a degenerative disease from which Bultitude suffered.[39]

In recent times it is remarkable to note how many contemporary bow-makers of distinction in England started their working life at Hills before setting up on their own. Although all these makers had their own individual characteristics, in most cases the 'Hill style' is discernible and the value to them of the training which they obtained at Hills must have been immense. For instance the contemporary Bristol bow-maker John Stagg, who obtained a degree in Engineering from Durham University, gives Desmond Hill great credit for employing him in the first place. 'I was a boat-builder and Desmond felt that it was closer to bow-making than cabinet making. He saw I had an eye for a curve, whether 30 ft. or 30 ins. It was an enlightened approach.'[40]

Total bow production of the firm of W. E. Hill & Sons up to its closure in 1992 is reckoned to be about 1,250 gold-mounted violin bows and 300 to 400 each of viola and cello bows. Silver-mounted bows in each category were about ten times the number for gold. As already stated, a gold-mounted bow bears under its nut a

[37] Inglis, 'Tales from the Chimney Corner', 540. [38] Ibid. 541. [39] Ibid. 540.
[40] Inglis, 'W. E. Hill & Sons', 298.

date, for example '63' = 1963, a serial number, for example 971, and a number indicating the maker, for example 8, stamped diminutively on the face. As a general rule a gold mounting should indicate a stick flawless in strength and flexibility, blemish-free, and designed for at least a century's playing.

As already indicated, those early makers whose work is not numbered have certain identifiable characteristics in their workmanship and mostly left identification marks on the bow: dots, dashes, and circles. Numbers started with Arthur Copley.

It must be added that the dissemination of what has hitherto been regarded as trade secrets obviously increases the risk of forgery. Buyers must therefore adopt a vigilant attitude and be prepared to take expert opinion on a bow's authenticity.

The Retford Collection

Hill bows are in constant use and are dispersed throughout the world. But after William C. Retford's death in 1970 Retford's tools and a number of bows in his possession, including those he was working on at the time of his death aged 95, were collected together and given to the Bate Collection housed in the Faculty of Music, Oxford University. Amongst these is an experimental tubular bow discussed in an article in the *Strad*.[41] The same article lists as being amongst the Retford Gift bows by Panormo, William Tubbs, Edward Dodd, a joint effort by Arthur Copley and Sidney Yeoman, A. R. Bultitude, and Samuel Allen as well as a number by William C. Retford himself. It is understood that this collection may be viewed by the public.

Other English Bow-Makers

A number of other English bow-makers are known from 1870 or thereabouts—in case it should be thought that there was a Hill–Tubbs monopoly. Many of them were also professional violin-makers: for example George Darbey and John Walker. These makers are mentioned in the Directory as appropriate.

Restoration Work and Dealing

William Ebsworth had established Hills' reputation as being one of the finest establishments in the world for restoration work. This side of the business, which was often in practice combined with dealing in fine instruments by buying,

---

[41] Jeremy Montagu, 'Tubular Bows', *Strad* (Mar. 1984), 803.

TABLE 3: *Bow-Makers at W. E. Hill & Sons* (Showing dates of work where available)

	Samuel Allen	(1848–c.1905) Work unmarked.
	William Napier	(1848–1930 or 1932) Born Forfar, Scotland. Work unmarked. Worked for Broadwoods, piano manufacturers. Joined Hills 1889.
	Sidney Braithwaite Yeoman	(1876–1948) Joined Hills 1885.
	William Charles Retford	(1875–1970) Joined Hills 1891, retired 1956.
	William Grieve Johnston	(1860–1944) Joined Hills 1894.
	William Richard Retford	(1900–60) See text.
	Frank Donald Napier	(1885–1969) Son of William above. Left Hills and bow-making 1930.
	Charles Leggett	(1872–1916) (Retford: 1880–1917).
	Arthur Scarbrow	(dates unknown)
No. 1	Arthur Henry Copley	(1903–?) Joined Hills 1917; finished bow-making 1959, continued as case-maker.
2	Edgar Bishop	(1903–42) (Retford: 1943) Joined Hills 1917.
3	Albert Leeson	(1903–46) Joined Hills 1919. Produced particularly fine work in the 1930s.
4	Leslie Bailey	(1905–?) Joined Hills 1920, left Hills and bow-making 1939 (Retford: 1940).
5	Arthur John Barnes	(1888–1945) Joined Hills 1919, left 1939.
6	Arthur Richard Bultitude	(1908–90) Joined Hills 1922, left 1961, became self-employed, retired 1982.
7	William David Watson	(b. 1930) Joined Hills 1945; left to become self-employed at Denham 1962.
8	J. Laidlaw	(dates unknown)
	Malcolm Maurice Taylor	(b. 1933). Joined Hills 1947; left 1973 to become self-employed.
9	Ronald Harding	(b. 1935) Joined Hills 1949; left Hills and bow-making 1960.
10	Arthur Allen Brown	(b. 1903) Joined Hills 1946; only made a few bows.
11	Allen Willis	(dates unknown) Joined Hills about 1940. Left about 1960.
12	Garner Wilson	Joined Hills c.1961; left to become self-employed 1966.
13	David Taylor	Left 1966; mainly bow repairs.
14	John Clutterbuck	(b. 1949) Worked 1964–71. Now self-employed.
15	Brian Alvey	(b. 1949) Worked 1966–78. Now self-employed.
16	Stephen Bristow	(b. 1952) Worked 1967–71. Became self-employed.
17	Ian Shepherd	Left bow-making 1976.
18	David Earl	Became self-employed 1981; died 1983.
19	Matthew Coltman	Left 1981. Became self-employed.
20	John William Stagg	(b. 1954) Left Hills 1983 to establish his own business in Bristol.
(21)*	Derek Francis Wilson	(b. 1962) Worked at Hills 1975–85. Became self-employed.
(22)	Timothy Gavin Baker	(b. 1962) Worked c.1981–4. Also worked at J. & A. Beare's.

* Numbers discontinued 1980.

Sources: John Stagg, bow-maker, Bristol; William Watson, 'English Bow Makers', *Journal of the Violin Society of America*, 6/2 (1982), 96; William C. Retford, *Bows and Bow Makers* (London, 1964); W. von Lütgendorff, *Die Geigen- und Lautenmacher*, iii, ed. Thomas Drescher (Tutzing, 1990); *New Grove Dictionary of Musical Instruments*; Andrew Hill.

TABLE 4: Early Hill Bow-Makers and their Marks

Maker		Maker
Sidney Braithwaite Yeoman		Arthur Scarbrow
William Charles Retford		Frank Donald Napier
William Richard Retford		Charles Leggett
William Grieve Johnston (before 1904)		Arthur Henry Copley
(after 1904)		

restoring, and selling them (with the immense advantage of a Hill Certificate of Authenticity where appropriate), continued healthily, bridging the periods when no new instruments were made. The reputation for fine restoration work started by William Ebsworth Hill was fostered particularly by Alfred Hill who was steeped in the Vuillaume–Mirecourt traditions.

Brian Parkinson, who learned restoration techniques as a Hills' apprentice, emphasizes that making and restoring appear to be two different disciplines, the proponents of which do not often talk to each other. This must partly be due to their working in different environments and it must have been an advantage of the Hill working system, rarely found elsewhere in Britain, that restorers, instrument-makers and bow-makers could more easily communicate with each other.[42]

[42] Brian Parkinson worked for a time for Ealing Strings, London, after leaving Hills and later became self-employed in Harrow, Middlesex. See Alburger, *Violin Makers*, pp. 201–11.

The Hills' achievements as dealers in fine Italian and many other makers of bowed string instruments, often selling after necessary restoration and meticulous setting-up, is mentioned in several parts of this book. Instruments taken into stock usually bear a stock number impressed on the end of the fingerboard, for example 'V70'. Either of the two successor firms, W. E. Hill of Aylesbury (Andrew Hill) or D. R. Hill of Great Missenden (David Hill), will presently (as a business transaction) reveal the old firm's description of an instrument bearing that stock number in its books. (It is understood that occasional mismatches are being revealed).

As an indication of the family's concern for the finest instruments going through their hands, staff would be instructed to conceal the existence of an instrument which might have been of interest to a customer if that customer had the reputation of not treating his possessions with proper care!

The Export Trade

When small firms or individual traders cease trading it is uncommon for their ledgers to be preserved—much to the chagrin of economic historians. Certainly in the case of the typical English violin-maker it is rare even for a list of buyers to be preserved—the Forsters being the partial exception. What follows is therefore necessarily somewhat speculative.

It seems inherently unlikely that most violin-makers in Britain until quite recent times seriously attempted to sell their goods abroad. Marketing was limited to advertising the availability of instruments from the maker's own workshop or to distribution of instruments through retailers in London and the other urban centres of musical activity. In the Forsters' list of buyers there are no indications that any were other than 'local'.

Where would the natural markets abroad have been? The USA would have been a primary candidate from the late nineteenth century onwards, noting that the somewhat punitive customs duties in the USA were lightened in 1909. But with the exception of the Hills' products on a limited scale (see below) all the evidence suggests that the American market was either for high-class, usually classic, Italian instruments or, through the mail-order catalogues, for the commercial productions of France and Germany.[43] At the same period, if an export market existed one would expect demand to develop in the old 'Dominions' with the necessary non-tropical climate. Trade connections with the UK were already

---

[43] See Ehrhardt, *Violin Identification*, Bk. 2, being copious extracts from such catalogues. Jay C. Freeman writing in the Foreword to John H. Fairfield, *Known Violin Makers* (Athens, Ga., 1942), states that in about 1908 and because of the Dingley Tariff Act, all violins, etc. made prior to 1801 paid no duty, whereas previously they bore 40%. As a result 'we have in the United States today the major portion of existing 16–18th century good Italian, French and other instruments'.

strong and growing cities sustained some significant musical activity—particularly in Australia, New Zealand, Canada, and South Africa. But although the occasional English instrument did find its way to these countries (sometimes with corners pinned against the effects of excessive heat and humidity in pre-air-conditioned days in tropical parts of the Empire, particularly India), there is precious little evidence of this happening on a systematic basis. This was not because of transportation difficulties—particularly as regards violins and violas. These had been imported into England from Italy as early as the seventeenth century and by the mid- to late nineteenth century France and Germany were exporting huge numbers of instruments, efficiently packed and shipped, to other European countries and the USA.

Possible partial exceptions were Charles Harris of London (*fl.* 1800), who is said to have used his overseas contacts through his work as a customs officer, and George Smart of London (*fl.* 1700) who apparently exported a quantity of cellos to Holland. But with the exception of the Hills, English instruments remained little known outside the UK, and still suffer from this lack of international recognition. The Hills were able to use their high standing with other internationally respected dealers such as Wurlitzer (the Rudolph Wurlitzer Co.). In 1922 Wurlitzer's issued the following advertisement:

VIOLINS OF
Messrs. W. E. Hill & Sons
London, England

We have to announce with great satisfaction that we have been appointed the sole representatives for the United States for the sale of the Violins of Messrs. W. E. Hill & Sons.

Messrs. Hill have occupied a pre-eminent position for many years as Violin and Bow makers. As the leading Old Violin Experts of Europe they have for more than a century enjoyed unique opportunities for the study of the world's finest violins.

Mr. Alfred Hill, present head of the house, since his youth has devoted much of his time to the making of violins. His knowledge and rare skill have made possible the production of the finest violins which have been produced anywhere during the past quarter of a century. It is safe to say that not since the time of Nicolas Lupot have violins of such high quality been produced.

We have been awarded a certain quota of violins by Messrs. W. E. Hill & Sons, but unfortunately the supply is exceedingly limited, as they are not made in commercial numbers.

No. 1—Made upon the model of Stradivarius of 1713–18, beautiful in wood and varnish, artistic workmanship and finish. Price $400.00

No. 2—Made upon the model of Stradivarius of 1713–18, superior wood and varnish, most artistic workmanship and finish. Price $600.00

It should be noted by way of comparison that in *c.*1922 'Wurlitzer Cremona Violins' of unspecified origin were for sale for between $50 and $100 and in the same year the highest-grade cello from L. Mougenot of France ('entirely made by hand') was $350. The cheapest product of Amadée Dieudonné fils was $35. Rather earlier, in 1903–4, Lyon and Healy of Chicago advertised bows by a variety of distinguished makers, including silver-mounted by A. Vigneron ($20), C. R. Weichold, Dresden ($20, also silver-mounted), and W. E. Hill & Sons, London: 'round and octagon. Beautiful trimmings and workmanship, perfect balance, pure silver trimmed; used largely by artists, $30; the same in gold mountings—$50.' A further advertisement mentions Hill bows in four grades from $30, the best gold-mounted, for which 'the best sticks are reserved'—$55. The bows of James Tubbs are also available: 'only his choice and best bows, selected in person by our connoisseur' for $38 ('dark finish, round, pure silver mountings').[44]

As the Wurlitzer advertisement indicates, Hill violins, etc. were not made in commercial quantities and their impact on the US import trade is unlikely to have been significant. These catalogues mention no other English maker at all, so the Hills' comparatively modest effort was probably unique. Their bows were rather a different matter and, of course, much easier to despatch abroad (or to be picked over by American 'connoisseurs'). Ultimately, success in these overseas markets depended upon large-scale factory production of which, as we have already seen, the French and German entrepreneurs had a virtually inviolable monopoly. The comparatively high cost of the Hills' products and their obvious popularity is a tribute to the quality of workmanship involved. In addition, the Hills preferred to sell to the customers direct. There was a feeling that intermediaries were inclined to make excessive profit out of the connection. Direct sales were clearly more simply made within the UK.

If there is little evidence of the exporting of British instruments and bows, with the above exceptions, a distinctly more common phenomenon was for makers themselves to emigrate to the USA or the Dominions. For example, Peter Davidson (the Scottish maker and author), the double bass specialist William Tarr (the latter for a time), and Tarr's son Joseph (d. 1926) emigrated to the USA.

Other *émigrés* whose work was a loss to Great Britain were, in particular, George Duncan (discussed in Chapter 8), who emigrated to Canada in 1892; John Smith, who went from Falkirk, Scotland to Winnipeg, Canada in the early part of the twentieth century where he established a fine reputation; Thomas Mitchell, born in Dundee in 1852 and who went to Canada in the 1880s, working in Toronto with great success; John A. Gould (1866–1944), who was trained at Liverpool and went to Hamilton, Canada and then on to the United States; a clutch of makers who followed Arthur Edward Smith (b. 1880) to Melbourne, Australia in the early years of the twentieth century; Adam Mackie, who worked in Aberdeen from 1893

---

[44] The rate of exchange in 1929 was 1 US dollar for 4s. 1½d., or in decimal currency 21p.

to 1899 and then settled in Johannesburg, South Africa, via Australia, New Zealand, and Tasmania;[45] and H. H. Saby, who left Northamptonshire in 1890 to set up a successful business at 75 Plein Street, Cape Town, South Africa (where he won a gold medal at an industrial exhibition). Some makers developed their expertise after arrival, such as Henry James Shrosbree who set up in Adelaide, South Australia, after what Meredith Morris calls 'a seafaring life' from 1872 to 1880. Shrosbree won a number of awards for his work in Adelaide.

In all it is possible to identify about thirty makers who between about 1850 and 1920 emigrated to the Dominions from England or Scotland. Few could match the misfortune of David Colville, who worked at Cupar, Scotland, between 1845 and 1885. Henley describes him as a hypochondriac who hated drink, tobacco, and women, but not canaries, which he trained to come at his call. He emigrated to Canada with a large number of violins which were destroyed by becoming submerged in one of the lakes. He then wandered all over America, New Zealand and Australia before being sent back to Scotland—insane.

---

[45] He wrote a small booklet on *The Secret of Italian Tone*, according to Henley.

Chapter Ten

🜚 Eminent Dealers, Collectors, and Connoisseurs

The London Dealing Fraternity — Collectors — The Gillott Collection

The London Dealing Fraternity

BY the beginning of the nineteenth century, as the Hill brothers remark:

With but few exceptions, all the notable players of the day had acquired and were playing upon [Stradivari's] instruments; amongst others, La Houssaie, Kreutzer, Rode, Bailliot, Habeneck, Lafont and Bouchet; in England, Viotti, Mori, Kiesewetter, Loder, Salamon, Libon, Raimondi, Cotton Reeve, and Alday.[1]

The Guarneri influence, stimulated by Paganini's playing in the second quarter of the nineteenth century, came rather later. The desire of players and collectors at that time to get their hands on a genuine Stradivari and the comparative prosperity prevailing in Great Britain in the nineteenth century provided the conditions whereby supply could meet demand in London. The Hills regarded the Betts family, having a business at the Royal Exchange in London, as the foremost dealers of the early nineteenth century, others being Dodd, Forster, and Davis. They speculate that Betts may have been in direct communication with similar firms in Paris, such as Pique, Lupot, Köliker,[2] or Gand, which seems likely, though it is unascertained. There were also well known city merchants, such as the Cazenove and Rivaz families, with transcontinental business interests and who, through the agency of members of those families who were keen amateurs, brought in fine instruments to Great Britain.[3]

After the end of the Napoleonic wars in 1815, a continuous period of peace brought increasing prosperity and further demand for Stradivari and other fine Italian instruments. From 1830 onwards trade between London and France,

---

[1] Hill, *Stradivari*, 258. [2] Köliker was, in the Hills' view, 'especially reputed as a dealer' (ibid.).
[3] Ibid. 260.

particularly Paris, became much more established. During the mid-nineteenth century the Hills give the principal dealers in England as A. & J. Betts, Corsby, John Hart, Davis, Fendt & Purdy, John Alvey Turner, and W. E. Hill. The foremost was Hart, but perhaps the most enterprising was Turner, who, taking John Lott (that is, 'Jack' Lott the violin-maker (1804–71)) with him as adviser, paid periodical visits to Paris to make purchases. Lott could understand French and must have had an exceptionally keen eye and retentive memory.

These nineteenth-century dealers operated businesses in one of the two centres of the violin trade in the world and at a time of great interest in the work of the Italian masters by players and collectors. The business should have been immensely profitable, but this proposition is not as obvious as it may seem. A good witness must have been Edward Heron-Allen, who, writing in the August 1894 number of the *Violin Times*, of which he was joint editor, states:

Arthur, Alfred and William Hill are old and valued friends of mine: we were boys together, and I have sometimes reproached them for the prices with which their names are connected, but they assure me that it is through no fault of theirs, and that . . . it is to their commercial disadvantage. It is a well-known fact that on the sale of 'Le Messie' violin for £2,000 their profit did not amount to one copper cent. The instrument passed through their hands, the prestige of the negotiation was theirs, and that is all. In the case of the Stradivari violoncello belonging to M. Batta, they paid for it 51,000 francs (£2,040) and sold it for £2,200. It may, therefore be conceded that in the making of such prices, the dealers have had no hand. On a violin which is readily saleable at £300 to £500 a clever dealer can make a handsome profit; beyond that the profits become small by degrees and beautifully less. The responsibility for this condition of things lies with the great players; so long as [they] insist on playing only on the violins of Stradivari the prices of Cremona violins will be maintained and wax higher yet; and the modern maker will starve.[4]

As has been mentioned before, the person most responsible for bringing the majority of the fine Italian instruments presently in circulation out of Italy in the first place was Luigi Tarisio (1790–1854), whose strange and romantic life story has been told many times, one of the earliest versions being by George Hart.[5] George Hart, probably speaking from family memory, recalls an episode occurring during one of Tarisio's visits to England and his ability instantly to recall the many instruments which had passed through his hands:

In the year 1851 Tarisio visited England, when Mr. John Hart, being anxious that he should see the chief collections of Cremonese instruments in this country, accompanied him to the collection, amongst others, of the late Mr. James Goding, which was then the finest in Europe. The instruments were arranged on shelves at the end of a long room, and

---

[4] *Violin Times*, 1 (1894), 150.
[5] *The Violin: Famous Makers* (1885 edn.), 331–43; see also Farga, *Violins and Violinists*, ch. 9. A biography is William Alexander Silverman, *The Violin Hunter* (London, 1957; repr. 1972).

far removed from them sat the genuine enthusiast, patiently awaiting the promised exhibition. Upon Mr. Goding taking out his treasures he was inexpressibly astonished to hear his visitor calling out the maker of each instrument before he had had time to advance two paces towards him, at the same time giving his host to understand that he thoroughly knew the instruments, the greater number having been in his possession. Mr. Goding whispered to a friend standing by, 'Why the man must certainly smell them, he has not had time to look.' Many instruments in this collection, Tarisio seemed never tired of admiring. He took them up again and again, completely lost to all around—in a word, spell-bound. There was the 'King' Guarneri—the Guarneri known as Lafont's—the beautiful Bergonzi Violin—the Viola known as Lord Macdonald's—General Kidd's Stradivari Violoncello—the Marquis de la Rosa's Amati—Ole Bull's Guarneri—the Santo Serafino 'Cello—and other remarkable instruments too numerous to mention.[6]

As the twentieth century arrived and progressed the firm of W. E. Hill & Sons of New Bond Street consolidated its reputation as one of the world's leading suppliers of great Italian masterpieces. Many lesser instruments went through their books too, and taken together with their workshop products from Hanwell and their immense reputation and practice as restorers, the firm must have become highly profitable. Such success in dealing does not come easily and the market, apparently so tempting, is difficult to enter for those without the necessary know-how. Great experience in the identification of often deceptive instruments is a *sine qua non*. The proprietors must be prepared for large slices of their capital to be tied up for uncertain periods. Buyers internationally must want to beat a path to the shop door. Certificates of guarantee must be accepted by the international fraternity. The Hills built up their reputation over the centuries and never allowed it to tarnish. The only other business to rival its reputation in more recent years has been that of John and Arthur Beare in Soho, London, the proprietors of which have demonstrated similar qualities. The history of this latter firm is summarized in the Directory.

Collectors

There was a necessary connection between London dealers and private, wealthy collectors whose activities had a significant effect on demand for fine instruments. Hart[7] thought that probably the first collector of Italian violins in England was William Corbett who, being a member of the King's Orchestra in the late seventeenth century, went to Italy in 1710 where he accumulated a collection of music and musical instruments. It is possible that he was a government spy, watching 'the Pretender'. When he died in 1748 he bequeathed his 'Gallery of Cremonys and

---

[6] Hart, *The Violin: Famous Makers*, 340. [7] Ibid. 351.

Stainers' to the authorities of Gresham College in London with a view to their being permanently exhibited. Unfortunately his wishes were not carried out because the instruments were later disposed of by auction.

Hart also mentions other early collectors in England as being the Duke of Hamilton, the Duke of Cambridge, the Earl of Falmouth, the Duke of Marlborough, Lord Macdonald, and (later) Mr Andrew Fountaine.[8] Hill adds to this list the names of Goding, Plowden, Gillott, and John Adam. Peter Davidson in his book on *The Violin* (1881) calls the collection of John Adam of London 'the largest and finest assemblage of instruments ever brought together at any time, or in any country'.[9] The collection embraced sixteen violins, seven of which were by Stradivari, four by Joseph Guarneri del Gesù, one by Carlo Bergonzi, and examples by Nicolò Amati, Rogeri, Stainer; four violas, one by Stradivari, two by Carlo Bergonzi, and one by the brothers Amati; three cellos, one by Stradivari, and two by Carlo Bergonzi. There were a number of other Italian instruments.

The collection of James Goding, of Belgrave Square, referred to above, was auctioned in 1857. Hart makes it clear that what was disposed of by auction at Christie's was the remnant of Mr Plowden's collection since he had at one period owned twelve Stradivari violins 'and nearly the same number by Guiseppe Guarneri'.[10] The auction included, as regards violins, three Stradivaris, five examples of the work of Guarneri del Gesù (one being formerly the property of Ole Bull), two Nicolò Amatis, and the MacDonald Stradivari viola; there were three cellos, of which one was the 'General Kyd' Stradivari and another by Sanctus Seraphin. Of these various instruments a Guarneri, formerly the property of Rode, achieved the top price at £260.

In examining the nexus between supply and demand of these fine instruments, we are reminded by the Hills that a number of famous players also clearly augmented their income by dealing. One of these was Dragonetti, the famous double bass player, and others included Paganini and Ole Bull who was 'quite notorious for such dealings in his day'.[11] But there is one character in this scenario who was not known as a player or as a dealer, but clearly played an important part in these mid-nineteenth-century activities, and this was the author and dramatist, Charles Reade.

Reade (1814–84) was a scholar and Fellow of Magdalen College, Oxford and subsequently became a barrister of Lincoln's Inn, London. His fame rests on his novels, in particular *The Cloister and the Hearth* (1861), founded on the life of Erasmus. Of particular interest to violin enthusiasts is 'Jack of All Trades' (1858), a

---

[8] Hart, *The Violin: Famous Makers*, 353.
[9] Davidson, *The Violin*, 220.
[10] Hart, *The Violin: Famous Makers*, 354.
[11] Hill, *Stradivari*, 261. The line between 'investing' in instruments and 'dealing' in them is a narrow one, but many legal and tax consequences hinge on the distinction nowadays. See further the analysis in Harvey, *Violin Fraud*.

scarce title (from *Cream*, including also *The Autobiography of a Thief*) founded on the life of Jack Lott (discussed in the following chapter). The Hills say that Charles Reade between 1840 and 1860 'took a keen interest in old instruments. He travelled a good deal in France, where he frequently met Tarisio, and purchased there Italian instruments, including Stradivarius and Guarnerius, which he re-sold to the London dealers, principally to Hart and Corsby. He also had transactions with Mr. Gillott, the penmaker, whom he materially aided in forming his collection.'[12] Why Reade chose to keep his violin-dealing activities *sub rosa* must be a matter of speculation—perhaps it was an early example of income-tax evasion! Reade did however contribute a celebrated series of articles to the *Pall Mall Gazette* in 1872, 'Cremona Fiddles', which was designed to accompany the Loan Collection of Instruments at the South Kensington Museum, now the Victoria and Albert Museum, London, which important exhibition is discussed later. In these 'Letters' he shows a great knowledge of Italian makers and making techniques and Reade's lively prose still makes stimulating and interesting reading. His opinions are looked at again in the context of the discussion of this exhibition.

It will be inferred from the names of the collectors picked out by Hart, Hill, and Davidson that the earlier ones tended to be of aristocratic connection, many of the instruments probably being acquired in the course of a grand tour (as discussed in Chapter 1). This is substantiated by an interesting letter of Antonio Stradivari, the grandson of the maker, addressed to the Turin dealer G. M. A. Brita, dated from Cremona 31 June 1776—'The violins of the Amati, as well as those of Stradivari, are gone after as if they were bread; three weeks ago there were two English Lords lodging at the Columbina who were looking for 8 violins of ours; they sent persons to ask me if I had some, and I answered to them no, that I did not have any more, saying that I had made only one contract, with you.'[13] But by the middle of the nineteenth century, although there was still plenty of wealth in aristocratic hands, it was the successful entrepreneur and businessman who seemed to have the resources and the will to put together fabulous collections of classical Italian instruments. An astonishing example of this breed was Joseph Gillott of Birmingham.

The Gillott Collection

Gillott was born in 1799 in Sheffield and having been trained in cutlery manufacture came to Birmingham to make buckles. The buckle industry was then in decline and so, working from humble quarters, he adapted his then simple

---

[12] Hill, *Stradivari*, 264. For the Gillott collection, see below.
[13] Ernest N. Doring, *The Guadagnini Family of Violin Makers* (Chicago, 1949), 222.

machinery to the making of pens—particularly steel pen-nibs. His business grew and he ran it in a humane and paternalistic manner from the 'Victoria Works', or 'Gillott Manufactory' in Graham Street, Birmingham, near the jewellery quarter. He was the friendly rival in business of the wealthy philanthropist Josiah Mason, the founder of the University of Birmingham, but Gillott was undoubtedly the pace-setter for what became a world-wide industry. His nibs were cheap and efficient. By 1866 Birmingham claimed to have established itself, not without reason, as the pen-shop of the world. There were twelve pen factories in the city employing 240 workers and Gillott produced literally millions of pens and nibs per week with his steam-driven machinery. Prices for nibs accordingly fell from 5s. per gross in the 1830s to $1^{1}/_{2}d.$ per gross in the 1860s. The makers were mainly women and girls with a few highly skilled and comparatively well-paid men.

Gillott moved his residence from Newhall Street, in the middle of the city, to Edgbaston and turned his house there into something of an art gallery, the great artist J. M. W. Turner being a personal friend. Gillott was also closely acquainted with Charles Reade who wrote the whole of his book *It is never too late to mend* with a single steel nib presented to him by Gillott.

George Hart, who was called in to value and dispose of Gillott's collection on his death in 1872, gives a vivid description of this operation in his book on *The Violin*.[14] Hart explains that in point of number Gillott's collection exceeded all others. He had upwards of 500 instruments, the chief part of which belonged to the Italian school. The disposal of his stringed instruments in April 1872 by Christie's was less than half the number originally owned by Gillott. Gillott was not an active musician or even particularly interested in music, though he was keen on fine art.

As Hart explains, Gillott's collection started with a picture deal. He was arranging for an exchange of pictures with Edward Atherstone, poet and novelist (1788–1872), who collected both violins and pictures. There was a balance unaccounted for and Mr Atherstone suggested that one of his fiddles should be thrown in as a counterpoise. 'That would be to no purpose', remarked Mr Gillott, 'for I have neither knowledge of music nor of the Fiddle.' 'I am aware of that,' rejoined his friend; 'but Violins are often of extraordinary value as works of art.'[15] So Gillott accepted Atherstone's fiddle as a makeweight and from then on instruments followed one after the other to such an extent that Hart was of the opinion that he was the master of the largest number of Italian instruments ever owned by a single individual. However, Gillott abandoned this interest as suddenly as he had acquired it and, disposing of a great number of instruments, stored most of the remainder in his steel-pen works at Birmingham where they remained undisturbed for more than twenty years.

[14] Hart, *The Violin: Famous Makers*, 355–61.   [15] Ibid. 355.

It fell to George Hart to catalogue the collection and, walking through the factory to the accompaniment, as he relates, of

countless machines busy shaping magnum-bonums, swan-bills and divers other writing implements, I was about to feast my eyes on some of the choicest works of the old Italian Fiddle makers . . . In the centre of the room was a large warehouse table, upon which were placed in pyramids upwards of seventy Violins and Tenors, stringless, bridgeless, unglued, and enveloped in the fine dust which had crept through the crevices of the cardboard sarcophagi in which they had rested for the previous quarter of a century. On the floor lay the bows. The scene may not inappropriately be compared to a post-mortem examination on an extended scale.[16]

Wondering why there were no cellos, Hart was then conducted into another warehouse where amongst unused lathes, statuary, antique pianos, parts of machinery, pictures, and picture-frames were fifty cellos in five rows, each ten deep. 'They looked in their cases like a detachment of infantry awaiting the word of command. Years had passed by since they had been called upon to take active service of a pacific and humanising nature in the ranks of the orchestra.'[17] Amongst the cellos were examples by Bergonzi, Amati, Andrea Guarneri, Cappa, Grancino, Testore, Landolfi, and others.

Hart was then told that there were yet more instruments at Gillott's residence in Edgbaston and on arrival there he was pointed to a long, glazed mahogany case. In this were Gillott's prizes, all in their cases, and amongst the sixteen examples were six Stradivari, two Guarneri, one Bergonzi, two Amati, and five other high-class violins.

The Sale by Christie's on 29 April 1872 comprised 153 lots and realized a total of £4,195. 29s. 6d. The catalogue reveals both the prices and the buyers. Amongst the most choice items, a 1737 Stradivari violin went for £160 to Hart. Hart also bought a J. B. Guadagnini for £28, a Lupot violin for £10. 10s. 0d., an Amati violin for £31, and a Guarneri cello (unclassified) for £121. Hill (presumably W. E. Hill) bought a 'Guarnerius model' violin for £5. 10s. 0d., a J. B. Guadagnini viola of 1733 for £20, an Amati cello for £22, and a Landolfi violin for £11, together with some French instruments and a cello by Peter Wamsley for £6. It is interesting to see that lot 117, 'a silver-mounted bow, and one other', went to 'Tubbs' for £2, and Charles Reade was a conspicuous purchaser of a Guarneri violin for £105, a Lupot violin for £21, a 'fine old Italian violin' for £27, and another such for £23. Reade also bought 'a very perfect tenor, by Carlo Bergonzi', lot 139, for £50, and a 'fine old Italian violoncello' with case for £42. Other well-known names amongst the purchasers were G. Chanot and Boullangier.

[16] Ibid. 357.   [17] Ibid. 358.

Amongst Gillott's instruments there were few English ones, though 'a violin, by Vincenzo Panormo—in capital preservation', lot 104, was bought by Joyce for £61, a tenor by William Forster was bought by Lord Harrington for £5. 10s. 0d., and an old English viola da gamba went to Lord Gerald Fitz-gerald for £2. 2s. 0d.—the latter buyer also buying the only double bass in the collection, by Gasparo de Salò, 'formerly Signor Dragonetti's with well-made case' (lot 48), for £41.

One buyer who was not present was Vuillaume. As Haweis says:

Down to the end of his life Vuillaume was a great dealer, and he hurried over to London when quite an old man to attend the sale of Mr. Gillott's fiddles. He mistook the date, and arrived the day after the sale. He came into Mr. Hill's shop in Wardour Street, and gave vent to his disappointment. Mr. Hill, whom he always visited when in London, had bought several instruments, and had a second deal with Vuillaume then and there, much to the Frenchman's gratification. It is interesting to catch this glimpse of the two greatest dealers and artificers of the age face to face for one moment, and in such friendly and characteristic relations.[18]

Peter Davidson[19] mentions a number of Scottish collectors owning Stradivaris and Guarneris in particular based not only, as one would expect, in Edinburgh and Glasgow but also scattered throughout Scotland including the Highlands. Davidson also mentions a disposal by auction in 1876 of the Thornley collection (John Thornley of Preston, Lancashire) and the Parera collection (P. R. Parera of Manchester) in 1877. Both these collections included fine Stradivaris and Guarneris. But not all these glamorous attributions were what they seemed. One so-called Strad cello, 1713, in the Parera collection and formerly in the possession successively of King George IV, the Duke of Cambridge, and Corsby, was the cause of a legal action when it became reclassified as a Rogeri.[20]

Of the many other collectors in the British Isles during the nineteenth century, too numerous to mention, one stands out for particular generosity to future players. John Rutson (1826–1906) used his private wealth as a patron of the arts and became Director of the Royal Academy of Music. He gave a priceless collection of instruments to the Royal Academy in 1890. These included four Stradivaris, one being the 'Archinto' viola of 1696, three instruments by the Amati family, a Pressenda (1833), a Cappa (1690), and a Rota (1800). These instruments are illustrated in David Rattray's book *Masterpieces of Italian Violin Making 1620–1850*.[21]

[18] Haweis, *Old Violins*, 117.   [19] *The Violin* (1881 edn.), discussed in Ch. 8.   [20] Ibid. 226–7.
[21] (London, 1991).

Chapter Eleven

The Great Copyists of Nineteenth-Century London

The Stradivari Influence — The Fendts — The Lotts — Forgery and the Criminal Law — Retrospect

The Stradivari Influence

IT is perhaps to be expected, in the light of the great interest shown by players and collectors in the instruments of Stradivari and Joseph Guarneri in particular, that there should be a market for new instruments made to look like those of classic Italian makers. Before 1800 there was little evidence of any systematic attempt to make new instruments look like those of an old master. Doubtless this happened occasionally, and some makers are reputed to have baked or chemicalized their wood to try to give the effects of age, but it is a feature of all the major English instrument-makers thriving in the eighteenth century and mentioned in the text that there is something distinctively English in their style which could hardly be mistaken by any experienced critic for classical Italian work. There were, of course, some makers such as Daniel Parker who went against the trend of copying the Stainer–Amati models then so prevalent, but even in his work the wood, probably the tooling techniques used, and other details of his work are unmistakably English.[1]

The importance of the arrival of Vincenzo Panormo in London in 1798 (in John Betts's workshop) has already been emphasized. He brought with him not only a deep knowledge of Italian violin-making technique but a deep respect for the work of Stradivari in particular. Within the next decade or two London had started to be a source of convincing facsimiles of the Italian instruments of a century earlier.

---

[1] Seventeenth-century English instruments, though still distinctive, were not infrequently relabelled as Italian.

The Fendts

In this connection there are two families who were at the centre of this trend, the Fendts and the Lotts. To take the Fendts first, the founder member of the family was Bernhard, born in the Tyrol in 1776. He was the nephew and pupil of François Fent of Paris, but he came to London in 1798 to work in the workshop of Thomas Dodd. Significantly, one of his colleagues there at the same time was John Frederick Lott (I), who later founded his own business in King Street, Seven Dials, London. Bernhard, who died in 1832, worked on the Strad and Amati models and is particularly renowned for his double basses (mentioned in Chapter 1). Bernhard had three sons, Bernhard Simon (1800–52), Martin (1812–45), and Jacob (1802–49). All these were distinguished makers but Jacob was particularly renowned for his facility as a copyist. Henley calls his production 'modern antiques, superlatively finished instruments (even to the worn appearance of the varnish), which would have constituted in themselves ... an important pictorial gallery of English art, if he had not indulged in the practice of counterfeiting by putting in fictitious labels, etc.' Nevertheless, his replicas of Stradivari, Guarneri, and Amati won him renown in his lifetime and possibly some wealth.

The first son, Bernhard Simon, who later became a partner of George Purdy, is usually regarded as pre-eminent in this family. He is described by Morris as:

as clever and ingenious a workman as ever handled gouge and callipers in this country, and, in my opinion, as unscrupulous as he was clever. He made scores of counterfeited 'Strads' and 'Josephs.' Hart says that he made some hundreds of copies of Guarneri alone. These were not all 'fakes', it is true, but very many of them were, and they have been sold time and again as the genuine work of the masters whose forged labels they carry. All the Fendts were counterfeiters, more or less—generally more, not less—and in so far as they departed from the paths of 'righteous dealing' they deserved nothing but the execration of posterity and the contempt of the historian, a cleverness notwithstanding. Cleverness does not atone for fraud.

Nowadays, the work of Bernhardt Simon and Jacob can usually be identified by experts without too much difficulty, but this has not always been so. The Fendt family extended to three generations and is further discussed in the Directory.

The Lotts

The Lott family is equally remarkable. The founder, John Frederick, was born in Germany in 1775 but joined Thomas Dodd's workshop in 1798. Morris states that 'he was a cabinet maker at first, but under the influence of Fendt he before long discarded that trade for the more congenial one of violin-making'. He established the unsullied reputation for himself of being possibly the finest London maker of double basses (see Chapter 1). His models were on Stradivari principles though his varnishing is often criticized as being below par for this quality of work. John Frederick had two sons. One was George Frederick (1800–68), who worked for many years for Davis of Coventry Street, London. He was, as Morris says, 'a very clever workman, and a very clever imitator—too clever, indeed'. Henley provides the ingenious justification that he 'regarded his work as a duty incumbent to the man who has a scrupulous appreciation for the model he imitates'.

The greatest of this family was undoubtedly the other son, the fascinating John Frederick (II), usually called 'Jack' Lott. His name has been mentioned before in this book and it will be recalled that Charles Reade wrote Lott's thinly disguised biography in his novel *Jack of All Trades: A Matter-of-Fact Romance*. From this depiction it is clear that Lott was a man of great talent, ingenuity, and initiative. The novel is of a picaresque character, and much of it describes Lott's career as an unsuccessful fireworks organizer (his rockets tended to travel horizontally, setting fire to the clothes of the onlookers) and elephant-trainer whose charges tended to run amok. These activities were made necessary because 'the fiddle trade took one of those chills all fancy trades are subject to'.

The novel also recounts Lott's adventures in the orchestra of the Adelphi Theatre in London, where, owing to a connection with one of the players whose violin he 'used often to repair and doctor', he was recruited as a second violin. The conversation is reported as follows: 'How can I do that?' 'Why I often hear you try a violin.' 'Yes, and I always play the same notes, perhaps you have observed that too?' 'I notice it is always the slow movement—eh? never mind, this is the only thing I can think of to serve you—you must strum out something—it will be a good thing for you, you know.' The resolution of this episode by Lott was ingenious. He took his instrument, 'a ringing one', and tuned up 'the loudest of them all'. But he also carried with him a bow which was soaped and which he substituted for the rosined one as soon as the music began. What then appeared to be vigorous playing to observers failed to produce any sound 'and in this manner for two months I gesticulated in that orchestra without a soul finding out that I was not suiting the note to the action'.

So far as his violin-making activities were concerned, he received initial tuition from his father who had established his own business in King Street, Seven Dials, by 1809, although still working primarily for Thomas Dodd. His father adopted the same course as he had with his son George Frederick, and Jack Lott was sent to work for R. W. Davis of 31 Coventry Street, London, from 1820. (Davis was a well-known dealing firm whose predecessor had been Norris & Barnes and whose successors became Withers.) It was during this period with Davis that in all probability Jack Lott learned the difference between the demand for old-looking and new-looking violins. It is said that he made two violins, 'dirtied them up', put them in old cases, and took them to an auction where they were sold for 60 sovereigns. His father, on the other hand, was not able to sell two new-looking violins at auction at all.[2]

In 1852, on returning from the adventures described in *Jack of All Trades*, Lott established his own business at 60 Wardour Street and began the work on which his fame rests. Experts acknowledge Lott's debt to Bernhard Simon Fendt in particular, the pioneer of 'the reproduction technique' which he adopted. But Jack Lott was one of the first of these superb copyists who favoured the Guarneri del Gesù model over that of Stradivari (preceded, probably, only by Jacob Fendt). This is not to say that Lott made no violins in the style of Stradivari and, occasionally, Amati—he did. But Jack Lott's fame largely rests on his Guarneri copies.

There are, however, perceptible differences. One is that Lott's instruments tend to be fractionally larger than most of del Gesù's—most of Lott's instruments are of a body-length of about 14 in. (356 mm), whereas Guarneri del Gesù exceeded a body-length of $13^{15}/_{16}$ in. (354 mm) in only about a quarter of his violins (on the Hills' assessment). Lott's varnish, though convincing, is not of the original Cremonese recipe, although John Dilworth has pointed out that under ultraviolet light the ground varnish is fluorescent, very like the Cremonese, whilst the coloured areas show as unreflective. John Dilworth is convinced that Lott used high-grade dragon's blood at a time when its use was becoming obsolete by artists because of its tendency to become colourless with time. However, the evidence is that Lott was astute enough to identify and avoid inferior grades having this tendency. Given natural wear to the artificial wear already built in by the maker, the end result remains very convincing. Lott also used excellent wood and carefully graduated thicknesses, which does much to account for the fine tonal reputation that these instruments have.

How accurately did Lott copy the idiosyncrasies of Guarneri? Clearly, working in London and associating with the leading dealers there and in Paris (Vuillaume in particular), Lott had the opportunity of seeing several fine instruments of the Italian master. One Jack Lott Guarneri copy was recently noticed by the author to have had unevenly placed soundholes, which was a feature (amongst others) of the so-called 'Pig Guarnerius', the solo instrument of Prosper Sainton whose London activities are described in Chapter 7. But defenders of the Lott reputation, which now stands much higher than it did when Morris wrote his rather deprecating comments about this maker, point out that Lott did not make exact copies but rather variations on the Guarneri theme.

---

[2] See John Dilworth, 'Lotts of Value', *Strad* (Oct. 1988), 801, an invaluable article to which the author is much indebted.

It is nevertheless a pity that the maker who is now regarded by many as the finest of all English makers of the violin should have disdained individuality to such an extent that his work was frequently confused with the originals he copied. John Dilworth in the article cited above states that there is no evidence that Lott sold his own work dishonestly. There is, in fact, no evidence either way, but inferences can legitimately be drawn from the fact that Lott's own label, though it does exist, very rarely appears in his instruments. He may have satisfied his conscience, as other makers in a similar position have done subsequently, by not making any positive representations about the actual maker of instruments being sold but leaving buyers to make their own judgement. This, of course, only passes the problem down the line when the instrument enters the market in later years.

Forgery and the Criminal Law

It is instructive to see how nineteenth-century criminal law would have regarded selling a musical instrument which purports to be by a maker other than the real one—not forgetting that whereas there is evidence that the Fendts did this, the Lott copies were apparently without any label.

In 1812 forgery was defined as 'the fraudulent making or altering of a writing, to the prejudice of another man's right'. Offences in the eighteenth and nineteenth centuries were usually laid down by statute and amplified by the common-law decisions of the judges. In the case of forgery, one of the most seriously regarded offences was the forgery of deeds, charters, sealed writings, court rolls, or wills. These matters were dealt with by the statute of 5 Eliz. 1, ch. 14 which enacted that

> if any person upon his own head and imagination, or by false conspiracy and fraud with others, shall wittingly, subtilly, and falsely force or make, or subtilly cause, or willingly assent to be forged or made, any false deed etc . . . and shall be thereof convicted, he shall pay to the party [wronged] double costs and damages, and be set in the pillory, and have both his ears cut off, and his nostrils slit and seared with a hot iron, and shall forfeit the profits of his lands during life, and be imprisoned also during life.

A number of other statutes of later date extend the ambit of forgery and counterfeiting (a felony without benefit of clergy) to the forgery or counterfeiting of bank bills or notes, bonds, lottery tickets, marriage licences, and the like. Felonies where no specific penalty was laid down were generally punishable by death by hanging or some lesser sentence such as, particularly in the nineteenth century, transportation to Tasmania or New South Wales, Australia.

If these punishments had been the likely result of violin 'counterfeiting', the Fendts and the Lotts might have been more circumspect. But it was established as a result of *R* v. *Closs* (1858)[3] that painting an artist's name in the corner of a false picture in order to pass it off as an original picture by that artist was not a forgery. The reason, in brief, was that a forgery must be of some document or writing.

What in fact had happened was that Thomas Closs, a dealer in pictures and 'being a person of fraudulent mind and disposition and devising and contriving and intending to cheat and defraud' had in 1857 and on other frequent occasions made copies of original paintings and forged the name of the artist. Defence counsel argued that the defendant was only making a faithful copy down to the original, including the signature, and there was no proof that he had passed off the picture as the original or the signature as a genuine signature. The court did not take so light a view as to the inference of dishonesty but Chief Justice Cockburn held that there was no forgery. 'A forgery must be of some document or writing; and this was merely in the nature of a mark put upon the painting with a view of identifying it, and was no more than if the painter put any other arbitrary mark as a recognition of the picture being his.' After a careful examination of the authorities the court decided that if a person, in the course of his trade openly and publicly carried on, were to put a false marker or token upon an article, so as to pass it off as a genuine one when in fact it was only a spurious one, and the article was sold and money obtained by means of that false mark or token, that would be a cheat at common law. The court gave as an example the case of a man selling a gun with the mark of a particular manufacturer upon it, so as to make it appear like the genuine production of the manufacturer.

Accordingly, if it could have been proved that any of these makers actually passed off their instruments as those of the original Italian makers of which they were copies, two possible offences might have been committed. The first one was the statutory offence of obtaining property by false pretences, introduced by legislation in 1757. There was also the common law offence of 'cheating', referred to above and which still exists. These offences were not, however, felonies, that is serious crimes carrying the death penalty or some other condign sentence, but misdemeanours punishable by fines, pillory, or a comparatively short term of imprisonment.

The modern law of forgery was reformed by the Forgery Act 1913 which defined the offence as 'the making of a false document in order that it may be used as genuine'. The Act went on to make specific provision for the forgery of wills, deeds, bank notes, and other documents relating to title to property. But there was a long-standing debate as to what other 'documents' came within the definition of the Act. One writer suggested that the real test of a document was whether it is a writing which conveys to the mind of all persons able to read it the same message

---

[3] Dears. and Bell Reports, 460.

as the spoken word. Only a 'writing' could be forged by being rendered 'false', that is, when it tells a lie about itself. A picture was regarded as not a 'document' because, although it might convey an idea or message to a spectator, it would not necessarily convey the *same* message to all spectators.[4]

It had also been held in *R. v. Smith* in 1858[5] that where the prisoner had sold his baking powder and egg powder in printed wrappers resembling the wrappers used by another established trader (with one sentence omitted) the offending wrapper was not a 'document'. 'It is elevating a wrapper of this kind very much to call it a document or instrument.'[6] This would apply in a similar way to violin labels even under the current law which is contained in the Forgery and Counterfeiting Act of 1981. However, forgery of a certificate of authenticity relating to an instrument would be quite a different matter and would, it is suggested, for many years have been, as it is still, within the ambit of the law of forgery. Currently, false labelling is taken care of primarily by the Trade Descriptions Act 1968 and this legislation is discussed in detail in the author's book on *Violin Fraud*. Active false labelling is likely now to attract a custodial sentence. In the nineteenth century, as can be seen, comparatively little stigma seems to have attached to it. It was almost as if the 'art world' was exempted from the consequences of behaviour which in other circumstances would roundly be condemned.

The legacy of the Fendts and Lotts is an equivocal one. Examples of their work which are brilliant imitations of the classical Italian makers continue to command a great following and high auction prices. Since they showed the way, many other makers have, at least for part of their production, also produced clever imitations of much older and intrinsically valuable instruments. Examples, discussed in the Directory as they arise, include Wulme-Hudson, the Voller brothers, and John Wilkinson. Many others have deliberately antiqued their varnish without in any way disguising their authorship. Such work has always found ready buyers.

Modern makers are divided about the ethics and intrinsic artistic desirability of continuing to produce 'antiqued' instruments. Wilfred Saunders, the distinguished contemporary maker, compares this practice to trying to sell someone a new car made to resemble an old car with chipped paintwork. On the other hand, buyer psychology still seems to enable makers who offer both new-looking and old-looking instruments to sell the old-looking ones at an enhanced price—indeed, they take longer to make. One suggestion made to the author by one maker was that professional orchestral players with shiny new instruments tend to get picked out by the conductor in a rehearsal! An outstanding modern copyist is Roger Hargrave who had the distinction of having one of his copies of a 1740 instrument

---

[4] See *Russell on Crime*, 12th edn., ed. J. W. C. Turner, at p. 1218. Also Glanville Williams, 'What is a Document?', *Modern Law Review*, 11 (1948), 150.

[5] Dears. and Bell Reports, 566.
[6] Per Pollock, CB.

by Joseph Guarneri filius Andreae offered for sale at an Austrian auction in Vienna with a reserve of 800,000 schillings. The instrument was also tricked out with a genuine certificate from a respectable source which actually related to another instrument. All Hargrave's internal brands had been removed. The instrument was eventually withdrawn, but only with some difficulty.[7]

It should not be thought that English nineteenth-century makers had a monopoly of this type of copying activity. The great Parisian maker Jean Baptiste Vuillaume produced some consummately skilful 'copies'. Jack Lott was a French-speaker and a friend of Vuillaume. As Towry Piper remarks, Lott 'was occasionally employed by J. B. Vuillaume, to whom he is said to have imparted information (little needed one would have supposed) on the methods employed in making facsimiles of old Italian work'.[8] Another consequence of all this during the later nineteenth century and the early twentieth century was the production on a large-scale basis of 'imitation old' instruments in French and particularly German factories, retailed at very cheap prices throughout Europe and the United States. Some were supplied complete with fake cracks and neck grafts plus facsimile labels. Whilst these commercial productions could hardly mislead any informed person, they were presumably enough to convince the next-door orchestral player, particularly in an amateur orchestra, that the owner was well-heeled enough to be able to afford an old and Italian-looking instrument.[9]

Retrospect

Looking back over the features of nineteenth-century London work picked out in this book a very different atmosphere to that prevailing in the eighteenth century can be discerned. There was a far wider realization of the value of classic Italian instruments. London had developed itself into one of the leading cities for the supply of these instruments, rivalled only by Paris. The dealers mentioned, including the redoubtable William Ebsworth Hill, soon established an international reputation for their expertise, their ability to identify any particular instrument, and certainly in the case of Hill the ability to restore damaged instruments in a sensitive way. Although the margin on the turnover of many of the finest instruments is said to have been relatively modest (see the preceding chapter), one assumes that the foundations of some extremely profitable businesses were laid by the third quarter of the nineteenth century. It could hardly be otherwise, since demand for these fine instruments increasingly outstripped supply, remembering that demand

---

[7] See 'How wrong you can be . . .', *Strad* (May 1992), 396.

[8] Moya and Piper, *Violin Tone*, 204.

[9] The danger of contravening the Trade Description Act 1968 when reselling these instruments is discussed in detail in Harvey, *Violin Fraud*, 204.

came not only from players but from wealthy collectors. And collectors and players alike greatly valued the certificate of authenticity obtained on purchases from the Hills in particular. A valuable violin was (and is) much more difficult to resell without its 'papers'.

On the making side, the fortunes of the Hill family have been outlined. In the nineteenth century those makers within the Hill family who had a significant production made fine instruments modelled on the Italian masters but without false labels (so far as we know) or 'antiquing'. A more prolific stream of distinguished instruments was produced by the great copyists, particularly the Fendts and the Lotts. The influx of workers from Italy, France, and Germany brought a valuable genetic strengthening to the English violin-making tradition although, perhaps unfortunately, in the process some 'Englishness' was lost. It can be said as a justifiable generalization that by 1800 the Old English School, particularly renowned for its cellos, was effectively dead and any maker worth his salt would be producing copies of (usually) Stradivari or Guarneri, 'straight' or 'antiqued' according to taste.

At the same time the trade was being threatened by the cheap importation of factory-made products from Germany and France, which was widely thought by nineteenth-century writers such as Sandys and Forster virtually to have killed off the English violin-making. That this was an exaggerated view can be seen by perusal of the Directory, since there were quite distinguished makers such as Craske (1791–1881), and a number of other makers of less renown, continuing to turn out a large number of well-constructed hand made instruments for which there was obviously a demand. Nevertheless, from a relatively low base there was a mushrooming of interest in violin-making in England and Scotland from about 1870, and the reasons for this are discussed in the following chapter.

Chapter Twelve

❧ Some Leading Lights in the Victorian Gloom

Was there a Dark Age? — Two Victorian Makers of the North Country — The Life and Fortunes of Walter Mayson — William Atkinson — Violin-Makers: Saints or Sinners?

Was there a Dark Age?

AS indicated in the last chapter, Heron-Allen, in revising the article on the 'Violin Family', for vol. V of the 1910 edition of Grove's *Dictionary of Music and Musicians* (ed. J. A. Fuller Maitland) took a somewhat gloomy view of the British scene. The only makers that Heron-Allen sees fit to mention in the same breath as the giants of the earlier part of the century—the Forsters, Tobin, John Furber, Harris, Henry Lockey Hill, Samuel Gilkes, Bernhard Fendt the elder (known as 'Old Barney', and accounted 'the best maker of violins since the golden age of Cremona'), Panormo, and Carter—were those of the Hill family, J. A. Chanot, and Béla Szepessy. He adds:

> There are a great many secondary makers whose names it would be invidious to mention, who if the truth be told hardly rank above amateurs, and there are several dealers who could make fiddles but who do not find it worthwhile. The most prominent amongst these are Frederick and George Chanot and Dykes of Leeds. All the makers, professional and amateur, are recorded, with little sense of proportion, in Rev. Meredith Morris's work, *British Violin-Makers* (London, 1904).[1]

Heron-Allen was very much brought up in, and always influenced by, the Chanot school, and perhaps he learned from that source a marked lack of respect for those makers who had not been through a proper training or apprenticeship.

Some of Heron-Allen's ire may have been directed against Meredith Morris's

---

[1] Edward Heron-Allen, 'Violin Family', in *Grove's Dictionary of Music and Musicians*, 2nd edn., ed. J. A. Fuller Maitland (London, 1910), v. 308–9.

book because in its first edition Morris completely omits any mention of the Chanot family. This was probably because he did not regard these makers as 'British'. Neither edition of his book mentions Béla Szepessy. But in his second edition, published in 1920, Morris does make amends for the former omission. He starts, in the Preface to the second edition, by suggesting that an improvement has been made 'in every way; for one thing it shows a better sense of proportion and a truer appreciation of the relative merits of makers, past and present'. There is also a new and fairly lengthy entry for G. A. Chanot, as established in Manchester. 'The Chanots are Anglo-French, but have been so long settled in this country as to become regarded as almost pure-bred Britons.'[2]

Morris goes on to remind his readers that the Chanots exerted an influence upon other violin-makers of their time to an extent which is not, perhaps, realized. This was partly because they were the trainers of quite a number of men who became first-class artists themselves. Morris then adds:

For a considerable size of the second half of last century, Georges Chanot was almost the only really first-class and properly trained violin maker in this country. William Ebsworth Hill and George Hart (senior) made few new instruments, and there were only the Withers (father and sons) and some two or three besides. Chanot came to London to work under Maucotel in 1851, full of enthusiasm for his art; in 1858 he started business on his own account, and it was not long before he was recognised as *facile princeps* of a small band of fiddle makers in this country . . . The revival of violin making in England dates from about the time when Chanot (Père) had reached his high water mark.[3]

Morris links this with the creation of Heron-Allen's 'brilliant series of articles', issued in 1882, which became the book *Violin-Making: As it Was, and Is*. Various influences gathered into one force at this juncture, and these articles (which embodied the Chanot tradition) 'acting like a telegraph wire conducted them in the right direction'.

A key part of this thesis depends upon the justice of demoting a very large number of other makers to the secondary rank—little better than amateurs. Although there is no doubt about the high quality of the work of Chanot, Szepessy, and the Hills, the modern verdict must surely be that these pessimistic sentiments were much over-generalized.

The point can be illustrated thus. If a purchaser were looking in 1880, for example (before the 'renaissance' got under way), for a new home-made violin in Scotland, a glance at the Directory would confirm that the purchaser would have had a huge choice. But disregarding makers of no obvious merit, if the fiddle search had taken place in Glasgow, the purchaser could have chosen instruments

---

[2] Morris, *British Violin Makers*, 120. A letter exists in the library of the Royal College of Music to Heron-Allen humbly admitting the validity of Heron-Allen's criticism of the first edition.
[3] Ibid. 120.

from John Anderson, Hugh W. Cooper, George Duncan, James Gilchrist, John Mann, and Alexander Smillie. If in Edinburgh he could have gone to visit the establishment of James Hardie or to Henry Anderson. Elsewhere in Scotland he could have found James Findlay at Padanaram, Alexander Mallas at Leith, John Marshall at Aberdeen, Archibald Richie at Dundee, and even so far north as Orkney he would have found James Omond. The auction prices of good specimens of most of these makers on the London market at present would in many cases run into four figures. The work of George Duncan, John Marshall, and Alexander Smillie is particularly appreciated. But none of them is apparently worthy of mention by Heron-Allen who in the 1893 issue of the *Violin Times* (which he edited) pours cold water on the claims of James Gilchrist in particular, but also of George Duncan and Alexander Mann.[4]

England, too, offered an abundance of choice at this period. In the London area there would have been the instruments of, for example, William Atkinson (he made his first violin in 1869), John Day, or something from the Voller brothers (if they could be found), to name but a few makers whose instruments have for the most part stood up well. Elsewhere in England George Craske was producing prolifically in various cities, and a glance at the Directory will show that there was hardly one city or even a remote rural county where there was no source of new instruments. Heron-Allen's answer might have been that all these 'hardly rank above amateurs', but even if this were so it is misleading to suggest that the Hills, J. A. Chanot, and Béla Szepessy were the only makers in England 'devoting themselves to the art'. In fact, the early years of the twentieth century saw a tremendous growth in interest by amateur or semi-professional violin-makers in England and Scotland. The volume increased, even if quality was erratic. But by way of re-emphasizing the point that there was far from a desert before that 'renaissance' of interest, a glance at the working lives of four makers, whose careers began before 1880 and who were either professional or semi-professional, might be illuminating.

Two Victorian Makers of the North Country

The work of Job Ardern illustrates the point that English violin-making was rich in eccentric characters whose output was significant but whose working methods did not conform to the professional stereotype. In fact, very little is known of Job Ardern's life, and perhaps there is little to know. Henley, drawing on the small booklet issued in about 1934 on this maker by the firm of W. E. Hill, and written by a 'friend', credits him with over 500 instruments. He worked where he was

---

[4] *Violin Times*, 1/8 (1893), 123–4 (signed 'Observer'). This polemic is referred to in Ch. 8.

born, in the village of Wilmslow in Cheshire. There he spent the whole of his 86 years (he died in 1912), working in the shade of a giant holly tree in front of his workshop window. The Hills' booklet contains a portrait of him: a bespectacled gentleman who might have been taken for the family doctor, bearing, apparently, a resemblance to Tennyson. He made little attempt to sell his instruments in his lifetime and on his death Hills acquired his stock, put any necessary finishing touches to them, and in the 1930s marketed them at prices of between £10 and £20. Henley says many were dispatched to Canada, and that instruments are numbered on the wide end of the fingerboard.

Ardern's work has stood up well over the years. The varnish that he used, which varies in tone through golden-brown to brown-red, has worn remarkably well. The workmanship is precise if often rather long in the body for modern taste, the model influenced by the Italian (Henley describes it as 'Amatese') but without losing the necessary Englishness about it. Many players testify to satisfactory tonal results from these instruments.

Henley states (quoting in fact from the Hills' booklet) that Ardern was a carpenter by trade but being in affluent circumstances had no need to sell his instruments to any great extent. His work brought him its own reward and he took pleasure in seeing his creations accumulating round him on shelves, walls, hanging from attic rafters, and the like.

There appears to be no memorial to Ardern's work. Nor is it know by whom, if anyone, he was taught. His name either does not appear or obtains the most inadequate of mentions in the major French and German dictionaries and he is entirely omitted by Morris. Only Henley has anything to say about him and his final sentence in this context is perhaps prophetic: 'The future should give Ardern an honoured place among nineteenth century makers.'

In contrast to Job Ardern, John Askew is one of the very few British violinmakers to have his own biography.[5] Askew was perhaps lucky to live in an area in which Egglestone, who was primarily a local historian, had a particular interest. It is not apparent from the biography that Egglestone had any particular prior interest in the violin, though he writes enthusiastically about Askew's work and collected it. It is partly the effect of this book which has led to the grossly exaggerated belief in some quarters that Askew might have been one of England's greatest makers (see the Directory). In fact, Askew's violins are rare (he appears to have made about twenty or thirty in all) and many of them he disowned. He said that he only made about ten or twelve 'really perfect ones'.[6] But Askew did obtain some expert and enthusiastic followers during his lifetime and at the International Inventions Exhibition in London in 1885 he obtained a bronze

---

[5] William Morley Egglestone, *John Askew, The Stanhope Violin Maker* (Stanhope, 1914). [6] Ibid. 66.

medal, Béla Szepessy obtaining the silver medal and George Duncan of Scotland the gold.

John Askew was born in 1834 in Stanhope, County Durham, some 27 miles from Newcastle upon Tyne. He was apprenticed to the trade of his father, that of cordwainer (or shoemaker). His hobbies were fishing in the nearby River Wear and playing the alto saxhorn in the Stanhope Band. Amongst the musical fraternity locally was James Benson, a schoolmaster keen on the making of violins and an excellent violinist. Benson encouraged Askew to study the violin and then attempt to make an instrument. The tools of the cobbler's trade were to hand and he became adept in the use of the cobbling knife and sharp razors. Benson enabled him to obtain suitable wood, some of it coming from old buildings locally. Later on, when Askew received the occasional commission, one eminent sponsor was Towry Piper. In 1893 Piper asked Askew to make a 'long Strad' copy and provided the wood (and better tools) for him.

Given the very primitive learning and working conditions it is amazing that Askew's work was apparently so successful. In later life he stated that he learned the rudiments of making from such books as Hart and old Italian and French works. His difficulty with the latter was that he knew no Italian or French, but his schoolmaster friend was able to help him with the translation. Askew also claims that a Newcastle friend lent him a very fine Strad to copy, though this may in fact have been a Strad copy by N. F. Vuillaume. Certainly this was what he had before him when making the 'long Strad' copy which Piper passed on to the leader of the orchestra he then conducted at Barnard's Castle—the verdict being that the copy turned out 'fairly well'.

Askew claims to have got his recipe for his varnish out of an Italian book. 'It was an exciting hour when I first put it on a violin but it was the right thing.'[7] He is later thought to have used Whitelaw's proprietary varnish, which generally proves to have degenerated, producing a craquelled surface.

Egglestone's biography goes through the known violins of Askew, starting with one made in 1877. The instrument which Morris saw and described, the 'Van Gelderen' (after its first purchaser, a surgeon-dentist and violinist of Newcastle upon Tyne) was made in 1884 and won a first prize at the Jubilee Exhibition, Newcastle upon Tyne, in 1887. The front and back views are illustrated in Egglestone's book. Morris says of this instrument that it 'was on the Strad model, with golden amber varnish of a slightly reddish tint, very transparent and lustrous. The workmanship showed the master-hand of a born fiddle maker, and the tone was full, responsive, and mellow.' Throughout these years Askew combined his

---

[7] Egglestone, *The Stanhope Violin Maker*, 66.

cobbling trade with that of making one violin or so every year with some intermissions. His last instrument is dated 1895, the year of his death.

Unfortunately, owing to the very small output of this maker, any contemporary judgement is difficult. Henley remarks on his 'master-hand workmanship and scroll work, purfling and sound-holes,' and his 'very transparent and lustrous' varnish. He rates the tonal quality as warmly sonorous and brightly responsive. The overall verdict is that he was 'skilful and clever though not a genius'. This is probably fair, but perhaps the most remarkable feature of Askew's life is that it should have been possible for someone with virtually no appropriate books, no expert tuition, and a few primitive tools, together with unlimited enthusiasm, to make instruments which stood up to professional competition at the time.

As with many other British violin-makers in like circumstances, the exercise of his craft clearly brought Askew great pleasure. The price for which he sold his instruments is not clearly established except that he sold his first one for 30s. (£1.50). The money from his main trade enabled him to follow the 'dream of my life'[8] and he was able to avoid the grinding poverty which was the curse of the life of Walter Mayson, his contemporary and a truly professional maker.

The Life and Fortunes of Walter Mayson

Mayson's life is a study in Victorian social history. We know more of the details of his life and thinking than of most nineteenth-century violin-makers partly because Mayson himself was a talented writer, not only about himself and the violin but also of poetry and fiction. But the major source of information is W. Meredith Morris's biography published in 1906 (and now a rarity).[9]

Mayson was born near Manchester in 1835, one of a family of eleven children. Morris traces his violin-making genes through his mother who was artistically inclined and the daughter of William Green, painter of Lakeland country scenes and a friend of Wordsworth, near whom he is buried in Grasmere churchyard. Mayson's father fell on evil days by reason of a debt which he had to discharge for a relative and the family was brought up in some hardship, rescued only by his mother's accomplishments as a teacher. Mayson's schooldays were marked by excellence in English composition in particular but he also became interested in music. The high point of his musical youth was an evening in Manchester listening to a performance of the *Elijah* (Mendelssohn) which made a deep impression

---
[8] Ibid. 64.
[9] W. Meredith Morris, *Walter H. Mayson: An Account of the Life and Work of a Celebrated Modern Violin Maker, with Numerous Illustrations* (Maesteg, 1906).

upon him. (How sparse was the musical stimulation provided to the young in those days, but perhaps each occasion was valued the more.)

When he was about 17 Mayson also became interested in the use of carving tools and his interest in violin-making was stimulated by his purchase on the open market of the instrument used by his grandfather, William Green. This was labelled 'Jacob Stainer' but was in fact apparently a fine specimen of the work of Richard Duke.

In the mid-nineteenth century early mortality was to be expected and several brothers and sisters died during Mayson's adolescence, closely followed by their father. His mother survived, and remained for many years the linchpin of the disintegrating family. Mayson married in 1863 but his first wife died shortly afterwards in premature childbirth. In 1866 he married again, this time to a lady who had two children from a former marriage. As Morris remarks, Mayson thus increased his expense threefold in one day: 'a thing ill-warranted by his slender income'.[10] In fact, Mayson had been apprenticed to a firm of shipping merchants in Manchester and the earlier part of his life was made comparatively comfortable from a seemingly secure position in this trade.

It was not until the age of 39, in 1873, that Mayson made his first violin. There was the usual problem with finding any proper instruction book at this period. Added to this, there was considerable scepticism amongst his friends as to whether anyone could make a go of it at the age of 39. Mayson had, though, been a collector of instruments for some years. As he himself says:

It was on the 16th October, 1873 that I jointed back and belly of my No. 1 fiddle. Yes! and the joints were by no means bad, and show out well today, for the instrument is left by Will to my son Stansfield, and so is ever by us. It is on the lines of 'Joseph' and eminently the work of an amateur—a lover of what he does I take that to mean—and fairly well finished, purfled, and covered with amber coloured oil varnish. From the very first I was determined to use no spirit varnish,—that would be a destroyer of all good tone. The tone of my No. 1 was only moderately powerful, but the quality was good, and one George Crompton said I should never make a better instrument. Absurd! My mother said he did not want me to.[11]

Shortly afterwards Mayson was made redundant at the establishment of the Manchester shipping merchants and decided to become a professional violin-maker and repairer. He managed to sell his second fiddle for £10 but the income from the trade was insufficient to keep his growing family and Mayson brought his pen into service. His essays and poems were published in the leading Manchester papers. They are well written and show an eclectic and literary mind.

---

[10] Morris, *Mayson*, 23.   [11] Ibid. 22.

What next became apparent was the social stigma that was attached to violin-makers. When Mayson was in a good position with a large firm of merchants and able to entertain freely he had numerous friends. But as soon as he became a professional fiddle-maker he was left only with a 'faithful few'.[12] He was encouraged, though, by the verdict of William Ebsworth Hill to whom a friend of Mayson's had shown some of Mayson's work. 'This man is a born fiddle maker, and it is really refreshing to find, in these days of copying, one who dares to be original. If I had this man for three months he would beat B—— and the rest of them into mummies.'[13] W. E. Hill in fact put his finger on one of the key features of Mayson's work: it never descended to slavish copying. In fact it was his desire to impart 'character' to his instruments which probably depressed his reputation subsequently.

Unfortunately, although Morris does not say so directly, Mayson's business was adversely affected by G. A. Chanot's arrival in Manchester in 1879. This event lost him a great deal of trade and scorn was poured on his work which was thought not to bear comparison with that of the professionally trained French family. Mayson also made the fatal mistake of sending about twenty of his violins to Puttick & Simpson's auction-room in London where they sold for little more than the cost of the wood. Naturally, his patrons who had bought his instruments at a proper retail price felt cheated. But Mayson saw this as the only way of staving off bankruptcy.

He moved to a humbler workshop in partnership with his stepson and recovered some of the ground lost. In fact he was sufficiently optimistic to decide to build a house with the assistance of a building society, a decision which, as Morris remarks, 'cost Mayson the peace of mind and earthly comforts of a life-time'.[14] Furthermore his stepson died within a short time and sales again fell off. He therefore sold his house (without discharging his full indebtedness) and rented a cottage near Windermere in the Lake District. Here he was able to live in beautiful surroundings and rather more cheaply.

In 1883 he exhibited a case of violins at the Cork Exhibition and in 1885 a quartet at a similar exhibition in London, in both cases earning a silver medal. He also sent a case of violins to the Melbourne Exhibition in 1888 and was awarded a gold medal—never received because the organization went bankrupt. Nevertheless, public and impartial critics were seen to think well of Mayson's work, though he never exhibited instruments after 1888. He lost confidence in the ability or integrity, or both, of 'musical' juries.

The year 1887 was a bad one for Mayson: he sold not a single instrument for nine months and had to spend his last penny of capital on wood for future use.

---

[12] Ibid. 33.
[13] We may speculate as to the identity of B——. Would it have perhaps been Buckman, Béla Szepessy, or Boullangier?
[14] Morris, *Mayson*, 36.

Help came unexpectedly. The family were about to sit down to a very frugal dinner when two unknown people from Liverpool knocked on the door. They had come to see his fiddles and after being shown a number of instruments and trying their respective merits, selected one and paid £20 in cash. The gold coins meant bread for a few months longer. But, in Mayson's own words, 'The incubus of the house I have built at Manchester still clung to me, for of course, I was liable at any moment to be called upon to meet any and all losses, and much correspondence had already passed between me and the building society on the subject.' Furthermore his mother then died at the age of 85 and was buried in the ancient church near Windermere which Mayson subsequently mentioned in his novel *The Stolen Fiddle*. The building society lost patience and threatened to sell the house unless it could be tenanted or owner-occupied. So reluctantly he left his lovely cottage in the country, Croft House, and returned to Manchester. There he made a workshop out of the upper floor of the house but still could not meet the demands of the building society. He was obliged to vacate the house and move to another address in Manchester where he stayed from 1890 till his death in 1904.

It is to this period, or more precisely 1889–99, that Morris assigns the greater part of Mayson's best work. He made on average one instrument per week, working rapidly but carefully.

He would go over the tables of his high-class instruments 15 or 20 times, gauging and working the thicknesses to the nth according to the principle of graduation which he had adopted. He was wont to say that 'at a push' he could make from first to last four scrolls a day, allowing three hours for each scroll, but that it was his rule never to 'throw' more than one scroll in the same day, owing to the mental and nervous fatigue which the work involved. Sound-hole cutting was his chief delight. He would sometimes spend half a day in carefully cutting the ff, paying due regard to the angle of inclination in its relation to the model.[15]

Mayson's idiosyncratic soundholes in fact provide one of the main features of his distinctive instruments. Morris also asserts that Mayson laid on some fifteen to twenty very thin coats of varnish, as described in his book, and only during the summer months—the temperature had to be at least 64° Fahrenheit.

By 1893 his children had grown up and done well for themselves. Two of his sons had started on their own account in music, Stansfield becoming an accomplished violin teacher and an occasional maker. The daughters helped him with his shop which sold general instruments and accessories as well as violins. A Swedish buyer bought a quartet of instruments for £75. This transaction itself attracted interest from others and Mayson was able to improve the quality of his wood which he imported from Italy and the Tyrol.

[15] Morris, *Mayson*, 50.

TOOLS FOR VIOLIN MAKERS.

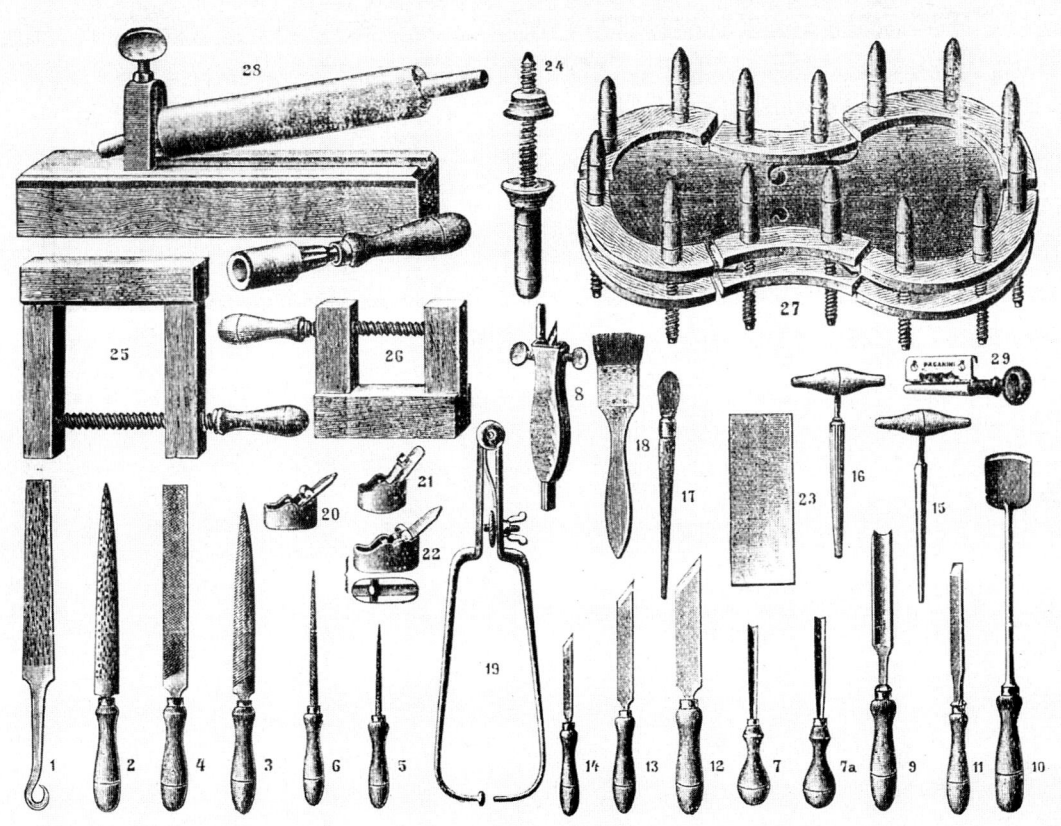

The above Tools are exactly the same as used by the leading Italian and Continental makers. Every article is of the best quality, and a necessity for every Violin-maker. Messrs ERNEST KOHLER & SON keep a very extensive Stock of all Fittings, Strings, &c., pertaining to the Violin. They are enabled to supply everything at lowest possible prices for cash. All orders and enquiries by post receive prompt attention.

No.				£	s.	d.	No.				£	s.	d.
1	Rasp, flat	(by post, 3d. extra)		0	2	4	18	Varnish Brush, flat	(by post 1d. extra)		0	1	0
2	Rasp, curved	,,	3d. ,,	0	1	4	19	Callipers	,,	2½d. ,,	0	6	0
3	File, curved	,,	1d. ,,	0	1	0	20	Plane, flat	,,	1½d. ,,	0	0	8
4	File, flat	,,	2d. ,,	0	1	4	21	Plane, curved	,,	1d. ,,	0	4	6
5	File, round	,,	1d. ,,	0	0	8	22	Plane, for Sound-posts	,,	1½d. ,,	0	5	4
6	File, larger, round	,,	1d. ,,	0	0	8	23	Scraper	,,	1d. ,,	0	0	6
7	F Hole Borer	,,	1d. ,,	0	1	0	24	Wood Cramp, for repairing	,,	1d. ,,	0	0	6
7a	F Hole Borer, larger	,,	1d. ,,	0	1	0	25	Wood Cramp, for gluing on Bass Bars					
8	Purfling Tool	,,	5d. ,,	0	4	10		(by post, 5d. extra)			0	1	4
9	Chisel	,,	1½d. ,,	0	1	6	26	Wood Cramp, for gluing on Necks and Finger					
10	Chisel	,,	1½d. ,,	0	2	0		Boards	(by post, 4d. extra)		0	1	2
11	Chisel	,,	1d. ,,	0	0	10	27	Wood Cramp, for gluing on Backs and Fronts,					
12	Knife, broad	,,	1d. ,,	0	1	4		per set of six	(by post, 6d. extra)		0	5	4
13	Knife, Medium	,,	1d. ,,	0	1	4	27a	Wood Cramp, for ditto, superior,					
14	Knife, small	,,	1d. ,,	0	1	0		(by post, 6d. extra)			0	8	0
15	Peg-Hole Cutter	,,	1d. ,,	0	3	10	28	Bending Iron, for Ribs			1	2	6
16	Peg-hole Rimer, fluted	,,	1d. ,,	0	7	0	29	Violin Peg Cutter, two sizes					
17	Varnish Brush, round	,,	1d. ,,	0	0	9		(by post, 1d. extra) each			0	1	2
							30	Mould (Outside) Strad or Storioni					
N.B.—Wood Cramps for Violoncello, same								Model	(by post 6d. extra)		0	10	6
	as No. 27	(by post 6d. extra)		0	10	6							

ERNEST KOHLER & SON, 101 LEITH STREET, EDINBURGH.

[Over.

PLATE 1. 'Tools for Violin Makers' (Ernest Kohler & Son, Edinburgh, leaflet, c.1900).

VIOLIN WOOD and FITTINGS.

THOROUGHLY SEASONED OLD WOOD OF VERY BEST QUALITY.

A COMPLETE SET OF WOOD & MATERIALS
Embracing Everything Required in Making a Violin, including Set of Strings.
Good Quality. :: **Post Free, 10s. 6d.**

FRONTS, Finest Pine—9d., 1/-, 1/6, 2/-, 2/6
FRONTS, One Piece—4/-, 6/6
BACKS, Sycamore—Good Quality, 1/6, 2/-, 2/6, 3/6
   "   "   Beautiful Figure, 4/6, 5/6, 6/6
   "   "   Very Old Selected Wood, 7/6, 8/6, 10/-, 12/-
   "   "   One Piece, Cut on Slab or Quarter --
                            5/-, 7/6, 10/-, 12/-, 15/-
BIRD'S EYE MAPLE BACKS—10/6
   "   "   Whole or Slab, 12/6
   "   "   NECK & SCROLL, Cut, 4/-
   "   "   RIBS, Per Set, 1/-
NECK GRAFTS—Each 1/-, 1/6, 2/-
NECK AND SCROLL BLOCKS—
        Each 9d., 10d., 1/-, 1/6, 2/-, 2/6, 3/-, 4/-
NECKS (Neck and Scroll), ready shaped out—
        Each 1/-, 1/6, 2/-, 2/6, 3/6, 4/-, 5/-, 6/-, 7/6, 10/-
   "   "   Three-quarter and Half Size—1/6, 2/-
RIBS—Per Set of Three, 6d., 9d., 1/-, 1/6
PURFLING or INDENTING—Best Quality—
        1d. per Length. Sufficient for One Violin, 4d.
BLOCKS—Set of Six, also Linings, Bent, 1/6
BASS BAR—3d.
SOUND POSTS, Seasoned Wood, each 1d. Very Old, 3d.
SOUND POST SETTERS—1/-
NUT EBONY, for top Finger-board, 1d.
   "   "   to go under Tailgut, 1d.
FINGER-BOARDS—9d.; Best Ebony, 1/-; Close Grain, 1/6, 2/-
TAILPIECES—Ebony, 6d., 9d., 1/-, 1/6
   "   Inlaid with Pearl—1/6, 2/-, 3/-, 4/-, 5/-
TAILPIECE GUT for One Violin, 1d.
PEGS—Per Set, 4d., 6d., 8d. Ebony, 1/-, 1/4
   "   Boxwood, yellow, per Set, 4d., 8d.
   "   Rosewood, per Set, 1/-, 1/4
BRIDGES—Each 1d., 2d., 3d., 4d., 6d., 1/-
TAILPINS (End Pin) 1d.; Ebony, 2d.: Rosewood, 2d.
STRINGS (Violin) Best Quality, 1st, 2nd 3rd, 4th—
        Each 3d., 4d., 6d., 9d.
   "   Special 4th String, real Silver, 6d., 9d., 1/-, 1/6
GLUE, Best Scotch, per Cake, 3d. and 4d., or 2/- per lb.
SANDPAPER, Fine Quality, per Sheet, 1d.
PREPARED PUMICE SURFACING POWDER—
    Per Box, 6d.
PREPARED TRIPOLI (FINISHING) POWDER—
    Per Box, 6d.
VANDYKE STAIN—per Bottle, 6d.
HARD SPIRIT VARNISH—per Bottle, 6d.

WHITELAW'S CREMONA AMBER OIL VARNISH
    —All Colours in Stock—Single Bottle (any Colour), with Box of Surfacing and Tripoli Powders and Pale Amber for first coat, 5/3
AMBER OIL VARNISH—Made with real Amber in Solution—Colours: Brown, Dark Red, Dark Orange, Light Orange, Golden, Ruby, Clear Amber. Per Bottle, 3/3 post free.
OIL AMBER VARNISH (KOHLER'S)—2/6 per Bottle.
VIOLIN VARNISH (SPIRIT)—per Bottle, 2/-
VIOLA—Necks and Scrolls—2/6, 5/6, 7/6
    Neck and Scroll Blocks—1/6, 2/-, 2/6
    Purfling—1d. per length.
    Backs, Sycamore—2/6, 4/-, 7/6, 10/-
    Fronts, Swiss Pine—1/6, 2/6, 4/-, 7/6
    Sound Posts—2d. each.
    Ribs, Sycamore—2/- per Set of Four.
    Bass Bars—6d. Top & Bottom Blocks, 10d. pair.
    Linings, Swiss Pine—2/- per Set.
    Finger-Boards—Best Ebony, 1/-
    Tailpieces—Ebony, 8d. Bridges—2d., 3d.
    Pegs—per Set, 8d. Ebony, 1/- Rosewood, 1/4
VIOLONCELLO—Necks and Scrolls, 5/-, 10/-, 15/-, 20/-
    Neck Scroll Blocks—4/-, 6/-, 10/6, 14/-
    Backs, Sycamore—10/-, 15/-, 20/-, 30/-
    Fronts, Swiss Pine—5/-, 7/-, 10/-, 14/-, 21/-
    Ribs, Sycamore—3/-, 4/-, 5/- per Set.
    Bass Bars—1/- Top & Bottom Blocks—2/6 pair.
    Finger-Boards—Ebony, 5/-, 7/6, 10/6
    Linings, Swiss Pine—3/- per Set.
    Tailpieces—Ebony, 2/-, 3/-
    Bridges—6d., 9d., 1/-, 1/6, 2/-, 2/6
    Pegs—per Set, 2/-, 2/8, 3/-, 4/- Rosewood or Ebony, 4/- Set.
    End Pins—Metal, 2/-, 2/6, 3/-, 5/-
    Strings—1st, 6d.; 2nd, 8d.; 3rd, 10d.; 4th, 1/-
    Nut Top Finger-Board—4d.
    Nut (below Tailpiece)—4d.
    Purfling—2d. per length. Tailpiece Gut—3d.
    'Cello Machine Heads—9/- and 12/-
DOUBLE BASS—Necks and Scrolls—
    Beech, 7/6; Maple, 12/-; Sycamore, 15/-, 22/6
    Tailpieces—Ebony, 6/-, 7/6
    Backs—12/6, 17/6, 21/-, 42/-
    Fronts—10/6, 12/6, 15/-, 30/-
    Ribs—5/-, 6/-, 7/6 per Set. Bass Bars—2/-
    Finger-Boards—Ebony, 9/-, 12/6
    Linings, Swiss Pine—3/- and 4/- per Set.
    Machine Heads—3 String—Iron, 5/-; Brass, 9/6, 12/-
    Machine Heads—4 String—Iron, 6/6; Brass, 11/-, 13/6
    Bridges (Full or Three-quarter Size)—Each 2/-
    Strong Tailpiece Fastening—7d.

VIOLIN MATERIALS ALREADY SHAPED OUT FOR AMATEURS TO PUT TOGETHER. Prices Moderate.
All Fittings kept in Stock for small size Violins.

THE VIOLIN: HOW TO MAKE IT.
With Plates and Diagrams.   By J. BROADHOUSE.   Price 3/6 net.   Post, 2d. extra.

Violins & Other Stringed Instruments, How to Make Them. Edited, PAUL N. HASLUCK. 1/- Post, 2d.
DIAGRAMS OR OUTLINES—STRAD, GUARNERIUS, AMATI, GASPARD da SALO. Models, each 1/-
'CELLO DIAGRAM - - 2/6
VIOLINS SPECIALLY MADE FOR EXTREME CLIMATES. Superior Quality. From £4.
VIOLINS IN THE WHITE (UNVARNISHED) 10/6, 12/6, 15/-, 21/-, to 60/-

Artistic Repairers of all Stringed Instruments.   *Valuable Old Violins Repaired and Restored.*
ESTIMATES GIVEN FREE OF CHARGE.

ERNEST KOHLER & SON, VIOLIN MAKERS and STRING MANUFACTURERS, **101 LEITH STREET, EDINBURGH**
[Over.

PLATE 2. 'Violin Wood and Fittings' catalogue (Ernest Kohler & Son, Edinburgh, leaflet, *c*.1900).

PLATE 3. Frontispiece from catalogue of W. E. Hill and Sons (*c.* 1920).

PLATE 4. John Askew

Your servant for Jesus' sake Wm Atkinson

PLATE 5. William Atkinson

Plate 6. J. W. Briggs

Plate 7. Georges Chanot

PLATE 8. George Craske, from a watercolour by John H. Leatherbrow, 1876 (reproduced by courtesy of Phillips, London).

PLATE 9. J. J. Gilbert

PLATE 10. George Hart

PLATE 11. Thomas Earle Hesketh

Plate 12. William Ebsworth Hill

Plate 13. Walter Mayson

PLATE 14. John W. Owen

PLATE 15. H. H. Saby, with his Fendt bass.

PLATE 16. Alex Smillie

PLATE 17. James Tubbs

PLATE 18. Edward Withers

PLATE 19. Edward Heron-Allen, FRS, 1928 (from a painting by Hardman).

PLATE 20. W. Meredith Morris

PLATE 21. Towry Piper

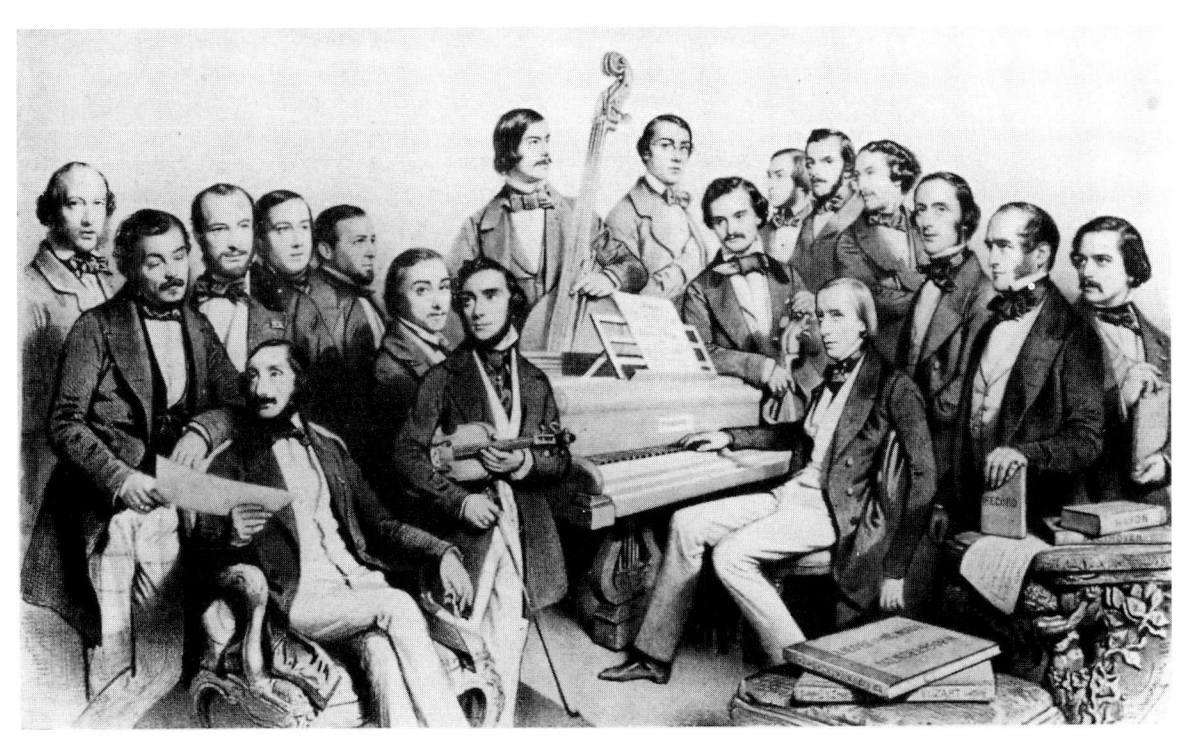

PLATE 22. The Musical Union Artists of the 1851 Season. *Left front* Ernst (seated), Sainton (looking over Ernst's paper), Sivori (with violin); *left back* (left to right) Eckhert, Vieuxtemps (decoration on lapel), Deloff, Hill, Laub (behind Sivori); *centre* (around pianoforte) Bottesini (with double-bass), Pauer, Piatti (with cello), Halle (at the keyboard); *right* (right to left) Baugniet (the artist, pencil and pad in hands), Ella (holding book, 'Record'), Sterndale Bennett, Seligmann, Menter (tall), Pilet (in background)

PLATE 23. J. T. Carrodus

PLATE 24. Marie Hall

PLATE 25. Beatrice Harrison

PLATE 26. Albert Sammons

PLATE 27. John Bunyan's violin (reproduced by courtesy of the Trustees of Bunyan Meeting, Bedford).

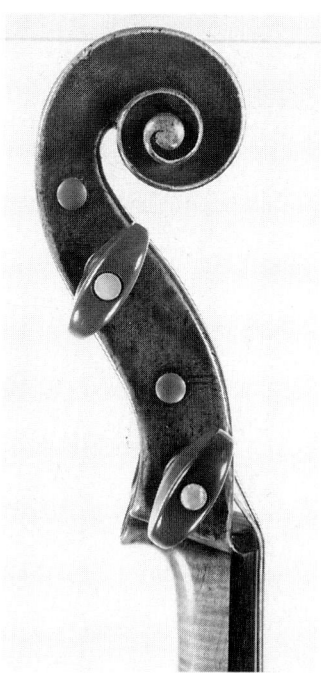

PLATE 28. Head of William Forster's 'Royal George' cello (reproduced in full on the front cover).

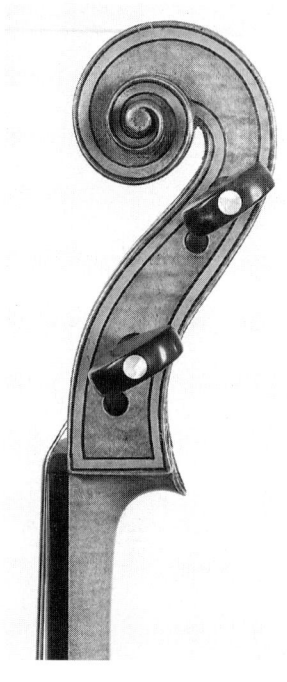

PLATE 29. B. S. Fendt, decorated cello head, c. 1840 (SEE PLATE C).

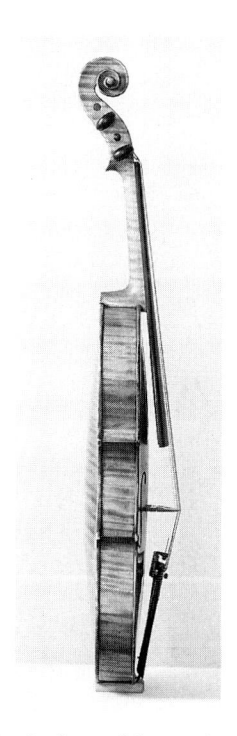

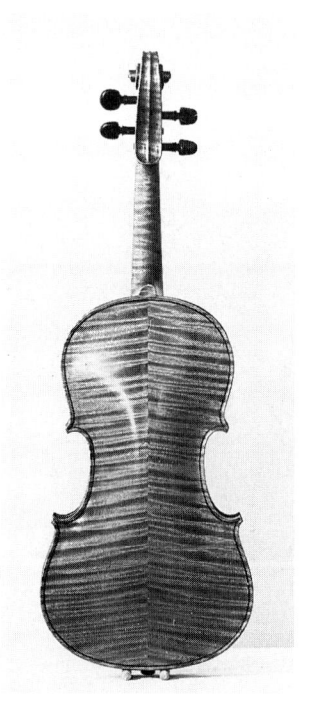

PLATE 30. Front, side, and back of one of the two known violins made by Edward Heron-Allen when a pupil of Georges Chanot in London, c.1886, Strad model (reproduced by courtesy of Pat Naismith, London Guildhall University).

Economic circumstances nevertheless obliged him to make instruments in different qualities, primarily depending upon the wood. His price-list of about 1893 from 62 Oxford Street, Manchester, indicates five 'styles' of violin, the cheapest at £5 'made of good old sycamore and pine, flat edges, purfled and varnished', through to the best, 'made of the very Finest Wood, and finished in a style to bear comparison with any' at £15. Violas were one-third extra and cellos from £20 to £35. Purchasers could choose 'Strad', 'Guarnerius', or 'Mayson' models. He was also beginning to attract favourable notices from the periodicals. The *Strad* in its issue of May 1891, for example, described the workmanship of one example as 'fine, the selection of the wood, the rich golden varnish, the shape of the f holes, all prove that the maker must be a thorough master of his art. The tone is exceptionally fine, especially on the E and A strings. If Mr. Mayson continues to turn out such work, his violins may, indeed, one day replace the masterpieces of some of the old Italian makers, which must one of these days become a thing of the past.'[16]

The path of the artist continued, nevertheless, far from smoothly. He made an especially fine instrument to present to the eminent player Lady Hallé (Madam Norman-Neruda), but this admittedly unsolicited gift was never even acknowledged. In fact her husband, Sir Charles Hallé, commented publicly at a rehearsal that he was greatly annoyed at the impertinence of people who made bold to send instruments for their acceptance. Mayson, who was a genuinely Christian and good-hearted man, bore no grudge. Rather the reverse, because he constructed a special instrument to commemorate Sir Charles Hallé after his death in 1895, which was the subject of very favourable comment in the *Violin Times* for April 1896.[17] Mayson also constructed several instruments with carved backs, the carving being in bas-relief with a surface of about 1/40th (0.6 mm) of an inch raised. One fine example, the 'Old Windsor', made in 1893, depicts Windsor Castle.

Despite the successes Mayson's struggle with the building society had not been resolved. He had merely postponed final settlement. One morning he received a letter from the building society's solicitors informing him that the property had been sold at a heavy loss which he was required to make good forthwith. Mayson had no means of raising the necessary £150. So, in his own words,

I fell on my knees for guidance, and did not ask in vain. On staring the position in the face, I decided to adopt the course of begging the people to accept instalments of £5 per month—a course to which they agreed—and £135 out of the £150 loss was punctually so paid by me; the Society, in acknowledgment of my probity and of my heavy previous loss, remitting £15 with a few nice words of approbation . . . Providence tempered justice with mercy, in that the whole of the penalty was not visited upon me at once.[18]

[16] Quoted ibid. 55.
[17] See the quotation from the review of this instrument, ibid. *Mayson*, 57. It is also illustrated there.
[18] Ibid. 64.

Unfortunately Mayson was to make an even greater financial error. He decided to open a branch workshop in London. He was now 64 and chose an existing centre of fiddle-making. He also acted contrary to the advice of his friends. In July 1899 he took a room on the second floor of 256 High Holborn where there was a strong, steady north light. He brought with him thirty selected specimens from his accumulated stock at Manchester. Almost immediately he was struck down by severe illness which involved his absence for several days from his workshop. The only 'friend' who bothered to call on him was Edward Heron-Allen—'That prince of writers on the king of instruments—and right glad was I to see his kind face. I was sad and weary, and my pocket grew lighter every day.'[19]

After three months trial of this abortive and disastrous enterprise, Mayson left London and returned to Manchester a sadder and a wiser man. Morris regards this as having been a blessing in disguise because he speculates that Mayson would have been diverted from violin-making into repairing and dealing. 'Stradivari himself would starve in modern London, unless he could make old "Cremonas" and turn out factory fiddles at 30s. per dozen.'[20] In fact the only violin made by Mayson in London was the infelicitously named 'Elephanta', though Heron-Allen saw this instrument and pronounced it to be 'very fine'.

The year 1899 brought a commission of a different sort. Mayson had always relied on his pen to help eke out a living. His works of poetry and fiction published in his lifetime include *The Stolen Fiddle*, the *Heir of Dalton*, *Corrazzi*, and *Poems and Dramas*.[21] But this time there was a commission from Harry Lavender, the editor of The *Strad*, to write a series of articles on the art of violin-making. The terms proposed were not generous. They involved 5s. per column plus 2d. per copy royalty on the book when it was reprinted.

Mayson felt himself obliged to accept the deal though he shrewdly added the rider that all plates of photographs and other illustrations should count as 'copy'. He was of course aware of the publicity value of the projected work. Mayson recalled the verdict of John Ruskin whom he knew personally: 'In every flock there are a few black sheep, but in the flock of publishers there are few white ones.'[22] The truth of this caustic remark was confirmed in that although Mayson saw copies of the subsequent book in public and private libraries he did not in fact receive any royalties. The book itself, *Violin Making*, appeared as No. IX in the Strad Library in 1902, and the author's son Stansfield Mayson prepared a second edition published in 1909. The text itself, though unsurprisingly somewhat idiosyncratic, reads well and was on the whole favourably received. It is written very much as a personal account as to how Mayson himself proceeded, outlining the various traps to be avoided and speaking as if to someone at his elbow.

[19] Morris, quoting Mayson, ibid. 68. [20] Ibid. 70. [21] Ibid. 75. [22] Ibid. 74.

The period from 1900 to his death in 1904 was, in Morris's view, Mayson's 'third period' when he made his most mature and satisfactory instruments. His work in the *Strad* brought him into contact with other makers and gave him further encouragement. Mayson also derived inspiration from what might be called mysticism, a belief that 'there exists now an invisible order of things intimately connected with the present, and capable of acting energetically upon it—for, in truth, the energy of the present system is to be looked upon as originally derived from the invisible universe, while the forces which give rise to transmutations of energy probably take their origin in the same region'.[23]

Mayson was also very attached to the work of Ruskin, lengthy passages of whose work he would recite aloud, 'becoming oblivious to his surroundings'.[24] 'He was no great believer, however, in the necessity of any set form of prayer or praise, although an adherent of the Established Church, but preferred a species of mystical prayer—a sort of still communion with the Father of Spirits which transcends the imperfect offices of expressed praise or prayer. To exercise faith meant to him to listen to the voices within the veil.'[25] Mayson was convinced that growth in the ability to make and design a fine instrument could only be accomplished by living a more 'ideal' life. He regarded himself as having been 'born again'. But, on the ground, there was much jealousy of Mayson's achievements, particularly in Manchester. Morris contrasts this petty jealousy between makers with the amity with which the great Cremonese makers managed to live cheek by jowl.

Luckily in 1903 Mayson's depression was lifted by an invitation to stay at the house of a well-known London doctor who purchased 'Elephanta' from him together with another instrument, and ordered four more violins to be specially made. Mayson allowed £50 against a Pressenda violin taken in part-exchange, but later regretted the bargain since the instrument had 'a cracked voice, and I was glad to get rid of him at £20'.[26] At this time, too, he was invited to Bristol to meet the promising young violinist Marie Hall, Mayson's opinion being valued not only on violin-making but violin-playing. Mayson was astute enough to recognize this player's 'remarkable execution, fine phrasing, intelligent rendering of passages of great individuality—her superb mastery of the bow, whether in the delicate manipulation of *adagio* or the abandon of *allegretto* or in the power and grip of the chords of Bach's *Chaconne*'.[27]

These interesting excursions and the comparative economic success of Mayson's business allowed him to spend his last years in comparative ease. Morris rather fancifully sees evidence of this contentment in the design of the soundholes in the instruments made in this final period.

[23] Ibid. 81.   [24] Ibid.   [25] Ibid. 84.   [26] Ibid. 87.   [27] Ibid.

The ultimate accolade on Mayson's work was perhaps the formation of a committee of prominent Manchester citizens and other admirers to raise funds to purchase a number of his best instruments for presentation to selected museums. Mayson's life and the business at Oxford Street, Manchester, were written about in the Manchester newspapers and, as Morris states, 'an honest effort to heal the wound caused by 30 years' neglect' was made.[28] Unfortunately even this venture did not properly succeed. The committee managed to realize only enough to purchase one instrument, a carved-back violin named 'Coronation' to commemorate the crowning of Edward VII, and made in 1902. This instrument was accepted by the Peel Park Museum in Salford near Manchester, but is now in the Ordsall Hall Museum, Taylorson Street, Salford. It is currently displayed in a re-creation of a Victorian music shop.

Mayson had never really recovered from the severe illness he had suffered in London. In 1902 he was seized with a severe pain under his left shoulder which medical treatment, diagnosing a rheumatic complaint, exacerbated rather than alleviated. This then turned out to be ischaemic heart disease, but a local doctor treated him with great care so that he made a slight recovery. The doctor (Dr Moore) would take no payment for his services or the plentiful drugs supplied, but Mayson got him to accept two of the etchings of Ambleside done by his grandfather, William Green. In November and December 1904 Mayson suffered two paralytic seizures and after the second stroke he died on 31 December 1904. He was buried next to his father at St Paul's, Kersal, near Manchester. He had attained 70 years and his gravestone included the sentence: 'A workman that needeth not to be ashamed.'

In his biography, Morris lists all Mayson's known instruments, to which Mayson almost always attached a name. (This was partly whimsy and partly an anti-forgery device.) Some of these names were inspired by current political events. During the Boer War, for example, instruments made in 1900 included 'Sir Redvers Buller', 'Mafeking', and 'Baden Powell'. In 1902 seventeen instruments were made, all violins except one viola, and these included the names 'Kitchener' and 'Sir A. Milner'. Mayson's faithful biographer got some reward in that one of Mayson's last instruments, finished in the white on 12 August 1903, was called 'Meredith Morris'.

In all Mayson produced what Henley calls 'the astounding total' of 810 instruments. Of these there are twenty-seven violas and twenty-one cellos. Many, but not all, of Mayson's violins are of a large pattern, $14\frac{1}{4}$ in. (368 mm) not being an untypical body length. Large-size instruments of this sort are no longer particularly in fashion and it is perhaps this factor, together with Mayson's reluctance to

---

[28] Morris, quoting Mayson, 108.

follow exactly established models, that prevents his work being valued in the auction-room as highly as the work of some of his contemporaries and successors. Nevertheless Mayson's later instruments, the thicknesses of the plates of which were very carefully gauged, do generally seem to be tonally satisfactory, at least for orchestral or chamber-music purposes. Henley in his *Universal Dictionary* would put it higher than this: 'splendidly full tone, which will become magnificent when the necessary years of playing have matured it'.

Mayson's life is also instructive because it shows the great difficulty which attended anyone with an English name setting up as a violin-maker in the provinces in the nineteenth century. Mayson worked very hard to produce the number of instruments that he did, and had it not been for the fruits of his ability as an author the enterprise would probably have been impossible. Whether it was the death of near relatives which occurred at frequent intervals during his earlier life or regular economic blows of fortune, Mayson needed character to survive. This he clearly had. His bearded face and powerful forehead suggest a man of great fortitude, breadth of mind, and gentleness of character. Even allowing for a certain element of hagiography in Morris's work, Mayson seems to have lived a life of almost irreproachable rectitude. His fault was to have too great a faith in his ability to market his own products. He put his own and his family's economic welfare on the line and all must have suffered considerable hardship for much of Mayson's career as a violin-maker.

William Atkinson

The preceding vignettes depict three makers who, in their own way, could be described as Eminent Victorians. William Atkinson's career is different in that his working life spans a period from 1869 to the year of his death, 1929. His mature work, therefore, belongs to the reigns of Edward VII and George V, though his formative years lie squarely in the nineteenth century.

There was sufficient interest in Atkinson's life for biographical snippets to be published before his death in local newspapers. We have, too, the benefit of the accounts drafted by the indefatigable Meredith Morris, who did a profile of this maker for the *Strad* of November 1900[29] and then reused much of his material in the biographies contained in the two editions of his book on *British Violin Makers*. The present author had the additional advantage of the reminiscences of Atkinson's living granddaughter, Daphne Bradley, for whom Atkinson made one of his best violins. Atkinson has been selected because, in the present author's

[29] p. 203.

opinion, he is one of the most refined makers of the turn of the century period in England and, unlike some of his professional rivals, made every part of his instruments himself, down to the purfling.

William Thomas Reed Atkinson was born in Stepney, London, on 23 October 1851. He had the advantage of a 'pay-school' education at a grammar school in Mile End Road, Stepney, until the age of 11.[30] Atkinson always maintained that he made his early acoustical and varnish experiments at school. The family then moved to Liverpool and Atkinson was put to work behind the bar of his uncle's public house near Birkenhead. Morris states that this was much against the boy's inclination, but he had no choice.

When he was a little older Atkinson joined the Merchant Navy where as a teenager he served as second steward on board several steamships. His granddaughter says that on one occasion Atkinson's ship took in tow the encased and floating Cleopatra's Needle, now standing on the Thames embankment at Westminster, which had broken away in a storm from the ship chartered to bring it to London.

Atkinson's parents then moved back to London and Atkinson left the Merchant Navy to become apprenticed to a joiner. His first instrument, dating from 1869, was made at this time. He married in 1880 and shortly afterwards moved to Tottenham, to the north of London and not connected to the metropolis as it is now. (Development at Tottenham occurred partly because the rail service from Liverpool Street to Enfield went through that area.) Atkinson took a double-fronted shop in Church Road which was a general hardware and dry-salter's stores selling, as his granddaughter remarks, 'most things from a pin to a pitchfork: oils, pigments and varnishes were a speciality'. The shop also displayed specimens of Atkinson's work: violins, violas, and cellos which were fashioned in the workshop to the rear.

The marriage produced three sons, one of whom died and another of whom eventually took over this shop from his father. Atkinson worked there until 1911. The building no longer survives but Harringay Council, having compulsorily acquired it, made in 1972 what is perhaps a unique gesture for any local authority by naming a nearby precinct for the elderly (thirty-nine one-bedroomed flats) after a British violin-maker: William Atkinson House.

Early in the 1900s Atkinson suffered a serious accident while helping his brother-in-law, the builder (Arthur Porter) who was responsible for both some local churches and the first stand to be created in the Tottenham Hotspur football ground. Atkinson's leg had to be amputated below the knee and for the rest of his life he had to wear a wooden prosthesis.

---

[30] Morris states this was until the age of 14 but there is an extant prize for 'good conduct' on leaving school in 1862.

Atkinson set great store by his varnishing. In an interview with a reporter from the *Southend Standard* in October 1928 he is quoted as saying: 'If I were asked what was my greatest gift, I should say it was to make a violin, but I would not spend five minutes on it if I had not got the varnish I use. That varnish is my own, and I would stake my life it is the same varnish which the Old Masters used.' This oil-based varnish took a long time to dry. Atkinson said that he could make a violin in a fortnight, but he would need two years in which to dry it.

Finding the Tottenham air, with increased urbanization, too smutty to be satisfactory for varnish-drying al fresco, in 1911 he moved to the village of Paglesham, near Southend-on-Sea, Essex. This village remains comparatively unspoilt and Atkinson's end cottage,[31] where he ran the local Post Office and general stores, remains, though converted into a simple house. His granddaughter remembers its oil lamps, uncarpeted winding stairs, and primitive toilet and washing facilities.

Atkinson also became churchwarden of St Peter's church in the village, and that was an important part of his life. He continued to combine violin-making with running his modest business with the help of his wife. Presumably a significant amount of Atkinson's time was actually taken in making, his family running the other side of the business.[32] This had the great advantage that he never felt economically pressured in the way that the unfortunate Walter Mayson did. He was able to take time to make instruments completely to his satisfaction and was ruthless in rejecting anything which did not come up to scratch. Atkinson was also liable to strip off the varnish if it was not perfect. It is thought that he made about 300 instruments in the white but only about 250 (including four violas and nine cellos) are accounted for. The obituary in the *Strad*[33] states that he had in his later years sought out and destroyed many examples of his early work which did not reach his mature standard of excellence.

Atkinson clearly continued to experiment with varnish for many years but essentially the oil varnish was put on in between eighteen and twenty-four coats, each having to dry before the next coat was put on. In the summer the instruments were dried by the simple expedient of stringing the violins up between two poles in the garden—the tall poles being thought by many of the villagers to be something to do with a wireless aerial. The natural colour goes from pale straw to deep red-brown. Poidras states that there was no added colouring matter in the varnish and Atkinson thought that it was similar to the varnish used by Italian painters of oils.[34]

As with so many English makers of this period who experimented with oil varnish, the results are sometimes not entirely satisfactory. At least one instrument

---

[31] It had a large garden which Atkinson enjoyed cultivating.

[32] Atkinson also repaired clocks and watches, his workshop having a huge picture window giving the light necessary for both activities.

[33] (Feb. 1930), 566.

[34] Poidras, *Dictionary*, ii. 76.

has been seen where there has been noticeable deterioration and craquelure. But in most cases it seems to have survived fairly well, although its soft texture means that the upper layers are easily rubbed off by vigorous or careless usage.

Atkinson never revealed the secret of his varnish to anyone. The contemporary newspapers report a death-bed attempt to convey the recipe to his son. 'The old man realised too late that he was dying, and tried to impart the secret to his son, but the effort was too much for him. He fell back on his pillow, dead.'[35]

Morris did a detailed analysis of Atkinson's violin construction and the following is taken from his profile in the *Strad* of November 1900.[36]

He works on two original models. The measurements of model No. 1 are as follows:

Length of body	$13^{15}/_{16}$ [354 mm]
Width across upper bouts	$6^{5}/_{8}$ [168 mm]
Width across middle bouts	$4^{3}/_{8}$ [111 mm]
Width across lower bouts	$8^{3}/_{16}$ [207 mm]
Depth of ribs at bottom	$1^{1}/_{4}$ [32 mm]
Depth of ribs at top	$1^{3}/_{32}$ [27 mm]
Length of soundholes	$3^{1}/_{32}$ [77 mm]
Distance between soundholes at top	$1^{19}/_{32}$ [41 mm]
Elevation from ½ inch to	$^{5}/_{8}$ [16 mm]

The measurements of model No. 2 are the same, except that at the top, middle, and bottom bouts, it is $^{3}/_{32}$ inches [3 mm] narrower . . .

Mr. Atkinson's wood is excellent. The figure of his maple is, as a rule, of medium width. His pine, which is from Berne, is simply perfect, having a 'reed' rather under medium width, perfectly straight and well defined. His outline is in the best Italian style. It is gracefulness incarnate. A very strong expression, but a true one. As the form of the gazelle is to that of the ordinary antelope, so is the outline of Atkinson to that of the ordinary fiddle. The Scroll is a masterly conception and of Pheidian beauty . . . The first turn parts suddenly from the boss, as in the best examples of Stradivari. The edges are softened down gently, with black lines to emphasize the extreme outline.

The button is nearly semi-circular, with toned-down edge, and in perfect keeping with the contour. The margin is one-fifth [inch] [5 mm] wide. The edges are strong and rounded; but the 'rounding' is not over-pronounced. The elevation of the edge above the purfle-bed is almost imperceptible. The margin and edges present a delicately refined appearance. In fact, everything about the Atkinson violins betokens aristocratic refinement. The purfling is one-sixteenth [inch] [1.6 mm] wide, the inner strip having a width which is slightly greater than that of the outer ones combined.

The varnish is beautiful, ranging in colour from pale straw to light ruby, and of the most delicate tints. On a specimen recently seen by me, and which had been examined and most flatteringly commented upon by the late Duke Saxe-Coburg-Gotha, the varnish was straw

---

[35] *Daily Express*, 24 Dec. 1929. [36] p. 203.

coloured and of the richest and tenderest hue. It is perfectly transparent and elastic, and soft as velvet to the touch. It is laid on in very thin coats and dried in the open air. Sometimes as many as twenty coats are given, but the final thickness of varnish is scarcely more than one-sixty-fourth of an inch [0.4 mm].

Mr. Atkinson's tone is quite remarkable. It is not exactly like the tone of any other maker, classical or post classical, that I am acquainted with. The size of the instrument would lead one to expect a tone of small volume, but such is not the case. The tone is strong without being loud, penetrating without being piercing. One need not go to Atkinson for mere loudness. His is a mellow tone with a silver ring. Its echo in a large hall is like the sound of an anvil struck at a distant smithy and borne by the breeze. It is the tone of the dulcimer magnified, clarified, beatified. It is a delicious tone! For this reason the Atkinson fiddles are pre-eminently solo instruments. For a similar reason it would not be wise to furnish the same orchestra with them throughout. That the gods rain honey on flowers is a kind provision; if they did it on grass they would spoil the world.

Atkinson normally branded his instruments just below the button with his monogram. His label is written in the copperplate he undoubtedly learned at grammar school in Mile End Road, Stepney, and is varnished over to preserve it.

During his life the quality of his instruments was well recognized and in his earlier years he won a bronze medal in Paris in 1889 and a silver medal at Edinburgh in 1890. As Morris says, 'Since 1890, he has developed his ideas considerably, and has freed himself entirely from the trammels of the French school.'[37] The Duke of Saxe-Coburg-Gotha took an active interest in his work and Atkinson's catalogue reproduces commendatory letters from Joseph Joachim (12 November 1904): 'I have seldom met with new instruments that pleased me so much, and I think that they would also carry in a large room', and from the well-known expert J. M. Fleming: 'The design and execution are the work of an artist, the degree of excellence displayed in any one point being maintained under every aspect that the instruments present . . . the tone is really exquisite.'

Consistently with his policy of strict quality control, and as a consequence of his not having to rely on selling every instrument, Atkinson made instruments in one quality only and charged £15 for violins, £20 for violas, and £30 for cellos. (The Directory gives current auction prices.)

William Atkinson survived until 1929, losing heart when his wife died. A contemporary local press report quotes him as saying: 'There is no pleasure in the work for me now. A little time ago my wife died on her birthday and she was the "best man" about the shop.'[38] Atkinson's working regime and honest business practices sprang from a character of considerable strength and colossal integrity. He is buried with his wife and a son who died as a child in Tottenham Cemetery.

[37] Morris, *British Violin Makers*, 1st edn., 68.   [38] *Southend Standard*, Oct. 1928.

By this time other makers of the early twentieth century were applying very much more commercial principles to their making and marketing and were not necessarily so scrupulous about making every part of their instrument themselves.

Violin-Makers: Saints or Sinners?

It might be thought that the lives of all the violin-makers picked out in this chapter seem too good to be true. Certainly there is little material which would have been of any interest to the script-writer of a modern soap opera. If there were any scandal in their lives, no one picked it up, and it seems unlikely, in any event, that there was. In the latter part of the nineteenth century a strict moral code was applied in many families of the sort that these makers belonged to, usually associated with a firmly held religious creed. Religion then was in its undemythologized state and beliefs and their moral foundations were not questioned so freely or simply ignored, as became the case subsequently. Every school taught the Ten Commandments and the Sermon on the Mount. Mayson, who as a boy cheated his mother out of ½d. change, was not chastised but made to fall on his knees to beg for divine forgiveness. He always remembered the experience.[39] And 'free-thinkers' such as William Tarr (1808–91) applied to their lives a moral code equally stringent.

Craft workers such as these, who worked on their own or as a small family unit, and stayed clear of commercial activities in the dealing market, managed to preserve an innocence sustained by a genuine love of their craft. Mass production takes away from the worker one of the most rewarding aspects of work: the fulfilment of seeing a beautiful artefact created with one's own hands. This was one of the underlying principles of the Arts and Crafts Movement, so opposed to the degrading effects of factory mass-production in search of greater profit but at some human cost. Of course, going a little further back into the nineteenth and late eighteenth centuries a more Hogarthian picture emerges. Alcoholism was a frequent problem and ethics flexible. John Dodd, the bow-maker, virtually destroyed himself by drinking and died in Richmond Workhouse. Richard Tobin ended in the Shoreditch Poor House for similar reasons and a number of Scottish makers of the early nineteenth century developed too great an affinity with the whisky bottle. The Fendts and the Lotts sailed very close to the wind, blurring the dividing line between copies and forgeries.

Comparing the very different social conditions and religious enthusiasm prevailing at the time Morris wrote and Mayson and his colleagues worked, it is possible

---

[39] Morris, *Mayson*, 17.

to see why Morris blamed the problems of some of the older English makers on, amongst other things, 'Latitudinarianism in ecclesiastical polity'.[40] It was on this spirit of greater seriousness in life, art, and morals, that the various elements making up the British 'renaissance' worked. Anyone with sufficient steadfastness of purpose and manual dexterity needed only to be bitten by the violin bug to feel the challenge.

So, stimulated by exhibitions, Heron-Allen, spectacular Stradivari auctions, the monthly violin magazine, and memories of the sound of the 'King of Instruments', a small army of British enthusiasts, including doctors, lawyers, vicars, surveyors, architects, accountants, engineers, plasterers, policemen, military men, two identifiable females, and quite a few hopeful professional makers, repaired to their workshops to re-create the glories of Cremona.

[40] *British Violin Makers* 2nd edn., 5.

Chapter Thirteen

❦ Great Exhibitions and Victorian Values

Nineteenth-Century Developments — Motivating Factors — Technical Instruction — The Great Exhibitions — Collecting British Violins

Nineteenth-Century Developments

THE disturbed period of the Napoleonic Wars at the start of the nineteenth century also accompanied the emergence of some of London's finest families of makers: for example the Forsters, the earlier Hills, the Betts, and the senior Lotts. This had little or nothing to do with the stemmed flow of imports from continental Europe, though there must have been some who welcomed the temporary absence of cheap German and French products. War or peace, so long as war did not actually extend inside the homeland's shores, seemed to make little difference to the activities of the British violin-maker. The 'industry' emerged at the end of the Wars in the same shape as before—primarily family businesses with little division of labour and still less mechanization. It was no more ready to compete, makers of the time showing little inclination to become involved in the mass-production methods developing abroad.

Economic prosperity must have had some beneficial effect on violin-making, as on every other trade, but it has to be remembered that potential purchasers in the form of professional musicians were throughout the century towards the bottom of the economic pile unless they were eminent soloists—and these would have regarded it as *de rigueur* to play a classic Italian instrument. Professional musicians were not represented by union leaders fighting their corner until the 1890s. The leading category of ordinary player would receive, if he played at the opera or theatre, about £6 to cover six or seven performances plus rehearsals. During the century the fee for playing one 'classical' concert was traditionally one guinea, which fell to 15s. because supply so far exceeded demand. A lesser grade of player who made a living from private receptions and balls, perhaps dressed as a

Hungarian bandsman à la mode, would typically receive a fee of a guinea, less the agent's commission of 3s. Many players naturally augmented their meagre income by teaching. By 1894 it was said that only one leader of a provincial theatre orchestra earned as much as £2. 15s. 0d. per week.[1] As far as this type of musician was concerned there was little 'trickle-down' effect from the country's general prosperity.

Even so, any conclusions to be drawn from the low status of professional musicians would show only a small part of the picture. There was great interest by 'amateurs' in the violin throughout the century, and theatre orchestras, innocent of any trade union rules, would happily encourage 'amateurs' to play along with the professionals. Theatre orchestras were in any event very often a rag-bag of instruments. The French horn was scarcely ever used and woodwind, particularly oboes and bassoons, were uncommon. As regards strings, cellos were rare and violas virtually unknown. The ubiquitous piano filled in the missing parts. But although the state of the professional string-player remained parlous, as has been shown in Chapter 7, the violin throughout the century became more and more acceptable as an instrument for a gentleman or, a little later, a lady to play, and John Lott's own adventures (see Ch. 11) suggest that theatre audiences were not discriminating as to standards. Amateurs would therefore find plenty of outlets for their energies both in wholly amateur undertakings and in mixed bands of professionals and amateurs. This is a theme which will be explored further in the context of later nineteenth-century books and periodicals mainly for the amateur player and the amateur maker.

This picture is also reflected in one of the first English biographical dictionaries, *Violins and Violin Makers* by Joseph Pearce, published in 1866, in which the author states:

In the present age the cultivation of Music forms one of the most general and most refined sources of amusement and pleasure. All ranks of people are now privileged to join in its delightful enjoyments. Even the cottage of the artisan is now often elevated by the elegant practice of music, through the increased facilities for producing instruments at a cheap rate. The consequence is that in the present age there is a more general study and a finer perception of what is good and beautiful, and their elevating tendencies are doing much for the mental cultivation and refinement of all classes.[2]

Pearce then goes on to remind his readers of concerts involving a chorus of several thousand voices supported by hundreds of instruments to be held at the People's Palace, Sydenham[3] and elsewhere, and that 'these orchestras are chiefly selected from the ranks of the people, of whom the artisan is the chief contributor'. And he adds:

[1] These details are taken from Ehrlich, *Music Profession*, ch. 7.
[2] Pearce, *Violins and Violin Makers*, 10–11.   [3] See Ch. 7.

The Pianoforte and the Violin are the most general instruments, and they have alike participated in the improvements effected, in becoming cheaper by the advance of science... We are a profoundly commercial nation, and it is delightful to see that in our greater wealth and prosperity, rational amusements and more especially music, go on increasing step by step with our more businesslike occupations. This class of amusements must exercise a humanising and refining influence on the habits and manners of the people, and they should be, therefore, patronised and encouraged by all those whose means are large and their example powerful.[4]

Pearce identifies what was seen by others as the depressing effect of the Free Trade era. Free Trade undoubtedly helped heavy industry, but as has been pointed out previously,[5] throughout the nineteenth century English violin-making faced increasingly severe competition from the mass-produced products of France and Germany. Free Trade was not seen by some as Fair Trade. Nineteenth-century authors such as Heron-Allen blamed it for the loss of much of England's violin-making industry. This is almost certainly wishful thinking. Unit costs of 'trade' German and French factory stringed instruments were so low that an *ad valorem* duty of 10 per cent or even 20 per cent would hardly have dented the price advantage as against the handmade English instrument. The USA imposed duty of $1.25 + 35 per cent on each violin (*c*.1926) without apparently stemming the flood.

Heron-Allen in some of his writing seemed to show a particular animus against French products (now regarded by most people as often superior to their German counterparts). His verdict on the factories at Mirecourt was that 'these turn out many thousands of crude "noise boxes" annually, ... extraordinary for their quantity and cheapness'. Heron-Allen then quotes a report on the cost of instruments from the firm of Thibouville-Lamy as being: wood for back 2*d*., wood for belly 2*d*., manufacture of same 1½*d*., wood for neck ½*d*., making same 1½*d*., fingerboard (stained) 2*d*., cutting 1½*d*., moulding back and belly 12½*d*., varnish 10*d*., fitting up strings and tailpiece, bridge, etc., 7½*d*.—Total 4*s*. 2*d*.[6] But 'cheap and nasty' though in some quarters they were thought to be, many consumers were happy enough with the product (which, of course, varied in quality and price), and instruments from continental Europe were imported into all parts of the British Isles in their thousands. Ironically, many years later one of England's best contemporary makers, William Luff, recommended amateur makers 'to beg, borrow or buy ... a good Mirecourt fiddle, and try to make one like it. You'll never make a better fiddle than a good Mirecourt fiddle, and in the making or even in just looking at it you'll acquire a style and you'll see what you have to do'.[7]

---

[4] Pearce, *Violins and Violin Makers*, 12.   [5] See particularly Ch. 6.   [6] *Violin-Making*, 85.
[7] Quoted in Alburger, *Violin Makers*, 58.

Motivating Factors

Is there, then, a theme which can be said to run through nineteenth-century violin-making? It will in fact be suggested that there are several—none obvious and some seemingly perverse. One is the undoubted psychological fact, observable in the careers of many of the makers mentioned in the Directory, that violin-making brings its own reward. There is something exceedingly satisfying in the making of a stringed instrument, particularly if the maker is free from economic pressure. Professional makers were able to augment their violin-making income by the proceeds of dealing (unless, as is the case with a few of them, they rigorously refused to be involved in this trade), and amateur makers were, by definition, not dependent upon the income from their instruments. The 'industry' in England developed on the basis of love rather than money.

Secondly, as will be explained in more detail, there were two contrary influences at work throughout the century, both opposed to each other, but both benefiting in a rather perverse way the development of the violin-making culture. The first was the pride with which Great Britain showed off its manufacturing ability to the rest of the world. This perhaps reached its apogee in the Great Exhibition at the Crystal Palace in 1851. Thirdly, as a reaction against the perceived crudeness of design of much of this work and the increasing soullessness of mass-production methods of manufacture, the Arts and Crafts movement, under the extraordinary inspiration of William Morris in particular, exerted a powerful influence in favour of traditional craftsmanship and appreciation of beautiful artefacts—of which, of course, the violin was a prime example, though apparently unnoticed by Morris himself.

Technical Instruction

The century also saw a number of attempts, for example in the Mechanics' Institutes, to provide education for the artisan and interest him in arts and sciences. Evening classes were established to develop appreciation of or participation in music. A 'stringed instrument' class was established at Birkbeck College in 1839 for players. These educational experiments were far from uniformly successful but it can be said with some assurance that there was a general feeling as the century progressed both amongst the middle classes and amongst the 'artisan' class that such 'hobbies' as woodwork were elevating and worthwhile for their own sake. This had been by no means always the case. To make violins professionally would hitherto have been generally regarded as little better than an activity for the poorly-educated manual labourer. It was to elevate the minds of such people that Mechanics' Institutes were established. The low status of professional makers continued until long afterwards—certainly well into the twentieth century. This is one reason why biographical information is so often sparse.

In the violin-making world what people needed was technical instruction. This was hardly available at all at the beginning of the century. Those who wanted to make an instrument would normally have had to attach themselves to an established business, perhaps under a formal apprenticeship. There were few such businesses and in any case the amateur did not want an apprenticeship. There were no known evening classes and, as will be seen, a paucity of literature. This latter deficiency was met with increasing success as the century progressed and culminated in the epic work of Heron-Allen, *Violin-Making as it Was, and Is*, first published as a book in 1884 (though previously in a periodical, as will be explained).

Furthermore, interest in the violin as an instrument was stimulated not only by the visits of Paganini and other leading artists from the Continent, together with a general increase in interest in music as Pearce has already pointed out, but also in the number of exhibitions which took place in the latter part of the century, some of which allowed people to see the masterpieces of Stradivari and Guarneri at close quarters for the first time.

The Great Exhibitions

So far as the influence of exhibitions on violin-making in Great Britain is concerned, confusion can be caused unless it is appreciated that these exhibitions were of two types. First there were what we would now probably call trade fairs which gave exhibitors a chance to show their newest products to the public and, in most cases, to a jury (goods being grouped into classes for judging purposes). Secondly, there were the far less common loan exhibitions, often held in a museum and designed to educate. The instruments demonstrated would be of historical interest and, particularly, would in the main have been lent to the exhibiting museum for the purpose.

The first major national exhibition of the trade fair variety is thought to have occurred in France in 1798, sponsored by the Ministry of the Interior to show the superiority of French goods against their major trading rivals, those of England. Napoleon ordered a repeat of this type of exhibition in 1801, 1802, and 1806. At the end of the Napoleonic Wars the exhibitions were repeated at four-yearly intervals from 1819.[8]

---

[8] See E. J. Shillitoe, 'Violin Making at the Great Exhibitions', *Strad* (Feb. 1979), 911, and subsequent articles in this series.

In Britain, Prince Albert, the Prince Consort, had encouraged a body of like-minded people to mount the largest ever such exhibition at a new building, the Crystal Palace, erected for £80,000 on 26 acres of Hyde Park. The exhibition primarily promoted newly designed or manufactured goods, though some articles of interest were also lent to the exhibition by the Queen and others. The size of the exhibits can be gauged by the fact that the official catalogue comprised four large volumes divided into thirty classes under four main heads: raw materials, machinery, manufactures, and fine arts. Amongst these exhibits were over 1,800 musical instruments.

Entry was open to all countries of the world and in the plucked and bowed instrument categories violins were exhibited by, amongst others, Enrico Ceruti, Claude-François Darche of Brussels, Derazey of Mirecourt, Jacquot of Nancy, Herzlied of Gratz, and G. &. A. Klemm of Markneukirchen. Perhaps the most outstanding foreign entries were, however, those of Joseph Rocca of Turin (who contributed two violins, one Guarneri model and one Stradivari model) and J. B. Vuillaume who contributed a complete set of bowed instruments, with bows made by patent machinery. The jury found, looking at Vuillaume's work, that the style and workmanship of the famous Italian makers of Cremona had been imitated 'with surprising truthfulness and beauty, and the appearance of age and wear given with remarkable exactness'. Only the varnish seemed deficient in richness and brilliancy.

There were a number of English makers represented. Arthur Betts contributed two violins (see Pl. 38). M. W. Dearlove of Leeds contributed a miniature Strad model violin and a miniature double bass. Edward Dodd of 112 Vauxhall Walk, Lambeth supplied a violin, a cello, and a double bass, and James Dodd bows for the violin, tenor, and cello, mounted with gold and tortoiseshell. Simon A. Forster of Soho Square produced a violin, a viola, and a cello made according to modern improved gauges and after the models of the exhibitor's grandfather. Purdy and Fendt of 74 Dean Street, Soho contributed violins, cellos, and a double bass. The comment on the latter's work was that without servilely copying the old Cremona makers, they had succeeded in producing very beautiful models. There was no attempt at artificial seasoning or colouring of the wood by baking it, and saturating it in lime, to cause effects which only age would give. The wood was in no way weakened or impaired, but left in its natural state and appearance.[9]

Trade fairs of this sort inevitably tend to swamp such a small section as stringed instruments with numerous other exhibits, and would hardly be the best forum to attract interest in the violin as such. Those interested in the development of the technology of piano-making, harp-making, and brass-instrument making, for

---

[9] See Peter and Ann Mactaggart, *Musical Instruments in the 1851 Exhibition* (being a transcription of the entries of musical interest) (Welwyn, 1986).

example, would be more likely to see something of novelty. Of a very different character was the Special Exhibition of Ancient Musical Instruments at the South Kensington Museum in 1872, the first such exhibition, so far as is known, to be devoted wholly to musical instruments. (The South Kensington Museum is now the Victoria and Albert Museum, Kensington, London.) Although the organizing committee was under the chairmanship of the illustrious Duke of Edinburgh, a keen violin enthusiast, much of the credit for the idea and certainly the work involved in it must be due to the distinguished musical historian Carl Engel. Engel himself was a keen collector of ancient musical instruments and in 1882 his private collection was acquired by what is now the Victoria and Albert Museum.[10] Engel contributed the introduction to the catalogue which is illustrated with sixteen photographic plates.

The Exhibition occurred in June, July, and August 1872 on terms which included lenders of musical instruments being admitted free to the Exhibition. All instruments had to be made before 1800.

Stringed instruments played with the bow formed class 2 and were numbered 54 to 204. The majority of these, so far as the violin family were concerned, were examples of Amati, Stradivari, and Guarneri (particularly 'Joseph'). The 'Hellier' inlaid Strad of 1679 lent by Capt. T. B. Shaw-Hellier was No. 85. A Strad of 1709 'La Pucelle' ('conservation parfaite') and the 1716 Stradivari 'Le Messie', Nos. 90 and 91, were lent by Vuillaume, who wrote the relevant catalogue notes in French. G. Chanot and John Hart were amongst the dealers who lent instruments, but the majority of exhibits were the property of private collectors.

English instruments, rather surprisingly, played a very subsidiary role, though there were examples of violins by Banks, Aireton, and Duke, three bows by Dodd, violas by Panormo, Fendt, Banks, and Forster, and cellos by Banks (1797), Forster (1772; the property of Lieut.-Gen. Sir J. Hope Grant, mentioned in Chapter 6), and the Royal George cello of Forster (discussed in chapter 7). All the double basses save one were by or ascribed to Gasparo da Salò and most were associated with 'the late Signor Dragonetti'.

This exhibition, certainly one of the most remarkable of its type ever assembled, caused some controversy amongst the cognoscenti. Four 'Letters' written by Charles Reade for the *Pall Mall Gazette* in successive weeks from 19 August 1872 provide a vividly written commentary of the background to and features of many of the exhibits but not without the occasional side-swipe at a misattribution. Charles Reade himself came in for some criticism by H. R. Haweis in his book on *Old Violins and Violin Lore* (London, 1898). Haweis blamed Reade for persuading

---

[10] See Carole Patey, *Musical Instruments at the Victoria & Albert Museum: An Introduction* (London, 1978). Heron-Allen regarded Engel with some distaste since Engel 'borrowed' without acknowledgement some of Heron-Allen's theories on the origin of the violin, later reproduced in Heron-Allen's *Violin-Making*.

Gillott to purchase a Guarneri ('The Red Knight') adjudged by William Ebsworth Hill to be a 'Landolpho', and No. 140 in the South Kensington Exhibition, also one of Gillott's, was adjudged 'a very dubious Strad tenor'.[11] He continues:

> The most impudent fraud or the most blatant delusion which has ever come under my notice was the so-called Maggini exhibited by Mr. J. W. Joyce (No. 110). It was made by Bernhardt Fendt ... but it was not removed, neither was the Amati tenor (No. 147), labelled and hung as Maggini, ever re-labelled, nor was a Klotz fiddle which bore a Stainer label ever corrected. The only fraud I succeeded in dislodging was a spurious Bergonzi—also sent up by Mr. J. W. Joyce—which after my attack on the South Kensington collection of 1872 disappeared ... These be among the humours of your loan collections! But we must be indulgent. Some mistakes are sure to be made, but it is only fair to remember that the fiddle world is vastly indebted to these grand fiddle exhibitions all the same.[12]

We may infer from this that the usual problem of attribution reared its head, with experts arguing about this until well after the event and with collectors eager to get the imprimatur of the Exhibition's attribution on their property. It is not clear who made the attributions in the catalogue of the 1872 Exhibition—Vuillaume was merely asked to see to the arrangement of the Italian instruments. One name conspicuously missing from the proceedings was that of W. E. Hill.

There was a further, though less well-known, exhibition in South Kensington in 1885 where matters were differently arranged, W. E. Hill this time playing a leading part. Perhaps because of this the showing of English instruments was very much better. There were instruments by Ford, Duke, Wamsley, Tobin, Lott, Joseph Hill, Lockey Hill, Banks, and an Urquhart dating from 1666.

A further loan exhibition was held at the Crystal Palace in 1900, but this did not compare in interest to the Music Loan Exhibition organized by the Worshipful Company of Musicians, under Royal patronage, at the Fishmongers' Hall in June and July 1904.[13] The motivation was described as 'To enable all interested in music under its various aspects to contrast, as a fruitful means of instruction, its past with its present condition—to estimate its growth and development, and to observe what progress has been made in the work of the instrument maker, composer, player and music printer.'[14] This was in fact a far more scholarly exhibition than anything hitherto and it was said with some pride in the Introduction to the catalogue that the delightful concerts of old music played on ancient instruments given at the South Kensington Exhibition in 1885 were by musicians who came to England for that purpose from Brussels and Amsterdam. 'Fortunately we have no

---

[11] p. 217.

[12] Haweis himself later came under attack by Morris for inaccuracies in the Dictionary with which Haweis's book concludes. See W. Meredith Morris, 'Some Strictures on the Rev. H. R. Haweis's New Work on Fiddles', *Strad* (Apr. 1899), 371–2, and, further on Haweis, Ch. 14 of this book.

[13] A lavishly illustrated catalogue was issued by Novello & Co., (London, 1909) in an edition of 500 copies: *An Illustrated Catalogue of the Music Loan Exhibition, Fishmongers Hall*, 1904.

[14] Arthur F. Hill, ibid., pp. xiv–xv.

longer to seek such players abroad; we can find them at home, although as yet we have no society or regular body of professional players who devote themselves solely to the study and mastery of the many instruments that are no longer heard, except on rare occasions.'

The Exhibition was singularly successful in combining the comprehensive collection of rare printed music, starting with Johannes Gerson's *Collectorium super Magnificat* (Esslingen, 1473), with manuscripts, portraits, and musical instruments. Lectures and musical illustrations were delivered daily by invited experts. The bowed string instrument section in the catalogue is preceded by a useful explanatory essay by W. W. Cobbett and the instruments of the violin family are a well-judged mixture of Italian classical instruments and a number of English ones. Primarily due to the loans of W. E. Hill & Sons and J. T. Chapman, English violins include examples by Christopher Wise, London, 1650; Jacob Rayman, London, 1657; J. Urquhart, London, 1666; Pamphilon, London, 1680; Baker, Oxford, 1683; Robert Cuthbert, London, 1690; Barak Norman, London, 1719; John Sexton, London, 1720;[15] Daniel Parker, London, 1720; Nathaniel Cross, London, 1731; John Barrett, London, 1740; P. Wamsley, London, 1742; John Marshall, London, 1754; Joseph Scott, Hallcliffe, 1760; Pearson Gardner, London, 1760; Joseph Hill & Sons, London, 1770; Thomas Powell, London, 1780; and William Forster, London, 1800. The nineteenth century was represented by works of J. & H. Banks, Lockey Hill, John Morris of Bath, T. Dodd, J. F. Lott, C. Harris, B. S. Fendt, and George Romney's carved instrument of 1830. There is also an English viola by William Baker, Oxford, 1683. The catalogue states that this and the Baker violin of the same date, both lent by T. W. Taphouse, were part of a 'Chest of Viols' by Baker, formerly in the possession of the Music Schools, Oxford. And in a rather disappointing cello section, out of four instruments one was by Joseph Hill, London, 1787.

Enough has been said to show that this was a magnificent slice of the history of English violin-making to 1830 which members of the Hill family, particularly Arthur F. Hill, were primarily responsible for organizing. It is a great tragedy that in no known museum or other single place can such a collection of English instruments be seen today.

Exhibitions of the trade fair variety were held in many of the cities of England and Scotland during the nineteenth century and the Directory mentions various examples of makers entering their products and obtaining gold or silver awards. Exhibitions of the other sort, educational in object, also occurred outside London: the Glasgow Exhibition of 1901, for instance, having the dubious honour of exhibiting the notorious forgery known as the 'Balfour Strad', now known to be by

---

[15] 'The Violins of Sexton are of extreme rarity and considerable merit. Only two have been seen by Messrs. W. E. Hill & Sons during the last 50 years.' *Illustrated Catalogue of the Music Loan Exhibition* 156.

the Voller brothers. (The history of this affair is outlined in the author's *Violin Fraud*).[16] Outstanding more recent examples were the Festival of Britain Exhibition of British Musical Instruments in 1951, under the auspices of the Galpin Society in association with the Arts Council, and another one in 1986 to celebrate the Society's fortieth birthday.

But by the end of the nineteenth century the evangelical work had been effectively done. The effect of the 1872 Exhibition was particularly profound. The maker Joseph Withers, describing his working life to Meredith Morris, said: 'I was a regular visitor at the Great Exhibition of stringed instruments held at South Kensington in 1872 . . . The "Messie" Strad fascinated me above all other instruments; it held me spellbound, and it was with difficulty that I could tear myself away from it. That fiddle has pursued me all through my life since I first saw it, and haunted me in all my dreams. I have worked at my fiddles under its spell, and have tried to catch some of its spirit in order to imprison it in my work.'[17]

Collecting British Violins

The significant feature of the great collections discussed in Chapter 10 was the predominance of classic Italian instruments. The collection of Gillott, for instance, seems only by chance to have included an occasional English violin. On the other hand, the fine display of early English instruments at the Music Loan Exhibition of 1904, mainly contributed to by the Hill family and J. T. Chapman, suggests that there was by that date a burgeoning interest amongst at least a small circle of collectors in the Old English School of violin makers. By the time Morris came to write the second edition of his book on *British Violin Makers* he was able to illustrate in his Frontispiece a quartet of Old English instruments consisting of violins by Daniel Parker and Richard Duke, a viola by Benjamin Banks, and a cello of 'Old' William Forster. Morris enthuses particularly about the Parker violin, 'one of the most superb specimens of this fine old maker's work in existence'. The collection was owned by J. E. Smith of Bayswater, London.

Whilst one would expect the Hills to take a particular interest in old English work, it is clear that a few collectors were discriminating enough to see that the creation of these instruments was of social, economic, and musical interest and that, as an investment, as well as something to play, these were instruments of considerable interest. One well-known book by J. H. Yoxall, MP, *The ABC about Collecting* (London, 1908), devoted a small section of the text to the virtues of

[16] pp. 16–19.
[17] W. Meredith Morris, *British Violin Makers* (2nd edn., 1920), 293. In 1879 Withers was awarded first prize for musical instruments at the Westminster Industrial Exhibition, which prompted him to start making professionally.

collecting British violins. The author specifically advises against trying to find a classic Italian instrument. 'The days for collecting fine Italian violins cheaply are over. But old British-made violins may still be found by a searcher, and bought for a few pounds.' The author particularly 'backs' instruments by Parker, Forster, Duke, Dodd, Norris & Barnes, Tobin, William Tarr, and a few others.

There are more genuine 'Dukes' in existence than there are 'Banks' and 'Forsters' put together, but they are not to be found in dealers' shops. They are fossilising in dust heaps in the garrets of country mansions. There were hundreds of fine amateur players among the gentle folk of those days, when the facilities for attending music halls, opera houses &c were so few and far between . . . A fine 'Parker' fiddle was once found on the wall of a cobbler's shop at Ecclesfield in Yorkshire; it had been left, in exchange for a pair of boots, by a wandering musician . . . Pawnbrokers' shops are quite a good place in which to search for good old fiddles . . .[18]

The message of all this was twofold. British violins were undervalued, and they were obtainable by the sort of informed search that collectors enjoy.

Writing in c.1914 for the second edition of Grove's *Dictionary of Music and Musicians*, Heron-Allen usefully contributes a list of old makers and prices for which their instruments were obtainable just before the First World War. On the quality of the makers listed, Heron-Allen states:

Taken in the mass, the instruments which have been produced in London are equal in general quality to those of any city north of the Alps. Until the time of Lupot, the English makers were unquestionably equal as a school to the French, though they were rivalled by the Dutch; and Lupot himself might have shrunk from a comparison with the best works of Fendt and Panormo. Whether the art of violin-making in England will ever recover the blow which it has received from Free Trade, remains to be seen.

When studying the Heron-Allen's table (reproduced here as Table 5), it is useful to know that Heron-Allen also gives then current prices (c.1910) for Stradivari and 'Joseph' Guarneri—up to £2,000, Amati School—up to £1,000, Brescian School—up to £500, Guadagnini—up to £400, and other Italians such as Testore—up to £200. Good French violins and violas from Gand & Bernadel were priced at £20 to £24.

Heron-Allen's last-quoted sentence makes the suggestion, much rehearsed in the later part of the nineteenth century, that Free Trade was the death of the British violin industry. He had made it his business to investigate the workings of the factories of Mirecourt, Mittenwald, and Markneukirchen, the sources of the cheap violin so helpful to the British violin pupil but unhelpful to British violin-makers. Heron-Allen ascribes the birth of the 'trade fiddles' (*violine dozzinali*) to

---

[18] Yoxall, *ABC*, 130–2.

TABLE 5: *Heron-Allen's Table of Prices*

Maker	Violins and Tenors Average (£)	Violins and Tenors Fine (£)	Violoncellos Average (£)	Violoncellos Fine (£)
Rayman	20	50	—	—
Urquhart	20	50	—	—
Pamphilon	20	40	—	—
Norman	15	40	15	50
Wamsley	20	40	20	60
Betts	15	30	15	45
Duke	12	40	—	—
Fendt	20	70	25	70
Tobin	20	50	—	—
Kennedy	15	30	15	30
Forster, W.	20	25	30	100
Forster, S. A.	—	—	30	50
Lott, J. F.	30	100	—	—
Dodd	20	60	30	80
Hill (Joseph)	15	40	—	—
Hill (Lockey 1)	15	40	—	—
Hill (Lockey 2)	15	50	15	50

Italy itself. He suggests that cheap instruments of coarse construction were probably made by German workmen and sold 'by the dozen' in Italy in the eighteenth century.[19] Germany itself soon took over this mass-production idea, initially at Mittenwald in Bavaria with the Klotz family, later in Groslitz. France followed suit early in the eighteenth century at Mirecourt in Lorraine. He assigns the origin of the Markneukirchen industry in Saxony to 'recent times'. Referring to *le violon à cent sous*, costing to make 4s. 6d. as already seen, Heron-Allen confesses that 'one of these fiddles, if carefully set up, can be made to discourse very tolerable music'.[20]

Heron-Allen states that the manufacture of these 'shop-fiddles' was initially done by hand. 'A good workman could make two fiddles in a week and had to be paid 16 francs or marks for each one.' In inspecting the various factories at the end of the nineteenth century Heron-Allen realized that the trade was by then 'full of secrets'. 'The writer ... has never succeeded in seeing the whole of the processes by which the cheap fiddles of today are made.' He had seen backs and bellies pressed into shape under heat, and for the better instruments gouged inside and

---

[19] Edward Heron-Allen, 'Violin Family', in *Grove's Dictionary of Music and Musicians*, 2nd edn., V. 308.
[20] Ibid.

out by rotary carving tools, ribs bent a dozen at a time by machinery, but excepting in one room in each factory where a man or two sits and works on the old principles, he had never seen a man or a woman (for many women are employed) make more than one part of a fiddle. One would make sides, another backs, another necks, another scrolls, and so on. Not one of them could make an entire fiddle, and he recalled to mind the fair Bavarian girl whose business it was, day in and day out, to cut f-holes. She was a 'skilled worker' and highly paid. 'She received one halfpenny for each *f* hole . . . We believe that the only actual manufactury in England today is that of Messrs W. E. Hill & Sons, who are compelled to charge £30 to £35 for the first-quality fiddles, and £20 for a second-quality instrument as they leave their works at Hanwell.'

The only other makers of any consequence that Heron-Allen could identify at this time were: 'Joseph Anthony Chanot who charges £10 to £21 for a new violin, and Szepessy Béla who charges £20. There are a great many secondary makers whose names it would be invidious to mention, . . .'

Heron-Allen's account makes a sceptical reference to the first edition of Morris's work which, in his view, in listing all the 'secondary makers' showed 'little sense of proportion'.[21] This conveniently leads us on to the question whether there really was a renaissance in English and Scottish violin-making in the early part of the twentieth century. With this there is the associated question whether the earlier twentieth-century makers dwelt on by Morris matched up to the standards we now expect of the highly trained and professional contemporary makers operating in Great Britain in the second half of the century. The next two chapters attempt to answer these questions.

[21] See Ch. 12 n. 1, and Ch. 8.

Chapter Fourteen

🙵 The Power of the Pen: Heron-Allen and his Legacies

Working in a Vacuum — Periodical Literature — Earlier Books — A Violin-Makers' 'Bible' — The Hidden Heron-Allen — From Fiddles to Fossils and Fantasy: Assessing Heron-Allen's Achievements — Tailnote to Heron-Allen — Towry Piper — William Meredith Morris and William C. Honeyman — William Henley

Working in a Vacuum

IT will have been noticed that the four makers whose lives have been outlined in Chapter 12, Ardern, Askew, Mayson, and Atkinson, had no formal tuition. They depended upon copying existing instruments (often themselves copies, not always accurate, of classic Italian models), and on what they could pick up by conversation with other makers and studying the sparse existing literature. Atkinson, who lived near London, was probably in a better position to see a wide range of original instruments in the shops of the big London dealers and in the exhibitions periodically mounted in London. Atkinson's work spans the period of the 'renaissance' in England as does, to a less extent, that of Mayson's. But Ardern and Askew must have worked in something of a vacuum. It is in these circumstances creditable that their work is as good as it is.

Periodical Literature

Corroborative evidence of the burgeoning of interest in England and Scotland in the violin as a musical instrument comes from the number of periodicals for violinists and violin connoisseurs that sprang into life at the end of the nineteenth century. The *Strad* was born in May 1890. But there was also the *Violin Times* which first appeared in November 1893 under the distinguished editorship of

Eugene Polonaski (author of violin tuition books, examiner to the College of Violinists, and late editor of the *Strad*) together with the celebrated Edward Heron-Allen. Heron-Allen's joint editorship lasted only a year—he felt that his other obligations made it impossible to devote the necessary time—but the first volume of the *Violin Times* is full of his fascinating contributions.[1] Then to the list must be added *The Violin Monthly Magazine* ('for all lovers of the instrument') which came out between 1890 and 1894, *The Violin*, published between 1889 and 1894, *Cremona* (incorporating *The Violinist*) (17 December 1906 to 16 December 1911), and *Violin and String World* (January 1908 to January 1913, when it merged with *A Musical Standard* which continued to January 1933). These were the primary periodicals for players and makers of instruments of the violin family but there were also a number of other periodicals, such as *The Musical Times*, of general musical interest and a number of magazines specializing in or including articles on woodwork, including how to make a violin. It was in one of the latter, *Amateur Work Illustrated*, that Heron-Allen first wrote the foundation of his famous book on *Violin-Making*. This is mentioned under his name later.

Of these British violin periodicals the *Strad* has proved the most enduring and though inevitably standards of contributions to its monthly numbers have been variable, series by such writers as Arthur Dykes (of the former firm of Dykes and Sons) and Frank Thisleton (see Chapter 15) still make interesting reading. The Strad Library also published a series of short monographs including Walter Mayson's book on *Violin Making*, studies of *Stradivarius* and *Guarneri* by Horace Petherick and *Chats to 'Cello Students* by Arthur Broadley.

Earlier Books

None of the above periodicals appeared before 1890, but books on the violin go back much earlier into the nineteenth century. As Hidalgo Moya pointed out: 'Books on violin making are of two kinds: those that instruct and those that amuse. Fortunately the last are few, but still plentiful enough to cause trouble—not because the writers were unskilled in their art, but because the reader is told very much less than enough of some matters and too much of others.'[2]

When William Honeyman investigated Scottish makers (see Chapter 8), several mentioned that they worked according to the principles laid down by Otto.[3] This is a reference to the treatise on the *Construction, Preservation, Repair, and Improvement of the Violin and all Bow Instruments* (*Together with a Dissertation on the Most Eminent Makers, Pointing out the Surest Marks by which a Genuine*

---

[1] See Brian Harvey, 'Heron-Allen's Fidiculana', *Strad* (May 1993), 484–6.
[2] Moya and Piper, *Violin Tone*, 65.   [3] See e.g. James Cannon, Dumfries.

Instrument may be Distinguished) by Jacob Augustus Otto, instrument-maker to the Court of the Archduke of Weimar. This book appeared translated from the German, with notes and additions by Thomas Fardely, Professor of Languages and Music, Leeds, and was published in London in 1833. As the translator said in his preface: 'It has frequently been a matter of deep regret amongst professional men that there exists an immense stock of valuable information on almost every art or science which is to many completely lost and hidden from their sight, as it were, by being couched in languages of which they have not had opportunities of acquiring a knowledge . . . Knowledge as Lord Bacon laconically, yet emphatically observes, is power.' Otto had published the first version of this work in Halle and Leipzig in 1817. In 1833 the translation of it appears to have been the first book in English to deal specifically with constructional principles. Otherwise the intending maker would have had to delve into the works of Félix Savart (*Mémoire sur la Construction des Instruments à Cordes et à Archet* (Paris, 1819)) or even possibly Antonio Bagatella's *Regole per la Costruzione de' Violini, Viole, Violoncelli et Violoni* (Padua, 1786). From what he says, John Askew and his schoolmaster friend struggled with one or two of these texts.

The descriptions given by Otto of 'constructional principles' are of a very general character. The author does little more than list the fifty-eight different parts of the instrument which he identifies, and give general advice about quality of wood; the actual instruction about how to make the body of the instrument is covered in two short pages. Nothing at all is said about the intricacies of carving out the neck or scroll. Subsequent editions were edited by John Bishop of Cheltenham, who consulted such authorities as Georges Chanot of Wardour Street, London, thus improving its usefulness. The fourth edition (c.1880) has pull-out diagrams which, though not to scale, do indicate such matters as plate thicknesses.

Shortly after the appearance of the English translation of Otto, George Dubourg's book on *The Violin* came out in London in 1836. This book falls into the category of 'amusement' rather than 'instruction'. George Dubourg was the grandson of Matthew Dubourg, already mentioned, who often played for Handel when in Dublin and had been one of England's first infant prodigies. Dubourg's book mainly talks about makers and players, though it includes a short and entirely inadequate chapter on the construction of the violin. It appeared in many subsequent editions revised and enlarged by John Bishop of Cheltenham.

The work by William Sandys and Simon Andrew Forster on *The History of the Violin and Other Instruments Played on with the Bow from the Remotest Times to the Present: Also an Account of the Principal Makers, English and Foreign, with Numerous Illustrations*, appeared in London in 1864. This book made considerably more impact than either of the previous works and is referred to frequently in this text. It managed to combine, sometimes slightly uncomfortably, what was for those times a detailed and diverting history of the instrument (very largely contributed by William Sandys) together with a Dictionary of Makers with a great deal of detail on the Forster family, contributed by Simon Andrew Forster.

William Sandys (1792–1874) was the first of a succession of lawyers who have taken a particular interest in the instrument and written about it.[4] He was educated at Westminster School, and became a solicitor in 1814. Between 1861 and 1874 he was senior partner of the firm of Sandys & Knott in London. He was also a Fellow of the Society of Antiquaries and an enthusiastic musical amateur. He had learned the cello under Robert Lindley. He had also written books on the *History of Freemasonry* (1829) and *Christmas Carols* (1833). His co-author Simon Andrew Forster was the last of the instrument-making Forster family, whose work is frequently referred to in this text. The book was very successful and reprinted frequently. Although in places its accuracy has been doubted, the authors were closer to the time of some of the major makers in England that they discussed and they had access to a manuscript work of Henry Hill, the viola-player and member of the distinguished Hill family of violin-makers. To the intending maker, however, there would have been little or nothing by way of actual instruction on how to make the instrument.

Similar remarks apply to George Hart's major work on *The Violin, its Famous Makers and their Imitators* (London, 1875), which appeared in numerous subsequent editions. This too contains material of great value from the historical point of view but nothing on the constructional side.

The honour of writing the first detailed account in English of how to make appears to belong to Peter Davidson, whose book on *The Violin* is discussed in Chapter 8. This was published in 1871 and went through four editions to 1881. By the time Morris wrote his work on *British Violin Makers* Davidson's work was, as Morris states, already 'scarce'. It had obviously fulfilled a much-felt need and although only a small part of the book (mainly chapters V and VI) actually deals with practical construction, Davidson includes useful diagrams and detailed measurements. There was, though, still a great deal which had to be left to the imagination and the violin-making world had to wait a little longer for an authoritative and comprehensive text.

Other writers whose work achieved great popularity in their lifetimes, but which could be classed as 'amusing' rather than 'instructional', include James M. Fleming, a writer and violinist born in Glasgow in 1839. Besides his tutorial works on violin playing he wrote *Old Violins and their Makers* (1883) and *The Fiddle Fancier's Guide* (1892). Both these books have information of value to the researcher

---

[4] After Sandys came, for example, Edward John Payne, barrister (*Grove* contributor), Edward Heron-Allen, and Towry Piper (both solicitors). Charles Reade, the novelist, playwright, and violin expert, was also a barrister.

but, as was usually the way in such books at that period, sources are rarely given and fact too easily degenerates into anecdote. James Fleming also wrote a short monograph on the Stradivari violin 'The Emperor' in 1891 and survived until the early years of the twentieth century.

Another popularizer was Hugh Reginald Haweis (1838–1910) who was the incumbent of St James, Marylebone. He achieved considerable renown for his work on *Music and Morals* (1873) and his autobiography, *My Musical Life* (1884). His fundamental tenet was the belief in music as a civilizing force if it could be introduced into the lives of the masses. (It was, a little under a century later, but it is doubtful if Haweis would have accounted the activities of modern rock groups either music or civilizing.) Haweis was also a talented violinist. Reference in this book has already been made to his work *Old Violins and Violin Lore* (1898). This undoubtedly further helped with the popularizing of the instrument, but (as mentioned in the preceding chapter) Morris, reviewing the work in 1899,[5] castigates it for numerous inaccuracies in the Dictionary of Makers which the book contains.

Haweis had progressive views in some respects. *The Illustrated London News* of 20 August 1892 contains an article by Haweis and a photograph showing him and his newly formed 'mixed' choir of male and female voices. Apparently his whole (male-voice) choir left him a few weeks before and so he rapidly substituted the new mixed choir. He states that he was glad to be rid of the boys with their 'dirty nails, messy ways, interminable sweet-sucking and dog-earing of the Psalters, their sniggering and whispering and stretching and kicking and fidgeting and sleeping; ruin of hassocks, surplices, and choir stalls'.[6]

A Violin-Makers' 'Bible'

An authoritative and detailed text on the details of making was eventually provided by the publication of Edward Heron-Allen's book *Violin-Making as it Was, and Is* which was published by Ward Lock in London in 1884. The instructional parts of the book had previously appeared in the pages of the same publisher's *Amateur Work Illustrated*.[7] The book rapidly went into a second edition in 1885 with some corrections and many subsequent reprints.

Since Heron-Allen's work is probably the most important and comprehensive book on violin-making and its history ever to have been written it deserves a more detailed look. The extraordinarily versatile author had contributed his own diagrams and drawings to the text which contains full-size pull-out illustrations of

---

[5] See 'Some Strictures on the Rev. H. R. Haweis's New Work on Fiddles', *Strad* (Apr. 1899), 371.

[6] Quoted in Scholes, *Mirror*, 539; and see pl. 76 thereof.

[7] Vols. 1–3 (1882–4).

the form of a Stradivari and a Guarneri violin. The earlier part of the book deals with the ancestry of the violin and of the bow, together with short biographies of the major makers of Europe and an account of the various experiments which had occurred with the shape and structure of the violin. Part II explains the theoretical considerations relating to the wood, the interior and exterior of the instrument, the varnish, and the fittings and appliances needed. Part III—'Practical'—deals with the tools, the moulds, and how to proceed in actually making the instrument. There are a number of appendices including a comprehensive bibliography founded on Heron-Allen's own renowned library of violin books and on the separately published *Bibliography of the Violin* mentioned below.

Violin-Making was so successful that it has remained in print ever since and is to be found in all English speaking countries with a violin-making tradition. A number of other books were subsequently published in many countries containing similar detailed instructional advice but Heron-Allen's work has always been regarded as the pathfinder. Heron-Allen's *Bibliography of the Violin*, another major work, was published in parts from 1890 by Griffith Farran & Co. and then in two quarto volumes in 1894.

Some of the details of the birth of Heron-Allen's violin-making book are given in the first edition of Morris's work on *British Violin Makers*. This relates that Heron-Allen had himself found, on leaving Harrow in 1878 and becoming an articled clerk in the family firm of solicitors in Soho, that to make a violin as a hobby was not easy. Such works as Otto, Dubourg, and Sandys and Forster were interesting on the history and theory but practically useless on how to *make*. Quickly developing his knowledge, he began to lecture and write on *Violin-Making*, having become a 'casual' apprentice of Georges Chanot. Ward Lock & Co. knew of his interest and encouraged Heron-Allen to contribute to their monthly magazine, *Amateur Work*. Heron-Allen agreed to supply the publishers with a series of articles on practical violin-making for amateurs, being tempted by the remuneration of 7*s*. 6*d*. per page—probably a small fortune to an articled clerk who would normally have been unpaid in those days (though his father actually made him an allowance of £150 per annum). The deal, however, was a sterner one than Heron-Allen then realized. The copyright and all rights of reprinting the articles in book form were to belong absolutely to the publishers without further payment. As Morris states, 'It need hardly be said that Messrs Ward, Lock have never made him any payment in respect of the many editions they have issued since 1884. Indeed, a few years ago, when the author offered to revise the book for a small fee, they stated that they did not feel justified in incurring the expense!'[8] This state of affairs must have been very galling for Heron-Allen who was a stickler for accuracy.

---

[8] Morris, *British Violin Makers*, 1st edn. (1904), 60.

After writing *Violin-Making* Heron-Allen continued his series of short monographs under the title *Opuscula Fidicularum* (1882–95), a collection of eight. It was many years before he came back to writing on the violin, with the exception of his revision of the articles on the violin and its makers for the second edition of *Grove's Dictionary of Music and Musicians* which came out between 1904 and 1910, and some contributions to the *Dictionary of National Biography*. In 1941, two years before his death, *Opusculum IX* was published, in a limited edition of 100 copies, on *The 'Nefer' Sign*. This is a learned monograph on the hitherto accepted identification of an Egyptian hieroglyph as an instrument of music, and corrects a passage on page 43 of his text on *Violin-Making* which suggests that the hieroglyph in question is one of the first depictions of a stringed instrument. Reviewing the authorities and the fruits of modern research Heron-Allen comes to the conclusion that 'We must now accept the fact that the derivation of any stringed instrument from the Egyptian Hieroglyph is purely imaginary and must disappear from the work of later musical historians.'[9] For bibliophiles, as Heron-Allen himself was, the publication of this late *Opusculum* poses a challenge to those lucky enough to have copies of the first eight such pamphlets, all of which were issued in severely limited editions. It is almost as though Heron-Allen, in the dark days of the Second World War, deliberately tested the capacity of future collectors of his works. He left his own magnificent collection of books and articles on the violin to the Royal College of Music in London.

Heron-Allen bestrides British turn-of-the-century violin-making like a colossus. Yet despite the by now international interest in his book, the absence of information hitherto about his extraordinary life is regrettable and some attempt must now be made to redress the deficiency.

The Hidden Heron-Allen

In the annals of early twentieth-century English polymaths and eccentrics the name of Edward Heron-Allen should stand high. The continued availability in print of his classic study of violin-making ensures that his name remains well known to successive generations of violin-makers and enthusiasts. Going through Morris's Dictionary (and the Directory in this book) it is quite clear that a number of makers who started their work in about 1890 or subsequently were greatly influenced by Heron-Allen's work. Even some distinguished living makers, such as Wilfred Saunders, acknowledge their debt to his book. It is natural, therefore, that violin enthusiasts should connect Heron-Allen's name almost exclusively with the violin. But as will be seen, this is to do him a serious injustice. Although many

[9] p. 12.

people would have been quite happy to achieve what Heron-Allen did purely in the world of writing about the violin and violinists, this was a small part of his total scholarly activity.

When the distinguished writer Jan Morris wrote an article in *The Times Saturday Review* of 3 August 1991—'Leaves from Other Lives'—about 'books that had messages written in them, or objects stuck in them, or were in general what booksellers liked to call association copies', she ended with a description of the most thoroughly personalized book in her library 'and the one that will most please my great grandchildren'. 'It is the copy of Augustus Hare's *Venice* which Edward and Marianna Heron-Allen bought during their visit to Venice in the spring of 1895.' The volume had been re-bound to incorporate photographs and mementos of this visit in a fascinating and attractive way. 'I love the book. I bless the Heron-Allens, whoever they were, for projecting the pleasure of their days in Venice so intimately . . . I bought it in Brighton, I see, in 1959, for 15 shillings . . .'

This perhaps unguarded comment brought forth a torrent of correspondence sent to Jan Morris by a wide variety of people anxious to enlighten her on the identity of Edward Heron-Allen, and Jan Morris was kind enough to make this correspondence available to the author. What comes out is that few of the correspondents saw Heron-Allen in the round—he was either an eminent writer on violins, or an eminent local historian, or a scientist, or a 'science-fiction' (or occult) book writer, or a protozoologist, and so on. Few people who knew his work well in one area seemed to know of it in another. This is understandable because the range of his achievements is almost unbelievable.

To begin at the beginning. Heron-Allen was born in London on 17 December 1861, christened Edward Heron, and spent his secondary education at Harrow School which he left in 1878. His father was a solicitor practising in his own firm of Allen & Son at 17 Carlisle Street, Soho, London. The firm had been founded by his ancestor Emanuel Allen in 1788, and he held many county and parochial appointments which descended down the family to Heron-Allen himself in due course. These included from 1900 the appointment of his firm as Solicitors and Parliamentary Agents to the City of Westminster, and for a time Heron-Allen took charge of what he described as the difficult and onerous work of the Parliamentary Practice of the City. Heron-Allen's father, George Allen, had taken his eldest son George M. Allen into partnership in 1884 but the latter died in 1889. In 1892 George Allen constituted a new firm under the old name of Allen & Son and Edward Heron-Allen became the senior partner. By the time that his book on *Violin-Making* was published (1884) its author clearly wished to be known as Edward Heron-Allen, with the hyphen.[10]

---

[10] The firm's successors practise as Allen & Fraser in Dean Street nearby. I am grateful to the senior partner, Mr F. D. Lavender, for his assistance in research.

To get to that point Heron-Allen had had to serve articles (or an apprenticeship) with his father for about five years from 1878. During this time articled clerks had to take professional examinations until their eventual admission as a solicitor. The life of an articled clerk tended to be relaxed—partly because parents were intended to maintain children in articles and so no salary was paid. The value of the job was learning the skills. Nor was it then traditional to go to university to read Law (or anything else), particularly for future solicitors (as opposed to barristers). It was thought that the professional training involved was a sufficient discipline and brought sufficient status with it without the necessity of a degree. His early steps did not, therefore lead him in the direction of Oxford or Cambridge, for better or worse. Armed with a mind sharpened in the sixth form of Harrow School he effectively educated himself thereafter.

During his years of apprenticeship he developed his interest in the violin. He had become keen on it at school from the age of 10 and studied under Otto Peiniger whilst at Harrow. With his allowance of pocket-money he collected books on music, specializing in books on the violin. In May 1882 Carl Engel's library was sold by auction and, to Heron-Allen's disappointment, most of the library was bought over his head by Bernard Quaritch, the well-known antiquarian bookseller. Heron-Allen called on Mr Quaritch and a friendship developed. Seeing Heron-Allen's enthusiasm for violin books, Quaritch kindly passed most of them on to him at virtually his purchase price. Part of the bargain was that Heron-Allen was to write a short treatise on the violin and deliver it, as the guest of Quaritch, at a meeting of the club called the 'Sette of Odd Volumes' founded in 1878. Heron-Allen duly delivered his lecture on 2 June 1882 before an audience which included Capt. Sir Richard Burton, the explorer and writer. Sir Richard encouraged him further to develop his interest in the literature of the violin and to study the instrument itself. The lecture became No. 1 of his series of short monographs on the violin, subsequently more elegantly restyled as *De Fidiculis Opuscula*, already referred to.

Soho was an area rich in violin-making and dealing establishments. In a book published about Soho[11] Heron-Allen contributed a piece on the 'Violin Dealers of Soho'. He mentions that eighteenth-century makers included John Holloway of Gerrard Street (*c*.1769), John Marshall of Covent Garden, John Morrison of Princes Street (*c*.1760), the Forster family in St Martin's Lane, and various members of the Hill family, particularly William Ebsworth Hill in Wardour Street. And besides these there were the son of Benjamin Banks at Golden Square, Thomas Dodd in St Martin's Lane, and Bernhard Simon Fendt in Dean Street. His contemporaries working in Soho when he wrote included Messrs Beare and

---

[11] J. H. Cardwell, H. B. Freeman, and G C. Wilton, *Two Centuries of Soho, Its Institutions, Firms and Amusements* (London, 1898).

Goodwin, Béla Szepessy, Joseph Anthony Chanot, Hart & Son, James Tubbs & Son, and the old-established business of Edward Withers, successors to Norris & Barnes (originally at 31 Coventry Street), all at various addresses in Wardour Street.

It was not surprising, therefore, that Heron-Allen found himself tempted into one of the local workshops, and the one that he chose, as mentioned above, was that run by Georges Chanot. He arranged to pay the sum of 10s. 6d. for every hour he worked in the shop, then a high fee, and Chanot also supplied Heron-Allen with wood. In fact Chanot patiently taught his pupil step by step along with his own son, Joseph. Some sceptical commentators who have perhaps felt threatened by the sheer professionalism of Heron-Allen's book on *Violin-Making* have doubted whether the author had actually made a real instrument. Heron-Allen himself, writing in the *Violin Times* in 1894,[12] stated:

Twelve years ago when I undertook the production of my book on *Violin Making* I apprenticed myself to one of the greatest makers of the day, George Chanot: in his workshop I worked hard for *two* years and produced *two* violins. One of these, copied exactly from the later Prosper Sainton's Guarnerius, has been more or less continually played upon ever since, and—it may be from parental pride—I would rather play today upon this instrument than upon any other that has passed through my hands, not being one of the master violins to which reference has been made. But it must be remembered that few new violins have the luck, if I may so call it, to be thus played upon during the first ten years of their existence. During the last two years my violin has been played upon and submitted to every tone test by Joachim, Wilhelmj Piatti, Simonetti, and Wolff, among other virtuosi, and they have unanimously volunteered the highest encomia upon this 'amateur fiddle'.

It was these two instruments that Heron-Allen describes in his book, the Guarneri model and the Strad model. Morris states, in the first edition of his book, that the materials used were the best procurable. The measurements were those given in the *Violin-Making* book and they were varnished with fifteen coats of a tender amber-coloured varnish with a glint of rose in it. This was laid on a coat of bright yellow saffron stain which gave a speck of fire wherever the oil varnish had chipped or worn. Heron-Allen himself warned against violin varnish recipes being interpreted canonically. He told Morris that it was just like making claret-cup or punch—one begins with a rough formula, and tastes and adds this and that as it seems required, until it is all right. So far as is known, these were the only two instruments made by Heron-Allen, though Morris infers that there might have been more. He states that 'Mr. Heron-Allen's labels are drawn in pen and ink, and each one differently. The instruments he has made are at his own and

[12] p. 150.

at his father's residence. They were not made for sale, and no price is put upon them; in fact, he would not part with them for any consideration.'[13]

Both the *Violin-Making* book and Vol. 1 of the *Violin Times*, of which he was joint editor, were dedicated to HRH Alfred Ernest Albert, Duke of Saxe-Coburg and Gotha, the Duke of Edinburgh, to whom reference has already been made in this text. The Duke (1844–1900) was the second son of Queen Victoria and Prince Albert, and followed a career in the Navy. The *Dictionary of National Biography* describes him as 'passionately fond of music and a good performer on the violin' but of a 'somewhat reserved disposition'. Heron-Allen was lucky to have a royal patron so interested in the violin and its music.[14]

By the end of 1894 Heron-Allen was well launched into legal practice but had virtually exhausted his interest in violin-making, it seems. He had also married in 1891. His wife, Marianna, was the daughter of the painter Rudolf Lehmann and her name appears with her husband's in the articles in the 1894 *Violin Times*, subsequently republished as a separate pamphlet, and as the co-translator and co-editor of *The Arts and Crafts-Book of the Worshipful Guild of Violin-Makers of Markneukirchen, 1677-1772*. She was also his companion in the Venice expedition to which Jan Morris's copy of Hare's *Venice* refers. Unfortunately Marianna became a complete invalid and her husband nursed her with great devotion until her early death. He married again in 1903, his wife Edith being the daughter of William Brown Pepler, a doctor of medicine. He had met her during a three-month tour of Egypt.

Meanwhile in 1893 he became interested in 'cheirosophy' (chiromancy or palmistry) and he published with Ward Lock the first scientific works on the subject: *A Manual of Cheirosophy* (1885) and *The Science of the Hand* (1886), both going into many subsequent editions—Ward Lock again taking the copyright of the *Manual*. Heron-Allen was also one of the earliest members of the Society for Psychical Research and attended occult seances throughout his life. He claimed to have exposed the blind medium Husk and the popular medium 'Miro'. He said that he never witnessed any phenomena that he could not himself reproduce as 'parlour tricks'.

In November 1886 he accepted an invitation to go on an extended lecture tour of America, his subject being 'Cheirosophy'. As one might expect, this was so well received that Heron-Allen described the tour as being extraordinarily successful,

---

[13] Morris, *British Violin Makers*, 1st edn. (1904), 62. The two instruments were left by will to the Royal College of Music but unfortunately sold shortly after the end of the Second World War when there were severe economic difficulties. The Strad copy is now owned by a distinguished professional maker and player in England. It is illustrated in this book (Pl. 30).

[14] Some of this information is based on short autobiographical notes, compiled for Heron-Allen's own obituary notice, kindly loaned to the author by Heron-Allen's grandson Ivor Jones. There is much more to be unearthed from Heron-Allen's own journals. The *Times* Obituary appeared on 30 Mar. 1943.

both financially and otherwise. His practice in Soho clearly managed without him for some time, since he led a literary and Bohemian life for three years from 1887, writing several novels and volumes of short stories and verses, normally under pen-names. He returned to his family firm in 1889, though he was always able to combine legal practice with his other literary, musical, and scientific interests.

His musical expertise led to his being appointed Special Commissioner of the Music Section of the Colonial Exhibition to Italy in 1885 which in turn led to his appointment as a Fellow of the Accademia of St Cecilia in Rome.

Although he had no formal training as a scientist he had had from his early school days a strong affinity for and interest in marine biology and protozoology, and this was encouraged by his move from London to a large house which he built (now unfortunately demolished) in 1906–7 near Selsey Bill in Sussex. (This occurred when he was 45; he retired from his legal practice at the age of 50.) He published a *Study of Chalk Foraminifera* in 1893 and other studies of the foraminifera of Selsey Bill between 1908 and 1911.[15] Many similar studies of his were published in scientific periodicals and it was no doubt in recognition of this, and of his presidency of the Microscopical Society between 1916 and 1918, that he was given the supreme honour for a British scientist of being elected a Fellow of the Royal Society in 1919. The large and important 'type slide' collection (made with Arthur Earland) was presented to the British Museum between 1926 and 1943. It is regarded as one of the two most important classified collections of 'recent' foraminifera extant in England.[16] Heron-Allen also succeeded in writing what he probably regarded as his finest scholarly work of this sort, *Selsey Bill: Historic and Prehistoric*. This was published by Duckworth in a large quarto edition in 1911.

The First World War saw Heron-Allen's attachment to the Intelligence Department of the War Office; prior to this he had served as a lieutenant in the Sixth Volunteers Battalion of the Royal Sussex Regiment, serving in France in 1918. He had also founded the West Sussex Boy Scout troop in 1911 at the request of Lord Baden-Powell himself (the founder of scouting, and hero of the Boer War), and his scouts were trained to act as a type of Home Guard during the war years.

His extraordinarily wide interests did not stop at science. Heron-Allen was also an accomplished linguist. His violin books frequently make Latin quotations which he rarely vouchsafed to translate to his no doubt often bewildered readers. He was a talented Persian scholar and became fascinated by the question of

---

[15] Foraminifera (from the Latin, 'hole-bearing'), constitute an order of minute animals, or protozoa, with a simple or complex shell perforated by pores (whence the name).

[16] See R. L. Hodgkinson, 'The Heron-Allen & Earland Type Slide Collection in the British Museum (Natural History)', *Journal of Micropalaeontology*, 8/2 (1989), 149–56.

whether Omar Khayyam was a mere voluptuary or a sublime philosopher. He was also convinced that the *Rubaiyat* of Omar Khayyam had not been exactly translated or understood. He published new scholarly editions in various versions of the *Rubaiyat* from 1898 to 1908.[17] These remain much sought-after rarities in the bibliophile world, as is his translation of *The Lament of Baba Tahir* (1901) from an almost unknown dialect of Persian known as Luri.

There was yet another string to Heron-Allen's bow. In his *Who's Who* entry he makes a somewhat terse reference to the writing of 'fiction and verse (chiefly under various pseudonyms)'. It is most probable that not all these works have been identified, but *Who's Who in Horror and Fantasy Fiction*[18] traces to Heron-Allen the pseudonyms 'Christopher Blayre' and 'Flavius'.[19] His first novel, involving psychic vampirism, was the *Princess Daphne* published in 1888. There was also *The Purple Sapphire* (London: Philip Allan & Co., 1921; 8 shillings), a collection of prototype science fiction stories with a tinge of horror. One of the stories was entitled 'The Cheetah Girl', but this was omitted from the volume and the subsequent expanded edition (*The Strange Papers of Doctor Blayre*, 1932) because it was thought that it might offend against the then current obscenity laws. It dealt with the offspring of a prostitute and a cheetah. That story had been published privately in 1923 and only twenty copies are thought to exist. The 'Purple Sapphire' title story is based on the premise that fact is stranger than fiction. The actual stone, with its well-documented evil powers, was in Heron-Allen's possession and was left on his death, with every possible precaution, to the Natural History Museum in London where it may still be found.[20] The other stories involved such matters as unfinished classics being completed by their dead authors. There was a later sequel, *Some Women at the University*, in 1934.[21]

He also wrote, for the Sette of Odd Volumes, *Madame de Sévigné* (1928) and *The Gods of the Fourth World* (1931) (springing from his deep interest in Buddhism). All these books are also of great scarcity value to collectors, particularly of occult fiction. It is frustrating that so little is known about the thinking that went into them by the author, but clearly he had a mind fascinated not only by exploration of the known, using the methodology of the microscopist, but also of the unknown and unknowable. The opportunity to do an address before the distinguished membership of the Sette of Odd Volumes clearly caused a good many of these disparate seeds to germinate initially.

---

[17] See *Second Edition of Edward Fitzgerald's Rubaiyat of Umar Khayyam*, edited, with an introduction and notes, by Edward Heron-Allen (London, 1908).

[18] Mike Ashley (London, 1977). See also George Locke, *A Spectrum of Fantasy* (London, 1980).

[19] There were in fact many others, usually anagrams of Heron-Allen's name: for example, Ronald Redhew Neal; Darrell O'Dennahew; Nora Helen Warddell. Two novels published in America were *sub nom.* 'Selina Dolaro'; also 'Dryasdust'.

[20] Heron-Allen's grandson, Ivor Jones, confirmed to the author that the family were forbidden to inspect it in his grandfather's lifetime. It was actually an amethyst looted from a temple during the Indian Mutiny.

[21] 'Christopher Blayre' is described by the author as 'Sometime Registrar of the University of Cosmopoli'.

Heron-Allen died on 28 March 1943 at his house, Large Acres, Selsey Bill, Sussex, having listed his recreations in *Who's Who* at that time as 'Persian literature; marine zoology; meteorology; heraldry; bibliography; occasional Essays and Scientific Romances; Auricula and Asparagus culture'. Such obituaries as there were in the darkest days of the war, with the notable exception of *The Times*, are primarily in specialist journals and deal almost exclusively with the interest which the journal covered: local history, local archaeology, and the like.

One of Jan Morris's correspondents remembered the Heron-Allen family from her childhood days. This correspondent[22] states that her family spent many summer holidays in a cottage in the grounds of Heron-Allen's house, Large Acres. She describes Heron-Allen as 'a brilliant, extraordinary, unusual, eccentric, man'. He had built a museum in his garden full of an incredible diversity of objects and his garden also included a maze designed by himself and an archery ground from which children were prohibited. In the centre of the lawn stood his specially designed barometer. The house also had accommodation for his 12,000-volume library. To the children he seemed rather frightening and odd and they all noticed his smooth, scented, white cheeks. Heron-Allen obviously still liked children around—he helped bring up one of his grandchildren during the early years of the Second World War and was also associated with the bringing up of Oscar Wilde's second son, Vyvyan Holland.

Edward Heron-Allen's entry in *Who's Who* is not very explicit about his family. However, the *Times* obituary baldly states that he had two daughters, the younger of whom predeceased him. This was in fact a tragic episode which almost put a stop to his creative work. The younger daughter's name was Armorel Daphne, born in 1908 to Heron-Allen and his second wife. She was a brilliant and beautiful girl who spent four years at Lady Margaret Hall, Oxford between 1926 and 1930, obtaining First Class Honours in Natural Sciences (Zoology)—obviously following in her father's footsteps in that respect. In the year that she went down she became engaged but on 3 July 1930, within a fortnight of her graduation, a wheel came off the elderly car that she was driving (contrary to her parents' wishes) and she was killed, at the age of 22. The Heron-Allens established a scholarship and holiday bursary in her name which was augmented by his will. This presently yields sufficient income to provide useful scholarships and book grants as well as support for a Heron-Allen Fellow in the Zoology field. There is also a portrait of Armorel in Lady Margaret Hall.[23] The College takes great pride and pleasure in its enduring links with the Heron-Allen family.

---

[22] Miss Elvira Hobson of Chichester, W. Sussex.
[23] The other daughter's name was 'Itha', an acronym for Ianthe Theodora Heron-Allen, who married and had children.

Heron-Allen's earliest known photographic portrait appears as the frontispiece of his book on *Violin-Making* and shows him, suitably accoutred in an apron and holding a violin body, as a young man aged about 22.

From Fiddles to Fossils and Fantasy: Assessing Heron-Allen's Achievements

In the light of all this astonishing activity, there are two ways in which one may view Heron-Allen. He could be regarded as a rich dilettante with the means to indulge every passing interest, be it violin-making, palmistry, marine biology, antique silver, or learning Middle Eastern languages, to name far from all of them. There is evidence that he was so regarded by some people. It may be asked: where is the CBE and where, indeed, are the honorary degrees for this amateur scientist, who was nevertheless an accomplished lecturer who visited both Oxford and Cambridge and had many friends in university circles? Honours of other kinds there certainly were, not least his Fellowship of the Royal Society—of all honours perhaps the most worth having—but the absence of honorary degrees is strange. He was certainly tetchy, resigning from a number of his scientific societies when an article of his was rejected (though subsequently published by the Smithsonian Institute, Washington). He also fell out with his scientific partner Arthur Earland, apparently on a matter of principle. He almost certainly thought that his work was not sufficiently recognized, with some justification in retrospect.

A second, and fairer, view would be to honour him as one of the most widely gifted Englishmen of his time. Any doubts are effectively answered by the sheer enduring quality of his work. His book on *Violin-Making* remains, over a century later, one of the best ever expositions of the subject and is still in print. The Hills always recommended it to their clients. His work on scientific matters is recognized as being meticulous and pathfinding; his collections in museums are an apt memorial to these qualities. The Selsey Bill work remains a classic of local history, though as a solicitor–local historian he is at least equalled by that other 'uncommon attorney', Reginald Hine of Hitchin (see Chapter 3 and the discussion of Bunyan's violin)—but Hine had no pretensions to be a musician, scientist, or novelist as well. Heron-Allen's pioneering translations of and commentaries upon Persian poetry are much sought-after. There is an 'occult' market for his novels which has made them collectors' items, few associating their author 'Christopher Blayre' with the sober protozoologist Heron-Allen.

Such multifaceted talent is bound to attract envy and jealousy from the professionals whom he seemed effortlessly to outshine in so many different fields. He was fortunate to inherit wealth, but his own activities built on this rather than frittering it away. His legacy to the society in which he lived was the fruit of his intellect, and who can legitimately quarrel with his policy decision to use his investment income to pursue scholarly activities for which there would ordinarily have been insufficient time in the busy working life of a lawyer?

Heron-Allen was perhaps not quite a genius but it is time that he was more generously given his due as one of the most brilliant and enigmatic polymaths of the late nineteenth and early twentieth centuries in England, adding lustre and illumination to every area that he touched.

Tailnote to Heron-Allen

After the preparation of much of this material the present author was invited to peruse some of the voluminous material in the nature of daily records of Heron-Allen's life, rescued by a family member from Large Acres, his home in Selsey Bill, when shortly after the Second World War it was demolished.

Amongst the surviving volumes is one devoted to the memory of Armorel, with the moving letters written to her family when she was killed in the car crash in 1930, aged only 22, as described above. There, in an envelope which had been sealed with her name on, was a chilling sentence in Heron-Allen's handwriting written on a clipping from the top of a page from *The Times* newspaper: 'I have accidentally seen Armourel's hands, and if there is a true scientific basis for cheirosophy she will die by a violent death between the ages of 20 and 23. E.H.A.' The extract from *The Times* bears the printed date, 'Friday, November 15, 1918'.

Towry Piper

Heron-Allen's violin writing comets shone so brightly in the sky that it is easy to overlook the importance of subsequent British writers on the instrument. Of these it would be wrong not to mention another lawyer, Alfred Towry Piper, since, although he lacked the rich diversity of talent of Heron-Allen, he nevertheless made significant and always scholarly contributions to violin literature, particularly in the pages of the *Strad*.

Towry Piper was born in 1859, the son of a doctor. Apparently his own ill-health dissuaded him from following medicine and he chose the law instead. He practised as a solicitor in London (mainly in the Strand–Chancery Lane area) between 1884 and about 1890. He then moved north to Barnard's Castle where he practised for many years. Meanwhile he cultivated his hobby of the violin and on retirement devoted himself exclusively to it. He became known as an accomplished writer, lecturer, and expert judge of violins including the Cobbett Violin Competition. As a player he was a pupil of Carl Jung and attained considerable proficiency. He joined the staff of the *Strad* in 1911 and contributed regularly to that periodical until illness forced him to retire from that too. His articles on the double bass are referred to earlier in this book. His last article in the *Strad* of 1925[24] was on 'A Viola by Jacob Stainer', written, his obituary mentions, some time before his illness became acute. He died on 15 May 1925.

Apart from his articles, Towry Piper's literary works include a new edition (1909) of Hart's *The Violin: Its Famous Makers and their Imitators*, and the biographical section on violin makers in Hidalgo Moya's *Violin Tone and Violin Makers*. His comments on instrument-making are pungent, scrupulous, and perspicacious. He was probably a more profound judge than William Henley (discussed below).

William Meredith Morris and William C. Honeyman

The other major writer of the early twentieth century, William Meredith Morris, a Welsh scholar also of many dimensions, is discussed in the context of Wales in Chapter 8. The two editions of his book written before his premature death remain of pioneering importance for students of British violin-making. Though not quite in the same league, perhaps, William Honeyman's contributions were also significant, particularly on the Scottish scene. His work is also described in Chapter 8.

William Henley

A glance at the Directory and the rest of this book makes very clear the author's indebtedness to William Henley, the compiler of *The Universal Dictionary of Violin and Bow-Makers*. Whether we can agree with Cyril Woodcock's verdict in the Introduction to that work: 'William Henley—one of the greatest names in the musical history of England' is questionable but he was undoubtedly another remarkable man. He was born at West Bromwich on 28 January 1874 and began his violin studies at the age of 6, taught by his father. Five years later he became the pupil of T. M. Abbott at Birmingham. In 1886, at the age of 12, he launched his public career with a concert tour of Gloucestershire and playbills were displayed proclaiming him the 'Wonder boy Paganini'. In fact William Henley was born exactly 100 years after Paganini, their birth-dates being the same, and Henley

[24] May, p. 61.

apparently believed he was Paganini's reincarnation. (One living violinist who heard Henley in concert described his playing to the author as 'fantastic', but a search of the National Sound Archive, London, disappointingly reveals no recordings by Henley.)

After his first concert Henley toured France in 1887 as leader of the D'Oyly Carte No. 1 Company and he returned to England with sensational success in the provinces. He started to study in London, becoming a pupil of Henry Holmes and Willy Hess. He is said to have declined the leadership of the Hallé Orchestra and from 1893 commenced study under the great master Wilhelmj who took an almost paternal interest in Henley's progress.

During his career as a player, which, according to Cyril Woodcock, involved playing before all the crowned heads of Europe, Henley could claim two other significant strands in his career. One of these was the development of his composition talents which led to his becoming both a Professor of Composition and Principal of the Violin at the Royal Academy in London.

Little is now known of Henley's compositions—and many of them were little more than salon pieces. But Henley's own permanent String Quartet performed Henley's Quartet (Op. 47) which van der Straeten says 'met with great praise'.[25] Henley is said by Woodcock to have composed two string quartets and three concertos as well as about 100 solos for violin and piano. His pedagogical studies and exercises for the violin are today his best-known work. The British Library *Catalogue of Printed Music*[26] lists a number of salon pieces, arrangements, and studies but few works of any apparent substance. There is the impressively polyglot 'Concertstück pour Violon avec accomp. de piano', Op. 22 (London; Schott & Co., 1910) and the Violin Sonata No. 1 in G minor, Op. 56 (London; J. Williams, 1914,), this latter piece being dedicated to Thomas Beecham (not the conductor) and advertised at the end of Henley's *Dictionary*. There is no mention of quartets or concertos, but the opus numbers are not fully accounted for.

The second strand of his work was that over a period of some sixty years he devoted a considerable amount of time and money to the preparation of his *Universal Dictionary*, which had involved visits to dealers and makers all over Europe. This monumental work, which deals with virtually all the known makers from every country in the world, was eventually produced from the author's notes under the editorship of Cyril Woodcock. It was originally published in five volumes by Amati Publishing Ltd. of Brighton in 1959–60, but came out in a new one-volume edition in 1973. This has 1,267 pages and approximately 9,000 biographical details of makers. The editor and well-known dealer Cyril Woodcock

---

[25] Van der Straeten *History of the Violin*, ii. 306. See also, for contemporary accounts of Henley, the *Strad* (Nov. 1892), 116 and (Aug. 1906), 129.

[26] Hee–Hoek, *Catalogue of Printed Music in the British Library to 1980*, xxviii (London, 1984).

himself brought out a complementary volume, *Dictionary of Contemporary Violin and Bow-Makers*, in 1965, published by the same firm. Unlike Henley's work, Cyril Woodcock's volume, though far from comprehensive and somewhat barbarously written, is illustrated photographically, and although the majority of instruments depicted are American there are interesting examples of the work of Dennis Plowright, Alfred Langonet, Cyril Jacklin, and W. E. Hill & Sons, including (pl. 112) the beautifully carved head of a lira da braccio, 'made entirely by Andrew Hill, son of Desmond'.

Henley's verdicts on some of the violin-makers discussed in the Directory of this book are mentioned under the appropriate entry. His prose style can be irritatingly flamboyant and there is often a demonstrable inability to call a spade a spade. But nevertheless the achievement is an extraordinary one, seriously flawed only by the failure to give any references to sources, some of which, when tracked down, prove to be copied inaccurately. Henley obviously did draw heavily on existing sources, particularly (as regards British violin-makers) Morris and Honeyman. But there is ample evidence that he must have examined instruments of most of the makers discussed and used his considerable technical expertise to judge their tonal capacity. His music remains an enigma. It is never performed these days and awaits, perhaps, an enterprising player or ensemble to blow the dust off a considerable output.

William Henley died in 1957 at Kew, Surrey. During his playing days Henley's own choice of instrument had been a Vuillaume, though Henley did not disabuse members of his audiences who thought it was a Strad. It was apparently such a true copy that 'even experts who were permitted to examine the instrument were fooled'.[27]

[27] Woodcock, *Dictionary*, 6.

Chapter Fifteen

The Twentieth Century: Prospect and Retrospect

Introduction — Amateur or Professional? — The Example of James Parkinson — The Early Twentieth Century — The Judgements of Frank Thistleton — A British Tour — Victor Fidicularum? — George Wulme-Hudson — T. E. Hesketh — John Owen — Arthur Richardson — Alfred Vincent — The Challenge from the Continent — How to 'Cheat' — The Contemporary Scene — Retrospect and Prospect — Survey of English Instruments used in Professional Orchestras in Britain

Introduction

UNSURPRISINGLY the fruits of the British 'renaissance' of interest in violin-making became apparent at the same time as the so-called 'renaissance' in national musical life. This has been outlined already in Chapter 7 and an attempt made to show that in the latter part of the nineteenth century musical education started to improve. Music colleges became more efficient, it became much more fashionable to learn a stringed instrument, and in England in particular the overwhelming blanket of the oratorio tradition was lifted to allow some fresh air to get into the scene. Stanford, Parry, and a few other usually German-educated British composers led the way. Later, when Edward Elgar reached his maturity in the early years of the twentieth century, music in England started to regain its self-respect. Further than this, Edward Elgar and William Walton, two essentially self-taught English composers, between them account for two violin concertos, two cello concertos, and a viola concerto, all of which form an important part of the late romantic international repertoire.

Although the economic difficulties of professional musicians continued, the number of interested amateurs playing chamber and orchestral music for their own pleasure and still, on occasion, joining the professionals in some theatre orchestras, greatly increased. In much more recent times, the number of pupils taking the Associated Board's exams in violin more than doubled between 1970 and 1990.[1]

This burgeoning scene gave the necessary encouragement to professional violin-maker and amateur alike. It has never been particularly easy for most makers to sell their new instruments. Only a lucky few can boast of a waiting-list. But provided prices were kept reasonable—and the price of a new violin rarely exceeded £30 before the Second World War—players were always open to the argument that it was more sensible to buy a new handmade instrument rather than a much more expensive old one which might be structurally questionable owing to the number of repairs previously carried out on it. It has probably always been the case that the best salesmen (or saleswomen) for living makers are the existing buyers of their instruments. Word of mouth is the best advertisement. Where it was necessary to advertise as well—and many professional makers did—the periodicals mentioned in the last chapter, and particularly the *Strad*, proved a convenient vehicle.

There is very often an element of speculation by the buyer when a new instrument is acquired. Will the value of the maker's work increase as time goes on? Will the maker really be regarded as a latter-day Stradivari in due course? Knowledgeable buyers could already see the quite recent work of the leading late nineteenth-century and early twentieth-century Italian makers improving in value, particularly once the makers had died. Was there any reason why the same thing should not happen to English or Scottish instruments? As we shall see, economic factors were sometimes overtly suggested in contemporary advertising for British instruments.

Amateur or Professional?

Dictionaries such as Henley's frequently attempt to categorize makers as 'amateur' or 'professional'. As the Directory in this book attempts to point out, this distinction can be very misleading. Obviously there were a large number of pure amateurs—people who made for pleasure and probably without intending to sell any, or at least their earlier, instruments. But the test of a good maker, amateur or professional, was not whether the occasional flash in the pan could be produced. It was whether the quality of the instrument was maintained over a significant run. To acquire the technique required for consistency, a systematic and well-thought-out approach was needed. Thicknesses and other measurements must be exact. The wood chosen must consistently be acoustically good as well as visually attractive. Varnish must be consistently applied. The instrument must 'work' for the average player.

[1] See the figures given in Ch. 7.

In a number of cases, what started off as 'amateur' work developed professionally as word got round that a certain maker's instruments were worth having. The maker would then often quote a set price for his work and there would be no inherent difference then between the status of that maker's instruments and any other professional maker's. Once instruments are made for the purposes of trade, amateurism goes out of the window. It may well have been the position in many cases that the maker had retired from some other vocation or combined the one with the other. The unpredictable nature of the market for new violins made it wise, in any event, not to be too reliant on their sale. The way that William Atkinson worked is a case in point.[2]

Even where, like Heron-Allen, a particular maker never sold his instruments in his lifetime, they would almost inevitably find their way on to the market sooner or later. Sometimes this would be through the agency of an auctioneer such as Puttick & Simpson (later Phillips) of London or Sotheby's or Christie's. This would assume, of course, that the inherent quality was good enough to justify a sale in a London sale-room. Otherwise the instrument might find its way into a music shop, a general second-hand 'antique' shop, or a local auction. But in any of these events the instrument would then belong to a third party who perhaps knew nothing of the maker and would have been curious to find out some basic information. First Morris and then Henley's Dictionaries went a good way to supplying this need. Both writers eliminated any mention of a maker who only produced the occasional instrument (with a few exceptions) but a glance at the Directory in this book, and particularly at those makers flourishing between 1900 and 1950, shows a huge volume of work that was produced in these years by amateurs and professionals alike.

The Example of James Parkinson

An interesting example of an amateur–professional was James Parkinson of Llandudno. Parkinson made his first violin at the age of about 60, having previously taken no interest in violins whatsoever. But whilst in the workshop of a professional violin-maker Parkinson questioned that maker's use of his tools. The maker replied that creating a violin was a great deal more than 'cabinet-making'. Parkinson retorted that as far as he could see it was the same thing. This led to a friendly challenge to make a violin, which Parkinson accepted.

Parkinson was in fact well qualified to start the work since he owned a famous firm of cabinet-makers in Liverpool and was one of the leading experts on timber

[2] See Ch. 12.

in England, for many years lecturing on timber and its uses. Parkinson then applied his cabinet-maker's mind to the works of the great Italian masters. Stradivari's workmanship was adjudged, in his eyes, as exquisite but the same could not be said of that of Joseph Guarnerius, which he regarded as often poor and sometimes very amateurish.

Parkinson looked at the violin as traditionally designed and decided to make one or two minor structural improvements internally. These 'improvements' affected the corner and neck blocks which were strengthened without affecting the vibrating area of the table. He obtained his linings from old cricket bats and continued them round the blocks to add to the general strength. He put his purfling directly over the ribs so as not to weaken the wood at its edge. He adopted a model which was a cross between a Stradivari and a Joseph Guarneri. The top half was on Guarneri lines, with sloping shoulders facilitating the fingering in the higher positions, whilst the bottom bouts were of the more rounded Strad outline. He was in a position to choose beautifully figured wood and he usually exercised this choice.

His violins became very successful. Albert Sammons, probably England's leading violinist at the time, owned one. So did several members of the Hallé Orchestra, and Arthur Catterell and William Primrose played solos on them. All spoke to the fine quality of tone.

Although Parkinson sold his violins he handed the proceeds to Dr Barnardo's homes, the National Children's Home or, crippled children's homes—though if the purchaser had strong views the money would instead go to any charity selected by that purchaser.

This saga illustrates the hermaphrodite status of these amateur–professional transactions. In the one sense a sale was certainly involved but in Parkinson's case, at least, no profit (or even contribution to expenses) was apparently obtained by the maker. Nevertheless Parkinson's output was extensive enough (and sufficiently well thought of) to make it remarkable that his name is entirely omitted from Henley's *Dictionary*.[3]

The Early Twentieth Century

The Directory at the end of the book includes some makers at the turn of the century or shortly afterwards certainly worthy of a mention in the abbreviated Roll of Honour dogmatically called by Heron-Allen in the quotation set out in Chapter 13. For instance, T. Jacques Holder (d. 1922) of Wardour Street, London, and

---

[3] See 'James Parkinson Violins', *Strad* (July 1929), 134.

Blackheath, Kent was a good maker and the mentor of George Wulme Hudson (mentioned in more detail later). The extraordinary 'facsimiles' emanating from the Voller brothers, including the famous 'Balfour' fake Stradivarius, also merit serious consideration. The violas of Percy Lee (1871–1953) have a high reputation but came too late for Heron-Allen. It is surprising, though, that he did not mention the products of the Hart and Withers workshops in London. And there were others whose work has stood up well.

It is hoped that the Directory at the end of the book is sufficiently comprehensive to record early twentieth-century makers of importance in enough detail for their work to be identified and appreciated. In many cases they will already have been scrutinized and described by Morris, Henley, and, more recently, a few selected later ones by Mary Anne Alburger (1979). Earlier twentieth-century makers of significance in Britain are also likely to have been the subject-matter of an article in the *Strad*. Where this has occurred, the relevant reference should be found in the Directory.

Nevertheless, it would be wrong in a book of this kind not to attempt to outline the contribution of those makers whose work is regarded as being outstanding by the standards prevailing during the period approximately 1900–40, but viewed from the perspective of the last decade of the twentieth century.

The Judgements of Frank Thistleton

Frank Thistleton was a well-known violinist in the early part of the twentieth century, having been a pupil of Wilhelmj. His main claim to fame was as a teacher and his books included *The Art of Violin Playing* and *Modern Violin Technique*. But Thistleton was clearly also knowledgeable about the craft of violin-making and anxious to encourage British makers who he thought were wandering guideless in the desert. As he wrote:

Thus it is that in nearly all the violins I have looked at by British makers I regret to say that I have seen promise rather than fulfilment. The reason for this is not far to seek ... our makers have no English School, no model or no tradition worth mentioning, to which they can look for guidance. Violin making as a serious industry does not exist in England and never has done. We have had a number of isolated makers ... but there is very little in the history of violin making in the country either to inspire or serve as a guide to modern makers. As violin making doesn't pay and is therefore seriously practised by few, the sources at which knowledge can be obtained are remote.[4]

[4] *Strad* (May 1928), 22.

This is an over-pessimistic assessment of nearly 300 years of admittedly variable work. But Thistleton's fundamental point may really have been that there was no tradition of systematic teaching of violin-making through the apprenticeship system, as already noted in this book. A few makers were apprenticed to one of the few other skilled practitioners in the art in Britain or, perhaps, abroad. More commonly, and certainly in more recent times, it was often a question of reading an instructional book such as Heron-Allen's or Walter Mayson's, learning by trial and error, and possibly also copying someone else's instrument.

Thistleton therefore ran a series of articles in the *Strad* from 1928, 'Modern British Violin Makers', which encouraged British makers to submit their work for assessment. Amongst the first to do so was Reginald Gordon Price of Kingston upon Thames who submitted his eighth violin but with the varnishing incomplete. Thistleton spoke quite highly of the work though he made the point that the tone, though excellent, might be completely changed when the varnishing process was completed. Price had been guided in his efforts by the experienced maker William Glenister of Beak Street, London, and was charging £15 for the instrument submitted. There was also a William Robinson of Liverpool (not to be confused with the better-known maker of the same name who worked at Plumstead). Thistleton was quite complementary about this former cabinet-maker's work and although Henley subsequently described him as an 'amateur', by 1929 he had made twenty-eight instruments and was charging £20. Thistleton suggested one or two improvements to the design. William Walton of Preston, who at that time[5] had made seventy-three instruments, avoided any hostile criticism except in respect of certain 'undercutting' in the scroll 'and one or two what I regard as too pretty curves'. The two samples submitted were adjudged to have excellent tone and an effective oil-based varnish. Walton told Thistleton that he had disposed of all his instruments without difficulty at prices from about £20 to £25.

A month later Thistleton had a chance to assess the work of the other William Robinson, of Plumstead, London.[6] By this time Robinson had made over 200 violins, ten violas, and ten cellos. Robinson submitted two violins, one a 'Strad' model and the other a 'Joseph', both made in 1927. Thistleton reacted to these instruments with an enthusiasm that had hitherto been rather lacking. He regarded Robinson as being a maker of 'outstanding merit'. The scrolls of the two instruments submitted were 'beautifully cut and ... full of character'. The thicknesses of the plates had been carefully thought out and the soundholes were beautifully cut, whilst the fitting up had been perfectly carried out to the smallest detail. Robinson had used Millington's varnish. Tonally, Thistleton found himself unable to speak too highly of it—a judgement echoed by some modern players. Robinson told

[5] *Strad* (June 1928), 102. [6] *Strad* (July 1928), 152.

Thistleton that he had sold all his instruments at prices varying from £25 to £50. Thistleton commented that 'if they are all like the new instruments submitted the purchasers have been lucky'.

One of the few other makers of the time to attract the same degree of enthusiasm as William Robinson of Plumstead was Jeffery J. Gilbert of Peterborough. He submitted a quartet of instruments for inspection together with the first violin which he had ever made, over fifty years before.[7] Although Gilbert was entirely self-taught he had made by then 355 instruments including thirty violas and twelve cellos (many of his instruments being used professionally). Gilbert was then in his 79th year. His hands had lost none of their cunning. Scrolls, corners, and purfling were adjudged perfect, the wood carefully chosen, the fitting up on all four instruments of the quartet excellent. The varnish was good, though on the soft side. 'This is a hopeless climate in which to try and dry oil varnish and the only thing is to be patient and just bide one's time,' remarked Thistleton. The tone of the viola, a few months older than the violins, was adjudged the best of the quartet and 'a joy to play on', and the cello 'beautifully resonant and deep throated'. Gilbert was then asking £30 each for the violins and the viola and £60 for the cello.

Two further makers of distinction were mentioned at the end of 1928.[8] These were William Glenister, late of Beak Street, London (and just a few months older than J. J. Gilbert), and John Walker of Solihull, Birmingham. Glenister was then towards the end of his career and had made 200 violins, ten violas, and fifteen cellos. Again he was entirely self-taught. Thistleton was astonished at the quality of the work, considering that he had never been connected with any trade or craft dealing with the use of tools and that his early life was spent at gardening or in the corn trade. Thistleton reminded readers that Glenister had already had testimonials from Morris, Fleming, and Towry Piper (and others too numerous to mention). Of the two instruments submitted for inspection he found the violin to have 'excellent tone', whilst the viola was regarded as 'altogether exceptional'. It was responsive, full, and round, whilst there was plenty of wood in both the front and back plates. Glenister had won the second prize in the Cobbett Competitions in 1918 and 1919. He charged £20 for violins, £25 for violas, and £35 for cellos.

John Walker was described as one of the few dealers and repairers who also made violins. This, Thistleton stated, was unusual because making did not usually repay the makers for their trouble. Thistleton was quite enthusiastic about the quality here but thought that Walker might have left a little too much wood in his model, a judgement still made by connoisseurs, though particularly about his later work. Nevertheless everything had been executed with the utmost care. Walker was asking £40 for the particular instrument inspected.

[7] *Strad* (Nov. 1928), 384.   [8] *Strad* (Dec. 1928), 448.

By a coincidence, the same *Strad* issue contained news that the University College of Southampton had started a violin class. It was thought to be the only University Institution to include violin-making in its curricula. The practical side was linked to the instrumental and aesthetic. Andrew Kiddle was the teacher responsible. This development was seen as one of the first steps in meeting Thistleton's criticisms that many makers were suffering from a lack of guidance and systematic training. But as Thistleton's articles progressed the author was clearly surprised by the number of makers submitting their work for his inspection and, in many cases, by its quality. It is also a noticeable feature of this exercise that although the economy was far from buoyant at the time, most of the makers of any reputation seem to admit to no difficulties in selling all their instruments.

A British Tour

One way of demonstrating the point that Thistleton had been unduly pessimistic when starting his series of articles is to trace the steps of an enthusiastic purchaser investigating the various outlets throughout England for new handmade British violins.

In or about 1930, as our putative buyer started his search in London he would naturally have been attracted to the New Bond Street shop of the Hills. He could also have gone to William Acton (handmade and modestly priced instruments), Joseph or John Chanot, William Glenister, George Wulme-Hudson, Alfred Vincent, Cyril Jacklin, or John Wilkinson (working through J. & A. Beare's—Italian 'look-alikes' for £10), to name but a few. Almost no English city was without its local violin-maker or makers. John Alexander, also a professional violinist, worked in Birmingham and John Walker (see above) was close by. In Bristol our buyer would have just missed George Darbey, a maker with an outstanding reputation at the time. Had he pursued the search across the river Avon and into Devon and Cornwall he would have found Arthur Richardson at Crediton and Albert Coad at Penzance. J. J. Gilbert could be found, going east, in Peterborough. In the north there was John Owen at Leeds and, one of the few female workers at the time, his daughter Ivy Rimmer Owen. In Manchester there were the major establishments of Thomas Earle Hesketh and the Voigts. In Liverpool one of the more obvious places to go to was Rushworth & Dreaper where workshop violins were made in the 'Ardeton' range under the supervision, and in some cases personally by, Richmond Bird. In Scotland, particularly in Glasgow where James Briggs and Andrew Smillie were well established, there was also a reasonable choice of maker, though probably not in such profusion as some fifty years earlier. All these individuals are discussed in more detail in the Directory.

Victor Fidicularum?

Of the many talented makers flourishing in the years up to the Second World War the question is often asked whether any individuals particularly stand out. As a general rule a good fifty years should be allowed to pass before a maker's quality is assessed with any degree of definitiveness. Some instruments which look fine when made, positively deteriorate with age and are revealed to have been poorly varnished, perhaps too thinly or thickly wooded (but usually the latter, making them heavy in the hand), and in other respects not to have fulfilled their initial promise. Nevertheless some attempt must now be made to pick out possible candidates for Britain's twentieth-century *corps d'élite*.

George Wulme-Hudson

A maker much patronized in his lifetime whose reputation has, if anything, increased is George Wulme-Hudson (1862–1952). Wulme-Hudson was amongst the band of makers who were also good players. Heron-Allen, Towry Piper, and other commentators have often praised the virtues of makers who are also competent players. How else can they test the tone of their instruments?, they ask. Whether this theory is completely sustainable is another matter. Being a good player is undoubtedly an advantage, but the point can be taken too far. Few violinists, for instance, would be competent to give a cello that they had made a thorough tonal test, but a good violin-maker will also usually make a good cello. We do not know in many instances whether the older makers were players or not. It seems likely that many had little or no competence. They could still make very fine instruments. The answer is probably that being able to play is an advantage but not essential. (Whether playing ability is there or not, having an ear which can identify tonal colour and quality is even more desirable.)

The young Wulme-Hudson studied the violin at the Birkbeck Institute in London and later with Arthur Payne at the Guildhall School of Music there. He was also apprenticed to a pawnbroker at the age of 12 and a few years later he used to sit on the counter after business hours in his nightshirt playing folk-tunes on the violin, accompanied by a variety of other instruments which happened to be available in the pawnbroker's establishment. Wulme-Hudson afterwards learned the banjo and other instruments but always preferred the violin. Later he entered the jewellery trade as a salesman but finding this irksome, and seeking inspiration from Heron-Allen's book, he succeeded in constructing his first violin in 1897. Thomas Jacques Holder of Blackheath, London, renowned for his clever copies of old Italian violins, gave Wulme-Hudson invaluable advice.

Wulme-Hudson then set out on the first step of a long career which involved both making very clever copies of Italian instruments, sometimes being purported incarnations of non-existent Italian makers if the label were to be believed, and also 'straight' work, unantiqued, but in the Italian tradition. Some samples of his work have suffered from varnish deterioration but on the whole it has lasted well and his reputation stands high. More details of his career will be found in the Directory.[9]

T. E. Hesketh

Outside London, Thomas Earle Hesketh (1886–1945), a pupil of G. A. Chanot, had a brilliantly successful career. He undertook a 'proper' apprenticeship involving five years and a further year as a journeyman. In 1891 he commenced business on his own account in Lower Mosley Street, Manchester. Morris, when writing his first edition, obviously researched Hesketh very thoroughly though much of this detail is missing from the second edition. Morris praises in particular a viola, being a copy of A. & H. Amati of 16⅝ in. (422 mm) and made to the order of Rawdon Briggs, a player in the Hallé Orchestra and a member of the Brodsky Quartet. Briggs considered this to be a superb instrument. In fact Hesketh made instruments for eminent players throughout his life, a series in the 1930s (Guarneri copies) for such players as the Bohemian virtuoso Ottakar Ševčík (who also taught at the Guildhall School of Music in London) and the instrument (probably) made for Leonard Hirsch (Pl. 66), being fine examples of his work at this time. Hesketh must have had a very enthusiastic following. Morris gives him 'a place among the elite of modern productions, and a high seat even amongst the mighty'. He adds that the work is nearly all personal. He employed one journeyman, Robert Elliot Keen, and also, for two years, a workman from Mirecourt who left in 1898. His repairing activities were sufficiently extensive to inhibit large-scale production of new instruments. Hesketh played well on both the violin and the viola. His charges were from 12 guineas to 15 guineas for a violin, 15 guineas for a viola, and 25 guineas for a cello (c.1900).

Instruments made towards the end of his life have the reputation of being either workshop instruments or possibly bought in from other makers or from abroad. Henley indicates that he had an association with Voigt. In fact Ernest Voigt confirmed to the author (in 1993) that he believed that his father, Paul, made instruments for Hesketh as early as 1906. This is, in fact, substantiated by other sources. On arrival in Manchester Paul Voigt in effect became a member of Hesketh's

---

[9] See also Albert Cooper, 'Trade Secrets', *Strad* (Feb. 1985), 753–9, a comprehensive and well-illustrated account of his life and work.

workshop, as mentioned by Vannes and other dictionary authors. It has been suggested, too, that Hesketh's eyesight became poor in his latter years and therefore he must have needed help. Nevertheless, there is little, if any, evidence of falling-off in quality, and if Hesketh expanded his workshop so that his products became less personal, he was by no means alone in doing this.

Hesketh died on 27 December 1945. His obituarist, John F. Russell, writing in the *Strad* in 1946, said that he was still capable of, and doing, excellent work. He used a stock of wood which had belonged to Craske who in turn had obtained it from the Forsters. He paid particular attention to tonal qualities, careful craftsmanship, and finish. 'I have never seen anything from his hand that was not a thing of beauty as well as an excellently contrived musical instrument.'[10] Admirers of his work included conductors particularly associated with the north of England: John Barbarolli, Thomas Beecham, Hamilton Harty, and also Jan Kubelík, the violin virtuoso and composer.

Obituarists sometimes feel the need to observe the dictum *de mortuis, nil nisi bunkum*, but statements of fact such as that relating to his doing excellent work to the end of his life would be too easily verifiable to risk an untruth. Did he buy in instruments from Continental sources? German or French *trade* instruments should be easily enough recognized by any expert from the construction methods used, the making of the scroll, button, and ribs, the purfling characteristics, and so on, even if coated with a seductive and alien varnish. Also one should be able to find similarly stereotyped models from other retailers purchasing from the same source, and critics should ask themselves whether they have identified any such 'look-alikes'. (It is pointed out later in this chapter that violins in the white were readily available, even by mail order.) Of course, there are intermediate positions, such as having instruments built to a set design by order. This then begins to raise philosophical problems of definition. If, say, Hesketh had removed his workshop to Munich but otherwise worked in the same manner and with the same materials, would his instruments cease to be 'English' and instead become 'German' with all the pejorative implications that, justly or unjustly, that statement of nationality conveys? Climates may differ, but is there something distinctive about English, German, or Italian air? The proposition is patently illogical. Similarly, there are shades of significance, rather better founded, if a maker's workshop is staffed by workers steeped in, say, the Mirecourt or Mittenwald or Cremona making traditions. In any event, ultimately it is more sensible to judge each instrument on its merits: workmanship, aesthetics, and tone. On these fundamental criteria Hesketh's instruments score highly as his obituarist points out, and as an apparently enthusiastic following at the present time confirms.

[10] *Strad* (Feb. 1946), 225.

John Owen

In Leeds, John Owen had a successful business as both a repairer of over 4,000 instruments and builder of about 200. He died in 1933 at the age of 81 and his work, highly professional as it is, shows some of the French influence acquired when he went to France to train as a young man. He used an oil varnish which has lasted well and although in the auction houses his work does not obtain spectacular prices, as a maker he was amongst the most successful of his time.

Arthur Richardson

Another maker, mentioned in various places in this text, whose work was greatly esteemed in his lifetime and still maintains something of a reputation was Arthur Richardson of Crediton. Richardson was particularly associated with the development of the 'Tertis' model viola of 16¾ in. (425 mm) now no longer universally in favour. Although much used professionally his instruments are also said by some rather to lack 'punch'. Richardson won the first prize for the best-toned violin at a competition in London in 1919 and was the prize-winner for a quartet of instruments in London in 1923. He attracted the enthusiastic support of both Meredith Morris and Towry Piper and his work was undoubtedly very fine. Richardson charged from £28 to £30 for violins and violas and £40 for cellos according to his pre-Second World War published catalogue.

Alfred Vincent

Another maker of the same period who is unaccountably omitted from many dictionaries was Alfred Vincent (1877–1947). An engineer by training, he made over 300 instruments of such quality that it was entirely appropriate for him to bequeath a quartet to the Royal Academy of Music in London. He was dubbed the 'English Stradivari' as a result of a competition in March 1919 held in the Aeolian Hall, London, being the final stage of the Cobbett Competition for British makers of stringed instruments. Alfred Vincent was awarded the first prize of £25 and three consolation prizes of £10 each were awarded respectively to William Robinson, Arthur Richardson, and William Glenister. The winning instruments had been heard in performances by the adjudicators (who included Albert Sammons and W. W. Cobbett himself), and the Vincent violin and a Stradivari were played behind the screen. The audience were invited to indicate their preference by a show of hands. There was a clear majority in favour of the Vincent instrument. Sammons subsequently performed the Elgar Violin Concerto at Queen's Hall using the Vincent violin.

Unfortunately Vincent is one of several successful makers of this period about whom it is said that a significant number of his instruments are imported German trade instruments, varnished up and sold with his own label. This theory is also discussed above in the context of T. E. Hesketh. The truth of the allegation remains to be established.

Vincent was himself a fine violinist, being leader of the orchestra at His Majesty's Theatre.[11] He worked in Great Poultney Street, Soho, London and was later assisted by his brother, H. Vincent.

The Challenge from the Continent

It is clear from their own accounts that most of the English makers whose work is reviewed by Frank Thistleton had little difficulty in selling their instruments. Prices varied from maker to maker but in general a violin would cost between £10 and £25 in the 1920s and 1930s. As will have been seen in Chapter 6 dealing with prices, these had changed little for two centuries until the Second World War. As far as the twentieth century goes, this was in large part because most of the inter-war years were years of depression. Handmade instruments had to compete with the mass-produced products of France and Germany. Some of these were well enough made and, for example, the violins of Ernst Heinrich Roth of Markneukirchen, Germany were, in 1929, retailed by the dealers Hawkes & Son, London, W1 (also of Manchester and Glasgow) at £9 for Strad copies and £6 for Amati copies, each payable by twelve equal monthly payments if desired. Even more seductive were Italian 'look-alikes' such as the handsome productions of 'Paolo Fiorini', in fact made in Munich and distributed through Beare & Son.

There was also the Italian challenge. Although popular mythology has it that Italian violins were never the same after the Cremona School faded out in the mid-eighteenth century, individual Italian makers such as Pressenda and the Roccas of Turin, the Degani family at Naples, the Bisiach family in Milan, Hannibal Fagnola (Turin), and many others continued the finest traditions of Italian making throughout the nineteenth and early twentieth centuries. Their best instruments are magnificently made and their tonal characteristics appealed to professional orchestral players, including those who played in cinema and theatre orchestras. Heron-Allen writing in *Grove*[12] includes the Bisiachs and Carlo

---

[11] Scholes, *Mirror*, 366.
[12] Edward Heron-Allen, 'Violin Family', in *Grove's Dictionary of Music and Musicians*, 2nd edn., ed. J. A. Fuller Maitland (London, 1910), v. 309.

Oddone amongst the list of 'makers of superior merit', adding that 'the Guadagnini Bros were not makers'. Carlo Oddone, though domiciled in Turin, had worked in London for F. W. Chanot and elsewhere between 1898 and 1901. His name was therefore well known to Heron-Allen. Another Italian challenge on the doorstep was the establishment of Giovanni Gaida in Castle Street, Long Acre, London, in 1925, having for the preceding twenty years or so worked for F. W. Chanot and others in London. He was later assisted by his son, Cesare. Both makers made it clear that they were born at Ivrea in Italy, and so were regarded as producing 'Italian' instruments.

Where a choice between a new English instrument and a new Italian instrument was being made, there were two factors weighing against the Italians. One was the price differential. Although prices were rarely advertised in the periodicals (because dealers no doubt had some discretion in the matter, unlike the case of a maker selling his instruments direct from a priced catalogue within the country) all the evidence points to these instruments being significantly more expensive than their English rivals. An English violin might be £20 whereas its Italian counterpart might be £40. (It has to be said that had the purchaser chosen well and adopted one of the Italian makers mentioned above, this price differential would have been more than maintained in contemporary conditions.) The other advantage in favour of English makers was that it was comparatively easy to market their instruments and many advertised in the pages of the *Strad* in particular.

There was also a concerted drive to persuade buyers of the merits of purchasing a new instrument. Hawkes & Son, the dealers mentioned above, took full-page advertisements which included the following two sentences: 'An increasing amount of attention is to-day being given to new violins, possibly because the price of old instruments is increasing; but the real reason we believe is due to violinists realising that it is possible for present-day makers to build good, reliable instruments. The prejudice against new violins is gradually being broken down—the modern violin is receiving its well deserved reward.'[13]

The implication in this advertisement that new violins are more reliable than old—that is, presumably, structurally sounder—is palpable and no doubt had its effect. Makers such as Cyril Jacklin, Alexander Hulme, Alfred Vincent, and George Wulme-Hudson, all working in or near London, Robert Alton of Liverpool, William Robinson of Plumstead, William Acton of Forest Gate, London, John Walker of Solihull, Birmingham, and William Walton of Preston, Lancashire, were amongst the makers who regularly advertised in the *Strad* at this era. Furthermore some makers were enterprising in securing the 'sponsorship' of leading players such as Albert Sammons (1886–1957), who appears to have

---

[13] e.g. *Strad* (Jan. 1930), 463.

performed on violins by Vincent, Robinson, and a number of others, and Albert Sandler (1906–48).

Italian makers had the advantage that the market for their products was worldwide. In particular, in more recent times many were imported into the USA whose buyers appreciated the fact that the Italian makers made only in one quality—the best.[14] But a mixture of price, accessibility, and pride in native craftsmanship probably swung the balance in favour of English makers in the minds of enough local purchasers to cause demand to equal supply. The same considerations apply to the rival products of the diminishing number of fine individual makers in France and Germany, such as Pierre Hel of Lille and Eugen Gartner of Stuttgart (whose work gets never a mention in the advertisement pages of the *Strad*).

How to 'Cheat'

In the eighteenth century it can normally be safely assumed that a correctly attributed instrument will have been made by the maker indicated or in his workshop and under his supervision. In the nineteenth century the practice started of buying in products from abroad and putting on a domestic label or brand. Earlier, while the labelled maker was not necessarily the 'real maker', the instrument was normally not imported. As the nineteenth century progressed it also became quite common practice for some makers, doubtless working under too much pressure, to buy in the body or the neck or scroll of an instrument, usually unvarnished, from one of the German or French manufactories. It is still possible to do this today.[15] The 'maker' then merely adds finishing touches, such as varnish. Heron-Allen, as editor of the *Violin Times* in 1893–4, drew attention to this practice, pointing out that if the label wrongly indicated that the instrument was 'made by' the stated English maker, those responsible contravened the criminal law, then the Merchandise Marks Acts. Since 1968 this would clearly be a false trade description under the Trades Descriptions Act 1968 (which has replaced and clarified the old law). 'Made by' would indicate to the average purchaser that the instrument has been built and varnished by the stated maker.

It is probably to draw attention to what was happening that some rival makers advertising in the *Strad* emphasized that the instrument was handmade by the maker *throughout*. Robert Alton of Liverpool uses these very words. William J.

---

[14] See Marlin Brinser, *Dictionary of Twentieth Century Italian Violin Makers* (Irvington, NJ, 1978), esp. p. 96, where Brinser reproduces his article 'A Case for Italian Made Violins' from *American String Teacher*, Mar.–Apr. 1961. Also, for an analysis of the distinctiveness of Italian violin-making, Carlo Vettori, *Linee Classiche Della Liutera Italiana (The Classic Lines of Italian Violin Making)* (Pisa 1980) (with Eng. trans.).

[15] See Pl. 2 illustrating tools and equipment which includes whole instruments in the white.

Acton states that 'My instruments are my personal work in every detail', and Alexander Hulme made a similar claim for his instruments.

Those makers in Britain who did obtain help from Germany or France were in good international company. Heron-Allen unequivocally states in his article in *Grove's Dictionary* discussed earlier that the then living Guadagnini family were not actual makers. The great Hannibal Fagnola is widely thought to have adopted a similar practice to that described above with regard to his later instruments. At the opposite extreme were those makers who encouraged purchasers who had placed an order to watch them making the relevant instrument, where this was practicable, and be present at the birth.

The Contemporary Scene

The Directory gives the names and, in some cases, short particulars of many, though by no means all, contemporary violin-makers in Britain, but assessments of modern instruments have to be made with great caution. Instruments need to have been played upon and exposed to the rigours of time for a reasonable period before anything approaching an authoritative judgement is possible.

There are clearly a number of recently deceased makers such as Clifford Hoing and William Luff, whose work is outstanding. As more training has been given and the work of the luthier has been approached with a great deal more seriousness and method than was necessarily the case in earlier years, a very much higher general standard of craftsmanship has emerged. This is sometimes at the expense of a certain adventurousness of spirit. Nevertheless, the gradual increase of night classes (the one started by Frank Howard at the Northern Polytechnic, London, being an outstanding example and responsible for many pupils) has undoubtedly been of the greatest importance. The London teaching tradition has been preserved in the violin-making department of the London College of Furniture (now part of London Guildhall University, formerly the City of London Polytechnic) which runs a full-time course on musical instrument technology.[16] The violin-making class was until 1994 under Patricia Naismith. For some years Local Education Authorities have been supporting part-time violin-making courses in various places in the country. Successful summer schools are held in Cambridge and other centres by experienced teachers such as Juliet Barker.

For intending full-time professional makers the establishment of the specialist Newark School of Violin Making in Nottinghamshire in 1972 was a development of great importance. The School was established by the late Maurice Bouette,

---

[16] See Alix McSweeney, 'London College of Furniture', *Strad* (Sept. 1981), 338.

himself a night-school pupil of William Luff. This was at a time when the old purchase tax, at rates of around 30 per cent, was imposed discriminately on new instruments, thus giving a great economic advantage to old and second-hand ones. Purchase tax had been imposed as a 'temporary' tax during the Second World War but proved very far from temporary and had clearly dampened the market for new instruments. Value Added Tax, as its name suggests, taxes purely the added value on new and old instruments alike. The establishment of the Newark School was well timed to take advantage of the new VAT regime introduced in 1973. It was also fortunate in securing teachers of the quality not only of Maurice Bouette but also of Wilfred Saunders and Glen Collins, two of the most eminent of living English makers.

A similar development for a time occurred in Wales (see Chapter 8), though Welsh students were very much in the minority. Bow-making also thrived in the post-war years, a glance at Chapter 9 showing how many Hill-trained makers have subsequently set up on their own.

The *Facta Britannia* Competition, started in 1981, is a forum in which contemporary makers can have their instruments and bows assessed comparatively by experts and played upon by professionals. Awards in 1981 went to such established or up-and-coming makers as Rowan Armour-Brown, Helen Michetschläger, Rod Ward, and Colin Wills.[17] The intention was to repeat the Competition annually, and the *Strad* contains a number of annual reports. It recently appears to have fallen into desuetude.

The anxiety in the 1990s is whether current economic conditions really permit so many of the younger generation of makers to make a reasonable living. The violin-makers of the 1920s and 1930s seemed to have had little difficulty in selling their instruments. There may still be a number of contemporary makers who are in this happy position. But it cannot be by any means universally so, particularly where the cost of time and materials will often put the purchase price up to four figures. The future of these makers will inevitably to some extent depend upon the continued popularity of the violin family as an instrument to learn. Chapter 7 attempts to investigate the current position and the outcome seems to be that whilst public spending on musical education has been significantly reduced, the violin has traditionally been a 'middle-class' instrument and parents so far show no less inclination than hitherto to support their children financially while they learn—and to acquire for them a decent instrument. Nevertheless it would, of course, be a national tragedy if the wide socio-economic base from which young instrumentalists are recruited, extended since the end of the Second World War, was narrowed again due to these financial stringencies. It becomes all the more

---

[17] See Gillian Lomas and Terence Kennedy, 'Facta Britannia '81', *Strad* (Sept. 1981), 345.

important for those who understand the great value of a practical and theoretical musical training for children, whatever their subsequent vocation, to bring this message home to the politicians.

Retrospect and Prospect

The long and varied story of the violin and its makers in the British Isles which has been traced in this book is difficult to summarize. Many past authors have made the point that English work has been consistently underestimated by opinion outside the islands (and sometimes within them) and the same certainly applies to the best of Scottish work. Irish work is remarkable only for its scarcity, Thomas Perry standing out like a church spire. Wales has still to produce a maker of any real eminence. The reason for these internal disparities lies in the cultural differences of the four communities. Scotland's productivity is astonishing and much of it is attributable to the popularity of the violin for the purposes of dancing and other social activity. A similar tradition applied in Wales, but with dissimilar results, and Ireland maintains perhaps the most vigorous continuous tradition of folk-based music-making—but also with dissimilar results to those of Scotland as regards the qualities of most of its makers.

There is little doubt that these differences could rapidly vanish since there is now no fundamental economic or musical difference between the various populations. Music is taught to as high a standard in Dublin, Glasgow and Edinburgh, Cardiff and Swansea, as it is in London or Birmingham. Enthusiasm to learn an instrument for orchestral purposes is approximately the same in all major cities of the British Isles. This should mean that demand is met in the same way by the production of instruments of equally high standard, and perhaps this is now happening. But many more years will need to pass before a final assessment is made.

Looking at the English scene specifically, the quality of making was very high when the story started to all intents and purposes at the Restoration of Charles II in 1660. They are often beautifully wrought and rich, if small, in tone. The eighteenth and nineteenth centuries saw a few makers of great merit such as Daniel Parker, the erratic Peter Wamsley, Richard Duke, Benjamin Banks, the Forster family, the Hill family, and the great copyists of the earlier part of the nineteenth century. There was also a great deal of indifferent work, much of it still in circulation and primarily responsible for dampening the reputation of English makers in the eyes of those who only see part of the scene. Whether this can be attributed to a lack of seriousness in the character of the race during the eighteenth and early nineteenth centuries, as Morris would have us believe, is debatable. It was certainly not helped by the comparatively enervating musical climate for much of that time, as this book tries to show. Inevitably supply is tied up with the demand for instruments and although this was much greater than many have previously thought, if (as Van der Straeten suggested) music is relegated to something rather less interesting to do than fox-hunting by those who have the money to indulge, the consequential effect is bound to be depressing.

The absence of any widespread apprenticeship system, of any useful books, and of opportunities for those in the provinces to view fine instruments, were all until comparatively recently factors militating against quality of production. When in the late eighteenth century the French and German factories got to work it was natural for the majority of purchasers to be attracted to the apparent bargains available. That there were as many good, and in a few cases, excellent, makers as there were during the eighteenth century is surprising in these circumstances.

Perhaps the most enduring achievement of eighteenth-century making was the production of the English cello. English makers put their best into the cello. Their instruments are a fine memorial to them. Native wood and English styling seem to suit the instrument better than the violin, in many cases. The cello was also much more favoured by the aristocracy and gentry, as the text points out. The violin was by no means ignored but it took a succession of virtuosi, particularly Viotti and Paganini, to cause English people to forget its vulgar associations and succumb to the mystique of the instrument.

The viola has attracted some interesting twentieth-century makers, earlier ones tending to make their instruments too small for present-day purposes—though 'the debate' about optimum size and air volume still continues. The double bass attracted a few outstanding makers whose work is discussed in Chapter 1.

During the latter part of the nineteenth century the challenge of making something which might, perhaps, equal the masterpieces of Cremona was one which more and more people felt inclined to take up. Some were inspired by the exhibitions which became quite common during the second half of the nineteenth century and allowed people to see, for the first time, fine examples of the work of Stradivari, Guarneri, and the other classic Italian makers. Books started to be written which were of real value and these culminated in the work of Edward Heron-Allen. Partly as a result of his book and partly of more professional teaching, the general technical standard of making greatly improved in the twentieth century, but perhaps at the expense of 'character'.

Looking at the post-classical era of approximately 1880–1950 more specifically, there was a smallish core of highly professional makers such as the Chanots, William Atkinson, T. Earle Hesketh, Alfred Vincent, John Owen, Arthur Richardson, the Hill family's workshop makers, and George Wulme-Hudson. They learned either by being properly apprenticed and trained or by extensive experience and observation of the work of the masters. Below them came an army of what Heron-Allen would call 'amateurs'—ironically many being there because of the inspiration of his book. There was the feeling, often associated with the English as observed from across the Channel, that 'gentlemen' did not need the training of an artisan. 'Gentlemen' were, after all, quite the equal of professional 'players' on the cricket pitch. Give them the tools and a snippet or two of instruction and they could match the best of Italian makers. There were indeed a few brilliant and erratic successes. There were also numerous heroic failures.

After 1950 there was a greater realization in many areas of endeavour in Britain that if foreign competition were to be bettered there was no substitute for a proper foundation and skilled on-the-job tuition. Schools of violin-making functioned in a serious way and the general standards of educated craftsmanship, designed to produce consistent quality in the light of the lessons of the past, rose significantly. The abundance of individual makers of violins and bows emerged from this background. Whether abundance will become superabundance will depend on the maintenance, and if possible, increase of demand from up-and-coming players. It appears that workshops with sufficient equipment and tools can be set up without prohibitive capital expense, and the problems of slow turnover of expensive new instruments can be mitigated by 'bread-and-butter' income from repairing and restoration, sale of accessories, and the like. Conditions in recent years have not been easy, however.

An encouraging factor for modern makers is the growth of interest in, and audience support for, 'authentic' performance of music of the seventeenth, eighteenth, and even nineteenth centuries. It seems not an unreasonable prognosis that the freelance string-player will need to practise baroque and modern performing techniques interchangeably. This is likely to increase demand for reproduction (or converted back) baroque (or 'classical') instruments and bows, to be used alongside conventional ones.

From the maker's point of view, structurally the violin has remained little changed since its birth a little before 1550.[18] Its secrets remain as elusive as ever. That remains the fundamental reason for the fascination of the subject to so many devotees.

Survey of English Instruments used in Professional Orchestras in Britain

As a tailnote to this chapter, an interesting way of testing the possible thesis that, at least as regards violins and violas, instruments by modern English makers are

---

[18] Experimentation with guitar-shaped or trapezoid structures has not found favour with most players, but it continues—see, for instance, Antonio Pace, 'A Baroque Queen Embalmed', *Strad* (Jan. 1993), 88. There is also considerable experimentation with electric violins, in effect mute violins with a built-in amplifier.

better represented than may have been thought in the string sections of British orchestras is to survey the instruments actually in use. This information is not altogether easy to come by, partly for security reasons, but three typical orchestras have kindly co-operated by making their (very sparse) insurance records available. Too much should not be read into these results since they show the instruments used on tour. In most cases this will be the instrument used permanently, but some players use two instruments and may leave a more valuable, or perhaps more fragile, one behind.

The general picture shown is that twentieth-century British instruments in the violin and viola section are much in favour, and the choice of cello and double bass shows equal preference for nineteenth- or late eighteenth-century British instruments, where a British instrument is used at all. Violas as a section have a consistently high percentage of British to non-British, approximately 65 per cent. The average percentage of all strings, British to non-British, is still a very creditable 45 per cent, approximately.

Three sample orchestras were taken. Orchestra 1 is one of the 'big five' London orchestras. Orchestra 2 is a highly distinguished orchestra in the provinces of England. Orchestra 3 is one of the professional Scottish orchestras.

Where known, further particulars of the makers listed will be found in the Directory.

Orchestra 1

Violins
Harris, Nigel (contemporary)
Dodd (London, c.1800)
Moon, George (contemporary)
Cross, Nathaniel (London, c.1720)
Fawcett, James (contemporary)
Ayres, Paul (1991)
Luff, William (1988)
Harris, Nigel
Highfield, Ian (contemporary)
Ayres, Paul (see above, 'after Guarneri')

Violas
Harrild, Paul (contemporary)
Unsworth, Victor (contemporary)
Smith (no details)
Ayres, Paul
Beard, John (contemporary)

Kudanowski, Jan (contemporary)
Castle, William (contemporary)
England, Rex (contemporary)
England, Rex

Cellos
Watkins, John (no details)
Dodd (London, c.1800)
English, unlabelled
Norman, Barak (London, c.1710)
Forster, S. A. (London, c.1850)
Banks, Benjamin (Salisbury, c.1780)

Double Bass
Fendt (presumably Bernhardt, London, c.1800)
Hill (no other details supplied)
Theress, Charles (London, c.1850)

Orchestra 2

Violins
Oliver, P. K. (no details)
Hepplewhite, Karl (contemporary)
Hepplewhite, Karl
Hepplewhite, Karl
Hill, W. E. & Sons (London, c.1920)
Johnson, John (London, c.1750)
Hull, Robert (contemporary)

Violas
Saunders, Wilfred (contemporary)
Crocker, Laurence (c.1950)
Walker, John (c.1940)
Hoing, Clifford (contemporary)
Solomon, Gimpel (contemporary)
Luff, William H. (contemporary)
Voigt (modern, but no further details)
Standen, John (no details)

Cellos
Luff, William (contemporary)
Hill, Lockey (London, c.1780)

Hepplewhite, Karl
Betts, John (London, c.1790)

Double Basses
Kennedy family (London, c.1830)
Kennedy family
Kennedy family
Hill, Joseph (London, 1780)
Martin, Thomas (contemporary)
Booth, William (Leeds, c.1820)
Highfield, Ian (contemporary)

Orchestra 3

Violins
Conkerton, E. R. (c.1940)
Briggs, J. W. (Glasgow, c.1900)
Smith, John (London, 1740)
Solomon, Gimpel (contemporary)
Craske, George (c.1860)
Nicholls, Colin (contemporary)
Duke, Richard (London, c.1760)
Rost, Franz (London, c.1930)
Hill, Lockey (Islington, London, 1794)
Hesketh, T. E. (Manchester, c.1920)

Violas
Craske, George
Saunders, Wilfred (contemporary)
Luff, William (Suffolk, 1988)
Rattray, Brian (Edinburgh 1979)
Robinson, Alfred G. (1947)
Rowe, Chris (1991)
Sanderson, Derek (Glasgow, 1966)
Forster (London, c.1800)
Topham, C. (1979)

Cellos
Kennedy (London, 1825)
Irving, Colin (1976)
Hill, Joseph (London, 1760)
Prentice, Ronald (1979)

Hill, W. Lockey (London, 1827)
Dodd (London, *c*.1820)

Notes
1. For technical reasons returns may not have given all Scottish, Welsh, or Irish instruments. A few Scottish instruments were returned, but the survey would not accurately show the use of instruments made outside England but within the British Isles. The percentages suggested may therefore *understate* the true position.
2. There were two double basses by Hawkes and Sons (*c*.1910) included in the returns to the author. The firm were primarily dealers and importers but apparently had a workshop so the instruments could be English (see Vannes). Without further details they were excluded *ex abundante cautela* (as was a violin by 'Colin Mezin'!).
3. Information in parentheses was either supplied by the orchestra or rests on the author's hypotheses, or a mixture of both.

London Map 1800
based on a Plan of London by George Cary

Showing the streets of some leading violin-makers of the Old English School in London

1. The old London Bridge had houses and shops on it, probably like the Ponte Vecchio in Florence. Urquhart and Pamphilon probably had shops there.

2. St Paul's Churchyard—a number of makers were based here, including Barak Norman and the Thompson family.

3. Blackman Street and Borough High Street in Southwark where Rayman and Lockey Hill had establishments.

4. In about 1730 Peter Wamsley moved the centre of violin-making westwards from the City to Piccadilly, where Edmund Aireton also later worked.

5. Soho was the primary area of violin-making in nineteenth-century London. Princes Street and Wardour Street were the main areas, though there were important businesses in Coventry Street and Leicester Square. B. S. Fendt worked in Dean Street, Soho.

6. The Hill family business moved from Wardour Street to New Bond Street before moving out of London in 1976.

7. John Joseph Merlin's establishment was in Queen Anne Street East. He later moved to the fashionable Hanover Square.

8. Richard Duke's establishment was at Holborn.

9. William Forster moved from the nearby St Martin's Lane South East to the Strand in 1784. The Preston Family also worked in this area. Thomas Dodd's business moved to St Martin's Lane in 1809.

10. Royal Exchange, where the Betts and Simpson families worked.

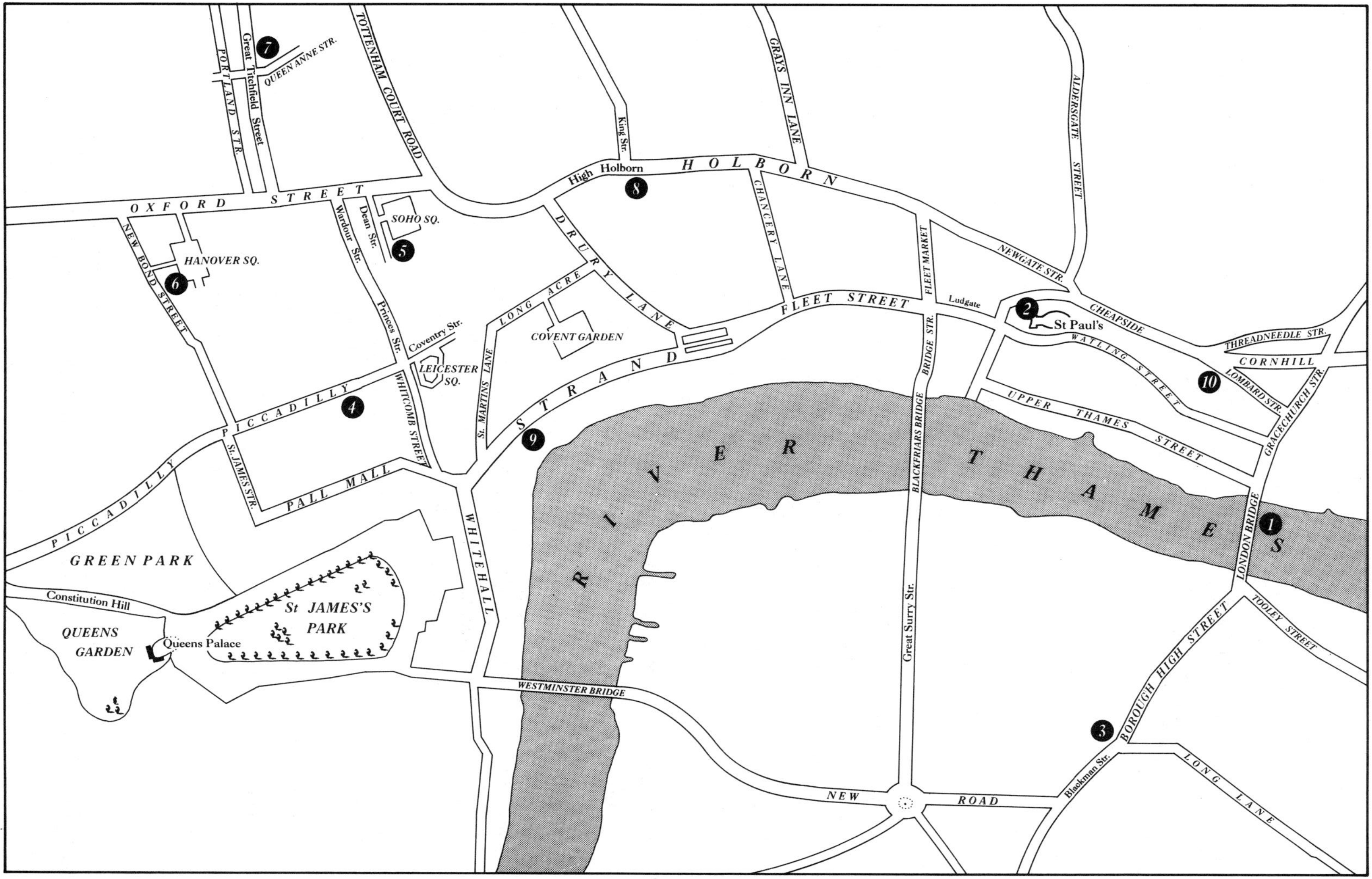

PORTLAND STR.
Great Titchfield Street
QUEEN ANNE STR.
TOTTENHAM COURT ROAD
King Str.
GRAYS INN LANE
ALDERSGATE STREET
OXFORD STREET
High Holborn
HOLBORN
SOHO SQ.
Wardour Str.
Dean Str.
NEW BOND STREET
HANOVER SQ.
CHANCERY LANE
FLEET MARKET
NEWGATE STR.
DRURY LANE
LONG ACRE
COVENT GARDEN
FLEET STREET
Ludgate
St Paul's
CHEAPSIDE
THREADNEEDLE STR.
CORNHILL
LOMBARD STR.
WATLING STREET
Princes Str.
Coventry Str.
LEICESTER SQ.
St. MARTINS LANE
STRAND
BRIDGE STR.
BLACKFRIARS BRIDGE
UPPER THAMES STREET
GRACECHURCH STR.
PICCADILLY
WHITCOMB STREET
St. JAMES STR.
PALL MALL
WHITEHALL
RIVER THAMES
LONDON BRIDGE
GREEN PARK
Constitution Hill
St JAMES'S PARK
QUEENS GARDEN
Queens Palace
WESTMINSTER BRIDGE
Great Surry Str.
TOOLEY STREET
BOROUGH HIGH STREET
Blackman Str.
NEW ROAD
LONG LANE
1
2
3
4
5
6
7
8
9
10

APPENDIX I

A Directory of Violin- and Bow-Makers in the British Isles

Sources (with abbreviations)

Alburger	Mary Anne Alburger, *The Violin Makers: Portrait of a Living Craft* (London, 1979).
Hart	George Hart, *The Violin: Famous Makers and their Imitators* (London, 1885).
W.H.	William Henley, *Universal Dictionary of Violin and Bow Makers*, 2nd edn. (Brighton, 1973).
Hill Archive	Manuscript notes c.1900–30 of Hill family on instruments made in the British Isles; Ashmolean Museum, Oxford.
W.C.H.	William C. Honeyman, *Scottish Violin Makers* 2nd edn. (Dundee, 1910).
Jalovec	Karel Jalovec, *Encyclopaedia of Violin-Makers* (London, 1968).
vL	Willibald Leo Frh. v. Lütgendorff, *Die Geigen- und Lautenmacher* (with supplement by Thomas Drescher) (Tutzing, 1990).
W.M.M.	W. Meredith Morris, *British Violin Makers*, 2nd edn. (London, 1920).
NGD	*The New Grove Dictionary of Music and Musicians*, ed. Stanley Sadie (20 vols.; London, 1980).
NGDI	*New Grove Dictionary of Musical Instruments*, ed. Stanley Sadie (London, 1984).
Piper	Hidalgo Moya and A. Towry Piper, *Violin Tone and Violin Makers* (London, 1916) (with Dictionary by Piper).
Poidras	Henri Poidras, *Dictionnaire des Luthiers* (trans. A. Sewell, *Dictionary of Violin Makers*) (2 vols.; Rouen, 1928–30).
Retford	William C. Retford, *Bows and Bow Makers* (London, 1964).
Vannes	René Vannes, *Dictionnaire Universel des Luthiers* (3 vols.; Brussels, 1951, 1959, with supplement by Claude Lebet, 1985).

Other sources as referred to in the text.

* Makers' names bearing an asterisk have a facsimile label reproduced in App. 2.
† Makers' names bearing a dagger have a sample of their work illustrated.

A Note on the Sources

Of the sources emanating from Britain, Morris (W.M.M.) is scrupulous in its scholarship and it is clear that the author met or made personal enquiry of many of the makers with whom he was a contemporary (*c*.1900). Meredith Morris's enthusiasms were somewhat indiscriminate and have by no means always stood the test of time, but on facts rather than opinions he was pretty accurate. Similar remarks apply to Honeyman (W.C.H.) on Scottish makers. I have used these sources as the primary ones. Henley's remarkable work (W.H.) is indispensable but, perhaps inevitably in such a huge *opus*, not always to be relied upon and derivative to some extent from Morris and Honeyman. Vannes has improved since it first appeared in 1932 (when the Hill brothers were prompted to comment that they had never come across a book more full of inaccuracies), but the material on British makers is largely derivative from the above sources; (a supplement by Claude Lebet (1985) is particularly useful on contemporary makers). Similar guarded remarks apply to Vol. II of Von Lütgendorff, but Vol. III compiled by Thomas Drescher (1990) is quite a different matter. This amends and adds to the previous volumes, examining many of the published sources which, perhaps uniquely up to that time, are properly acknowledged in the text. A questionnaire was also administered and many modern British makers included. I am greatly indebted to this work which is a model of its kind. In absorbing these sources translations from the French (Vannes) and German (von Lütgendorff) have been mine, and I hope that I have not misunderstood the sometimes idiomatic modes of expression.

Poidras clearly corresponded with some contemporary British makers and occasionally sheds some light on the scene. Towry Piper was a scrupulous commentator whose knowledge commands great respect. Sandys and Forster, Hart, and other nineteenth-century writers, being in many cases the first historians of the British field and closer to many makers of importance than other dictionary compilers, are significant for that reason. *The New Grove Dictionaries*, which contain articles by a selection of contemporary experts on British makers, are also of immense value.

Karel Jalovec produced his *Encyclopaedia of Violin-Makers* in 1965 and this also includes short descriptions of the work of many British makers plus, often, a snap judgement on quality. The two-volume *Encyclopaedia* seemed to the author, as regards British makers, to be both slapdash and too obviously derivative to be much use for present purposes, but this judgement may in specific instances be unfair and future researchers are advised at least to check entries in the Jalovec work to which occasional reference is made in the present Directory.

The Directory also contains the fruit of my own observation of hundreds of British instruments in workshops, auction-rooms, and private collections over the last twenty years—not long enough, of course, but perhaps just sufficient to add a little 'inside knowledge' here and there. I have also benefited from many discussions with professional dealers, restorers, and connoisseurs such as Charles Beare, John Dilworth, Hamilton Caswell, Norman Rosenberg, the late John Dyke of Malvern, amongst many. There are upwards of a thousand makers who qualify as working or having worked in the British Isles—an astonishing total. Their output was variable: anything from a dozen or so to, in cases such as Craske, 2,000 or more. Most professional makers produce at least 300 instruments. But if we average it at fifty instruments per maker it will be seen that there are something in excess of 50,000 British instruments of the violin family theoretically in circulation—and

Britain is not known for its commercial production as compared to France and Germany. The vast majority of these instruments were handmade with loving care (if not always with a great deal of insight).

The Directory tries to be comprehensive but inevitably cannot fully succeed. There are undoubtedly more makers than appear here, but most of them are likely to have made only the occasional instrument, often as a hobby activity. Conversely, quite a few makers appear for the first time, usually because I have come across their work by chance, and research on others (see for instance, John Joseph Merlin, Joseph Scott, or Rushworth & Dreaper) has shown up the perpetuation of myth by each Dictionary following (usually) an erroneous source.

I did think of omitting any maker adjudged to be too obscure. Early on I identified Robert Ballantyne of Edinburgh ('workmanship bordering on mediocrity'—W.H.) as one of them. This was while I was working on the Directory, with ever-increasing foreboding as to its length, and making a viola in summer day-classes under the tolerant tutelage of Juliet Barker in Cambridge. The very next day in conversation with a class-mate I was told that his son played on a violin by a Scottish maker by the name of Ballantyne! The chances of this occurring at that moment were infinitesimal but it taught me to be careful. I can only apologize to those players the maker of whose British instrument is absent. Those adjudged merely repairers or dealers have, however, been omitted. As it is I think there is little prospect of my offending against the Trade Descriptions Act 1968 if I state that the Directory is the most comprehensive list ever published to date of British makers, but equally I again acknowledge my debt to the sources quoted, particularly Morris, and Henley and various articles in the *Strad*. These sources remain indispensable, not least for the greater detail often given. For reasons of space I have had to confine myself to bare essentials in most cases. The Directory here is designed to be merely an appendix to the main text, not to dominate it.

The work of the Newark School and other factors has resulted in many new young makers working in Britain in recent years. I have done my best to mention them, but have to a large extent relied on vL, Vannes/Lebet, Alburger, and the *Strad* (including its annual Directories). I have not conducted any formal questionnaires but in some cases have applied my personal knowledge of the work of the maker mentioned. In other cases contemporary makers have kindly supplied details to me in response to an open invitation in the *Strad* (May 1993) to do so. (The extent of the detail depends on the information so vouchsafed.) There will nevertheless be some inevitable omissions in the circumstances. ('Workshops' as such have not normally been included).

Assessments of all non-living makers are offered in the light of modern opinion. There are numerous references to relevant articles in the *Strad* or other periodicals. Modern auction prices are appended when these are representative and an unequivocal instrument of a non-living maker was actually sold. These prices often say more about the real standing of a maker than any number of words.

Auction Houses (with date of sale and lot number)

C	Christie's
P	Phillips
S	Sotheby's

Example: P 11/88/135 = Phillips, November 1988, lot 135.

Author's Note

NB: All prices quoted include buyer's premium (but not VAT thereon). Condition can vary enormously and this can radically affect prices. Prices are for violins unless otherwise indicated. Readers should as a general rule assume auction prices are equivalent to wholesale prices. Dealers reselling have to meet the cost of putting instruments into good playing order so that statutory guarantees of fitness for purpose, etc. are fulfilled, and this element is reflected in price differentials. VAT usually has to be added too. (Occasionally Lots are subject to VAT on the hammer price, which is here adjusted, where possible, accordingly).

I was unfortunately not able to obtain relevant information in time from another firm of London specialist auctioneers, Messrs Bonhams.

Do not treat these prices as 'auction records'. The intention is to indicate the value of good representative specimens, many of which I saw in the auction-rooms. But few instruments of any age are exactly alike. ALWAYS CHECK THE AUCTIONEER'S CATALOGUE ENTRY FOR DESCRIPTIONS AND VERIFICATIONS.

Directory

ABDY, William. Worked in London 1768–1800. Klotz modelling, mediocre work.

ABEL, David. Little or nothing is known of his work. Thought to have worked in London during first half of 19th cent.

ABSAM, THOMAS (c.1810–49). See 'Abson' below. Wakefield, Yorks. W.H. suggests Tyrolean descent. W.M.M. states that he made chiefly for Pickard, a dealer in Leeds. Label: Made by | Thomas Absam | Wakefield, Feb. 14 | 1833 (Hart).

ABSON, Thomas. One viola seen so labelled and 'Leeds, late from London, 1813' added, all in MS. (The instrument looked French.) Probably the same as Thomas Absam (*sic* in other Directories). P 3/93/133, viola 15⅜ in. (392 mm), Leeds, 1813, £1,760.

ACTON, William John (1848–1931). Worked in London—unpretentious, solid work with durable varnish. W.M.M. lists 210 violins, 19 violas, 29 cellos, 21 double basses, and 250 bows. Also made viols. MS label: William John Acton | Maker | Forest Gate London 1898 (W.M.M.).

ADAMS, Cathune (*fl.* 1775–1805). Worked in Garmouth, Scotland. Made kits, violins, and cellos, some with decorated fingerboards. Amati modelling. 'The tone is excellent' (W.C.H.). Handwritten label.

ADAMS, Colquhoun (*fl.* 1875). Worked at Garmouth, Scotland. W.H. praises scroll. Dark brown varnish.

ADAMS, Henry Thomas (*c.*1904–20). Worked at Plumstead, Kent. Copied classical Italian instruments. Praised by W.H. who says that he used Scotch sycamore. P 7/90/115, £1,835.

ADDISON, William (*c.*1660). Worked in London. Mainly a viol-maker. Label: William Addison | in Long Alley | over against Moorfields 1670 (W.M.M.).

AGUTTER, Ralph (*c.*1700). See text. Mainly music publisher. Violins bearing his label: 'Ralph Agutter living in the Strand over against York Buildings' exist. If he made his own instruments, he deserves the credit that W.H. gives.

†AIRETON, Edmund (1727–1807). Worked in London and thought to be a relative of the composer Edmund Ayreton (*sic*) (1734–1808)—see vL. Followed the Stainer and Amati modelling after school of Peter Wamsley. W.H. states that he made cheaper models for Norris and Barnes. His father is thought to have had the same name and to have been employed by Peter Wamsley. His better specimens are now quite highly valued. Often unlabelled. The Hill Archive states that 'The work of this maker that we have seen bears a great resemblance to the style of Thomas Smith. It is probable, therefore, that Aireton had some connection with him.' S 11/90/96 (ascribed to), £3,740. S 11/88/179, cello, £6,380. (See also Robert Donnington, *Galpin Society Journal*, 3 (1950), 27–45.)

AIRETON, Edmund (jun.) (*fl.* 1790). This London maker is thought to be the son of the above. The Hill Archive mentions a 15¼ in. viola stamped 'Aireton' under the button with a contemporary German head. They remark that it is like the work of Joseph Hill.

AIRTH, William (*c.*1860–81). Worked in Edinburgh. 'Fair workmanship and tone' (W.M.M.). Married daughter of James Hardie 'from whom he learned the art' (W.C.H.). Emigrated to Australia 1881.

ALEXANDER, John (1871–*c.*1930). Cruden, Aberdeenshire. W.H. notes about 14 violins. Signed internally. P 9/91/81, £176.

ALEXANDER, John (*fl.* 1917–40). Pupil of Thomas Simpson and J. Brierley of Birmingham. Professional violinist in Birmingham Symphony Orchestra. His instruments have a good reputation.

ALEXANDER, Richard (*fl.* 1810). Kilmarnock, Scotland.

ALLEN, Edward HERON- (1861–1943). Distinguished author and connoisseur, discussed in text. Made two instruments in his early years under the instruction of Georges Chanot. Heron-Allen himself states that that one of a Guarneri model was particularly successful tonally and had been tried by such artists as Joachim. Also a London solicitor, cheirosopher, novelist, local historian, linguist, and scientist (FRS 1919). (Ch. 14 contains the only biography so far attempted.)

ALLEN, Samuel (1848–1905). Primarily a distinguished bow-maker, first for W. E. Hill & Sons, about 1880–91, where he was an important influence in the characteristic style of Hill bows (see Retford) and later established his own business in 1891 in London. Few bows bear his stamp. According to *NGD*, best known for his cello bows after the style of Tourte. W.H. also credits him with a few violins.

ALLKIN, Edwin William (1887–c.1925). Worked in Nottingham. Some 15 violins and several violas up to 1924 noted by W.H. who speaks moderately well of the workmanship. Instruments signed in ink on the back with name and address.

ALLWOOD (*fl*.1800). Sheffield. Both W.H. and W.M.M. speak well of tone and fairly good workmanship.

ALLWOOD, Thomas (19th cent.). Barnstaple. 'His work is said to be fairly good' (W.M.M.).

ALLWOOD, Thomas (*fl*. 1847). Glasgow. See P 12/81/272.

ALTON, Robert (1881–c.1950). Violin- and bow-maker and restorer, working in northern cities and also Brixton, London. Author of a well-known book on *Violin and Cello Building and Repairing* (London, 1946). Also bows.

ALVEY, Brian (b. 1949). Bow-maker with W. E. Hill's until 1978, when established own business. See *NGDI*.

ANDERSON, Henry (1839–c.1900). Edinburgh. According to W.C.H. made about 100 violins mostly on the model of Guarneri. No label, but sometimes written inscription. Bronze medal, Glasgow, 1890.

ANDERSON, James (*fl*. 1860). Worked in Paisley, Scotland, often using old wood. High prices paid in the past for good specimens.

ANDERSON, John (1829–83). Aberdeen. Reputed to have made two violins a month in his working days, but W.M.M. expresses some scepticism about this. Pupil of Matthew Hardie. Specialized in small Stradivari model (13⁷/₈ in., 353 mm).

ANDERSON, John (1856–c.1900). Son of John Anderson (above), though W.M.M. and W.H. disagree on the genealogy: W.M.M. and W.C.H. say that he was the son of John Anderson and W.H. gives James Anderson. This John Anderson, a violinist himself, achieved quite a prolific output mainly on the Stradivari model. He is regarded as one of the better Scottish makers (see text). Label: Made by | John Anderson | Bon-Accord Violin Maker | Glasgow, 18.., blue ink on white paper, printed.

ANDREWS, Edward (1886–c.1951). Violins labelled from Great Yarmouth. Also made bows.

ANDREWS, Martin Paul (b. 1962). Wales. Diploma with Merit, Newark School, 1980–3. 21 violins, 8 violas, and 2 cellos to date, prices £2,500–£3,000 for violins, £3,000–£3,500 for violas. Now self-employed working in Bristol.

ANGELL, Frederick Stanley (1886–1926). Amateur, but W.H. speaks well of his 'refined workmanship'. Worked in Bristol from c.1920. Well known for his proprietary varnish which several other contemporary makers used.

ANGELL, Sidney E. (1883–1926). W.H. credits him with about 70 violins and violas. A colleague of Joseph Chanot in Wardour Street, London. Fair workmanship.

ANKERS, James (*fl*. 1880). 'Workmanship disgustingly rough' (W.H.).

ANYON, Thomas (*fl*. 1896). Manchester. Amateur maker, being a chartered accountant, but credited by W.H. with excellent workmanship such as few British makers could equal. 'Very beautiful instruments' (W.M.M.). Some varnish deterioration seen on otherwise attractive violin.

APPLEBY, Joseph (late 19th cent.). Worked at Wednesbury. Poor reputation.

ARCHER, Charles (b. 1904). Chelmsford. Art Professor at the Royal College of Arts and influenced by the work of Arnold Dolmetsch. Viols, violins, violas, and cellos.

†ARDERN, Job (1826–1912). See text. Worked at Wilmslow, Cheshire, making over 500 instruments. Many of these were acquired by W. E. Hill & Sons at his death. They are often attractive instruments with golden-brown or deep red-brown varnish which has often worn well. Tonally his violins are usually pleasing. One of the better English makers during this period, so wedded to his craft that he disdained to sell many of his instruments. Instruments branded with a number at end of fingerboard (W.H.). P 6/90/103, £1,100; P 9/91/106, £750; S 11/92/317 (1885), £660.

ARDETON. See Rushworth & Dreaper, and in text.

ARMOUR-BROWN, Rowan (b. 1948). Distinguished contemporary violin-maker. Studied in Cremona and with Gimpel Solomon. See also under Network Group. See Alburger and vL.

ARMSTRONG, Alexander (*fl.* 1880). Amateur working in Smethwick, near Birmingham. Made over 100 instruments (W.H.).

ARNE, Nicholas (*fl.* 1850). Poor work.

ARNOLD (*fl.* 1871). Burnley. Ordinary workmanship.

ARNOLD William Thomas (*fl.* 1770). One of the few older Welsh makers, he worked at Newport. Poor reputation.

ASHTON, John, (1859–*c.*1920). Amateur working at Bury, Lancs. Made at least 8 violins.

ASKEW, John (1834–95). See text. Formerly a shoemaker, he worked at Stanhope, Durham and attained a fine reputation in his lifetime. The subject of a biography by W. M. Egglestone (1914). Won a diploma at the International Exhibition, London, 1885. Made about 30 violins, 12 of which he regarded as really satisfactory. Vannes makes the astonishing statement: 'il était un des premiers maîtres luthiers de l'Angleterre' which is hardly likely to be the case where the maker is self-taught with little to copy. But to be fair, his few instruments are rarely seen. 'Skilful and clever but not a genius' (W.H.).

ASKEY, Samuel (*fl.* 1782–1840). Associated with Morrison and Corsby in London, but not of the same class. Some instruments labelled. P 6/91/326, £682. Died by falling down a cellar. (Given as Astley, 1785, by Sandys and Forster, 274.)

ASPINALL, James (*fl. c.*1915). Amateur working near Sheffield. 'Commendable work' (W.H.). Used Whitelaw's oil varnish (which is often a recipe for future disaster).

ATKINS, James (*fl.* 1904). Worked in Cork, Ireland. Stradivarian modelling with varnish praised by W.H. 'Good workmanship and . . . a full, clear, and responsive tone' (W.M.M.).

ATKINS, John (1848–1919). Worked in Sheffield. Enthusiastic player, connoisseur, and collector who made full-time after retirement from being an engineer. Produced over 20 violins. Branded under tailpiece button, and labelled with number.

ATKINSON, John H. (*fl.* 1920). Credited with a number of violins and violas with oil varnish (W.H.). Another enthusiastic British maker to be influenced by the 'Messie' Strad.

*†ATKINSON, William (1851–1929). See text. Worked at Tottenham, London, until 1911 when he moved to Paglesham, Essex (better-quality air for drying varnish outdoors!). Combined making with being a postmaster, a sensible *modus operandi* and in no way

compromising his professionalism. Made about 300 violins, violas, and cellos, rejecting anything not matching up to his exacting standards. One of the finest English makers of this period whose instruments have generally lasted well. Varnish usually successful (18–24 coats of oil varnish) but sometimes deterioration has occurred. Slightly varied Strad modelling. W.M.M. praises him very highly and, on this occasion, this is well deserved. 'Highly finished workmanship in every detail. Made all his own instruments, down to the purfling' (W.H.). 'Careful work, good tone.' (Jalovec). Violins, violas, and cellos originally priced respectively at £25, £30, and £50, in one quality only. 'The tone is remarkably clear and responsive, it is powerful but withal mellow and silvery.' (W.M.M.). Copperplate MS over-varnished labels. Monogram branded on back under button. P 6/90/199, £2,750; S 6/91/27 £2,860.

AUBREY, Philip (*fl.* 1840). Gloucester. Poor work. (W.M.M.).

AYRES, Paul and Karen. A contemporary firm in Didsbury, Manchester—makers, repairers, and dealers.

BACON, T W. (*fl.* 1900). W.H. states made pochettes, but also violins known. Worked in London.

BAILEY, Leslie (*fl.* 1920–39). Bow-maker during these years with Hills.

BAINES (*fl.* 1780). Mentioned by W.M.M. as pupil and employee of Matthew Furber in London. W.H. praises varnish and tone.

BAIRD, Neil. Contemporary maker and restorer working in Glasgow.

BAKER, Timothy Gavin (b. 1962) Contemporary bow-maker trained at Newark school, then with Hills under John Stagg, and later worked with J. & A. Beare in London. Enjoys a high reputation. (vL)

*†BAKER family. Distinguished early family of viol- and violin-makers centred in London and Oxford. *William* of Oxford (*fl.* 1673–83) is credited with one of the earliest English cellos (C11/89/212 (1672)); his son *John* worked in Oxford and John's brother (probably), *Francis*, in London (St Paul's Churchyard). Instruments seen suggest Tyrolean influence. P 4/91/168 (violin by William Baker), £1,540.

BAKER, William (*fl.* 1820–40). Worked at George St., Brighton. Variable workmanship. P 11/91/74, £1,320.

BALLANTYNE, Robert (*fl.* 1840–60). Glasgow and Edinburgh. Indifferent reputation.

BALMFORTH, Leonard Geoffrey (1881–1936) and Leonard Percy (1909–66). Leeds. Father and son. Proprietors of well known firm of dealers; both combined instrument-making with restoration work. See *Strad* (Dec. 1955), 296, and *Strad* (Dec. 1966), 307.

*†BANKS, Benjamin (1727–95) and family. See text. *Benjamin* (sen.) worked in Catherine St., Salisbury—'the English Amati'. Also influenced by Stainer (then fashionable), Stradivarius, and other classic Italians. One of the most distinguished makers of the 'Old English School'. Also son *Benjamin* (1754–1820)—a few instruments from Golden Sq., London. His other sons *James* (1756–1831) and *Henry* (1770–1830) ran the Salisbury business to 1811 and then established their business in Liverpool to 1831. Their instruments are variable—excellent at their best, descending to 'trade' quality. According to Sandys and Forster, *Henry's* activities were confined to piano-tuning. *James* was the violin-maker and repairer in what was a successful business. It has also been suggested

that most of the instruments were merely finished at Liverpool having been previously begun at Salisbury (but this seems unlikely). A fine cello with a full and powerful tone by J. & H. Banks is described by Sandys and Forster as owned by Charles Lucas, then the principal cello at the Royal Opera, Covent Garden. Benjamin Banks sen.: S 11/89/463, £4,180; S 4/93/327, viola, 15⁵⁄₁₆ in. (388 mm), Salisbury, 1780, £3,220; S 11/88/189, cello, £17,600. James & Henry Banks: S 3/91/88 (fine violin), £9,350.

BANKS, James & Henry. See under Banks, Benjamin, above.

BARCLAY, Alexander (1856–1918). Worked in Dundee. Indifferent work.

BARKER, George (*fl.* 1920). Worked in Chesterfield. 'Excellent Stradivarian modelling' (W.H.).

BARKER, Juliet (b. 1934) (also known as Juliet Beament, being wife of Prof. Sir James Beament, FRS). Works in Cambridge. Distinguished for her violas in particular; also as a teacher. Trained in Mittenwald. 21 violins, 35 violas, and 4 cellos (per vL). See Alburger. Now works with her son, Christopher Beament.

BARLOW, Arthur (*fl.* 1920). Worked mainly in Braunton, N. Devon. Produced about 35 instruments in Stradivari and Guarneri modelling. A chemist by primary trade.

BARNES, Arthur John (1888–1945). Bow-maker with Hill's.

BARNES, Robert (*fl.* 1770). Apprenticed with Thomas Smith in Piccadilly and then a partner of John Norris, 1765–80. Probably employed others. Labelled as from Windmill St., Haymarket, London.

BARNES, and MULLINS (*fl.* 1905–30). Employed workmen to enable them to say 'made in London by hand'. Mainly traders.

BARRETT, John (*fl.* 1714–33). See text. Worked in London, one of the more commonly met of the early English makers. Work variable, often descending to unattractive models with ink lines instead of purfling. Stainer modelling. Worked at the Harp and Crown in Piccadilly. A few violins and cellos of fine quality. C 4/91/190, violin, 1734, £6,050; S 6/91/115, cello, 1741, £6,050. S 4/93/456, violin, London 1738, £2,415.

BARRETT, Kershaw (*fl.* 1930). Labelled as from Marshlands, or Moor House, Oxenhope; also from Haworth, 1909. Several quite attractive Stradivarian violins and a viola seen—typical English work of the period.

BARROW, Francis (*fl.* 1920). St Helens, Lancs.

BARRY, Frederick Drennan (1870–1926). Pupil of Frank Howard and professional string-player. Made instruments as from Wood Green, London, and also bows. W.H. suggests popular with orchestral players.

BARTON, George (*c.*1772–1810). Worked at Elliot Court, Old Bailey, London. A guitar-shaped specimen is reported as being in the Museum in Markneukirchen (vL).

BARTON, John (*fl.* 1780–1810). Brother of George (above). Employed by C. & S. Thompson from 1784 (W.H.). The Hill Archive states that he 'made violins for Preston'. Variable workmanship. One specimen labelled as from Shipyard, Temple Bar, London, 1791.

BARTON, John Edward (1846–*c.*1920). Worked in Llanelli, S. Wales. W.M.M. speaks highly of him—made all his own tools and used an original model 'of excellent material, workmanship, and tone'. Modern opinion does not appear to bear out this enthusiasm. P 10/91/175, £308.

BASFORD, John. Contemporary maker, restorer, dealer, player, and expert appraiser based in Sheffield. One of the few in the trade with a music degree (from Sheffield University).

BASTON, Victor. Contemporary maker working in Southall (also Beaconsfield, 1977). Some Tertis model violas.

BATEY, Brian M. and Julian. Contemporary makers, restorers and dealers of Whitchurch, Shropshire.

BATHO, W. J. (*fl.* 1860). Somewhat obscure, but both W.H. and vL mention good double basses. Also cellos. Place of work (in England) not known.

BEAMENT, Christopher. Contemporary. Works with Juliet Barker (q.v.) in Cambridge.

BEAMISH, John (*fl.* 1910). London. W.M.M. mentions that he made a few instruments while working at the 'Peasant Art Guild' of 17 Duke St., Manchester Sq.

BEARD, John Sebastian (1919–92). Modern English maker who worked in London. Formerly professional viola-player and brother of Paul Beard, sometime leader of the BBC Symphony Orchestra. Studied with W. J. Piercy who himself was trained in the Mirecourt tradition. In 1979 charged £1,050 for a violin and £1,200 for a viola. Instruments, particularly violas, used professionally. See Alburger; vL.

BEARDSMORE, Adèle (b. 1966). Studied at the Newark School 1984–7, then worked successively in Cornwall and Holland (at Contrada Musica, Amersfoort, mainly on restoring, including bows). Established in Cambridge in 1992. Has made about 18 instruments including violas and two cellos, before moving to Australia.

BEARE, J. & A. Internationally known firm of makers and dealers in Soho, London. Bows stamped with their name. The brief history of the firm is that John Beare (1847–1928) divided the firm in 1892 into Beare & Son, with his son Walter, and Beare, Goodwin & Co. The former firm was (and is) associated with dealing in new instruments and accessories. The latter firm, in conjunction with Edward Goodwin, specialized in fine and ancient instruments. It became John and Arthur Beare. Associated with the latter firm was Arthur Beare (1875–1945), younger son of John Beare. William Arthur Beare (b. 1910) was the son of Arthur, trained in France, and besides having a fine reputation as a restorer and connoisseur also made instruments of excellent repute. Charles Beare (b. 1937), the stepson of William, was trained in Mittenwald and worked with Rembert Wurlitzer in New York and with S. F. Sacconi. Undoubtedly one of the world's leading experts on all aspects of violin-making and appraisal, he is also a distinguished author. His son Peter (b. 1965) trained in Salt Lake City, USA, and with Vatelot in Paris and Spidlen in Prague, now makes and restores with the firm too. A number of distinguished modern makers and restorers have worked at Beare's. See generally Alburger; *NGD*; *Strad* (Feb. 1987), 128; and vL.

BECKETT, John (*fl.* 1880–96). Worked at Faversham, Kent.

BEDFORD, Thomas (*fl.* 1880). Worked in Huddersfield in, according to the Hill Archive, the Betts–Forster style.

BEE, F. L. (*fl.* 1910). Shiremoor, Northumberland. Nothing known. (W.M.M.)

BEEMAN, Henry W. (*c.*1858–1940). See P 6/94/92.

BÉLA SZEPESSY. See under Szepessy, Béla.

BELL, A. (*fl.* 1920). Worked at Camborne, Cornwall. Violins and cellos—'really good tone' (W.H.).

BELL, John M. (*fl.* 1910). Birkenhead.

BELLINGHAM, Thomas J. (1853–1927). Worked at Leeds, enthusiastic amateur. Self-taught and did not believe in templates or other conventional methods of making. Achieved respectable recognition in his day (W.H.).

BELLIS, Andrew. Contemporary bow-maker working in Worcs. (vL).

BERRY, Arthur (*fl.* 1910–25). Succeeded in making violins whilst serving in the First World War as some of his labels indicate. Worked at Great Harwood, Lancs. where he was an ironmonger.

BERRY, Peter (1879–?). Kircaldy, Scotland. An amateur maker of talent, not afraid of departing from tradition by, for example, cutting his button in the form of a shoe. 'The material is excellent' (W.M.M.).

BERTRAM, William (*fl.* 1790–1810). Scottish amateur maker producing instruments suitable for Strathspey outdoor work (W.H.).

†BETTS family. See text. Founder of the dynasty was 'Old' *John* Edward Betts (1755–1823). Although he made a few instruments himself he is mainly known for having the perspicacity to employ Panormo, Fendt, and Tobin. The Betts firm produced instruments showing strong Cremonese influence and of a very high standard. Both John Edward and his nephew and partner *Edward* (known as 'Ned'; d. 1817) were trained by Richard Duke. Instruments are often branded 'Betts London' on button. Label: John Betts, No. 2 North Piazza | Royal Exchange, London, fecit . . .' The Betts firm were also one of the first such to specialize and profit by the trade in old Italian instruments. Other makers such as Isaac Newton (*fl.* 1775–1825) and John Carter also worked for the firm as employees or outworkers. Forgeries abound. *Arthur* Betts, brother of John Edward, succeeded to the business. Again, he employed very talented workmen. A violin made by the firm of Arthur and John Betts for the Great Exhibition, 1851, (illustrated), made £6,600 (P 11/91/142). Also P 4/91/137, £8,800; Cello, S 11/90/324, *c.*1800, £17,050. S 4/93/66, £5,980.

BEVAN, Thomas (*fl.* 1860–1900). West Bromwich. 'Made about 30 preposterous-looking fiddles from any woods he could lay his hands on.' (W.H.).

BEVERIDGE, William (1821–92). Worked at Tough, Scotland. Credited with a large number of instruments in his spare time. Instruments labelled and branded.

BICKHAM, Richard (*fl.* 1816). Southampton. Indifferent work.

BICKLE, Paul (b. 1945). A Newark-trained maker given as working at Alton, Hants. (also the USA) with about 160 instruments by 1985 (vL). It is understood that he died recently.

*BIDDULPH, Harry (1866–1949). Born in Wales and proud of his nationality, he worked in London. Well thought-of in his day. (See particularly W.H.).

BIDDULPH, Peter. Contemporary luthier and expert having a business in London. Formerly associated with P. & W. Moes (until 1981). See *Strad* (Oct. 1991), 870; Vannes/Lebet.

BIGGAR, John (*fl.* 1850). Worked at Stewart Blainslie, Scotland. (Not mentioned elsewhere.)

BIGNON, François (b. 1957). Born in Laval, France. Maker and restorer now working in Birmingham. Specializes in smaller-size instruments.

BINLEY, Thomas (*fl.* 1780). Worked in Desborough.

BIRCH, Thomas (*fl.* 1840–60). Hereford. Average work.

BIRD, Richmond Henry (*fl.* 1920). Born in Walsall in 1869 and worked for many years as chief craftsman for Rushworth & Dreaper (q.v.) at Liverpool from 1914. Good reputation as a craftsman. An attributed Ardeton violin fetched £1,320 (P 6/91/110) but research reveals that he made the firm's violas, not violins.

BISHOP, Edgar (1904–43). Bow-maker with Hills. See Retford, 74.

BLACK, James (*fl.* 1841). Dundee. P 1/92/102, £374.

BLACK, Jno. (i.e. John) (*fl.* 1890). Worked in Edinburgh. One well-made small viola seen.

BLACKSTONE, J. (*fl.* 1760). Instruments rare, but supposed to be good old English School (W.H.).

BLADE, Gilbert George (*fl.* 1955). Basildon. Not otherwise recorded. P 7/92/186, £88.

BLAIR, John (*fl.* 1790–1820). Edinburgh and Aberdeen. He might have worked with Matthew Hardie (perhaps his teacher) and his Stradivarian modelling is similar (W.C.H.). Poor spirit varnish. Wrote name on interior of table; also stamped 'J.B.'

BLAIR, William (1793–1884). Scotland. Played Strathspeys for Queen Victoria. Allegedly pupil of Matthew Hardie at Edinburgh. Indifferent work.

BLAKEMORE, George (*fl.* 1920). Worked in Walsall, Staffs.

BLIGHT, R. (*fl.* 1830). Exeter. 'Very good work' (W.M.M.).

BLYTH, Williamson (1821–97). Worked in Edinburgh. 'Turned out about 2,000 wretched violins' (W.H.)—an over-generalized comment. P 3/90/136, violin, 1895, £329; P 4/92/89 'good violin', Edinburgh, 1890, £385.

BOARDMAN, Peter. Contemporary violin-maker working in Donaghadee, County Down, N. Ireland. First Prize-winner, Royal Dublin Society musical instrument competition, 1984, 1986.

BOOTH, Charles (*fl.* 1882–95). Burnley. Ordinary work.

BOOTH, Joseph (*fl.* 1880). Manchester. 'Fair orchestral tone' (W.H.).

BOOTH, William (*fl.* 1809–56). Worked at Leeds. Amati modelling. 'Fairly good work and tone' (W.M.M.).

BOOTH, William (1816–56). Son of the above. Also worked in Leeds. 'Good workmanship superior to that of father' (W.H.).

BOOTHROYD, Norman (*fl.* 1940). London.

BOTHWELL, William (*fl.* 1870–85). Aberdeen. Indifferent work. 'Charged a guinea for each specimen' (W.H.).

BOUETTE, Maurice K. (1922–92). Distinguished contemporary maker and particularly renowned as a teacher and founder of the Newark School of Violin Making (1972). See *Strad* (June 1967), 46; *Strad* (Nov. 1982), 500; Alburger.

BOUETTE, Martin Graham (b. 1951). Son of the above. Trained at Mittenwald and later with J. & A. Beare. Also a distinguished teacher of violin-making. (vL)

†BOULLANGIER, Charles (1823–88). A French immigrant maker working in London from 1856. Generally a very high standard of craftsmanship, but there is some evidence that in

some cases he bought violins from Mirecourt in the white and varnished them. Worked at Charlotte St. and Frith St. in London. P 4/91/120, violin, 1850, £4,840; S 3/91/146, £4,730. His son, also *Charles*, carried on the business for a short time after 1888—also a distinguished maker.

BOURKE, Thomas (*fl.* 1896–1924). Born in Ireland, then worked as a cabinet-maker in London. Made a number of instruments with oil varnish; classic Italian modelling. Exhibited two instruments at the Wembley Exhibition (1924). Highly regarded by W.H.

BOWER, Andrew (*fl.* 1890). Worked at Grangemouth, Scotland. 'Fair success' (W.H.).

BOWERS, Paul Arthur (b. 1946). Newark. Contemporary maker of the younger generation, associated with Newark School. *Strad* (Oct. 1977), 478; *Strad* (July 1983), 211; Alburger; vL.

*BOWLER, Arthur (b. 1867, *fl.* 1900). London. Very highly regarded by W.H. and W.M.M., the latter writing about him in *Strad* (Apr. 1900), 363. He was apprenticed to J. A. Chanot and gathered great experience in restoration work on fine Italian violins. Credited with at least 40 violins of his own, and violas and cellos. 'A rare conjunction of perfect tonal maturity and unimpaired structural solidity' (W.H.). Unfortunately his work surfaces too rarely to make a contemporary judgement, but one well-built cello, sale-room estimate c.£3,000, seen.

BOWMAN, Alfred John (*fl.* 1920). Peckham, London. Pupil of William Robinson (q.v.). Credited with about a dozen averagely conscientious instruments.

BOYER, J. A. (*fl.* 1880). Aberchirder, Scotland. Made about 30 violins as an enthusiastic amateur.

BOYLE, W. F. (*fl.* 1925). Clergyman who made violins at Inniskerry, Ireland, after retirement. Apparently good modelling spoiled by disastrous varnish in most specimens (W.H.). This is a familiar story with the less professional British makers of this time. Boyle was unsuccessful in the use of linseed oil.

BRADDYLL, H. Stanley (*fl.* 1934–c.1951). London. Royal Navy Commander. Credited with several violins, violas, and cellos of 'splendid workmanship' (W.H.).

BRADLEY, E. J. (*fl.* 1921–51). Resident in Shirley, Warwicks. 'Twenty coats of amber varnish' (W.H.). Fair workmanship.

BRAUND, Frederick T. (1890–c.1980). Well-regarded instruments made in Colchester. Learned with F. W. Chanot and credited with over 70 instruments up to 1980. Instruments used by professional orchestral players. See *Strad* (Oct. 1980), 748. P 3/92/61, £462.

BRAY, F. (*fl.* 1930). Middlesbrough.

BRAYSHAW, James (*fl.* 1840–60). Worked in Lancaster.

BRECKINBRIDGE, John (1790–1840). (W.C.H. gives 'Breckinridge'.) Worked in Glasgow. Poet and amateur maker of whom W.H. in particular speaks highly: 'Beautifully made instruments'.

BRETTELL, William Macduff (*fl.* 1920). West Bromwich. Highly regarded by W.H.

BRIDGEWOOD & NEITZERT (Contemporary). A partnership between Gary Bridgewood (b. 1962) and Thomas Neitzert (b. 1959), both Diploma holders of the former London

College of Furniture (now London Guildhall University). They work in London N16. Production to 1994 includes all instruments of the violin family, both in modern and period set-up, Renaissance and baroque viol and plucked instruments, and a few bows.

BRIERLEY, J. (*fl. c.*1900). Birmingham.

BRIGGS, Henry B. Son and successor to the businesss of J. W. Briggs (below).

*†BRIGGS, James William (1855–1935). See text. Born Wakefield, Yorks. of an English Quaker family, educated in Rawdon, W. Yorks., and worked at first from Wakefield but spent most of his working life (i.e. after age 21) in Glasgow. Pupil of William Tarr of Manchester. An important and increasingly highly regarded maker credited with over 300 instruments of all four varieties including a cello made for Pablo Casals. Earlier Stradivari and Guarneri models boldly modified to his own design—violins' body-length often 14³⁄₁₆ in. (363 mm); later instruments often smaller, at 14¹⁄₁₆ in. (357 mm). Gold medal, Leeds Exhibition, 1890 and diplomas at Paris and Vienna. W.M.M. mentions that some of the table wood was obtained from an old church in Warsaw. Briggs also became an experienced dealer, operating on the continent of Europe and acquiring a deep knowledge of classic Italian instruments some of which he copied in facsimile. W.M.M. states (1st edn., 84) that all his work is personal with the exception of the scrolls of his later instruments which were carved by his son Harry (or Henry). However, William Smith, who was Briggs's pupil, believes the Markneukirchen-born Philipp Schreiber, who is known to have worked with Briggs in Glasgow from 1895, with some intervals, made many of Briggs's instruments other than the heads. He used his own golden-brown oil varnish (laid on direct without any sizing), but in W.M.M's 2nd edn. it is implied that he also used Whitelaw's varnish. (Unfortunately instruments are often seen with considerable varnish wear.) Handwritten label: James W. Briggs | Glasgow, 1889. *Strad* (Aug. 1957), 126. S 11/91/161, £5,060; S 11/92/245, £3,080; S 11/92/319, £2,860.

BRISTOW, Daniel. Contemporary maker and dealer of Tetbury, Glos.

BRISTOW, Richard. Contemporary maker and dealer working in George Darbey's former shop in Bristol. Diploma from Welsh School of Violin Making.

BRISTOW, Stephen (b. 1952). Bow-maker of Hill School established in Bicester. Some bows stamped 'J. S. Rameau'.

BRITTEN, David. Contemporary maker of violin family at Northampton.

BROOKFIELD, Edward (*fl.* 1900). Worked with his son at Southport—'some particularly nice violins and bows' (W.H.).

BROUGHTON, Leonard W. Contemporary. Southampton.

BROWN, Alexander (*fl.* 1845–64). Worked in Glasgow. Stradivarian modelling. 'Excellent both in tone and in workmanship' (W.C.H.).

BROWN, Andrew. Contemporary maker of instruments and bows—also restoration. Works in Devon. (vL)

BROWN, Arthur Alan (*fl.* 1946). A bow-maker with Hills.

BROWN, Charles F. (*fl.* 1912–25). Worked at Wakefield.

BROWN, J. (*fl.* 1827–86). Worked at Huddersfield, Yorks. Poor reputation except, perhaps, for double basses. P 3/91/125, £440; P 7/92/45, £440.

BROWN, J. (*fl.* 1855). Worked at Wakefield, Yorks. 'Tone soon wears out and becomes dead' (W.H.).

BROWN, James. There were three generations of makers of this name. The eldest was born in London in 1759 and worked with John and Thomas Kennedy and in Wheeler St., Spitalfields, London. Died 1834. Variable work. His son, born 1786, was apprenticed to his father and then worked in White Lion St., Norton Folgate, London. Taught Lambert who in turn taught Joseph Withers (q.v). Died *c.*1860. Similar work. The grandson worked in London 1833–8. Similar work. S 4/93/45, violin, London, *c.*1820, Hill certificate, £2,300.

BROWNE, John (*fl.* 1728–43). Worked at the Sun in Cornhill, London. Amati–Stainer modelling; often indifferent work. P 3/93/163, 1732, £1,045 + VAT.

BRUCE, A. B. (*fl.* 1920). Credited with 60 violins and 2 cellos to 1924. Worked in Glasgow. 'Sterling workmanship' (W.H.).

BRUCE, Arthur (*fl.* 1900–10). Worked in Belfast. 'Considerable ability and skill' (W.M.M.).

BRUNSKILL, J. (*fl.* 1880–1901). Worked at Berwick-on-Tweed and Newcastle upon Tyne. Highly regarded by W.H.: 'Several Gold Medals at exhibitions'. Stradivari modelling.

BRUNTON, Elliot B. (1949–94). Contemporary maker of Newark School, based in Aylesbury. Trained as restorer at Hills (see text). (vL)

BRUTON, James (1800–62). Worked at Thornbury, Glos. No instruments known.

BRYANT, Percival Wilfred (*fl.* 1920–32). Bow-maker with Withers in London, then at Brighton. Stamped 'P. W. Bryant'. Bows used professionally. See *NGD*.

*†BUCKMAN, George Hutton (1845–1925). Worked in Dover without being financially dependent upon it and had a high reputation in his day. Produced about 50 instruments. Stradivari and Guarneri models. 'The workmanship is accurate and beautifully finished down to the smallest detail.' (W.M.M.) Varnish deterioration now noticeable on specimen seen. P 7/92/83, £308.

BULTITUDE, Arthur Richard (1908–90). Distinguished bow-maker associated with Hill & Sons and William Retford. See text. Had own business in Hawkhurst, Kent from 1961. Credited with nearly 2,000 bows stamped 'A. R. BULTITUDE'. Fine work. See *Strad* (Sept. 1975), 359, *Strad* (June, 1990), 430 (obituary illustrating engraved gold-mounted bow); Alburger; *NGD* C 11/90/207, silver-mounted bow, £660; S 11/90/56, gold and tortoiseshell bow, £1,760.

BURLING, Alfred James (*fl.* 1890–1925). Worked in London. Produced about 40 Guarnerian model violins.

BUTCHER, S. A. (*fl.* 1905). Manchester.

BUTTON (*fl.* 1800–30). Primarily a dealer and associated both with Purday at 75 St Paul's Churchyard, London, and with John Whitaker. Generally associated with violins of the lower class of workmanship. Probably used outworkers.

BUXTON, Henry (*fl.* 1845). Worked at Chester. Indifferent workmanship.

BUXTON, James (*fl.* 1813). Worked in Bristol. Indifferent workmanship.

BYRNE, Leo F. Contemporary maker and dealer at Hoylake, Wirral.

BYROM, George (1870–1928). Primarily a repairer but made a few violins of some reputation. See also his brother John below.

BYROM, John (d. 1929). Brother of George, above, and worked primarily as an outworker for his brother. Some instruments are under his own label and have a good reputation.

BYRON, H. (*fl.* 1800). Worked at Bristol. Fair work. (W.M.M. refers to a Humphrey Byron of similar date working at Oxford on Amati model.)

BYWATER, Henry (*fl.* 1800). Worked at Bristol on Duke model. (W.M.M.)

CAHUSAC family. Business *fl. c.*1755–1800 near St Clement's Church, Strand, London. *Thomas* Cahusac senior ran a general music-publishing and instrument business in the Strand where his two sons (*Thomas* and *William Maurice*) also established a business (at 196 Strand). The Cahusacs very likely used outworkers and were significantly connected to the Banks family in Salisbury. Most instruments are poor commercial specimens of Teutonic build but there undoubtedly exist a few much better specimens. See *Galpin Society Journal*, 41 (1988), 24. P 6/90/445, £660. Piper praises those with Amati outline and attractive varnish and thinks the Cahusacs may also have been actual makers.

CAIN, Nial (b. 1958) and CAIN AND MANN. After graduating with a Fine Art Honours degree, N. Cain was apprenticed to D. Barry Oliver. He went into partnership with *David Mann* (b. 1951) in 1990 at Hexham, Northumberland, Mann also having been a pupil of Oliver. One viola and 11 violins, mainly Strad models with boxwood centre for purfling and high-quality wood, to date. Instruments labelled 'Cain & Mann, Anno 19—, Fecerunt HEXHAM, ENGLAND', in decorative border.

CAIRNS, Peter (*fl.* 1900–20). Worked at Portobello, Edinburgh, and indulged in experiments of modelling and wood.

CALOW family. *William*, the elder, (1847–1910) worked in Nottingham. Specialized in double basses. Fair reputation. Two sons, *Francis William* and *Thomas*, both made in Nottingham *c.*1900. Thomas 'committed suicide by hanging himself from a double bass string in 1905, when only 37 years of age' (W.H.). *Francis William* also has a fair reputation as a violin, cello, and double-bass maker in Nottingham. (There was also a grandfather, *Thomas*, working at Tansley, Derby, 1833–52.)

CANNON, F. C. (*c.*1920). Canterbury. Pupil of Frank Howard. Fair work.

CARR, John (1839–1918). Worked in Falkirk, Scotland. Violins and a few violas, cellos, and double basses. Used Whitelaw's varnish.

CARR, Richard (*fl.* 1920). 'About 20 violins—neat workmanship.' (W.H.).

CARROLL, James (*fl.* 1855–1913). Worked with his son in Manchester. Fair reputation—some violins bearing forged Italian labels (W.M.M.).

CARSWELL, William (*fl.* 1917). Worked in Birkenhead. Unrecorded elsewhere. One specimen seen using bird's-eye maple, but nothing outstanding. P 1/92/50, £154.

CARTER, John (*fl.* 1770–90). One of John Betts's (I) talented employees in London. His own label is from Wysh St., Drury Lane, London—'Violin, Tennor and Bass Maker', though most of his work is labelled as Betts's. Instruments, if in good condition, can be valuable (particularly cellos).

CARTER, William (*fl.* 1930). London. Neat work of good quality. P 3/93/95, £990.

CARTWRIGHT, William John (1836–1919). Worked at Yeadon near Leeds. 'Workmanship of exemplary finish and exactitude' (W.H.). Produced over 1,000 instruments. Tone questionable. (W.H. gives 'Cartright'.)

CARY, Alphonse and Co. (*fl.* 1890). Primarily dealers, London and Newbury.

CASTLE, William. A viola used professionally (see text); no other details known.

CASWELL, Hamilton. Contemporary. Proprietor of large retail establishment (with workshop) in Bristol. Professional double-bass player. See also Irving, Colin.

CAVE, Barry. Contemporary maker working in Warkton.

CHADWICK, John. Contemporary. Hale, Cheshire.

CHALLONER, Thomas (*fl.* 1750). Worked in London. Shows influence of Peter Wamsley.

CHANNON, Frederick William (1862–1946). Worked at Plymouth, London, Byfleet, and Weymouth successively. Has reputation of being one of the finest of his generation of makers in England. Believed to have made all his own instruments by hand (which cannot always be assumed). 'Irreproachable workmanship' (W.H.). Usually Stradivarian modelling, sometimes Guarneri. C 4/91/118, £990.

*†CHANOT family. First 'English' member was *Georges*, son and pupil of the distinguished Parisian maker of the same name. In 1851 he joined Charles Maucotel in London. Established his own business in Wardour St., London, 1858. 'For a considerable slice of the second half of last century, Georges Chanot was almost the only really first-class and properly trained violin maker in this country.' (W.M.M.) Strongly connected to the English 'Renaissance', if such it can be called, not least because he taught Edward Heron-Allen and the latter's famous book on *Violin-Making* is founded on the author's experience under Chanot. Also made bows. His eldest son was *Georges Adolphus* (1855–1923). Established his business in Manchester. Another very fine maker, though some may have been superior 'workshop' products. Gold medals at various exhibitions. Followed classical Cremona modelling. Also bows. The younger brother, *Frederick William* (1857–1911), was a pupil of his grandfather in Paris and worked in London. Three grades of violins made, 20 guineas, 15 guineas, and 10 guineas respectively (W.H.). The third son was *Joseph Anthony* (1865–1936). He succeeded to the family business in Wardour St. and became one of London's highest-regarded experts. Fine violins produced, including copies of Prosper Sainton's 'Pig' Guarnerius (W.H.). Also bows stamped 'J. A. Chanot'. Credited with over 150 instruments. See *Strad* (Jan. 1937), 393 (obituary). Employed Giovanni Gaida (q.v.) for some years before the latter's establishment on his own in 1925. See on this *Strad* (Aug. 1937), 393. His two sons *William Arthur* (1899–1966) and *John Alfred* (1904–81) continued the family business. C 3/90/174, Georges Chanot, London, £1,100; S 11/90/181, G. A. Chanot, Manchester, 1887, £4,180; S 11/90/184, F. W. Chanot, London, 1893, £4,400; S 11/88/83, J. A. Chanot, London, 1922, Voigt certificate, £4,620.

CHAPPELL, Lewis (*fl.* 1900–27). Violin- and bow-maker in London. W.H. particularly praises his bow-making abilities (he learned from James Tubbs): 'equal in balance to any French bow of any period'. He was also an instructor at the short-lived British Violin Makers' Guild in Hampstead, 1915–18, in instrument- and bow-making. (See also Roberts, Albert J., below.)

CHESTER, W. (*fl.* 1640–50). W.H. states that he worked in Watford 1640–50 but no other references are known. Possibly a viol-maker.

CHILD, Francis (*fl.* 1750). Worked in Littlejohn St., Goulden Sq., London—the Hill Archive remarking on the Stainer style. They saw an instrument brought in by the Earl of Wemyss with walnut wood stained and spirit-varnished.

CHILTON, William Hallam (*fl.* 1920). Amateur working at Cricklewood. Copied his John Furber violin.

CHRISTIE, James (*fl.* 1827). Worked in Dundee. Fair reputation.

CHRISTIE, John (*fl.* c.1840). Worked at Kincardine-on-Forth, Scotland. Influenced by the work of Matthew Hardie. 'His work would be excellent if he had used oil varnish.' (W.M.M.).

CHURCHYARD, T. (*fl.* 1800–35). Worked in Devon—produced about 50 violins. A folk-violinist himself. 'Neat workmanship.' (W.H.).

CLARE, Harry (*fl.* 1920). English-born, he worked in Wales (Merthyr Tydfil). Highly regarded by W.H. after whom he named one of his violins.

CLARK, James (*fl.* 1779–1810). A pupil of Matthew Furber. He worked at Turnmill St., Clerkenwell, London. Instruments typical of period.

CLARK, Julian (b. 1937). Contemporary bow-maker of Banbury.

CLARK, William (*fl.* 1800–20). Worked at Exeter. Commonplace instruments.

CLAUDEL, Didier. Contemporary bow-maker. Works in London.

CLOUGH, George (*fl.* 1920). Worked at Blackburn.

CLUTTERBUCK, John (b. 1949). Contemporary bow-maker of the Hill School. Associated with bows marked 'J. S. Rameau' (See also Stephen Bristow).

COAD, Albert (*fl.* 1916–30). Worked in Cornwall at Camborne and Redruth. Highly spoken of by W.H.: 'praiseworthy workmanship'. Influenced by work of Walter Mayson. Instruments labelled, inscribed, and sometimes branded. P 11/88/133, £550.

COATH, Martin (b. 1959). Maker and restorer working at Oxford. Makes in the Cremonese style using his own-recipe spirit varnish.

COCKCROFT, William (*fl.* c.1860). Worked in Rochdale. One very well built and beautifully varnished violin seen dated 18.3.1851. Obviously virtually unknown to W.M.M. and W.H.—identical uninformative entries.

COCKER, Lawrence (1912–82). Much-respected modern maker who worked in Derby. Credited with about 200 instruments and noted perhaps most for his violas. Also made bows using unconventional wood. See *Strad* (Oct. 1965), 195.

COCKMAN, F. C. (*fl.* 1910). Worked in London—experimentally shaped violins.

COHEN, Brian (b. 1952). Professional maker working at Guildford, Surrey. Awarded Crafts Council Bursary, 1986. Charges currently: violins £3,200, violas £3,800, and cellos £7,500 plus VAT.

†COLE, James (*fl.* 1845–92). Worked in Manchester, pupil of William Tarr. Uneven work but at their best his instruments can be quite valuable, particularly cellos. P 9/91/163, cello, £4,180. P 3/92/72, violin, £1,550.

COLE, Thomas (*fl.* 1680). London. Little known. Mainly viols, but violas known of rough workmanship (W.H.).

COLLIER, Samuel (*fl.* 1740–60). London, at Corelli's Head on London Bridge. Stainer modelling.

COLLIER AND DAVIS (*fl.* 1770–80). A firm working in London (No. 7 Fish-Street-Hill, according to the label). Quite rare, but of good repute. 'Fairly flat models of splendid outline' (W.H.).

COLLINGWOOD, Joseph (*fl.* 1725–50). Worked in London at the 'Golden Spectacles', London Bridge. An underestimated maker discussed in the text. Instruments rare, no doubt because of mislabelling.

COLLINS, Glen Alan (b. 1947). Nephew of William Luff and distinguished contemporary. Associated with Newark School of Violin Making. Made a cello for the Prince of Wales (1982). See Alburger; *Strad* (Aug. 1982), 243 (Prince of Wales's cello); *Strad* (May 1984), 24.

COLLINS, H. E. Contemporary. London. Pupil of P. Naismith.

COLLINS, Paul (b. 1963). Trained at Newark, graduating in 1984. Now works in Tollesbury, Essex. Has made 23 violins, 25 violas, and 3 cellos, and his instruments are used in London orchestras and colleges of music.

COLLINS, Roy (b. 1933). Bow-maker in Acton, Sudbury, Suffolk. A pupil of Arthur Bultitude, he has made 189 violin bows, 151 viola bows, 158 cello bows, and 60 baroque and miscellaneous bows.

COLLINS, William Henry (*fl.* 1900). Born in 1860 and worked at 21 Poland St., Soho, London. Produced mainly Stradivari-model violins from 1891. 'Thoroughly good workmanship' (W.H.). 'Beautifully finished throughout, and tone is of very good quality' (W.M.M.).

COLTMAN, Matthew. Contemporary bow-maker, Ealing, London.

COMBES, Malcolm C. Contemporary maker, Portsmouth; first instrument 1958. Another maker who originally used Heron-Allen's book as his sole guide. See *Strad* (Dec. 1968), 314 (viola, 1964).

COMINS, John (*fl.* 1790–1808). Worked in London—pupil of William Forster in similar style.

CONKERTON, E. R. (*fl.* 1920–40) 'Excellent violins and violas' (W.M.M.). Little known, but at least one violin used professionally.

CONWAY, William (& Son), also William (jun.). Father (*fl.* 1736–58) and son (*fl.* 1760–1810), London. Fair reputation.

COOPER, Albert (b. 1913). Best known as a dealer, connoisseur, and author of the monograph on Benjamin Banks and of numerous articles in the *Strad*. Trained as an engineer but started as a luthier professionally in 1947. Resident in Winchester.

COOPER, Hugh William (*fl.* 1893–1920). Made about 100 violins working in Glasgow (75 Dundas St.). Models on Stradivari and Guarneri with Whitelaw's varnish, often craquelled.

COPLEY, Arthur Henry (b. 1903). Bow-maker with Hills. Also made cases.

CORSBY, G. (*fl.* 1850). There seems to be a remarkable disagreement about dates, W.H. giving his working life in London as 1785–1830, and W.M.M. giving 1785–1800. Joseph Pearce, writing in 1866, says 'Now and for a long time a dealer in Violins, etc, in Princes' Street, Soho, London'. Piper states that he employed others to make instruments for him: 'Another Corsby of Northampton made some good double-basses.' This was probably his brother who worked c.1780. George Corsby accumulated a valuable collection of classic Italian instruments auctioned in Jan. 1874. This included a Strad violin, viola, and cello (1700), and cellos by Forster sen., Vincenzo Panormo, Dodd sen., Fendt sen., and Benjamin Banks were also included. (See P. Davidson, *The Violin* (1881), 225). P 3/91/293, unpurfled cello, 1819, £633.

Cox, Gilbert. Contemporary maker and restorer at Brighton.

Cox, Henry (*fl.* 1838). Worked in Dublin. Mediocre reputation.

Cox, Henry (*fl.* 1925). Worked in Hants.

CRAIG, John (*fl.* 1860–1920). Amateur maker in Edinburgh 'but his work is excellent' (W.M.M.).

CRAMOND, Charles (*fl.* 1800–33). Worked in Aberdeen. Indifferent reputation. (W.H. gives 'Crammond'.) W.C.H. states that he emigrated to Canada in 1834 in disgust at amateur competition. Instruments labelled and branded on button.

†CRASKE, George (1795–1888). Worked in various places including Bath, Leeds, Sheffield, Birmingham, Manchester, and Stockport. W.H. credits him with 2,050 violins, 300 violas, 250 cellos, and 20 double basses. Born in Bury St Edmunds, his father having been brought over from the Continent (presumably Germany) as Bandmaster to Duke of Grafton, George Craske was sent to learn the trade from William Forster ('Old Forster') in London and some of his early instruments were made for the retail establishments of Muzio Clementi and Thomas Dodd. London trade during this time (c.1820) being badly affected by contemporary fashion for the pedal-harp (particularly Erards), he removed to Bath. Craske's skill and reputation soon spread and enabled him to study the fine Italian instruments of a few well-connected customers such as Sir Patrick Blake of Langham Hall, Suffolk. Undoubtedly a clever and accomplished workman, particularly fond of 'Joseph' Guarneri models, his large stock passed into the hands of George Crompton of Manchester on Craske's death and then on Crompton's death the residue was marketed by Hills (who published a brochure on him mainly by George Crompton, repr. in 1982). Joseph Pearce, writing in 1866, states that some of his instruments acquired Italian labels, though not through any fault of Craske. His instruments have an equivocal reputation as regards tone, but a number are used professionally. 'Tone generally disappointing' (W.H.). His instruments were made in different qualities and Hills on selling them charged £20, £25, and £30. P 6/91/202, violin, c.1840, £3,300; S 11/92/269, £2,750; C 3/90/228, cello 1830, £4,180.

CRAWFORD, R. C. (*fl.* 1915). Worked in Glasgow. Apparently hitherto unrecorded. P 3/92/38, 1915, (14⅛ in., 357 mm), £770.

CRAY, Philip. Contemporary. See Nework Group.

CREHAN, Kieran. Contemporary. Works in Dublin, Ireland.

CRESWELL, John. Contemporary. Works at Sutton Coldfield near Birmingham on baroque and modern bowed stringed instruments. Prize-winner in Facta Britannia competitions. Also sings bass in a professional choir.

CROFT, W. H. (*fl.* 1871–92). Worked at '16½ Summer Lane, Birmingham'. Violin teacher. Also made violins, violas, cellos, and basses.

CROLL, Peter A. Contemporary maker working in Handsworth, Birmingham. Work not personally seen but one report indicates that it has a high reputation for workmanship and varnish.

CROMPTON, Edward (*fl.* 1870). Work little known but obtained Bronze Medal at Edinburgh in 1886 (vL).

CROSS, Colin (b. 1957). Trained at Newark School (1986–9) and has made to date 15 violins, 5 violas, and 2 cellos. Works in Disley, Cheshire.

†CROSS, Nathaniel (*c.*1689–1751). Worked in London, one of the finest of the old English makers of the first half of the 18th cent. Discussed in text. One label: Nath Cross next door to the George Inn in Aldergate Street, fecit, London, 1731. P 6/91/157, 1725, £3,080. S 6/90/330, cello (Hill certificate), £9,900. P 1/92/110 (violin), £3,080.

CROUCH, John (*fl. c.*1680). The Hill Archive mentions a specimen of this maker from about 1682 in London. The Hills describe the work as being decent and in good style after Amati, but slightly influenced by Stainer. They give the label as 'John Crouch at ye 3 Lutes in Drury Lane Nere Princes Street, London, 1682'. The author knows of no other example.

CROWTHER, John (*fl.* 1760–1810). Said primarily to have been an employee of the Kennedy family. Worked at Haughton St., Clare Market (London). 'Work of average merit' (W.M.M.).

CUMMING, Andrew (*fl.* 1890). Worked in Kirkcolm, Scotland. Made about 50 violins after 1892 (W.C.H.).

CURRIE, A. W. (*fl.* 1958). Liverpool.

†CUTHBERT, Robert (*fl. c.*1690). Early maker of considerable merit—discussed in text. Small Amatese modelling. W.M.M. mentions some specimens influenced by Maggini. Fine varnish. Worked at the 'White Horse' in Russell St., Covent Garden, London. Work rarely met with. Neatly written MS label. The Hills long had in their possession an instrument by this maker labelled 'Made by Robert Cuthbert in Russell Street, Covent Garden, 1690'. They described the work as 'very neat and good. The varnish is pale yellow like the Amatis.' The Hills also saw a cello from the Harp & Crown, Russell St., double purfled, like the work of Barak Norman with 'black–brown' varnish, and which they described as 'very interesting'. The Hill Archive quotes the Daily Courant of 18 May 1714, as advertising Mr Corbett's collection of music and instruments with 'some fine single and double Cases made by old Mr. Cuthbert'. It is not certain, of course, whether the two are the same. There is contemporary evidence that Cuthbert was also a music seller from Russell Street, Covent Garden.

CUTTER, Edwin (*fl.* 1890–1925). Ordinary workmanship with some original features. Resident near Bristol.

DALGARNO, Thomas (*fl.* 1860–70). Worked at Aberdeen. Attributed with about 20 violins and some cellos. Criticized as having the wood too thin, being influenced by Otto's *Treatise on the Violin* (1833). W.C.H. states 'tone is excellent' but other authorities disagree (see W.H., vL).

DALTON, T. (19th cent.). Worked in Leeds. Virtually unknown.

DARBEY, George (1849–*c.*1920). (Also 'Darby'.) Worked at Cremona House, Bristol. A highly regarded maker in his day, both W.M.M. and W.H. comparing Darbey's work with that of the finest French artists of the time. Also made highly esteemed bows. 'He employs no assistants of any kind . . . He has no pupils and no workmen. All the work, including the making of the purfling, the fittings for the bows, etc. is made by his own hands, so that instrument and bow alike, from start to finish, are the handiwork of George Darbey.' (W.M.M.) Orange-red oil varnish used. For some reason his instruments have rarely come on the market recently. S 11/88/349, silver-mounted bow, £330.

DAVIDSON, K. (*fl. c.*1875). Worked at Huntley, Scotland. Few instruments, with a poor reputation.

DAVIDSON, Peter (1834–1901). Worked in Forres (Scotland) before emigrating to USA in 1886. Author of the book discussed in the text on *The Violin: Its Construction Theoretically and Practically Treated*, which was very popular in its time but which, according to W.M.M., is 'a very interesting but wholly unreliable work'. (The book is now very scarce). In a sense he was an amateur, being an excise officer by profession, but he made a number of instruments on the Stradivarian–Guarnerian model of which W.H. speaks approvingly. He was also a composer and player. His importance as a precursor to Heron-Allen is often overlooked.

DAVIDSON, William (1827–1902). Worked at Edinburgh. Large production of instruments on Stradivarian model. One ugly, crude specimen seen. P 7/92/36, £154.

DAVIES, T. (*fl.* 1890). Instruments labelled and branded from Birmingham. One viola seen, 1880, numbered 9, 16⁵⁄₁₆ in., 413 mm.

DAVIES, Vincent (*fl.* 1910). Worked at Erwood (W.M.M.).

DAVIS, A. W. E. (*fl.* 1940). Worked at S. Kensington, London. Guarneri modelling with golden-brown varnish. (W.H.).

DAVIS, Charles John (*fl.* 1895). Worked at Milford Haven. Credited with invention of a new form of bow (vL).

DAVIS, Richard (1775–1836). Associated with the London firm of Norris and Barnes, to which he succeeded on the death of Norris in 1816. This firm employed others to make instruments in its name. See text.

DAVIS, William (*c.*1790–1850). Cousin (W.M.M.) or nephew (W.H.) of the preceding Richard. As the successor in business in Coventry St., London, his employees included Charles Maucotel. Sold business in 1846 to Edward Withers (q.v.). See text.

DAVY, William (*fl.* 1920). Bolton, Lancs. Amateur whose instruments W.M.M. praises tonally. Viola dated 1938 sold P 10/81/32.

DAY, John (1830–1905). Worked in London and one of the more underestimated makers in the standard dictionaries, being misdescribed by W.M.M. He was in fact one of the few distinguished violin-makers of the nineteenth century who were also first-rate players, being a pupil of De Bériot. In 1845 he made his debut with De Bériot's Second Concerto at a Philharmonic Concert in London. In 1847 he became a member of the Queen's Band and played as soloist to Queen Victoria. He was also organist at a London church. (See van der Straeten, *History of the Violin*, ii. 299). His work is now recognized as being in the first rank and is much sought after. He played on a Guarnerius which he copied. Work of this standard gives the lie to the notion that there was a sudden renaissance in the later part of the nineteenth century: John Day was making fine instruments from the 1850s. Possibly his problems have been caused by dubbing him an 'amateur', but the distinction between amateurism and professionalism is meaningless in this context. It has been suggested that some of his work is too close for comfort to that of George Craske! The author, however, implies nothing in the absence of more research. Jalovec states that he always made gifts of his instruments. Label (printed): John Day: Londinii, Mus.Doc | Violinist in Her Majesty's | Private Band. Fecit | anno 1872 No. 25. P 4/91/139 (1884), £2,860; P 7/92/97 (1872, No. 25), £2,530.

DAY, William Samuel (1862–c.1924). Father and son of same name, the son being born 1887. Worked in London and Plymouth. W.H. writes enthusiastically about their work, which includes bows. Little contemporary evidence available. P 6/82/32, £462.

†DEARLOVE family. *Mark* worked at Leeds, 1808–49 (W.H.). Son was *Mark William*, also of Leeds, 1836–76. Exhibited at the Great London Exhibitions of 1851 and 1862. *Joseph Anthony* was the son of Mark William and succeeded to his business in 1876. Mark sen. was associated with Thomas Absam, John Gough, and John Fryer. The work of the family is of average quality for provincial makers of this period and a number of the violins branded 'Dearlove' are thought to have been made by others. Of the family, the work of Mark William is the best regarded. Label: Dearlove and Fryer | Musical Instrument Manufacturers | Boar Lane Leeds. 1836. P 11/88/79 ('good viola' 15$^{3}/_{16}$ in. (385 mm)), £1,045; Mark Dearlove, P 9/92/194, £682.

DEAS, John (19th cent.?). Worked at Lilburn. (See W.H. who mentions flat arching with Stradivarian outlines.)

DEIGHTON, J. R. Worked at Newcastle upon Tyne. Nothing known. (See W.H.)

DELANY, John (*fl.* 1795–1812). Worked in Dublin. See text. Small Amati models.

DELUNET, Auguste Léon (1867–1939). A Mirecourt-born and trained employee of Hills for 33 years when he set up on his own in Norwood, London, having worked for a short time in Canada and New York. Mainly an expert restorer but made a few good imitations.

DENNIS, Jesse (1795–1860). Worked in London, mainly for Matthew Furber.

DE SOUZA, Cosmo (*fl.* 1903). Worked in Birmingham (vL).

DEVEREUX, John (*fl.* 1850–1920). Worked in London with B. Simon Fendt until emigrating to Melbourne, Australia, in about 1864. Best known in Australia for his double basses.

DEVIS, William (*fl.* 1760). London. Watchmaker by trade. Stainer–Tyrolese modelling typical of this time. W.H. suggests some instruments relabelled as made by Klotz.

DE VONEY, Frank (*fl.* 1900). Travelled widely but mainly worked at Blackpool. Made many instruments 'on an original model, strongly built but rather roughly made ... They have a powerful but rather harsh tone.' (W.M.M.) Wrote a book on *The Acoustics of Violin Making* (Edinburgh, 1893). Emigrated to USA C 4/91/150, £176.

DEWARS, William. Born at Brechin, Scotland 1878 but emigrated to USA. 'Very promising' (W.M.M.). Stradivari and Guarneri modelling.

DICKENSON, Edward (*fl.* 1760). Worked 'At the Harp and Crown in the Strand | Near Exeter Change | London' according to the label. Stainer modelling of poor reputation.

DICKENSON, Henry (*fl.* 1900). Made several double basses at Burton-on-Trent.

DICKESON, John (1725–*c.*1780). Worked in London and Cambridge—Amati-pattern instruments with a good reputation but rarely seen. Sometimes also 'Dickson'.

DICKIE, William (*fl.* 1880). Worked at Rotherham.

DICKSON, George (*fl.* 1910). Medical practitioner working in Edinburgh. 'The maker of the beautiful amber oil varnish' (W.M.M.).

DICKSON, John. See under Dickeson.

DILWORTH, John Edwin (b. 1954). Trained in the Newark School and worked for some time with J. & A. Beare in London. Highly regarded, not least for his many scholarly contributions on distinguished makers of various nationalities in the pages of the *Strad*.

DINWOOD, P. (*fl.* 1900). Worked in Glasgow. One cello seen, with marquetry inlay.

DIPPER, Andrew John (b. 1949). Pupil of Central School of Art and Design in London, has also worked in Cremona. Also a writer, particularly on the classical Italian school.

DITTON (*fl.* 1700). The only reference to this maker seems to be as one of the instruments in the estate of Thomas Britton (see text).

DIX, David. Contemporary maker who has been working in London since at least 1960. Good violins and violas known.

DIXON, Alfred Thomas (*fl.* 1920). Established in Kent and Sussex. Mainly a violinist and teacher. P 3/90/198, £484.

DOBBS, Harry (1916–76). Commenced making only in 1960 on a self-taught basis. Made over 100 instruments (mostly violas) with considerable success. Worked at Peopleton, near Evesham, Worcestershire. See Alburger. P 9/91/93, £638.

*†DODD family. One of the most prominent bow-making, instrument-making, and dealing families in London at the turn of the 19th cent. See text. The earliest was *Edward*, *c.*1705–1810, who moved from Sheffield to London and flourished as a bow-maker. Most of his bows are unmarked. He had three sons, John, James, and Thomas. *John* (1752–1829) is widely regarded as the finest bow-maker in England before the Tubbs family and as the English 'Tourte'. W.M.M. refers to his frequent bacchanalia bringing many troubles on his head and causing him to descend into shoddy workmanship to pay the bills. His bows are slightly shorter than Tourte's. There are many testimonies to the strength, balance, and elasticity of these bows which often have ivory frogs with 'DODD' stamped on the frog or stick. He is said to have cut the sticks to the required sweep straight out of the block without bending by heating. Unfortunately many ungenuine and comparatively worthless products are also so stamped. Despite some help from wealthier friends he ended his days in the workhouse. He worked at Kew, near London. *James* was also a distinguished bow-maker and died in 1857. *Thomas* (*fl.* 1786–1820) is best known as an instrument-maker and dealer in London. He in fact made few, if any, instruments himself but had the perspicacity to employ John Lott (sen.) and Bernhard Fendt. Thomas acquired a deep knowledge of Italian instrument-making and prided himself particularly on his varnish. His label ran 'DODD, Maker | 92 St. Martin's Lane | Perfect copies of Stradivarius | Amati, Stainer & C. Note—the only possessor of the recipe for preparing the original Cremona oil varnish. Instruments improved and

repaired.' Thomas Dodd also went into the harp and piano market. *James* Dodd (II) was the son of James Dodd (above). He was born in London in 1792 and died there 1865. With his brother, another *Edward*, he ably continued the Dodd family bow-making tradition. He also used the stamp 'J. DODD'. See *NGDI*. P 4/91/155, Thomas Dodd, fine violin, c.1810, £11,000; S 6/90/365, Edward Dodd, ivory violin bow, c.1780, £1,650; S 11/91/68, John Dodd, silver-mounted violin bow, £770; S 6/90/228, James Dodd, gold and tortoishell violin bow, c.1850, £2,200.

DODDS, Edward (*fl.* 1817–96). Produced about 300 instruments working from 1 Charlotte Place, Edinburgh. Work seen is pretty in the French manner—very un-Scottish. W.H. makes some deprecatory comments.

DOLMETSCH, Arnold (1858–1940), workshop current). This maker and his well-known family of Haslemere specialized in early musical instruments made 'authentically' long before this became fashionable. Some fine instruments have emerged. Violin no. 23 reached by 1931; see P 93/12/152, £897.

DONALD, W. (*fl.* 1870). Scotland. One instrument seen thus branded.

DORANT, William (*fl.* 1800–26). Worked at Spitalfields, London. Ordinary work.

DOYLE, Paul. Contemporary. Violins and viols. Galway, Ireland.

DUCKWORTH, Frank Stanley (*fl.* 1925). Worked in Blackburn, Lancs. Respectable work.

DUFF, William (1810–92). Worked at Dunkeld, Scotland. Crude work.

DUGLHEY, John (*fl.* 1760). Worked at Leicester. Poor reputation.

†DUKE, Richard (*fl.* 1750–85). See text. It is uncontroversial to say that Richard Duke deserves his reputation as one of the finest of English 18th-cent. violin-makers, though the exceptional enthusiasm that his work elicited in the 19th cent. has not persisted into the latter half of the 20th. This is probably because, as with most English makers of the 18th cent., the tone, though pleasant, round, and even, can lack brilliance and power. He also ran a retail business and employed workmen. Nevertheless, the fine craftsmanship which this maker shows at a time when this quality was not particularly evident in London is extremely creditable. Duke adopted anglicized versions of the Stainer and Amati models, occasionally venturing into approximate copies of the Long Strad. Typical good quality English varnish of the period, normally of a deep brown colour. Considering his eminence, it is surprising that so little is known about his life. Modern opinion suggests that he may have been a pupil of Wamsley or Thomas Smith. He certainly had distinguished pupils, teaching Joseph Hill, John and Edward Betts, and his son *Richard* (*fl.* 1768–90) whose ability was not comparable to his father's. Duke also made violas of an experimental variety and cellos, sometimes of a quite small pattern. Writers over the years have frequently warned of the numerous cheap imitations of 'Duke' instruments. Many copy the brand 'Duke, London' which the maker put under the button on the back. W.H. suggests that 'Duke' alone identifies the forgery. Many of such instruments were German trade copies. Label: Richard Duke | Maker | Near opposite Great Turnstile | Holborn, London | 1769 (and others). (Jeremy Bentham, the early 19th-cent. philosopher, owned a Duke violin.) See *Strad* (Aug. 1972), 162; *Strad* (Mar. 1994), 249; *NGD*. S 3/91/145 (1763), Hill certificate, £3,850; P 11/92/100, £3,080; Richard Duke jun. P 6/91/165 (1777), £2,090.

Duke, William (*fl.* 1730). Worked at Holborn Bars, London. Possibly father of Richard (W.H.).

Duncan, George (*fl.* 1880). See text. Worked in Glasgow. Emigrated to Canada 1892. Fine reputation in his day, and his instruments can still command considerable respect. Obtained Gold Medal in London, 1885. Made about 40 violins in Scotland before leaving, 'all of them of the highest standard of excellence' (W.M.M.). S 6/91/36 (Glasgow, 1888), £2,090; S 11/91/323 (Glasgow, 1891), £2,530.

Duncan, James (*fl.* 1920). Resident at Kirkcaldy, Scotland. After 1919 indulged in a number of experimental models, claiming in 1951 the 'world's best-toned violins' (W.H.). This claim does not seem to have been substantiated.

Duncan, James (*fl.* 1900). Worked at Cluny, Aberdeenshire. Specimen seen suffered from varnish deterioration. Solidly made instruments about which W.H. is quite enthusiastic. P 7/92/38, £330.

Duncan, Robert (*fl.* 1760). Worked in Aberdeen. Highly arched, ordinary work.

Dunlop, Alexander (*fl.* 1890). Worked in Broxburn, Scotland. 'Excellent Strad modelling' (W.H.).

Dunthorne, John (*fl.* 1790). East Burg, Suffolk. Work of plain wood and ink-purfling variety. (Not mentioned in other dictionaries.)

Dyke, John (Contemporary). Trained at London College of Furniture. Has made a number of good instruments including 2 cellos.

Dyker, George (*fl.* 1910). Worked in Forres, Scotland. Credited with about 40 violins and several cellos. Stradivarian model. 'Workmanship perfect' (W.H.).

Dykes, Arthur W. (*fl.* to 1950). Ultimate proprietor of the firm of Dykes & Sons at Leeds (see below). Important contributor to the *Strad*. See *Strad*, (Apr. 1976), 887, a comprehensive assessment (Robert Lewin).

*Dykes, George Langton (1884–1922). Worked in Leeds and London, son of *Harry* Dykes, of Dykes and Sons, 84 New Bond St., London; pupil of Paul Bailly. According to W.H. made 'exactly corresponding' copies of Cremonese and other Italian models; also instruments of the viol family. 'A born artist' (W.M.M.). Vannes admits to an error in saying that he came to Mirecourt and Paris (as does W.M.M.). Father of Arthur Dykes, above. Well known as an expert in his day. W.M.M. was sufficiently impressed to dub him the 'High-Priest of Fine Art'.

Ealing Strings. See under Sadler, Malcolm.

Earl, David J. (d. 1983), Bow-maker, formerly with Hills, self-employed from 1981. Worked at Greenford, Middx (vL).

Edwards, David Van. See under Van Edwards.

Eglington (*fl.* 1810). Worked in Drury Lane, London. Little known.

Eisenman, H. (*fl.* c.1890). Worked in London. Neat work and well-varnished instruments; varnish has proved durable. Rather stereotyped work, perhaps, but not to be despised. Labelled as from London. P 9/92/130, £550.

Elliot, William (*fl.* 1910). Worked in Hawick, Scotland. Credited with over 100 instruments by 1920. Highly thought of by both W.M.M. and W.H. 'The work of this artist is bound to come to the front.' (W.M.M.) P 6/90/108 (1910), £1,430: P 6/91/246 (1914), £506.

EMERY, Julian (b. 1940). Contemporary maker. Worked in Sussex and Wilts. and currently Aberystwyth, Dyfed. Originally inspired by Heron-Allen's book and so taught himself, learning by trial and error. See Alburger. To date made about 110 violins, 90 violas, and 50 cellos.

EMPSALL, John K. (*c*.1860–1910). Amateur violinist who experimented with varnish, earlier instruments being bought in in the white. Worked in Ben Rhydding, Yorks.

ENGLAND, Rex. Contemporary. Violas used professionally (see text); no details known.

ERVINE, Robert (*fl.* 1893–1925). Worked in Belfast. Stradivari modelling quite well thought of by W.H.

EVANS BROS. (*fl.* 1920). Apparently two brothers who built violins on the Guarneri model. Worked at Shildon, Co. Durham.

EVANS, David. Contemporary. Trained in Miltenwald. Known for his teaching of violin-making and proprietorship of Sydney Evans Ltd., an old-established Birmingham business specializing in the supply of violin-making wood, tools, and accessories, as well as instruments.

EVANS, Isaac Probyn (*fl.* 1910). Worked at Merthyr Tydfil, Wales. A cellist who made a few instruments on Amati or Guarneri modelling.

EVANS, John Michael. Contemporary. Clwyd, Wales.

EVANS, Richard (*fl.* 1750). Worked first in Anglesey and then in London. Made *crythau* (Welsh folk stringed instruments), harps, and a few violins.

EWAN, David (1838–1912). Worked at Cowdenbeath, Scotland. Formed and wrote Scottish dances and made over 100 violins and 20 cellos. Instruments branded. Variable work.

EXCELL, Dominic Andrew (b. 1955). Works in Brighton. Pupil of Newark School (vL).

EYLAND, Robert (b. 1951). Works in London specializing in lutes and gambas.

EYLES, Charles (1844–*c*.1925). Wangford and Bournemouth, etc. Credited by W.H. with about 200 'hobby-specimens', based on Guarneri in the main. 'The violin I saw and tried was beautifully made, and had a wonderfully bright, sweet, and pleasing tone.' (W.M.M.)

EYLING, Thomas (*fl.* 1810). Gloucester. Amatese modelling. 'Instruments doomed to be shelved' (W.H.).

FAHERTY, Martin. Contemporary. Works in Cork, Ireland.

FAIRFAX, Andrew (b. 1953). Studied at the Newark School and in Holland. Associated with the firm of J. & A. Beare in London. Specializes in restoration. Also wife, *Anneleen*, maker and repairer. (vL)

FALKNER, Arthur (*fl.* 1920). Worked in London. Not listed elsewhere. S 3/91/66 (viola), London, 1923, £770.

FALLOWFIELD, Frank. See under Rushworth & Dreaper.

FARQUHARSON, Ian (*fl.* 1920). Worked in Edinburgh. Poor work.

FARRELL, William James (1870–1926). Worked in London (Farrell & Co., 181 Caledonian Rd.) before emigrating to Australia. Greatly interested in experimentation, he is the subject of a long encomium by W.H. Wrote a book *The True-Tone Violin* (1921). Such contemporary evidence as there is does not seem to support W.H.'s enthusiasm. He was certainly not afraid of unorthodox wood (including Australian native timber) and bold experimentation.

FAWCETT, James (and Sylvie). Contemporary. Diploma with Distinction from Newark School. Works at Eye, Suffolk.

FEAR, Harry (*fl.* 1900). Worked at Handsworth, near Birmingham. Indifferent work.

FELL, William James (*fl.* 1900). Worked in Caledonian Rd., London. 'Especially good tone. Splendid woods.' (W.H.).

†FENDT family. Discussed in text. Founder was *Bernhard*, born in Innsbruck, Tyrol, 1776, thought to have been the nephew and pupil of François Fent of Paris. Arrived in London and worked for Thomas Dodd in 1798 (with J. F. Lott). From 1800 employed by John Betts. Dodd was thought to have applied the varnish on Fendt's instruments. 'Nearly all the Amati models of John Betts owe their creation of fine contour to the ingenuity of Fendt.' (W.H.) Double basses have particularly fine reputation. His instruments are not labelled. Clearly important in the transfusion of a more sophisticated Italianate style into London making at the turn of the 19th cent. His son *Bernhard* (or Bernard) *Simon* (1803–52) 'was as clever and ingenious a workman as ever handled gouge and calipers in this country, and, in my opinion as unscrupulous as he was clever. He made scores of counterfeited "Strad's" and "Joseph's."' (W.M.M.) This maker was amongst the first to start the London industry of clever imitations of Italian masterpieces. It was obviously what the market wanted. But as is the case with John Lott, Fendt's instruments are normally also of excellent tonal quality. Some instruments labelled—e.g. 'Bernard S. Fendt, junr., 1831'. These instruments are valuable. Fendt went into partnership with *George Purdy* (Purdy & Fendt) from 1832 onwards. Bernhard's second son, *Martin*, (1812–45) was also an excellent workman associated with Arthur Betts. Bernhard's third son was *Jacob* (1802–49), apprenticed to his brother Bernhard Simon and employed by Davis of Coventry St., London and others. He became well known for his splendid copies of Italian master violins with all the appearance of age and fictitious labels. 'In some respects the best maker of the family.' (W.M.M.) *Francis* (*fl.* 1850), the fourth son, produced undistinguished work in London and Liverpool. *William* (1833–52) was the son of Bernhard Simon. Despite his youth, he produced very talented work. S 6/89/III, violin *c.*1830 of Jacob Fendt (Hill certificate), £7,700; P 9/91/160, cello, London, *c.*1830, £14,300; S 6/90/275, viola, Bernard Fendt, 1833 (Hill certificate), £9,350.

FERBER, N. (1805–15). According to W.H. (the only reference known to this maker) rather good instruments with Stradivarian modelling, pretty wood, and good tone.

FERGUSON, R. (*fl.* 1840–48). Worked in Aberdeen. Indifferent work.

FERGUSON (or FERGUSSON), William (*fl.* 1815). Worked in Edinburgh 'showing much of the style and artistic refinement of Perry of Dublin' (W.C.H.). Violins and cellos.

FERRIER, William (*fl.* 1880). Worked in Dundee. Mainly a photographer; poor reputation.

FIDLER, Joseph Charles (*fl.* 1920). Worked at Reading. Guarneri modelling with own oil varnish (W.H.).

FINDLAY, James (1815–96). Worked at Padanaram, Scotland. Credited with between 400 and 500 violins usually of crude workmanship and plain wood. 'Findlay was a capital violin player ... in Strathspey playing especially, hard to beat, and was much in request at country gatherings and balls.' (W.C.H.) Interesting because he illustrates the ability of Scottish makers in particular to knock up work quickly to meet local demand for dancing purposes.

FINGLAND, Samuel (*fl.* 1890). Resident in Glasgow. Indifferent reputation.

FIRTH, George. Father and son of this name. Father (*fl.* 1840) worked at Leeds and son (*fl.* 1880) at Bradford. Both produced very ordinary work.

FIRTH, Thomas George (*fl.* 1920). Pupil of William Robinson and worked at Plumstead, London. Fair reputation.

FISHBURN, Ralph E. (*fl.* 1920). Worked near Durham, a coal-miner and somewhat eccentric. Experimented as a result of claimed spiritualistic communication with Stradivari. (A number of British makers made similar claims, all with fairly disastrous results.)

FISHER, George (*fl.* 1820). Cheltenham. W.M.M. praises a specimen's tone.

FISHER, Leslie H. (b. 1903). Worked at Wallasey, Cheshire. Apprenticed at Rushworth & Dreaper, Liverpool, under Richmond Bird. Gave instruments female names, e.g. 'Ruth Sarah' (1930). (Not in W.H.)

FISHER, William, A. (*fl.* 1925). Worked at Erdington, Birmingham—Stradivarian modelling.

FIVAZ, Charles F. (*fl.* 1880). Worked at Islington Common, London. W.H. points to graceful design and neat finish with well-cut scroll picked out in black. Little is known of this maker but his work seems to be much appreciated. P 11/91/132 (1892), £5,429.

FLECK, William (1852–1914). Worked at High Wycombe where he had been a medical practitioner. Used Stradivarian–Guarnerian modelling for violins, violas, and cellos which have a good reputation. His wife, *Ethel*, varnished some of her husband's instruments and made on her own account. 'The workmanship is beautiful and delicately finished.' (W.M.M.)

FLETCHER, Joseph (*fl.* 1820). Worked at Hitchin, Herts. 'Good tone' (W.M.M.).

FLEMING, John (*fl.* 1818). Worked at Saltcoats, Scotland. Oil-varnished Stradivarian models. Name branded.

FLEMING, Michael. Contemporary. Working in Oxford. Also viols.

FORBES-WHITMORE, Anthony. Contemporary. Working in Harrogate, Yorks.

†FORD, Jacob (*fl.* 1780–95). Worked in London. See text. Generally regarded as following mixed Stainer/Amati models. His workmanship maintains a high reputation. Carefully chosen wood. Moulded edge is beaded with the purfling immediately before rise of the moulding of the edge. A wide inner strip of white wood is sandwiched between two narrow strips of black (rather than the usual three strips of roughly equal thickness). This is a feature of many English violins of this period (though by no means unique to them). The Hill Archive has some quite extensive notes on Jacob Ford, a maker regarded by the Hills as underestimated. They point out that he appears to have taken Amati as his model and that the finish of the edge and purfling is quite delightful. The wood on the backs is English sycamore, the curl being a very small figure and, as a rule, very prettily marked. 'The tone of a good Ford is of excellent quality and is fairly brilliant . . . a fine and original English maker.' Ford was in fact known to Arthur Hill's grandfather who had been heard to say that he was a gentleman's servant and lodging-house keeper. Few instruments were thought to bear his own name. 'The total number

of Ford's instruments known to us is certainly under 50.' The Hills mention that Sir William Hamilton had one labelled Omobono Stradivari, and many Fords have sailed under Italian labels. The Hills saw two labels printed, one from 'The corner of Davies Street and Barkeley Square, London' and the other from 'South Street, Grosvenor Square, London' with only the date being in manuscript. The Hills also thought Ford worked for Thompson's at St Paul's Churchyard. See *Strad* (Dec. 1954), 254 (with illustration of instrument *c.*1780). W.H. gives a label as 'Jacob Ford | Maker | London, 1792'. P 6/90/172 (attrib.), £2,860.

FORD, William (*fl.* 1924). Worked in Sunderland. Followed a not untypical pattern of being a joiner initially but under the inspiration of Heron-Allen's book started violin-making. Used varnish by Harris of Gateshead. 'Commendable designs and workmanship' (W.H.).

FORREST, E. (*fl.* 1924). Worked at Bradford.

FORRESTER, Alexander (*fl.* 1946). Worked at Fauldhouse, Scotland.

*†FORSTER family. See extensive discussion in text. One of England's outstanding violin-making families. The oldest was *John* (1688–1781). Started as a maker of spinning-wheels and guns at Brampton, Cumberland. Rough and unfinished workmanship. His son *William* (1714–1801) also made spinning-wheels and made violins at Brampton on the Stainer model. No great reputation. William's son, *William* (1739–1808), known as 'Old Forster', probably the greatest maker of the family and 'one of the greatest of all the old British makers' (W.M.M.). He made the move from Brampton to London in 1759 struggling initially, and his label gives an idea of the range of his achievements: 'William Forster | Violin, Violoncello, Tenor, and bow-maker | Also Music Seller to Their Royal Highnesses | The Prince of Wales and Duke of Cumberland | opposite the Church, St. Martin's Lane, London | N.B. The above instruments are made in the best manner | and finished with the original varnish, | and a copy of every Capital Instrument in England may be had | William Forster'. Thorough fine-quality work and brilliant marketing, soon became very fashionable. Particularly magnificent cellos, as discussed in the text. Variable model, but usually broadly Amati influence. Cellos with red varnish now more favoured than those varnished dark amber, the latter being initially preferred. Normally date and number are written in ink under the tail-pin. Some instruments branded internally, and/or signed, e.g. on bottom rib. The third *William*, 'Young Forster', was the son and pupil of his father. He was born in London in 1764 and died in 1824. His work is more erratic than his father but his best instruments were of some quality. Sometimes labelled 'William Forster Junr . . .'. His music warehouse was at 41 Lisle St., Leicester Sq., London. *Simon Andrew* (1801–70) was the son of William (III) above. He learned from his father and from Samuel Gilkes. His workmanship is not regarded as particularly good. 'All his work that I have seen reflects little or no credit upon the great name of Forster.' (W.M.M.) This verdict is clearly too harsh. He was also joint author with William Sandys of the still important book *History of the Violin*, (1864). P 4/91/207, cello by William (Old), £24,200; P 11/92/310, cello, body-length 29 in., 735 mm, *c.*1790, £20,900; S 3/90/196, violin by William (Young), 1796, £5,500; C 4/90/232, cello by Simon Andrew, £9,900.

FOSTER, George. Contemporary. Walsall, Staffs.

*FOUCHER family. Many dictionaries, including Henley, are confusing about this family. Only Vannes appears to be reliable on this point. The founder member was *Georges*, a French luthier born in the first half of the 19th cent. He was a partner in 1866 of the firm Haynes, Foucher & Co. in London, dealers with a good trade in Mirecourt instruments. He became Hon. Sec. of the College of Violinists and his published works include a short Treatise on the *History of Construction of the Violin* (edns. 1894, 1897, etc.) There were two sons, *Georges* (II), of whose work little is known, and *Felix* (b. 1888). Felix enlisted to fight in the Great War in 1916 and was killed in France in Aug. 1917. This was a tragedy since in his short life he is thought to have made over 250 violins and 2 cellos. 'The workmanship, more especially of his later instruments, is beautiful, evincing the artist mind and the trained hand in every turn of the chisel and gouge.' (W.M.M.) Morris discusses 'a magnificent copy' of a Gagliano and another 'exact copy' of a B. S. Fendt. Although it has not been suggested elsewhere, part of the explanation of the large output may stem from the family connection with Mirecourt makers, from whom in some cases Felix may have had some help. His instruments bear number and date on label.

FOWERS, Herbert (*fl.* 1900–25). Worked at Draycott, near Derby. Made violins, violas, and cellos on Stradivarian modelling with ruby-brown oil varnish (W.H.).

FOX, Isaac (*fl.* 1880–c.1905). A mystery here—W.M.M. states that he worked at 4 Upper Bridge St., Canterbury, primarily as a gun, etc. manufacturer but made violins and violas to 'a high standard of excellence'. W.H. gives him as working at Canterbury (New Zealand). There is agreement that he was born in Loath, Lincs., in 1856.

FOX, Joseph (*fl.* 1855–64). Worked in Leeds.

FOX, Richard (*fl.* 1920). Worked in London 'making violins during leisure time' (W.M.M.).

FRANCIS, Thomas Richer (*fl.* 1880). Mendlesham, Suffolk.

FRANKLAND (*fl.* 1776–95). Thought to have been a pupil of one of the Forsters and to have worked for 'young Forster' and at Robin Hood Court, Shoe Lane, London. 'Ordinary work' (W.M.M.).

FRETWELL, George H. (*fl.* 1910). Romney Marsh.

FRIESEN, Lydia Brigitte (b. Canada 1955). Worked with father Heinrich Friesen (who was trained at Moscow Conservatoire and Mittenwald) and graduated from Newark School of Violin Making in 1985. Worked in New York with Jacques Français and René Morel before becoming established in Cambridge with Jonathan Woolston (q.v.). Has made violins, violas, and cellos; also restores instruments.

FRYER, John Charles (*fl.* 1820). Worked in York and Leeds, becoming partner of Mark Dearlove. Similar work. P 3/93/323, cello signed on inner back, York, 1820, £4,840.

*FULLER, Henry (*fl.* 1910–29). Worked at Plaistow, London on the Stradivarian–Guarneri model, with a smaller one for ladies. 'Careful workmanship' (W.H.). Poidras indicates that he was self-taught and applied a varnish varying from gold-brown to red-brown. Used a manuscript label with the number of dots indicating the number of the instrument. A handsome instrument is reproduced in pl. xxvii of Poidras' work.

FULTON, Henry (*fl.* 1890–1915). Worked at Liverpool, making violins and cellos. W.M.M. obviously saw 'a very well made violoncello'. Nevertheless, reputation somewhat ordinary.

†FURBER family See text. An important family of violin-makers in London. *David* appears to be the founder, flourishing 1760–80 in London and stated to be a pupil of John Johnson (W.M.M.). Stainer modelling. His son *Matthew* died in 1770—'very little of his work is known' (W.M.M.). Matthew (I) had 3 sons. The oldest was *James*, probably not an actual maker. *Matthew* (II) was the second son (1780–1831) and is credited with 'a large number of instruments, some of which are very good' (W.M.M.). One label runs 'James and Matthew Furber, Clerkenwell Green, London, 1796' (MS). The third son was *John* (*fl.* 1810–45), pupil of his father and of John Betts. He was the most distinguished maker of the family and copied the Grand Amati model and the 'Betts' Stradivari when that was in the possession of Betts. 'His work is excellent in every respect.' (W.M.M.) Worked at '13 St. John's Row, Top of the Brick Lane, Old St., Saint Luke' (London), and at Cow Cross, Smithfield and Turnmill Street, Clerkenwell. W.H. refers to the 'sometimes pronounced grooving near the edge', and 'golden red varnish'. His instruments are also often branded on bottom rib or on linings. John's son and pupil was *Henry John* (1830–*c.*1868) who also made a large number of instruments on the classic Italian model. Hart, his contemporary, states that he has made several excellent instruments, 'and maintained the character for good workmanship which has been associated with the name of Furber for upwards of a century'. W.M.M. disagrees: 'I cannot say that I like his instruments very much ... perhaps it has not been my fortune to see the best of them.' There was also a *William*, genealogy not known, who worked in London 1820–40. 'Violins of the third-rate order' (W.H.). The most recent member was *Henry* (genealogy not known), who worked as a violin, cello, and double-bass maker at 185 Euston Rd., London, 1872–88 (W.H.). W.H. speaks well of neat workmanship, choice of wood, and reddish-orange varnish. Also made big violas. It can be seen that the family were essentially copyists and some of John's work no doubt appears under Betts labels. This leads to auctioneers attributing a number of instruments to the Furber family, either because they are unlabelled or because of the economic history of the family. P 6/91/269, cello, John Furber, London, *c.*1830, £6,380; violin, John Furber 1836, some worm restoration, £935; S 3/91/166, violin, Matthew Furber, London, *c.*1820, £3,190; S 6/90/329, cello, Henry Furber, London, 1886, £5,060; S 11/89/593, cello, Matthew Furber, London, *c.*1800 (Hill certificate), £12,100.

FURLOUGH, Henry (*fl.* 1800–26). Worked at Bath—fair reputation.

FURNOW, Walter (*fl.* 1790–1810). Worked at Cheltenham—Stainer modelling with a much exaggerated arch (W.M.M.).

GADD, Joseph J. (1895–*c.*1950). Started repairing in 1910 and took up his work again after serving in the Air Force between 1915 and 1919. Mainly a repairer, but with a good reputation for his violins after Guarneri, Maggini and Nicolo Amati. Used an oil varnish. Exhibited at The Hague, 1949, his first instrument dating from 1942. Worked at Brough, E. Yorks. Label includes signature. (See Vannes and W.H.).

GAIDA, Cesare (b. 1902). See next entry.

GAIDA, Giovanni (1862–1939). We can hardly claim this maker to be in any way British since he was born at Bollengo (near Ivrea), but he spent much of his working life in London, mainly working for F. W. Chanot. Many instruments bearing an 'F. W. Chanot' label were made by Gaida but varnished by Chanot. He also worked for the London firm of Dykes & Sons. In some of these instruments Gaida's initials 'G.G' are found on the label or branded inconspicuously inside. Naturally, the work is Italian in quality and highly regarded. S 3/90/167, *c.*1920 (Guivier certificate), £6,820; S 3/90/347, 1908, £8,800; S 4/93/16 London, *c.*1910 (Hill certificate), £8,050. See *Strad* (Mar. 1972), 490. There were 2 sons, *Cesare* (above) and *Silvio* (below), both of whom made a few instruments of good quality. Cesare Gaida, S 11/91/188, 1930 (Hill certificate), £7,150.

GAIDA, Silvio (1899–1952). See preceding entry.

GAMBLE, Ernest (*fl.* 1880–1920). Worked at Leicester. Thought to have put his own label in Saxon factory instruments. A son, Howard, continued the business (W.H.).

GARDEN, James (*fl.* 1880). Worked in Edinburgh. W.H. says 'made fine violins and a viola', whereas W.C.H. probably more accurately states 'made *five* violins and one viola on the Stradivarian model'.

GARDINER, Pearson (*fl.* 1758–90). An interesting and little-known maker working in London after the Amati modelling of Duke. W.H. speaks well of tonal qualities. There was one in the 1904 Exhibition discussed in the text. 'P. Gardiner' branded internally and externally, and occasionally labelled.

GARDNER, Charles (*fl.* 1868–95). Worked in London—ordinary work.

GARNER, Hugo (*fl.* 1860–84). Worked at Chelsea, London. Ordinary work.

GARNER, Joseph (*fl.* 1820). A few ordinary violins.

GASKIN, George H. (1856–1913). Worked at Bromley, Kent, primarily as a policeman. In his lifetime obtained considerable distinction for his instruments, one being endorsed by the violinist Jan Kubelík. Also won Gold Medal at Crystal Palace Exhibition. S 11/88/279, small violin, £319.

GAY, Wilfred (*fl.* 1905–15). Worked at Bristol, pupil of Henry Lye of Camerton. 'Several excellent instruments' (W.M.M.).

GEARY, William George (*fl.* 1920). A pupil of W. B. Prince of Tooting and rated by W.H. as a violin- and bow-maker 'adding to the lustre of London's roll of honour'.

GENTLE, Roland (1931–86). Distinguished Cambridge bow-maker and teacher. See *Strad* (Aug. 1986), 227, obituary.

GIBBONS, Arthur William (b. 1914). Up to 1959 had made 4 violins which 'owing to fine tonal quality ... were sold as soon as completed' (W.H.). Pupil of W. J. Piercy, himself an experienced former employee of Messrs Hills. Worked at Skeyton, near Norwich.

GIBBS, G. W. (*fl.* 1920–8). Worked at Hendon, London, and Wisbech.

GIBBS, James (*fl.* 1820). London. Employee of Morrison, Corsby & Gilkes in the early 19th cent. No separate instruments known.

*†GILBERT, Jeffery James (1850–1942). See text. Son of another Jeffery Gilbert of Kent who also made violins and cellos, this maker worked at Peterborough and is credited

with over 350 violins, some 40 violas of varying measurements (but, particularly, large ones), and about 12 cellos. One of the most distinguished English makers of his generation. He was helped by experts and connoisseurs of the period, particularly Charles Reade, George Hart, Dr John Day, and George Withers, but was essentially self-taught. Gilbert told W.M.M.: 'Every instrument that is worthy of the name has individuality and a temper all its own, and must be studied as you would a child, if you would form a thing of beauty that will sing with the voice of melody.' Though he worked on an original model, the length of body is usually 14 in. (317 mm) and Gilbert used a varnish which W.M.M. describes as 'brilliant, elastic and transparent, the colours ranging from light amber to a very deep and rich red. It is, of course, an oil varnish but not linseed nor any other heavy oil, which destroys all that is good in colour' (W.M.M., quoting Gilbert). Gilbert won a number of prizes including a Gold Medal at the International Exhibition, Edinburgh in 1890. According to W.H. used Czechoslovakian sycamore for his backs. W.H. states that the number of the instrument is placed at the back of the neck under the fingerboard and also on the upper block inside. Poidras states: 'the scrolls are particularly well carved and the soundholes recall those of Stradivarius. The ample and free tonal quality of his instruments is due, partly, to a tender varnish varying from light amber to dark red.' His instruments have stood up quite well to the test of time, though prices have not appreciated as one would have expected from these descriptions. There are three stringed instruments of his in the Peterborough City Museum—see Clifford Bevan (ed.), *Musical Instrument Collections in the British Isles* (Winchester, 1990). Instruments labelled and autographed. P 4/91/73, 1898, £1,210; C 4/91/90, viola, £1,980; C 3/90/208, viola, 1919, £2,420. S 6/89/73, cello, 1928, £3,300; S 4/93/14. viola, 16¹/₁₆ in. (407 mm), Peterborough, 1905, £1,840.

GILCHRIST, James (1832–94). Worked in Glasgow. See text. Highly thought of in his lifetime and undoubtedly fair work, with typical length of back 14³/₁₆ in. (360 mm). Made about 90 violins, violas, and cellos reputed to have a strong and brilliant tone. Label: James Gilchrist | Rothesay, 1886. A specimen at P 9/92/97 sold at £495; S 4/93/19, Glasgow, 1889, £782.

*†GILKES, Samuel (1787–1827). One of the most distinguished makers of the first part of the 19th cent. in London. Initially worked for William Forster and some of his labels run 'Gilkes from Forster's . . .'. A reputation for fine acoustical wood and responsive tone. He is related to the maker Charles Harris and was his pupil. About 1820 he made Amati and Stradivari copies—'excellent in every way' (W.M.M.). Worked as from '34 James Street, Buckingham Gate, Westminster' (thus labelled) and may be branded inside and on bottom block. Some poorer instruments for dealers are attributed to him. P 4/91/141, 1820, £6,600.

GILKES, William (1811–75). Son of Samuel, worked in London. Regarded as not achieving the quality of his father but was particularly successful with his double basses. These are often on the Brescian model with double purfling. Instruments often branded and name sometimes spelt 'Gilks'.

GILL, Lovett (*fl.* 1920–30). London. Architect by training. Credited by W.H. with 30 instruments reaching a high level of design and workmanship.

GIRVAN, Thomas (*fl.* 1865–1900). Worked in Edinburgh, producing about 20 violins on the Stradivarian model. Poor tonal reputation.

GLADSTONE, Robert (*fl.* 1870). Worked at Newcastle upon Tyne but thought to be French or German products (W.H.).

GLENDAY, James (*fl.* 1870). Worked at Padanarum, Scotland, of the school of James Findlay (q.v.). Credited with about 20 violins on the Guarnerian model—work rough and commonplace according to W.C.H.

*GLENISTER, William (1850–*c*.1936). Worked in London, 1887–1936, producing about 70 instruments. Has a high reputation amongst early 20th-cent. English makers. 'Capital workmanship' (W.H.). W.M.M. cites him as being 'only an amateur' (as does Jalovec) but this has no meaning where a large number of violins, violas, and cellos were made and advertised for sale in music papers. Glenister was as professional as anyone else. Towry Piper in the *Strad* (June 1915), 49, wrote that 'so far as tone is concerned these instruments will bear comparison with any new fiddles I have tested in recent years, one of the white examples, made in 1914, being quite remarkable for the beauty and quality of its tone'. Glenister has maintained his reputation in today's market conditions, but not everyone will be over-impressed by the sometimes 'squashed' scroll and some specimens seen suffer from varnish deterioration. Obituary with portrait: *Strad* (Sept. 1936), 216. S 11/90/190, 1905, £1,760.

GLOAG, John (*fl.* 1900). Worked at Galston, Scotland. Stradivarian modelling of fair reputation.

GODLIMAN, Martin (b. 1949). Contemporary maker having been trained at Hill & Sons. Established on his own since 1977 at London. 1978, viola obtained a prize at Newark. Has made over 120 instruments, including cellos, violas d'amore. See *Strad* (Aug. 1981), 268; Vannes; vL.

GOFTON, Robert (*fl.* 1854–90). Credited with 30 good-toned violins from Whitby, Yorks. P 3/90/108, £715.

GOLD, Joseph J. (*fl.* 1940). Brough, E. Yorks.

GOLDSMITH, Melvin (b. 1968). Grandson of Charles Archer. Works at Chelmsford, Essex. To date has completed 25 violins, 13 violas, and 3 cellos.

GOLDSMITH, William (b. 1908). This maker also sometimes signs his labels 'William Smith'. He was a pupil of J. W. Briggs at Glasgow where he worked for 16 years before moving to Chelmsford and Braintree, Essex. 'Fine maker and repairer of violins'. (W.H.). Also father of Bernard Gregor Smith, cellist of the Lindsay Quartet, who prizes one of his father's cellos.

GOODMAN, James (*fl.* 1850). W.M.M. mentions a maker of this name at Brentford.

GORDON, Hugh (*fl.* 1850). Irish maker born at Stoneyford and worked at Belfast. Died 1854. 'Commonplace workmanship' (W.H.).

GORDON, M. E. (b. 1910). Physician and surgeon who worked in Plymouth, his profession being one where violin-making often seems to be a serious hobby. (In fact he won First Prize at the Doctors' Hobbies Exhibition In London, 1958.) This labels him as an 'amateur' but 'probably finest Amateur Maker in England today.' (W.H.). But since his instruments show evidence of high market values for their time, little significance attaches to this apparent stigma. Credited with 14 instruments up to 1958—Strad modelling with red, gold, and golden-brown varnish. 'Careful and neat workmanship ... Powerful and clear tone' (W.H.). Also made good-sized violas (16⅝ in. (422 mm)). Instruments labelled and branded externally and internally.

Goss, Philip (*fl.* 1890). Worked in Plymouth, Devon. No. 33 dated September 1887. See P 6/94/97.

Gothard, F. (*fl.* 1860–95). Worked at Huddersfield, Yorks. Ordinary workmanship (W.H.).

Götting, Christoph (b. Wiesbaden, Germany, 1948). Apprenticed at Violin Making School, Mittenwald (1964–7) and worked in London for J. & A. Beare 1969–74. Also obtained Gold Medal, Bayerische Handwerkskammer, Mittenwald (1974). Now self-employed in Romsey, Hants. Specializes in copies of a Stradivari instrument of 1705 and intends also to make violas and cellos. Instruments used professionally.

Gough, John (*fl.* 1845–70). Worked at Thornbury, Glos. Very little known about him, but W.M.M. finds some evidence of his being a distinguished maker. W.H. says 'violins visually rather attractive, but very poor tone'.

Gough, Joseph. London, 1816 (Davidson, *The Violin*, 238).

Gough, Walter (*fl.* 1820–40). Worked at Leeds—poor reputation.

†Goulding & Co. Name of a dealing firm in London 1785–*c*.1800 and thereafter to mid-19th cent. as Goulding, D'Almaine & Co. The consensus of opinion is that all instruments were made for the firm and Vannes states that for the most part such instruments had a German or French provenance. The firm certainly traded with Mirecourt and Saxon producers. But some instruments look more typical of fairly ordinary or sometimes good-class English work of the period. W.H. refers to good-class instruments generally having golden-red varnish. 'Goulding London' is branded under the button. In fact Sandys and Forster state, apropos of Thomas Kennedy, that after his retirement in June 1849 'he was much employed by Messrs. Goulding, D'Almaine & Co., and other music houses' (p. 353); also, possibly, Henry John Furber. See text. P 4/91/242, £330; P 9/92/55, £638; S 4/93/420, cello, 29 in. (737 mm), London, *c*.1800, £2,990.

Graham, R. (*fl.* 1910). Learned violin-making in Carlisle. Little known but W.H. says 'admirable designs and workmanship'. Worked at Cadoxton.

Grater, Thomas (1843–*c*.1925). Worked mainly in Birmingham, being an enthusiastic violinist himself. 'Copied classic Italian models, violins and cellos which he sold for £10 and £15 respectively—modest prices.' (W.H.) P 2/90/274, £968.

Gray, J. (*fl.* 1813–22). Worked at 51 South St., London, his instruments having a fair reputation.

Gray, John (1862–1950). Worked at Sunderland. Another maker inspired by Heron-Allen's book. Made about 20 violins and a few violas. Fair reputation.

Green, Miranda Karol (b. 1947). Contemporary maker working in Harwell, Oxon. Studied at London College of Furniture under Patricia Naismith and was Director of Welsh School of Violin Making. Instruments from Cardiff labelled 'Miranda Karol | Luthier | Cardiff | 1983' (vL).

GREENWOOD, George William (1885–?1930). Worked at Rochdale, Lancs., being a pupil of T. E. Hesketh at Manchester. 'Perfection of finished workmanship pervades the entire structure.' (W.H.) 'Workmanship . . . magnificent' (W.M.M.).

GREGSON, Robert (1871–?1920). Worked at Blackburn, Lancs., with a short period at Montreal, Canada. Credited with about 100 instruments of Stradivarian modelling. Label: Arte et Labore | Robert Gregson | Blackburn | Anno 1913.

GRICE, John (*fl.* 1700–40). Thought to have worked in London and Edinburgh. An interesting maker discussed in text and about whom little is known. Henley suggests that he might have been one of the first to adopt a Stradivarian model, but no evidence of this has been seen. An instrument labelled 'Made by John Grice in Antwarpen From London 1743' was sold in 1990—P 3/90/147, £550.

GRIFFIN, William (*fl.* 1925). Worked at Blackheath, London, somewhat experimentally.

GRIFFITHS, A. V. (*fl.* 1910). London. Good reputation (W.M.M.).

GRIME, Harold (*fl.* 1900–20). Worked at Accrington, Lancs. 'Ordinary workmanship' (W.H.).

GRIMES (19th cent.). Worked at Sherborne. Little known.

GUASTALLA, René Michel Bruno (b. 1957, Paris). Trained in France before becoming a partner in Oxford Violins, Oxford. About 20 instruments to 1994, modelled closely on classical examples.

GUITON, R. (*fl.* 1900). Worked at Cork, Ireland. 'An excellent amateur who has made several beautiful violins on the models of Stradivari and Guarneri' (W.M.M.).

GUNTER, Henry (*fl.* 1850). Scarborough. Poor reputation.

GWYTHER, Henry (*fl.* 1830–50). Worked at Gloucester and mentioned only by W.M.M.: 'Rather rough work, but tone very fair'.

HAINSWORTH, Charles (*fl.* 1920). Norwich.

HALES, Hubert Sidney (1873–1946). Coventry. Theatre and opera violinist who mainly repaired but made a few indifferent violins.

HAMBLETON, Joseph (*fl.* 1850). Worked at Salford, Lancs. Indifferent reputation.

HAMILTON, William (*fl.* 1890). A Scottish engineer who worked at Uddingston making violins and also violas on the Gasparo da Salò model. 'Well finished workmanship' (W.H.). Used Whitelaw's amber varnish.

HAMILTON, W. T. R. (*fl.* 1900). Worked at Edinburgh.

*HAMMETT, Thomas (1872–?1930). Worked at Plumstead, London, from 1923. Good reputation for his carefully crafted instruments. Button crowned with ebony. 'Well chosen wood of splendid figure' (W.H.). Labels are in hand-done Gothic lettering with name and date. Initials are engraved near the soundpost and filled with black wax. Used Millington's varnish. P 11/90/173, 1924, £638.

HAMMOND, John (1870–*c.*1950). Worked in West Burton, Wensleydale, Yorks. A Heron-Allen addict whose living came mainly from farming but who produced about 25 instruments by 1950.

HANCOCK, George (1851–?1920). Stoke-on-Trent. Classified as 'amateur' but as usual this is misleading. Produced at least 20 instruments which both W.M.M. and W.H. describe as being of fine workmanship. Classic Italian modelling.

*Hancox, Arthur James (*fl.* 1920–30). Worked at Deddington, Oxon. Fair work.

†Handley, Henry (1839–1931). Worcester's finest maker, continuing his trade well into his old age. An enthusiastic violinist and said to have been a 'friend' of Sir Edward Elgar (W.H.). He certainly knew Elgar, repaired his violin and those of the Elgar family's shop in Worcester. Handley had a workshop in the Lychgate, near the Cathedral, which was unfortunately demolished in the redevelopment of this area in the 1960s. Worcester disappointingly has no memorial of this interesting citizen, but there are a few surviving photographs. Handley spent much of his time repairing and restoring but he made 105 violins, 10 violas, and 1 cello up to 1927 when he retired. His date of death is queried in other directories. It was in fact 9 Oct. 1931. His instruments vary in quality somewhat. His violas, from the sample seen, are heavy and over-wooded. His violins show considerable individuality at their best, sometimes having unusual purfling patterns (but without exhibitionism). Whilst he mainly copied the Italian classical makers, he used his imagination and designed instruments in the English tradition. In some cases he had problems with the varnish which never really dried. However, there are many satisfactory instruments amongst his output, undoubtedly entirely handmade by him and with a good, durable varnish. The tone is certainly acceptable for orchestral purposes and can be quite powerful. His better instruments should be ranked in terms of value with those, say, of Job Ardern—that is, just below the best makers of this time but as serious instruments which should appreciate. Obituary in *Strad* (Nov. 1931), 388. Label: Henry Handley | Fiddle Restorer and Maker | Worcester | 1919. No. 101. (W.H.).

Hansell, Roger. Contemporary maker and dealer at Leyburn, N. Yorks.

Harbour, Jacob (*fl.* 1760–90). Worked at Duke St., Lincoln's Inn Fields, London, and Holborn, London. Violins have poor reputation, but his cellos, though scarce, are regarded as better, as are his viols.

Harbour, William (*fl.* 1764–99). London. Brother of Jacob. As with his brother, used very highly arched models for his violins with ugly varnish. Violas regarded as much better.

Harday, Henry (18th cent.). London. Nothing known.

Hardie, Alexander. Two makers of this name, father dying in 1852 and son dying in 1890, both working in Scotland. The father's instruments may be branded 'Hardie Maxwelltown'. The son worked at Galashiels. Stainer and Amati modelling.

Hardie, James (I) (*fl.* 1830–56). One of two violin-makers of this name, he worked in Edinburgh and is not related to other makers of the same surname. 'Very good work' (W.M.M.). Label: James Hardie fecit | Edinburgh, 1839 (neat calligraphy) (W.H.).

Hardie, James (II) (1836–1916). Established with his three sons in Edinburgh as one of its leading musical businesses. Educated at university in Aberdeen and initially became a schoolmaster. Violin making was in his blood, being the second son and pupil of Peter Hardie. Credited with over 2,000 instruments which he claimed to have made with his own hands assisted only by his sons. W.H. particularly praises his instruments on the Maggini model, duly double purfled and sometimes ornamented on the back. Gold Medal at International Exhibition, Edinburgh, 1890. There appear to have been forgeries of his work, though since he produced two new instruments every week

(W.M.M.) which, in his own words, were 'rattled up in haste, and sold for a few shillings, to keep the pot boiling', his work is uneven in quality. W.H. warns against copies of German or French origin. Label: James Hardie & Sons | Makers | 117 Nicholson Street, Edinburgh (and others) (W.H.). P 2/90/100, £455.

HARDIE, John (*fl.* 1875). Another worker of this surname at Edinburgh. Good reputation.

*†HARDIE, Matthew (1755–1826). See text. Working at Edinburgh from 1796 he is often termed the 'Scottish Stradivari'. He came to a sad end, being buried in the pauper's part of the churchyard of Greyfriars' church—his grave duly being identified by the indefatigable Meredith Morris. W.C.H. suggests that part of the problem was economic—his business was already being adversely affected by the importation of cheap German fiddles. He was confined to Calton gaol for debt where 'it is even said that he made some of his best violins' (W.C.H.). W.M.M. rightly laments that Scotland's finest maker is not more properly remembered. Comparable perhaps to Benjamin Banks but basing his work on Stradivari in the main, though occasionally Amati, the work has survived well. His instruments are much sought after, though, as indicated in the text, the work is somewhat uneven. 'The Hardies' ... varnish is a spirit one, yellow in colour or faded to pale brown, but not a very hard one, and so thinly laid on that the tone is not materially hampered by this covering.' (W.C.H.) 'In his best instruments the workmanship is very fine. The scrolls ... have the stamp of genius upon them. The buttons are usually longer and more oval than those of Amati or Stradivari. The soundholes are just a fraction short, but are of good outline and clean-cut. The margins are moderately full, but the edges might be slightly stronger than they are. The modern taste has improved upon that of the old makers in respect to the strength of the edges.' (W.M.M.) Label: MADE BY | MATT HARDIE, EDINBURGH | 1810 (and others). The last two figures of the date are handwritten. P 4/91/171, Edinburgh, 1815, £3,740; P 6/91/167, cello, Edinburgh, 1822, £9,350.

HARDIE, Peter (1775–1863). Went to Edinburgh University and then studied under his cousin, Matthew Hardie. Also skilled violin-player, learning with Niel Gow (see text). Higher arching than Matthew Hardie and neat purfling. 'The tone is usually large and mellow.' (W.C.H.) 'Tonal quality often nasal, seldom really mellow' (W.H.). 'P. Hardie' stamped below the button.

HARDIE, Thomas (1802–56). Son of Matthew Hardie. For one apprenticed to such a good maker at the age of 10 great things would be expected, but the general consensus is that this maker's instruments are usually tonally disappointing. He needed a quick turnover and is thought to have had an ineradicable whisky-drinking and laudanum-taking propensity, the cause of his falling down the stairs of his house and dying from his injuries. Charles Reade's novel *Christie Johnstone* (1850) contains a character 'Thomas Harvey', a man of great ability but broken and debased through drink and stamped in the direst poverty, based (according to W.C.H.) upon Thomas Hardie. He is said to have baked his wood to get quick but ephemeral results. Label: Thomas Hardie | fecit | Edinburgh | anno 18 . .

HARDING, Phil. Contemporary maker at Newent, Glos.

HARDWICK, John Edward (1886–*c*.1964). Pupil of George Wulme-Hudson, working at

Ashted, Surrey. Credited with over 100 violins by 1964, some with elaborate decorative work. See *Strad* (May 1964), 19.

HARDY, B. (*fl.* 1820). Worked at Pocklington, Yorks.

†HARE, John (*fl.* 1680–1725). See text. Stainer modelling and his work generally has a poor reputation. Label: John Hare at ye Viol and Flute | near the Royal Exchange | in Cornhill, London. 1704 (W.H.). See *Strad* (Dec. 1986), 574 (John Dilworth).

HARE, Joseph (*fl.* 1700–33). Son of John—see text. As Joseph Pearce says, writing in 1866, this maker 'is said to have been the first in England to introduce the flat model'. Certainly a more interesting maker than his father John and one prepared to experiment, probably having seen good Italian models. Those seen are usually quite highly arched but do show the influence of northern Italy rather than of the Tyrol. Various labels, some as per John Hare, another at ye Golden Viol in St Paul's Churchyard, London, and another 'at the Viol and Hautboy over against Urchin Lane in Cornhill, London, 1723'. The Hill Archive and an extract from the *Daily Post* of 26 July 1728 make it very clear that Joseph Hare was the son of John Hare, the father dying in about 1725 and Joseph dying in 1733. The business was carried on by Elizabeth Hare and then John Simpson. (See also discussion of Daniel Parker in text.) P 4/91/169, £1,540.

HARFORD, Patrick (*fl.* 1750). Mentioned by W.H. as working in Dublin 1730–52 with instruments indicating Rome or Cremona origins, attractive with clear Tyrolean brown varnish. Very scarce.

HARGRAVE, Roger Graham (b. 1948). Works in Bremen, Germany. One of the most eminent of the middle generation of contemporary English makers, using fine-art techniques to make uncannily accurate facsimiles of classical Italian models (as mentioned in the text) as well as 'straightforward' instruments. He was taught at the Newark School 1976–9 and subsequently became connected with the Hills in London for two years before moving to Machold's in Bremen to specialize in high-grade restoration work. His instruments bear multiple brands, some in hidden places, but may also have convincing facsimile labels. He has won many prestigious prizes and has contributed a number of scholarly articles on the Amatis and similar topics to the *Strad*. His lectures and answers to questions at the Sixth Tiverton Violin Conference (1992) on the techniques and ethics of the copyist were published by the *Strad* as part of the Conference Proceedings and repay careful study by those interested in the making and varnishing techniques involved. See also *Strad* (June 1986), 116 and, generally, vL.

HARHAM (or HARKHAM) (*fl.* 1760–90). London. Indifferent work.

HARLOW, Frank. Contemporary (2nd prize Cremona Triennale, 1979). Working at Sheffield. See *Strad* (Oct. 1983), 394.

HARRILD, Paul V. Contemporary. Working at Newark on Trent, Notts. Member of Nework Group.

†HARRIS, Charles (I) (*fl.* 1780–1825). Though employed as a Customs House officer, a truly professional maker with a high reputation. One of the first English makers to adopt flatter modelling as standard, based loosely on Amati and Stradivari. Inevitably, some of his instruments were passed off as Italian in subsequent years. He rarely used a label but his signature may sometimes be found written in ink inside. He worked at

Cannon Street Row, Ratcliffe Highway and 69 Parsons St., Ratcliffe, London. The Hill Archive suggests that he worked in Oxfordshire in the latter part of his life, like his son (below). Some players say that his models were too flat to be tonally completely satisfactory, but this must be a matter of opinion. An article in the *Strad* (Aug. 1970), 150, states that 'his violoncellos especially are among the finest ever made here'. Much of his work appears to have been done for the 'trade', and this may have been a rare example of a maker exporting instruments abroad, perhaps exploiting business connections made in his job. He employed Samuel Gilkes as an apprentice and assistant, and also his son Charles (with whom W.M.M., amongst others, appears to confuse him). The author and maker Peter Davidson had an 'excellent specimen' of this maker. Davidson states: 'The archings of the backs of his violins are formed in a peculiar manner, with a deep undulation or scoop all round the inner parts from the indenting; the bellies, or tables, are generally made from wood of good quality. Some of his violins have the backs made of rosewood, others of walnut etc.' One violin 'possessed a delicacy and fullness of tone seldom or never obtained in the old instruments of common-place English makers' (Davidson, *The Violin*, 241).

HARRIS, Charles (II) (*fl.* 1791–1851). Eldest son of the above, he worked with his father and then with John Hart in London. Much of his work dates from the period when he moved to various places in Oxfordshire: Adderbury, Steeple Aston, and Woodstock. He does not have the excellent reputation of his father, but nevertheless many of his instruments are well-made and attractive affairs. Auction particulars sometimes fail to discriminate between the two makers. William Ebsworth Hill worked with him at the start of his (Hill's) career. The Hill Archive states that Harris was more interested in being regarded as a man of property and Lord of the Manor of Steeple Aston than a violin-maker, and so he and his apprentice, W. E. Hill, had a fine time of it. (The Hill family obviously thought sufficiently highly of the Harris family to choose them as apprentice-masters.) Charles Harris, jun. died impoverished—he was not a man of business—in Oxford in 1851. P 6/91/120, Adderbury, 1819, £840; P 11/91/206, cello, Woodstock, 1817, £4,840. NB It is not clear whether these instruments come from father or son. The general assumption is that instruments labelled from Oxfordshire are the work of the son.

HARRIS, Griffith (*fl.* 1810–40). Ordinary workmanship emanating from Swansea, Wales.

HARRIS, John Edward (1860–1951). Pupil of Georges Chanot in London, but most of his work comes from Gateshead-on-Tyne from 1908 onwards. Credited with over 200 violins of excellent workmanship. W.M.M., writing *c.*1920, states that he used the Strad model of handsome wood, well made and beautifully finished. 'Tonal quality always very responsive, often quite brilliant' (W.H.). Brought out his own special varnish preparation, sold at 4*s.* per bottle. Widely used by other professional makers at the time. Labels as from Nile St., Gateshead, with number, model, and date.

HARRIS, Nigel (b. 1939). New Zealand-born contemporary maker, credited with 40 violins, 10 violas, and 6 cellos to 1986. Given as working in Wells, Somerset (vL).

HARROD, Jack (*fl.* 1880). Worked at Burton-on-Trent—average merit.

HARROD, Robert (*fl.* 1760–1820). Worked in St Peter's Churchyard, Exeter, and in London. His work is said to resemble that of Richard Duke (W.H.). W.M.M. states that he worked in Oxford (possibly confusing Exon with Oxon).

*HART family See text. The founder was *John Thomas* (1805–74) who established the firm of Hart & Son in Princes St., Leicester Sq., London (later Lower Wardour St.). He was apprenticed to Samuel Gilkes but made few instruments, 'though excellent of their kind' (W.H.). Piper writes: 'John Hart and Georges Chanot I of Paris, were in their day the most renowned judges of fiddles in Europe, and the former was instrumental in forming some of the more notable collections of violins that have ever been brought together.' (186) His son *George* (1839–91) also became an expert of the highest eminence and wrote *The Violin, Its Famous Makers and their Imitators*, for long a standard work of reference. He was himself a good musician, learning the violin under Sainton and also the piano. George's son, also *George* (1860–*c.*1931), followed in the family tradition and became a very successful dealer and maker from 28 Wardour St., London. He employed workshop makers, trained in either France or England, who were responsible for the instruments labelled 'Hart & Son', and the Voller brothers (q.v.) were used as outworkers. Very high standards were imposed and all these instruments are sought after. Also bows with an excellent reputation. George (II) was succeeded by his son *Herbert* (1883–1953) who was also thought to have bought in instruments made by the Voller brothers, probably the cleverest copyists of Italian work in England this century. The firm closed in 1939. (*NGDI*, W.H., and Piper) S 11/336/91, George Hart, London, *c.*1860, £3,520; P 3/91/113, Hart & Son, *c.*1890, £1,980; S 11/90/35, Hart & Son, 1926, £3,080.

HART, Harold J. (*fl.* 1945). Exeter.

HARVEY, Ernest (*fl. c.*1890). An amateur maker who worked in Penarth, Wales. Italian modelling and though W.M.M. says 'of very good workmanship' modern opinion does not seem to endorse this verdict. P 7/91/219, £308. He had two sons, *E. Victor* and *Eugene*, both of Dinas Powis, and mentioned by W.M.M. as makers.

HARVIE, Robert (*fl.* 1850). Worked in Berwick-on-Tweed. Excellent modelling but pedantic workmanship according to W.H.

HARWOOD, J. A. (*fl.* 1920). Worked at 59 Oban Rd., Newcastle upon Tyne.

HASLAM, Dr W. D. (*fl.* 1900–12). Worked at Croydon, Surrey. Another doctor who took up violin-making with some success. 'Workmanship quite up to the standard of the best professional work' (W.H.). Strad modelling, a few being 'imitation old'.

HAWKINS, John J. (*fl.* 1800). Worked in London on an experimental model without sides or back—'utterly absurd innovations' (W.H.).

HAXTON, George (1878–*c.*1925). Worked from Glasgow and made about 70 instruments. 'Excellent modelling after Stradivarius, but mostly after Guarnerius' (W.H.). Fair reputation. P 3/93/41, 1910, No. 9, £605.

HAY, James (*fl.* 1920). Worked from Guildford. Trained as an engineer but credited by W.M.M. with 'several lovely instruments'.

HAYNES, H. (*fl.* 1900). According to W.M.M. and W.H., made a large number of violins from Malvern and Southsea on the Guarneri model. Concentrated on tone rather than appearance.

352 APPENDIX I

HAYNES, Jacob (*fl.* 1745–55). Worked in London—commonplace Stainer modelling.

HAYNES, W. (*fl.* 1900). One instrument seen numbered 37 of 1897 from 14 Grays Inn Rd., London.

HEALE, Michael (Contemporary). Works in Guildford, Surrey, specializing in viols with exotic wood and other baroque instruments.

HEAPS, Alfred Walker (1854–1906). Emigrated from Leeds to Sydney, Australia, in 1876 where most of his work was done.

HEAPS, John Knowles (*fl.* 1840–55). Worked at Leeds and was prone to experimentation which appears to have got him nowhere.

HEARNSHAW, Francis (*fl.* 1870–96). Worked in Nottingham.

*HEATON, William (1827–1905). Worked from Hill Top, Gomersal, near Leeds. Credited with over 200 instruments and a few cellos of Italian modelling 'some of which reached a high standard of excellence' (W.M.M.). Prices in 1900: violins, £12–£15; cellos, £20–£30. See *Strad* (July 1900), 140; *Strad* (Oct. 1905), 203. P 7/91/46, 1896, £528; S 11/92/255, 1897, £220.

HEBDEN, Herbert (*fl.* 1905). Worked at West Green, London. Moderate praise from W.H.

HEESOM, Edward (*fl.* 1750). London. High Staineresque modelling. Instruments labelled and branded.

HEFFER, Michael (b. 1929). Works in Cambridge—taught in the Welsh School of Instrument Making and has produced 10 violins, 6 violas, 4 cellos to date. Certificates of merit for professional violin and viola tone, Facta Britannia, 1982.

HEMMINGS, George. See under Rushworth & Dreaper.

HENDERSON, D. G. (*fl.* 1890). Worked in Edinburgh. 'Beautiful work; Strad model; pale red varnish . . . sweet, mellow tone' (W.C.H.).

HENDERSON, John (1842–?1920). Worked on retirement as an engineer as a professional maker at Broxburn, Scotland (W.M.M.).

HENLEY, Joseph (*fl.* 1920). Worked in Wednesbury, Staffs.

HENLEY, William H. T. (*fl.* 1924). Amateur working in London. 'Several passable violins' (W.H.).

HEPPLEWHITE, Lionel Karl (b. 1936). Contemporary violin-maker and restorer who is also a competent player (and formerly a government scientist in acoustics research). His instruments are used by professional players. He first made a violin in 1955 and recommenced in 1974, obtaining a Diploma for viola tone quality at the Newark Competition in 1978. Selected by the Crafts Council of Britain in 1982 for inclusion in their Selected Makers Index. Output to date is approximately 12 cellos, 20 violas and 82 violins. He works in Malvern, Worcs. See *Strad* (Sept. 1978), 406. His son, *Michael Anthony Hepplewhite*, (b. 1961), also makes.

HERON-ALLEN, Edward. See under Allen.

*†HESKETH, Thomas Earle (1866–1945). See text. One of the most highly regarded violin-makers of this era in England. He worked in Manchester, from 1891. He is one of the comparatively few British makers of this time who did a proper apprenticeship, namely five years with G. A. Chanot from 1885. He favoured primarily Guarneri and less often

Stradivari modelling with violas also of classic Italian modelling. Paul Voigt worked for him in Manchester before establishing his own workshop there in 1905. Hesketh's instruments throughout his output maintain a sound reputation for careful and aesthetic build combined with fine tonal qualities. P 3/90/99, 1929, £2,860. P 11/91/108, 1935, £4,840; P 3/93/187, 1933, £4,620.

HEWITT, A. W. (*fl.* 1895). Worked at Shanklin, Isle of Wight. 'Satisfactory workmanship' (W.H.).

HEWITT, John (1733–98). Feltham, Middx. Clergyman and graduate of St John's College, Cambridge. He also made some Stainer-influenced violins which W.H. suggests might have received foreign labels later on.

HICKS, George Herbert (*fl.* 1910). First worked with G. A. Chanot in Manchester but made about 60 Stradivari-influenced violins from 1910. 'Successful in every detail of workmanship' (W.H.). Worked in Oxford. Label: G. H. Hicks | Violin and Violoncello Maker | Oxford.

HICKS, H. W. (*fl.* 1910). Early 20th-cent. maker working in Bromsgrove. 'Very good workmanship' (W.H.).

HICKS, Johnson (*fl.* 1877). Worked in Torquay, Devon. Very high praise from W.H.: 'We can designate no other English productions of the same period more worthy of approval.' His work is largely unknown today.

HIGHFIELD, Ian K. (b. 1946). Originally trained as architect and sculptor. Works in Birmingham and has made 127 instruments to date, including 6 basses and some gambas. Uses his own brand of oil-based varnish. Instruments used professionally.

*†HILL family. The full discussion in the text will not be repeated here. The major makers of England's most distinguished family of violin- and bow-makers were: *Joseph* (1715–84) who was apprenticed to Peter Wamsley of London. Especially renowned for his cellos, and his instruments are of the Amati–Stainer variety in vogue at this time; *Lockey Hill* (1756–1810), again one of the best London makers of this period; *Henry Lockey Hill* (1774–1835), probably the finest maker of all the Hills and employed by John Betts for many years. He was one of the first London makers to adopt the Stradivari model which became more fashionable in London at this time; and *William Ebsworth Hill* (1817–95), whose scarce but excellent work is fully discussed in the text. In 1880 the firm of *W. E. Hill & Sons* was established in Wardour St., and then from 1887 in New Bond St., London, first at No. 38 and in 1895 at No. 140. The firm has a world-wide reputation not only for its instruments but also for its bows coming from the firm's workshop mainly in Hanwell London (from 1890), but more recently (since 1974) from Great Missenden, Bucks., until the closure of the firm in 1992. Joseph Hill: S 11/89/477, *c.*1770, £2,640; S 3/90/182, cello, *c.*1760, £13,200; S 11/91/304, cello, £8,250. NB Auctioneers do not always distinguish between Lockey Hill and his son Henry Lockey Hill whose dates overlap. Lockey Hill: P 4/91/147, *c.*1777, £2,420; P 4/91/153, *c.*1790, £4,180; S 3/89/59, viola, *c.*1800, £6,050; Henry Lockey Hill: P 9/91/134, *c.*1820, £5,500; P 9/91/127, (attributed), £6,820; William E. Hill: P 6/91/162, viola, *c.*1845, £7,150; W. E. Hill & Sons: C 7/91/69 £4,180; P 3/92/155, £5,428; Bows: S 11/91/255, silver and tortoiseshell, £1,760; S 11/91/85, gold and tortoiseshell, £2,420; S 3/91/114, gold and tortoiseshell,

London, 1954, £2,310; C 4/91/83, gold and tortoiseshell, £2,420; S 11/92/78, silver and ebony, 1933, round stick, 62 g, £2,200. NB Hill bows and their stamps and markings are fully explained in the text.

HILL, Hugh (*fl.* 1930). Worked in Belfast, taking up violin-making when struck by illness. Copied classic Italian modelling and made about 20 instruments.

HILLARD, Allen (*fl.* 1654–84). Mentioned by W.H. as working in London and producing a few instruments of the Brescian type. No other record.

HILSDEN, Martin J. (b. 1948). Contemporary maker, ex Hills. Now works in Oxford. See Alburger; vL.

HILTON, Thomas James (*fl.* 1888). Worked at Gorleston, Norfolk. Credited with about 50 violins, many on the Strad or Bergonzi model. 'The tone is excellent.' (W.M.M.)

HINDS, Frederick (*fl.* 1740–76). Apparently made viols, English guitars, and zithers as well as a few violins. Some viols may have been converted into cellos. Worked at Ryder's Court, Leicester Fields, London, and so labelled. W.H. speaks quite highly of this maker. (Note: There is an English Guitar of 1786 branded 'F. Hintz' in the Hill Collection, Ashmolean Museum, Oxford, described in Boyden, *Hill Collection*, 42–3. Quite possibly this is the same maker.)

HIORNS, James (*fl.* 1920?). Worked at Olton, near Solihull, near Birmingham.

HIRCUTT. The first mention of this maker appears to be in Pearce, *Violins and Violin Makers* (1866): 'English maker, about 1600'. This entry is substantially repeated by the other dictionary authors, e.g. Fleming, W.M.M., and W.H. The latter states 'high arching and perpendicular soundholes'. The date sounds improbably early and the style sounds more typical of a century later. Instruments apparently branded. The maker remains something of a mystery.

HODGSON, David Ian (b. 1956). Contemporary maker trained in the Newark school. Given as working in York (vL).

*HOFMANN family. Georg William, b. Markneukirchen 1879, d. Dublin 1963, worked in London and Dublin, associated with Charles Meinel and later with his son *William M. Hofmann* (b. 1929, Dublin). The father is credited with 20 violins and 1 cello between 1906 and 1940. William Hofmann, member of ISVB, works at Greystones, Co. Wicklow.

*HOING, Clifford A. (1903–89). A distinguished modern maker who worked at High Wycombe, Bucks. Originally trained as a wood-carver but became during his lifetime one of the most respected violin- and viola-makers. Credited with about 150 handmade instruments with choice wood. Followed classical Italian modelling with one or two of his own features. Diploma of Honour, The Hague, 1949. Instruments signed and branded. See Alburger, and *Strad* (July 1990), 558. S 11/92/240, 1958, £1,705.

HOLDER, Ernest L. (*fl.* 1892–1914). Brother of Thomas Jacques (below) and also made successful copies of Italian models. Worked in Lee Rd., Blackheath, near London.

HOLDER, Thomas Jacques (1842–1922). A high reputation for his copies of Italian instruments. He worked in Wardour St., London and at Blackheath nearby. Father and teacher of Thomas James Holder (below) and teacher of George Wulme-Hudson. 'Seldom labelled with his name' (W.H.).

HOLDER, Thomas James (1874–1926). Though born in Cardiff he spent most of his working life in Paris (1913–29). As with other members of the family, a successful copyist of Italian instruments. (See Vannes on this family generally.) Label: T. J. Holder | Luthier | Paris. Also branded.

HOLE, A. P. (*fl.* 1870). Apparently worked at Leicester (W.H.).

HOLLARD, George (1812–94). Rustic violin-maker resident at Compton-Dundon (W.M.M.).

HOLLOWAY, John (*fl.* 1775–95). Worked at 31 Gerard St., Soho. 'Indifferent work' (W.M.M.).

HOLMES, Stanley (*fl.* 1905–24). Worked in Liverpool. Initially in clerical work, he was another maker 'converted' by Heron-Allen's book and he evolved into a reasonably successful maker. Original model influenced by Stradivari but using a varnish of his own.

HONE, P. A. (*fl.* 1901–*c.*1950). Made over 20 violins of 'robust construction' (W.H.). Worked in Coventry.

HOOTON, John (*fl.* 1925). An amateur (b. 1873) who worked at Ashton-in-Makerfield (near Manchester).

HOPKINS. (*fl.* 1850–75). Resident in Worcester. Poor reputation.

HOPKINS, E. (*fl. c.*1940). Worked in Portsmouth. 'Nice workmanship and tone' (W.H.). Printed label with handwritten name.

HORRIDGE, Walter Percival (*fl.* 1925). Resident at Stamford (Lincs.), b. 1875. 'An amateur who makes lovely violins on the Strad model' (W.M.M.). Pupil of Scholes of Rushden.

HOSKINS, James (*fl.* 1840). Worked at Camerton, Somerset.

HOUSE, William J. (b. 1932). Works at Worle, Weston-super-Mare. Trained at Welsh School of Musical Instrument Making and Repair. Has made to date 6 violins.

†HOWARD, Frank Herbert (1868–1930). Born in Nottingham but settled in London from 1917. Originally trained as a cabinet-maker, he commenced making violins at the age of 17 and did so professionally from 1894. He also taught violin- and bow-making at the Northern Polytechnic in London (Holloway) from 1919 and hence had a number of pupils, including William Luff, who appear in this Directory. Credited with about 100 violins and several violas and cellos of classic Italian modelling. 'Excellent workmanship though not the acme of refinement' (W.H.). Instruments labelled, branded, and numbered. P 6/91/266, 1920, £605; S 4/93/54, London, 1919, £1,610.

HOWARTH, H. (*fl.* 1925). Primarily a player, though credited with a few instruments from Bury, Lancs. (W.H.).

HOYLE, Edward (*fl.* 1900). Worked at Todmorden, Yorks. Formerly a cabinet-maker, W.M.M. credits him with 73 violins. W.M.M. enthuses but W.H. does not.

HUDSON, George (1859–1916). Worked at Skegness, Lincs. Credited with about 100 instruments, each one being numbered. Used oil varnish. 'Workmanship entirely satisfactory' (W.H.). His father was Richard Hudson, 'well known in parts of Lancashire as Dick O'New-laith, a famous country fiddler' (W.M.M.). George Hudson (not to be confused with George Wulme-Hudson) labelled, branded, and numbered his instruments.

†HUDSON, George Wulme- (1862–1952). One of England's most distinguished makers of the first half of the 20th cent. See text. A very talented copyist and known to the trade by his pen-name of 'Carressi'. The late John Dyke, of Malvern, an expert on English

violin-makers, summarized George Wulme-Hudson's career in general terms to the author as follows: 'His early works were 'fakes', with antiqued varnish but carried the brand 'G.W.H' internally and on the corner of the label. His middle period instruments were labelled 'Carressi' and some suffered from varnish deterioration. From 1937 onwards his work was largely 'straight'—instruments labelled with his own name.' He was a pupil of Thomas Jacques Holder in Blackheath and as a young man worked for the firm of Edward Withers. He was also a lively writer, particularly for the *Strad* in the 1930s. He is credited with about 800 instruments, a few of which were violas, but no cellos are known. Born, worked, and died in London. See *Strad* (Feb. 1949), 230; *Strad* (Feb. 1985), 753 (Albert Cooper). C 7/91/105, £4,180; S 6/90/103, viola, 1931, £4,400.

HULL, Robert (b. 1938). Works in Liverpool. Up to Mar. 1993 had made 36 violins, 129 violas, 23 cellos, and 6 baroque or 'classical' violins/violas. Instruments used in many of the professional orchestras in Europe. Robert Hull originally trained as a musician and teacher and became a full-time maker in 1985.

HULME, Charles Darley (b. 1895). Worked initially at Manchester and with Béla Szepessy in Soho before emigrating to Australia in 1889 as violinist and violin-maker. Good reputation.

*HUME, Alexander (c.1860–1941). Born in Scotland he was one of the few British makers of this time who were professionally trained in Germany, having already studied the violin with Prosper Sainton in London. Started in Dumfries, then worked at Peterborough from 1915 and London from 1917. Undoubtedly a competent and professional maker of this era with his 'Class A' instruments having a particularly good reputation. Poidras points out that he stopped the making of models 'B' and 'C' sometime before 1925. Also made bows. W.H. has a full description of his varnishing methods. His varnishes look durable, though there is often slight craquelling, so common with oil varnishes of this period. His reputation now seems to have faded somewhat, but may perhaps revive. C 11/92/71, cello, London, 1921, £1,980.

HUMPHREYS, Robert (*fl.* 1890). Worked at Timberland, near Lincoln. Average work.

HUNTER, Harold (c.1893–1983). Trained with John Byrom (q.v.) and worked in Liverpool. Also a performing violinist. Ran a shop in Liverpool until about 1966 primarily as a restorer and dealer but also as a maker. The contemporary maker Michael Johnson (q.v.) was his pupil.

HURSCROFT, E. (*fl.* 1930). See text. Worked in London and for Beare and Son. Marketed his instruments for £14. (His name is absent from other dictionaries.)

INGRAM, David (*fl.* 1800–10). Worked at Edinburgh. Mediocre work.

INGRAM, Henry (*fl.* 1820). Worked at Durham. Mediocre work.

INGRAM, Walter (*fl.* 1830). Worked at Bristol. Poor reputation because he allegedly 'chemicalized and baked the wood' (W.H.).

INGRAM, William (*fl.* 1925). Worked at Linlithgow, near Edinburgh. Employed as a weights and measures inspector but a fair amateur player and maker as well. Produced instruments from 1920.

INVERARITY, James R. (*fl.* 1925). Worked at Aberdeen and 'made a large number of violins, violas, cellos, and double basses' (W.H.). Quite well thought of by W.H.

IRESON, Frank Herbert (*fl.* 1900). Worked at Bishop Auckland. Average work.

IRVING, Colin J. (b. 1945). Ash Green, Surrey, and now with Hamilton Caswell, Bristol. Originally an engineer but began to take string instrument restoration and making more seriously at age 22. Trained with Dolmetsch and then Gimpel Solomon. By 1978 had produced 25 violins, 10 violas, 26 cellos, and a double bass, plus baroque instruments. His work is now well known and much respected. See Alburger; vL; Vannes/Lebet.

IRWIN, E. J. (*fl.* 1901). Worked at Bradford. 'Praiseworthy designs ... and satisfactory tone' (W.H.). Instruments numbered.

JACKLIN, Cyril William (1902–88). One of the most interesting and distinguished of modern British makers. He came to the art not from playing the violin but from woodwork and having an interest in the sale-room. He then studied with Frank Howard (q.v.) for three years and carefully read Heron-Allen's book when he was 18. In 1921 he became a partner with Frances Ciesla and in 1927 worked on his own in London, also being principal repairer to the bow-maker James Thompson Wilson (one of the best pupils of James Tubbs). He moved his workshop to Loughton, Essex on being bombed out of his London premises in 1940. In 1949 he became a director of the firm of Albert Arnold Ltd. in London but when that business closed down in 1956 he moved back to Loughton. He is credited with rather over 60 violins, 20 violas, and a cello following classic lines. According to the account in Alburger he worked very quickly, making one instrument a week in the white. He had a no-nonsense approach to making. He did not use a mould at all—just a flat board. He claimed that his instruments consequently had a certain individuality, rather than looking 'as if it's come off a machine, like so many of the French instruments' (Alburger, 101). He always sprung his bass bars. In his earlier years he worked for some time with a large firm of manufacturing chemists where he was able to effect research upon varnishes (see Poidras). This no doubt stood him in good stead—his varnishes have frequently been compared to those of the Italians. He also made bows in his earlier days. In 1965 he became an expert consultant for Sotheby's and had an international reputation as both a restorer and an expert with a fabulous memory. See *Strad* (Apr. 1982), 894; *Strad* (June 1988), 445; Alburger. Instruments labelled with signature.

JACKLIN, T. (*fl.* 1910). Worked at Hull. 'Very good workmanship' (W.H.).

JACKSON, S (*fl.* 1830). Askam, Lancs.

JAMES, Rhys Price (*fl.* 1948). Formerly a miner (born 1909), he learned violin-making after the Second World War. Made many instruments for schools, working at Bridgend, Wales (W.H.).

JAMES, Stephen (*fl.* 1800). Worked from Bristol. 'Average work' (W.M.M.). Amati modelling.

JAMIESON, Thomas (*fl.* 1830–45). Worked at Aberdeen. Good and neat workmanship.

*J'ANSON, Edward Popplewell (*fl.* 1840–75). Worked at Leeds and Manchester. One of the most mysterious of 19th-cent. British makers since so little is known about him despite his obvious talent. 'Truly superb modelling of "Italian types"' (W.H.). 'The instruments that still have his label in them (few though they may be in number) bear abundant testimony to his consummate skill.' (W.M.M. ranks J'anson with Tobin and Collingwood as amongst the least properly appreciated English makers.) It is widely believed that many of his instruments have been re-labelled with Italian names. A cello seen by the author with a Langonet certificate bears these opinions out. The violin described below was also attractive but with quite short, upright soundholes. S 11/89/290, violin labelled 'Edward P. J'anson fecit Manchester, anno 1884', 13^{15}/$_{16}$ in. (354 mm), £2,860.

JAY, Henry (*fl*. 1640–70). Also spelled 'Jaye'. A London viol-maker mentioned by Mace. W.H. praises his skilful workmanship, fine purfling, and rich varnish. There is a tenor viol (1667) in the Victoria & Albert Museum, London. One attributed violin seen.

†JAY, Henry (*fl*. 1740–76). London. Chiefly renowned as a maker of kits. (These were miniature violins used by dancing-masters.) Also made violins and cellos, the latter for Longman & Broderip labelled as from Long Acre, London. The Hill Archive suggests that Jay was a pupil of Wamsley and worked extensively for J. & J. Simpson. S 11/90/208, 1776, £880.

JAY, Thomas (*fl*. 1690–1720). Worked in London—'honest true bred English violins of the period' (W.H.).

JEFFREY, John (1841–1918). Worked at Chirnside, Berwickshire, Scotland. Credited with about 50 instruments, the later ones having a fine oil varnish and tonal quality about which W.H. enthuses. Based on this, this maker should be put in the front rank of Scottish makers of the late 19th and early 20th cents. Unfortunately his work is not often available for inspection.

JEFFREYS, Arthur (1898–1980). Worked with the firm of Hills in London, primarily as a restorer.

JENKINS, Thomas (1819–90). Resident at Haverfordwest, Wales. Credited with a large number of instruments on various models—'enthusiastic amateur workmanship' (W.H.).

JERMY, Arthur (*fl*. 1900). Resident at Kingsland, near London, and born 1867. 'Said to be a clever artist' (W.M.M.).

JERVIS, Frank (*fl*. 1800). Worked at Belfast, Northern Ireland. Neat Amatese modelling.

JOHN, William (contemporary). Makes, restores, and deals from Ealing, London. There is a fine illustration of this maker's copy (1987) of the 'Betts' Stradivari of 1704 from Ealing Strings in their publication *The Stradivari Influence* (London, 1987), 137.

JOHNSON, David Bruce. Contemporary maker and restorer (also of fretted instruments) working in Birmingham. Also makes electric violins for Nigel Kennedy and others.

*†JOHNSON, John (*fl*. 1750–62). See text. One of the most prominent of the mid-18th-cent. London makers, using broadly Stainer modelling. As explained in text, he obviously used workshop labour. His work nowadays is quite well respected. Worked at Cheapside, London. P 9/91/107, *c*.1750, £2,090; S 12/91/172, £2,750.

JOHNSON, Joseph (*fl*. 1900). Worked in Backworth. P 9/91/80, £220.

JOHNSON, Michael (b. 1948). Works at Penrith, Cumbria. Number of instruments to date: 32 violins, 12 violas, and 2 cellos.

JOHNSON, Stanley (1927–1991). Retired headmaster who worked in Redditch. Produced a few well-crafted instruments. Also a collector, restorer, and competent violinist.

JOHNSTON, James. (*fl*. *c*.1880). Mentioned by W.M.M. as turning out some of the best specimens of violin-making in Scotland at the time. Worked at Pollokshields.

JOHNSTONE, William John (*fl.* 1975). Resident at Edinburgh. Used carefully made Italian modelling.

JONES, David (*fl.* 1800). Worked in Merthyr Tydfil, Wales. Ordinary work.

JOWETT, Patrick. Contemporary. Lecturer at Newark School. Works at W. Bridgford, Nottingham.

JUBB, William (*fl.* 1935). Worked at Horsforth, Leeds.

JUDGE, Michael J. (*fl.* 1900). Worked in Dublin. W.H. remarks on longer than customary soundholes. Spirit varnish. Won award at Royal Dublin Society Exposition, 1923.

JUKES, N. (*fl.* 1925). A tinsmith by trade, credited with rough and inelegant work. Instruments branded. (W.H.)

KAROL, Miranda. See under Green.

KEARNS, Michael Lloyd (b. 1953, Manitoba, Canada). Studied at Newark School. Partner in Oxford Violins, Oxford. About 35 instruments to 1994.

KEEBLE, Jowett R. (*fl.* 1925). Made on a composite model of his own from Cirencester, Glos. Prepared his own varnish.

KEEN, W. (*fl.* 1790). London. Thought to have worked with Charles and Samuel Thompson. P 9/90/76, viola (small), 1796, £660.

KEENAN, Edward (*fl.* 1920). An Irish maker, born 1876 and worked in Dublin. Both W.M.M. and W.H. obviously rate him quite highly. Boldly modelled and full-toned instruments generally after Stradivari, but sometimes Guarneri. Experimented with native woods from time to time. Printed label with signature against a black background. C 4/91/155, 1917, £1,320.

KELLEWAY, Arthur Ernest (b. 1903, *fl.* 1925). Worked in Southampton, based on Stradivari with various shades of oil varnish. Self-taught. 'Excellent modelling' (W.H.).

KELMAN, James (*fl.* 1890). Worked at Auchintoul, Banffshire, Scotland. W.C.H. credits him with 36 violins on the Stradivarian model, influenced by Davidson's book (see text). Handwritten or printed labels.

KENDAL, George (late 19th cent.). Mentioned by W.M.M. without further detail.

KENDLE, Philip (*fl.* 1820). Worked in Hereford. Ordinary work.

KENNEDY, Alexander (*fl.* 1910). Worked at Wallsend, Tyne and Wear. 'Excellent tone' (W.H.).

†KENNEDY family. See text. They were really expatriate Scots since the first Kennedy, *Alexander*, was born in Scotland in 1695 (W.C.H.). The family is well known because of its prolific output. Alexander worked in Oxford Market, London between about 1730 and 1785. W.H. finds the earliest-dated instrument to have been 1743. The influence of the high-built Stainer modelling is obvious, but the instruments tend to be well made and with well-figured wood. He is generally regarded as one of the better London makers of the mid-18th cent. His nephew and pupil *John* (1730–1816) is regarded as having made mainly cheap violins for others. What W.H. calls 'the commonplace old English violin of superficial structure', i.e. roughly made and unpurfled, often comes from his hands if attributed to one of the Kennedys. The most important maker was *Thomas*, son and pupil of John (1784–1870). He initially worked for Thomas Powell and William Forster. Amazingly prolific, he is credited with about 2,000 instruments. He tended to

drop his high standards in the interests of making a quick turnover and so his work is very uneven. There are believed to be about 300 cellos mainly made on the Amati model. At its best Thomas Kennedy's work is exquisite and is valued accordingly. Worked mainly at 364 Oxford St., London; also at 19 Princes St., Westminster (1811). Sandys and Forster significantly remark that he was much employed as an outworker by Messrs Goulding and other music-houses. James Brown, the maker at Spitalfields, London, was associated with the Kennedy family, particularly Thomas. W.H. says John's varnish is 'invariably light reddish'. Thomas Kennedy: P4/91/146, 1844, £4,400; P 11/92/168, £2,640; S 3/91/94, cello, 1813, £8,800.

KESSLER, Dietrich (b. 1929). Swiss-born and trained maker who arrived in England in 1950. Associated with the firm of Edward Withers in London from 1969 to 1987. Specializes in the making of early stringed instruments. Fine reputation.

KILBURN, W. D. (20th cent.). Gateshead.

KIRKWOOD, Robert (19th cent.). Edinburgh. 'Made a number of lovely violins' (W.M.M.). Not mentioned by W.H.

KNAPTON, James (early 18th cent.). Little-known maker working near St Paul's Churchyard, London. (Omitted by W.H.)

KNIGHT, Alfred (*fl.* 1810). Worked at Worcester. Undistinguished.

KNIGHT, Frank R. (*fl.* 1925). Worked at Reigate making over 30 instruments. Pupil of W. Glenister (and so labelled).

KNIGHT, Philip David. Contemporary. Graduated from London College of Furniture. Works in Chelmsford.

KUDANOWSKI, Jan (b. 1940). A Polish violin-maker trained in Cremona; has for some years been working in Birmingham as an esteemed restorer and maker. See Alburger.

LABRAM, Leonard (b. 1933). A contemporary violin-maker resident in Nuneaton. He also designs and makes ingenious violin-making tools.

LAIDLAW, J. M. (*fl.* 1950). Associated with the firm of Hills, a 'much esteemed' violin-maker and repairer (W.H.).

LAIDLAW, John William (*fl.* 1925). Worked at East Boldon, Newcastle upon Tyne. Used his own preparation of oil varnish. 'Workmanship satisfactorily accurate' (W.H.).

LAING, William R. (20th cent.). Folkestone.

LAMB, John (*fl.* 1880). Resident at Shiremoor. Indifferent work.

LAMB, John (*fl.* 1925). Son of the preceding and also from Shiremoor. Credited with about 60 violins of indifferent quality.

LAMBERT, John (*fl.* 1850). An associate of James Brown in Spitalfields, London. Taught Joseph Withers. Instruments may be branded at top of back.

LAMBERT, J. F. (*fl.* 1814). Worked at Mile End Rd., London. Possibly identical with preceding maker.

LAMBERT, Jonathan (*fl.* 1750). Worked in St John's Madder Market, Norwich, apparently with little aesthetic success. 'Hideously ugly soundholes' (W.H.).

LANCASTER, Arthur Cotton (*fl.* 1900). Worked in Colne, Lancs. 'The workmanship is beautiful, and the tone bright, sweet, and responsive.' (W.M.M.) He achieved some fame by making an instrument to commemorate the sinking of the *Titanic* in 1912.

LANGONET family. *Charles François* (1861–1929) was born in Mirecourt and joined the firm of Hills in 1880. He remained there for nearly 50 years. He trained many other makers including his son, and was undoubtedly highly influential in the French-influenced production of this firm. His son, *Charles Frank* (1888–1963), was also apprenticed in Mirecourt and then worked with Hills. He established his own business in 1946 with his son in London. Widely known and respected as a fine maker and expert. His son *Alfred Charles* was born in 1917 and after working with Hills became a highly respected maker and expert. See *Strad* (Apr. 1961), 438; *Strad* (Sept. 1956), 142.

LANT, Ernest F. (*fl.* 1950). Worked at Sevenoaks, Kent.

LAPWOOD, Ronald E. (b. 1904). Worked in London and encouragingly spoken of by W.H.

LATTEN, H. G. (*fl.* 1925). Worked at Lewisham. Pupil of Frank Howard. Average work.

LAUGHER, William (*fl.* 1890). He made steel and plated pins by trade at Redditch (a town renowned for this). Well praised by W.H. Made about 50 violins and 10 violas.

LAURENCE, K. M. (*fl.* from 1934). One of Britain's first women violin-makers. Started in 1934 at Worth Maltravers, Dorset.

LAZARE, Robert (20th cent.). London.

LEADER, James Henry (*fl.* 1830). Worked in Bristol. 'Commendable workmanship' (W.H.).

LEAKE, H. (*fl.* 1820). Worked at Huntley, Scotland. Fair reputation.

LEE, H. W. (*fl.* 1925). Violins and double basses from Blackheath, near London. Fair reputation.

LEE, Percy (1871–1953). Professional maker and viola-player. Made about 50 instruments, specializing in violas and viols, from Cricklewood. 'One of the ablest representatives of the modern British school of violin making ... Violas are magnificently made and beautifully finished.' (W.M.M.) C 11/90/74, viola, 1917, £3,080.

LEGGAT, Charles (1880–1917). Distinguished bow-maker with Hills who died in First World War. See Retford, 80.

LENTZ family. The founder was *Johann Nicholaus* (*fl.* 1800–13), emigrating to London from the Tyrol and thought to have been a pupil or associate of Bernhardt Fendt. Good work with varnish similar to Dodd and J. F. Lott, but less transparent (Jalovec). (Piper states that he was first employed as a butler and became friendly with J. F. Lott.) Worked in Chelsea. One son was *Jacob* (*fl.* 1820), chiefly famed for 'a fairly large number of magnificent double basses' (W.H.), unfortunately unlabelled. He apparently 'antiqued' his instruments. Another son was *John Frederick* (*fl.* 1820), who, like his father, worked from Lower Sloane St., Chelsea, London. The work of these makers is not often seen or, perhaps, recognized.

LESLIE, Christopher Julian (b. 1956). Contemporary maker given as working in Adderbury, Oxon. (vL).

LEWER, James (*fl.* 1760). Moorfields, London.

LEWIS, Edward (*fl.* 1680–1740). One of the most distinguished early violin-makers in London. See text. Earliest labels, as from 'St. Paul Allay' in London—see *Strad* (June 1966), 46. Also 'over against Earls Court in Drury Lane, London' (cello, 1732, P 11/92/328, in well-formed MS).

LEWIS, Thomas (*fl.* 1820). Thought to be a cobbler, resident in Gloucestershire.

*LEYDEN, John (*fl.* 1915). Luithouse, Glasgow.

LIESSEM, Remerus *(or Remerius)* (*fl.* 1750). Worked in London. W.H. describes his violins as 'invariably of small proportions', typically 13½ in. (334 mm) but Phillips catalogues one (branded) of the usual 14 in. (355 mm). Also lutes and citterns.

LIGHT, George (*fl.* 1790). Worked at Exeter on the Amati model.

LINDSAY, David (*fl.* 1900). Worked at Edzell, Tay, Scotland. Credited by W.M.M. with about 40 violins of good workmanship—Italian modelling.

LINDSAY, Michael H. (1860–1906). An Irish-born maker who worked at Stockton-on-Tees. W.H. praises his workmanship but not his tone.

LISTER, James (*fl.* 1905). Worked at Ilkley, Yorks. P 10/91/52, £152.

LISTER, John (*fl.* 1730). Worked at Leeds. Poor reputation.

LITTLEWOOD, Gerald. Contemporary maker working in Hollingworth-in-Longdendale.

LOCK, George Herbert (1850–c.1910). Primarily a mathematics teacher at Shrewsbury. Credited with about 60 violins and 3 cellos—'commendable designs and workmanship' (W.H.).

LOGAN, John (*fl.* 1890). Worked at Abington, Lanarkshire, Scotland. About 50 violins on Cremonese modelling.

LOMAX, Jacob (*fl.* 1920). A pawnbroker by trade, making over 30 violins. 'Fair workmanship' (W.H.).

LONGMAN & BRODERIP. A firm of dealers in 26 Cheapside, London, c.1740–1800. See text. Interesting because amongst their workers were Benjamin Banks, Henry Jay, and Joseph Hill, who W.H. states was responsible for their small-size violas. (Also (earlier) Longman and Lukey.) Violins frequently have ink simulated purfling. Also music publishers. The Museum of London has an exhibition of this firm's musical instruments, including a dancing-master's kit. Longman and Lukey: C 3/90/252, cello, London, £8,250. Longman & Broderip: P 9/90/142, violin with simulated purfling, c.1780, £638.

LONGMAN AND LUKEY. See above.

LONGSON, F. H. (*fl.* 1900). Worked at Stockport. Variable work. P 1/91/80 £550.

LONGSTAFF, Robert. Contemporary. Makes early stringed instruments at Abingdon, Oxon.

LONGSTON, J. L. (*fl.* 1880). Stockport.

LONSDALE, William P. (*fl.* 1880). Worked at Preston.

*†LOTT family. See the discussion in the text. The founder of the violin-making family was *John Frederick* (I), born in Germany in 1775, died in London in 1853. Particularly renowned for his double basses as discussed in the text. For much of his working life he was part of Thomas Dodd's London workshop (from 1798). *George Frederick* (1800–68) was John Frederick's eldest son. He was closely associated with Davis of Coventry St., London. 'Was an excellent judge of Italian instruments, and a clever imitator.' (Hart) The second son was *John Frederick* (II) (b. 1804, d. 7 June 1870 (Hill Archive)), or 'Jack' Lott, arguably the finest violin-maker in 19th-cent. London. Charles Reade's novel *Jack of All Trades* (1858) was based on Lott's extraordinary life and this is discussed in the text. The Hill Archive states that Reade was actually in partnership with Lott and that a

Deed existed. Lott and Reade went on trips abroad in order to buy and sell. As W.M.M. points out 'there is no doubt about it, . . . among the variety of talent he displayed was one for brilliant forgery. Some of his skilful counterfeits have deceived the ablest judges. I can only reiterate what I have said before that all the talent and skill of a craftsman of this sort has will not atone for a life of fraud.' This is one view of the matter. The fact is that his instruments today command high prices and all the evidence suggests that the tonal qualities satisfy good players. Instruments seldom labelled. Experts believe that there are a number abroad, particularly in USA, with false Italian labels. Particularly renowned for his Guarneri copies: 'No player should permit such a treasure to pass out of his hands.' (W.H.) See particularly John Dilworth in *Strad* (Oct. 1988), 801. S 11/91/217, *c*.1840 (Hill certificate), £17,600; S 6/90/210, *c*.1850 (Hill certificate), £24,200.

Low, W. F. (*fl*. 1885). Worked in Sunderland. P 1/92/282, copy of Sainton's Guarneri, £440.

*†Luff, William Henry (1904–93). See text. One of the finest 20th-cent. English makers with a very high reputation for his beautiful work; and who continued making up to his 90th, and last, year. He was born into a musical family and learned the violin. At 16 he became a pupil of Frank Howard in London and then joined the London workshop of Arthur Dykes (1920). There he worked under the supervision of Max Millant (who worked in London before opening his Paris business). Luff acknowledges his great debt to Millant, who had been Mirecourt-trained. He made about 30 instruments up to 1939, mainly copies of Guarneri which, in the maker's words, were 'given an appearance of age'. After the war, in which he served in the RAF, he worked for nine years with J. & A. Beare. During these years he also restored numerous classic Italian violins, etc. whose workmanship and style he carefully noted. He became independent in 1955. Awarded the MBE in 1979. The total to 1993 was 425 instruments, of which 59 were violas (from 15¼ in. to 17 in.) and one cello, 'a copy of Douglas Cameron's Montagnana, which he lent me for the taking of patterns, etc.' (See the maker's letter to the author, quoted in the text.) See *NGDI*; Alburger; *Strad* (Sept. 1973), 710; *Strad* (Sept. 1984), 340.

Lundie, William (*fl*. 1780). Worked in Aberdeen. Omitted from other dictionaries. An early Scottish maker. One violin seen. Very crude work. P 9/91/76, 1779, £242.

Luton, George (*fl*. 1850). Worked at Leicester. Undistinguished.

Lye, Henry (1832–*c*.1916). Employed as an estate carpenter at Camerton Court, Somerset. Spent all his spare time in constructions of violins, violas, and cellos and was still making at age 84. Credited with a very considerable number of instruments 'of uniform excellence, and the tone large, bright, and responsive' (W.M.M.). See *Strad* (Oct. 1956), 182.

MacAlister, Gavin (b. 1945). Graduate of Newark School of Violin Making 1989–92 (diploma with distinction), and working in Swanley, Kent. Has made 8 violins, 2 violas, and 1 cello to date.

MacCarthy, John Leader Temple (*fl*. 1925). Worked at Cambridge. Stradivarian modelling.

McClean, E. P. (*fl*. 1920). Dover.

McCurdy, Alec (b. 1914). Contemporary maker, formerly a local government solicitor. Works in Newbury, Berks. Specializes in the production of cellos. See *Strad* (Mar. 1982), 812.

MacGeorge, George (d. 1821). Associate of Matthew Hardie at Edinburgh and produced somewhat similar work. Spirit varnish.

MacGill, James Campbell (*fl.* 1895). Worked in Arran, Scotland.

McGregor, A. (*fl.* 1900). Worked in Edinburgh. Fair reputation.

M'Intosh, James (1801–73). W.C.H. suggests that he was an associate of Peter Hardie. Earlier models on Stainer form. Later ones more on the Amati–Stradivari model. He was also a skilful player. 204 violins, 10 violas, and 35 cellos.

MacIntosh, John (*fl.* 1900). Galston, Scotland. Made about 60 violins between late 19th cent. and 1926. W.H. speaks well of his later productions. Died in poverty. Sometimes decorated his instruments with oil vignettes—e.g. of Sir Walter Scott.

M'Intosh, John (*fl.* 1925). Worked at Edinburgh.

MacIntosh, William (*fl.* 1900). Worked in Dundee and labelled himself 'M'Intosh'. Fair reputation.

M'Kenzie, Malcolm (1828–1904). Considerable production from Dumbarton, Scotland.

Mackie, Adam (1871–*c.*1930). Worked at Aberdeen between 1893 and 1899 before emigrating to the Colonies, eventually settling in Johannesburg. Interesting work, his earlier violins made in Scotland not being labelled.

Mackintosh (or McIntosh), John (*fl.* 1820). A Scotsman who worked in Dublin and was a pupil of Thomas Perry. He succeeded to the business of Perry and Wilkinson. Instruments seen have not been impressive but he has a fair reputation. Instruments branded on back. P 9/92/82, 1815, £528.

M'Lay, William (1815–*c.*1885). Kincardine-on-Forth. Credited with about 50 violins, 6 violas, and 6 cellos of average workmanship (W.H.).

Macmillan, Hector (b. 1929). Works from W. Lothian, Scotland. To date has made 7 violins and 8 violas.

McNeill, John (1850–1923). Worked in Edinburgh and Dublin. Good reputation.

McNeill, Thomas (*fl.* 1910). Worked at Dublin, dying in 1917, brother of John above.

McNeill, William (*fl.* 1890). Worked at Edinburgh from 1876. P 4/91/66, £528.

MacNicol, Alexander (*fl.* 1860). Worked at Padanaram, Scotland. Credited with 45 violins on the Guarneri model of average workmanship (W.H.).

MacSivan, John (*fl.* 1900). Produced about 100 violins from Partick, Scotland.

Maghie, John Fisher (*fl.* 1900). Worked at Dalston, Cumberland. W.H. mentions strong but keen tone.

Mahoney, Frederick Daniel (b. 1880). Associated with the Chanot family in London and given as working in Lavenham in 1950 (W.H.).

Mallas, Alexander (1826–91). Worked at Leith, Scotland. An interesting maker who himself played using an Amati of 1689. A millwright by trade, his Stradivari and Guarneri models were produced in his spare time. 'A highly respected and amiable man, who, for many years, bore patiently the agony of an incurable disease' (W.C.H.).

Mann, John Alexander (1810–89). Worked at Glasgow. See text. Some of his instruments are thought to have been supplied by Vuillaume. 'I am not quite sure that Mann made all these violins with his own hands.' (W.C.H.)

MANN, Thomas Howell (*fl.* 1900). Worked in Cardiff. P 4/91/91, £495.

MANUEL, Evan (*fl.* 1820). Worked at Merthyr Tydfil, Wales. Crude work.

MARLAND, John and Septimus (*fl.* 1900). Worked at Hurst, Lancs.

MARNIE, John (*fl.* 1850). Made about 40 violins at Padanaram, Scotland.

MARSHALL, James H. (*fl.* 1920). An engineer, resident near Manchester, who produced a number of instruments on Guarneri modelling.

MARSHALL, John (*fl.* 1760). Worked in London on the Stainer model. Violins, violas, mandolins, and guitars. S 3/90/316, 1754, £1,980.

*†MARSHALL, John (1844–1919). Worked at Aberdeen. See text. One of the most distinguished Scottish makers producing about 300 instruments. His later instruments, particularly those which are copies of an Alessandro Gagliano that he had in for repair and carefully measured, are some of the finest Scottish violins of this era. Label of one specimen: 'John Marshall | Violin Maker | Aberdeen 1912' and in handwriting 'Coppy [*sic*] Alex Gaglianus'—also branded internally. P 6/92/59, 1912, £1,265.

MARTIN, Adam (*fl.* 1790). Worked at Hermitage Bridge, London. Little is known about this maker but one or two interesting and well-made instruments seen. Generally Amatese modelling. The Hill Archive states that he probably worked for Thompsons at St Paul's Churchyard. S 11/89/399, £1,540.

MARTIN, Henry (*fl.* 1800). Nottingham. 'Fairly good work, which would be better but for the exaggerated arching' (W.M.M.).

MARTIN, Paul K. Contemporary. Newark School trained. Tetford, Lincs.

MATTHEWS, Robert Ss (*fl.* 1930). A talented pupil of William Glenister of London. P 4/91/126, good violin, *c.*1935, £682.

MATHER (*fl.* 1720). Swanwick. W.M.M. praises a cello.

MATHER, Alexander (*fl.* 1900). Worked at Plumstead, Kent.

MAUCOTEL, Charles (1807–69). A French maker usually employed by Gand who was engaged by W. Davis of Coventry St., London, and arrived in 1844. Shortly afterwards he became self-employed. He produced extremely distinguished work of unmistakably French character. He cannot really be claimed as a 'British' maker. P 11/91/172, 1858, £8,800.

MAW, John Harrison (b. 1956). Contemporary bow-maker in Hill tradition (vL).

MAWBEY, Frederick H. (*fl.* 1900). Worked in Nottingham. Fair reputation.

MAXWELL, Edwin C. (*fl.* 1940). Wimbledon, London.

MAY (*fl.* 1745). Worked in London. Almost unknown, but W.H. enthuses—'lovely work'.

*†MAYSON, Walter H. (1835–1904). Worked at Manchester. One of the best-known late 19th-cent. English maker whose biography was written by W.M.M. and is fully discussed in the text. His work is attractive in its own way but these days often looks too idiosyncratic to be in the mainstream of the market. He is credited with 810 instruments, many of them named (for example, 'Cleopatra'). He was also a writer. Instruments tend to be rather large but very often have acceptable tone, at least for the amateur player. This is no doubt a tribute to his careful workmanship. P 4/91/76, 1891, £440. P 9/90/88, £792.

MEAD, L. J. (*fl.* 1947). Worked in Portsmouth. 'Excellent workmanship and varnish' (W.H.).

MEAD, L. J. (*fl.* 1957). Worked at Cosham. P 2/90/21, £308.

MEARES, Richard (*fl.* 1700). A good early English maker mainly known for his viols. Worked at Bishopsgate, London. Assisted by his son of the same name. The Hill Archive states that Pamphilon was undoubtedly his pupil.

MEEK, James (*fl.* 1920). Born 1862 and worked at Carlisle and Birkenhead. Produced about 80 violins and some violas. W.H. rates this maker highly, as does Poidras: 'Very fine and promising modern make'.

MEGGISON, Alfred (*fl.* 1800). Worked in Manchester. Indifferent work.

MEINEL, Gustav (*fl.* 1910). Worked in London and Dublin, as did his son *Charles* (1890–1945), a pupil of Léon Mougenot and from 1919 to 1924 partner in the Dublin firm Meinel and Hofmann. Subsequently established in London (vL).

MELCHIOR, Arthur A. Contemporary. Work labelled as from Epsom Downs, Surrey.

MELLIN (*fl.* 1750). Worked in London. Little known.

MENTIPLY, Andrew (*fl.* 1890). Violin- and bow-maker working at Ladybank, Fife, Scotland. Employed as a railway worker. 'Loud tonal quality appealing to Scottish dance-players' (W.H.).

MENZIES, John (*fl.* 1830). Worked at Falkirk, Scotland. Large, Stradivarian modelling. No particular distinction.

MEREDITH, L. (*fl.* 1730). Worked at St Paul's Churchyard, London—described by W.M.M. as adopting a large model somewhat on the lines of Maggini.

†MERLIN, John Joseph (1735–1803). Worked in London—'The Ingenious Mechanick'. Fully discussed in text. Instruments attributed to him are of well-made Tyrolean modelling. It seems unlikely, for reasons given in the text, that he made any of the instruments bearing his label. They were probably made by other London makers on an outworker basis. The former Greater London Council put on an exhibition of his work, which included 'gouty' wheelchairs, roller-skates, money scales, watches, and 'pianoforte-harpsichords', in 1985. There is a splendid portrait of Merlin by Thomas Gainsborough. P 3/89/144, 'Josephus Merlin, Cremonae Emulus Londini 1778, No. 97, 66 East Portland Chapel', 13⅞ in. (352 mm) (Hill certificate), £1,980.

MESSING, Frederick James (1755–98). Apparently labelled instruments which he had repaired rather than made (W.H.).

METCALF, R. (*fl.* 1900). Worked in Newcastle.

MICHEL, Aleth (b. 1958). After initial study at the Sorbonne, Paris, eventually found a place at the Welsh School of Musical Instrument Making 1983–6, obtaining Diploma with Merit, and was encouraged to become self-employed in 1986, working in Montpelier, Bristol. Specialist in high quality-work and does not advertise or deal. Has made 15 violins, 11 violas, and a bass gamba, with 5 others in course of construction. Instruments used by professionals. Also plays violin and does restoration work. See generally *Strad* (May, 1992) 434.

MICHETSCHLÄGER, Helen T. (b. 1959). A London-born maker trained in the Newark school. Has also made some interesting experimental models in smaller form. Has now established a fine reputation. To May 1993 has made 52 violins, 35 violas, and 18 cellos from Stanton Harold, near Ashby de la Zouch, Leics. See *Strad* (Dec. 1991), 1088.

MIGGE, Otto (b. 1857, Coblenz; *fl.* 1900). This German maker worked in London, 1896, and Eastbourne, 1908, establishing a reputation. Wrote a book, *The Secret of the Celebrated Italian Violin Makers* (1894). Towry Piper sardonically observes apropos of the discovery of this 'secret': 'violins by him seen by the writer certainly did not justify the claim'. (Piper, 214).

MILES, George (*c.*1860–1912). Worked at Erith. W.H. suggests modest artistry but good tone.

MILES, Ralf (*fl.* 1930). Worked at Royal Forest of Dean and Stroud; well thought of in his time.

MILLAR (1813–77). Worked at St Andrews. 'The work is very good, but the tone often disappointing' (W.M.M.).

MILLER (*fl.* 1750). Worked in London. Little known. See text.

MILLER, George (*fl.* 1760). Worked at London, mainly on viols.

MILLER, John (*fl.* 1890). Worked at Dundee and credited with 40 violins on Strad model (W.H.).

MILLINGTON, Ernest (*fl.* 1910). Borrowash. 'Clever amateur' (W.M.M.).

MILNE, Patrick Gordon (1873–1949). Credited with about 70 violins from Aberdeen and later Glasgow. 'He is one of the best of present-day Scottish makers.' (W.M.M.) Models on the Guarneri and Strad patterns. Used an oil varnish. Instruments used professionally, according to W.M.M.

MILNER, Frank (*fl.* 1925). Worked at Sheffield—apparently talented. Mainly a violinist and conductor.

MILTON, Louis Frank (1898–1947). Well-known English maker resident at Bedford. Good robust work with, from samples seen, durable varnish. P 9/91/87, £646. P 3/89/79, £1,100.

MINSHULL, Ernest Frederick (*fl.* 1910). Worked in Manchester, associated with G. A. Chanot there. Later worked at Leeds (1924). Fair reputation. Instruments signed on back.

MITCHELL, George (1823–97). Credited with about 100 instruments of varying quality. Worked at Edzell, Scotland.

MOCKETT, Brian H. Contemporary bow-maker. Worked for W. E. Hill & Sons. Now works in Chesham, Bucks.

MOFFAT, J. W. (*fl.* 1960). Worked in London in the Kennedy style.

MOLYNEUX (*fl.* 1770). Of French Huguenot extraction, worked in Dublin, an example of his esteemed work being in the Museum there. Italianate modelling. Rare.

MONK, John King (*fl.* 1890). With a few instruments he experimented with a new bass-bar system which was not successful. Also prolific output of traditional instruments. P 7/91/193, £132.

MOODY, George Thomas (*fl.* 1930). Southampton.

MOON, George. Contemporary maker working in Croydon.

MOORE, Alfred (*fl.* 1900). Worked in Douglas, Isle of Man. Produced violins, violas, and cellos. Good reputation. 'Very conscientious worker' (W.H.) S 3/89/352, viola, 1910, £1,870; S 11/92, violin, 1901, £2,090.

MOORE, Anthony John (*fl. c.*1900). Worked at Sunderland. His label mentions wood 200 years old. Fair work. (Also an artist.)

MOORE, J. G. (*fl.* 1910). Liverpool.

MORGAN, William (*fl.* 1890). Worked at Dunnottar Castle, Scotland, where he was a caretaker. Made over 100 violins not renowned for their refinement but whose tone W.H. praises.

MORRIS, Clive. Contemporary. A fine cello of his was sold by Phillips in November 1989 for the benefit of the Jacqueline du Pré Memorial Fund Appeal.

MORRIS, Henry (*fl.* 1900). Made at Darlaston where he was in business. Made 12 replicas of a Guarneri model of Joseph Chanot. Named his instruments after the signs of the zodiac.

MORRIS, John (*fl.* 1800). Worked in Bath. The Hills exhibited one of his violins in the 1903 Exhibition discussed in the text. Omitted by W.H. Work obviously rare, but interesting. The Hill Archive suggests that he might have learned from one of the Banks family.

MORRIS, Martin. Contemporary. Works at Kidlington, Oxford. See *Strad* (June 1986), 106.

MORRIS, William Meredith (1867–1921). See text. Primarily a clergyman and an author much mentioned in this book, but on a few occasions he practised what he preached with a respectable violin. P 4/91/84, £1,100.

MORRISON, Archibald (1820–95). Worked in Glasgow, initially for John Mann. Followed Guarneri modelling for his later instruments. 'Suitable for ballrooms' (W.H.). P 4/91/33, £550.

MORRISON, James (*fl.* 1890). Worked at Dunfermline.

MORRISON, John (1760–1827). London. Made largely for the trade but his cellos in particular have a good reputation. Some instruments so labelled are German. The Hill Archive notes two cellos with lines across the two-piece backs done in burnt cork to simulate maple. They thought his cellos 'quite well made' but suffering from poor materials.

MORTIMER, J. W. (1857–?1926). Worked in Cardiff. Best known for his double basses.

MOWBRAY, David C. (1868–?1920). Leith, Scotland. Mainly a repairer.

MOYA, Hidalgo (?–1927). Trained in Mirecourt and worked from Leicester where he achieved a fine national reputation. Strad or Guarneri modelling, with very neat purfling. Many coats of oil varnish. From 1920 an invalid. Wrote, with Towry Piper, *Violin Tone and Violin Makers* (London, 1916). P 11/88/95, 1918, £2,090; P 4/91/115, £2,200.

*MUMBY, Ernest (*fl.* 1925). Worked at Tottenham, London. Pupil of Emmanuel Whitmarsh. P 4/91/55, £572.

MURDOCH, Alexander G. (1815–91). Prolific output of somewhat ordinary work from Aberdeen. Wrote *The Fiddle in Scotland* (London, *c.*1880), containing sketches of players and makers (W.H.). Rather undistinguished work.

MURPHY, Bartholomew (*fl.* 1800). Worked at Cork, Ireland.

MURPHY, Denis (*fl.* 1830). Worked at Dublin, Ireland.

MURPHY, John (*fl.* 1830). Worked at Cork, Ireland.

MURRAY, Alexander (*fl.* 1850). Worked at Morpeth, Northumberland. Made 'a considerable number of violins' (W.M.M.).

MURRAY, Daniel (*fl.* 1900). Edinburgh.

MURRAY, David (*fl.* 1880). Gorebridge. P 3/93/120, 1889, £935.

MURRAY, James (*fl.* 1880). A railway-engine driver by trade. Worked at Milldamhead, Dumfries, Scotland. P 7/91/223, £154.

MURRELL, Reginald Frank (b. 1933). Self-taught. Vannes/Lebet lists 2 violins, 12 cellos, and 3 violas. Two prizes, Facta Britannia 1983.

MUST, Frederick (*fl.* 1800). Worked at Shrewsbury.

MUYLLAERT, Jan. Contemporary. Works at Navan, Co. Meath, Ireland.

MYALL, Norman (Contemporary). Works in Hackney, London, specializing in Renaissance and baroque stringed instruments.

MYLES, Francis (*fl.* 1840). Worked at Cardiff. Poor work.

NAISBY, Lawrence (*fl.* from 1929). Worked in Liverpool. Maker, restorer, and dealer.

NAISBY, Thomas Henry (1878–1927). Worked at Sunderland, Co. Durham. By trade a plasterer and professional footballer. Modified praise from W.H.

NAISMITH, Patricia C. (b. 1932, New Zealand). An accomplished violinist and violist, she came to England with a scholarship to the Royal Academy of Music in London, then studied part-time in London with William Luff, becoming a distinguished teacher herself at what was then the London College of Furniture, now part of London Guildhall University. See text. Has a special interest in violas. See Alburger.

NANCE, William Edwin (*fl.* 1890). Penarth. A prosperous coal merchant in Cardiff, he made about 100 violins as a hobby, using local wood.

NANETTE (*fl.* 1865). A French maker who worked in London.

NAPIER, William (1848–1932). Employed by Hills as violin- and bow-maker. See Retford. His son *Frank Donald Napier* (1884–1969) also worked for Hills as a bow-maker for a time.

NASH, Thomas (*fl.* 1900). Worked at Ayr, Scotland. Ordinary work.

NAYLOR, Isaac (*fl.* 1780). Worked at Headingly, near Leeds, a pupil of Richard Duke to whom his work was similar if not quite as good.

NEITZERT, Thomas (b. 1959). See under Bridgewood and Neitzert.

NELSON, George (*fl.* 1900). Worked at North Seaton, near Blyth, Northumberland. 'I have reliable evidence that some of his violins have remarkably fine tone.' (W.M.M.)

NELSON, James (*fl.* 1890). Glasgow.

NELSON, John (b. 1939). Formerly senior teacher of design technology now doing full-time making at Gresford, near Wrexham. Particularly interested in varnish. 12 violins to date (price £1,500).

NEMES, George. Distinguished contemporary maker working in London. Son of Stefan Nemes (b. 1908, Budapest); the family escaped from Hungary during the 1957 uprising and joined the workshop of Cyril Woodcock. See *Strad* (Aug. 1980), 262.

NEWORK GROUP A co-operative of contemporary luthiers: Rowan Armour-Brown, Paul Bowers, Paul Harrild, Philip Cray, Malcolm Siddall, and Patrick Jowett, established in 1989. See *Strad* (Aug. 1990), 606.

NEWBURGER, Henry (*fl.* 1820). Worked at Axbridge, Somerset.

NEWMAN, J. H. (*fl.* 1900). Worked at Croydon.

NEWTON, Isaac (*fl.* 1800). W.M.M. states that he made mostly for the trade, particularly for Betts. W.H. thinks little of most of his work.

NEWTON, Thomas (*fl.* 1745). Worked in Southampton St., Covent Garden, London, in the Tyrolean style. Indifferent work.

NICHOLLS, Colin G. Contemporary. Apprenticed to and worked with Hills 1966–77, then establishing himself at Northolt. Makes on Goffriller and Amati models (Vannes).

NICHOLSON, J. (*fl.* 1880). London. Another medical doctor with a strong interest in violins. Mainly experimental work to do away with the soundpost (W.H.).

NICHOLLS, Claire. Contemporary. Trained at Newark School and works at Heaton, Newcastle upon Tyne.

NISBET, William (1828–1902). Worked at Lint Mill, Prestonkirk, Scotland. 'An extraordinarily versatile man' (W.M.M.). Made 120 violins, some on the Maggini and some on the Amati model. 'The workmanship is excellent, and the tone very good.' (W.M.M.) Bronze medals at Edinburgh International Exhibition, 1886. Also a Strathspey player. Inscribed in pencil on inner back.

NOON, T. M. (*fl.* 1910). Amateur who worked in Cardiff.

NORBORN, John (*fl.* 1720). Worked in London. Label: Maker London 1723. Indifferent reputation. P 3/92/127 £605.

*†NORMAN, Barak (1688–1740). One of the most distinguished of the early English makers. See text. Also made viols. Worked at 'The Bass Viol in St. Paul's Alley London'. In partnership with Nathaniel Cross for some years. The Hill Archive gives an auction catalogue entry for 1874 (Foster's) for 'a fine violoncello of Barak Norman, 1710 . . . bearing Prince of Wales' crest. This violoncello was the favourite instrument of His late Majesty, George, IV.' S 11/91/134, *c.*1720, £1,100.

NORRIS, John (1739–1818) and NORRIS AND BARNES. Widely thought to have been a pupil of Thomas Smith but mainly a trader in partnership with Robert Barnes, Coventry St., London. His bows are thought to have been made by Dodd (W.H.). P 3/91/140, *c.*1770, £605.

NORRIS, Robert (20th cent.). London.

NORRIS, William (1727–98). Clergyman working at Wood Norton, Norfolk. Spent some time in Germany and visited Mittenwald. Has a reputation for refined workmanship on the Klotz modelling. Instruments branded 'N', but W.H. states that many now have a Klotz label within.

NOWAK, Steffen (b. 1958). Born in Bremen, Germany. Works at Totterdown, Bristol. Trained at the Welsh School of Musical Instrument Making and Repair. To date has made over 50 instruments, including violins, violas, and cellos, both modern and baroque.

NUTLAND, James (*fl.* 1777). Worked at Huntingdon. Hitherto unrecorded. One viola seen with ink purfling and in style of Stainer, body-length 15⅛ in. (384 mm).

O'CONNOR, Gerry. Contemporary. Ravensdale, Co. Louth, Ireland.

O'DUBHLAIODH, P. Contemporary. Trained at Welsh School of Violin Making. Works at Hibernian Violins, Malvern, Worcs.

O'HALLORAN, James F. Contemporary. Diploma, Cork School. Works at Carrigaline, Co. Cork, Ireland.

OLD, William (*fl.* 1880). Worked in Falmouth, Cornwall. P 7/91/20, £209.

OLDFIELD, W. (*fl.* 1870). Westmorland.

OLDHAM, Thomas (*fl.* 1820). Worked in Tewkesbury, Glos.

OLIVER, Barry, D. (b. 1946). Contemporary violin-maker working in Washington, Tyne and Wear. As a young man he worked with Lawrence Naisby in Liverpool (q.v.) and thereafter studied in Cremona, particularly with Morassi. See Alburger; also vL.

OLIVER, James (*fl.* 1820). Worked at Reading. Thought to have chemicalized his wood.

O'MAHONEY, James (*fl.* 1890). Worked at Michelstown, Cork, Ireland. A contractor and builder by trade credited with 60 violins in his spare time. W.M.M. speaks quite highly of this work. W.H. states mordantly that his violins 'satisfied violinists in Southern Ireland'.

OMOND, James (1833–1907). Credited with about 300 violins, violas, and cellos working from Stromness, Orkney, Scotland. 'He would have obtained a larger tone if he had given his plates a greater taper.' (W.M.M.) Work seen is solidly well-crafted with durable varnish. P 3/93/311, cello, 1898, £1,540.

O'NEILL, Gerard. Contemporary. Works at Corbally, Limerick, Ireland.

OPIE, A. J. (*fl.* 1910). Portsmouth. Naval scientist, credited with violins of 'beautiful workmanship' by W.M.M.

ORCHARD, Joseph (*fl.* 1850). Thought to have worked in Worcester.

ORR, William (*fl.* 1910). Broxburn.

ORTON, Philip (*fl.* 1850). Worked at Hereford. Ordinary work.

OSBORNE, Henry (*fl.* 1860). Worked at Sherborne. Mediocre work.

OSBORNE, Samuel (*fl.* 1890). Leamington Spa. A cabinet-maker who made a few instruments.

OSMOND, William (*fl.* 1820). Worked at Evesham. Variable work.

OTTLEY, Jacob (*fl.* 1800). Worked in Bristol. Little known but good reputation. 'Excellent modelling' (W.H.).

OUTRAM, Frederick (*fl.* 1820). Wrote his name in ink on the wood. Residence not known. W.M.M. saw 'a well-made instrument with a good tone'.

OWEN, Ivy Rimmer. (1883–?) Daughter of J. W. Owen, below. She pre-dates K. M. Laurence (q.v.) and may therefore have the distinction of being the first recorded British female violin-maker. Little is known of her work but W.H. speaks highly of it. One specimen violin seen was neat but rather heavy in the hand. P 11/922/245, 1905, No. 3, £568.

*†OWEN, John William (1854–1933). Worked in Leeds. One of the most distinguished professional violin-makers of this period. After a start in engineering he became enthusiastic about violins and went to France and visited one of the larger workshops there. French influence is obvious in his work, if not in his varnish which was oil of his own formula. Classic Italian modelling. 'A fine maker. Faultless work.' (Jalovec). Credited with about 200 violins, violas and cellos and repaired over 5,000 instruments. Prices in 1904 were for violins, from £12, violas, from £15, and cellos, £20. Printed label: 'J. W. Owen | Leeds' (date on bare wood after the maker's autograph). His work has lasted well on the whole. Also produced bows. Discussed further in text. P 9/90/125, Leeds, 1898, £1,320; P 3/93/188, No. 74, 1907, £2,310.

OXFORD VIOLINS: see under Guastalla, Kearns, and Yakoushkin.

OXLEY, Joseph (*fl.* 1800). Worked in Cambridge. 'Long, high-built instruments with a good, penetrating tone' (W.H.). Instruments branded.

PADDAY, Tony and Louise. Contemporary, working in Yeovil, Somerset.

PADDON, W. R. (b. 1905). Worked at Bingley, Yorks., where he was an art master at the Grammar School. Later worked at Shipley. Harris's brown oil varnish and modelling after Stradivari and Amati. Produced over 20 violins. Handwritten label, dated and numbered labels.

PAGE, Arthur Lewis (*fl.* 1910). Made at Uxbridge on Stradivarian modelling.

†PAMPHILON, Edward (*fl.* 1670–90). Worked on London Bridge (or so tradition has it) and discussed in the text. The family came from Essex as noted in the Hill Archive and recently exhaustively traced by Michael Coyne in *Pamphilon: An Essex Family* (1992). Edward had contemporary violin- or instrument-making relatives including an unrecorded Nicholas (d. 1727) and the family is traced back at least to the 15th cent. in Essex. As W.M.M. states 'his model is a sort of cross between the Brescian and Tyrolese types'. Some models double-purfled. Good reputation for his oil varnish. Reputation for tone is that it is clear, sweet, and responsive, if small. (Coyne's book suggests that Pamphilon also stuck his own labels into nondescript Italian instruments; see p. 91.) P 4/91/166, c.1680, £3,300.

†PANORMO family. A distinguished Italian family of luthiers, some members of which settled in London. See text. 'Founder' was *Vincenzo Trusiano*, 'old Panormo' (1734–1813). Sicilian in origin, he went to Paris in 1753 and then to Dublin in 1789 on the French Revolution breaking out. There he was associated with Perry. In 1791 he came to London and worked with John Betts. Here the Italian influence he brought to London making of the time was very significant. As a maker he is rated highly by the best Italian standards, but we can clearly only call him 'British' by adoption. C 6/90/335, £30,800. S 11/91/400, c.1790 (Hill certificate), £33,000. S 11/92/152, 1791, £33,000. Vincenzo's eldest son was *Joseph* (1768–1834). He worked in London with his father and family and also in King St., Soho. Brilliant and versatile, he died in poverty. High-quality instruments were produced and also some of the finest guitars ever made. A son of Vincenzo was *George* (1777–1845), who made fine Stradivari-pattern violins and cellos, and over 2,000 guitars. Another son, *Louis* (1784–1862) worked with Betts and subsequently in Bloomsbury. Again, well known for his guitars. He also made esteemed bows. He died in Auckland, New Zealand (vL). *Edward Ferdinand* (1811–91) was the son of Joseph. He was more of a guitar-maker. *George Louis* (or Lewis) (1815–77) was the son of George. He worked with his father and uncle, again specializing (but not exclusively) in guitars. See *NGD*; *NGDI*; *Strad* (Apr. 1986), 932 and (May, 1986), 34 (John Dilworth). George Panormo: S 11/90/109, c.1800 (Hill certificate), £6,600. Joseph Panormo: P 4/91/140, c.1800, £9,020.

†PARKER, Daniel (c.1680–?1730 or 1760). London. See text for the controversy about the dates and other features of this maker who is usually regarded as the finest representative of the Old English School. One of the earliest English makers to copy the long Strad pattern, usually 14¼ in. (362 mm) violin body-lengths. Some instruments have

been found with reported ink-written labels, but their authenticity is not established. High reputation for tone, as discussed in the text. Fritz Kreisler owned and periodically played a Daniel Parker. P 4/91/159, c.1750 £9,900. See *NGD*; *NGDI*; *Strad* (Dec. 1986), 371 (John Dilworth); *Strad* (Feb. 1994), 124 (John Dilworth).

PARKER, George Arthur (*fl.* 1920). Worked in London on Stradivari modelling. Also made strings from 1914.

PARKINSON, Brian B. Contemporary Hills-trained restorer of Harrow, mentioned in text.

PARKINSON, James (*c.*1858–1930). Llandudno. Interesting 'amateur' maker discussed in the text. Credited with at least 64 violins and 4 violas. See *Strad* (July 1929), 134. P 4/91/99, 1920, £672.

PATERSON, James (1834–98). Edinburgh maker well thought of by W.C.H. Copied the Count Cessol Stradivari. Formerly a cabinet-maker.

PATTERSON, William D. Contemporary. Medal from Crafts Council of Ireland. Works in Fermoy, Co. Cork, Ireland.

PAUL, Adam (b. 1945). Woodbridge, Suffolk. Trained at Cambridge and then for four years in Cremona, Italy, and with Sacconi. Also does fruit-farming. In an interview in *The Times* (20 July 1990) he stated that his violins were £1,000 +, violas £1,800, and cellos (taking two months to build) £2,500 +. Has an international clientele. See Alburger; vL.

PAYNE, Alan E. Contemporary. Montgomeryshire, Wales.

PAYTON, F. and W. C. (*c.*1925). Worked in Islington Green, London.

PEARCE, George (1820–56). London. Worked as an employee of Simon Andrew Forster, graduating from errand-boy. Sacked in 1844 for neglect of duties. Died in 1856 'through his own act and deed by swallowing poison' (Sandys and Forster, 348). He was capable of first-class work and occasionally an instrument with his own name appears. S 3/90/193, *c.*1840, £2,420.

PEARCE, James (*fl.* 1790). Saffron Hill, London. 'Shocking perpetrations in stiff looking outline' (W.H.).

PEARCE, Sleightolme (*fl.* 1929). Worked in Lincoln. Stradivari modelling.

PEACE, Thomas (*fl. c.*1800). Worked in London with his brother James (above). Similar work.

PEARCE, William (*fl.* 1835). Worked with Forster's and violins so labelled. Fair work.

PEARCE, William R. (*fl.* 1885). Worked in London. Indifferent reputation.

PEMBERTON, Edward (*fl.* 1660–1700). An early London maker whose varnish has a better reputation than his instruments.

PEMBERTON, J. (*fl.* 1585). Credited with a strange violin-like instrument owned by the Victoria and Albert Museum, perhaps once a cittern. This attribution is now thought to be incorrect. It is unlikely that there is any ascertainable violin-maker working so early in London.

PENERIO, Francesco (*fl.* 1924). Possibly an Italian maker working in London (or fictitious?). P 9/92/208, £494.

PERHAM, Walter James (b. 1883). Pupil of F. W. Channon and made in Newhall, Surrey, producing about 30 violins on Italian modelling.

PERKINS, John (*fl.* 1915). Northampton.

PERRY, James (*fl.* 1800). Worked at Kilkenny, Ireland and cousin of Thomas Perry (below). A large production of usually indifferent work.

PERRY, Joseph (*fl.* 1800). Worked in Dublin. Another cousin of Thomas, below. High reputation: 'modelling and varnish considered equal to the English Banks' (W.H.).

PERRY, Leonard Alwyn (b. 1921, Darlaston). Professional maker since 1950. Originally an engineer, then trained with John Alexander of Birmingham. In 1949 he won a diploma at The Hague. By 1993 he had made and sold world-wide 82 violins, 128 violas, 11 cellos, and several viols. Prices (1993): violins, £1,500; violas, £1,500; cellos, £4,250 (information by maker to author). Works in Deganwy, Gwynedd, North Wales. See Alburger; vL; (also entry in W.H.).

*PERRY, Thomas (?1744–1818). See the discussion in the text. Worked on his own and later with William Wilkinson in Dublin. Ireland's most renowned maker. Instruments branded 'Thomas Perry' or (probably only after Perry's death) 'Perry and Wilkinson', and some bear a label and a number. There are many crude German forgeries. The firm appears to have made over 4,000 instruments. Samples of his work are in the National Museum, Dublin. See also *NGDI*. P 11/91/106, *c.*1800, £1,760; S 11/92/342, Perry and Wilkinson, Dublin, No. 4421, £990; P 3/93/182, Perry and Wilkinson, branded 'Perry Dublin', 1804, £3,520.

PETHERICK, Horace William (1839–1919). Made a few instruments from Croydon. Best known as author of somewhat unreliable books on Stradivari and Guarneri.

PHILBRICK, Benjamin (*fl.* 1800). 'Bizarre, rough workmanship' (W.H.). Residence unknown.

PHILIP, William (*fl.* 1890). Made at Bathgate, Scotland. Good reputation.

PHILIPS, David (*fl.* 1900). Made at Haverfordwest, Wales.

PHILLIPS, John (*fl.* 1920). Made at Ynysbwl, S. Wales. Good reputation for Stradivarian modelling. Gold medal at Welsh Eisteddfod, 1920 for best Welsh violin.

PHILLIPSON, Edward (*fl.* 1900). Evangelist minister working in Cumberland and self-taught. Later instruments on Stradivarian model and completed one yearly. P 2/90/82, £278.

PICKARD, Handel (*fl.* 1862–75). Worked in Leeds before ill-health caused him to change occupation to innkeeper. Conscientious work, though thought to have chemically impregnated his wood.

PIERCE, Frank Allen John (b. 1908). A cabinet-maker by trade, he is given as working in Eastbourne. 'Excellent modelling' (W.H.).

PIERCY, W. J. (d. *c.*1963). Modern English maker who worked for 18 years for the Hill firm before becoming self-employed. (See also Beard, John; Vannes.)

PILLING, James (*fl.* 1915). Liverpool.

PIPER, William James (b. 1948). Contemporary English maker who learned his craft under the aegis of the Birmingham firm of Sydney Evans and was later associated with Thomas Smith Ltd., also of Birmingham. Credited with 185 instruments (see Vannes/Lebet, 1985), he has also taught over 100 pupils in a violin-making class at Colton Hills College, Wolverhampton. Currently working in Hanbury, Worcs.

PLANE, Walter (1848–79). Worked in 21 Brunswick Place, Glasgow, having access to one of David Laurie's Strads (see text). P 3/92/73, £1,034.

PLATT, A. W. (*fl.* 1920). Worked at Bradford, Yorks. 'Amateur' (W.H.).

PLOWRIGHT, Dennis. G. (b. 1925). Contemporary maker with an established reputation working in Exmouth, Devon. Originally trained as a chartered mechanical engineer. Since 1952 has completed 26 cellos, 90 violas, and 43 violins. Pays particular attention to gradation of thickness of back for tonal purposes. Uses oil varnish only.

POLLARD, Edwin (*fl.* 1920). Made primarily in Blackpool. 'Standard of workmanship never fluctuates from the good "honest" kind.' (W.H.) Also bows.

PORTER, Charles (*fl.* 1920). Worked in Wolverhampton.

POWELL, Thomas and Royal (late 18th cent.). Initially worked in Forster's workshop. Then worked at Clements Lane, Clare Market (London), *c.*1770 and St John's Sq., *c.*1800. Careful work, but rather weak tone (W.M.M.).

PRENTICE, Ronald (b. 1932). Contemporary maker working near Taunton, Somerset. Credited with over 200 instruments, violins, violas, cellos. Italian-styled double basses. Originally studied in Mittenwald. See Alburger; vL.

PRESCOTT, George (*fl.* 1885). Worked at Dublin. Credited with some excellent cellos (W.H.).

*PRESTON, James and John (*fl.* 1800). There is some mystery surrounding this name. It seems to be associated with an early 19th-cent. firm of publishers with a son Thomas. John Preston worked at 97 The Strand, London in the late 18th cent. and the variable, somewhat prolific work suggests more than one hand. There are 2 English guitars by a J. N. Preston, stated to be working 1734–70, in the Hill Collection, Ashmolean Museum, Oxford, and both stamped 'Preston Maker London' on back of pegbox. (Boxden, *Hill Collection*, 40–1.) There was also a maker of this surname in York, *c.*1790. Attractively engraved labels.

PRETTS, A. (*fl.* 1851). Worked in London with S. A. Forster. High praise from W.H., but work little known.

PRICE, Albert Henry (*fl.* 1890). Bow-maker in London. Pupil of Tubbs. (W.H. suggests simply a repairer.)

PRICE, Reginald Gordon (*fl.* 1935). Worked at New Malden, Surrey. See text. Pupil of William Glenister.

PRIDDEY, J. (*fl.* 1950). Worked in Handsworth, Birmingham. Hitherto unrecorded. One specimen still had sticky varnish 40 years after making. Underlying work good, though tone questionable.

PRIESTNALL, John (1819–99). Rochdale. Credited with 300 violins, 30 violas, 6 cellos, and 8 double basses. 'Reasonably good workmanship' (W.H.). 'He stamped his name on the back of his instruments under the button, and the number is punched on the button itself—a very tasteless method.' (W.M.M.)

PRINCE, W. B. (1856–1926). Worked in Upper Tooting, London, and thus labelled. Taught W. G. Geary (q.v.).

PRINGLE, David (*fl.* 1850). One violin from the north of England seen dated 1857 of somewhat rustic, baroque appearance. Probably would have been dubbed 'village carpenter' by the Hills, working from a long-superseded design. Not recorded elsewhere.

PROCTOR, Joseph (*fl.* 1845). Labelled as from Croft. Very flat modelling.

Pryce, Jonathan (*fl.* 1815). A clergyman who worked at Whixall, Shropshire.

Pryor (or Prior), William (*fl.* 1720). Worked at Gateside, Co. Durham. (Gateshead was commonly called Gateside at this time.) Interesting early English maker (or possibly put his labels in the work of others); discussed in the text.

Pullar, E. F. (*fl.* 1920). Plumstead, Kent. Born in Jamaica in 1872 of Scottish descent. Modified Guarnerian model with an oil varnish much praised by W.H., who gives the pure linseed-oil-based recipe.

Purday, T. E. (also Purdy) (*fl.* 1805–64). London. Primarily a dealer and music publisher, associated first with Button and then with Fendt. Instruments made by 'Purdy and Fendt' have an excellent reputation. See *NGD*.

Purvis (*c.*1790). North Shields. A violin so labelled seen which looked like good late 18th-cent. English work. Not recorded elsewhere.

Pycroft, Ernest (*fl.* 1875). Worked in Manchester.

†Pyne, George (1852–1921). Worked in Wardour St., London. One of the most successful of the makers of this period. Worked for 20 years with Edward Withers. 'An out and out patriotic Englishman, spiritually and mentally so much as to sometimes render his independence injurious to his bank book' (W.H.). Part of his character was never to descend to the unscrupulous copying of old Italian instruments or inserting fictitious labels. Also consistently praised English makers as being underrated. He specialized in producing well-made instruments at a price orchestral players could afford. His work is somewhat variable, but excellent at its best. Made every instrument personally. Credited with about 500 violins and violas. Classic Italian modelling. Pyne was also a violinist in various theatre orchestras. C 7/91/100, 1891, £2,200.

Radcliffe, A. H. (*fl.* 1925). Amateur who worked in Liverpool.

Rae, John (1847–?1920) Born in Scotland and made in London after 1883. Made two or three new instruments every year after many experiments in acoustics. Particularly known for his use of Californian pine (*sequoia gargantua*) for the tables of a number of his instruments. 'Immaculate workmanship attached to every detail' (W.H.). 134 instruments by 1924 (see P 10/81/37). Also a few violas and cellos. Instruments often numbered and dated.

Raeburn family. A family of Scottish makers, the best known of which are *Alexander* (1841–1907) who worked at Leven, Fifeshire; his brother *George R.* (1846–1918) also worked at Leven and at West Calder, near Edinburgh; also *John*, (1833–1910), eldest brother of Alexander and a coal-miner by trade, and *George* (1846–1918). John, also a poet and artist, worked at Largoward, St Andrews, and is enthusiastically described by W.H. Bronze medals Glasgow and Edinburgh Exhibitions. Violins sold for £5. John Raeburn: P 9/91/27, St Andrews, 1897, £1,100.

Raistrick, John W. (*fl.* 1905). Worked at Bradford, Yorks. 'Very good workmanship' (W.H.).

Raitt, J. (*fl.* 1900). Worked at Carphin, Fifeshire, Scotland.

Ramsay, William (*fl.* 1900). Worked at Biggar, Scotland. Above average. One attractively figured violin with exceptionally well-preserved varnish seen—sale-room estimate *c.*£600.

RATCLIFFE, Harry W. (mid-20th cent.). Worked in Lockwood.

RAWES, James M. (b. 1961). Works at Stanwix, Carlisle. Trained at Newark School of Violin Making and worked for W. E. Hill & Sons. To date has made 13 violins, 3 violas, and 4 cellos.

RAWLINS, Henry (also Rawlings) (*fl.* 1780). Worked in London and associated with the Italian virtuoso violinist Giardini who led the Italian Opera orchestra at the time. Some of his labels mention this. S 3/89/350, £1,540.

*†RAYMAN, Jacob (*fl.* 1650). The earliest clearly identified London violin-maker, discussed in the text. Of Tyrolean extraction and showing Tyrolean characteristics in his making, which could well have had a pervasive influence. Labels first from Blackman St., Southwark, London and then Bell Yard, Southwark.

RAYMANT, A. F. (*fl.* 1920). Worked in Bow, London. Classic Italian modelling.

RAYMOND, Robert John (b. 1911). Distinguished contemporary maker with 84 instruments to his credit comprising 37 violins, 39 violas, 3 mute violins, and 5 cellos. Formerly a local government officer who made his first instruments *c.*1959. Works in Colchester, Essex. See *Strad* (July, 1979), 206.

READ, John R. W. (*fl.* 1930). Worked in London. Talented pupil of George Wulme-Hudson. 'Excellent workmanship' (W.H.).

REDFERN, William (*fl.* 1830). Worked in London. Ordinary work.

REED, Joseph (*fl.* 1920). Worked in Barrow-in-Furness. Classic Italian modelling with oil varnish.

REEGAN (*fl.* 1805). Amateur who worked in Limerick, Ireland.

RETFORD, William Charles (1875–1970). One of England's finest bow-makers. See text. Employed for sixty-four years by W. E. Hill & Sons (1892–1956). Jalovec mentions that during his retirement he continued to produce the occasional specimen. His book, *Bows and Bowmakers*, was published in 1964. See also *NGD*. His son *William Richard* (1899–1960) worked with him at Hill's for a time.

RICHARDS, Don Louis (1859–94). Son of Philip, below. Worked in Wardour St., London. Very high praise from W.H. but his instruments are little known.

RICHARDS, Frederick George (1876–?1947). Made over 30 violins and 10 violas as a hobby. Stradivarian modelling. Resident at Eastbourne, Tunbridge Wells, and Torrington, Devon.

RICHARDS, Philip (*fl.* 1850–83). Father of Don Louis above. Worked in Wardour St., London from 1850 and then from 1880 in Noel St. Exhibited at the Great Exhibition in London, 1851, 4-stringed double basses. Reputation for conscientious work (W.H.).

*†RICHARDSON, Arthur (1882–1965). One of the most distinguished of England's makers of the first half of the 20th cent., working in Crediton, Devon. See text. Originally trained as a wood-carver and draughtsman. Won first prize in the Cobbett Competition, best-toned British violin, 1919 (and other prizes). Used particularly Millington's varnish. Associated with Lionel Tertis in the design of the Tertis model viola discussed in the text, a model not universally liked nowadays. See *Strad* (Aug. 1981), 271; *Strad* (Aug. 1984), 254; *NGDI*. P 3/91/92, viola, 1924, £715; P 6/90/204, violin, 1929, £2,200.

RICHARDSON, George (*fl.* 1890). Worked in Nottingham. Credited with 'some beautiful viols' (W.H.).

RICHMOND, Malcolm F. (*fl.* 1920). Worked in Falkirk. Pupil of Smillie of Glasgow. Fair work.

RIDGE, Eric V. (*fl.* 1950). Worked in Cheltenham and Gloucester, inexplicably omitted from other dictionaries. Also made guitars (see *Guitar News*, Mar./Apr. 1958). Neat workmanship and good tone. S 3/89/258, Gloucester, 1944, £572; P 4/91/43, 1947, £550.

RIMBAULT, H. E. (*fl.* 1900). Worked in Cardiff. 'Gentleman amateur' (W.M.M.), with fair reputation.

RINGWOOD AND WHEATLEY (*fl.* 1800). Ringwood worked with Perry in Dublin and formed a dealing partnership with Wheatley in the early 19th cent.

RIPPENGAL, C. W. (*fl.* 1940). Worked in Leicester and advertised his violins and 17 in. violas as 'personal work throughout'.

RIPPON, Alfred Ferdinand (*fl.* 1870). Worked in Reading. Stradivarian model, and a yellow-brown varnish. Used his own labels and facsimile Cremona labels.

RIPPON, John (*fl.* 1840) Worked at Peterborough, carving woodwork in the Cathedral. Some violins have fancy heads—fair reputation.

RITCHIE, Alexander (*fl.* 1925). Worked at Battersea Park, London. 'Capital workmanship, subtle varnish and very satisfactory tone' (W.H.).

RITCHIE, Archibald (1833–1902). Worked at Dundee, making about 200 instruments. Used Guarneri model, enlarged. 'The instruments look heavy, although the workmanship is beautifully finished.' (W.M.M.) Both W.M.M. and W.H. have some reservations about tone. Instruments labelled, numbered, and branded.

RITCHIE, John. Worked at Aberdeen and Dundee, probably late 19th cent. 'One viola named "Thistle" ' (W.H.).

ROBERTS, Albert J. (*fl.* 1915). London. According to W.H., originally a maker of reeds for woodwind instruments, but made about 20 good violins. It seems more likely that these are achievements of Alexander Roberts below. W.M.M. more reliably describes him as the founder of the Violin Makers' Guild established in the early 20th cent. at 35 Southend Rd., Hampstead, London, and discussed in the text.

ROBERTS, Alexander (1873–?). W.M.M. gives him as being born at Primrosehill, Fettercairn, Scotland, and it is possible that W.H. confuses him with the preceding maker.

ROBERTS, Derek (b. 1948). Trained at the Welsh School of Instrument Making and Repair. To date has made 14 violins, 8 violas and 1 cello. Works at Leamington Spa.

ROBERTS, John (*fl.* 1690). Given as working at Shrewsbury at this very early date. Work almost unknown.

ROBERTS, Lewis (1868–1917). Worked in Morriston, Swansea. 'He was the only Welshman whose efforts in violin making have assumed any very definite proportions.' (W.M.M.) He is credited with a large number of violins of indifferent quality, the later ones being on the Strad model.

ROBERTS, William (20th cent.). York.

ROBINS, F. (*fl.* 1830–90). Worked at Pilton Common, near Barnstaple before emigrating to Canada from which he returned later in life. Amateur work.

ROBINSON, Alfred George (*fl.* 1940). Worked at Willingdon, Sussex. 'Really splendid

Strad. modelling' (W.H.). First class workmanship ... good oil varnish.' (Jalovec). Diploma of Honour, International Exhibition, The Hague, 1949.

ROBINSON, James W. (b. 1948). American-born maker who trained in Cremona. Worked for a time in London, particularly with Ealing Strings and Cranston Workshop Ltd. (both in London). Subsequently worked in S. E. Asia, Hawaii, and the USA and is presently established in Sydney, Australia. See Alburger.

ROBINSON, Stanley. Son of William, below. Made at Abbey Wood, London.

†ROBINSON, William (1873–1960). See text. Worked in Plumstead, London. One of the more important makers of the first half of the 20th cent. in England. Produced instruments from 1908. He received encouragement from the London firm of dealers, Dykes and Sons, Bond St., but was largely self-taught. His work is very neatly executed, though the varnish has not always worn particularly well. Classic Italian modelling. Has a reputation for better tonal quality than some of his professional contemporaries—Albert Sammons is reputed to have used an almost new Robinson for one of his recordings. Credited with 430 violins, 40 violas, and 15 cellos. (See vL.) See also *Strad* (June 1982), 122. Label: William Robinson | Plumstead, London. | 1890 .. no. . WR. P 4/91/40, London, 1923, £880; S 11/91/137, Plumstead, 1931, £990; P 4/91/118, viola, London, 1944, £1,430.

ROBINSON, William (*fl.* 1930). An 'amateur' maker working at Liverpool, born 1882. Instruments have a good reputation. He charged £20 per instrument. See text. Label: Made by | Wm. Robinson | 2 Silverdale Terrace, Carmoyle Road | Liverpool | date.

ROGERS, George (*fl.* 1910). Worked at Conlig, Co. Down, Ireland. Credited with 'a number of fine instruments on the Stradivarian model' by W.M.M., who under his name writes a short encomium of Irish violin-making (or the comparative lack of it).

ROMNEY, George (1734–1802). London. See text. One of England's great portrait painters, he was also a fine cabinet-maker and wood-carver 'and he made a number of violins, which were ornamented with carved figures' (W.M.M.). He was also a good amateur violinist. One specimen was in the ownership of the Hill family. See *Strad* (Aug. 1940), 106, for illustrations of his ornamented instruments.

ROOK, Joseph (*c.*1770–1852). A good reputation for a few good-toned violins and cellos. Associate of the Forster family in Carlisle, where he was a Vicar-choral at the Cathedral (see Sandys and Forster, 292 and under Scott, Joseph, below). P 9/91/73, *c.*1850, £935.

ROPE, Alfred James (*fl.* 1925). A prolific maker who enlisted as a soldier aged 17 in 1879 and succeeded in making his first instrument at Aldershot Barracks, in 1890, which in itself deserves a medal. Credited with over 200 instruments, not enthusiastically reviewed by W.H. Worked in Woolwich. P 1/92/240, 1919, £165.

ROSE, James. Contemporary. Worked for W. E. Hill & Son. Works at Carlisle.

ROSE, John, father and son (*fl.* 1560–1610). Also 'Ross' and 'Rosa'. Early London makers of viols. The father worked in the mid-16th cent. in Bridewell and is sometimes known as the father of English viol-making. John Rose, jun. has an even finer reputation. See text. W.H. mentions a viola of 1598. If correct, this is the earliest English viola known by many years. It is more likely to have been a conversion of an instrument originally of the viol family. See also J. Stow, *Annales*, cited in D. Gill, 'An Orpharion by John Rose', *Lute Soc. Jnl.*, 2 (1960), 33.

Ross, Donald (1817–1901). Worked at Edinburgh. A forestry inspector by profession, he is credited with about 50 violins, generally on the Maggini model, of fair workmanship. Instruments apparently anonymous.

Ross, Rowland. Contemporary. Distinguished English maker specializing particularly in baroque instruments. Makes about 12 instruments a year. Works in Cowplain, Hants. (vL). See *Strad* (Sept. 1983), 309.

Rost, Franz Georg (20th cent.). 44 Lexington St., London, in 1953. Sound work. P 3/93/93, 1923, £1,100.

Roth, Paul Edwin (b. 1930). A German-born maker who worked for a time with the firm of Sydney Evans in Birmingham and then on his own, 1964–73, before returning to Germany. P 11/92/215, viola, Tertis model, 1957, £672.

Rowe, John (*fl.* 1880). An art master working at Taunton, Somerset, credited with about 12 well-made violins.

Rowe, Malcolm. Contemporary maker working in Leicester with an established reputation for his cellos in particular.

Rowe, Thomas A. (b. 1909). Produced some instruments from the Isle of Wight from 1941. Boat-builder by trade. Hand-drawn labels.

Rowinski, Stanislav (*fl.* 1920). A Pole who set up in London from 1882. Much of his work was done for the trade and none dates from later than 1922. Also made bows for the trade. His son, *Herbert* (b. 1895), worked similarly.

Rowley, Arthur John (*fl.* 1930). Worked in Coventry where he was born in 1880 and taught the violin. Credited with 100 violins up to 1930. Fair reputation. P 6/91/71, 1932, £440.

Roy, Andrew (*fl.* 1835). Thought to have worked in northern England. Little known. P 4/91/162, £1,430.

Rubio, David Joseph (b. 1934). A distinguished modern maker specializing in guitars and early string instruments as well as fine instruments of the violin family, used professionally. Initially studied medicine in Dublin. Also a distinguished writer. Based in Cambridge. A valuable account of his current working practices can be found in *Strad* (July 1993), 669. This describes, amongst other things, how, by combining craftsmanship with modern technology, Rubio is able to make 20 violins, 5–6 violas, and 5 cellos a year as well as a few guitars. He has no assistants. Initially he copied many historic instruments, having at least 40 moulds. He has now amalgamated them into a model of his own. He charges £3,750 for violins, £4,000 for violas, and £9,000 for cellos. See also *NGD*; vL; *Early Music*, 3/4 (1975), 355.

Ruddiman, Joseph (1733–1810). Worked at Aberdeen. W.C.H. suggests that because of his relatively early date he should be regarded as 'The father of Scottish violin makers'. Worked on the Stainer–Stradivarian model. 'A true artist' (W.C.H.). 'Wretched spirit varnish' (W.H.). Also made guitars, etc. Engraved label.

Ruiseal, Conchubhar. Contemporary. Diploma, Cork School. Works at Greystones, Co. Wicklow, Ireland.

RUNNACLES, Harry E. (Contemporary). Works in Stowmarket. A cello dated 1980 was numbered 56 and signed and dated internally. See P 6/94/334.

*RUSHWORTH AND DREAPER. This Liverpool-based firm, now Rushworth's Music House Ltd., was established in 1828 and its letterhead indicates: 'Five Generation Family Music House—the largest in Europe'. Their well-known 'Ardeton' stringed instruments were made between 1920 and 1943, mostly by an individual maker who was a member of a workshop team. Contrary to widely held belief, the violins were made by Richard S. Williams and Frank Fallowfield (who worked for the firm for over 60 years), Richmond ('Dickie') Bird made the violas, and cellos were made by George Hemmings. All craftsmen were trained by Bird. Varnishing was mostly by George Hemmings from his own recipe and the timber and fittings were from Germany. There were some 162 violins, 7 violas and 25 cellos. The name 'Ardeton' comes from 'A. Rushworth-Dreaper, made in Islington' (courtesy Garth Hennie, Manager, Violin Dept.). (Instruments labelled 'Apollo' are thought to have been imports.) 'Ardeton' violins sold for £20 in c.1930, new, and cellos £40 new. S 6/90/69, Ardeton, Liverpool, £2,090; S 11/92/28, Ardeton, 1925, £770; S 11/92/316, Ardeton, Liverpool, 1925, £880.

RUSSELL, George (*fl.* 1680?). W.H. gives an old English maker of this name.

RYLANDS, John. (*fl.* 1800). W.M.M. mentions him as a Bristol maker.

SABY, Henry Humphrey (1860–1930). Born in Burton Latimer, Northants. Saby was a capable performer and also studied violin-making with W. Calow of Nottingham. After emigrating to Cape Town, South Africa, in 1890 he enhanced his professional reputation. One of England's exports of talent—see text. Gold medal, Cape Town, 1904. See Pl. 15.

SADLER, Malcolm. (d. 1993). Expert (ex-Hills) and formerly senior proprietor of the large retail establishment Ealing Strings, London. Contributed to Jalovec.

SANT-CROIX, Ralph de (*fl.* 1910). Worked in London. Somewhat undistinguished work.

SAINT-GEORGE, George (*fl.* 1880). A violin and viola d'amore teacher who also made, particularly viols. Labelled as from London. His son *Henry*, also a violinist, wrote books for the Strad Library, his work on *The Bow* being the best known.

SAINT-JOHN (*fl.* 1870). Worked in Dublin. About 40 instruments, using wood from staircases of old houses.

SANDERSON, Derrick M. (b. 1932). Alva, Scotland. Formerly professional violinist with CBSO and BBC Scottish Orchestra. Has made copies of classic instruments including the Strad 'Archinto' viola and 'Messie' violin. Uses proprietary German varnishes, usually yellowish-brown. See Alburger; vL.

SAUNDERS, Stephen (*fl.* 1900). Worked at Twickenham. Worked for the London & South Western Railway and an enthusiastic string-player. 'A large number of violins of considerable merit, some of which were on the "long Strad" model' (W.M.M.). Handwritten labels and sometimes branded.

SAUNDERS, Wilfred George (and family) (b. 1927). One of the most distinguished of contemporary English makers, working in Nottingham. Trained as a joiner, he had always been interested in music and learned the violin. Motivated by a reading of Heron-Allen's book. Self-taught, but obtained help from distinguished makers such as Arthur

Richardson and the Hill family. Particularly renowned for his violas which are used professionally and internationally. This maker inserts a precautionary brand on the butt end of the neck beneath the fingerboard. He is also a distinguished and enthusiastic teacher, associated with the Newark School. See Alburger; vL; *Strad* (Aug. 1984), 252, illustrating his Tertis model violas. His son *Jacob N.* (b. 1959) works independently in Austria and is credited with 12 violins and 2 violas (see Vannes/Lebet).

SAXON, John (*fl.* 1815). Mentioned by W.M.M. as working in Stockport.

SCARFE, Roland (*fl.* 1925). Worked at Bexhill-on-Sea.

*SCHOLES, Arthur, L. (1870–? post 1926). A well-respected maker in his time and also teacher of a number of other English makers. Worked at Rushden, Bedford, and London. 'I have tried only one violin of this maker, which was a fine instrument with a large and brilliant tone.' (W.M.M.) 'An esteemed modern English violin-maker ... of German birth.' (Jalovec). Printed label with number of instrument and date handwritten.

SCHREIBER, Philipp (b. 1875, Markneukirchen, d. ?1930). Worked for J. W. Briggs at Glasgow before and after First World War and, according to William Smith, Briggs's pupil, Schreiber made many of Briggs's instruments except the heads. Also a clever mathematician and submarine designer.

†SCOTT, Joseph (*fl.* 1795). Instruments labelled as from Haltclife (or Hattcliff), Near Hesketh, New Market. The Hills give this as Cumberland (1904 Exhibition catalogue—see text) rather than 'Cambridge', per W.H. A maker who seems to be constantly mis-described in the dictionaries, W.H. dating him 1865–96. Regarding the maker Joseph Rook of Carlisle (q.v.), Sandys and Forster (350–1) state that he 'in 1795 worked as a farm-servant to a Mr. Scott, of Haltcliff, near Hesket New Market, who was also an amateur fiddle-maker, and from whom some knowledge was gained'. There were two well-made specimens, with somewhat elongated heads, in the Hill collection sold at Phillips in Apr. 1991. Approx. 200 instruments, all numbered. P 4/91/149, £1,870; P 4/91/150, £1,650.

SEXTON, John (*fl.* 1720). A rare London maker. See text. According to the Hill Archive he worked at London Bridge *c.*1728–47. The Hills only saw three examples of his work. They commented: 'General style and work show the influence of Parker, Barak Norman and Cross.'

SEYD, Ernst August (1866–*c.*1920). A good musician of German origin who worked in London both on a Stradivarian and original model. Fair reputation.

SEYMOUR (*fl.* 1890). Worked at Warwick and Leamington. Indifferent work. Instruments branded.

SHACKLETON, Daniel (end of 19th cent.). Worked in Bedford. A few good violas.

SHAKESPEARE, Michael. Contemporary. Working in Blackheath, London. Also teaches making with Pat Naismith (q.v.).

SHAW, John (*fl.* 1680). Early London maker. Famous for his fine viols. The Hills mention violins seen of 1656 and 1674 in the Urquhart style. They quote a label as 'John Shaw at the Goulden Harp and Hautboy nere the Maple in the Strand—1656'.

SHAW, John (*fl.* 1910). Worked at Hulme, near Manchester. A double-bass player whose instruments were favoured by orchestral players in Lancashire (W.H.).

SHAW, Thomas (*fl*. 1895). W.C.H. credits him with 11 violins made at Cove, Dumbartonshire. 'Good average ability' (W.M.M.).

SHELLEY, Jan (b. 1962). Graduate of Newark School. Makes, restores, and deals in Liverpool.

SHEPHERD, H. G. (*fl*. 1910). Worked at Brighton.

SHEPHERD, William N. (1932–84). Professional maker who worked at Shepherd's Bush, London, making his first instrument in 1949. Made about 120 instruments in all, mostly violas, for which he charged £850. Used oil varnish. It took him about 55–60 hours to make an instrument. Modified Strad modelling. See Alburger; *Strad*, (June 1984), 84.

SHERDON, Daniel (*fl*. 1850). Worked in Gloucester. Poor work.

SHIELDS (*fl*. 1890). Designed new type of bow from Manchester.

SIDDALL, Malcolm. Contemporary maker and restorer working at Llandovery, Wales. Diploma from Newark School.

SILCOCK, John (*fl*. 1730). The Hill Archive mentions an instrument from this maker labelled 'Instrument maker in Middle Row in Broad St. Giles, London 1731'. It was in the manner of Wamsley with dark golden-brown varnish.

SIMPSON, Frank Thomas (*fl*. 1925). Worked at Dunmow, Essex. Praised by W.H.

SIMPSON, George (*fl*. 1807). Worked in London.

SIMPSON, George S. (*fl*. 1925). A builder who made instruments in Crail, Scotland. Some instruments were decorated. Fair reputation.

SIMPSON, John and James (*fl*. 1735–90). A well-known 18th-cent. workshop whose instruments are branded. Fair 'old English' work. The Hills give as the earliest date 1735 from the Viola and Flute, Swithin's Alley, near the Royal Exchange, London. The Hills said that Lockey Hill worked for John Simpson. Worked from Sweeting's Alley, opposite the east door of the Royal Exchange, London. Co-founders in 1794 of Puttick and Simpson, the London auctioneers now part of Phillips. Discussed in text. P 4/91/145, *c*.1780, £2,860; P 11/92/207, *c*.1800, £2,640.

SIMPSON, Octavius (*fl*. 1825). Worked at Kelso, Scotland. Produced imaginatively decorated instruments. Otherwise, undistinguished work.

SIMPSON, Robert. (*fl*. 1925). An amateur who worked at Belfast.

SIMPSON, Thomas (1864–1933). Initially a piano repairer at Walsall, Staffs., but became established as a violin-maker in Handsworth, Birmingham. Spent his final years at Brixham, Devon. Credited with 80 violins of varying refinement. 'His later instruments are on the Strad model, and show much better work.' (W.M.M.) Also a fine reputation as a repairer in Birmingham. Also bows, stamped 'Simpson, Birmingham'.

SINCLAIR, William (1836–*c*.1900). Produced about 40 instruments. Mainly on Guarneri model, some experimental. Worked at New Pitsligo, Aberdeenshire.

SIRRELL, S. H. (*fl*. 1938). Stratford-upon-Avon.

SKEFFINGTON, William Kirkland (*fl*. 1890). Worked in Glasgow. Indifferent reputation.

*SKINNER, John Walter (1868–after 1930). A cabinet-maker who worked in Sheffield and produced a number of instruments well thought of by W.H. Labelled as from Sheffield, numbered and dated. P 7/91/81, Sheffield, 1921, £220.

SKRILEVICIUS, Vaitekus (b. 1921, Scotland). Works in Coventry. Has to date made 10 violins. Also a folk-violinist.

SLADE, Joseph. (*fl.* 1920). Mainly a flower-painter and horticulturist. Made instruments from 1886 on classic Italian modelling. 'Everything extremely well finished' (W.H.). Labelled as from S. Godstone, Surrey.

SLOUS, Gideon. (*fl.* 1840). Produced violins and violas in London which are signed below tailpiece. Work virtually unknown.

SMART, George. (*fl.* 1700). Worked in London, and particularly known for his cellos, many of which were exported to Holland. Unpurfled work redeemed by fine application of orange varnish. Instruments stamped 'G. Smart' under button (W.H.).

SMART, John. (*fl.* 1700). Worked in London producing violins, violas, cellos, and double basses. Instruments labelled as from Oxford Rd., London and sometimes branded below button.

SMILLIE, Alexander (1845–1918). Worked in Glasgow. Self-taught, but regarded as one of Scotland's finest makers. Credited with a large number of violins, violas, and cellos on the Stradivarian–Guarnerian models. Used Whitelaw's amber varnish. 'His instruments many years ago ranked, in my opinion, with the best that are made in Great Britain today.' (W.M.M.) Also an authority on Persian carpets (W.H.). Labelled as from Crosshill, Glasgow. Dated and numbered. C 11/90/334, Glasgow, 1905, £2,090.

†SMILLIE, Andrew Young (1878–1948). Son of Alexander above. Credited with 200 violins and some violas and cellos. Classic Italian modelling. 'Magnificent instruments' (W.H.). 'Handsome flat violas.' (Jalovec). Initially worked with his father.

SMITH, Alexander Howland (*fl.* 1900). Credited with about 50 instruments of ordinary quality, working from Edinburgh.

SMITH, Arthur Edward (*fl.* 1905). Initially worked at Morden, Essex and associated with the firm of Jeffreys and Sons of Morden. Migrated to Australia in 1909.

SMITH, Bert (*c.*1910–73). Worked in the English Lake District, mainly at Coniston. Copied classic Italian models, particularly the 'Messie' Strad—also large violas, and bows. A good reputation in his lifetime. P 10/91/105, 1953, £572; P 3/93/94, 1954, £1,430.

SMITH, James (*fl.* 1730). Little-known maker who worked in London in the early part of the 18th cent.

SMITH, James (*fl.* 1925). Worked at Chapelhall. Tone praised by W.H.

SMITH, James (*fl.* 1947). Worked at Coaltown-of-Wemyss, Scotland (W.H.).

SMITH, John (*fl.* 1800). Worked at Whitchurch, Shropshire. Amatise modelling.

SMITH, John (*fl.* 1850–1923). Worked at Teddington, London. Careful if undistinguished work. P 7/91/51, £616.

SMITH, John (1859–1941). Made some instruments in Falkirk and Glasgow before migrating to Winnipeg, Canada. Influenced by Davidson's book (see text). 'The work is beautifully finished . . . His scrolls are magnificently carved. The tone is large' (W.M.M.).

SMITH, John E. (b. 1867, fl. 1925). A pupil of the distinguished maker William Glenister (q.v.) and worked at 23 Beak St., London. Fair reputation.

SMITH, Nathaniel (*fl.* 1830). Worked at Bristol.

SMITH, Pye (*fl.* 1850). Worked in Hereford. Poor reputation.

SMITH, Robert (*fl.* 1910). Worked at Coatbridge, Scotland.

†Smith, Thomas (*fl.* 1740–90). Well known later 18th-cent. maker in London. He worked with and succeeded Peter Wamsley. 'Made many violoncellos of merit. Instruments of Stainer build. They are very like the work of Wamsley and are not unfrequently sold as his.' (Piper) W.M.M. remarks about his cellos: 'Such as I have tried had a hard, rasping tone.' This is probably uncharitable. 'Dirty amber or brownish yellow' varnish (W.M.M.). Various labels, one being 'Made by Thomas Smith | at the harp and hautboy in Pickadilly | London, 1759' (W.H.). P 3/91/202, 1783 (Hill certificate), £2,640; P 6/90/360, cello, London, 1760, £1,980.

Smith, Thomas (*fl.* 1922). Worked in Larkhal, Scotland. Mainly a farmer but produced about 40 instruments on classic Italian modelling.

†Smith, William (*fl.* 1780). An interesting maker whose work is little known. The best opinion is that he worked in London from about 1770 and then in Stockport and Sheffield (in Sycamore St.). (See Davidson, *The Violin*, 252.) The label given below suggests that he also made for the trade. Although the Hill Archive suggests that this Smith's instruments were all inlaid in the Sheraton manner (see illustration) and had obviously seen several such, John Basford, the Sheffield maker and connoisseur, tells the author that he has seen a number of 'ordinary', undecorated, instruments from this maker. Credited with a fine cello from Sheffield, labelled and branded 'Smith Sheffield' and dated 1782 (formerly in the Hill collection). Some instruments labelled 'Wm. Smith | Real Maker | London, 1771' (W.H.).

Smith, William (*fl.* 1800). Worked in Hedon, Yorks. and probably different from the preceding William Smith. Indifferent reputation.

Smith, William. See under Goldsmith.

Smith, William Edward (*fl.* 1900). Wetherby, Yorks.

Solomon, Gimpel (b. 1934). A talented maker born in New York and working in Bridgwater, Somerset. Known particularly for his violas and fine restoration work. See *Strad* (June 1982), 112.

Somny, Joseph Morris (*fl.* 1888–1931). A Mirecourt-trained maker who worked for Hills at Hanwell for 22 years before opening his own workshop there. Later worked from George St., Baker St., London. Variable work.

Sorrel, Frank (1920). Amateur who worked at Wesley, Essex and Great Bentley. Poor reputation.

Soubeyran, Ariste Marc (b. 1957). A contemporary maker now working in London and trained in Brienz. Worked with Dietrich Kessler at E. Withers Limited before setting up on his own.

Southgate, W. (*fl.* 1890). Worked in Birmingham.

Sowerby, A. L. (*fl.* 1910). Worked from 87 Fitz George St., Manchester, as professional maker and repairer. 'Good modelling and varnish' (W.H.).

Spicer, John (*fl.* 1660). Generally thought to have been a dealer in viols and violins.

Spicer, William (*fl.* 1860). Worked in London (W.M.M.).

Stagg, John William (b. 1954). Distinguished contemporary bow-maker who worked with Hills until 1983. Currently working in Bristol. See text.

Stanley, Robert A. (*fl.* 1915). Manchester. Fair reputation. P 11/90/198, 1917, £825.

STEDMAN, Royston. (*fl.* 1870). Worked at Leyton, Essex. Fair reputation.

STEELE, James (*fl.* 1925). Worked at Wallington, Surrey. Born Cumberland, 1878. Started making in 1920, particularly influenced by the 'Messie' Strad. Well thought of by W.H.: 'Flawless workmanship'.

STEELE, Kelvin. Contemporary. Newark-trained. Works at Nottingham.

STENT, E. (*fl.* 1914). London.

STEPHENS, G. D. (*fl.* 1870). Worked in Bristol. 'Very fair work' (W.M.M.).

STEVENSON, Samuel. Contemporary, working in Co. Antrim, N. Ireland.

STEWART, N. (*fl.* 1850). Previously unrecorded. S 3/90/178, cello (mid-19th cent.), £7,620.

*STIRRAT, David (*fl.* 1810–20). Worked in Edinburgh. Workmanship is thought to be good but used spirit varnish thinly applied. 'His workmanship is finished with extreme care and delicacy' (W.M.M.). Name, place, and date usually written on bare wood with a hard pencil. Suffered from ill health and died prematurely. S 6/90/403, £2,610.

STOCKDALE, William (*fl.* 1910). Worked at Acklington, Northumberland. Guarneri modelling preferred.

*STONEMAN, Henry (*fl.* 1920). Born in Devon in 1856. He made his first violin in 1903, being a joiner and cabinet-maker by trade. Worked in Exeter and named his instruments. 'Very worthy productions' (W.H.). Usually used seasoned Italian wood. Instruments labelled, named, and numbered.

STOPPANI, George (b. 1949). Contemporary maker working in Manchester and credited with 70 instruments to 1985 (vL).

STOTT, George Theodore (1870–1953). A professional maker working in Liverpool who produced about 60 instruments to 1925. Stradivarian modelling. Oil varnish. Instruments labelled as from Liverpool and dated.

STRONG, John (*fl.* 1640). A viol-maker.

STRONG, Matthew (*fl.* 1870). Worked in Huddersfield.

STROUD, Cyril Charles (20th cent.). Peterborough and Etwall, Derby (1974).

SWANSTON, Leo (1868–1906). Amateur who worked in Newcastle upon Tyne (a cabinet-maker by trade). Made about a dozen violins (W.H.).

SWEETING, T. (*fl.* 1900). Worked in Horsforth, Leeds. (Not mentioned elsewhere.)

SYKES, Kevin. Contemporary. Works at Galway, Ireland.

SYMINGTON, George (*fl.* 1880). Worked in Kilmarnock, Scotland. Previously unrecorded. P 6/90/347, cello, 1883, £770.

*†SZEPESSY, Béla (1856–1925). A distinguished Hungarian maker (whose name is often reversed by dictionary writers, etc.) who worked some forty years in London. Trained under Nemessanyi and in Vienna, he made some of the finest violins available in London during these years which have maintained their superb reputation. He cannot in any sense other than the residential be said to be 'British', but he exercised a beneficent influence on other London makers of the time. It is extraordinary that W.M.M. should omit him entirely. He is credited with rather more than 300 violins and around 2 dozen larger instruments. As would be expected from such a prolific maker, not all his instruments are of the same quality or finish but they are without exception well con-

structed and have always been popular with players for their tonal qualities. See text. Also *Strad* (Oct. 1946), 166. P 9/91/144, 1885, £6,380; C 7/91/104, 1896, £7,150.

TARR, Aubrey James (*fl.* 1945). Amateur working at Exmouth, Devon.

TARR, Joseph C. (d. 1926). Son of William Tarr, below, who worked at Manchester before emigrating to New York.

TARR, Thomas (*fl.* 1880). Worked at Sheffield and made violins and 'several orchestral double basses of strong tone' (W.H.). Probably son of William (below).

†TARR, William (1809–92). See text. One of England's most prolific double-bass makers, working from Manchester. Credited with at least 200 double basses, but also made violins, violas, and cellos. His reputation rests primarily on the larger instruments.

TAYLOR, A. Contemporary violin-maker; instruments labelled as from Ash Vale.

TAYLOR, B. (*fl.* 1750). Worked in London. 'Very fair work' (W.M.M.).

TAYLOR, David W. (b. 1940). Bow-maker, apprenticed with Hills in 1956 and became their principal restorer—he is reported to have restored a Tubbs bow in 13 pieces! Self-employed since 1966 in Norwood Green, near London. (See Vannes.) Work of the fine quality and character which one would expect from someone with this background. Stamped 'D. W. Taylor'.

TAYLOR, Edward (*c.*1820). Worked in Hull.

TAYLOR, Malcolm M. (b. 1933). Contemporary bow-maker initially working with Hills under Arthur Bultitude and W. C. Retford. Fine reputation. Given as working in Barnstaple, Devon. See *NGDI*; vL.

TAYLOR, Michael (b. 1949). Bow-maker (and also violin-maker) who has produced distinguished work and is associated with the firm of Ealing Strings in London. His copy (1987) of the 'Hellier' inlaid Stradivari is illustrated in the firm's publication *The Stradivari Influence* (London, 1987), 140–1. See *NGDI*; vL.

TAYLOR, Robert (*fl.* 1917–46). Worked in Leicester. A professional maker who achieved a fine reputation for his instruments, particularly violas, and also bows. Used his own brand of oil varnish. Original models based on modified Italian classical design. P 10/91/96, 1912, £682.

TAYLOR, Stephen Oliver (*fl.* 1920). Worked at Leicester specializing in cellos. 'His cellos are really the finest things in the way of new instruments that I have seen.' (W.M.M.) A reluctant seller in his lifetime, it seems.

TAYLOR, Thomas Duxbury (*fl.* 1880). Credited with 10 violins from Bolton (W.H.).

TAYLOR, William (*fl.* 1790). Assistant of Panormo, working in Drury Lane, London. Particularly esteemed for his double basses. Label: Gulielmus Taylor, 1798 (and others). Instruments sometimes branded. W.H. draws attention to possible fakes.

TAYLOR AND TAYLOR (*fl.* 1885). Worked in London on an experimental, but unsuccessful 'Duplex String Violin' (W.H.).

TEALE, John (*fl.* 1825). Worked in London. Fair work.

TEMPLE, George (*fl.* 1945). Worked in Morpeth and Broomhill, Northumberland. Classic Italian modelling—'competent workmanship' (W.H.). Also Tertis model violas. His brother *William* is credited with a number of bows.

TENNANT, James (1790–?1860). A strathspey player working in Lesmahagow, Scotland, who also made violins, violas, and cellos in his later life. Indifferent work.

THERESS, Charles (*fl.* 1845–60). Born in Mirecourt, France, but worked with Maucotel in London, 1845, and in King St., Soho, 1848–60. (W.H.).

THIRLBY, C. S. (*fl.* 1910). Romsey.

THOMAS, R. J. (*c*.1900). Worked at Darlington, England.

THOMAS, Watkin (1849–1908). Worked at Swansea, Wales. His erratic reputation is mainly for poor-quality work.

†THOMPSON family (*fl. c*.1746–1805). The importance of this London family of putative makers lies not in the quality of their instruments (see the discussion in the text) but in their prolific production. Since this production is so variable in quality, it is likely that the 'makers' in the family either ran a workshop or used outworkers. As Piper says, 'there were several makers, or rather instrument dealers, in business in St. Paul's churchyard. Instruments vary, and the violoncellos are often better than the violins. The latter are generally a sort of mixture of the patterns of Stainer and Amati, with red or yellow varnish, and of no particular character.' (p. 265). The firm were also music-sellers and publishers and general dealers in musical instruments. The earliest Thompsons were *Robert* and *Peter*, the former working from about 1746 to 1785 'At the Bass-Violin in St. Paul's ally c/o St. Paul's Churchyard'. *Peter* worked from about 1746 to 1757 and was succeeded by his widow Ann and his son Charles. *Charles and Samuel* Thompson worked in St Paul's Churchyard *c*.1770–90 and instruments bearing their joint names are common. *Peter* (*c*.1779–94) and *Henry* (*c*.1793–4) also worked with Samuel, and Henry continued the business after Samuel's death. By 1805 the business seems to have been taken over by Button and Whitaker. The above genealogy is based on vL and *NGD*; W.H. gives a rather different account of this family and includes a *Simon* (1790–1802) and a *John* (J. M. A.), 1753–9. There is little dispute, however, that the instruments were sold for the lower end of the market, some being unpurfled and crude, but others are, as W.H. says, 'never wholly indifferent but also never high class'. Some scrolls will be found unduly petite. Violas were made by Charles and Samuel generally to a body length of 15¾ in. (400 mm). S 3/90/217, *c*.1780 by Charles and Samuel Thompson, £1,430; P 11/92/122, 1810, C. & S. T. (labelled and branded), £682; P 11/92/175, 1770, similar, £792.

THOMPSON, Edward Fernleigh Maurice (1892–after 1960). Worked in Worthing, Sussex, and Cornwall. Made a small number of Guarneri-model violins. Emigrated to New Zealand late in his life.

THOMPSON, James (*fl.* 1830). Worked in Crookham. Indifferent work. Instruments branded 'J.T'.

THOMPSON, James (*fl.* 1865). Worked in Whitehouse, Scotland. W.H. speaks well of his work—'modelling almost exquisite'—or is this faint praise? Little known.

THOMPSON, James (*fl.* 1930). Worked at Old Heaton.

THOMPSON, Phil (b. 1943). Contemporary maker working in Altrincham, Cheshire. Has a degree in mechanical engineering and was taught violin-making in part by S. G. Lowe of Hale, Cheshire. 6 violins and 5 violas (plus some guitars and a viola d'amore) since 1974.

THOMPSON, William (*fl.* 1880). Worked at Bishop Auckland. Indifferent work.

THOMSON, James (*fl.* 1848). Worked at Berwick-on-Tweed. 'A talented and enlightened maker' (W.H.).

THOMSON, W. M. (*fl.* 1920). Worked at Dysart, Kirkcaldy, Scotland. A cabinet-maker who made a few good-looking but indifferent-sounding instruments.

THORBURN, S. W. (*fl.* 1910). Symington Mill.

THORLEY, N. (*fl.* 1850). Worked at Failsworth, Manchester. Orchestral player who produced a fair number of violins and cellos for his orchestral colleagues. S 6/91/122, cello, £1,540.

THORLEY, Thomas (*fl.* 1870). Worked at Manchester, being the son of the above.

THORN, William (*fl.* 1875). Worked at South Molton, Devon. W.H. remarks on his cellos of excellent sonority.

THOROWGOOD, Henry (*fl.* 1750). Worked at 'The Violin and Guitar' under the North Piazza of the Royal Exchange (in London). Instruments rare.

THOW, John (*fl.* 1870). Worked at Dundee, Scotland. Respectable instruments on classic Italian lines. Instruments branded and date-stamped on scroll.

TILLER, C. W. (*fl.* 1895). Cabinet-maker working at Boscombe and Bournemouth. Often one-piece backs. Oil varnish (W.H.). P 11/90/296, Boscombe, 1915, £374.

TILLER, Wilfred (20th cent.). Martock.

†TILLEY, Thomas (*fl.* 1770). An interesting London maker, whose work is little known. W.H. remarks on the 'accurate and neat workmanship, admirable tinted varnish'. (This is a beautiful golden-brown colour.) It may be that he mainly worked for the trade. He used a manuscript label 'Market Lane, St. Jameses', London. The Hill Archive comments on the likeness of Tilley's instruments and those of Joseph Hill ('our ancestor'). The Hills were of the view that Joseph's production of cellos was suspiciously high and thought that Tilley probably worked for Joseph Hill. P 6/92/192, cello (one-piece slab-cut back), 1768, £5,060.

TIPPER, J. W. (*fl.* 1918). Worked in Derby.

†TOBIN family. *Richard* Tobin (1777–1841) is discussed in text. Initially he worked in Dublin with Thomas Perry and then went to London *c.*1798 to work for John Betts (primarily) until his death in Shoreditch Workhouse in 1841. As W.M.M. states: 'The few instruments which have been recognised as the undoubted work of Tobin are acknowledged to be of a very high order of merit—i.e. "very high" relatively to the work of the Old English school. I know of three Tobin violins, of the Grand Strad model, which I consider to be superior in point of workmanship to anything ever made in this country.' Tobin worked at a time in London when, under the influence of Panormo and others, his own 'Old English style' changed from being dominated by the Stainer–Amati influence to one far more modelled on Stradivari in particular and allegedly Guarneri (though this seems anachronistic). Tobin has been particularly praised for his scrolls, but enthusiasts have pointed out that, at his best, all points are superbly done. He could also produce indifferent work, a trait traditionally attributed to dissolute habits and alcoholism. Though he made largely for others, some instruments are branded internally. Readers are referred particularly to a detailed survey of his work by John Dilworth in

Strad (May 1985), 44. Tobin's son, *James*, worked in London c.1830–50. W.H. places his work at the same level as his father. Tobin, Richard: P 6/91/159, London, c.1824, £4,400; S 11/91/276, cello, early 19th cent., £2,860.

TODD, G. (*fl.* 1898). Worked at Tweedmouth, Scotland.

TODD, John (*fl.* 1795). Worked in York. Unrecorded elsewhere. Typical Old English work of no great distinction. (1 viola seen.)

TOLLEY, William Henry (*fl.* 1925). Worked at Miles Platting, Manchester. Strad modelling.

TOLMIE, G. (*fl.* 1900). Worked at Hanwell, Middx. An amateur whose work W.H. praises as being very respectable.

TOOMEY, Timothy (*fl.* 1920). A serious maker whose early work comes from Bolsover, Derbyshire (up to 1897) and then from London. Made violins, violas, and cellos with steadily improved varnishing results. W.H. speaks well of his work. Instruments numbered and labelled.

TOPHAM, Carass (b. 1930). Distinguished contemporary maker working in Radley, Abingdon, Oxon. Specializes in violas but has also made violins and cellos.

TOPHAM, John Carass (b. 1951). Son of the above and trained in Mittenwald and London. Established in Redhill, Surrey (vL).

TORR, Ernest (*fl.* 1920). Born in Bootle, near Liverpool, in 1871, this maker (overlooked by writers other than W.H.), having learned his trade with George Byron of Liverpool, is credited with 100 violins, 7 violas, and 5 cellos up to 1927. Preference for Strad modelling and made careful experimentation with plate thicknesses, weight of instrument, and varnishing. W.H. gives him 95 per cent for design, workmanship, and varnish for his later instruments. Label: Ernest Torr | Liverpool, 1927.

TRANTOR, Thomas (*fl.* 1900). Worked in Liverpool. Instruments branded. P 3/93/59, £396.

TRIMNEL, Joseph Henry (*fl.* 1890). Worked at Birmingham—amateurish work.

TRINGHAM, Henry (*fl.* 1840). Worked at Shrewsbury. Poor work.

TRUEMAN, Richard (*fl.* 1825). Very small production from Bath. 'Pretty design' (W.H.). Influenced by Amati.

TUBBS family. See discussion in text. The best-known is *James* Tubbs (1835–1921). This bow-maker is known all over the world and is often regarded as the equal, or almost the equal, of some of the great French bow-makers. His work is analysed in the text. James's father *William* (1814–78) worked at Thomas Dodd's in London before becoming self-employed elsewhere in London. In turn William's father was *Thomas* (c.1790–1860) who made in the style of John Dodd. Very high reputation. James's son *Alfred* (1863–1909) worked with his father. There were also other members of the family—for instance *C. E. Tubbs*. Bows stamped as indicated in the text. James Tubbs in particular was very prolific, making at least 10 bows per month. The sticks are generally round and of dark pernambuco. Tubbs, James: S 3/91/28, silver violin bow, £2,200; S 3/91/49, chased gold violin bow, £5,720; C 7/91/60, silver cello bow, £3,300; S 11/92/100, silver-mounted bow, plain ebony frog, 60 g, £4,400. Tubbs, Thomas: S 11/91/99, violin bow, early 19th cent., £1,100.

TUNNICLIFFE, Brian. A contemporary bow-maker. Works in London. Pupil of Arthur

Bultitude and makes in the classical French style. Also historical bows. Stamp: B. Tunnicliffe. See *Strad* (June, 1984), 104; vL.

TURNBULL, William (*fl.* 1876–89). Dundee. Scottish Guarneri modelling with 'fairly tasteful workmanship' (W.H.).

TURNER, John (1790–1862). Worked in London, being a dealer and importer. Instruments branded under button. They seem to emanate from Continental Europe with lion heads, etc.

TURNER, William (*fl.* 1650). Worked in London, being one of the early viol-makers of great distinction. W.H. reports two purported violins from his hand, but this seems doubtful.

TWEEDALE, Charles L. (*fl.* 1900–40). Vicar of Weston, Yorks. See text. A prolific maker who must be regarded as professional since he actively marketed his instruments and produced catalogues. Very influenced by spiritualism and was under the impression that he was in receipt of Stradivari's varnish recipe direct from that maker. The tatty appearance of many of his instruments now rather belies that theory. The workmanship is sound enough and a few nicely wooded instruments (he made in different grades) have survived quite well. He gave his instruments fanciful names and this information appears on a picturesque photographic label. P 9/90/182, 1924, £396.

TWEMLOW, S. P. (*fl.* 1925). Resident at Sandbach, Cheshire. Fair reputation.

*TYSON, Herbert William (*fl.* 1900). Worked at Louth, Lincs. Specimens seen suggest competent and attractive work. Very little said about him in the dictionaries. Italian modelling with varying shades of brown oil varnish. 'Good work.' (Jalovec).

TYE, J. (*fl.* 1850). Worked at 37 Agnes St., York Rd., Lambeth, London. Possibly also in Liverpool. Indifferent reputation.

UNSWORTH, Victor. A contemporary maker of standing. Works in Bristol area. See *Strad* (Nov. 1979), 321.

URQUHART, Alexander (*fl.* 1900). Made at Invergordon, Scotland. W.H. praises strong tonal sonority, if only average workmanship.

URQUHART, Donald (*fl.* 1895). A self-taught enthusiast who made in his spare time. Instruments, numbering about 20, labelled as from Tain, Scotland.

URQUHART, Thomas (*fl.* 1680). See text. His work comes from London (his workshop being on London Bridge). Thought by some to have come from Scotland at the invitation of Charles II. One of the first of the Old English School, with good reputation. Particularly praised for his oil varnish 'equal to the Cremonese in transparency and flexibility' (W.H.). (The Hill Archive disputes the theory that Urquhart actually came from Scotland, suggesting that this arose from a confusion of names.) P 4/91/174, (table off), £2,640.

VALE, Robert. Contemporary maker and restorer working at Droitwich, Worcs.

VALENTINE, William (*fl.* 1860). London. Not in W.H., or W.M.M. Hart says 'made many double-basses for Mr. Hart, which are highly valued'. Died about 1877. Probably something of an unsung hero, at least in the double-bass world; see also Ch. 1.

VAN EDWARDS, David (b. 1942). Self-taught. Works and teaches in Norwich, specializing in lutes and baroque instruments and early bows. Output to 1993 approximately 350 bows. Prices in 1993: £150–250. Besides pernambuco uses snakewood, ebony, greenheart, and partridge wood.

VAUGHAN, David Robert (*fl.* 1926). Worked at Chester. 'Excellent Strad modelling' (W.H.).

VAUGHAN, Derek (b. 1931). Formerly a professional viola-player and then associated with the Newark School. No. of instruments (violins and violas) to 1993: about 50. Works at Lynton, Devon. (vL).

VAUGHAN, J. (*fl.* 1895). Worked at Dublin.

VAUS, W. (*fl.* 1925). Worked at Hackney, London. Small production.

VEGTER, Hugo. Contemporary. Specializes in baroque, using traditional tools. Also bows. Works in Cobh, Co. Cork, Ireland.

VERNON (*fl.* 1825). Nephew of John Betts and thought to be purely a dealer.

VERNON, John Maurice (1901–70). A talented, apparently amateur, maker who was a close friend of George Wulme-Hudson. Bronze medal at the 1951 Festival of Britain competition. Owned some fine Italian instruments, including a J. B. Guadagnini, from which he made copies. Much respected by Arthur Hill. See *Strad* (Feb. 1985), 759 (Albert Cooper).

†VINCENT, Alfred (1877–1947). Often regarded as one of the finest makers in London of his era, he is inexplicably omitted by most of the dictionaries, including W.M.M., Vannes, and vL. W.H. devotes a short but useful paragraph about his 'beautiful workmanship'. Jalovec dubs him 'competent amateur violin-maker'. Discussed in text. Played as leader of the orchestra at His Majesty's Theatre. In 1923 he won the Cobbett Competition for British makers of stringed instruments, beating William Robinson, Arthur Richardson, and William Glenister into equal second place. His violin and a Stradivari were then played behind a screen by Albert Sammons and the audience voted by a clear majority in favour of the modern instrument. Vincent became known as the 'English Stradivari', slightly absurd to be sure, but an indication of the esteem in which his instruments were and continue by many to be held. (See Scholes, *Mirror*, 366). Vincent was originally trained as an engineer and was assisted in his work by his brother (H. Vincent). They worked at Great Pulteney St., Soho, London, but in later life Albert Vincent suffered from ill health and retired to Brighton. He is credited with over 300 instruments and he bequeathed a quartet to the Royal Academy of Music. C 11/91/113, 1922, £2,860; P 6/90/205, *c.*1910, £3,740.

VLUMMENS, Dominic C. (*fl.* 1925). Born in Antwerp in 1885, his father being a repairer. He worked in London, setting up on his own *c.*1925 (W.H.). Well thought-of classic Italian modelling. Label: 'Dominicus Vlummens | London 19– + O.C. S 6/90/103, London, 1925, £2,310.

*VOIGT family. One of the oldest violin-making families in the world, the line extending back to Adam of Markneukirchen in 1699. *Arnold* (1864–?1927) worked mainly in Markneukirchen but established himself in London 1885–90. He was both a skilful violin-maker and bow-maker. *Paul Arno* (1881–1970) joined the workshop of T. Earle Hesketh in Manchester in 1899 and established his own business in Manchester in 1905. His son *Paul* (1912–91) was apprenticed at Markneukirchen, then returned to his father's business in Manchester and subsequently established a business in Shaftesbury Ave.,

London, with his elder brother Ernst (b. 1911). *Peter Ernest* (b. 1943) is the son of Ernst and works in West Sussex (vL). Instruments produced by the English branches of this family have a high reputation for workmanship and tone. *Paul* jun. is remembered with respect also as a restorer and retailer in London. *Eric*, contemporary maker and restorer, works in Manchester. See *Strad* (May 1992), 454. P 2/91/102, Paul Voigt sen., Manchester, 1907, £607.

VOLLER brothers. Brothers were *William* (b. 1860), *Charles*, and *Arthur* who worked at Streatham, London, c.1885–1935. The Voller family is thought to be either of Dutch or English origin. In the 19th cen. they were particularly associated with Hart & Son and thereafter worked independently. Their instruments are occasionally labelled 'Voller, London' followed by number and date. Shadowy figures, they were so successful at imitating Italian work that much of it swiftly entered the violin underworld and acquired Italian labels. 'Appearance of wear and age marvellously accomplished' (W.H.). A few experts now reckon that they can readily identify the work of the Voller brothers, but the Vollers were perhaps the most successful of modern English makers in the art of exact imitation. Accordingly, when identified, their instruments can be very valuable though originally sold at £20 for violins, £25 for violas, and £36 for cellos (W.H.). They made well over 300 instruments. They are authoritatively believed to have made the so-called 'Balfour' Strad, a *cause célèbre* at the turn of the century. Jalovec adds that they made aptly named *Schwindelgeigen* for Hamma of Stuttgart, and also 'cannibalized' old instruments. The Hill Archive has some detail on the Voller family supplied by a correspondent writing in 1936 from Minehead (name illegible). This letter states that the father of the Voller brothers was a Shropshire farmer. The division of labour was that William Voller, who died in 1933, did most of the varnishing. Alfred Voller, who died at Salcombe in 1917 or 1918, was the scroll-cutter, and Charles Voller, still living in 1936, made the bodies. For a great many years they lived together at Streatham Hill and before that at Wormwood Scrubs (presumably 'outside' rather than 'inside'). Their varnish came from a recipe supplied by a Dr Duncan who found it in Cremona. They started by opening a shop in Notting Hill Gate after working with Frederick Chanot. All three were trained orchestral players, William on the viola, Charles on the violin, and Alfred on the cello. Alfred and Charles remained bachelors; William married and had two daughters. See W.H.; *NGDI*; vL; the author's book on *Violin Fraud* (Oxford, 1992); Albert Cooper, 'A Tale of Copies and Collusion', *Strad* (Jan. 1993), 48 (with colour illustration); Andrew Hill's illustrated article on 'The Balfour "Stradivari"', *British Antique Dealers' Handbook* (1988), 47. C 6/90/331, £14,300.

VRINT, Peter (*fl.* 1898–1933). Dutch father and son with establishment at Charing Cross Rd., London. Mirecourt-influenced production of large-proportioned instruments—loud but not lovely (infers W.H.). Also bows.

WADE, Joseph (*fl.* 1884–1900). Worked near Leeds producing 'well over 100 splendidly made instruments' for £15 and £20 (W.H.).

WAKE, Henry Sebastian (b. 1900). Born in Newcastle upon Tyne he became another British export, emigrating to Philadelphia, USA, and later San Diego, as cellist, author, and maker.

WALKER, Hector M. (1925). Amateur maker at Liverpool.

WALKER, Henry (*fl.* 1910). Worked at Stoke-on-Trent.

WALKER, Henry J. (*fl.* 1900). Worked at Whitby, Yorks. Described by G. Foucher, *Treatise on the History and Construction of the Violin* (London, 1894), as 'one of the most skillful scientific workmen of the present day ... His instruments are handsome copies of Stradivarius and of excellent tone.' (p. 52)

WALKER, John (*fl.* 1835). Rustic maker who lived at Martley, Worcs.

WALKER, John (1876–1957). Worked at Solihull, near Birmingham. Originally a professional violinist in Birmingham theatre orchestras. Credited with about 200 violins and one viola, he acquired a good reputation in his lifetime as maker, repairer, and dealer—also a good bow-maker. See *Strad* (May 1968), 6. P 3/91/219, 1944, £1,100.

*WALKER, William (1859–?1930). Worked at Broxburn, Scotland, also Mid Calder. Originally a hairdresser and tobacconist, he was practically self-taught and produced over 150 instruments on Italian modelling—'quite equal to professional handicraft' (W.H.).

WALL, Robert Frederick (*fl.* 1940). Worked in London and Channel Islands. Small production. Cinema violinist.

WALLACE, Alfred (*fl.* 1900). Worked in Guernsey, Channel Islands.

WALTERS, Philip (b. 1951). Left teaching in 1987 to become full-time maker, marketing instruments mainly via teachers and orchestral players. Output to date over 60 violas, 6 cellos, and 10 violins. Works in Bridewell Cottage, on the edge of Forest of Dean, Coleford, Glos.

WALTON, William (1860–1938). Worked at Preston, Lancs. Originally a station-master, he commenced violin-making in 1887, averaging two instruments each year. Attracted the favourable attention of the expert Towry Piper, and subsequently the well-known contemporary maker William Luff collected a number of Walton's instruments. 'His work is of a high order, and finished with extraordinary care. His scrolls are of a vigorous design and carved very beautifully. The tone is large, brilliant, and perfectly equal and responsive. His work places him in line with our first-class professional makers.' (W.M.M.). Instruments labelled, dated, and numbered. See *Strad* (Dec. 1958), 270. C 6/90/298, 1915, £495; S 6/91/215, Preston, 1902, £3,523; P 3/93/53, 1908, No. 27, £1,100.

*†WAMSLEY, Peter (*fl.* 1725–45). One of the best-known London makers of the first part of the 18th cent. Thought to have been a pupil of Nathaniel Cross. Normally followed the Stainer model. His work is strangely uneven, varying from excellent to fairly crude, with ink purfling lines. This variability may have been because he obviously had a workshop with apprentices. Also thought to have baked his wood or chemically treated it and over-thinned it, but some of his work is in professional use currently. Often regarded as one of the founders of the Old English Cello School. Also credited with violas of good size. See *NGD*; *NGDI*. Instruments labelled as from 'Ye Golden Harp in Pickadilly, London' or 'The Harp and Hautboy in Piccadilly'. S 3/90/336, London, 1748 (Hill certificate), £4,950; C 11/92/72, cello, 1732, £4,400.

WARD (*fl.* 1827). Worked at Warrington, Lancs.

WARD, Alan. Contemporary maker and restorer working (ex Hills) at High Wycombe, Bucks.

WARD, George (*fl.* 1710–50). Worked in Dublin and regarded as a maker of undoubted ability capable of instruments quite equal to those of Perry. Handsome wood and beautiful varnish. W.H. states that a specimen is preserved at Dublin Museum.

WARD, Robert (*fl.* 1938). Worked in Liverpool. One viola (15^{9}/$_{16}$ in., 395 mm) called 'The Plover', dated 1938, labelled and branded on back 'Bob Ward, Liverpool'. See P 12/93/73.

WARD, Roderick (b. 1946). A self-taught maker commencing in about 1970. Output to 1991 was 32 violins, 45 violas, 6 cellos, 1 violone, and 1 bass viol. Principally works on Strad pattern but modelled many violas after a 15^{3}/$_{8}$ in. (391 mm) Banks. Uses oil varnish.

WARDE, William (*fl.* 1865). Worked in London. Indifferent workmanship.

WARDLAW, Richard (*fl.* 1900). Amateur work from Cardiff.

WARHAM, Roderick. Contemporary maker and restorer working at Clyst St Mary, Exeter.

WAREHAM, H. F. (*fl.* 1920). Worked in Hornsea, London, producing 'Patonzi–Cremona' violins.

WARRICK, Alan (b. 1919). Son of Alfred, below. Known primarily as double-bass specialist in Southall, Middx.

*WARRICK, Albert E. (1863–*c.*1906). A serious maker who was a pupil of Chanot at Manchester. Worked at Leeds from 1889. Gold medal, Leeds Exhibition, 1895. Principally copied Stradivari and Guarneri. S 3/91/15, Leeds, 1893, £1,650.

WARRICK, Alfred (1890–1962). Son of the above and carried on his business until 1923, when he moved to London to work with Dykes & Son and then became self-employed at Ealing, London. (See Woodcock, *Dictionary of Contemporary Violin and Bow Makers*, 87).

WATERSTONE, J. P. (*fl. c.*1927). Worked in Mountshannon, Ireland. A few instruments on classic Italian modelling.

WATKINS, O. (*fl.* 1845). Flat model, splendid design, red-brown varnish (W.H.). Little known.

WATSON, Francis B. (*fl.* 1928). Amateur working at Sheffield.

WATSON, Frank (1866–*c.*1914). Violin- and bow-maker resident at Rochdale, Lancs. Credited with about 200 instruments. (No. 46 was made in 1902.) Quite highly thought of by W.H.

WATSON, John (*fl.* 1900). Presbyterian clergyman working in Lerwick, Shetland Islands. Credited with about 50 violins 'of good workmanship and tone' (W.M.M.).

WATSON, Michael. Contemporary. Working at St Leonards-on-Sea, E. Sussex.

WATSON, Thomas Kay (1883–*c.*1950). Worked in Edinburgh. Although an amateur, credited with workmanship of a very high order (W.H.). Immaculately handwritten labels.

WATSON, William David (b. 1930). One of England's most distinguished living bow-makers. See text. Trained and worked at Hills until becoming self-employed in 1962. He works at Great Kimble, Oxford. See Alburger; *NGD*. Published 'English Bow Makers', *Journal of the Violin Society of America*, 6/2 (1982), 96.

WATT, Alexander Stocks (1859–1908). Produced about 50 violins and a few violas from Edinburgh. 'Beautiful workmanship' (W.M.M.). 'Used magnificent wood' (W.H.).

WATT, Walter (1797–1826). Worked in Scotland making instruments for strathspey players of whom he was one.

WATT, Walter (*fl.* 1885). Worked at High Blantyre, Scotland.

WATT, William Reid (*fl.* 1925). An engineer who worked in Birmingham. Trained by Frank Howard (q.v.) and instruments dated from 1924. Fair reputation.

WATTS, John Ernest (b. 1936). Works at Ashover, near Chesterfield, Derbyshire. Studied in the 1950s under Arthur Richardson and received help from many London makers. Eventually left schoolteaching to become full-time self-employed maker and restorer. Finds a ready market for his products without advertisement. Output to date is 126 violins, 30 violas, 5 cellos, and 1 double bass. Also plays violin in local symphony orchestra and folk group. Bridges branded and label runs 'John Ernest Watts | Ashover 19—'.

WATTS, Michael. Contemporary. Working at Bristol.

WAYLETT, Henry (*fl.* 1765). Worked at Exeter Exchange, Strand, London. 'Clean and accurate workmanship' (W.H.). Some violas.

WEAVER, Samuel (*fl.* 1790). Worked in London. Poor reputation.

WEBB, Robert J. (1914–50). Worked in London. A high reputation attaches to small production of violins and violas (the latter on the Tertis model).

WEBB, William (*fl.* 1920). London.

WEBSTER, George (*fl.* 1940). Worked at Aberdeen. One instrument seen of very good workmanship. S 11/91/348, Aberdeen, 1942, £880.

WELLBY, Charles (*fl.* 1890–1930). 'Excellent instruments' on Strad and Guarnerian modelling, from Edinburgh and appreciated by orchestral players there (W.H.).

WELLER, Frederick (*fl.* 1930–52). Holmwood, Surrey. Originally a coffin-maker, he started with single-stringed violins from cigar boxes. Then graduated to playing his own instruments in orchestras, working in a shed at the bottom of his garden. Slowly became more professional and is credited with 200 instruments up to 1952. 'A maker who really dedicated his life to the art' (W.H.). P 4/92/42, Holmwood, Surrey, 1952, No. 154, £440.

WELLS, Mark (b. 1956). Contemporary working in Oundle. Credited with 7 violins, 8 violas, and 1 cello to 1985 (vL).

WERRO, Jean (1868–1938). A distinguished Swiss luthier who worked in Islington, London, c.1890–1914, before going to Berne. His son *Henry* (1896–1971) was born in and spent his early days in London. He became an international expert in Switzerland.

WESTCOTT, F. W. (*fl.* 1920). Worked at Newcastle upon Tyne 1910–23. Good reputation for small production.

WHEATLEY, John (*fl.* 1825). Worked in Dublin. Instruments branded.

WHITAKER, John (*fl.* 1820). Partner with Button in St Paul's Churchyard, London. Also 'John Whitaker & Co., 75 St. Paul's Churchyard'. Probably workshop instruments.

WHITBREAD, Walter William (*fl.* 1920). Worked at Southsea and area. Variable work. P 2/90/194, 1921, £190.

WHITE, Ernest E. (*fl.* 1925). Worked at Wednesfield, near Wolverhampton. Amateur.

WHITE, Henry J. (*fl.* 1924). A professional maker working at Ealing and later at Frith St., Soho, London. Also professional player.

WHITE, James (*fl.* 1870). Worked in Edinburgh. W.H.'s double negatives, if penetrated, suggest poor, thin tone.

WHITE, John (early 19th cent.). Worked in Camerton, Somerset (Vannes).

WHITE, S. T. Contemporary. Market Harborough.

WHITE, Wilfred. Contemporary. Instrument dated 1969 from Pudsey, Yorks.

WHITEHEAD, Gerald (*fl.* 1955). Worked at Southport. Model on Guarneri pattern.

WHITESIDE, Henry (1749–1824). Worked in Liverpool. Cumbersome instruments with backs of beechwood but W.M.M. describes him as 'a remarkable man and a clever craftsman'. (He built the first Smalls lighthouse and also made harpsichords, etc.)

WHITESIDE, Richard (*fl.* 1900). Amateur working in Lancashire.

WHITMARSH, Emmanuel (*fl.* 1856–*c.*1910). Worked in various places in London with his son Edwin. Responsible for a large number of violins sold for between £4 and £10. Work is therefore variable but good at its best. Medal at the Inventions Exhibition, London, 1885. P 9/91/91, London, 1889, £1,100; S 11/92/320, £825.

WHITAKER AND BUTTON given by W.H. as working in Leeds, 1805–30. Ordinary work. (Presumably connected with London makers of this name.)

WHONE, Adam (b. 1957). Started his career as one of the first pupils of the Newark School under Maurice Bouette, Glen Collins, and Wilfred Saunders (q.v.). Then became associated respectively with Ealing Strings, W. London, and with James Robinson and Martin Godliman at the Cranston Workshop (in London, 1978). Later he took over the well-known London firm of Edward Withers Ltd. from Dietrich Kessler in 1987. See vL and *Strad* (June 1988), 497.

WIGAN, David (*fl.* 1900). Worked at Shrewsbury. Amateur.

WILA, Frank (*fl.* 1910). Worked in Rochdale—'excellent workmanship' (W.M.M.).

†WILKINSON, Charles John (1889–1961). Worked in London. A shadowy, but talented, maker who escaped the attentions of W.H. (and all the other dictionary writers except the latest vL) entirely. This was partly because he never had a label printed nor introduced his own name into his work. The printed labels, 'John Wilkinson, London, [MS date]' that do occur were inserted by J. & A. Beare when selling his instruments (information of Charles Beare to the author). He was originally a professional violinist but was wounded in his left wrist at the Battle of the Somme in 1918. He then turned his attention to violin-making and went to Thomas Jacques Holder (q.v.) for advice. For nearly four decades, wearing an iron splint, he sold instruments through and carried out restoration work for the firm of John and Arthur Beare. As Albert Cooper remarks, he 'was probably the last of a very long line within the outworker system, stretching back as far as the 17th and 18th centuries, when key figures such as Peter Wamsley, Richard Duke, John Betts, the Forsters, and many more made full use of it' (see *Strad* (July 1985), 187). His work consisted of fine 'antiqued' copies of the Italian masters, including Guarneri del Gesù, Joseph Rocca, Pressenda, and Guadagnini. Experts can recognize his work by such indicia as slim side linings, small discrepancies between the size of the plates since he never used a mould, use of a thin glue, use of wood such as plain maple for the scroll and beech for the ribs when makers such as Testori are being copied, and tool-marks on the scroll volute. He also used a fictitious label stating 'Gennaro Lanari fecit Napoli Anno 19—' occasionally. It is estimated that he produced over 900 instruments of which over 100 are violas. His work improved with time and his prices went up from £4 for a violin in 1939 to about £25 for a violin or viola in the 1950s. See vL, and

Albert Cooper, 'Against the Odds', *Strad* (July 1985), 186. (His son *John* (b. 1924) also worked for J. & A. Beare between 1938 and 1962. S 6/91/229, London, 1930, £2,860; S 11/92/20, c.1930, £2,680.

WILKINSON, J. T. (*fl.* 1925). Worked on the Guarneri and Stradivari models. Harris's varnish. 'Workmanship quite satisfactory' (W.H.).

WILKINSON, Samuel Blakely (1853–95). Worked in Leeds. Instruments variable and generally of no great distinction.

WILKINSON, William (*fl.* 1818–39). The apprentice of Thomas Perry (q.v.), became his son-in-law and successor in business. W.M.M. stresses that Perry had no hand in the making of the instruments which bear the dual name 'Perry & Wilkinson'. It is widely thought that Wilkinson may have antedated some of those made after about 1818 but the position is clearly confused. Wilkinson is widely regarded as being a much inferior workman to Perry, though a good businessman. P 4/91/176, Perry & Wilkinson, Dublin, 1809, £2,750.

WILLIAMS, Arthur (*fl.* 1925). One of Frank Howard's many pupils. Stradivari and Guarnerian modelling. 'A very painstaking and skillful craftsman with an artist's eye for beauty' (W.H.).

WILLIAMS, Benjamin (*fl.* 1810). Worked at Aberavon, Wales. Credited with about 80 violins on the Amati model (W.H.). 'Very good workmanship' (W.M.M.).

WILLIAMS, R. J. (*fl.* 1920). A self-taught professional maker who had made 47 instruments by 1922. Silver Medal, Royal National Eisteddfod of Wales, Neath, 1918. Violins numbered and labelled as from Llandudno.

WILLIAMS, Richard (Robert according to W.H.) Stephen. See under Rushworth & Dreaper.

WILLIAMS, Robert Raikes (*fl.* 1920). Worked at Perth, Scotland. P 10/91/173, £187.

WILLIAMS, Thomas (*fl.* 1915). High reputation as an amateur working in Edgbaston, Birmingham. W.M.M. comments favourably on a Carcassi copy, 'a very clever bit of work'.

WILLIS, Allen. Contemporary bow-maker working c.1940–60 for Hill & Sons in London.

WILLIS, Charles Silk (*fl.* 1915). A leather merchant by trade, born in Walsall (the centre of this trade) in 1883. Had lessons from Chanot in London and then worked at Caversham.

WILLMORE, Josiah John (*fl.* 1920). Pupil of Frank Howard. Worked at Wood Green, London.

WILLS, Colin George (b. 1944). Distinguished contemporary maker of violins, violas, and cellos in modern and baroque style. Works from the 'Hare and Hounds', Exton, Somerset. Associated with the annual (until 1992) Tiverton Violin Conference. See *Strad* (May 1983), 27.

WILSON, Derek F. (b. 1962, Abingdon). Bow-maker and restorer. Worked for Hills 1978–85, then with Peter Benedek, Munich, 1985–91 before being self-employed on the Isle of Wight. Bows now stamped 'D. Wilson'.

WILSON, Fred (*fl.* 1910). Chelmsford. Violins of 'exquisite workmanship and beautiful tone' (W.M.M.).

WILSON, Garner. Distinguished contemporary bow-maker who worked with Hills for some years until 1968. Now one of the best-known of contemporary English bow-makers, working in Bury St Edmunds.

WILSON, J. Gordon (*fl.* 1880). Worked in Glasgow.

WILSON, James John Thompson (*fl.* 1890). Mainly known as a bow-maker. For some time an associate of James Tubbs. Worked in London. Bows stamped 'JJT Wilson'.

WILSON, James L. (*fl.* 1890). Worked at Greenock, Scotland, a pupil of Mann. Whitelaw's varnish.

WILSON, Joseph (*fl.* 1925). A dentist who made in Edinburgh and Glasgow. Copied the 'Alard' Strad and used wood taken from an ancient bridge at Genoa. He had a high opinion of his own work.

WILSON, Richard. Contemporary bow-maker with workshop next to Juliet Barker's, Cambridge.

WILSON, William (*fl.* 1925). Worked at Clydebank, Scotland. Also a fitter at the Singer Works in Glasgow. 'Instruments of excellent design' (W.H.).

WINFIELD, Frank E. (*fl.* 1924). A cabinet-maker who worked at Crewton, near Derby. Classic Italian modelling. Golden-brown oil varnish.

†WISE, Christopher (*fl.* 1660). An interesting early English maker discussed in text. Worked in 'Half-Moon Alley | Without Bishops-Gate, London'. Small, almost Italianate, modelling. Also made viols.

*WITHERS family The founding father was *Edward* (I) (1808–75) who bought the business of William Davis in Coventry St., Haymarket, London in 1843. He became recognized as one of the best makers England had produced in the 19th cent. according to W.M. and employed Maucotel and Boullangier (q.v.) for a time. His son, *Edward* (II) (1844–1915) learned with his father and with John F. Lott. He established the firm of 'Edward Withers and Sons' at 22 Wardour St., London in 1865. He achieved a fine reputation and was appointed maker to the Duke of Edinburgh in 1893. S 11/90/194, *c.*1880. £1,540. His sons *Edward Sidney Munns* (1870–1955), *Bernard Sidney Withers* (1873–1942), and *Douglas Sidney Withers* (1879–1962), were in turn then succeeded by their sons *Bernard* and *Edward Stanley*. In 1969 the business was sold to Dietrich M. Kessler and in 1976 to Adam Whone. *Edward* (II) is credited with about 200 good-quality instruments. See *NGD*; *Strad* (June 1988), 497. *George* (1850–1920) was the second son of Edward (I) and worked with his father for some years before establishing his own business, George Withers & Sons, in (eventually) Leicester Sq., London. This business attracted great fame until its closure in 1933. After 1900 the business was carried on by George's two sons, *Walter George* and *Guarnerius* Withers (the latter being a bold baptismal decision). Guarnerius was a fine violinist and also a maker praised by W.M.M. Both sons were trained in Mirecourt. Their oil varnish is often referred to on their labels. Also made bows stamped 'G.W. and S' or their full name, 'George Withers & Sons'. See *NGD*; vL.

WITHERS, Joseph (1838–1920). Worked in London. See text. Not related to the above. A pupil of Lambert, himself a pupil of James Brown of Spitalfields, in 1869. Particularly inspired by seeing the 'Messie' Strad. Made his last violin aged 80. Quite highly thought of by W.M.M. and W.H. 'Tone of rich reedy quality' (W.M.M.).

WOLFF brothers (from 1864). A well-known German firm of better-class 'trade' violin-makers which opened a branch in London for over 20 years from c.1885. Some instruments accordingly labelled as from London.

WOOD, G. F. (*fl.* 1900). Worked in London. Good reputation.

WOOD, George (*fl.* 1895). Worked in Liverpool. Had reached No. 38 by 1899.

WOOD, James (*fl.* 1928). Perth, Scotland. A cabinet-maker by trade.

WOODCOCK, Cyril (b. 1896). Worked in London and Brighton. Made a number of instruments modelled after the Italian masters. Best known for his published works, particularly as editor of W.H.'s magnificent *Dictionary*.

WOODROW, David Bernard (b. 1935). Initially worked in Cremona under G. B. Morassi. Makes after Stradivari model. Also a writer (vL).

WOODWARD (*fl.* 1830). Worked in Birmingham.

WOOLSTON, Jonathan W. (b. 1958). Graduated from Newark School of Violin Making in 1985. Worked in New York for Jacques Français under René Morel before becoming established in Cambridge in 1990 with Lydia Friesen (q.v.). Various prizes for tone and workmanship. Makes and restores violins, violas, and cellos. (Author examined one sample violin of impeccable workmanship.)

WORDEN, James (1839–1910). A multi-talented man who besides being a violin-maker was also a cabinet-maker, organ-builder, and practising musician. Credited with about 50 instruments mostly on classic Italian lines. Worked in Preston, Lancs. 'Good workmanship' (W.H.). Elaborate label referring to various Saints.

WORNUM, Robert (1742–1815). Music-publisher in London and claimed to make violins and cellos. Probably bought them in. Instruments branded.

WORTHINGTON, John (1820). Mediocre work from Hereford.

WORTHY, W. H. (*fl.* 1955). Mentioned by W.H. as established at Helmsley, York, 1953. Strad modelling. 'Very nice tone' (W.H.).

WOULDHAVE, John (*fl.* 1960). Worked at North Shields, Northumberland, but suspected to have resold German and French factory products.

WRIGHT, Daniel (*fl.* 1740). Work little known.

WRIGHT, Ebenezer (*fl.* 1880). Worked at South Shields, Northumberland.

WRIGHT, Haydn W. (*fl.* 1925). Worked from Brixton, pupil of Frank Howard.

WRIGHT, J. (*fl.* 1925). Worked at Slough. A boot-maker by trade. 'Violins which evidence thoughtful and careful procedure' (W.H.).

WRIGHT, Joseph (*fl.* 1890). Worked at Derby. Apparently merely added decorative paint-work to existing instruments.

WROZINA, Ignaz (*fl.* 1885). A Hungarian who was employed by Methven and Simpson at Edinburgh from 1885. Silver Medal at Edinburgh Exhibition. His son became a maker in USA.

WULME-HUDSON, George. See under Hudson.

WYMERS, John (*fl.* 1760). Worked in Cambridge. Little known.

YAKOUSHKIN, Mark (b. 1953, Oklahoma). Studied Art and taught himself bow-making. Joined Oxford Violins, Oxford in 1983 as partner. About 150 bows to 1994.

YATES, Richard (*fl.* 1900). Worked at Ardwick, Manchester and established for himself a good reputation in his day. Made a particular study of acoustics. Tended to use dark brown good-quality varnish on well-figured wood. 'Entire workmanship exonerates him from any charge of hurry or carelessness' (W.H.).

YEATES, J. J. (*fl.* 1925). Maker and musician at Weston-super-Mare.

YEOMAN, Sydney D. (1876–1948). A well-known bow-maker who was employed by the firm of Hill & Sons in London, 1885 onwards.

YOOLE, William (*fl.* 1850). Pupil of Hardie in Edinburgh. Credited with 8 violins and 2 cellos 'of exceptional merit' (W.H.).

YOUNG, James (*fl.* 1900). Worked at Edinburgh—Guarneri modelling.

YOUNG, John (*fl.* 1700). Thought to have been purely a music-seller. Inspired Purcell to set to music a rhyme which began: 'You scrapers that want a good fiddle well strung, | you should go to the man that is old while he's Young'.

YOUNG, John (1812–66). Worked in Aberdeen. Exaggerated Stradivari modelling with spirit varnish.

YOUNGMAN, Marshall (1860–1924). Worked in Halifax, Yorks. A chemist who became a professional maker having been inspired by Heron-Allen's book. Sound, Italian modelling. Credited with 50 violins, 6 violas, and 6 cellos, violins selling for £12, cellos for £25. Golden-brown oil varnish. 'Workmanship very accurate' (W.H.). See *Strad* (Feb. 1957), 342.

YOUNGSON, Alexander. Contemporary. Tertis model viola from Glasgow, 1974.

Cities and Towns in the British Isles where the Principal (and Other Selected) Makers Worked, 1650–1950

ABERDEEN (Scotland)
Anderson, John
Bothwell, William
Cramond, Charles
Dalgarno, Thomas
Duncan, James
Duncan, Robert
Jamieson, Thomas
Marshall, John
Milne, Patrick
Murdoch, Alexander
Ruddiman, Joseph
Young, John

ACCRINGTON (Lancs.)
Grime, Harold

ACKLINGTON (Northumberland)
Stockdale, William

AUCHINTOUL (Scotland)
Kelman, James

BATH (Somerset)
Craske, George
Furlough, Henry
Morris, John
Trueman, Richard

BEDFORD (Beds.)
Milton, Louis Frank
Scholes, Arthur L.
Shackleton, Daniel

BELFAST (N. Ireland)
Bruce, Arthur
Ervine, Robert

Gordon, Hugh
Hill, Hugh
Jervis, Frank

BERWICK-ON-TWEED (Scotland)
Brunskill, J.
Harvie, Robert

BIRMINGHAM (W. Midlands)
Alexander, John
Brierley, J.
Craske, George
Croft, W. H.
De Souza, Cosmo
Priddey, J.
Riley, Henry
Simpson, Thomas

Southgate, W.
Williams, Thomas
Woodward

BRIGHTON (Sussex)
Baker, William

BRISTOL (Avon)
Angell, Frederick S.
Buxton, James
Bywater, Henry
Cutter, Edwin
Darbey, George
Gay, Wilfred
Ingram, Walter
James, James Stephen
Leader, James Henry
Ottley, Jacob
Rylands, John
Shepley, George
Smith, Nathaniel
Stephens, G. D.

CAMERTON (Somerset)
Hoskins, James
Lye, Henry
White, John

CARDIFF (Wales)
Mann, T. H.
Mortimer, John William
Myles, Francis
Noon, T. M.
Rimbault, H. E.
Wardlaw, Richard

CARLISLE (Cumbria)
Meek, James
Rook, Joseph

CHELMSFORD (Essex)
Wilson, Frederick

CHELTENHAM (Glos.)
Fisher, George
Furnow, Walter
Ridge, Eric

COLCHESTER (Essex)
Braund, Frederick T.

CREDITON (Devon)
Richardson, Arthur

DERBY (Derbyshire)
Cocker, Laurence

DOVER (Kent)
Buckman, George Hatton

DUBLIN (Ireland)
Cox, Henry
Delany, John
Hofmann family
Judge, Michael J.
Keenan, Edward
Mackintosh, John
McNeill, John
McNeill, Thomas
Molyneux
Murphy, Denis
Panormo, Vincenzo Trusiano
Perry, Joseph
Perry, Thomas
Ringwood and Wheatley
Tobin, Richard
Ward, George
Wilkinson, William

DUMFRIES (Scotland)
Cannon, James
Murray, James

DUNDEE (Scotland)
Black, James

Christie, James
Ferrier, William
Macintosh, William
Miller, John
Noble, Hugh
Ritchie, Archibald
Turnbull, William

DUNFERMLINE (Scotland)
Morisson, James

DURHAM (Co. Durham)
Ingram, Henry

EDINBURGH (Scotland)
Airth, William
Anderson, Henry
Black, John
Blair, John
Blyth, Williamson
Craig, John
Davidson, William
Dickson, George
Dodds, Edward
Ferguson, William
Girvan, Thomas
Hamilton, W. T. R.
Hardie, James
Hardie, James I.
Hardie, Matthew
Hardie, Thomas
Henderson, D. G.
Ingram, Walter
Kirkwood, Robert
McGregor, A.
McNeil, John
McNeil, William
Paterson, James
Ross, Donald
Smith, Alexander Howland
Stirrat, David
Trimnel, Joseph Henry
Watt, Alexander Stocks

Wellby, Charles
Wilson, Joseph
Wrozina, Ignaz
Young, James

EDZELL (Scotland)
Lindsay, David
Mitchell, George

EVESHAM (Worcs.)
Osmond, William

EXETER (Devon)
Blight, R.
Clark, William
Light, George
Stoneman, H.

FALKIRK (Scotland)
Carr, John
Menzies, John
Smith, John

GARMOUTH (Scotland)
Adams, Cathune
Adams, Colquhoun

GLASGOW (Scotland)
Anderson, John
Ballantyne, Robert
Breckinbridge, John
Briggs, James William
Brown, Alexander
Cooper, Hugh William
Duncan, George
Fingland, Samuel
Gilchrist, James
Leyden, John
Mann, John Alexander
Milne, Patrick G.
Morrison, Archibald
Plane, Walter

Skeffington, William Kirkland
Smillie, Alexander
Smillie, Andrew Y.

GLOUCESTER (Glos.)
Aubrey, Philip
Eyling, Thomas
Gwyther, Henry
Ridge, Eric V.
Sherdon, Daniel

GOMERSAL (Yorks.)
Heaton, William

GREAT YARMOUTH (Norfolk)
Andrews, Edward

GREENOCK (Scotland)
Wilson, James L.

HALIFAX (Yorks.)
Youngman, Marshall

HAVERFORDWEST (Wales)
Jenkins, Thomas
Phillips, David

HEREFORD (Herefordshire)
Birch, Thomas
Kendle, Philip
Orton, Philip
Smith, Pye
Worthington, John

HIGH WYCOME (Bucks)
Fleck, Ethel
Fleck, William
Hoing, Clifford

HUDDERSFIELD (Yorks.)
Gothard, F.

Strong, Matthew

HULL (Yorks.)
Jacklin, T.
Taylor, Edward

INVERGORDON (Scotland)
Urquhart, Alexander

LADYBANK (Scotland)
Mentiply, Andrew

LEEDS (Yorks.)
Balmforth, L. G.
Balmforth, L. P.
Bellingham, T. J.
Booth, William
Booth, William
Craske, George
Dalton, T.
Dearlove family
Dykes, George Langton
Firth, G.
Fox, Joseph
Fryer, John Charles
Gough, Walter
Heaps, Alfred Walter
Heaps, John Knowles
J'anson, Edward Popplewell
Lister, John
Naylor, Isaac
Owen, John William
Pickard, Handel
Wade, Joseph
Warrick, E. A.
Whittaker and Button
Wilkinson, S. B.

LEICESTER (Leics.)
Duglhey, John
Gamble, Ernest
Hole, A. P.

Luton, George
Moya, Hidalgo
Taylor, Robert
Taylor, Stephen Oliver

LERWICK (Shetland Islands)
Watson, John

LEVEN (Scotland)
Raeburn family

LIVERPOOL (Lancs.)
Banks family
Bird, Richmond Henry
Byrom, George
Fendt, Francis
Fulton, Henry
Hull, Robert
Naisby, L.
Stott, George
Walker, Hector M.
Whiteside, Henry

LLANDUDNO (Wales)
Parkinson, James
Williams, R. J.

LLANELLI (Wales)
Barton, John Edward

LONDON
Acton, W. J.
Addison, William
Aireton, Edmund
Allen, Samuel
Angell, S. E.
Askey, Samuel
Atkinson, William
Baines
Baker family
Banks, Benjamin
Barnes, Robert
Barrett, John

Barry, Frederick
Barton, George
Barton, John
Beare family
Betts family
Boullangier, C.
Bowler, Arthur
Brown, James
Burling, A. J.
Button
Cahusac family
Carter, John
Cary, Alphonse
Challoner, Thomas
Chanot family
Channon, Frederick William
Clark, James
Cockman, F. G.
Cole, Thomas
Collier & Davis
Collingwood, Joseph
Collins, William Henry
Conway, William
Corsby, George
Cross, Nathaniel
Crowther, John
Cuthbert, Robert
Davis family
Davis, A. W. E.
Day, John
Delunet, Auguste Leon
Dennis, Jesse
Devereux, J.
Dickenson, Edward
Dickeson, John
Dodd family
Dorant, William
Duke family
Eglington
Eisenmann, H.
Evans, Richard
Farrell, William

Fendt family
Fivaz, G. E.
Ford, Jacob
Forster family
Foucher family
Fox, Richard
Frankland
Furber family
Gaida family
Gardiner, Pearson
Gardner, Charles
Garner, John
Gibbs, James
Gilkes family
Gill, Lovett G.
Glenister, William
Goulding & Co.
Griffiths, A. V.
Hammett, Thomas
Harbour, Jacob
Harbour, William
Hare, John
Hare, Joseph
Harham/Harkham
Harris, Charles
Hart family
Hawkins, John J.
Haynes, Jacob
Haynes, William S.
Heeson, Edward
Hill family
Hillard, Allen
Hinds, Frederick
Hircutt
Holder family
Holloway, John
Hudson, G. W.
Hume, Alexander
Hurscroft, E.
Jacklin, Cyril William
Jay, Henry
Jay(e), Henry
Jay, Thomas

Johnson, John
Keen, W.
Kennedy family
Knapton, James
Laidlaw, John M.
Lambert, John
Langonet family
Lee, H. W.
Lee, Percy
Lentz, Jacob
Lentz, Johann Nicolaus
Lentz, John Frederick
Lewis, Edward
Liessem, Remer(i)us
Longman & Broderip
Longman & Lukey
Lott family
Luff, W. H.
Marshall, John
Martin, Adam
Matthews, Kenneth S. R.
Maucotel, Charles
May
Meares, Richard
Meeson, Richard
Meinel, Gustav
Meredith, L.
Merlin, John Joseph
Migge, Otto
Miller
Miller, George
Moffat, J. W.
Morisson, John
Newton, Isaac
Newton, Thomas
Norborn, John
Norman, Barak
Norris, John
Pamphilon, Edward
Panormo family
Parker, Daniel
Pearce, George
Pearce, James and Thomas
Pearce, William R.
Pemberton, Edward
Powell, Royal and Thomas
Preston, James and John
Pretts, A.
Price, Albert Henry
Prince, W. B.
Purday, T. E.
Pyne, George
Rae, John
Rawlings, Henry
Rayman, Jacob
Read, John R. W.
Richards, D. L.
Richards, P.
Ritchie, Alexander
Roberts, A. J.
Robinson, William
Romney, George
Rope, A. J.
Rose, John
Rost, Franz
Rowinski, S.
Saint-George, George
Saunders, S.
Scholes, Arthur L.
Sexton, John
Seyd, Ernst
Shaw, John
Simpson, James
Simpson, John
Smart, George
Smart, John
Smith, James
Smith, John
Smith, Thomas
Smith, William
Somny, Joseph Maurice
Spicer, John
Spicer, William
Szepessy, Béla
Taylor, William
Theress, Charles
Thompson family
Thorowgood, Henry
Tilley, Thomas
Tobin family
Tubbs family
Turner, William
Urquhart, Thomas
Vincent, Alfred
Voigt family
Voller brothers
Vrint, P.
Wamsley, Peter
Waylett, Henry
Weaver, Samuel
Webb, Robert
Whitmarsh, Emmanuel
Wilkinson, Charles John
Wise, Christopher
Withers family
Withers, Joseph
Wood, G. F.
Wornum, Robert
Wright, Daniel
Wright, H. W.

MALVERN (Worcs.)
Haynes, H.

MANCHESTER
Anyon, Thomas
Booth, Joseph
Chanot, Georges Adolphus
Cole, James
Craske, George
Crompton, Edward
Hesketh, Thomas Earle
Hicks, G. H.
J'anson, Edward
   Popplewell
Mayson, Stansfield
Mayson, Walter Henry
Meggison, Alfred
Pyecroft, Ernest

Shaw, John
Sowerby, A. L.
Stanley, Robert A.
Tarr family
Thorley, N.
Thorley, Thomas
Voigt family
Yates, Richard

NEWCASTLE UPON TYNE
(Co. Durham)
Brunskill, J.
Deighton, J. R.
Gladstone, Robert
Laidlaw, John

OXFORD (Oxon.)
Baker, John
Baker, William
Hancox, Arthur
Harris, Charles (I)
Harris, Charles (II)
Hicks, G. H.

PADANARUM (Scotland)
Findlay, James
Glenday, James
MacNicol, Alexander
Marnie, John

PAGLESHAM (Essex)
Atkinson, William

PENARTH (Wales)
Harvey, Ernest

PETERBOROUGH (Cambs.)
Gilbert, Jeffery

PLYMOUTH (Devon)
Channon, Frederick
    William

PRESTON (Lancs.)
Lonsdale, William
Walton, William
Worden, James

REDDITCH (Worcs.)
Laugher, William

REDRUTH (Cornwall)
Coad, Albert

ROCHDALE (Lancs.)
Cockcroft, W.
Greenwood, G. W.
Priestnall, John
Watson, Frank

SALISBURY (Wilts.)
Banks family

SHEFFIELD (Yorks.)
Craske, G.
Dodd, E.
Milner, F.
Skinner, J. W.
Smith, William

SHREWSBURY (Shropshire)
Locke, George Herbert
Must, Frederick
Roberts, John
Tringham, Henry
Wigan, David

SOLIHULL (Warwicks.)
Walker, John

STANHOPE (Co. Durham)
Askew, John

STOCKPORT (Cheshire)
Craske, George
Longson, F. H.

Saxon, John
Smith, Thomas

STOCKTON-ON-TEES
(Co. Durham)
Lindsay, Michael H.

STOKE-ON-TRENT (Staffs.)
Hancock, George

STROMNESS (Orkney
Islands)
Ormond, James

SWANSEA (Wales)
Harris, Griffith
Thomas, Watkin

TAIN (Scotland)
Urquhart, Donald

WAKEFIELD (Yorks.)
Absam, Thomas

WILMSLOW (Cheshire)
Ardern, Job

WORCESTER (Worcs.)
Handley, Henry
Hopkins
Knight, Alfred
Orchard, Joseph

YORK (Yorks.)
Preston, John
Todd, John

APPENDIX 2

Facsimile Labels

WARNING: These facsimiles of labels of a miscellany of makers, some eminent and some relatively obscure, are reproduced with some hesitation, as there is a long history of nefarious people copying facsimiles from books and inserting them in alien instruments (see the author's book on *Violin Fraud*). Morris in fact reproduces many of these, so they are perhaps harmless by now. Makers frequently change their labels and many instruments bear false ones. NEVER RELY ON A LABEL ALONE.

William Atkinson in Tottenham 1903.

James W Briggs Glasgow. 1888

William Atkinson in Paglesham 1929.

Arthur Bowler
LONDON, FECIT 1940

William Baker
In Oxon
1672

GEO. H. BUCKMAN,
DOVER, 1899.

Benjamin Banks
Musical Instrument Maker
In Catherine Street, Salisbury 1779

A.E. CHANOT, Fecit.
LONDON, A.D. 1906

MOR O GÂN YW CYMRU I GYD
No 75. Y Symthegfed
GAN UN O FEIBION CYMRU
H Biddulph
19 LLUNDAIN 27

MADE BY
G.A. CHANOT.
VIOLIN, VIOLA, VIOLONCELLO &
BOW MAKER & RESTORER,
MANCHESTER. A.D. 1903.
No 255 Model of Amati

408 APPENDIX 2

George Darbey, Cremona House, Bristol. Anno 1902 [GD]
George Darbey

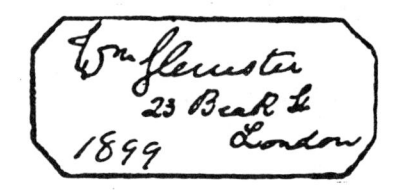

Wm Glenister
23 Beak St
1899 London

T. DODD,
VIOLIN, VIOLONCELLO
& BOW MAKER
New Street
Covent Garden

T. Hammett 1920

MADE BY
GEORGE L. DYKES,
LEEDS, PUPIL OF
PAUL BAILLY,
(PUPIL OF JEAN BAPTISTE VUILLAUME, OF PARIS)
No.

A. J. Hancox, :: Deddington, Oxon.
Fecit Anno Domini 1929.

William Forster
Violin Violoncello Tenor & Bow-maker
to their ROYAL HIGHNESSES the PRINCE of WALES
& DUKE of CUMBERLAND   London

MADE BY
MAT. HARDIE & SON,
EDINBURGH.
1821

F.F. No. 240.
Felix Foucher.
LUTHIER.
London. 1915.

HART & SON.
MAKERS
28 Wardour Street. W
18 LONDON. 99

Henry Fuller.
Plaistow.
1929

WILLIAM HEATON,
MAKER,
HILL TOP, GOMERSAL.
Nr. Leeds.

Jeffery J. Gilbert. Peterborough
Fecit. Anno MDCCCXCIX.

Thomas Earle Hesketh
Manchester Fecit 1900 [EH]

Samuel Gilkes
fecit London   1812

Joseph Hill. Maker.
at the Harp and Flute,
in the Hay Market.
17 LONDON. 66

FACSIMILE LABELS 409

JOSEPH HILL & SONS *MAKERS*,
at the *HARP* and *FLUTE*,
in the Hay Market.
LONDON   1771

Clifford A. Hoing,
High Wycombe,
Buckinghamshire

L. HILL.
VIOLIN & VIOLONCELLO
Maker.
Boro:
LONDON

A. HUME   LONDON
MAKER   Anno 19
Highest Awards, London. 1918-24-25

Willm Hill. MAKER
in Poland Street near Broad
Street Carnaby Market 1785

Edward P. I'anson. Fecit.
Manchester, Anno 1872.

WILLIAM E. HILL,
Maker. London.
—1850—

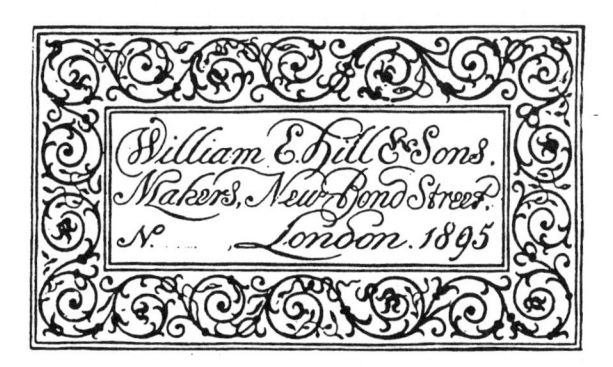

Made & Sold by JOHN JOHNSON
the Harp & Crown in Cheapside
LONDON 50

William E. Hill & Sons
Makers, Wardour Street,
London. 1882

ARTHUR E. KELLEWAY,
VIOLIN MAKER,
SOUTHAMPTON.
No. 10.   1914

John Leyden
Glasgow
No. 88.   1926

William E. Hill & Sons.
Makers, New Bond Street.
N°   London. 1895

J. F. LOTT,
MAKER
LONDON

G. WILLIAM HOFMANN,
Dublin. 1926.
G. W. Hofmann

William H. Luff
MAKER
London 1966.

410 APPENDIX 2

John Marshall, Violin Maker, ABERDEEN.

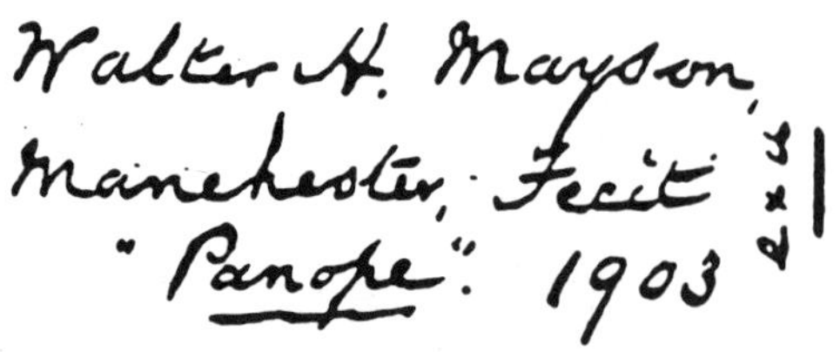

John Preston, York.

Walter H. Mayson, Manchester, Fecit "Panope" 1903

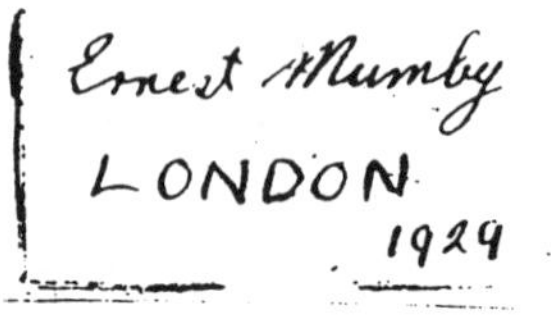

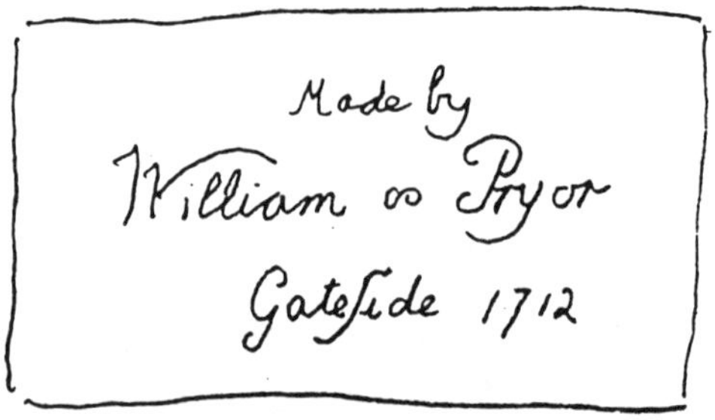

Made by William ∞ Pryor Gateside 1712

Ernest Mumby LONDON 1929

Jacob Rayman, at ye Bell yard in Southwark

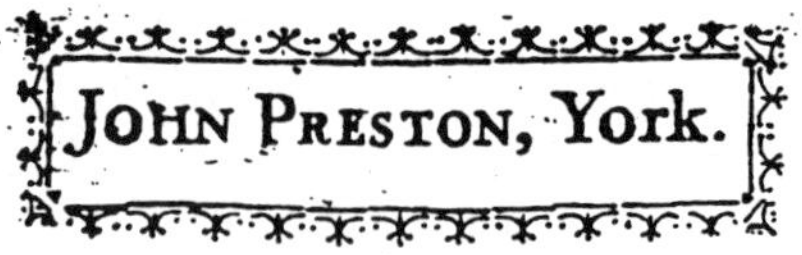

Barak Norman at the Bass Viol in St Pauls Church London Fecit

MADE BY Arthur Richardson CREDITON DEVON. 19·

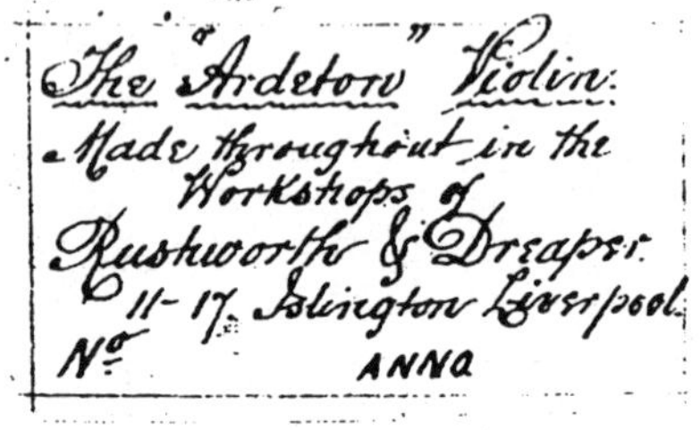

The "Ardetow" Violin. Made throughout in the Workshops of Rushworth & Dreaper 11-17 Islington Liverpool. No. ANNO

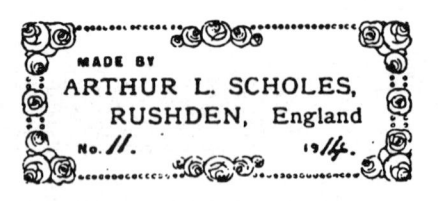

J. W. OWEN MAKER Leeds

MADE BY ARTHUR L. SCHOLES, RUSHDEN, England No. 11 1914

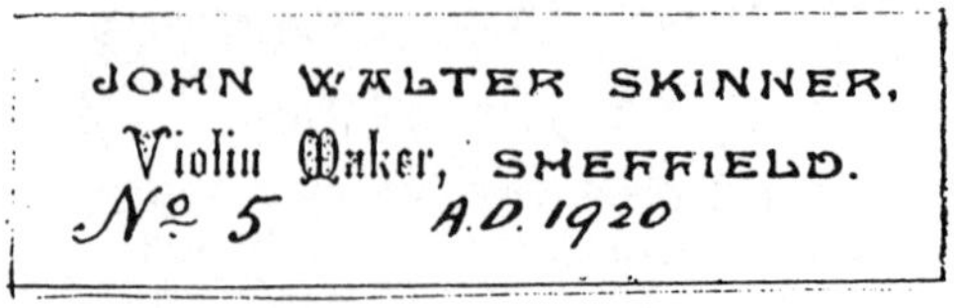

Preston Maker London

JOHN WALTER SKINNER, Violin Maker, SHEFFIELD. No 5 A.D. 1920

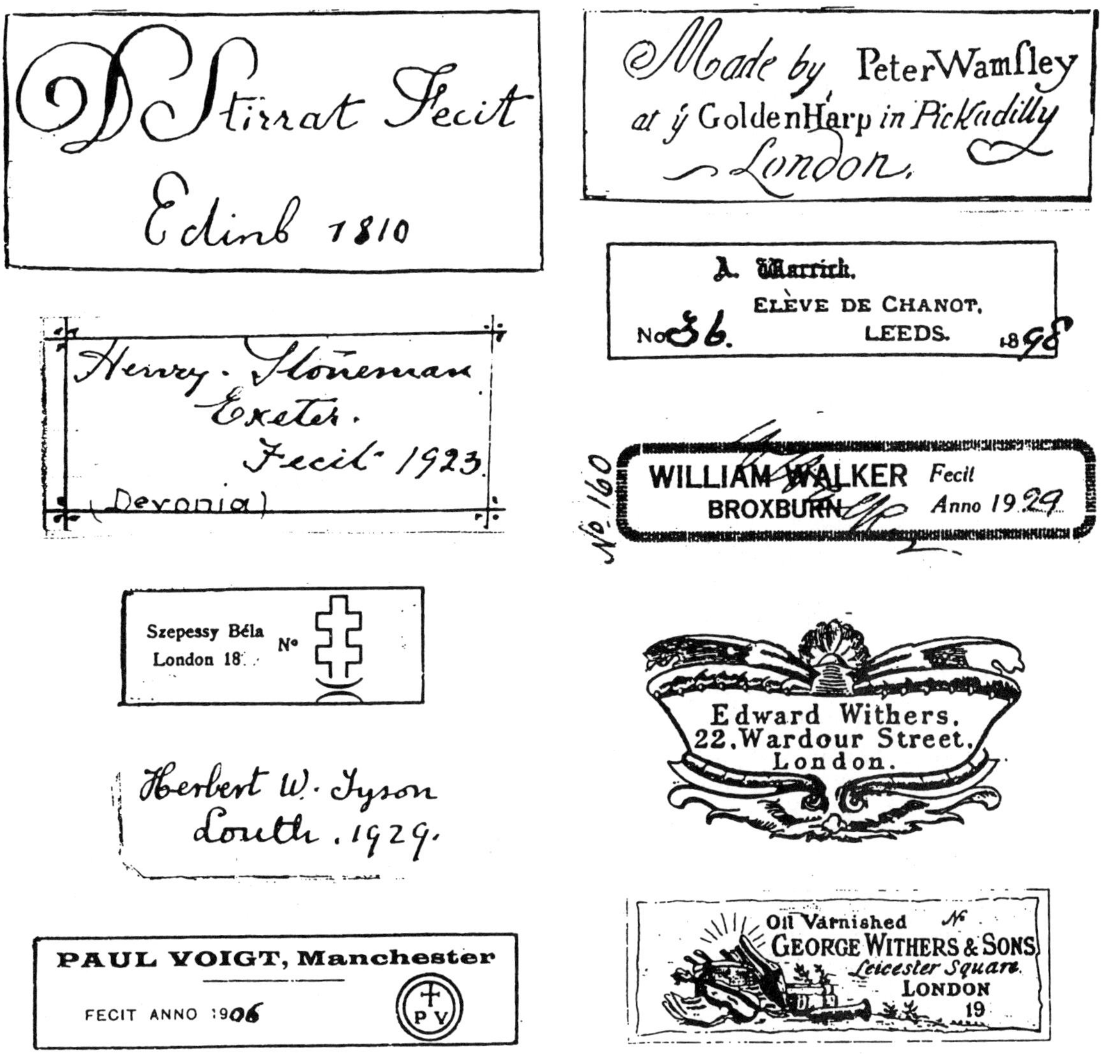

FACSIMILE LABELS 411

D Stirrat Fecit
Edinb 1810

Made by Peter Wamsley
at ý Golden Harp in Pickadilly
London.

Henry Stoneman
Exeter.
Fecit 1923.
(Devonia)

A. Warrick.
ELÈVE DE CHANOT.
No 36. LEEDS. 1898

N° 160
WILLIAM WALKER Fecit
BROXBURN Anno 1929

Szepessy Béla N°
London 18

Edward Withers.
22. Wardour Street.
London.

Herbert W. Tyson
Louth. 1929.

PAUL VOIGT, Manchester
FECIT ANNO 1906

Oil Varnished N°
GEORGE WITHERS & SONS
Leicester Square.
LONDON
19

Explanatory Notes to Plates

The colour and monochrome Plates noted here are designed to show the reader examples of the work of the leading makers of the British Isles. In a few cases two examples have been included. The author is only too aware that there are still some makers who are unrepresented despite the distinction of some of their work. This unfortunately is inevitable if the book is to be kept within budget. A glance at the number of makers mentioned in the Directory will show that agonizing selection decisions are likely to be unavoidable. Nevertheless, the Plates do illustrate, in alphabetical order (except within the Hill family, presented chronologically for clarity), an impressive array of British and Irish work and it is much to be hoped that this, together with the remarks in the text, will help to demonstrate the character and quality of these makers' work and bring it more prominently to international attention. The word 'character' is important; for instance, much English eighteenth-century work has recognizable national characteristics, great charm, and considerable tonal merit in many cases—particularly cellos. In recent years it appears that the market is beginning to appreciate this.

It will be apparent that the author is more than simply indebted to the generosity of Messrs Sotheby's, Christie's, and Phillips, from whose archives the majority of the photographs originate. All have been equally kind and helpful in assistance with this work and in allowing their photographs to be reproduced. The colour specimens from Sotheby's are particularly magnificent and greatly beautify this book. It is simply a fact that the majority of photographs come from the Phillips' stable and this may be something to do with the great knowledge and affection that Edward Stollar, for many years head of the Musical Instruments Department of that firm, has shown for British instruments. I am tremendously indebted to his knowledge and enthusiasm and also to that of his able successor, Philip Scott.

The descriptions of the instruments are primarily taken from the relevant catalogue entry. In some cases the material label was not directly quoted, and I have only underlined the legend on any particular label where I am reasonably sure that it is accurately given. Almost all the instruments are unequivocally attributed to a particular maker, many supported by Hill certificates or sold out of a collection of instruments of the British Isles owned by the former firm of W. E. Hill & Sons Ltd. and mainly sold by Phillips in 1991 ('the Hill collection'). In this connection it is sad to have to remark that many of the instruments of a historic character have now been dispersed and it would be a very uphill task to assemble such a variety again, were a long overdue effort made to obtain them for where they really belong—in a public Museum.

Cover FORSTER, WILLIAM (sen.), Cello, *c.*1790—'The Royal George'. LOB 28$^{7}/_{8}$ in. (734 mm), varnish of an orange to red-brown colour, labelled *William Forster, Violin, Violoncello,*

Tenor and Bowmaker to their Royal Highnesses The Prince of Wales and the Duke of Cumberland, and inscribed in gilt letters around the tailpin *William M. Forster Sr. London*. **Note**: The Hill family, in whose possession this instrument was for some years, described the model as being after Amati. The Arms of the Prince of Wales and his feathers are painted on the table and the words *Liberty & Loyalty* on the ribs.

Plate A   CROSS, NATHANIEL, Cello, London, 1733, LOB 28$^{5}/_{16}$ in. (719 mm), varnish of a light golden-brown colour. Hill certificate, 1938.

Plate B   PANORMO, VINCENZO, Violin, London, c.1790. LOB 14$^{3}/_{16}$ in. (359 mm), varnish of a golden-brown colour, unlabelled. Hill certificate, 1961.

Plate C   FENDT, BERNARD SIMON, Cello, London, c.1840. LOB 29$^{5}/_{8}$ in. (752 mm). **Note**: This unlabelled instrument is a copy of one by Andrea Amati known as 'Il Re' and made for Charles IX of France, the original instrument being in the Shrine to Music Museum, Vermillion, South Dakota. Arthur Betts made a similar copy in 1837. (Hills' letter, 17 July 1989)

Plate D   LOTT, JOHN FREDERICK, Violin after Guarneri del Gesù, London, c.1840. LOB 13$^{15}/_{16}$ in. (354 mm), varnish of a red-brown colour on a golden ground labelled *Joseph Guarnerius fecit Cremone anno 1732*. Hill receipt, 1931. **Note**: this instrument was sold for £17,600 in 1991.

Plate 31   AIRETON, EDMUND, Violin, London, 1761. LOB 13$^{15}/_{16}$ in. (353 mm), varnish of an orange-brown colour on a golden-brown ground, inscribed on inner back twice *Made by Ed. Aireton 1761*. **Note**: Hill certificate, 1969, numbered P4.

Plate 32   ARDERN, JOB, Violin, c.1890. LOB 14$^{1}/_{8}$ in. (359 mm), varnish of a clear orange colour on a light-brown ground, labelled *Job Ardern, Wilmslow, Cheshire*.

Plate 33   ATKINSON, WILLIAM, Viola, Tottenham, 1906. LOB 16$^{5}/_{8}$ in. (422 mm), varnish of a clear amber-brown colour, labelled *William Atkinson, Tottenham 1906* with branded monogram below button.

Plate 34   BAKER, WILLIAM, Cello, Oxford, 1672. LOB 28$^{3}/_{16}$ in. (716 mm), varnish of a golden-brown colour, labelled *William Baker | in Oxon | 1672*. **Note**: The scroll is said to be the work of John Hill. Receipt of W. E. Hill & Sons, 1903. Fingerboard numbered 8467. This instrument is thought to be one of the earliest English cellos in existence.

Plate 35   BANKS, BENJAMIN, Violin, Salisbury, 1751. LOB 14$^{1}/_{8}$ in. (359 mm), varnish of a golden-brown colour, inscribed on lower inner back *Benj. Banks Sarum Fecit 1751*. **Note**: This instrument is said to pre-date by four years the earliest previously recorded instrument by this maker—see *The Wurlitzer Catalogue* (New York, 1931).

Plate 36   BANKS, BENJAMIN, Cello, Salisbury, c.1780. LOB 29$^{5}/_{16}$ in. (744 mm), varnish of a golden-brown colour, labelled *Benjamin Banks | Fecit | Salisbury* and branded twice on the back. Fingerboard numbered F300.

Plate 37 BETTS, JOHN, Violin, London, 1814. LOB 14 in. (356 mm), varnish of a clear red-brown colour on a yellow ground, labelled *Betts, No. 2 North Piazza Royal Exchange, London 1814*. **Note**: From the Hill collection.

Plate 38 BETTS, JOHN & ARTHUR, Violin, London, 1850. LOB 14$^{1}/_{16}$ in. (357 mm), varnish of a golden-brown colour on a yellow ground. Maker's label at the Royal Exchange, London, 1850. **Note**: This violin was shown at The Great Exhibition in London, 1851.

Plate 39 BOULLANGIER, CHARLES, Viola, London, 1855. LOB 16$^{3}/_{16}$ in. (410 mm), varnish of a clear red colour on a yellow ground, labelled *Boullangier Fecit London, 1855*, with initials on upper back.

Plate 40 BRIGGS, JAMES W., Violin, Glasgow, 1884. LOB 14$^{1}/_{8}$ in. (359 mm), varnish of a red colour on a golden-yellow ground, handwritten label from Glasgow 1884.

Plate 41 BUCKMAN, GEORGE H., Violin, Dover, 1902. LOB 14$^{1}/_{16}$ in. (357 mm), varnish (oil) of a transparent orange colour on golden yellow ground, labelled with maker's label from Dover, 1902.

Plate 42 CHANOT, FREDERICK WILLIAM, Violin, London, 1897. LOB 13$^{15}/_{16}$ in. (354 mm), varnish of a red-brown colour, labelled *F. W. Chanot London Fecit AD 1897*.

Plate 43 CHANOT, GEORGES ADOLPHE, Violin, Manchester, 1906. LOB 14$^{1}/_{4}$ in. (362 mm), varnish (oil) of a transparent golden-brown colour, with the maker's label *G. A. Chanot, Manchester 1906*, Model of Stradivarius No. 326, Gold Medals 1885 etc., with maker's brand on the bottom rib.

Plate 44 COLE, JAMES, Double Bass, Manchester, c.1870. LOB 46 in. (1608 mm), string stop 42$^{1}/_{2}$ in. (709 mm), varnish of a golden colour, stamped at top of back *J. Cole, Manchester*.

Plate 45 CRASKE, GEORGE, Violin, c.1880. LOB 14$^{3}/_{16}$ in. (360 mm), varnish of a red-brown colour on a yellow ground, labelled *Made by George Craske (born 1795, died 1888) and sold by William E. Hill & Sons London*.

Plate 46 CROSS, NATHANIEL, Violin, London, 1743. LOB 14$^{1}/_{8}$ in. (359 mm), varnish of a golden orange-brown colour, labelled *Nathll. Cross, +, London, 1743*. **Note**: This instrument has its original neck, bass bar, and bottom saddle.

Plate 47 CUTHBERT, ROBERT, Violin, London, 1676. LOB 13$^{7}/_{8}$ in. (352 mm), varnish of a golden-brown colour, labelled *Robert Cuthbert at the White Horse in Russell Streete nigh Covent Garden 1676* (MS). **Note**: This historic instrument is one of the earliest English violins recorded and is pictured before subsequent restoration. The Cuthbert instrument in the Hill collection was dated 1690.

Plate 48 DAY, JOHN, Violin, London, 1884. LOB 14$^{1}/_{16}$ in. (357 mm), varnish of a red-brown colour on a yellow ground, labelled *JOHN DAY; LONDINII MUS DOC. VIOLINIST IN HER MAJESTY'S PRIVATE BAND fecit anno 1884*. **Note**: From the Hill collection.

Plate 49 Dearlove, Mark William, Viola, Leeds, 1847. LOB 15³⁄₁₆ in. (385 mm), varnish of a golden-brown colour, inscribed in pencil on the inner back and branded DEARLOVE MAKER LEEDS below the button.

Plate 50 Dodd, Thomas, Violin, London, c.1810. LOB 13⅞ in. (352 mm), varnish of a clear light red-brown colour on a yellow ground, unlabelled. **Note:** From the Hill collection.

Plate 51 Duke, Richard, Violin, London, 1777. LOB 14¼ in. (362 mm), varnish of a red-brown colour on a golden-brown ground, bearing the maker's label in Holborn Londonii fecit 1777 and branded DUKE, LONDON, below the button.

Plate 52 Fendt, Bernard Simon, Viola, London, 1833. LOB 15⅞ in. (403 mm), varnish of a rich golden-brown colour, labelled by maker in London, 1833. Hill certificate, 1980.

Plate 53 Fendt, Jacob, Violin, London, c.1830. LOB 13⅞ in. (353 mm), varnish of an orange-red colour, unlabelled. Hill certificate, 1949.

Plate 54 Ford, Jacob (attributed to), Violin, London, c.1770. LOB 14 in. (356 mm), varnish of a clear golden-brown, unlabelled. **Note:** See Phillips 6/90/172.

Plate 55 Forster, William (sen.), Viola, London, c.1790. LOB 15½ in. (394 mm), varnish of a clear orange-brown colour, labelled *Forster, Violin, Violoncello, Tenor and Bow maker, to their Royal Highnesses the Prince of Wales & Duke of Cumberland, London,* with signature. J. & A. Beare certificate, 1978.

Plate 56 Forster, William (sen.), Cello, London, 1782. LOB 29 in. (735 mm), upper bouts 13⅜ in. (340 mm), lower bouts 17¼ in. (440 mm), varnish of an orange-red colour on a yellow ground, labelled as preceding specimen and dated 1782, with signature. **Note:** From the Hill collection. Sold by Phillips in April 1991, this fine instrument attracted a hammer price of £22,000.

Plate 57 Furber, Henry, Cello, London, 1886. LOB 29½ in. (750 mm), varnish of a red-brown colour, labelled *H. Furber, Violin, Violoncello and Double Bass Maker, London 1886.*

Plate 58 Gilbert, Jeffrey J., Violin, 1931, LOB 14 in. (356 mm), varnish of a deep red-brown colour on a light-brown ground, labelled with maker's label in Peterborough, 1931, No. 371.

Plate 59 Gilkes, Samuel, Violin, London, c.1820. LOB 13⅞ in. (353 mm), varnish of a red colour on a yellow ground, name obliterated by a number on bottom rib. **Note:** Model after Stradivari. From the Hill collection.

Plate 60 Goulding & Co., Cello, London, c.1790. LOB 29⁵⁄₁₆ in. (742 mm), varnish of a golden-brown colour, branded GOULDING & CO. LONDON below the button.

Plate 61 Handley, Henry, Violin, Worcester, 1887. LOB 13¹⁵⁄₁₆ in. (354 mm), varnish of a golden-amber colour, labelled *Henry Handley | Fiddle Restorer and Maker | Worcester | 1887.*

Plate 62 HARDIE, MATTHEW, Violin, Edinburgh, 1815. LOB 14¹⁄₁₆ in. (357 mm), varnish of a clear golden-amber colour, labelled with maker's label in Edinburgh, 1815. **Note:** From the Hill collection.

Plate 63 HARDIE, MATTHEW & SON, Cello, Edinburgh, 1822. LOB 29⅝ in. (752 mm), varnish of a clear golden-brown colour, bearing maker's label in Edinburgh, dated 1822. **Note:** From the Hill collection.

Plate 64 HARE, JOSEPH, Violin, London, 1723. LOB 14¹⁄₁₆ in. (357 mm), varnish of a clear golden-amber colour, labelled *Joseph Hare at the Viol and Hautboy over against Urchin Lane in Cornhill, London 1723* (engraved except for handwritten date). **Note:** Another historic instrument from the Hill collection. The corners and chamfers of the scroll are outlined in black.

Plate 65 HARRIS, CHARLES, Cello, Woodstock, Oxfordshire, 1817. LOB 30⅛ in. (765 mm), varnish of a transparent golden-amber colour, inscribed on the inner back at Woodstock, Oxford, dated May 1817 (see P 11/91/206). **Note:** It is not entirely clear whether this exceptionally large and fine cello is the work of Charles Harris senior or junior. The authorities suggest that both worked in Oxfordshire for a time. Compare the instrument discussed and illustrated in *Strad* (Aug. 1970), 150.

Plate 66 HESKETH, T. EARLE, Violin, Manchester, 1934. LOB 13¹⁵⁄₁₆ in. (354 mm), varnish of a red-brown colour, labelled *Facsimile* JOSEPH GUARNERIUS DEL GESU. *Made by* T. EARLE HESKETH, MANCHESTER 1934, NO IX (and in ink) SPECIAL LEN H (Probably Leonard Hirsch). **Note:** This is one of a series of fine instruments made by Hesketh on the Guarneri model, often for eminent players, in the 1930s.

Plate 67 HILL, JOSEPH, Cello, London, 1774. LOB 28½ in. (725 mm), varnish of a golden-brown colour labelled *Joseph Hill at the Harp and Flute in the Hay Market London, 1774*. Hill certificate, 1912. **Note:** The model is stated to be after Stradivari.

Plate 68 HILL, JOSEPH, Violin, London, c.1790. LOB 13¹⁵⁄₁₆ in. (354 mm), varnish of a golden-brown colour, unlabelled. **Note:** From the Hill collection. The instrument has its original neck, bass bar, and saddle.

Plate 69 HILL, LOCKEY, Violin, London, c.1780. LOB 13¹⁵⁄₁₆ in. (354 mm), varnish of a transparent golden-brown colour, branded below the button LONGMAN & LUKEY No. 26 Cheapside, London. **Note:** This instrument, also from the Hill collection, is attributed to the work of Lockey Hill when working for the trade, particularly Longman & Lukey (later Longman & Broderip). Longman's used other London makers too. Their lesser instruments often have ink 'purfling'.

Plate 70 HILL, HENRY LOCKEY, Violin, London, 1820. LOB 14¹⁄₁₆ in. (357 mm), varnish of a red-brown colour on a yellow ground, labelled *Lockey Hill Violin and Violoncello maker, Boro' London, 1820*. **Note:** From the Hill collection. The catalogue description (P 4/91/154) describes this as 'a fine Violin by LOCKEY HILL.' but the date and Stradivarian style definitely indicates this to be the work of the son, Henry Lockey Hill.

PLATE A. Nathaniel Cross, Cello, London, 1733.

PLATE B. Vincenzo Panormo, Violin, London, *c.*1790.

PLATE C. Bernard Simon Fendt, Cello, London, *c.*1840.

PLATE D. John Frederick Lott, Violin after Guarneri del Gesù, London, *c.*1840.

PLATE 31. Edmund Aireton, Violin, London, 1761.

PLATE 32. Job Ardern, Violin, *c.* 1890.

PLATE 33. William Atkinson, Viola, Tottenham, 1906.

PLATE 34. William Baker, Cello, Oxford, 1672.

PLATE 35. Benjamin Banks, Violin, Salisbury, 1751.

PLATE 36. Benjamin Banks, Cello, Salisbury, *c.* 1780.

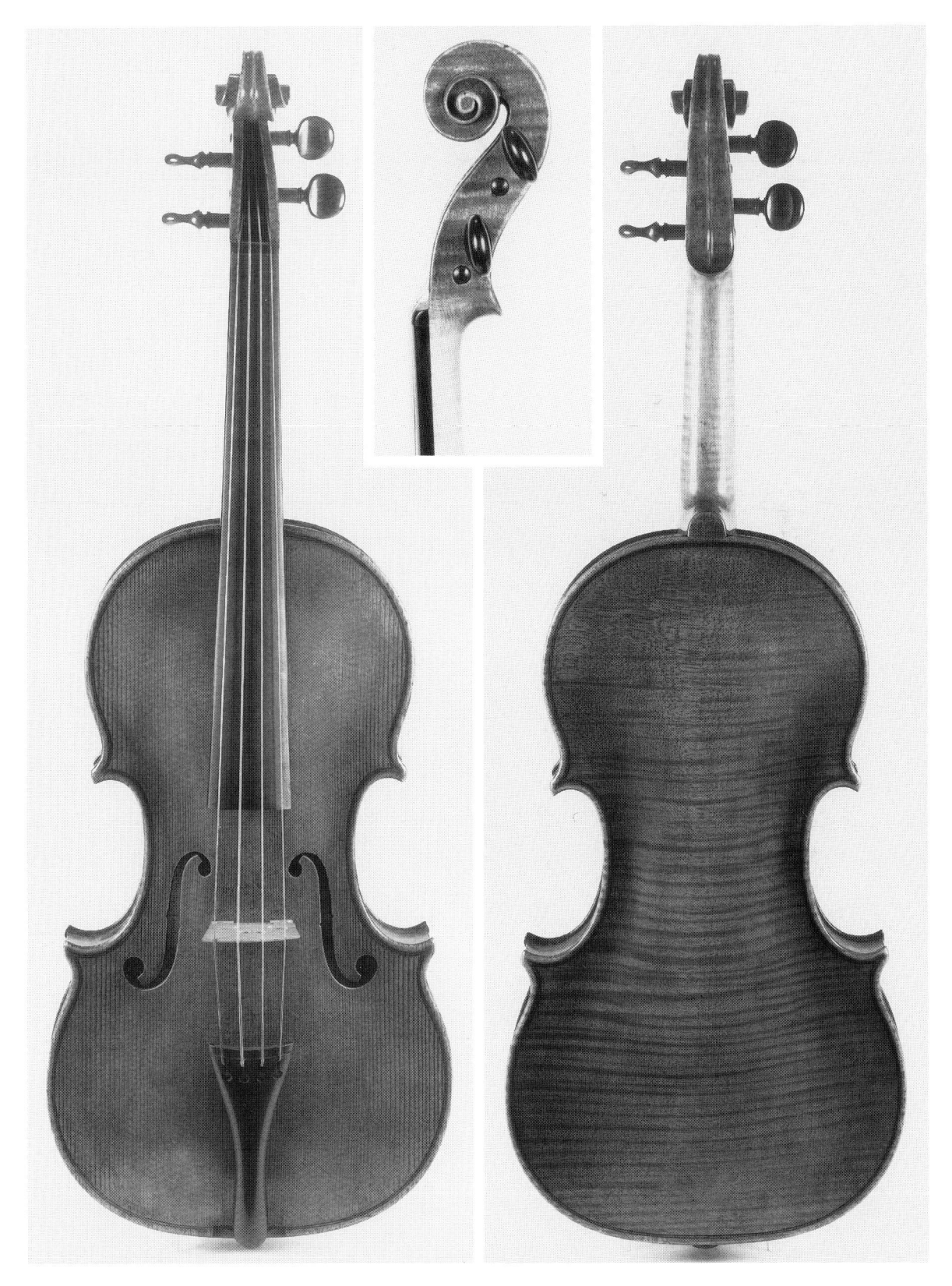

PLATE 37. John Betts, Violin, London, 1814.

PLATE 38. John and Arthur Betts, Violin, London, 1850.

PLATE 39. Charles Boullangier, Viola, London, 1855.

PLATE 40. James W. Briggs, Violin, Glasgow, 1884.

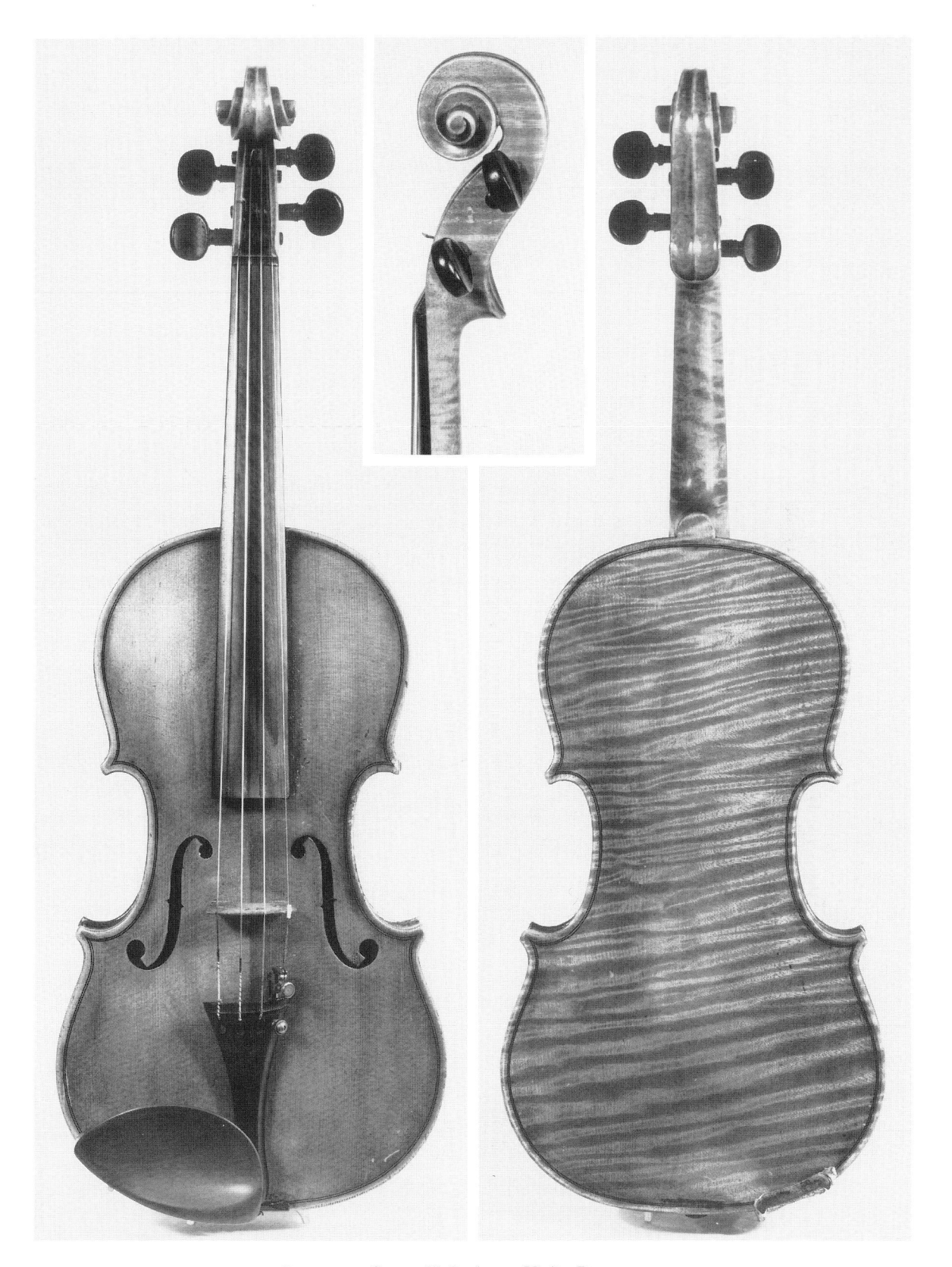

PLATE 41. George H. Buckman, Violin, Dover, 1902.

PLATE 42. Frederick William Chanot, Violin, London, 1897.

PLATE 43. Georges Adolphe Chanot, Violin, Manchester, 1906.

PLATE 44. James Cole, Double-bass, Manchester, *c.* 1870.

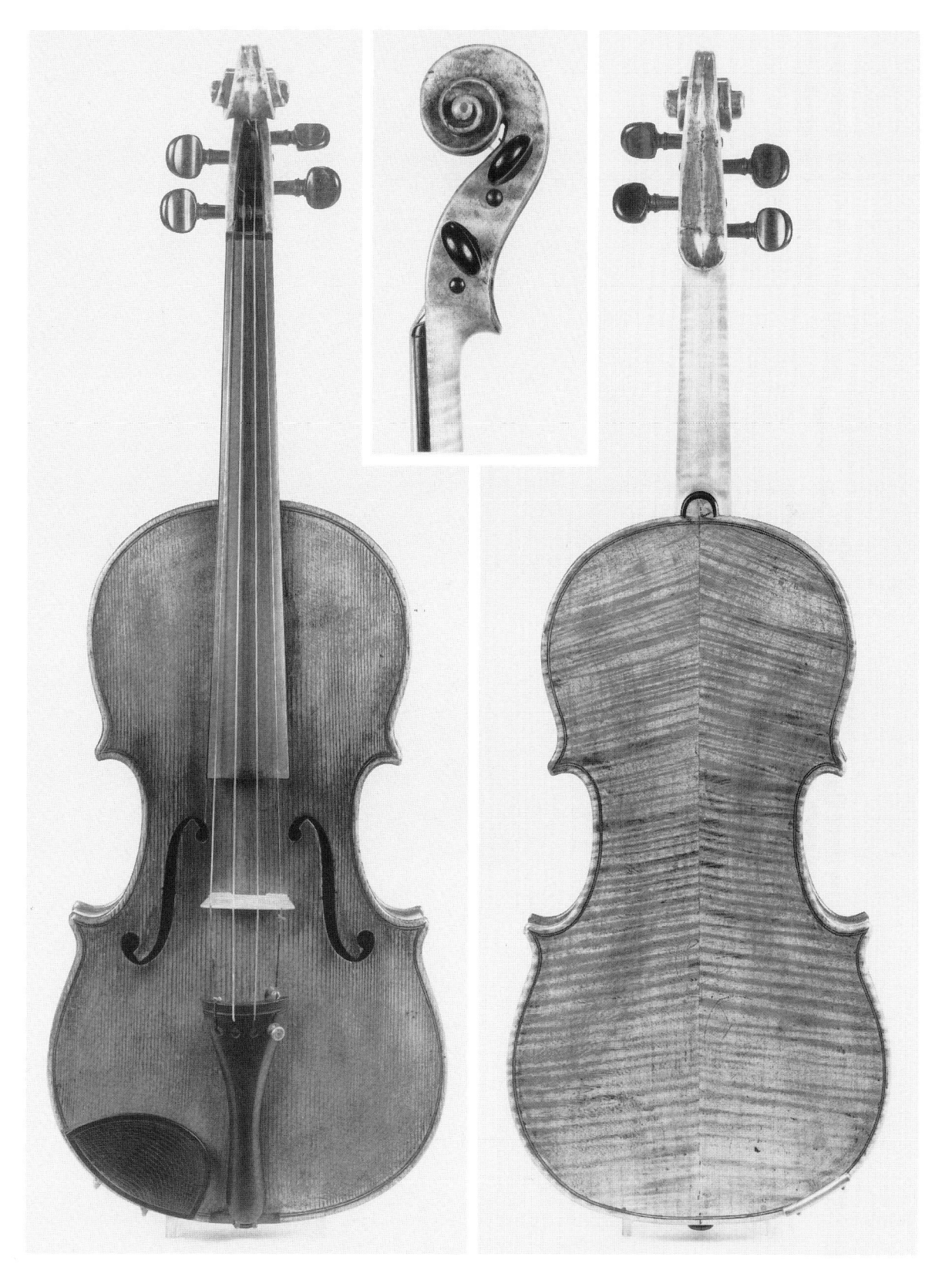

PLATE 45. George Craske, Violin, *c.* 1880.

PLATE 46. Nathaniel Cross, Violin, London, 1743.

PLATE 47. Robert Cuthbert, Violin, London, 1676.

PLATE 48. John Day, Violin, London, 1884.

PLATE 49. Mark William Dearlove, Viola, Leeds, 1847.

PLATE 50. Thomas Dodd, Violin, London, *c.* 1810.

PLATE 51. Richard Duke, Violin, London, 1777.

PLATE 52. Bernard Simon Fendt, Viola, London, 1833.

PLATE 53. Jacob Fendt, Violin, Lndon, *c.* 1830.

PLATE 54. Jacob Ford (attributed to), London, *c.* 1770.

PLATE 55. William Forster (senior), Viola, London, *c.* 1790.

PLATE 56. William Forster (senior), Cello, London, 1782.

PLATE 57. Henry Furber, Cello, London, 1886.

PLATE 58. Jeffrey J. Gilbert, Violin, 1931.

PLATE 59. Samuel Gilkes, Violin, London, *c.* 1820.

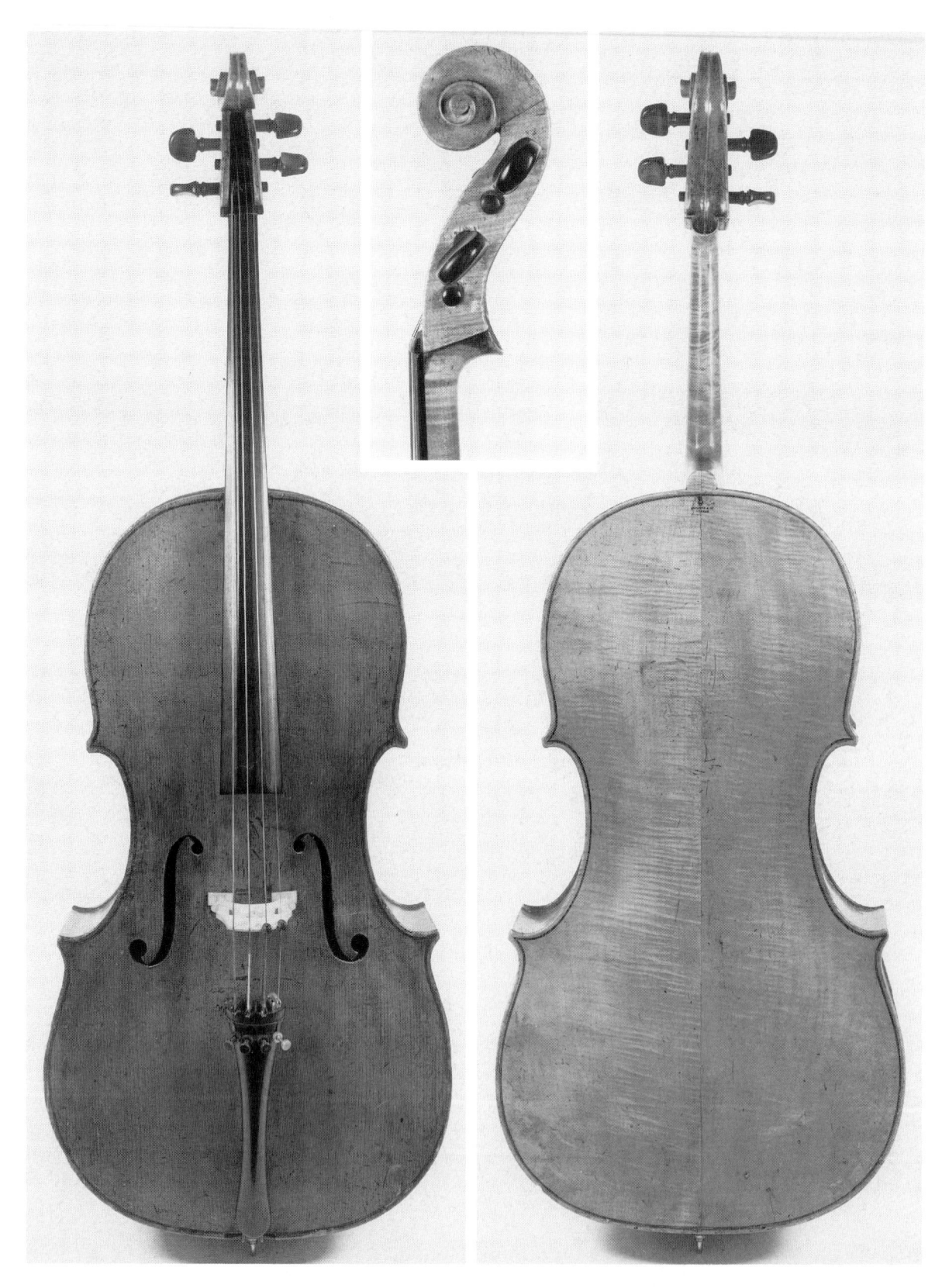

PLATE 60. Goulding & Co., Cello, London, *c.* 1790.

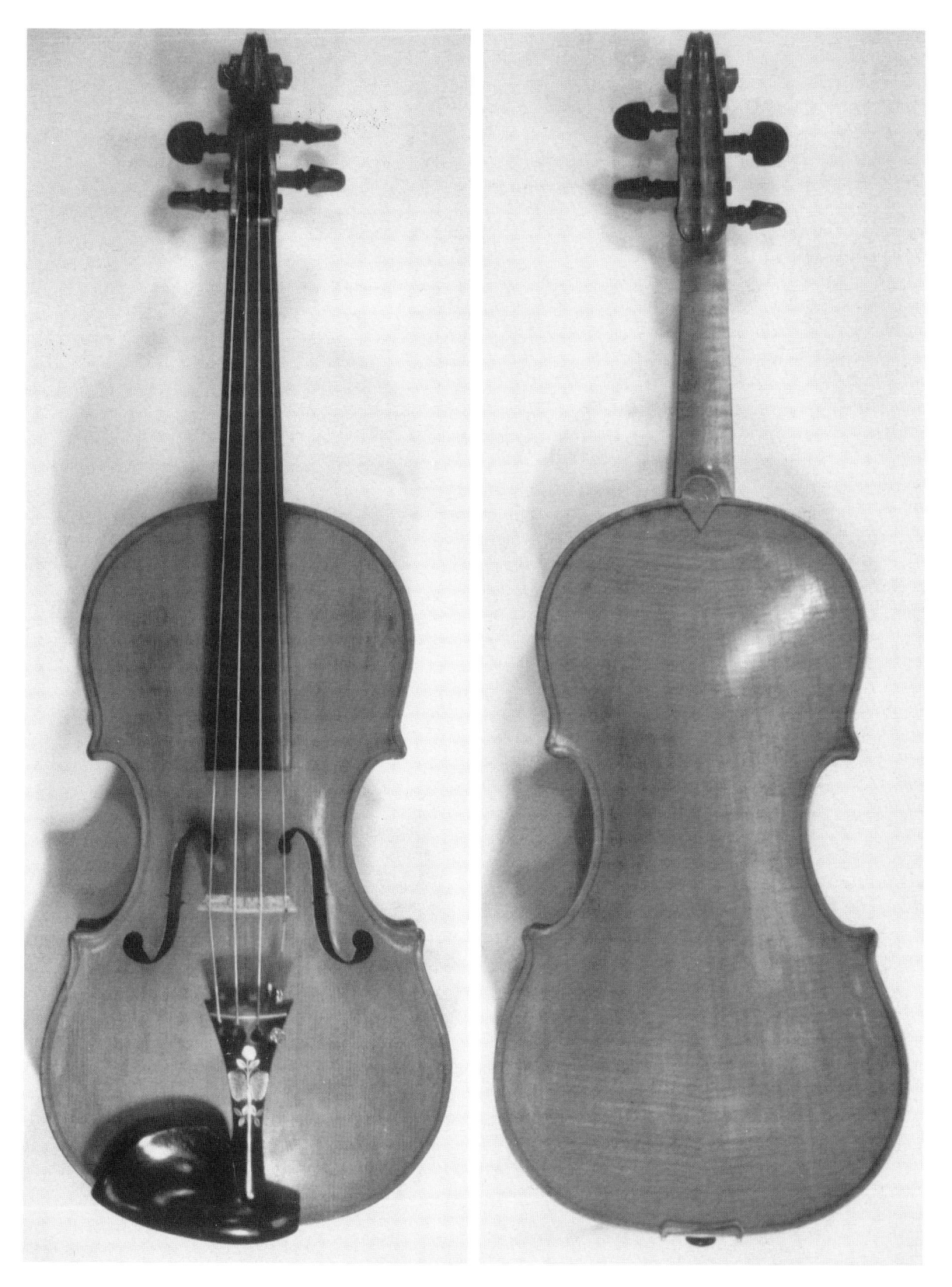

PLATE 61. Henry Handley, Violin, Worcester, 1887.

PLATE 62. Charles Harris, Cello, Woodstock, Oxfordshire, 1817.

PLATE 63. Matthew Hardie, Violin, Edinburgh, 1815.

PLATE 64. Matthew Hardie & Son, Cello, Edinburgh, 1822.

PLATE 65. Joseph Hare, Violin, London, 1723.

PLATE 66. T. Earle Hesketh, Violin, Manchester, 1934.

PLATE 67. Joseph Hill, Cello, London, 1774.

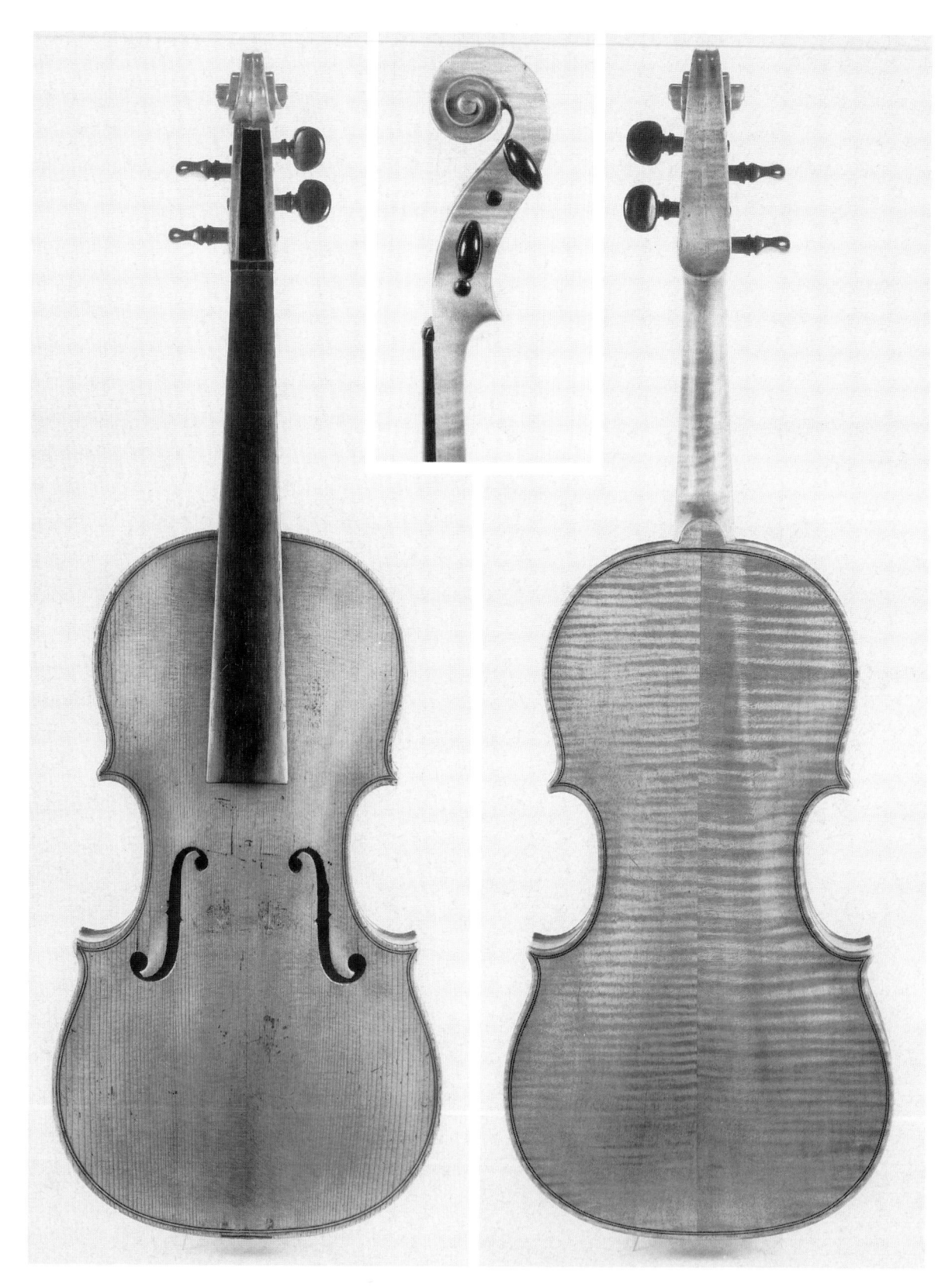

PLATE 68. Joseph Hill, Violin, London, *c.* 1790.

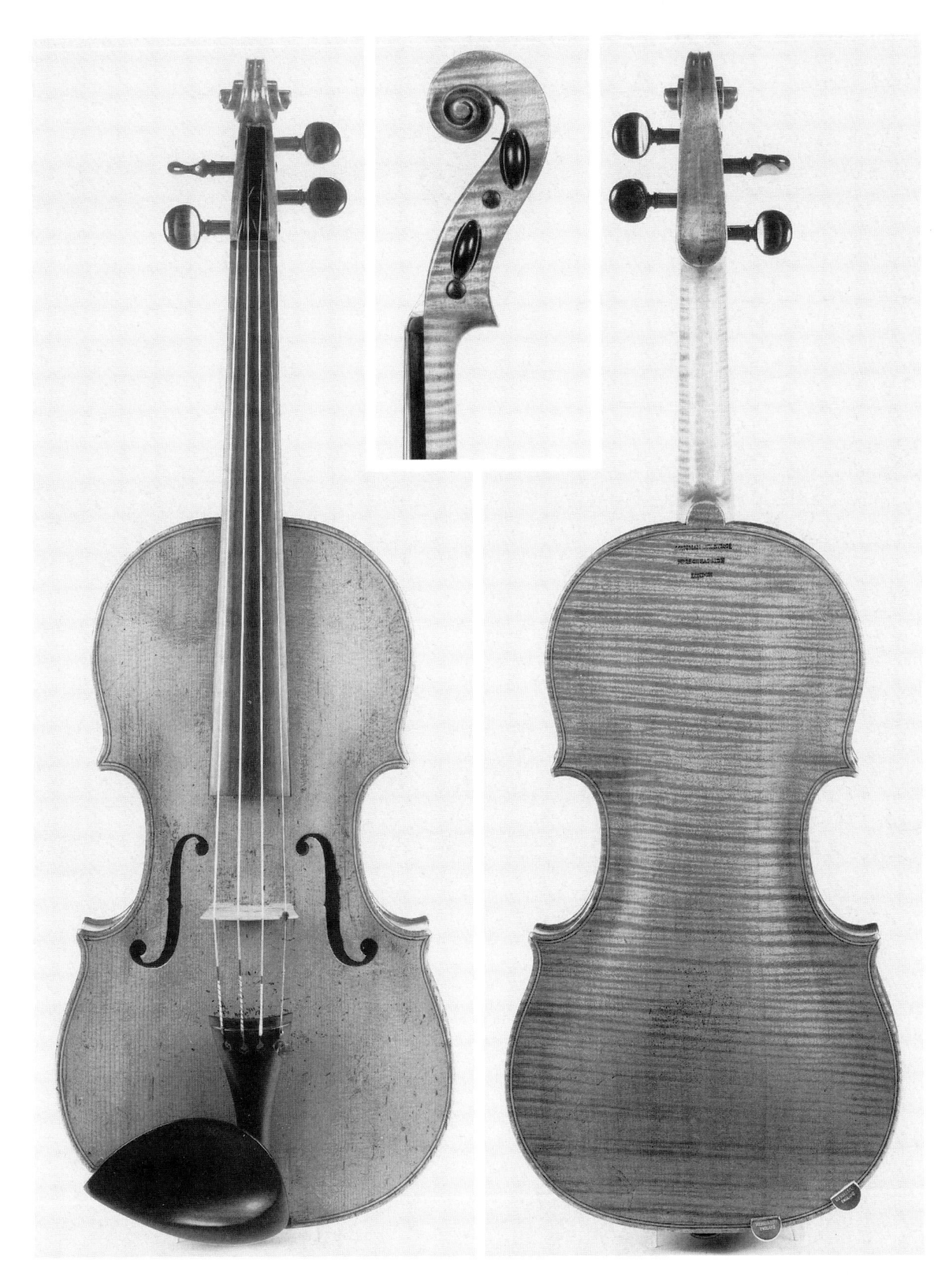

PLATE 69. Lockey Hill, Violin, London, *c.* 1780.

PLATE 70. Henry Lockey Hill, Violin, London, 1820.

PLATE 71. William Ebsworth Hill, Viola, London, 1845.

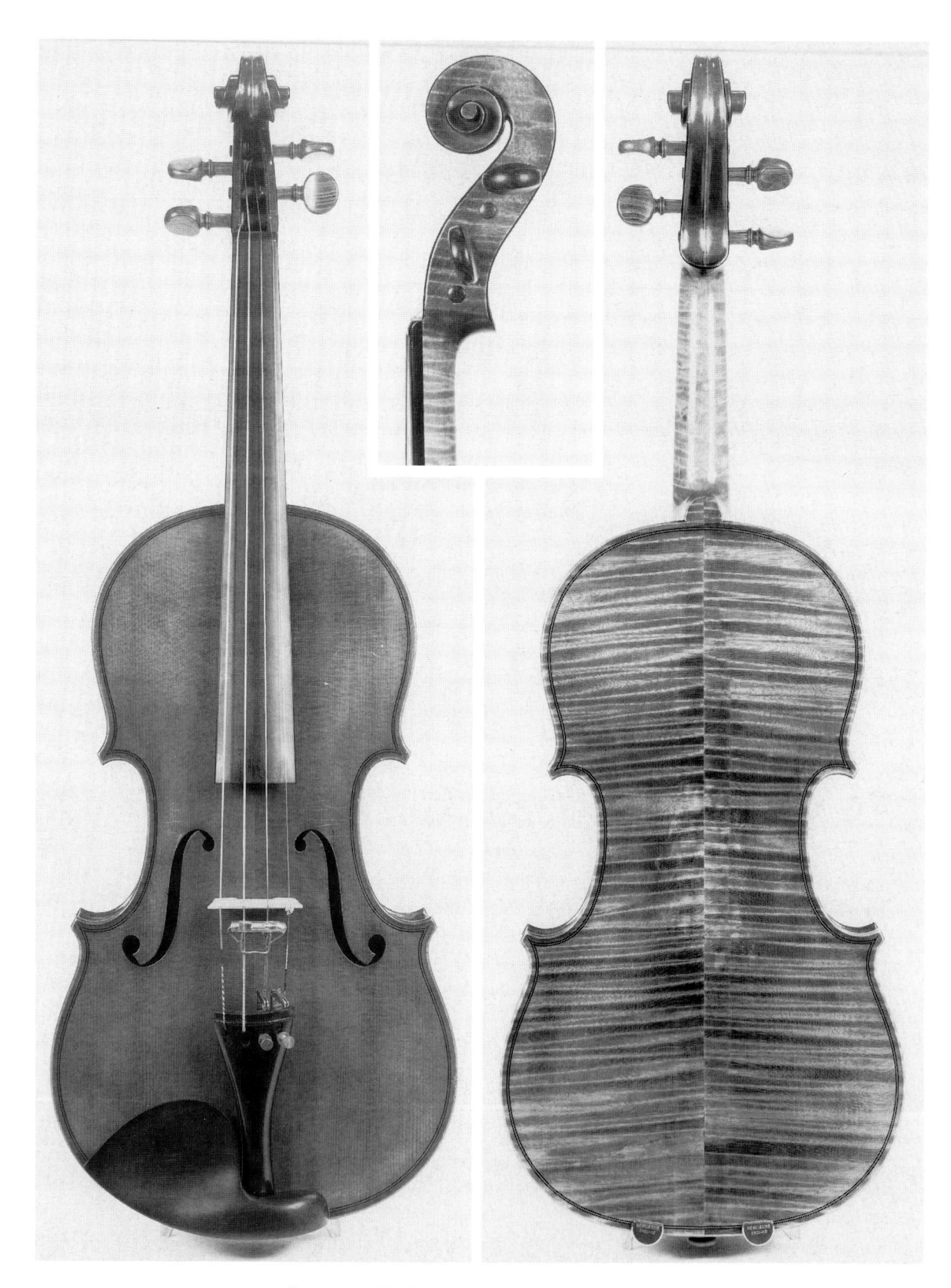

PLATE 72. W. E. Hill & Sons, Violin, London, 1918.

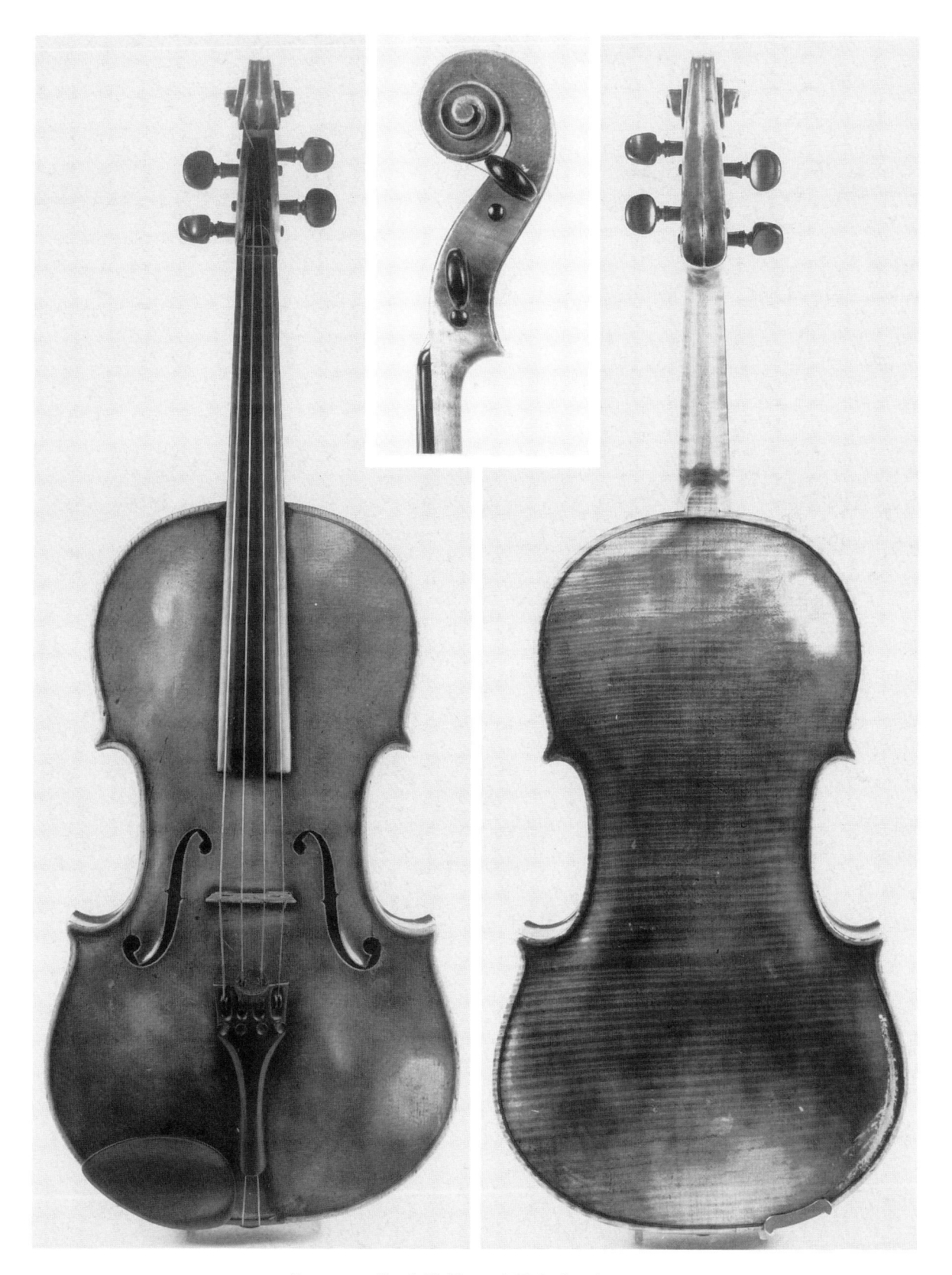

PLATE 73. Frank H. Howard, Viola, London, 1928.

PLATE 74. George Wulme Hudson, Violin, London, 1937.

PLATE 75. Henry Jay, Cello, London, 1757.

PLATE 76. John Johnson, Violin, London, 1759.

PLATE 77. Thomas Kennedy, Violin, London, 1844.

PLATE 78. John Frederick Lott, Violin, London, *c.* 1850.

PLATE 79. William H. Luff, Viola, London, 1973.

PLATE 80. John Marshall, Violin, Aberdeen, 1912.

PLATE 81. Walter H. Mayson, Violin, Windermere, 1885.

PLATE 82. Joseph Merlin, Cello, London, *c.* 1780.

PLATE 83. Barak Norman, Cello, London, *c.* 1720.

PLATE 84. John William Owen, Cello, Leeds, 1926.

PLATE 85. Edward Pamphilon, Violin, London, *c.* 1670.

PLATE 86. George Panormo, Violin, London, *c.* 1820.

PLATE 87. Joseph Panormo, Violin, London, c. 1800.

PLATE 88. Daniel Parker, Violin, London, *c.* 1720.

PLATE 89. Thomas Perry, Violin, Dublin, *c.* 1780.

PLATE 90. Thomas Perry, Cello, Dublin, 1785.

PLATE 91. George Pyne, Violin, London, 1914.

PLATE 92. Jacob Rayman, Viola, *c.* 1650.

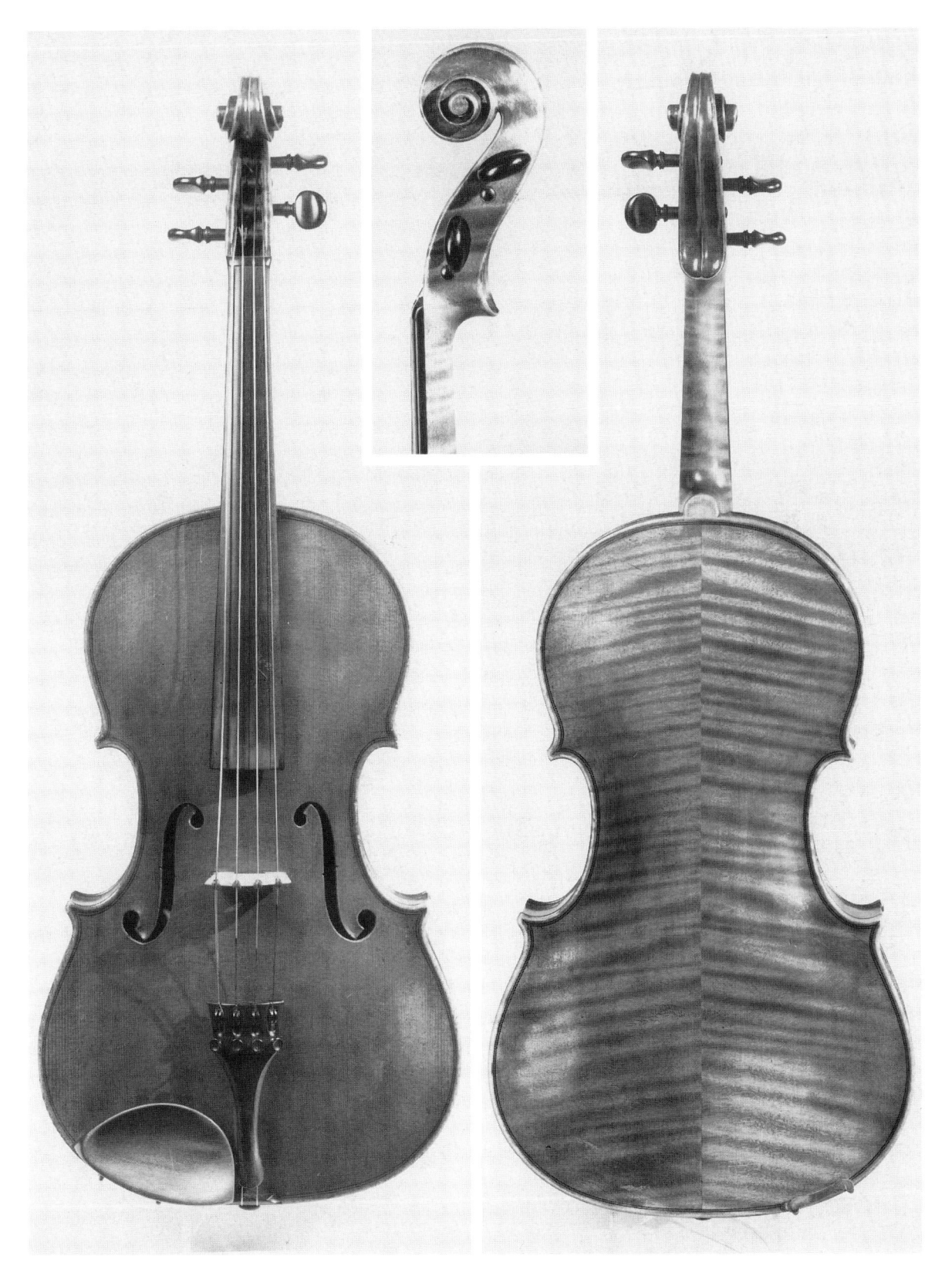

PLATE 93. Arthur Richardson, Viola, Crediton, 1938.

PLATE 94. William Robinson, Violin, London, 1929.

PLATE 95. Joseph Scott, Violin, Haltcliff, *c.* 1790.

PLATE 96. John Simpson, Violin, London, c. 1790.

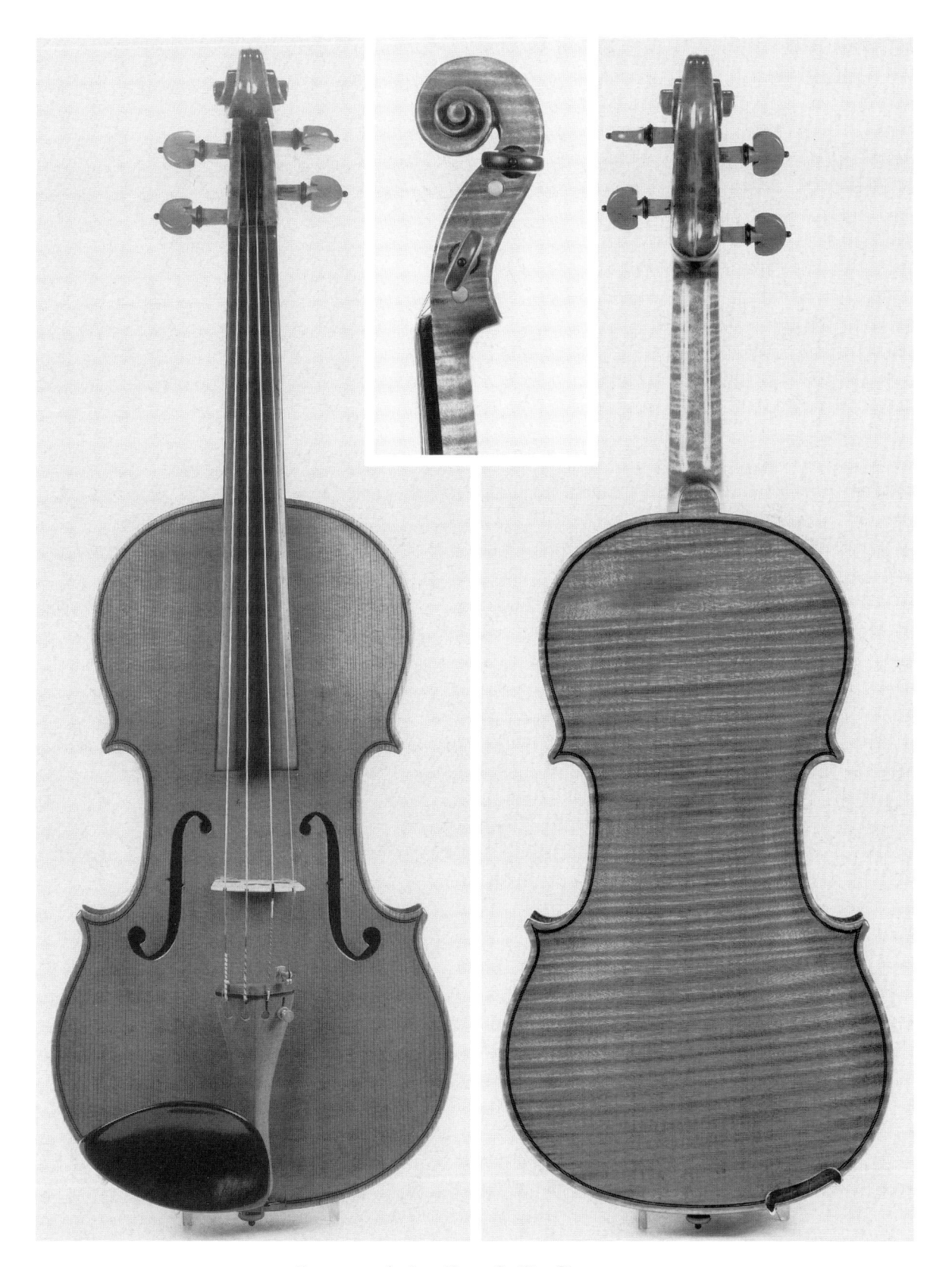

PLATE 97. Andrew Young Smillie, Glasgow, 1947.

PLATE 98. Thomas Smith, Violin, London, 1783.

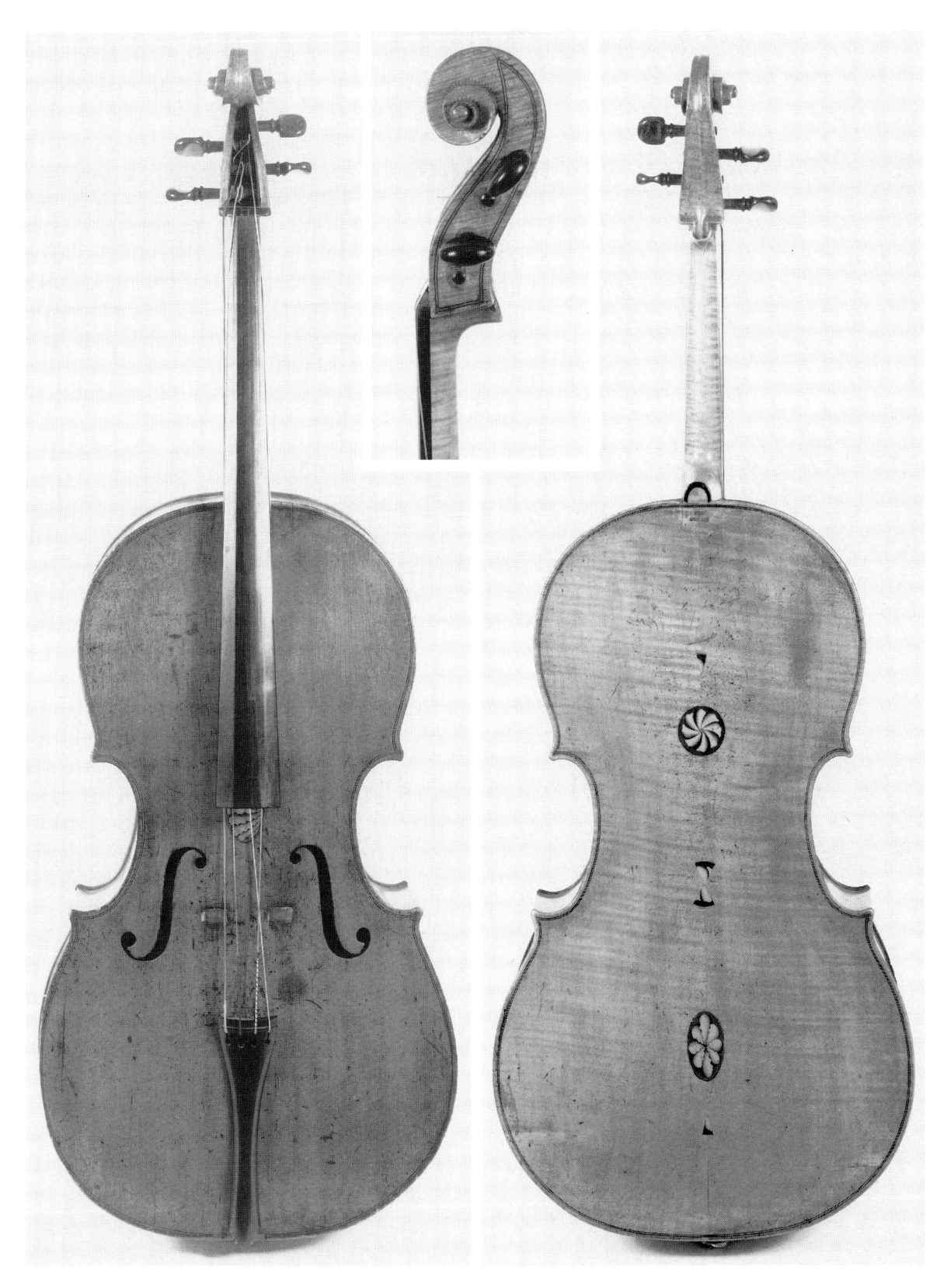

PLATE 99. William Smith, Cello, Sheffield, 1789.

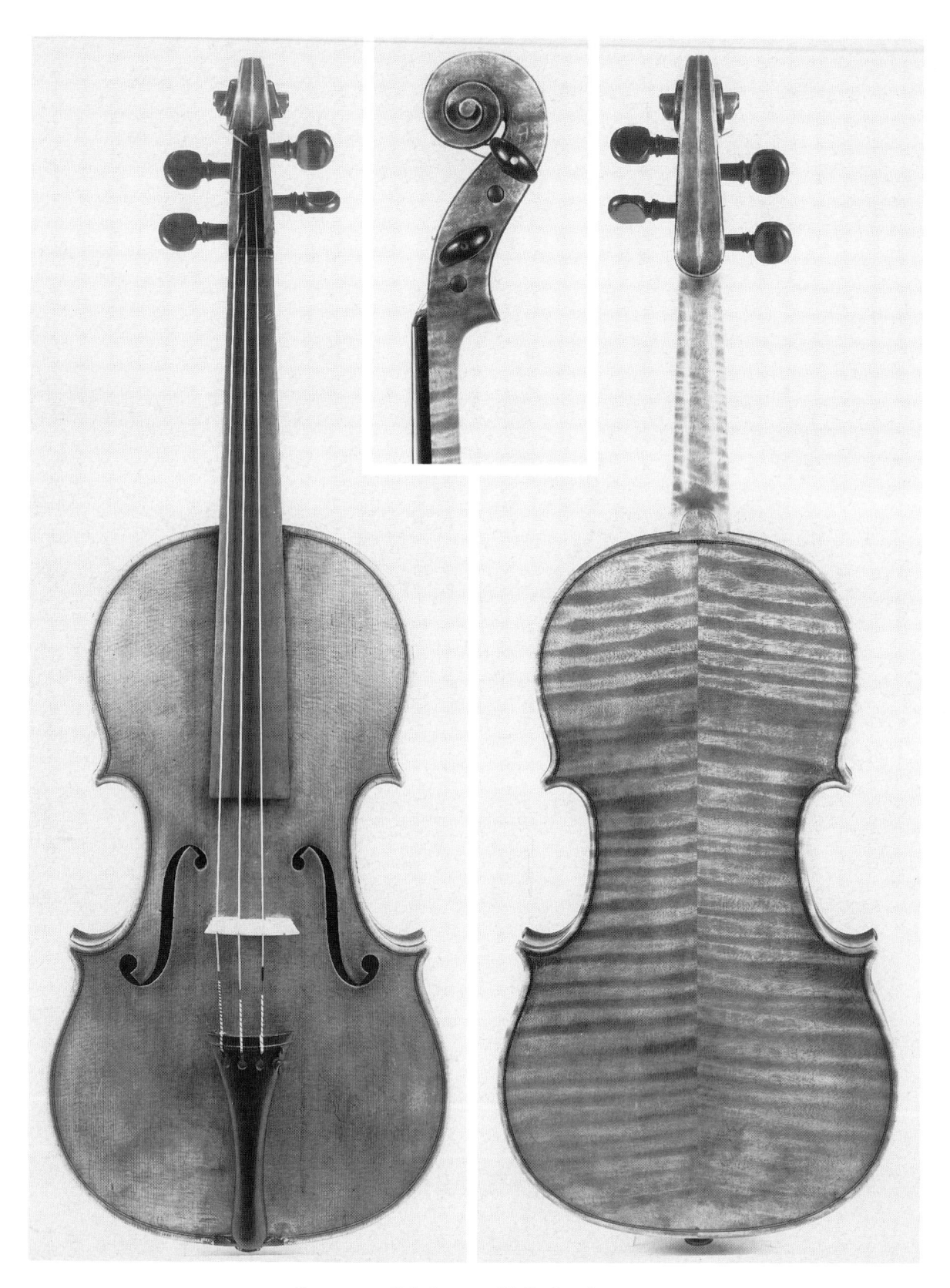

PLATE 100. Bela Szepessy, Violin, London, 1890.

PLATE 101. William Tarr, Violin, Manchester, 1876.

PLATE 102. Charles and Samuel Thompson, Violin, London, 1783.

PLATE 103. Thomas Tilley, Cello, London, 1768.

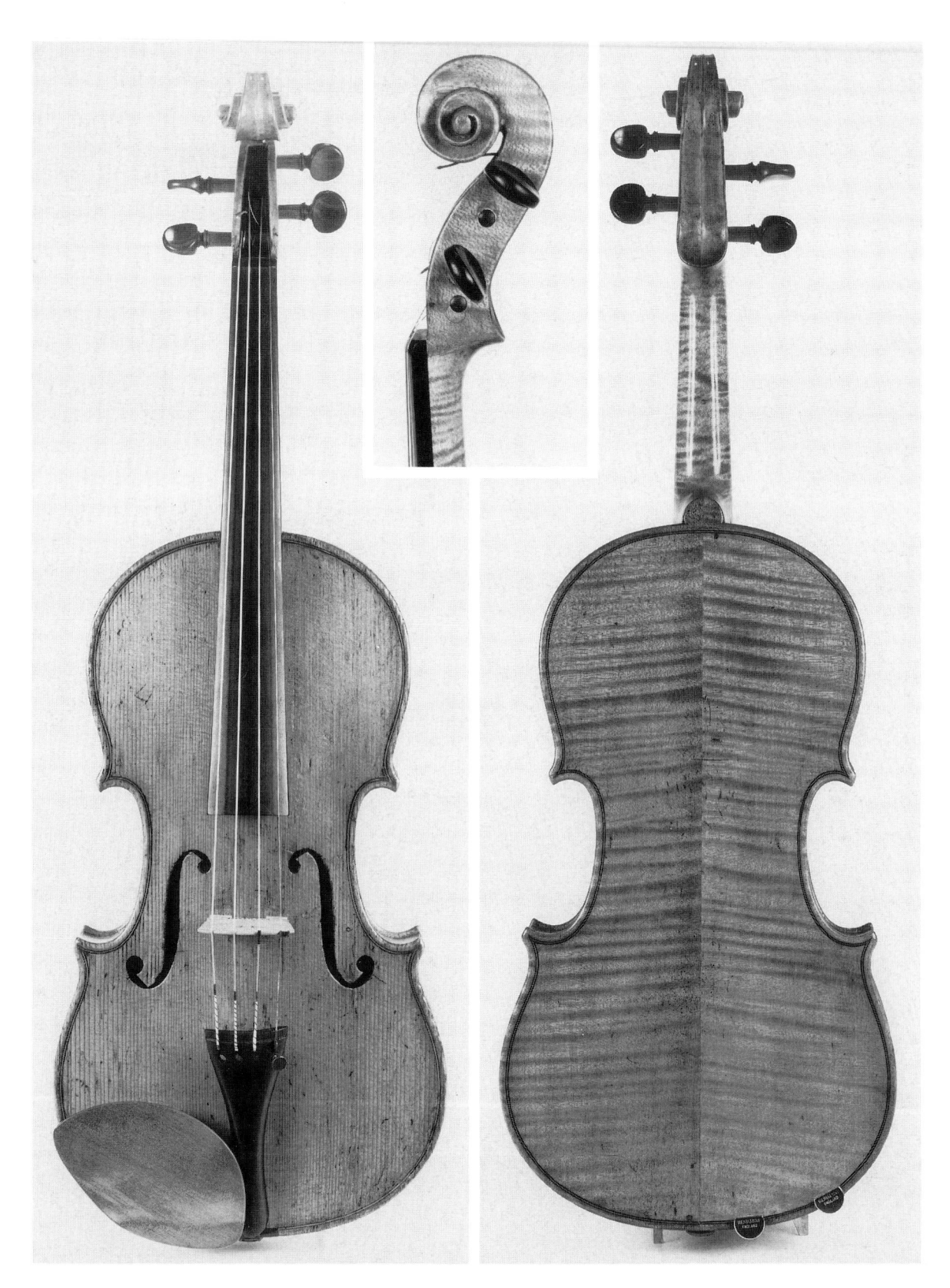

PLATE 104. Richard Tobin, Violin, London, *c.* 1820.

PLATE 105. Alfred Vincent, Violin, London, *c.* 1910.

PLATE 106. Peter Wamsley, Violin, London, 1748.

PLATE 107. Peter Wamsley, Cello, London, *c.* 1730.

PLATE 108. John Wilkinson, Viola, London, 1949.

PLATE 109. Christopher Wise, Violin, London, 1663.

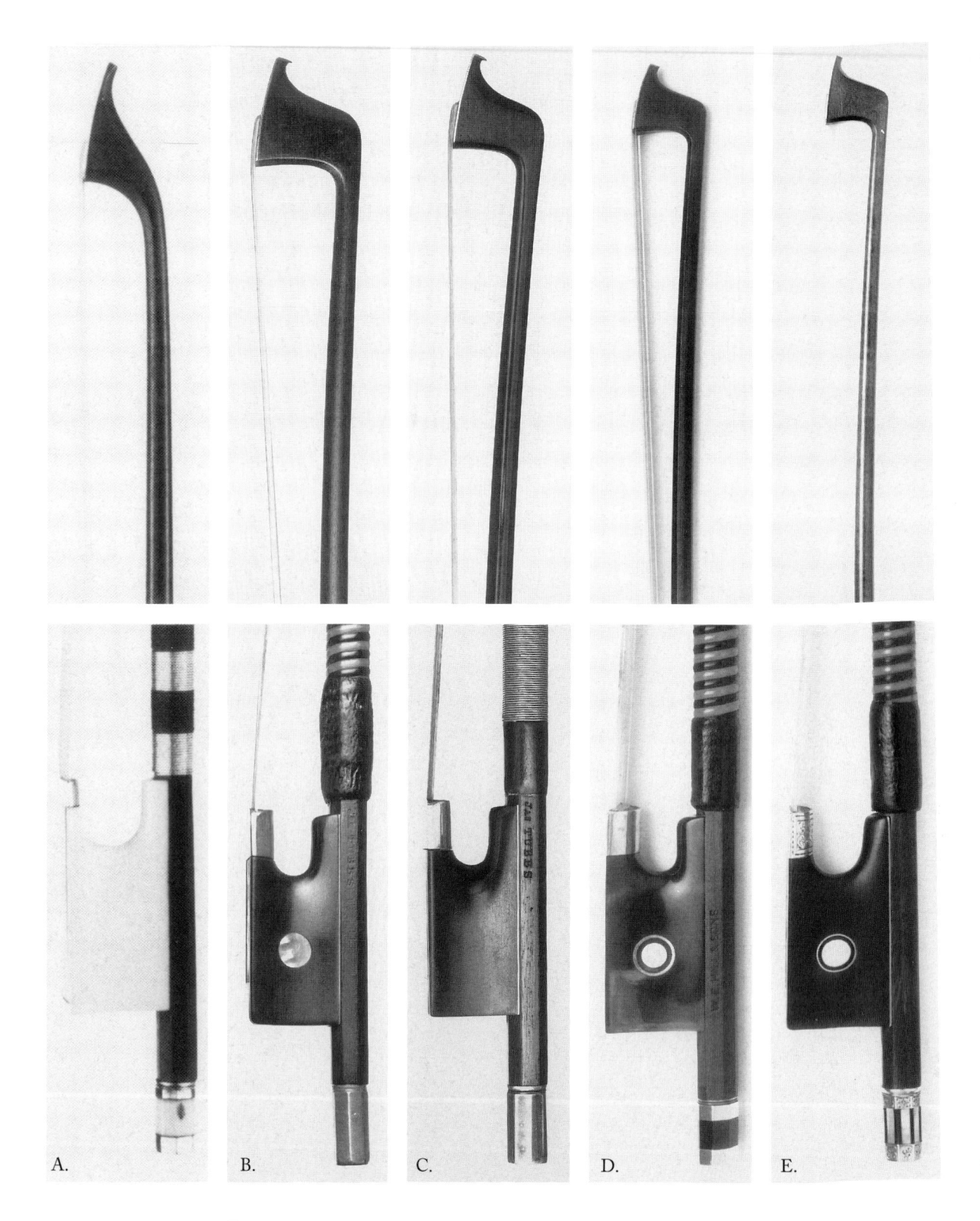

PLATE 110. Violin Bows. *a.* John Dodd, London, *c.* 1790; *b.* James Tubbs, London, *c.* 1900; *c.* James Tubbs, London, *c.* 1920; *d.* W. E. Hill & Sons, London, 1960; *e.* W. E. Hill & Sons, London, *c.* 1920.

Plate 71 HILL, WILLIAM EBSWORTH, Viola, London, 1845. LOB 15½ in. (395 mm), varnish of a transparent golden-amber colour, maker's manuscript label in Southwark, London, 1845. **Note**: A rare and magnificent instrument from the Hill collection.

Plate 72 HILL, W. E. & SONS, Violin, London, 1918. LOB 14 in. (356 mm), varnish of a red-brown colour, labelled *William E. Hill & Sons, Makers 140 New Bond Street, London, 1918, No. 303*. Hill certificate 1976, stating that 'the violin is one of our 1st quality instruments and is modelled after the MESSIE STRADIVARI of 1716'.

Plate 73 HOWARD, FRANK H., Viola, London, 1928. LOB 16⅝ in. (522 mm), varnish of deep red-brown colour on a yellow ground, maker's label in London, signed and dated 1928. **Note**: Frank Howard was an influential teacher at the Northern Polytechnic, London. William Luff was one of his early pupils.

Plate 74 HUDSON, GEORGE WULME-, Violin, London, 1937. LOB 14 1/16 in. (357 mm), varnish of a clear brown colour on a yellow ground, with maker's label *fecit London, anno 1937*.

Plate 75 JAY, HENRY, Cello, London, 1757. LOB 29½ in. (750 mm), varnish of a clear brown colour on a light-brown ground, maker's label in Long Acre, London, dated 1757.

Plate 76 JOHNSON, JOHN, Violin, London, 1759. LOB 14 1/16 in. (357 mm), varnish of an orange-red colour on a yellow ground, labelled *Made and Sold by John Johnson at the Harp & Crown in Cheapside, London, 1759*. **Note**: From the Hill collection.

Plate 77 KENNEDY, THOMAS, Violin, London, 1844. LOB 14⅛ in. (359 mm), varnish of an orange-red-brown colour on a yellow ground, labelled *Thos. Kennedy, maker, 364 Oxford Street, London, 1844*. **Note**: A fine specimen of this maker's work from the Hill collection.

Plate 78 LOTT, JOHN FREDERICK, Violin, London, c.1850. LOB 13 15/16 in. (354 mm), varnish of a rich ruby red colour on a yellow ground, bearing the label of Edward Withers, London. **Note**: Phillips state that this shows the hand of John Frederick Lott (II) who was connected with the Withers firm and its predecessor. This seems correct. See P 3/89/183 and compare Colour Plate D.

Plate 79 LUFF, WILLIAM H., Viola, London, 1973. LOB 16⅜ in. (416 mm), varnish of a light-brown colour on a golden yellow-brown ground with maker's printed label *William Luff, Maker, London, 1973*.

Plate 80 MARSHALL, JOHN, Violin, Aberdeen, 1912. LOB 14¼ in. (362 mm), oil varnish of a transparent orange-brown colour on a golden-amber ground, labelled *John Marshall, Violin Maker, Aberdeen* (and in MS) *1912, coppy Aless. Gagliano* [sic]; branded on upper inner back and top block.

Plate 81 MAYSON, WALTER H., Violin, Windermere, 1885. LOB 14⅛ in. (359 mm), varnish of a clear red-brown colour on a yellow ground, with the maker's signed label at Newby Bridge, Windermere, 1885, and named 'Second Echo'.

Plate 82 MERLIN, JOSEPH, Cello, London, c.1780. LOB 28 13/16 in. (732 mm), varnish of a golden-brown colour, branded *I. Merlin | London* below the button and on the pegbox.

Plate 83 NORMAN, BARAK, Cello, London, c.1720. LOB 28¼ in. (718 mm), varnish of a golden-brown colour, labelled *Barak Norman at the Bass Violin, St. Paul's Churchyd. London fecit 1720*. **Note:** Barak Norman's label is usually read as being 'at the Bass Viol in . . .' See S 11/92/288. Certificate of Waidela AB, 1961.

Plate 84 OWEN, JOHN WILLIAM, Cello, Leeds, 1926. LOB 29½ in. (750 mm), oil varnish of a red-brown colour on a yellow ground, bearing maker's label in Leeds, dated 1926, No. 48, and inscribed on the inner back.

Plate 85 PAMPHILON, EDWARD, Violin, London, c.1670. LOB 13¹⁵⁄₁₆ in. (355 mm), varnish of a golden orange-brown colour, unlabelled. **Note:** See P 11/80/171.

Plate 86 PANORMO, GEORGE, Violin, London, c.1820. LOB 14¹⁄₁₆ in. (357 mm), varnish of a golden-orange colour, labelled *Panormo fecit London*. Receipt of William Luff, London, 1964.

Plate 87 PANORMO, JOSEPH, Violin, London, c.1800. LOB 14¹⁄₁₆ in. (357 mm), varnish of a rich red-brown colour on a yellow ground. **Note:** From the Hill collection.

Plate 88 PARKER, DANIEL, Violin, London, c.1720. LOB 14⅛ in. (359 mm), clear varnish of an orange-red-brown colour on a yellow ground, unlabelled. **Note:** From the Hill collection. The controversy over this maker's correct dates is discussed in Ch. 5.

Plate 89 PERRY, THOMAS, Violin, Dublin, c.1780. LOB 14 in. (356 mm), varnish of a clear golden-brown colour, branded PERRY DUBLIN below the button and No. 2541 on the button. **Note:** From the Hill collection. Compare the corners of the upper bout of this instrument with those of Parker, preceding.

Plate 90 PERRY, THOMAS, Cello, Dublin, 1785. LOB 29⅞ in. (759 mm), upper bouts 13¾ in. (350 mm), lower bouts 16¾ in. (425 mm), varnish of a clear brown-amber colour, labelled *Thos. Perry No. 6 Anglesea Street, Dublin, 1785*. and branded below button PERRY DUBLIN.

Plate 91 PYNE, GEORGE, Violin, London, 1914. LOB 14 in. (356 mm), varnish of a light golden-brown colour, with maker's label in London anno 1914 and branded *G. Pyne, London* on inner back.

Plate 92 RAYMAN, JACOB, Viola, c.1650. LOB 16⁹⁄₁₆ in. (421 mm), varnish of a rich golden-brown colour, the head carved with multiple scrolls, labelled *Jacob Rayman, 1650(?)* (partly legible), with letters from W. E. Hill & Sons of 1935 and A. Smillie, Glasgow, of 1935, relating to the history of the instrument. **Note:** This historic viola was during this century played in the Hallé Orchestra by the late Sydney Errington. Although its date is not certain it appears to be the earliest instrument of the violin family, conventionally made, known by a London maker. The Brescian influence is manifest.

Plate 93 RICHARDSON, ARTHUR, Viola, Crediton, 1938. LOB 16¾ in. (425 mm), oil varnish of an orange-red colour on a yellow ground, with maker's label and signature in Crediton, Devon, dated 1938, stating specially designed in collaboration with Mr Lionel Tertis.

Plate 94   ROBINSON, WILLIAM, Violin, London, 1929. LOB 14 in. (356 mm), varnish of a clear orange-brown colour on a yellow ground, with maker's label in Plumstead, London, dated 1929, No. 224.

Plate 95   SCOTT, JOSEPH, Violin, Haltcliff, c.1790. LOB 14³⁄₁₆ in. (360 mm), varnish of a ruby red colour on a yellow ground, bearing maker's label at Haltcliff, Near Hestkett, Newmarket, No. 68. **Note:** From the Hill collection.

Plate 96   SIMPSON, JOHN, Violin, London, c.1790. LOB 14¹⁄₁₆ in. (357 mm), varnish of a golden orange-brown colour on a light-brown ground, labelled with the maker's label *Musical Instrument Makers at the Bass-Viol and Flute in Sweeting's Alley opposite the East door of the Royal Exchange London.*

Plate 97   SMILLIE, ANDREW YOUNG, Glasgow, 1947. LOB 14³⁄₁₆ in. (362 mm), varnish of a transparent orange colour on a yellow ground, maker's label from Glasgow, anno 1947.

Plate 98   SMITH, THOMAS, Violin, London, 1783. LOB 14¹⁄₁₆ in. (357 mm), varnish of a golden-brown colour, with the maker's label *Made by Tho. Smith at The Harp and Hautboy in Pickadilly London 1783*. Hill certificate, 1987.

Plate 99   SMITH, WILLIAM, Cello, Sheffield, 1789. LOB 29¼ in. (742 mm), varnish of a transparent golden-brown colour, with the maker's label *Made by SMITH Sycamore Street Sheffield, 1789* and branded Smith Sheffield below the button. Fingerboard stamped P 1215. **Note:** The Hill Archive has a note stating 'Mr. Tarr says that his instruments always bear the peculiar ornament of a Sheraton "Shell" in the middle of the back.'

Plate 100   SZEPESSY, BÉLA, Violin, London, 1890. LOB 14⅛ in. (359 mm), varnish of an orange-red-brown colour on a yellow ground, with maker's label in London, 1890, No. 62.

Plate 101   TARR, WILLIAM, Violin, Manchester, 1876. LOB 14³⁄₁₆ in. (360 mm), varnish of an orange-brown colour on a golden-brown ground, with maker's label in Manchester, No. 24, 1876.

Plate 102   THOMPSON, CHARLES AND SAMUEL, Violin, London, 1783. LOB 14 in. (355 mm), varnish of a clear red-brown colour, labelled *Made and Sold by Chas. & Saml. Thompson in St. Paul's Church Yard, London, 1783* and branded Thompson London below the button.

Plate 103   TILLEY, THOMAS, Cello, London, 1768. LOB 29½ in. (750 mm), varnish of a golden-orange colour with maker's original manuscript label *Thos. Tilley | Maker in Market Lane | St. Jameses | London 1768*. Hill's No. 131 stamped on the fingerboard. **Note:** Instruments by this maker, particularly cellos, are rare. (The Hill Archive suggests that he may have made for Joseph Hill.) The handsome one-piece back is cut on the slab.

Plate 104   TOBIN, RICHARD, Violin, London, c.1820. LOB 14¹⁄₁₆ in. (357 mm), varnish of a golden orange-brown colour, unlabelled. **Note:** from Hill collection.

Plate 105   VINCENT, ALFRED, Violin, London, c.1910. LOB 13¹⁵⁄₁₆ in. (354 mm), with maker's label in London.

Plate 106 WAMSLEY, PETER, Violin, London, 1748. LOB 14⅛ in. (359 mm), varnish of a red-brown colour, labelled *Peter Wamsley, Maker at the Harp & Hautboy in Picaddilly, London, 1748*, with Hill's receipt of 1933. **Note:** The violin is in 'baroque' specification.

Plate 107 WAMSLEY, PETER, Cello, London, c.1730. LOB 29¾ in. (730 mm), varnish of a golden-brown colour, labelled similarly to above.

Plate 108 WILKINSON, JOHN, Viola, London, 1949. LOB 16½ in. (420 mm), varnish of a deep red-brown colour on a yellow ground, with maker's label in London dated 1949.

Plate 109 WISE, CHRISTOPHER, Violin, London, 1663. LOB 13¹³⁄₁₆ in. (352 mm), varnish of a clear brown colour. Printed label: CHRISTOPER WISE *Vine Court without Bishops-Gate, London 1663*. **Note:** This historic instrument, one of the earliest known English violins extant, is from the Hill collection. It clearly shows Brescian influence. Compare Plate 92 (Rayman), also showing Brescian influence, and Plate 47 (Cuthbert), showing more the Amati influence.

Plate 110 Bows (*a*) DODD, JOHN, Silver- and ivory-mounted Violin Bow, London, c.1790. The round stick of a chestnut-brown colour with pike head and mother-of-pearl inlay in the ivory head plate, ivory frog, and button, the latter with two silver bands, stamped Dodd on the shaft and *L. Panor* [sic] on the frog. 54 g. (*b*) TUBBS, JAMES, Silver-mounted Violin Bow, London, c.1900. The round stick of a dark chocolate-brown colour, the ebony frog inlaid with pearl eyes, silver-overlaid ebony adjuster, stamped *Jas. Tubbs* on the shaft, 62 g. (*c*) TUBBS, JAMES, Silver-mounted Violin Bow, London, c.1920. The round stick of a chocolate-brown colour, plain ebony frog, silver-overlaid ebony adjuster, stamped *Jas. Tubbs* on the shaft, 60 g. (*d*) W. E. HILL & SONS, Silver- and tortoiseshell-mounted Violin Bow, London, 1960. The octagonal stick of a chestnut-brown colour, the tortoise-shell frog inlaid with silver rings enclosing pearl eyes, the ebony adjuster with two silver bands, stamped *W. E. Hill & Sons* on the shaft, 59 g. (*e*) W. E. HILL & SONS, Engraved gold-mounted Violin Bow, London, c.1920. The round stick of a chestnut-brown colour, the ebony frog inlaid with gold rings enclosing pearl eyes, the ebony adjuster inlaid with pearl facets and with two gold bands, all mounts including the gold head plate engraved with floral motifs, stamped *W. E. Hill & Sons* on the shaft, 56 g.

Acknowledgements to Sources

Photographs of instruments (plates 31 to 110) are reproduced by kind permission of Phillips (for all plates other than those listed below); Sotheby's (for plates 42, 44, 53, 57, 83, 86, 92, 106, and 110: Christie's (for plates 34, 36, and 82); Hamilton Caswell (for plate 34); and the author (plate 61).

Select Bibliography

ADELMANN, OLGA, *Die Alemannische Schule* (Berlin: Staatliches Institut für Musikforschung, 1990).
ALBURGER, MARY ANNE, *The Violin Makers: Portrait of a Living Craft* (London: Gollancz, 1979).
—— *Scottish Fiddlers and their Music* (London: Gollancz, 1983).
ARNOLD, DENIS (ed.), *The New Oxford Companion to Music* (Oxford University Press, 1983).
AUER, LEOPOLD, *Violin Playing as I Teach it* (London: Duckworth, 1921).
BAINES, ANTHONY, *The Oxford Companion to Musical Instruments* (Oxford University Press, 1992).
—— (ed.), *Musical Instruments Through The Ages* (Harmondsworth: Penguin, 1961).
BALFOUR & CO., *How to tell the Nationality of Old Violins* (London: Balfour & Co., 1900; repr. 1983).
BEVAN, CLIFFORD, *Musical Instrument Collections in the British Isles* (Winchester: Piccolo Press, 1990).
BLOM, ERIC, *Music in England* (Harmondsworth: Penguin, 1942).
BOYDEN, DAVID D., *Catalogue of the Hill Collection of Musical Instruments in the Ashmolean Museum, Oxford* (London: Oxford University Press, 1969).
BRINSER, MARLIN, *Dictionary of Twentieth Century Italian Violin Makers* (Irvington, NJ: Books on Music, 1978).
BROADHOUSE, JOHN, *The Violin: How to Make it* (London: Reeves, c.1910).
BURN, RICHARD, *Justice of the Peace*, (London, 1758).
BURNEY, CHARLES, *A General History of Music* (4 vols.; London, 1726–89).
CARDWELL, J. H., FREEMAN, H. B., and WILTON, G. C., *Two Centuries of Soho, Its Institutions, Firms and Amusements* (London: Truslove & Hanson, 1898).
CARRODUS, J. T., *How to Study the Violin* (London: Strad Library, 1895).
COATES, KEVIN, *Geometry, Proportion and the Art of Lutherie* (Oxford University Press, 1985).
COOPER, ALBERT, *Benjamin Banks, The Salisbury Violin Maker* (Haslemere: Ashford Publications, 1989).
COWLING, ELIZABETH, *The Cello* (London: Batsford, 1975).
COYNE, MICHAEL, *Pamphilon: An Essex Family* (Essex [sic]: Vine Press, 1992).
DAVIDSON, PETER, *The Violin: Its Construction Theoretically and Practically Treated* (London: Pitman, 1871; 1880; 1881; 1895).
DORING, ERNEST N., *The Guadagnini Family of Violin Makers* (Chicago, 1949).
DUBOURG, GEORGE, *History of the Violin*, 1st edn. (London: Henry Colburn, 1836); 5th edn. rev. John Bishop (London, 1878).

EGGLESTONE, WILLIAM MORLEY, *John Askew, The Stanhope Violin Maker* (Stanhope: W. M. Egglestone, 1914).

EHRHARDT, ROY, *Violin Identification and Price Guide*, Bk. 2 (Kansas City: Heart of America Press, 1978).

EHRLICH, CYRIL, *The Piano: A History* (London: Dent, 1976).

—— *The Music Profession in Britain since the Eighteenth Century* (Oxford University Press, 1985).

ELKIN, ROBERT, *The Old Concert Rooms of London* (London: Edward Arnold, 1955).

ELLIOT, KENNETH AND RIMMER, FREDERICK, *A History of Scottish Music* (London: BBC, 1973).

FAIRFIELD, JOHN H., *Known Violin Makers* (Athens, Ga.: Harold M. Chaitman, 1942, 1973).

FARGA, FRANZ, *Violins and Violinists* (London: Rockliff, 1950).

FARMER, HENRY GEORGE, *A History of Music in Scotland* (London: Henrichson, 1947; 1970).

FELLOWES, EDMUND H., *English Cathedral Music*, 5th edn., ed. J. A. Westrup (London: Methuen, 1969).

FLEMING, JAMES M., *The Fiddle Fancier's Guide* (London: Haynes, Foucher & Co., 1892).

—— *Old Violins and their Makers* (London: L. Upcott Gill, 1883).

FOUCHER, G., *Treatise on the History and Construction of the Violin* (London: G. Foucher, 1894; rev. edn. 1897).

FRASER, GEORGE MACDONALD, *Flashman and the Dragon* (London: Fontana/Collins, 1985; paperback, 1986).

FRY, GEORGE, *Italian Varnishes* (London: Stevens, 1904).

GALPIN, FRANCIS W., *Old English Instruments of Music* 4th edn., rev. Thurston Dart (London: Methuen, 1965).

GEORGE, M. D., *London Life in the Eighteenth Century* (London: Peregrine Books, 1966).

GILL, DOMINIC (ed.), *Book of the Violin* (Oxford: Phaidon, 1984).

Grove's Dictionary of Music and Musicians, 2nd edn., ed. J. A. Fuller Maitland (5 vols., London: Macmillan, 1904–onwards).

GWYNN, R. D., *Huguenot Heritage: The History and Contribution of the Huguenots in Britain* (London: Routledge, 1985).

HART, GEORGE, *The Violin and its Music* (London: Dulau & Co., 1881).

—— *The Violin: Famous Makers and their Imitators* (London: Dulau & Co. and Schott & Co., 1875).

HARVEY, BRIAN W., *Violin Fraud: Deception, Forgery, Theft, and the Law* (Oxford: Clarendon Press, 1992).

HAWEIS, H. R., *Old Violins and Violin Lore* (London: Reeves, 1898).

—— *My Musical Life* (London: Longman, 1902).

HAWKINS, SIR JOHN, *A General History of the Science and Practice of Music* (London: Novello, 1875).

HEAL, SIR AMBROSE, *The Sign Boards of Old London Shops* (London: Portman Books, 1957, repr. 1988).

HEE-HOEK, *Catalogue of Printed Music in the British Library to 1980*, xxviii (London: K. G. Saur, 1984).

HENLEY, WILLIAM, *Universal Dictionary of Violin and Bow Makers*, 2nd edn. (Brighton: Amati Publishing, 1973).

HERON-ALLEN, EDWARD, *Violin-Making as it Was, and Is* (London: Ward Lock, 1884).

—— *Second Edition of Edward Fitzgerald's Rubaiyat of Umar Khayyam* (London: Duckworth & Co., 1908).

HILL, W. H., A. F., AND A. E., *Antonio Stradivari: His Life and Work* (London: William E. Hill & Sons, 1902).

—— *The Violin Makers of the Guarneri Family* (London, 1931).

HINE, REGINALD, *Relics of an Un-Common Attorney* (London: Dent, 1951).

HOLMAN, PETER, *Four and Twenty Fiddlers* (Oxford University Press, 1993).

HONEYMAN, WILLIAM C., *The Violin . . . How to Choose One* (Dundee, 1893; 6th edn., repr. 1983).

—— *Scottish Violin Makers: Past and Present*, 2nd edn. (Dundee, 1910; repr. Bridgwater: S. A. Kellow, 1983; repr. with a new Preface by John Turner, Morgantown, Va.: Scotpress and Fiddletree Music, 1984).

HUMPHRIES, C. AND SMITH, W. C., *Music Publishing in the British Isles from Earlier Times to the Nineteenth Century* (London: Cassell, 1954).

Illustrated Catalogue of the Music Loan Exhibition, Fishmongers Hall, 1904, (London: Novello, 1809).

JALOVEC, KAREL, *Encyclopaedia of Violin-Makers* (London: Paul Hamlyn, 1968).

John Joseph Merlin: The Ingenious Mechanick (London: GLC, 1985).

JOHNSON, DAVID, *Music and Society in Lowland Scotland in the Eighteenth Century* (London: Oxford University Press, 1972).

LAURIE, DAVID, *The Reminiscences of a Fiddle Dealer* (London: T. Werner Laurie, c.1924).

LÜTGENDORFF, WILLIBALD F. VON, *Die Geigen- und Lautenmacher* (with supplement by Thomas Drescher) (3 vols., Tutzing: Schneider, 1990).

MACE, THOMAS, *Musick's Monument* (London, 1676; Paris: Centre National de la Recherche Scientifique, 1977 (facsimile of 1676 edn.)).

MACKERNESS, ERIC D., *A Social History of English Music* (London: Routledge & Kegan Paul, 1964).

MACTAGGART, PETER and ANN, *Musical Instruments in the 1851 Exhibition* (Welwyn: Mac & Me, 1986).

MCVEIGH, SIMON, *The Violinist in London's Concert Life 1750–1784: Felice Giardini and his Contemporaries* (New York, 1989).

MASON, LOWELL, *Musical Letters from Abroad* (New York: Mason Brothers, 1854; repr., New York: Da Capo Press, 1967).

MICHELMAN, JOSEPH, *Violin Varnish* (Cincinnati, Oh.: J. Michelman, 1946).

MITCHELL, B. R., and DEANE, P., *Abstract of British Historical Statistics* (Cambridge University Press, 1971).

MORRIS, W. MEREDITH, *Walter H. Mayson: An Account of the Life and Work of a Celebrated Modern Violin Maker, with Numerous Illustrations* (Maesteg: J. James, 1906).

Morris, W. Meredith, *British Violin Makers*, 1st edn. (London: Chatto & Windus, 1904); 2nd edn. (London: Robert Scott, 1920). (All references in text are to 2nd edn. unless otherwise stated.)

—— *Famous Fiddlers by the Reverend W. Meredith Morris*, ed. D. Roy Saer (Cardiff: Welsh Folk Museum, 1983).

Moya, Hildago, and Piper, A. Towry, *Violin Tone and Violin Makers* (London: Chatto & Windus, 1916).

Mozart, Leopold, *Treatise on the Fundamental Principles of Violin Playing* (Augsburg, 1756; Eng. trans., Edith Knocker, London: Oxford University Press, 1951).

New Grove Dictionary of Music and Musicians, The, ed. Stanley Sadie (20 vols.; London: Macmillan, 1980).

New Grove Dictionary of Musical Instruments, The, ed. Stanley Sadie (London: Macmillan, 1984).

Parke, W. T., *Musical Memoirs* (London, 1830).

Patey, Carole, *Musical Instruments at the Victoria & Albert Museum: An Introduction* (London: HMSO, 1978).

Pearce, Joseph, jun., *Violins and Violin Makers: Biographical Dictionary of the Great Italian Artistes, their Followers and Imitators, to the Present Time, With Essays on Important Subjects Connected with the Violin* (London and Sheffield: Longman & Co., 1866).

Peppin, A. H., *Public Schools and their Music* (Oxford: Oxford University Press, 1927).

Peterlongo, Paolo, *The Violin: Its Physical and Acoustic Principles* (London: Paul Elek, 1979).

Poidras, Henri, *Dictionnaire des Luthiers* (*Dictionary of Violin Makers*, trans. Arnold Sewell) (2 vols.; Rouen: Imprimerie de la Vicomté, 1928–30).

Praetorius, Michael, *Syntagma Musicum* (3 vols.; Wittenburg and Wolfenbüttel, 1614–20). Vol. iii trans. Hans Lampl (Los Angeles, Calif.: University of Southern California, 1957), microfilm.

Price, Bernard, *The Story of English Furniture* (London: BBC, 1982).

Rattray, David, *Masterpieces of Italian Violin Making 1620–1850* (London: Royal Academy of Music, 1991).

Raynor, Henry, *A Social History of Music* (London: Barrie & Jenkins, 1972).

Reade, Charles, *Cremona Violins* (Birchfield: George Muntz, 1873).

Remnant, Mary, *English Bowed Instruments from Anglo-Saxon to Tudor Times* (Oxford: Clarendon Press, 1986).

—— *Musical Instruments: An Illustrated History* (London: Batsford, 1989)

Retford, William C., *Bows and Bow Makers* (London: The Strad, 1964).

Riley, Maurice W., *The History of the Viola* (Ypsilanti, Mich.: M. W. Riley, 1980).

Rousseau, Jean, *Traité de la Viole* (Paris: 1687).

Sadie, Stanley (ed.), *The Cambridge Music Guide* (Cambridge University Press, 1988).

Sadler, Malcolm (ed.), *The Stradivari Influence* (London: Ealing Strings, 1987).

Sandys, William, and Forster, Simon Andrew, *The History of the Violin and other Instruments played on with the Bow from the Remotest Times to the Present* (London: J. R. Smith, 1864).

SCHOLES, PERCY A., *The Puritans and Music* (London: Oxford University Press, 1934).
—— *The Mirror of Music, 1844–1944* (London: Novello and OUP, 1947).
—— *Oxford Companion to Music*, 10th edn. (London: Oxford University Press, 1970).
SHAW, H. W., *The Three Choirs Festival* (Worcester: Ebenezer Baylis & Son for the Three Choirs Festival, 1954).
SILVERMAN, WILLIAM ALEXANDER, *The Violin Hunter* (London: Wm. Reeves, 1957; repr. 1972).
STAINER, ELIZA C., *Dictionary of Violin Makers* (London: Novello c.1896).
STOWELL, ROBIN (ed.), *Violin Technique and Performance Practice in the Late Eighteenth and Early Nineteenth Centuries* (Cambridge University Press, 1985).
—— *The Cambridge Companion to the Violin* (Cambridge University Press, 1992).
TAYLOR, JOSEPH, *The Principles of Violin Construction* (London: Curwen, 1926).
TEMPERLEY, N., *The Music of the English Parish Church* (2 vols.; Cambridge University Press, 1979).
TERTIS, LIONEL, *Cinderella No More* (London: Peter Nevill, 1953).
TROLLOPE, A., *The Warden* (1855; Penguin edn., Harmondsworth, 1982).
TWEEDALE, REVD C. L., *News from the Next World* (London: Spiritualist Press, 1940).
VAN DER STRAETEN, EDMUND S. J., *Romance of the Fiddle* (London: Rebman, 1911).
—— *History of the Violoncello* (London: Wm. Reeves, 1925).
—— *The History of the Violin* (London: Cassel, 1933).
VANNES, RENÉ, *Dictionnaire Universel des Luthiers*, i, ii (3rd edn., Brussels: Les Amis de la Musique, 1988); iii by Claude Lebet (Brussels: Les Amis de la Musique, 1985).
VETTORI, CARLO, *Linee Classiche Della Liutera Italiana* (*The Classic Lines of Italian Violin Making*) (Pisa: Giardini Editori E Stampatori, 1980).
Violin Family, The (The New Grove Musical Instruments Series; London: Macmillan, 1989).
WALKER, ERNEST, *A History of Music in England*, 3rd edn. by J. A. Westrup (Oxford: Clarendon Press, 1952).
WILSHERE, JONATHAN, *William Gardiner of Leicester* (Leicester: Leicester Research Services, 1970).
WOODCOCK, CYRIL, *Dictionary of Contemporary Violin and Bow Makers* (Brighton: Amati Publishing, 1965).
WOODFIELD, IAN, *The Early History of the Viol* (Cambridge University Press, 1984).
YOUNG, PERCY M., *The Concert Tradition: From the Middle Ages to the Twentieth Century* (London: Routledge & Kegan Paul, 1965).
—— *A History of British Music* (London: Ernest Benn, 1967).
YOXALL, J. H., *The ABC about Collecting* (London: London Opinion [*sic*] Curio Club, 1908).

Index

(Appendices, including Directory, are not included)

Abel, Carl Friedrich 137
Aberdeen 173, 175
Academy of Ancient Music 97
accessories 56–9
acoustic design 1
Acton, William J. 291, 299
Adam, John (collector) 218
Agutter, Ralph 22, 95
Aireton, Edmund 116
Alban, Mathius 69
Alburger, Mary Anne 288
alcoholism 250
Alexander, John 291
Allen, Samuel 206
Alton, Robert 297–8
amateurism 285–6, 303
Amati, Andrea 9
Amati family 9, 100, 114, 186–7, 262
Amati, Nicolò 155, 187
Amsterdam 27
Anderson, John 176
Anderson's Varnish 50
apprenticeship system 84–5, 256, 302
Ardern, Job 234–5, 265
aristocracy 98, 122
Armour–Brown, R. 300
Arts and Crafts Movement 250, 255
Ashmolean Museum 9, 11, 194, 200
Askew, John 176, 235–7, 265, 267
Associated Board (examinations) 163–4, 285
Atkinson, William 234, 245–50, 265, 286
attributions 119
auctioneers (London) 286
auctions 5, 221, 226
Australia 212, 213, 214, 227
authenticity 80–1, 298–9

Bach, Johann Christian 91, 99, 137
Baker, Francis 72 n.
Baker, John 72
Baker, William (of Brighton) 36
Baker, William (of Oxford) 33, 43, 72, 260
'Balfour' Strad. 260–1, 288
Baltzar, Thomas 16, 17, 21
Banister, John 18, 21, 23
Banks, Benjamin 4, 31, 32, 33, 40, 41, 48, 88, 89, 107, 13–16
Banks, James and Henry 115–16
Barker, Juliet 299
baroque instruments, demand for 59, 303

Barrett, John 33, 34, 56, 106
bass bar 43, 63, 64
Bate Collection, Oxford 208
Beare, J. & A. 217
Beethoven Quartett Society, 150
Berlioz, Hector 30, 149, 151
Betts, Arthur 257
Betts family 215, 216, 252
Betts, John Edward 90, 118, 166
Betts Strad, sale of 90
Bird, Richmond 291
Birkbeck College 255
Birmingham 220
Birmingham Festival (1852) 153
Birmingham School of Music 162
Bisiach family 296
Blagrove, Henry 148, 160
blocks 43
Blunt, Richard 74
body of violin 38–40
Boosey and Hawkes 159
Bouette, Maurice 299–300
bows 62, 146, 198, 199–209, 213
boxwood 58
Brescia 8–9, 10, 13, 37, 69, 75, 262
bridges 58, 63
Brienz, violin-making school 85 n.
Briggs 176, 291
British Isles, definition of 165
British violins (collecting) 261–2
Britten, Benjamin 22
Britton, Thomas 25, 28, 30, 75, 102, 186
Brown, James 36
Brunton, Elliot 198
Bull, Ole 146, 173, 218
Bultitude, Arthur 198, 204, 207
Bunyan, John 70–2
Burney family 91, 140
Burton, Sir Richard 273
button of violin 40–2
Byrd, William 7

Cahusac, Thomas 59 n., 68, 88
Cameron, Basil 98
Campoli, Alfredo 65
Canada 212, 213, 214
Carlisle Museum 9
Carlton House 141
Carrodus, J. T. 154–5

Carter, John 90–2
cello, introduction and special position of 32–4, 139–42
Cervetto the Elder 26, 139
Cervetto the Younger 122, 140, 142
chamber music 20–2, 149–51
Chanot family 233, 291
Chanot, G. A. 239
Chanot Georges 233, 274
Chanot, J. A. 232, 264
Chapel Royal 17
Chapman, J. T. 260–1
Charles II 16–17, 21
Charles I 7, 20
cheating, methods of 298
child's violins 24
chinrest 24 n.
church bands 33–4, 36
cittern 25 n.
City of Leeds School of Music 162
classes, violin making 299–300
Clementi, Muzio 137
Clifton College 157
Coad, Albert 291
Coates, Kevin 1, 41
Cobbett, W. W. 260, 295
collectors 180–1, 217–22
College of Violinists 162, 266
Collingwood, Joseph 116
Collins, Glen 300
Colville, David 214
competition, economic effects of 87, 126–9, 254, 262–4
concerts, development of 96–7
construction methods 37–40, 285
contemporary British makers 299–301
converting baroque violins 62–5
Coperario, John 7, 12
Copley, Arthur 204
copyists (London) 223–30
Corbett, William 28–9, 186, 217–18
Corelli, Arcangelo 22, 142
Corsby, George 216
Costa, Sir Michael 154
counterfeiting, see fraud
Cramer, Wilhelm 146, 201
Craske, George 234
Cremona 9, 10, 13, 16, 18, 27–8, 181, 186
criminal law 227–30, 298
Cromwell, Oliver 8
Crosdill, John 102, 130, 140, 141, 142
Cross, Nathaniel 33, 101–2, 103–5
Cross, Thomas 95
crwth 11, 14, 166–8
Crystal Palace 138, 255
customs duties 24, 87, 127–8
Cuthbert, Robert 79–80

da Salò, Gasparo 8–9, 26, 34, 35
Dando, J. H. B. 149–50

Darbey, George 291
Davidson, Peter 180–1, 213, 268
Davies, Sir Peter Maxwell 175
Davies, Sir Walford 169
Davis, Richard and William 94
Davis, Richard (dealer) 215, 216, 225–6
Day, John 234
De Comble, Ambroise 70
dealers 187, 215–17
Dearlove, M. W. 257
Degani family 296
Delany, John 185
Delius, Frederick 161
demand and supply 3, 26–9, 100, 121, 230–1
division of labour 86–7, 127
Dodd, Edward 200, 257
Dodd, family 146, 189, 200, 215
Dodd, James 257
Dodd, John 94, 146, 200–1
Dodd, Thomas 94, 224, 225
double bass 34–6, 141, 224, 225
Dowland, John 7, 12
Dragonetti, Domenico 34, 124, 142, 152, 218, 222, 258
du Pré, Jacqueline 163
Dublin 182
Dubourg, George 267
Dubourg, Matthew 25, 267
Duke family 88, 118–19, 189
Duke of Edinburgh 258, 275
Duke, Richard 70, 118–19, 238
Duncan, George 176–7, 179, 213, 234, 236
Dundee 175
Dykes, G. L. 232
Dykes, Arthur 266

Edinburgh 172, 173, 175
education 23–5, 155–9, 163–4, 300
electric violins 303 n.
Elgar, Sir Edward 98, 161, 283
Engel, Carl 167, 258
English making (retrospect) 301–3
Eton College 157
Evelyn, John 16, 17, 21
exhibitions 256–61
exports 122, 211–14

Facta Britannia Competition 300
factories, violin-making 85–6, 125–6, 263–4, 302
Fagnola, H. 296–9
fairs 68
Falkner, J. Meade 123
family craft businesses 88, 189
Fellowes, E. H. 158
Fendt & Purdy 216
Fendt, Bernard Simon 9, 224
Fendt, Bernhard 188, 224, 232
Fendt family 36, 145, 189, 224, 231
Fendt, Jacob 224

INDEX

Fendt, Martin 224
fiddlers, Welsh, Scottish and Irish 168, 171, 175–6, 183
fiddles (early) 10, 11
Finger, Gottfried 96
fingerboards 59, 63
Fleming, J. M. 14, 249, 268–9
Flemish construction methods 40
folk fiddle, *see* fiddle
Ford, Jacob 116–17
forgery 227–30
Forster family 34–5, 56, 87, 88, 122–3, 416, 187, 215, 232, 252, 258
Forster, Simon A. 35, 257
Forster, William II 34, 122, 137, 140, 141, 142, 151–2
Forster, William III 35, 129
France, *see* Mirecourt
fraud 7, 119–20, 227–30
Free Trade 126–7, 254, 262
frequencies (sound) 5–6
Furber family 189
Furber, John 232
Füssen 75 n.

Gaida, G. & C. 297
Galpin Society 261
Gand & Bernadel 262
Gardiner, William 137, 144
Geminiani, Francesco 25, 96, 97
George III 141
George IV 141
Germany, cheap imports from 87, 125–6, 183, 230, 231, 254, 263
Giardini, Felice de 96–7
Gibbons, Orlando 7, 12
Gilbert, J. J. 290, 291
Gilchrist, James 178
Gilkes, Samuel 89, 232
Gilling Castle 13
Gillott, Joseph 218, 219–22
Glasgow 173, 181
Glenister, William 289, 290, 291
glue 55
Goding, James (collector) 216–17, 218
Gould, John A. 213
Goulding and Co. 89
Gow, Niel 175
Grabu, Louis 21
grafts (neck) 41, 59, 63
Grant, Sir James Hope 123, 142, 258
Great Exhibition (1851) 257
Grice, John 69, 166
Grieg, Edvard 173
Guadagnini, J. B. 262
Guarneri, Andreas 114–15
Guarneri del Gesù 64, 116, 143–6, 155, 188, 215, 226, 262
Guildhall School of Music 160
guilds 82–3

Hall, Marie 161, 243
Handel, George Frideric 25, 95, 97, 98, 138, 267
Hanover Square Rooms 91, 140, 147, 149
Hardie, James 176
Hardie, Matthew 175, 176, 179–80
Hare, Joseph 70, 105–6, 109–10
Hare, John 105
Hargrave, Roger 5 n., 229–30
Harris, Charles 33, 89, 191, 212
Harris family 189, 232
Harris's Varnish 50
Harrison, Beatrice 161
Harrison, May 161
Hart family 58, 186–7, 189
Hart George 132, 186–8, 220–1, 268
Hart, John 216
Haweis H. R. 150, 155, 258–9, 269
Hawkins, Sir John 15–16, 17, 19, 75
Haydn, Joseph 30, 137, 141
Haym, Nicola 96
Helby v *Matthews* (1895) 160 n.
'Hellier' Strad. 257,
Henley, William 281–3
Heron-Allen, Edward 32, 38, 145, 167, 178–9, 195, 216, 232–3, 242, 266, 269– 80
Hesketh, Thomas Earle 145, 291, 293–4
Hill, Albert Phillips 196
Hill, Alfred Ebsworth 195
Hill, Andrew 283
Hill, Arthur Frederick 194, 195
Hill, Benjamin 189
Hill, Desmond 196, 207
Hill, family 88, 189–99, 231, 252, 260
Hill, Henry 30, 102, 122, 148, 149–52, 191, 268
Hill, Henry Lockey 32, 65, 190–1, 232
Hill, Joseph 70, 73, 89, 116, 189
Hill, Joseph (II) 189
Hill, Lockey 89, 189
Hill, Paul Ebsworth 196
Hill, W. E. & Sons 189, 191, 217
Hill, William 189
Hill, William Ebsworth 89, 191–3, 201, 216
Hill, William Henry 194, 195
Hine, Reginald 279
Hoing, Clifford 299
Holborne, Anthony 12
Holder, T. J. 287–8, 292
Holland 212
Honeyman, William C. 131, 166, 177–80, 281
Horsley, William 150
Huddersfield College of Music 162
Hudson, George Wulme 229, 291, 292–3
Hudson, George (composer) 18
Huguenots 67–8, 100
Hullah, John 156, 158
Hulme, Alexander 299
human voice 10
Humfrey, Pelham 19

Hutchinson, Colonel 8
Huttoft, William 88, 114

immigrants 66, 67, 69, 188, 231
imports of instruments 26–9, 87, 124, 187–8, 262–4, 296–8
India 212
inflation 133–5
influences (stylistic) 36, 145, 186–8
ink purfling 56
Ireland 144, 182–5, 301
Italian instruments, imports of 187–8, 296–8
Irvine, Robert 185

Jacklin, Cyril 283, 291
Jaye, Henry 6 n., 89
Jenkins, John 18, 23
Jewish immigration 27
Joachim, Joseph 150, 249
Johnson, John 117

Keenan, Edward 185
Kennedy family 189
Kennedy, Nigel 163
Kew Palace 141
kits (pochettes) 15 n.
Klingenthal 69, 86
Klotz family 27, 42, 263
Klotz, Matthias 85
Krouchdaler, Hans 76

labelling, false 119–20
Lady Margaret Hall, Oxford 278
Langonet, Alfred 283
Langonet family 195
Lanier, Nicholas 8
Laurie, David 51, 102–3, 176, 181
lawyers, as violin writers 268
'Le Messie' (Stradivari violin) 194, 195, 216, 258, 261
Lee, Percy 288
Lenton, John 23
Lewis, Edward 30, 33, 40, 78–9, 107–8
Lindley, Robert 35, 138, 142
Lindley, Thomas 148
linings 43
lira da braccio 9, 11
literature of violin 265–83
Little, Tasmin 65
Locke, Matthew 18, 20
London 72–3, 215, 217, 223, 242, 273–4, 291
Longman and Broderip 88, 89, 114, 189
Longman and Lukey 89
Lott family 145, 224, 225, 231, 252
Lott, John F. (Senior) 35, 224–5
Lott, John Frederick ('Jack') 7, 36, 65, 145, 216, 225–7
Luff, William 145, 254, 299, 300
Lyon and Healy (Chicago) 213

Mace, Thomas 6, 7, 13
Mackie, Adam 213
Maggini, Paolo 9, 100–1
Manchester, 244–5, 293
Mann, John A. 180 n.
maple 52–3
Markneukirchen 69, 86, 262, 263
Marlborough College 157
Marshall, John 177, 234
Mason, Lowell 153
Matteis, Nicolò 21, 27
Maucatel, Charles 94
Mayr, Ferdinand 24
Mayson, Walter 123, 161, 237–45, 265
Meares, Richard 74, 104
Mechanics' Institutes 159, 255, 256
mechanisation 87
Mell, Davis 23
Merlin, John Joseph 91–3, 137
Messiah (Handel) 98, 99, 154, 182
metal violins 71–2
Michetschläger, Helen 300
Miller 94
Millington's Varnish 50
Mirecourt 56, 69, 85, 86, 87, 124–5, 194–5, 254, 262, 263
Mitchell, Thomas 213
Mittenwald 69, 85, 86, 262, 263
Monteverdi, Claudio 15
Morley, Thomas 7
Morris, W. Meredith 4, 37, 170–2, 232–3, 281
Morris, William 255
Morris and Barnes 94
moulds, use of 38
Moya, Hidalgo 266
Mozart, Leopold 97
Mozart, W. A. 24, 30
music festivals 147
Music Loan Exhibition (1904) 259–60, 261
musical education 23–5, 155–9, 163–4, 300
musicians, social and economic condition of 124, 152, 153, 252–3
Napier, William 204, 207
National Youth Orchestra 163
neck 63
Neruda, Madam Norman (Lady Hallé) 161, 241
New Zealand 212
Newark School 299–300
Norman, Barak 32, 68, 70, 73, 100–2, 104, 151
Norris and Barnes 146
North, Roger 14
Norwich 99
nut, of violin 58

Oddone, Carlo 297
oil varnish 47–8
old versus new violins 5–6, 285, 297
Onslow, George 150
opera 97–8

INDEX

oratorio 98, 99, 284
orchestras 136–8, 147, 148–9, 152, 162, 303–7
Ordsall Hall Museum, Salford 244
origins of violin family 8–10
Otto, J. A. 266–7
Owen, Ivy Rimmer 291
Owen, John 291, 295
Oxford 99

Paganini, Niccolò 31, 121, 143–6, 188
Pamphilon, Edward 32–3, 68, 73 n., 77–8
Panormo, Vincenzo 34, 119, 166, 188, 223
Parker, Daniel 31, 37, 40, 58, 65, 70–1, 108–13, 186, 223, 261–2
Parkinson, James 286–7
Parry, Joseph 167
Pearce, Joseph 253–4
pegs 58, 92
Pemberton, Edward 73
Pemberton J. 71 n.
Pepusch, J. C. 96
Pepys, Samuel 19, 21, 26, 189
periodicals (violin) 265–6
Perry, Thomas 68, 166, 183–5
Philharmonic concerts 142
Philharmonic Society 31, 138, 143, 146–7, 152
piano industry 87, 159–60
Piatti, Alfredo 150–1
pine, British 53
Piper, Towry 236, 280–1
pitch 62
Playford, John 8, 22, 23, 95, 173
Plowright, Dennis 283
Polonaski, Eugene 178, 266
Price, R. G. 289
prices 125, 127, 128–35, 152–3, 187, 198, 285, 296
Prince of Wales 102, 141
provincial Colleges of Music 162
Pryor, William 107–8
Purcell, Henry 18, 19, 20, 22, 95
Purchase Tax 196–7, 300
Purdy & Fendt, *see* Fendt & Purdy
purfling 6, 44, 54, 55–6
Puritanism 8

Quaritch, Bernard 273
quartets 149–151

R. v. Closs (1858) 228
R. v. Smith (1858) 229
Rattle, Simon 163
Rayman, Jacob 27, 29, 31, 70, 71 n., 75–6
Reade, Charles 155, 218–19, 220, 225, 258–9
rebec 9
rehairing of bows 205
restoration work (Hills) 191–210
retailers and outworkers 89–90
Retford, William 198, 204, 206–7, 208

Richardson, Arthur 31, 50, 291, 295
Robinson, William (Liverpool) 289
Robinson, William (Plumstead) 289–90
Rocca, Joseph 257
Rose, John 6, 74
Roth, Ernst Heinrich 296
Rousseau, Jean 6 n.
Royal Academy of Music 155, 160, 161, 222, 282, 295
Royal College of Music 156, 160, 271, 275 n.
Royal Family 99, 140–1
Royal George cello 140–1
Royal Manchester College of Music 162,
Ruddiman, Joseph 176
Rural Music Schools 162
Rushworth and Dreaper 195, 291
Rutson, John 222

Saby, H. H. 214
saddle 58
Sainton, Prosper 148
Saloman, Johann Peter 137, 138, 147
Sammons, Albert 287–95, 296, 297–8
Sandler, Albert 298
Sandys W. & Forster S. A. 267–8
Sandys, William 268
Saunders, Wilfred 229, 271, 300
school music 156–9, 163
Scotland 145, 172–183, 233–4, 301
Schreiber, P. 176
scroll 40–2, 76, 240
seasoning wood 54
Shaw, John 74
Shetland Isles 173, 174
Shield, William 102
Shrosbree, H. J. 214
Simpson, James and John 117
Simpson, John 106
Skinner, John S. 175
slab wood 54–5
Smart, George 212
Smillie, Alexander 176, 234
Smillie, Andrew 291
Smith, Adam 127
Smith, Arthur Edward 213
Smith, John 213
Smith, William 93
Soho (London) 73, 273–4
soundholes 43
soundpost 63
sources 3–4
South Africa 212, 214
Southampton, University College 291
Special Exhibition (1872) 74, 123, 142, 219, 258–9, 261
spirit varnish 47–8
Spohr Ludwig 138, 160
Stagg, John 207
Stainer, E. C. 3–4, 5
Stainer, Jacob 16, 27, 64, 100, 186

Stainer, Sir John 158
Statute of Apprentices 84–5
Stirrat, David 176
Strad (magazine) 242–3, 265, 266, 281, 285
Stradivari 5, 16, 24, 26, 28, 64, 69, 70, 105–6, 109, 114, 119, 142–3, 145, 187–8, 193, 194, 215, 219, 223, 262
Straub, Frantz 76
strings 60–1
supply, *see* demand and supply
sycamore 53
Szepessy, Béla 176, 232, 233, 236, 264

tail–button 58
tail pieces 59
Tarisio, Luigi 188, 216–17
Tarr, Joseph 213
Tarr, William 36, 213
taste, English 186–8
technical instruction 255–6
Tertis, Lionel 31
Testore family 262
Thibouville–Lamy, J. 124–5, 254
Thistleton, Frank 266, 288–91
Thompson, Charles and Samuel 64
Three Choirs Festival 98, 155
Tieffenbrucker, V. 13
Tobin, Richard 41, 119, 166, 232, 250
Tolley's Case (1615) 85
Tomkins, Thomas 20
tone 5, 61–2, 64–5
tools 61
Tourte, François 146, 200–1
Tovey, Sir Donald F. 174
trade signs 73
trade routes 68
Trinity College of Music 160
Trollope, Anthony 123
Tubbs family 200, 204
Tubbs, James 201–4, 213
Turner, John A. 216
Tweedale, Charles L. 45
Twenty–Four Violins 16, 17, 19

Uppingham School 156–7
Urquhart, Thomas 76–7, 100, 166, 176
USA 211, 212–13

Valentine, William 36
varnish 44–52, 197–8, 240
VAT, introduction of 197, 300
Venice 10
Veracini, Francesco Maria 96

Victoria and Albert Museum, *see* Special Exhibition (1872)
Vincent, Alfred 291, 295–6
viola, introduction and development of 29–32, 149–52, 302
violin, introduction and early makers of 12–16, 71–2
violinists, Italian 96
Violin Makers' Guild (London) 86
Violin Times 178, 265
viols 6, 10, 11, 13–14
Viotti, G. B. 70, 142–3
Visconti, Gasparo 96, 109
Voigt family 291
Voller brothers 229, 234, 261, 288
von Lütgendorff 4
Vuillaume family 102–3
Vuillaume, J.–B. 34, 51, 180 n. 222, 230, 257
Wales 166–72, 300, 301
Walker, John 290, 291
Walker's Varnish 50
Walton, William (composer) 284
Walton, William (maker) 289
Wamsley, Peter 4, 73, 105, 114, 116, 189
Ward, Rod 300
Weelkes, Thomas 7
Welsh Folk Museum 168, 172
Welsh Violin Making School 172
Whitelaw, James (varnish) 45–6, 50
Wilkinson, John 229, 291
Wilkinson, William 184
Williams, Benjamin 170
Willis's Rooms 150
Wills, Colin 300
Wise, Christopher 79
Withers, Edward 94
Withers family 58
Withers, Joseph 261
women players 153, 160–1
Wood, Anthony 14
wood for violin and bow–making 52–5, 201
Woodcock, Cyril 282–3
Worcester Cathedral 10 n.
'workshop' instruments 294
Wulme–Hudson, *see* Hudson
Wurlitzer's 212–13

Yehudi Menuhin School 163
Yeoman, Sidney 104
Young, William 18
youth orchestras 163–4

Zoffany, Johann 139